THE ROUTLEDGE COMPANION TO MEDIA FANDOM

This companion brings together an internationally and interdisciplinarily diverse group of emerging and established fan studies scholars to reflect on the state of the field and to chart new directions for research.

Engaging an impressive array of media texts and formats, and incorporating a variety of methodologies, this collection is designed to survey, complicate, and expand core concerns. This second edition includes 20 new chapters, 11 revised chapters, and 12 reprinted chapters organized into four main sections: Methods, Ethics, and Theoretical Approaches; Fan Practices and Platforms; Identities; and Industry and Labor. Each section features a short introduction that discusses the section's scope and contributions, highlights the importance of the section's topic to fan studies, and offers suggestions for further reading.

This collection remains an essential volume for students and scholars interested in fandom and fan studies, popular culture, media studies, and film and television studies.

Melissa A. Click is Associate Professor of Communication Studies at Gonzaga University, USA. Her work on fans, audiences, and popular culture has been published in *Television & New Media*, the *International Journal of Communication Studies*, *Popular Communication*, and *Popular Music & Society*. She is editor of *Anti-Fandom: Dislike and Hate in the Digital Age* (2019), and the co-editor of *Bitten by Twilight* (2010).

Suzanne Scott is Associate Professor in the Department of Radio-Television-Film at the University of Texas at Austin, USA. She is the author of *Fake Geek Girls: Fandom, Gender, and the Convergence Culture Industry* (2019), and the co-editor of *Sartorial Fandom: Fashion, Beauty Culture, and Identity* (2023).

THE ROUTLEDGE COMPANION TO MEDIA FANDOM

Second Edition

Edited by Melissa A. Click and Suzanne Scott

Routledge
Taylor & Francis Group
NEW YORK AND LONDON

Designed cover image: archivector / Shutterstock

Second edition published 2025
by Routledge
605 Third Avenue, New York, NY 10158

and by Routledge
4 Park Square, Milton Park, Abingdon, Oxon, OX14 4RN

Routledge is an imprint of the Taylor & Francis Group, an informa business

© 2025 selection and editorial matter, Melissa A. Click and Suzanne Scott; individual chapters, the contributors

The right of Melissa A. Click and Suzanne Scott to be identified as the authors of the editorial material, and of the authors for their individual chapters, has been asserted in accordance with sections 77 and 78 of the Copyright, Designs and Patents Act 1988.

All rights reserved. No part of this book may be reprinted or reproduced or utilised in any form or by any electronic, mechanical, or other means, now known or hereafter invented, including photocopying and recording, or in any information storage or retrieval system, without permission in writing from the publishers.

Trademark notice: Product or corporate names may be trademarks or registered trademarks and are used only for identification and explanation without intent to infringe.

First edition published by Routledge 2018

ISBN: 978-1-032-43800-9 (hbk)
ISBN: 978-1-032-44608-0 (pbk)
ISBN: 978-1-003-37302-5 (ebk)

DOI: 10.4324/9781003373025

Typeset in Sabon
by Newgen Publishing UK

CONTENTS

List of Figures x
List of Contributors xii

Introduction 1
Melissa A. Click and Suzanne Scott

PART I
METHODS, ETHICS, AND THEORETICAL APPROACHES 7

1 The Ethics of Studying Online Fandom 11
  Kristina Busse

2 What Does the "Transnational" Mean for Fan Studies Today?
  Some Provocations 21
  Rukmini Pande

3 (Media) Fandom Is Not a Noun 31
  Katherine E. Morrissey

4 After Poaching and Negotiated Readings: Towards the Real-time
  Emergence (and the Temporary Pauses) of Fans' Co-decoding 41
  Matt Hills

5 Surveying Fandom: The Ethics, Design, and Use of Surveys in
  Fan Studies 51
  Lucy Bennett

Contents

6 Fandom and Disability: Expanding Theoretical Perspectives to
   Fan Studies   60
   Divya Garg

7 Transnational Media Fan Studies   71
   Lori Morimoto

8 When Platforms Fall: Scraping and Interpreting Fandom Data in
   Tumultuous Times   81
   Anastasia Salter and Bridget Blodgett

9 Archaeologies of Fandom: Using Historical Methods to Explore
   Fan Cultures of the Past   90
   Kathy Fuller-Seeley

10 Conversation on Studying "Toxic" Fans   100
   Kishonna L. Gray, CarrieLynn D. Reinhard, and Adrienne Shaw

PART II
FAN PRACTICES AND PLATFORMS   111

11 Where the Fans Are: Rethinking Fan Studies and Participatory Culture   115
   Rhiannon Bury

12 Fan Curators and the Gateways into Fandom   124
   Derek Kompare

13 The Roles of Language in Transcultural Fanfiction   132
   Clarice Greco

14 Fan Tourism and Pilgrimage: Revisited   142
   Rebecca Williams

15 Negotiating Fandom: The Politics of Racebending   151
   Henry Jenkins

16 Shifting, *Harry Potter*, and TikTok Fan Practices   164
   Claire Whitley and Katharine Perrotta

17 Tumblr Fan Aesthetics   175
   Louisa Ellen Stein

Contents

18 Accessing Platformed Fandoms: Disability and Digital Fan Practices 187
   Elizabeth Ellcessor

19 A Tale of Two Communities: The Polish Fandom, the Fandom in
   Poland, and the Internet's Influence on Fan Identities 197
   Agnieszka Urbańczyk

20 Navigating Online Ecosystems: Chinese Celebrity Fans'
   Participation across Social Media Platforms 207
   Qiuyan Guo

21 Vidding and Identity: A Conversation 216
   Francesca Coppa, Alexis Lothian, and Tisha Turk

PART III
IDENTITIES 227

22 The Invisible Bag of Holding: Whiteness and Media Fandom 231
   Benjamin Woo

23 The Queer Politics of Femslash 240
   Julie Levin Russo

24 Identity, Positionality, and Comics Fandom: Women of Color Fans 251
   Erika Chung

25 Finding the National in Transnational: Mapping Identities and
   Power in K-pop Fandoms 261
   Celeste Oon

26 Charting Latinx Fandom 270
   Jillian M. Báez

27 Everyday Costume: Feminized Fandom, Retail, and Beauty Culture 281
   Elizabeth Affuso

28 Watching the Series of the Enemy: The Reception of Turkish Soap
   Operas by Greeks 291
   Dimitra Laurence Larochelle

29 Aging, Fans, and Fandom 301
   C. Lee Harrington and Denise D. Bielby

30 Sounding Queer Fandom: Podfic and Nonbinary Theory 312
Olivia Johnston Riley

31 Boys Love Media across Asia: Theorizing the Role of Queer Affect in Transcultural Fandom 322
Thomas Baudinette

32 Advancing Transcultural Fandom: A Conversation 331
Bertha Chin, Aswin Punathambekar, and Sangita Shresthova

PART IV
INDUSTRY AND LABOR 341

33 Fans and Merchandise 345
Avi Santo

34 The Fanfiction Gold Rush 2.0: After/AI 354
Mel Stanfill

35 Fandom and the Politics of Cancel Culture 363
Eve Ng

36 Conspicuous Convention: Industry Interpellation and Fan Consumption at San Diego Comic-Con 373
Anne Gilbert

37 (Black Female) Fans Strike Back: The Emergence of the Iris West Defense Squad 384
Kristen J. Warner

38 Fantagonism, Franchising, and Industry Management of Fan Privilege 394
Derek Johnson

39 Friki Conventions: Comic-Cons, Expos, and Fandom in Mexico City 406
Guillermo Aguilar Vázquez and Ana Fabiola Vidal Fernández

40 Fannish Affect, "Quality" Fandom, and Transmedia Storytelling Campaigns 414
Melanie E.S. Kohnen

41	DAZN's Coverage Strategies of the UEFA Women's Champions League: Growing the Game Through Women's Football Fandom *Charlotte E. Howell*	424
42	The Bigger Picture: Drawing Intersections between Comics, Fan, and Industry Studies *Alisa Perren and Laura E. Felschow*	433
43	So Strike We All: Union Action and Cosplay on the Picket Line *Kate Fortmueller and Suzanne Scott*	444
	Index	456

FIGURES

16.1	A selection of TikTok videos which establish the elusivity of successful Shifting.	167
16.2	Stills from a TikTok video which demonstrate the creator using changes in casual clothing to signify different characters.	171
16.3	Stills from a TikTok video which demonstrate the use of continuity editing (shot-reverse-shot, eyeline match) to distinguish between characters.	172
17.1	Example of fan art image and accompanying poetic tag.	179
17.2	Tumblr tags can simultaneously occupy both the center and margins of a post.	180
17.3	Fannish tagging recontextualizes and thus transforms media objects such as this audio from the musical Hamilton.	181
17.4–17.6	Dynamic gifsets such as this embody Tumblr's affective multimodal aesthetic.	183
18.1	Screenshots as the author prepares to post a screen capture from the 2023 *Dr. Who* episode "The Giggle," which featured a character (and actress) who uses a wheelchair. The three screenshots show Mastodon's prompts, the writing of alt text, and the ALT badge on the final post.	190
36.1	Small comic book retail booth on the SDCC trade floor.	379
36.2	Warner Bros.' large-scale booth on the SDCC trade floor, during a signing for HBO's *Silicon Valley*.	380
36.3	Attendees study convention maps with their SDCC bags. Souvenir bags are sponsored by Warner Bros., and distributed to attendees at registration.	381
40.1	*Interview with the Vampire* activation at SDCC 2023. Photos by the author.	415
40.2	Panem October screenshot on the left, capitol.pn screenshot on the right.	419

List of Figures

43.1	Screengrab of themed picket schedule posted to the WGA's Instagram Stories.	449
43.2	Picketer dressed as Samara from *The Ring* during the 2023 horror-themed picket during the WGA strike.	451
43.3	Screengrab of WGA Instagram post coverage of the *Bridgerton* themed picket.	452

CONTRIBUTORS

Elizabeth Affuso is Academic Director of Intercollegiate Media Studies at the Claremont Colleges, where she teaches media studies at Pitzer College. She is co-editor with Suzanne Scott of *Sartorial Fandom: Fashion, Beauty Culture, and Identity* (2023) and with Avi Santo of "Films and Merchandise," a special issue of *Film Criticism* (2018). Her work on beauty, fashion, fandom, and consumer culture has been published in *Jump Cut*, *Point of Sale: Analyzing Media Retail*, and *Documenting Fashion*.

Jillian M. Báez is an Associate Professor in the Department of Africana, Puerto Rican, and Latino Studies at Hunter College, City University of New York. She is also on the doctoral faculty in Women's and Gender Studies at the CUNY Graduate Center. Báez is the author of *In Search of Belonging: Latinas, Media, and Citizenship*, recipient of the National Communication Association's Bonnie Ritter Award for Outstanding Feminist Book.

Thomas Baudinette is Senior Lecturer in Global Cultures at Macquarie University. A cultural anthropologist, his research focuses on queer media and its impacts on understandings of gender and sexuality across East and Southeast Asia. His first book is *Regimes of Desire: Young Gay Men, Media, and Masculinity in Tokyo* (University of Michigan Press, 2021). His second book is *Boys Love Media in Thailand: Celebrity, Fans, and Transnational Asian Queer Popular Culture* (Bloomsbury, 2023).

Lucy Bennett is a Lecturer at JOMEC, Cardiff University, UK. Her work on popular music fandom appears in journals such as *New Media & Society*, *Journal of Fandom Studies*, *Transformative Works and Cultures*, *Continuum*, *Celebrity Studies* and *Participations*. She is the co-founder of the Fan Studies Network and co-editor of *Seeing Fans: Representations of Fandom in Media and Popular Culture* (with Paul Booth) and *Crowdfunding the Future* (with Bertha Chin and Bethan Jones).

Denise D. Bielby is Distinguished Professor of Sociology, Emerita at the University of California Santa Barbara. She writes about film and television as culture-producing industries and has published on Hollywood screenwriters, the global television marketplace, and fandom. Her current research focuses on cultural authority and voice and examines discursive practices in film criticism.

Bridget Blodgett is an Associate Professor in the College of Arts and Sciences at the University of Baltimore. Her research analyzes internet culture and the social impacts thereof on offline life. Her current research takes a critical eye to online game communities regarding gender, inclusiveness, and identity. Much of her work is best summarized in *Toxic Geek Masculinity in Media* (with Anastasia Salter), which was released in 2017 by Palgrave MacMillan.

Rhiannon Bury is a Professor of Women's and Gender Studies at Athabasca University, Canada. She has been researching and publishing on online television fandom for over 30 years. Her two monographs were published by Peter Lang in 2005 (*Cyberspaces of Their Own: Female Fandoms Online*) and 2017 (*Television 2.0: Viewer and Fan Engagement with Digital TV*). Her most recent project focuses on fan reaction to queer and racebent adaptations: *The Last of Us* (HBO 2023–) and *Interview with the Vampire* (AMC 2022–).

Kristina Busse is an independent scholar and active media fan. She has edited several fan studies essay collections and is former cofounder and coeditor of *Transformative Works and Culture* (2008–22). Kristina has published widely on fanfiction and fan cultures, including *Framing Fan Fiction* (2017) and the forthcoming *Slash Fan Fiction and the Politics of Fantasy* with Alexis Lothian.

Bertha Chin is Senior Lecturer at the Department of Communications and New Media, NUS Singapore. She has published extensively on transcultural fandom, fan labor, subcultural celebrity, anti-fandom and fan-producer relationships. She is co-editor of *Crowdfunding the Future: Media Industries, Ethics and Digital Society* (Peter Lang, 2015) and *Eating Fandom* (Routledge, 2020). She is also co-Editor-in-Chief of *Popular Communication*.

Erika Chung is a PhD candidate in the joint Communication and Culture program at Toronto Metropolitan University and York University. Her research focuses on the intersectionality of race and gender in comics fandom, and the experiences of racialized women in popular culture. She has published in the *Journal of Cultural Analysis and Social Change*, *Canadian Journal of Communication*, *Panic at the Discourse* and *Women Write About Comics*.

Francesca Coppa is a Professor of English, Theatre, and Film Studies at Muhlenberg College. A founding member of the Organization for Transformative Works and the Archive of Our Own, she is the author of *The Fanfiction Reader: Folk Tales for the Digital Age* (2017), which won the Prose Award for Best Book in Media and Cultural Studies, and of *Vidding: A History* (2022), a multimedia history of fan music video and ACLS Open Access finalist.

Elizabeth Ellcessor is an Associate Professor of Media Studies at the University of Virginia. She is the author of several books related to media, disability, and access, including *Restricted Access: Media, Disability, and the Politics of Participation* (2016), and is co-editor of the *Journal of Cinema and Media Studies*.

List of Contributors

Laura E. Felschow is an Assistant Professor of Media Studies at the State University of New York at Oneonta. Her work has appeared in *Transformative Works and Cultures, Media Industries, Mediapolis,* and in a number of edited collections. Her research focuses on gender and production cultures.

Ana Fabiola Vidal Fernández is an independent researcher focusing on fans and creative classes in Mexico. She holds a Master's degree in Sociocultural Anthropology from the Benemérita Universidad Autónoma de Puebla (BUAP), with a thesis entitled "Los mixólogos y bartenders como intermediarios culturales en la promoción y el consumo de bebidas en México. El caso de Tehuacán Brillante."

Kate Fortmueller is an Associate Professor of Film and Media History at Georgia State University and is the author of books about media industries and labor including *Below the Stars: How the Labor of Working Actors and Extras Shapes Media Production* (2021), *Hollywood Shutdown: Production, Distribution, and Exhibition in the Time of COVID* (2021), and is co-editor of the anthology *Hollywood Unions* (2024).

Kathy Fuller-Seeley teaches media history in the Radio-TV-Film Department at the University of Texas at Austin. She's written about the history of American moviegoing in *At the Picture Show: Small Town Audiences and the Creation of Movie Fan Culture* (1996), *One Thousand Nights at the Movies* (2013) and other book chapters. She is completing a book project about silent Western films produced in San Antonio, Texas in 1910–1911.

Divya Garg is a Lecturer in the School of Culture and Communication at the University of Melbourne. Her forthcoming monograph explores transcultural fandom and disability through the case study of Marvel superhero media fandom (University of Iowa Press, 2025). Her work has also appeared in *Continuum: Journal of Media and Culture* (2024), *Queerbaiting and Fandom* (2019), *Fame and Fandom* (2022), and *Disability and the Superhero* (2023).

Anne Gilbert is a television market researcher based in Los Angeles. She holds a PhD in Media Studies from Rutgers University, and her work on fans and television has been published in *Television & New Media* and *Transformative Works & Cultures.*

Kishonna L. Gray is an Associate Professor in Writing, Rhetoric, & Digital Studies and in African-American and Africana Studies at the University of Kentucky.

Clarice Greco is a Professor at the Postgraduate Programme in Communications at Paulista University. She holds a PhD and a Master's degree from the School of Communications and Arts at the University of São Paulo. She is the coordinator of the Research Group for the Analysis of Audiovisual Products (GRUPA-UNIP). She has published essays in English on Telenovela Studies and Media Fandom in journals such as *Participations, Transformative Works and Cultures* and *Comunicación y Sociedad*. She is the author of two books in Portuguese: *Qualidade na TV: telenovela, crítica e público* and *Virou Cult: telenovela, nostalgia e fãs.*

List of Contributors

Qiuyan Guo is a scholar who received her PhD from the School of Information Sciences at the University of Illinois Urbana-Champaign. Her research interests include information literacy and readership, information behavior, fan participation and practices, and online cultural studies. Her work has appeared in *Transformative Works and Cultures*, *Library and Information Science Research*, *Celebrity Studies*, and *Feminist Media Studies*, and she has presented at multiple conferences in the US.

C. Lee Harrington is Professor Emerita of Sociology and Social Justice Studies at Miami University. Her research interests include soap operas (reception, production, narrative, worldbuilding, and critique), the global market for television, fan identities and communities, and issues related to culture, media, aging, and death. She has co-authored two books with Denise D. Bielby (*Soap Fans*, 1995 and *Global TV*, 2008), co-edited numerous anthologies, and published in varied media and fan studies journals and collections.

Matt Hills is currently teaching at Manchester Metropolitan University, and is an Honorary Professor at the University of Bristol. Until 2023, he was a Professor of Fandom Studies at the University of Huddersfield. Matt is the author of books such as *Fan Cultures* (Routledge, 2002) and *The Pleasures of Horror* (Continuum, 2005), as well as the co-editor of *Transatlantic Television Drama* (Oxford University Press, 2019), and most recently *Adventures Across Space and Time: A Doctor Who Reader* (Bloomsbury Academic, 2023). He has published widely on media fandom and *Doctor Who*.

Charlotte E. Howell is an Associate Professor of Film and Television Studies at Boston University. Her research has been published in *The Journal of Cinema and Media Studies*, *Critical Studies in Television*, *Television and New Media*, and *Celebrity Studies*. Her areas of specialization include television studies, media industry studies, sports media studies, and fan studies. Her book *Divine Programming Negotiating Christianity in American Dramatic Television Production, 1996–2016* was published in 2020.

Henry Jenkins is Provost Professor of Communication, Journalism, Cinematic Arts, Education and East Asian Languages and Cultures at the University of Southern California, is the editor or author of 21 books, including *Textual Poachers: Television Fans and Participatory Culture*, *Convergence Culture: Where Old and New Media Collide*, *Spreadable Media: Creating Meaning and Value in a Network Society*, *By Any Media Necessary: The New Youth Activists*, *Popular Culture and the Civic Imagination: A Casebook for Creative Social Change*, *Where the Wild Things Were: American Boyhood and Permissive Parenting in Postwar America*, and the forthcoming *Frames of Fandom* book series. Check out his "How Do You Like It So Far?" podcast.

Derek Johnson is currently Professor and Department Chair in Communication Arts at the University of Wisconsin-Madison. He is the author of *Media Franchising: Creative License and Collaboration in the Culture Industries* as well as *Transgenerational Media Industries: Adults, Children, and the Reproduction of Culture*.

Melanie E.S. Kohnen is an Associate Professor of Rhetoric and Media Studies at Lewis & Clark College. Her research focuses on the tensions among the contemporary media industries, audiences, and digital platforms. Specifically, she investigates the connections between the micro-level of media events, like the site-specific experiential marketing at San Diego Comic-Con, and macro-levels of cultural forces, like the platform economy and the algorithmic processing of human experience.

Derek Kompare is an Associate Professor of Film and Media Arts and an Associate Dean of Faculty in the Meadows School of the Arts at Southern Methodist University. He is the author of *Rerun Nation: How Repeats Invented American Television*, *CSI*, and co-editor of *Making Media Work: Cultures of Management in the Entertainment Industries*.

Dimitra Laurence Larochelle is an Associate Professor at the Université Sorbonne Nouvelle – Paris 3. Her research focuses on the reception of transnational TV series, audiovisual platforms, gender, and digital technologies. She is Secretary of the Research Committee 14 (Sociology of Communication, Knowledge, and Culture) of the International Sociological Association (ISA) and member of the board of the RC 37 (Sociology of Arts) of the ISA.

Alexis Lothian is an Associate Professor in the Harriet Tubman Department of Women, Gender, and Sexuality Studies at University of Maryland College Park. Her research centers on speculative fiction, digital media, and fan culture and their relationships to gender, race, and disability justice. She is the author of *Old Futures: Speculative Fiction and Queer Possibility* (NYU Press, 2018) and co-edits the Queer/Trans/Digital/Diaspora book series at NYU Press.

Lori Morimoto is an Assistant Professor at the University of Virginia. She does research on transcultural and transnational media fandoms, particularly in an East Asian context, and she serves on the editorial boards of the *Journal for Cinema and Media Studies*, *Velvet Light Trap*, *Transformative Works and Cultures*, and *Participations: Journal of Audience and Reception Studies*. Her work has been published in *East Asian Journal of Popular Culture* and *Mechademia: Second Arc*.

Katherine E. Morrissey is an Assistant Professor at Arizona State University. Her research focuses on representations of gender and sexuality in popular culture and the impacts of digitization on creative communities. Katherine has served as Review Editor for *Transformative Works and Cultures* and Communications Officer for the International Association for the Study of Popular Romance. Katherine's work has been published in the *Journal for Popular Romance Studies* and *Transformative Works and Cultures*.

Eve Ng is an Associate Professor and Associate Director of Graduate Studies in Media Arts and Studies and core faculty in Women's, Gender, and Sexuality Studies at Ohio University. Her publications include *Cancel Culture: A Critical Analysis* (Palgrave, 2022), *Mainstreaming Gays: Critical Convergences of Queer Media, Fan Cultures, and Commercial Television* (Rutgers UP, 2023), and numerous journal articles. She is an associate editor of *Communication, Culture & Critique*, and on the editorial boards of other journals.

List of Contributors

Celeste Oon is a PhD student in Cinema and Media Studies at the University of Southern California. Within the context of digital networks, she investigates how users negotiate power and intimacy, perpetuate discriminatory rhetoric, and develop platform-specific subcultures; she is especially interested in how these processes unfold in fan communities. Her work has been presented at conferences such as SCMS and PCA, and has appeared in *Transformative Works and Cultures*.

Rukmini Pande is an Associate Professor in Literary Studies at O.P Jindal Global University, India. She has been published in edited collections (*Wiley Companion to Media Fandom and Fan Studies* and *The Routledge Handbook of Popular Culture Tourism*) and peer reviewed journals (*Feminist Media History*, *Transformative Works and Cultures*). She has also published a monograph, *Squee From The Margins: Race in Fandom* (2018) and an edited collection, *Fandom, Now In Color: A Collection of Voices* (2020).

Alisa Perren is a Professor in the Department of Radio-TV-Film and Director of the Center for Entertainment and Media Industries at The University of Texas at Austin. She is co-editor of *Media Industries: History, Theory, and Method* (2009), author of *Indie, Inc.: Miramax and the Transformation of Hollywood in the 1990s* (2012), co-author of *The American Comic Book Industry and Hollywood* (2021), and co-founder and editorial collective member of the journal *Media Industries*.

Katharine Perrotta is an Associate Lecturer in Academic Language and Learning at Flinders University. Her PhD research is in the area of Screen and Media and explores the limits of lesbian representability in contemporary queer cinema, focusing on discursive constructions of industrial and authorial queerness. Her research interests also extend to contemporary fandom practices and digital media.

Aswin Punathambekar is a Professor at the University of Pennsylvania's Annenberg School for Communication, and Director of the Center for Advanced Research in Global Communication. His research and teaching address media and cultural change in post-colonial and diasporic contexts with a focus on South Asia and the South Asian diaspora. He serves as an editor of the peer-reviewed journal *Media, Culture and Society* and the Critical Cultural Communication series at NYU Press.

CarrieLynn D. Reinhard is a Professor in the Department of Communication Arts and Sciences at Dominican University. She is author, co-editor, and co-author of various articles, books, and book chapters regarding fan studies, audience studies, and reception studies, including *Fractured Fandoms: Contentious Communication in Fan Communities* (Lexington, 2018).

Olivia Johnston Riley is a graduate student in Media & Cultural Studies at the University of Wisconsin-Madison. They study disability and queerness in speculative media, as well as how fans of these media take up, interpret, and transform these texts.

Julie Levin Russo is a Member of the Faculty at The Evergreen State College, where she teaches media studies and arts in wide-ranging intensive or interdisciplinary contexts. Her research explores the collisions between media convergence, fan production, and remix culture and their reverberations within lesbian fan practices. Among numerous publications, she co-edited special issues of *Transformative Works and Cultures* on Fan/Remix Video (2012) and Queer Female Fandom (2017).

Anastasia Salter is a Professor of English and Director of Graduate Programs for the College of Arts and Humanities at the University of Central Florida, and the author of eight books that draw on humanities methods alongside computational discourse and subjects. This includes most recently *Playful Pedagogy in the Pandemic* (with Emily Johnson, 2022) and *Twining: Critical and Creative Approaches to Hypertext Narratives* (with Stuart Moulthrop, 2021).

Avi Santo is a Professor of Media Studies and Chair of the Department of Communication at the University of North Carolina at Chapel Hill. He is the author of *Configuring the Field of Character and Entertainment Licensing* (Routledge, 2023) and *Selling the Silver Bullet: The Lone Ranger and Transmedia Brand Licensing* (University of Texas Press, 2015).

Adrienne Shaw is an Associate Professor in the Department of Media Studies and Production, and a member of the Lew Klein College of Media and Communication Graduate Faculty, at Temple University. She is founder of the LGBTQ Game Archive and author of *Gaming at the Edge: Sexuality and Gender at the Margins of Gamer Culture* (University of Minnesota Press, 2014).

Sangita Shresthova researches digital fandom, participation, transmedia, and civic engagement. Her recent publications include three co-authored books: *Practicing Futures: The Civic Imagination Action Handbook*, *Transformative Media Pedagogies*, and *Popular Culture and the Civic Imagination: Case Studies of Creative Social Change*. Sangita is the Director of Research and Programs and a Co-PI of the Civic Paths Group at the University of Southern California where she oversees multiple initiatives that trace cultural and political participation.

Mel Stanfill is an Associate Professor with a joint appointment in the Texts and Technology Program and the Department of English at the University of Central Florida. Key focuses of Stanfill's work include fandom, platforms, and their intersection. They have published in *New Media and Society*, *Cultural Studies*, *Exploiting Fandom: How the Media Industry Seeks to Manipulate Fans* (University of Iowa Press, 2019), and *Fandom Is Ugly: Networked Harassment in Participatory Culture* (NYU Press, 2024).

Louisa Ellen Stein is an Associate Professor of film and media culture at Middlebury College. Louisa is the author of *Millennial Fandom: Television Audiences in the Transmedia Age* (University of Iowa Press, 2015) and co-editor of *A Tumblr Book: Platforms and Cultures* (University of Michigan Press, 2020), *Sherlock and Transmedia Fandom* (McFarland, 2012) and *Teen Television: Programming and Fandom* (McFarland, 2008). Louisa's work explores audience engagement in transmedia culture, with emphasis on cultural and digital contexts, gender, and generation. Louisa is mother of two fans, and in her spare time she edits fan video, video essays, and remix video.

List of Contributors

Tisha Turk directs the writing center at Grinnell College. Her fan studies scholarship has been published in *Transformative Works and Cultures*; *Music, Sound, and the Moving Image*; and *A Companion to Media Fandom and Fan Studies*. She has worked with the Organization for Transformative Works and the Electronic Frontier Foundation to win Digital Millennium Copyright Act exemptions granting vidders and other remix artists the right to break copy protection on media files.

Agnieszka Urbańczyk is a scholar working at the KEN University in Kraków, Poland. She received the "Diamond Grant" for her PhD project titled "Politics of the Science Fiction Genre in Fan Reception," and published a monograph on the subject in 2021. In her research, she focuses on political metaphors in science fiction and their fan reception.

Guillermo Aguilar Vázquez is a PhD student at Centro de Investigaciones y Estudios Superiores en Antropología Social (CIESAS – CDMX). His current thesis, "*Otakuology Mexican Style: Cultural Industry, Conventions, Fans, and Otaku Identity in Mexico City*," focuses on understanding how the consumption of anime and manga is redefined and appropriated by Mexican otakus, serving as the main driving force for establishing social relations and a sense of belonging and identity.

Kristen J. Warner is an Associate Professor in the Department of Performing and Media Arts at Cornell University. She is the author of *The Cultural Politics of Colorblind TV Casting* (Routledge, 2015). Kristen's research interests are centered at the juxtaposition of racial representation and its place within the film and television industries as it concerns issues of labor and employment.

Claire Whitley is an Associate Lecturer in Creative Arts at Flinders University. Her PhD research focused on gender and comedy in post-*Bridesmaids* Hollywood and examined the industrial response to heightened interest in media aligned with popular feminism. Her postdoctoral work has focused largely on fan practices in new media spaces and filmic backlash to heightened discourses of intersectional feminism in popular culture.

Rebecca Williams is an Associate Professor at the University of South Wales. She has published widely on media fandom, media tourism, and themed spaces. Her books include *Theme Park Fandom* (Amsterdam University Press, 2020), *Post-Object Fandom* (Bloomsbury, 2015), *Everybody Hurts: Transitions, Endings, and Resurrections in Fan Cultures* (University of Iowa Press, 2018), and *A Fan Studies Primer: Method, Research, Ethics* (University of Iowa Press, co-edited with Paul Booth, 2021).

Benjamin Woo is an Associate Professor of Communication and Media Studies at Carleton University (Ottawa, Canada). He is the author of *Getting a Life: The Social Worlds of Geek Culture*, co-author of *The Greatest Comic Book of All Time: Symbolic Capital and the Field of American Comic Books*, and co-editor of *The Comics World: Comic Books, Graphic Novels, and Their Publics*.

INTRODUCTION

Melissa A. Click and Suzanne Scott

As we finalized the table of contents for this second edition of *The Routledge Companion to Media Fandom* in the summer of 2023, media fan culture (and the pervasive coverage and theorization of it) was everywhere. Beyoncé fans circulated their favorite examples of the "Everybody on Mute" challenge from the *Renaissance* tour across social media platforms. Intergenerational audiences donned pink to attend screenings of the box-office smash of the summer, *Barbie*. The fan practice of designing and exchanging beaded friendship bracelets became so ubiquitous at Taylor Swift's Eras Tour that, by the fall of 2023, the Formula 1 United States Grand Prix in Austin, Texas had set up a booth for racing fans to make their own to share. Despite this moment of fannish ubiquity that spanned global audience demographics, journalists were quick to deem the summer of 2023 #BillionGirlSummer, referencing *Barbie*'s box office triumph and the unprecedented economic success of both Beyoncé's and Taylor Swift's summer tours.

In many ways, #BillionGirlSummer brings us back to some of the foundational foci and tensions of fan studies. As we noted in the first edition of this collection, many point to 1992 as the year that the field of media fan studies was officially established. Marked by the publication of Camille Bacon-Smith's *Enterprising Women: Television Fandom and the Creation of Popular Myth*, Henry Jenkins' *Textual Poachers: Television Fans and Participatory Culture*, and the edited collection *The Adoring Audience: Fan Culture and Popular Media*, edited by Lisa A. Lewis, the origins of fan studies can be traced back to a wide array of work within television studies, feminist media studies, queer theory, and (sub)cultural studies from the 1970s onwards. Fan studies represented a break from pre-existing work on audiences and reception on a number of key fronts: first, scholars actively sought to speak back to pathologized representations of fans within both journalistic and scholarly discourse (Jensen 1992). They accomplished this, secondly, by framing fans as resistant readers and media producers in their own right, focusing on both the communal and creative dimensions of fan culture. Third, and finally, this early work overwhelmingly focused on female fans, often suggesting that fan culture functioned as both a feminine and feminist space for commentary on popular media representations (Bacon-Smith 1992; Jenkins 1992; Penley 1992).

On one hand, #BillionGirlSummer might be read as a full circle moment, where the commercial value of women as a consumer group was finally acknowledged and feminized media objects were revalued as a result. Framed as an "undeniable triumph of women's creativity and ownership" as well as "the roaring return of big tent monoculture" by NPR commentator Bilal Qureshi (2023), #BillionGirlSummer seemed to mark a moment in which fandom had not only become fully mainstream, but *necessary* in an increasingly splintered media landscape: "Not a cruel, but a communal, collective, and yes, glorious summer." On the other hand, #BillionGirlSummer's emphasis on economic impact stands in contrast to some efforts within fan studies to focus on resistant or even explicitly anticapitalist modes of consumption. Emphasizing fans as impassioned consumers, first and foremost, reflects the growing centrality of fans as a desirable consumer bloc. While these tensions certainly existed in 2018 when the first edition of this collection was published, they have only become more prominent and complicated.

Accordingly, when it came time to choose the cover image for the second edition in 2024, we selected an iconic symbol of contemporary fan engagement: heart hands. In 2011, *The New York Times* described the gesture, which it noted was regularly flashed by young celebrities, as "a human version of those best-friends-forever lockets that break apart to be shared" (Meltzer 2011). The symbol is related to "finger hearts," popularized by K-pop and K-drama celebrities in the 2010s (Sharma 2023), through both gestures' expressions of love toward fans, and their regular use by celebrities and fans around the world. In 2011, as is the case in 2024, the heart hands gesture is largely attributed to Taylor Swift and her fans. *The New York Times* recounts how Taylor Swift used the gesture as a relatively unknown country singer trying to engage with her fans. Swift's first experience with the gesture was a positive one that encouraged her to continue using it: "she was in the middle of a song and decided to put her hands above her head in the heart shape. The crowd started doing it back and cheering" (Meltzer 2011). In 2024, of course, the gesture has become ubiquitous, appearing in advertising, reality and scripted programming, live events, and, of course, in social media. As an indication of its regular use, the heart hand became part of Unicode 14.0 and also became an emoji ("Heart Hands Emoji" n.d.) in 2021. Google even patented the heart hand gesture to allow users of wearable devices (like the now discontinued Google Glass) to make the gesture to "like" things in real life (and post your "like" to social media) (Vincent 2013). We believe the gesture's contemporaneity, along with its capacity to quickly connote the love, support, and connection in fan communities and between fans and their objects of affection, make it a worthy symbol of the cutting-edge work in our collection.

Our use of this gesture is not meant to obscure the ongoing friction between the profit-driven motivations of media producers to monetize what fans love, and fans' desires to consume, possess, and rework their favorite media. Likewise, we acknowledge the ongoing push and pull within and between fan communities which endures alongside the give and take between producers and fans over casting, social issues, and diverse representations. Since the first edition of this book was published in 2018, we have witnessed the emergence of numerous developments and controversies in the media landscape and in fans' responses to them. For instance, underscoring the maturation of the fanfiction-to-mainstream media pipeline (Morgan 2020) – and the growing influence and impact of fanworks – in 2019 Archive of Our Own (AO3), the Organization for Transformative Works' noncommercial and nonprofit hosting site for fanworks, won a Hugo award for "Best Related Work." Most notably, the Covid-19 pandemic and the resulting lockdown (beginning in March

2020) reshaped our habits of engagement with media and led to major changes in the popularity of the streaming industry and the social media platform TikTok. The widely shared video of the killing of George Floyd by Minneapolis police officer Derek Chauvin in May 2020, alongside the racial disparities made more visible by the pandemic, led to increased visibility for Black Lives Matter (BLM) and widespread reckonings around race in the United States and around the world. In the US, the Writers Guild of America and SAG-AFTRA struck for more than six months in 2023 to negotiate better pay and working conditions, and better job security in response to threats from Artificial Intelligence. Media fans' impactful and imaginative responses to industry changes and social and political injustices reflect that fandom's political project remains intact and that fan scholars will continue to have an abundance of topics and cases to explore into the future. Fans' political engagements also serve as reminders that fan studies scholars must push past comfortable topics and techniques to places that feel less familiar and less certain and that fan studies' task is to intervene in an already controversial, inevitably political endeavor involving emotion, identity, culture, and community.

As we noted in the introduction to the first edition, one of the primary challenges facing any effort to comprehensively cover the rapidly expanding and increasingly interdisciplinary field of fan studies is that, within our current "peak geek" media landscape, the definition of "fan" has become increasingly malleable and marketable in ways that are both necessary and productive, as well as potentially problematic. After all, who exactly qualifies as a "fan" once fan culture moves from the margins to the mainstream? Should the term be broadly used to describe anyone who is an avid, enthusiastic consumer of a media object (be it a television series, franchise, sports team, or celebrity)? Can someone who "lurks" in online discussions, following fan sites or celebrities on social media without engaging them directly be a "fan," or is active participation in a fan community (either digitally or through real-world events like meet-ups or conventions) required to claim that title? Is it simply anyone who claims that identity, describing themselves as a "fan?" Or, as many fan scholars suggest, is the designation of "fan" reserved for someone who moves beyond textual consumption to produce and circulate transformative fan works (such as fanfiction, fanvids, or fanart) in order to establish and strengthen fan communities of practice?

It is certainly not our intent to privilege any one definition of the term, and indeed one of our primary goals with the first edition was to interrogate efforts to delimit conceptions of fandom, fans, and fan practices. These challenges ranged from questioning the inherent limitations of focusing on overtly "participatory" or "productive" fans, to calls to expand the range of media objects and fan practices studied by fan scholarship. We also continue to believe that it is vital to maintain some conceptual differentiation between "fans" and "audiences" as an object of study. In other words, while many of the foundational binaries that the field of fan studies was built on have justifiably been challenged and dismantled over the past several decades, we need to be equally critical of abandoning the political valences of the term "fan" that accompanied these distinctions. This new edition further expands these efforts, most actively through the solicitation and inclusion of essays that move beyond Western fan cultures and objects.

Alongside the changing media landscape, fan studies has also grown and changed since 2018, as evidenced by the publication of a number of impactful collections such as Pande's (2020) *Fandom, Now in Color: A Collection of Voices*; Booth and Williams' (2021) *A Fan

Studies Primer: Method, Research, Ethics; and Kies and Connor's (2022) *Fandom, the Next Generation*. Our own projects on gender and convergence, *Fake Geek Girls: Fandom, Gender, and the Convergence Culture Industry* (Scott 2019), and anti-fandom, *Anti-Fandom: Dislike and Hate in the Digital Age* (Click 2019), have been published as well. As fan studies grows and matures, it is increasingly clear that no one collection can possibly represent all of the fields' long-standing foci and areas of innovation and development.

With this in mind, we have solicited 20 new chapters for this new edition and from the first edition we have included 11 revised chapters and 12 reprinted chapters. As in the first edition, this collection is designed to provide direction, explore fan studies' history and contributions, and to help shape this promising future by bringing together an internationally and interdisciplinarily diverse group of established scholars of media fandom to survey core concerns, evaluate the state of the field, and point to new directions of inquiry. This second edition contains 43 chapters that have been organized into four sections: Methods, Ethics, and Theoretical Approaches; Fan Practices and Platforms; Identities; and Industry and Labor. Each of the four sections begins with a short introduction that discusses the section's scope and contributions, and highlights the importance of the section's topic to fan studies. The section on Methods, Approaches, and Ethics seeks to fill the longstanding gaps in fan studies made by its resistance to conversations that could formalize methodological approaches and procedures; this revised section contains practical information for addressing methodological and ethical questions and also contains theoretical interventions and provocations for further developing the field. Recognizing that scholarship on transformative works is well-established in fan studies, the section on Fan Practices and Platforms explores established and emergent fan activities, and how these are shaped by the technological affordances and limitations of particular platforms, through a variety of case studies. The work contained in the section on Identities underscores the foundational and enduring influence of identity and representational politics on fan studies, and seeks to expand the range of familiar identity categories explored in the field with chapters on gender, sexuality, race and ethnicity, ability, nationality, and age. These chapters foreground questions of representation, inclusion, and exchange to offer models of exemplary scholarship. Finally, the section on Industry and Labor examines the power dynamics in fans' evolving relationships with media companies, workers, campaigns, and merchandise. Overall, we believe the collection will offer a wealth of innovative and diverse chapters on media fandom that will prove useful to students and scholars alike.

References and Further Reading

Abercrombie, N. and Longhurst, B. (1998). *Audiences: A Sociological Theory of Performance and Imagination*. London: Sage.

Bacon-Smith, C. (1992). *Enterprising Women: Television Fandom and the Creation of Popular Myth*. Philadelphia: University of Pennsylvania Press.

Baym, N. (2000). *Tune In, Log On: Soaps, Fandom, and Online Community*. Thousand Oaks: Sage.

Booth, P. and Williams, R. (eds.) (2021). *A Fan Studies Primer: Method, Research, Ethics*. Iowa City: University of Iowa Press.

Booth, P. (ed.) (2017). *A Companion to Media Fandom and Fan Studies*. New York: Bloomsbury.

Bury, R. (2005). *Cyberspace of Their Own: Female Fandoms Online*. New York: Peter Lang.

Click, M. (ed.) (2019). *Anti-Fandom: Dislike and Hate in the Digital Age*. New York: New York University Press.

Coppa, F. (2014). Fuck Yeah, Fandom Is Beautiful. *Journal of Fandom Studies* 2 (1): pp. 73–82.

Coppa, F. (2017). *The Fanfiction Reader: Folk Tales for the Digital Age*. Ann Arbor: University of Michigan Press.
Doty, A. (1993). *Making Things Perfectly Queer: Interpreting Mass Culture*. Minneapolis: University of Minnesota Press.
Fiske, J. (1989). *Understanding Popular Culture*. Boston: Unwin Hyman.
Geraghty, L. (2014). *Cult Collectors: Nostalgia, Fandom, and Collecting Popular Culture*. New York: Routledge.
Gray, J. and Sandvoss, C. and Harrington, C. (eds.) (2007). *Fandom: Identities and Communities in a Mediated World*. New York: New York University Press.
Gray, J. and Sandvoss, C. and Harrington, C. (eds.) (2017). *Fandom: Identities and Communities in a Mediated World (Second Edition)*. New York: New York University Press.
"Heart Hands Emoji" (n.d.). *Emojipedia*. https://emojipedia.org/heart-hands
Hellekson, K. and Busse, K. (eds.) (2014). *The Fan Fiction Studies Reader*. Iowa City: University of Iowa Press.
Hills, M. (2002). *Fan Cultures*. London: Routledge.
Howell, K. A. (2018). *Fandom as Classroom Practice: A Teaching Guide*. Iowa City: University of Iowa Press.
Ito, M. and Okabe, D. and Tsuji, I. (eds.) (2012). *Fandom Unbound: Otaku Culture in a Connected World*. New Haven: Yale University Press.
Jenkins, H. (1992). *Textual Poachers: Television Fans and Participatory Culture*. New York: Routledge.
Jenkins, H. (2006). *Convergence Culture: Where Old and New Media Collide*. New York: New York University Press.
Jenkins, H. (2007). *Star Trek* Rerun, Reread, Rewritten: Fan Writing as Textual Poaching. In *Fans, Bloggers, and Gamers: Exploring Participatory Culture*. New York: New York University Press.
Jensen, J. (1992). Fandom as Pathology: The Consequences of Characterization. In L. Lewis (ed.), *The Adoring Audience*, London: Routledge, pp. 9–29.
Kies, B. and Connor, M. (2022). *Fandom, the Next Generation*. Iowa City: University of Iowa Press.
Lewis, L. (ed.) (1992). *The Adoring Audience: Fan Culture and Popular Media*. London: Routledge.
Meltzer, M. (2011, 9 August). When Two Thumbs Down Are a Sign of Approval. *The New York Times*. www.nytimes.com/2011/08/11/fashion/hand-heart-gesture-grows-in-popularity-noticed.html
Morgan, E. (15 June 2020). Fan Fiction Goes Mainstream. *Medium*. https://medium.com/any-writers/fan-fiction-goes-mainstream-4069b6b674f
Pande, R. (ed.) (2020). *Fandom, Now in Color: A Collection of Voices*. Iowa City: University of Iowa Press.
Pande, R. (2018). *Squee from the Margins: Fandom and Race*. Iowa City: University of Iowa Press.
Penley, C. (1997). *NASA/Trek: Popular Science and Sex in America*. New York: Verso.
Penley, C. (1992). Feminism, Psychoanalysis, and the Study of Popular Culture. In Lawrence Grossberg, Cary Nelson, and Paula Treichler (eds.), *Cultural Studies*. New York: Routledge.
Qureshi, B. (14 August 2023). How three female artists lead this summer's billion-dollar pop culture revival. *NPR*. www.npr.org/2023/08/11/1193283472/barbie-taylor-swift-beyonce
Radway, J. (1984). *Reading the Romance: Women, Patriarchy, and Popular Literature*. Chapel Hill: Univ. of North Carolina Press.
Ross, S. and Stein, L. (eds.) (2008). *Teen Television: Essays on Programming and Fandom*. Jefferson: McFarland & Company.
Sandvoss, C. (2005). *Fans: The Mirror of Consumption*. Cambridge, UK: Polity.
Scott, S. (2019). *Fake Geek Girls: Fandom, Gender, and the Convergence Culture Industry*. New York: New York University Press.
Sharma, R. (2023, February 17). Finger hearts: Korean "love language" takes over the globe. *Times of India*. http://timesofindia.indiatimes.com/articleshow/97983285.cms?utm_source=contentofinterest&utm_medium=text&utm_campaign=cppst
Stanfill, M. (2024). *Fandom is Ugly: Networked Harassment in Participatory Culture*. New York: New York University Press.
Stein, L. (2015). *Millennial Fandom: Television Audience in the Transmedia Age*. Iowa City: University of Iowa Press.

Tulloch, J. and Jenkins, H. (1995). *Science Fiction Audiences: Watching Doctor Who and Star Trek*. London: Routledge.
Vincent, J. (18 October 2013). Google patents the heart hand-gesture to let you 'like' things with Glass. *The Independent*. www.independent.co.uk/tech/google-patents-the-heart-handgesture-to-let-you-like-things-with-glass-8887361.html
Williams, R. (2015). *Post-Object Fandom: Television, Identity, and Self-Narrative*. New York: Bloomsbury.

PART I

Methods, Ethics, and Theoretical Approaches

Introduction

Throughout its history, fan studies has been more focused on the analysis of fan communities and practices than on discussions of the methods, ethics, and theoretical approaches involved in the process of engaging fans and fandom through research. While fan studies scholars' protectivist orientation toward fan communities has made methods, ethics, and approaches a more prominent topic in conversations about scholarly practices (the September 2016 special issue of *Journal of Fandom Studies* and the 2021 book *A Fan Studies Primer*, are notable examples), the relative dearth of information about the methods of fan studies has made teaching challenging and learning to produce fan studies scholarship daunting. While we believe there is no true method, ethical stance, or theoretical approach one should adopt when studying fan cultures, the collection of chapters in this section raises important methodological, ethical, and theoretical considerations and discusses the kinds of information that can be gleaned about fandom when using particular tools and perspectives. Our hope is that these chapters will prove useful in the classroom as well as in the field.

This section contains two chapters reprinted from the first edition. Kristina Busse examines the ethics of studying fandom online; and through case studies and discussion of her own experience, she demonstrates the difficulties of crafting a universal list of best practices and underscores the need to continually evaluate the wealth of issues raised when studying fan cultures online. Using Sherlock Holmes fandom in East Asia as an example, Lori Morimoto asserts that the dearth of transnational scholarship in fan studies has resulted in an incomplete conceptualization of the complexities of fandom. The evidence that "ancillary" East Asian fans might have more official access to Benedict Cumberbatch than "central" UK and US fans strengthens Morimoto's claims that a greater engagement with transnational fandom and transnational scholarship can help fan studies develop a more expansive and sophisticated awareness of how fandoms emerge and circulate.

Additionally, this section includes two chapters from the first edition that have been revised and updated. Kathy Fuller-Seeley's discussion of historical fan practices reminds us that our knowledge of contemporary fans' relationships with media and celebrities are rooted in longstanding practices and orientations; through case studies and suggestions for finding historical evidence of fan practices, Fuller-Seeley argues that while the histories uncovered of previous fandoms will necessarily be partial, they are unquestionably valuable. Online surveys are the focus of Lucy Bennett's chapter, in which she considers the ethics, design, and distribution of this research tool through her own experiences; Bennett also offers suggestions to help improve representativeness and guide analysis of the data collected.

Finally, this section contains six new chapters. Rukmini Pande's chapter interrogates pervasive assumptions in fan studies through three case studies or "provocations," underscoring how all fandom is transcultural; overall, Pande demonstrates how scholars' lack of awareness about complex geopolitical issues in our contemporary global mediascape can have unanticipated impacts on fan studies scholarship. Next, pushing back on scholars' regular use of "fan" and "fandom" as nouns, Katherine Morrissey traces the development of the term "media fandom" to demonstrate how such terms reinforce biases and propagate false understandings in fan studies scholarship; Morrissey encourages scholars to break limiting habits and engage new terms and utilize more careful research practices to conceptualize "fan" as an active practice. Using Stuart Hall's "Encoding/Decoding" model as a starting point, Matt Hills encourages scholars to reconceptualize fans' decoding behaviors as practices that largely occur in real time with other fans through the continuous connectedness of social media; calling this decoding "multisocial co-decoding," Hills emphasizes that fan studies scholars must understand that fans often negotiate a text's meaning with other fans as well as with the text. Divya Garg connects fan and disability studies scholarship, insisting that the intersections where these research traditions meet provide a fruitful position from which to develop a transcultural, decolonial approach that can help fan studies scholars produce more thoroughly inclusive scholarship. Garg highlights the social model that conceptualizes disability as a social phenomenon, with attention to feminist disability studies and Crip theory. Anastasia Salter and Bridget Blodgett provide a primer on the ethical and logistical challenges of data scraping for preservation and discovery; their work includes a discussion of the need for cross-platform and multiplatform discourse analysis in our contemporary time of increased platform destabilization. Kishonna Gray, CarrieLynn Reinhard, and Adrienne Shaw conclude this section with an engaging conversation about the methods and ethics for studying "toxic" fans and fan practices. They discuss how they conceptualize toxicity in fan cultures; methods, challenges, and best practices for conducting research about toxic practices and communities; and advice for scholars embarking on this work with "toxic" research subjects.

For Further Reading

Anselmo-Sequeira, D. (2023). *A Queer Way of Feeling: Girl Fans and Personal Archives of Early Hollywood*, University of California Press, Berkeley.
AoIR. (2019). Internet Research: Ethical Guidelines 3.0. https://aoir.org/reports/ethics3.pdf
Barker, M. and Mathijs, E. (2012). Researching world audiences: The experience of a complex methodology. *Participations*, 9 (2), 664–698.
Bennett, L. (2014). Tracing textual poachers: Reflections on the development of fan studies and digital fandom. *Journal of Fandom Studies*, 2 (1), 5–20.
Bennett, L., Chin, B., and Jones, B. (2016). Between Privacy, Ethics, Fandom and Social Media: New Trajectories That Challenge Media Producer/Fan Relations, in A. Davisson and P. Booth (eds.) *Controversies in Digital Ethics*, Bloomsbury Press, London: pp. 107–122.

Busse, K. and Hellekson, K. (2012). Identity, Ethics, and Fan Privacy, in K. Larsen and L. Zubernis (eds.) *Fan Culture: Theory/Practice*, Cambridge Scholars Publishing, Newcastle: pp. 38–56.

Butsch, R. (2000). *The Making of American Audiences: From Stage to Television, 1750–1990*, Cambridge University Press, Cambridge.

Clemons, A. (2019). Enabling/disabling: Fanfiction and disability discourse. *Canadian Journal of Disability Studies*, 7 (3), 247–278.

Dervin, B. and Foreman-Wernet, L. (2003). *Sense-Making Methodology Reader: Selected Writings of Brenda Dervin*, Hampton Press, New York City.

Dirth, T. P. and Adams, G. A. (2019). Decolonial theory and disability studies: On the modernity/coloniality of ability. *Journal of Social and Political Psychology*, 7 (1), 260–289.

Dym, B. and Fiesler, C. (2020). Social norm vulnerability and its consequences for privacy and safety in an online community. *Proceedings of the ACM on Human-Computer Interaction*, 4 (CSCW2), 1–24.

Fazel, V. M. and Geddes, L. (2022). *The Shakespeare Multiverse: Fandom as Literary Praxis*, Routledge, New York.

Fowler, F. (2014). *Survey Research Methods*, 5th ed., Sage, London.

Fuller, K. (1996, 2001). *At the Picture How: Small-Town Audiences and the Creation of Movie Fan Culture*, Smithsonian Institution Press, rpt. Charlottesville, University of Virginia Press, Washington.

Garg, D. (2025). *Fandom and Disability: Global Fan Cultures and Marvel Superhero Fandom*, University of Iowa Press, Iowa Press.

Gray, J., Sandvoss, C. and Lee Harrington, C. (eds.) (2007). *Fandom: Identities and Communities in a Mediated World*, NYU Press, New York.

Hannell, B. (2024). *Feminist Fandom: Media Fandom, Digital Feminisms*, and Tumblr, Bloomsbury Academic, New York.

Hills, M. (2016). From Para-Social to Multisocial Interaction: Theorising Material/Digital Fandom and Celebrity, in P. David Marshall and Sean Redmond (eds.) *A Companion to Celebrity*, Wiley Blackwell, Malden: pp. 463–482.

Hine, C. (2000). *Virtual Ethnography*, Sage, London.

Jenkins, H. (1992). *Textual Poachers: Television Fans and Participatory Culture*, Routledge, New York.

Kwon, J. (2019). *Straight Korean Female Fans and Their Gay Fantasies*, University of Iowa Press, Iowa City. https://muse.jhu.edu/pub/165/monograph/book/64359

McDonald, T. and Lanckman, L. (eds.) (2019). *Star Attractions: Twentieth-Century Movie Magazines and Global Fandom*, University of Iowa Press, Iowa City.

McLelland, M., Nagaike, K., Suganuma, K., and Welker, J. (eds.) (2015). *Boys Love Manga and Beyond: History, Culture, and Community in Japan*, 1st ed., University Press of Mississippi, Jackson.

Pande, R. (2018). *Squee from the Margins: Fandom and Race*, University of Iowa Press, Iowa City.

Reinhard, C. D., Stanley, D., and Howell, L. (2021). Fans of Q: The stakes of QAnon's functioning as political fandom. *American Behavioral Scientist*, 66 (8). https://doi.org/10.1177/00027642211042294

Rouse, L., Condis, M., and Stanfill, M. (2024). Making fandom great again: Silencing discussions of racism in reactionary and transformative fandoms. *Popular Communication*. https://doi.org/10.1080/15405702.2024.2336254

Sannon, S. and Forte, A. (2022). Privacy research with marginalized groups: What we know, what's needed, and what's next. *Proceedings of the ACM on Human-Computer Interaction*, 6 (CSCW2), 1–33.

Wanzo, R. (2015). African American acafandom and other strangers: New geneaologies of fan studies. *Transformative Works and Cultures*, 20. https://doi.org/10.3983/twc.2015.0699

1
THE ETHICS OF STUDYING ONLINE FANDOM

Kristina Busse

Introduction: Fans First

Like many acafans of my generation, I came to fandom studies by being a fan first, and that model has remained my central ethical guideline. I engage with fandom as a participant–observer, who reveals her academic and fan status, and I share my academic writing in stages with not only my fannish friends but also anyone I reference or cite. If there is any conflict between the academic and the fannish self, the simple plan goes – the academic has to give way. In fact, when Karen Hellekson and I founded the first fan studies journal, *Transformative Works and Cultures* (TWC) in 2007, we established an editorial attribution policy that emphasized fannish community standards over traditional humanities conventions. In the submission policies, we "strongly recommend … that permission be obtained from the creator for any fan work or blog post cited in a submitted article" and encourage authors not to use direct URLs for fan blog sites. Two years later, we expanded and explained our decision in "Fan Privacy and TWC's Editorial Philosophy" (Hellekson and Busse 2009), which laid the groundwork for our "Identity, Ethics, and Fan Privacy" (Busse and Hellekson 2012). The reasons for this were manifold, but foremost it was TWC's affiliation with the fan advocacy nonprofit Organization for Transformative Works and our own identification as fans.

And yet there have been times when my clear moral imperative of "fans first" did not fully cover the intricacies of a given situation. After all, even with underlying guidelines of always placing other fans and fandom spaces first, our roles as fans, academics, teachers, and political and social beings, may interfere with and affect one another in ways that might not be immediately obvious. So, while the perceived objective neutrality of outside observers has clearly been shown to be erroneous (Clifford and Marcus 1986; Gertz 1988), being an academic insider creates its own difficulties – from our access and the way fans may engage with us, to specific text choices and the frameworks we chose to analyze them.

DOI: 10.4324/9781003373025-3

We may use pseudonyms and attempt to fully occupy different subject positions, but it behooves us as scholar fans and fan scholars to remain aware of all our various identities and how they may affect our fan engagement. Likewise, a decade later, I am not certain any more that our policy of encouraging, if not mandating, permission should be upheld, or whether an even more flexible set of recommendations might be needed.

In the following, I look at the ethical dilemmas ethnographic researchers face and how these debates translate into online fan studies research. My brief overview and discussion of human subject research illustrates how utilitarian approaches often harm the already most vulnerable, which indicates the superiority of clear rules like the ones endeavored by Internal Review Boards (IRBs). Nevertheless, such strict rules ultimately fail to fully account for the complexities of online interactions and the long-term involved role of participant observers that fan studies researchers occupy. Using case studies and personal experiences, I suggest that even personal imperatives can become detrimental when a strict set of rules fails in specific situations. The Association of Internet Researchers' (AoIR) ongoing concern about online ethical engagements offers a framework in which fan researchers can and should negotiate their own positions with their subjects, friends, and fellow fans. Shifting focus from universal rules to the particular situations of fan scholars and their interactions and relationships, this nod toward virtue ethics thus acknowledges the complexities and expanse that compound contemporary online fan studies research.

Overview: Ethical Concerns in Online Fan Studies

Whereas most earlier ethics guidelines remained restricted to anthropology and sociology, the Internet and its textual quality of social interactions and communications forced humanities scholars to confront ethical concerns (Thomas 1996; Ess 2002; Lotz and Ross 2004; McKee and Porter 2009; Whiteman 2012). AoIR's 2012 ethical guidelines point out how researchers have to take into account their own particular research situations and establish their own guidelines. Many of the rules governing IRBs do not apply to the online environment, which makes it all the more important to adapt the rules accordingly. Valuing flexibility over universality, the AoIR describes how "ethical decision-making interweaves one's fundamental world view (ontology, epistemology, values, etc.), one's academic and political environment (purposes), one's defining disciplinary assumptions, and one's methodological stances" (2012: 3). Fan studies scholars likewise draw from various disciplines, occupy a range of research positions, and employ diverse methodologies, all of which affect how they can successfully yet conscientiously study and engage fandom.

Potential Harm

Any discussion of ethical research must address the most infamous failures: medical research, such as the Nazi atrocities that initiated the Nuremberg Code and the Tuskegee syphilis experiments; social research, such as Stanley Milgram's 1963 obedience study (Herrera 2013), Laud Humphreys's 1970 tearoom trade research (Babbie 2004) and Philip Zimbardo's 1971 Stanford prison experiment (Zimbardo, Maslach, and Haney 2000); and, online research, such as Marty Rimm's 1995 cyberporn findings (Lee 2000) and the 2014 Facebook emotional contagion experiment (Hunter and Evans 2016). All these experiments caused bodily or emotional harm through the researchers' deceptive and manipulative behavior and the human subjects' lack of autonomy and consent.

While anything less than these notorious failures may feel safe, fan studies research bears its own potential exposure and jeopardy; like many other anthropological inquiries into subcultures and online communities, it must negotiate specific relationships, community norms, and disciplinary expectations. Fans have long feared legal and moral persecution: they often operate in a legal grey zone when they manipulate and transform copyrighted material owned mostly by big studios, and they often push the boundaries of local morality that frowns upon explicit sexuality, especially its non-normative versions. As a result, drawing attention to a vidding community in an academic essay may expose all its members to greater risk. Meanwhile, citing a fan story and directly linking to its author's site may expose that fan to unwanted scrutiny – they may have revealing details in other posts on their blog that they don't expect more than a handful of people to read, or their wallet name may be attached to their web site. While a cease and desist letter or a DMCA notification or a reprimand from one's boss may not be major issues, it is nevertheless harm that would not have occurred otherwise, and it behooves researchers to do their best to avoid putting any fan into such a position.

Informed Consent

One way to solve this issue is to require informed (and continuous) consent from all participants, but there are multiple types of scenarios where that is difficult. Online research often deals with anonymous or pseudonymous subjects, where consent cannot be verified. Historical research may not be able to track down current identities, which complicates consent. Finally, there is a place for covert research in cases where consent may not be possible yet the research is valuable and important (van Amstel 2013; Spicker 2011). Foregrounding an awareness of not abusing one's role as authority figure nor purposefully manipulating the subjects, informed consent needs to establish a modifiable ethical framework that challenges the less flexible IRB guidelines (Haggert 2004). Here more than anywhere, it is important to not follow a utilitarian ethics where the good of the many outweighs the good of the few, but "balance the rights of subjects (as authors, as research participants, as people) with the social benefits of research" (AoIR 2012: 5).This advice constitutes a basic mandate to remain considerate of the harm research can cause, and this potential harm applies both to the communities in general and to individual subjects.

Text or People

In qualitative online research, there are two specific concerns that complicate the ability to establish and evaluate potential harm an ethnographic researcher has to confront: one is the question whether online evidence ought to be viewed as a textual document or as an utter- ance by the person who wrote it; the other is the question whether a given online space, especially on social media sites, is public or private. Given that much of online interaction (at least before Tumblr) was textual and the focus of much of fan studies was on fan fiction, acafans were confronted with two opposing academic research models: whereas psychology and sociology would demand that studying online fandom be regarded as human subject research, language and art studies would instead see all openly accessible publications as texts. Shorthanded as "text or people," this debate remains central in terms of what ethical approach researchers should take (Whiteman 2012: 81–115). If online texts are testimonies of human research subjects, researchers need IRB permissions with informed consent, and even pseudonyms should be redacted. If online texts are artistic artifacts, however, researchers must properly cite them and acknowledge authorship.

Fan scholarship cannot easily separate the two, however: journals on LiveJournal, Dreamwidth, or Tumblr, often mix political and cultural commentary, episode reviews, fan works and personal narratives, which makes it difficult to determine when a researcher is dealing with a fan work or an intimate personal account. Whereas a story can easily be seen as an artistic creation whose author must be named (thus contradicting the sociological approach of offering researcher-chosen pseudonyms or offering quotes without authorial attribution), a personal anecdote might easily demand the inverse (thus contradicting a literary approach in which all text must be properly attributed). Not naming the fan of a text they authored may devalue the work and the person in ways that can be as unethical as exposing them and their community can be. In fact, the same journal entry may contain the public and the private: the fan work that must be cited and the personal information that must be protected.

Public versus Private

Accordingly, scholars studying online fan communities are often confronted with a model of semi-public spaces and expectations of privacy that are unlike many other online public blogs and forums (Whiteman 2012: 47–80). As AoIR explains, "Individual and cultural definitions and expectations of privacy are ambiguous, contested, and changing. People may operate in public spaces but maintain strong perceptions or expectations of privacy" (2012: 7). As we describe in "Identity, Ethics, and Fan Privacy" (Busse and Hellekson 2012), there are a complex set of circumstances as to why many online fan fiction communities have established expectations of privacy unlike those in regular publishing. In particular, we use the concept of "layered publics" to discuss the way fans often understand a shared fan space to be private even when it is accessible and thus public.

Fandom spaces have mostly thrived on limited access and clear community rules: from the pages of zines and con spaces, to mailing lists with list moms, interaction has often been controlled and self-policed. Unlike large areas of the Internet that publish with the intent to reach the widest audience possible, many, if not most, fans go to great lengths to control access. Many mailing lists are access restricted, archives often use spider and robot blocks, LiveJournal offers a complex system of controlling access, and fans gratefully employ all these features in varying degrees. Even as fan fiction has mainstreamed, fans often continue to want to limit and control access, both to secure the ability to delete their work if desired or necessary and, possibly, to retain its contextual framing within a fannish community (Busse 2017).

Moreover, across many fan fiction fandoms, the unspoken yet carefully policed rule has remained that fans can safely assume that their fannish pseudonyms remain separate from their wallet name. Even as fandom as a whole has become more public, privacy of personally identifying markers remains a central part of the fannish ethos. Where even a decade ago, fans still passionately debated the dangers of sharing their fan works openly, these discussions have all but become meaningless with central archives like AO3 and the shift to Tumblr as a popular fannish media platform. And yet, even on Tumblr, fans have created specific rules that indicate to their community that a certain post should be understood as private and not be re-blogged. Thus, fan scholars need to remain ever vigilant as they draw attention to particular fan works, especially when these exist in spaces (such as blogging platforms and social networking sites) where fans have an expectation of privacy due to the semi-public nature of their blogs and the mixing of public and personal material.

Caveat: Complicating Ethical Imperatives

The "fans first" position is one I've held for over 15 years, and it has mostly served me well. Yet, as fandom mainstreams and fannish platforms change, I contemplate my role as fan and academic, as canon creator and historian. Specifically, I return yet again to the ethics of how to study and publicly discuss fans, fan works, and fan communities. There are practical and theoretical reasons why a policy of always getting permission can be difficult. Moreover, with our role as embedded observer and our dual identification as fan and academic, it is important to confront the drawbacks of potential bias and conflict of interest. Confronting these questions is important to our research and, as a result, vital to the proper representation of our communities.

Access and Permission

Absence of proof is not proof of absence, and fan studies research that relies on textual evidence (as opposed to interviews or surveys) faces ephemeral interfaces and disappearing sites. Domains expire, stories get removed and blogs deleted, and vids and other fan works are taken down for supposed DCMA infringement. Furthermore, the pseudonymous nature of fandom often means that fans change their names and cannot always be tracked even if they remain in fandom. A hard permission rule effectively limits discussions and may exclude older fandoms, ideas, and discussions. 20-year-old mailing list posts and personal emails from the 1990s may long have been deleted or lost from one computer to another. LiveJournal posts get locked, accounts deleted and, with them, not only do fannish artifacts disappear but entire conversations and debates surrounding them. Even current conversations can be difficult to track and cite. Many blogging platforms with their expansive forking structures are anti-archival as are Tumblr and Twitter with their purposefully ephemeral interfaces.

To give just one example: for more than a decade, Fandom Wank functioned as archive and fannish commentary for disagreements and infighting in media fandom (Hellekson 2010; Lothian 2012). It was first founded on LiveJournal in 2002 and, after its deletion and several intermediary sites, found its home on the fannish LiveJournal fork, JournalFen. As of 2016, its site, as well as the one hosting the Fandom Wank wiki, have been down; years of detailed accounts of fannish wank have mostly disappeared. Even if a fan researcher had saved some of these discussions and descriptions, it might be nearly impossible to get permission. In fact, permission involving older stories or conversations can be quite difficult to obtain: fans leave fandom or pass away; they change pseudonyms or email addresses; or they merely don't answer emails or asks. In fact, as fandom continues to mainstream, its sense of subcultural identity with its mandate for secrecy changes. Some of the older fannish norms do not apply any longer – if they ever did.

Even where fans can be reached, the exchange in question may have been emotionally draining; in fact, looking back, some may want to forget or may even feel deeply embarrassed by their positions. The question for us as fan scholars then becomes whether we should simply ignore any potentially contentious topics and should limit our discussion to the quotes and references we can obtain. Or should the desire to establish a proper account of fandom and fannish history overrule an individual fan's privacy choices. For example, I recently wrote about the debates abbreviated as Haiti!Fail that were in response to an actor slash story set in the immediate aftermath of the devastating 2010 Haiti earthquake. Not only did the deaths of hundreds of thousands of Haitians become the backdrop for the fictional love affair of two white Americans, but the story was published mere months after the disaster and illustrated with photo manipulations that included actual images from the earthquake aftermath. Comments by hundreds of fans over dozens of journals took the story and its author to task for its ignorant premise and racist representation, its offensive setting and dehumanizing characterizations and its linguistic and metaphorical stereotyping. The author took down her journal and erased her online identity. Even if Haiti!Fail were not worth discussing in its own right, it was part of a changing attitude toward issues of race and ethnicity within media fandom and, as such, part of an important fannish event. Yet, even if I could track down the author, I doubt I would receive an answer, let alone permission.

Access and full immersion, moreover, create an entirely different sort of conundrum I've often thought of as the "fannish uncertainty principle": the more embedded fans are within a given fan community and are privy to its potential secrets, the less likely they are to want to write about it and to divulge those secrets, entwined as they are in personal interactions.

Being immersed in the inner workings of a group may give a scholar some of the personal motivations about why certain events happen in specific ways; at the same time, community loyalty or personal friendship ties may encourage the scholar to not share those insights. Many a canon debate or aesthetics disagreement or ethical kerfuffle may cover (or at least become entangled with) a cheated lover, roommate trouble, or financial disagreement. As amazingly supportive as fandom can be, both as an abstract creative community and as a personal emotional and intellectual support group, it also contains all the petty, mean, even vicious ways in which fans – like all humans – can interact. It is difficult for researchers both to separate out the personal from the fannish and to remain aware of their own personal feelings.

Personal Bias

Even when we consciously monitor our feelings about fannish topics and our relationships with other fans, it is important to acknowledge the personal bias and involvement as fans and how that affects our choices, and opinions. Given that access and permission are often difficult to obtain, it is all too easy to stick close to home, cite one's friends and acquaintances, and trust their sources, quotes, and recollections. Moreover, it is difficult to fully address how to use material that we have helped create. Of course, within autoethnographic reading it is possible to directly address this issue and theorize one's own subject position and fannish creation (Willis 2006; Farley 2013). In other cases, however, it is difficult to separate fannish and academic selves. I use quotes from discussions in which I participated because I know they exist, but I can't be sure what aspects of a discussion might have been triggered by my own comments. Likewise, I don't know if a specific story is the perfect example for one of my ideas, because it indeed was written in response to my own comments.

In a field like fandom studies the sheer wealth of material, the speed and ephemerality of information and the seeming endless number of fannish online spaces alone mean that any research is limited by definition to what the author knows, has access to and, frankly, is interested in. If we had world enough and time, we might be able to do comprehensive research on one archive, one fandom, one genre, but even then, at the very moment we concluded the study, dozens if not hundreds of new stories would be there the very next day. Choice and selection matters deeply, however. There is a tendency among acafans to showcase the richness and creativity of fandom by presenting the interesting and creative while sidestepping many of the more problematic issues and infighting. Moreover, as acafans we sometimes lean toward specific texts, not only because they may be popular and appealing to our academic value system, but also because we tend to be immersed in a community that is predisposed to academic discourses. This may limit the choices from which we draw, even when we discuss the fan works and fannish events with a clear eye to our personal biases.

Conflict of Interest

Likewise, performing my writing process in public can create dilemmas. Keeping the essays visible to all fans cited and giving them veto rights makes the work more collaborative and open. And yet, given the value fans place on participating in fannish conversation, I double my academic work with fannish contributions. There has been more than one backlash to not only the outside observer fan but also, specifically, the acafan. The criticism is twofold: acafans can oppress other fans by using their educational privilege and rhetorical abilities, and acafans deploy their fannish networks and friends to further their academic publications. While acafans do not profit financially, we do improve our scholarly reputation which, in turn, may affect employment and promotion. This does not mean necessarily that we are exploiting fandom and should stop researching it. It does mean, however, that we should not dismiss fannish discomfort and remain aware of potential privileges and rewards.

Ultimately, every acafan has to balance costs and benefits, but it is important not to ignore personal fannish and academic gains. In *Fangasm* (2013), Kathy Larsen and Lynn Zubernis recollect their interactions with other academics, fans and "The Powers That Be" (TPTB). In particular, they describe how their particular position gained them status with both the production team (as scholars) and in fandom (as people with access) even as they discuss with brutal honesty what it cost them: "the fence we were straddling between being fangirls like our friends and trying to do research (which, let's face it, was about being an insider as much as writing a book) led yet to more problems" (2013: 111–12). Their personal account reveals the sometimes not so noble motivations (in and out of fandom) all of us have at times, as well as the costs Larsen and Zubernis suffer, including the loss of marriage, fannish friends and a book deal with TPTB.

Meanwhile, other fan studies scholars have likewise advocated an approach that does not treat fannish utterances (or, even more problematic, only some fannish utterances) as in need of special protection. Instead they consider all public utterances as texts and therefore citable, the way journalists and most users treat the Internet. Anne Jamison (2015), for example, argues that "fannish practice/tradition doesn't dictate [her] pedagogy." She points out, however, how her selections try to minimize risk, readily admitting that "[t]here are many competing ethical and professional obligations." Francesca Musiani (2011) likewise addresses various theoretical concerns, namely that it places fan research apart from other forms of ethnography, giving the fan community undue power compared to other researched communities and restraining necessary analysis and potential criticism. Moreover, in so doing, it reshapes the researcher/research subject boundaries and singles out fan communities. As the AoIR guidelines illustrate, protecting communities is not restricted to fan studies, but it is worth acknowledging the complex situation fan researchers find themselves as they negotiate texts and people in semipublic spaces, and as they must confront their own biases.

Conclusion: Collectivity and Comprehensiveness

In the end, all of these theoretical concerns are ever present to fan researchers as they balance responsibility both to the fans and to the scholarship, to the community and some arbitrary sense of truth. I continue to revisit them as my positions as fan and as researcher change, and as the fields of online fandom and fan research grow and transform. Natasha Whiteman calls for a "localised production of ethical stances" (2012: 139), and this seems to be a better approach than trying to establish and impose universal guidelines even just for ourselves. Ideally, I want to correspond with all my sources and get explicit permissions for everything I discuss and cite, but as I've shown, there are both theoretical and practical concerns. I want to be an advocate for fandom and showcase its aesthetic achievements, but given that the subdiscipline is more than two decades old, it is more than time to add more critical voices, to look at the good and the bad.

Like feminist and queer studies, fan studies often makes the personal political and academic. Using personal narratives and experiences to argue theoretical points, it often acknowledges if not celebrates the fact that scientific objectivity can only ever be a falsehood, that any observation, description, and theory always carries the imprint of the researchers themselves. So, it may be that the solution is a form of self-awareness and autoethnography (Hills 2002; Monaco 2010; Driscoll and Gregg 2010), and I tried to model such an approach in this article. Or possibly the solution for fan studies scholarship must be envisioned not as an individual but a collective one: just like fan fiction at its best is deeply intertextual not only with the source text but with other stories and meta conversations, fan studies is a collective endeavor, where every article and book is but one part, where all of us create a growing body of research together (Hellekson and Busse 2006). Our different methodological and disciplinary roots, our different ethical approaches and degrees of embeddedness are not a drawback but rather a strength. Drawing from scholars with different interests and biases allows us to look at the same event from varying perspectives, to illuminate strange texts and small fandoms and to collectively contribute to a theory (and ethics) of fan studies.

References

AoIR (2012) "Ethical Decision-making and Internet Research 2.0: Recommendations from the AoIR Ethics Working Committee," http://aoir.org/ethics/.

Babbie, E. (2004) "Laud Humphreys and Research Ethics," *International Journal of Sociology and Social Policy* 24(3–5), pp. 12–19.

Boyd, D. (2014) *It's Complicated: The Social Lives of Networked Teens*. New Haven: Yale University Press.

Busse, K. (2017) "Intimate Intertextuality and Performative Fragments in Media Fanfiction," in J. Gray, C. Sandvoss and C. L. Harrington (eds.) *Fandom: Identities and Communities in a Mediated World*, 2nd edition. New York: NYU Press.

Busse, K. and Hellekson, K. (2012) "Identity, Ethics, and Fan Privacy," in K. Larsen and L. Zubernis (eds.) *Fan Culture: Theory/Practice*. Newcastle: Cambridge Scholars Publishing, pp. 38–56.

Clifford, J. and Marcus, G. E. (eds.) (1986) *Writing Culture: The Poetics and the Politics of Ethnography*. Berkeley, CA: University of California Press.

Driscoll, C. and Gregg, M. (2010) "My Profile: The Ethics of Virtual Ethnography," in E. Probyn and C. Evers (eds.) "Researching Intimate Spaces," special issue, *Emotion, Space and Society* 3(1), pp. 15–20.

Ess, C. (ed.) (2002) "Internet Research Ethics," special issue, *Ethics and Information Technology* 4(3).

Farley, S. K. (2013) "Translation, Interpretation, Fan Fiction: A Continuum of Meaning Production," *Transformative Works and Cultures* 14, http://dx.doi.org/10.3983/twc.2013.0517.

Freund, K. and Fielding, D. (2013) "Research Ethics in Fan Studies," *Participations* 10(1): 329–34, www.participations.org/Volume%2010/Issue%201/16%20Freund%20Fielding%2010.1.pdf.

Gertz, C. (1988) *Works and Lives: The Anthropologist as Author*. Stanford, CA: Stanford University Press.

Haggerty, K. D. (2004) "Ethics Creep," *Qualitative Sociology* 27(4), pp. 391–414.

Hellekson, K. (2010) "History, the Trace, and Fandom Wank," in H. Urbanski (ed.) *Writing and the Digital Generation: Essays on New Media Rhetoric*. Jefferson, NC: McFarland, 58–69.

Hellekson, K. and Busse, K. (2006) "Work in Progress," in K. Hellekson and K. Busse (eds.) *Fan Fiction and Fan Communities in the Age of the Internet*. Jefferson, NC: McFarland, pp. 5–32.

Hellekson, K. and Busse, K. (2009) "Fan Privacy and TWC's Editorial Philosophy," *Organization for Transformative Works*, http://transformativeworks.org/projects/twc-citation.

Herrera, C. (ed.) (2013) "Stanley Milgram and the Ethics of Social Science Research," special issue, *Theoretical & Applied Ethics* 2.2.

Hills, M. (2002) *Fan Cultures*. London: Routledge.

Hunter, D. and Evans, N. (eds.) (2016) "Facebook Special Issue," *Research Ethics* 12(1), pp. 2–52.

Jamison, A. (2015) "Since I and my class have been cited," *Tumblr*, February 23, http://annejamison.tumblr.com/.

Larsen, K. and Zubernis, L. (2013) *Fangasm: Supernatural Fangirls*. Iowa City: University of Iowa Press.

Lee, J. H-S. (2000) "Cyberporn: The Controversy," *First Monday* 5(8), http://firstmonday.org/issues/issue5_8/li/index.html.

Lothian, A. (2013) "Archival Anarchies: Online Fandom, Subcultural Conservation, and the Transformative Work of Digital Ephemera," *International Journal of Cultural Studies* 16(6), pp. 541–56.

Lotz, A. D. and Ross, S. M. (2004) "Toward Ethical Cyberspace Audience Research: Strategies for Using the Internet for Television Audience Studies," *Journal of Broadcasting and Electronic Media* 48(3), pp. 501–12.

McKee, H. and Porter, J. (2009) *The Ethics of Internet Research: A Rhetorical, Case-Based Process*. New York: Peter Lang.

Monaco, J. (2010) "Memory Work, Autoethnography and the Construction of a fan-Ethnography," *Participations* 7(1), pp. 102–42, www.participations.org/Volume%207/Issue%201/monaco.htm.

Musiani, F. (2011) "Editorial Policies, 'Public Domain,' and Acafandom," *Transformative Works and Cultures*, 7, doi:10.3983/twc.2011.0275.

TWC Editor (n.d.) "Submissions," *Transformative Works and Cultures*, https://journal.transformativeworks.org/index.php/twc/about/submissions.

Thomas, J. (1996) "A Debate about the Ethics of Fair Practices for Collecting Social Science Data in Cyberspace," special issue, *Information Society* 12(2), doi:10.1080/713856145.

van Amstel, H. (2013) "The Ethics and Arguments Surrounding Covert Research," *Social Cosmos* 4(1), pp. 21–26.

Whiteman, N. (2012) *Undoing Ethics: Rethinking Practice in Online Research*. New York: Springer.

Willis, I. (2006) "Keeping Promises to Queer Children: Making Space (for Mary Sue) at Hogwarts," in K. Hellekson and K. Busse (eds.) *Fan Fiction and Fan Communities in the Age of the Internet.* Jefferson, NC: McFarland, pp. 153–70.

Zimbardo P. G., Maslach, C. and Haney G. (2000) "Reflections on the Stanford Prison Experiment: Genesis, Transformations, Consequences," in T. Blass (ed.) *Obedience to Authority: Current Perspectives on the Milgram Paradigm.* Mahwah, NJ: Lawrence Erlbaum, pp. 193–237.

2
WHAT DOES THE "TRANSNATIONAL" MEAN FOR FAN STUDIES TODAY? SOME PROVOCATIONS

Rukmini Pande

It is always an honor to be invited to be part of edited collections such as this one, which seek to, and I take the liberty of quoting from the email I received from the editors here, "establish the core concerns, evaluate the state of the field, and point to new directions of inquiry." It was initially suggested that I contribute to the focus area of "transcultural fandom." As I have previously argued that *all* fandom is transcultural (Pande 2021a), I decided to use this space to think through some of the effects the usage of these categories have had on the core concerns and current state of the field. Further, what new directions of enquiry could open up if these categories are questioned and what that could mean for fan scholars in practice. I have therefore taken the opportunity presented by this volume to pose a series of interconnected methodological provocations that touch on key issues in fan studies as I conceive of them today.

Before I go further, I would like to acknowledge that all such categorizations are always imperfect and that I have wrestled with the problematics of them myself many times, as they hold the power of definition. However, as I noted in *Squee From The Margins*, the category of transcultural fandom as a whole is a persistent one and usually signifies that the fan cultures under discussion are, "outside the dominant paradigm that grants certain texts and fandoms canonicity, either by geographic location or language, or both" (Pande 2018a: 6). Multiple scholars, both within this volume and outside of it have complicated this assumption, but the ways in which the category continues to circulate is still significant. I argue that this is illustrative of two aspects – firstly, that the default for "universal" fans and fandoms remains located in the Global North, and secondly, that even when non-anglophone fans and fandoms gain attention of the discipline, it is only because certain cultural products, be they media texts or individual celebrities, are seen to be somehow exceptional and set apart from their larger generic or industrial context. However, this rarely leads to sustained interest as academic attention moves on quickly. This cycle was seen in the context of the uptick of interest in Chinese Danmei texts (webnovels featuring intimate relationships between male characters and their television adaptations) amongst anglophone fans during the height of the pandemic. This led to a bit of a rush of publications and conference panels but those remained focused on the texts that were the most popular, with less attention being paid to the larger complex history of the genre in the region.

Further, due to the sectioning off of these fandoms, scholarship on them is rarely seen to be relevant to broader conceptualizations of the discipline and such work rarely attains canonicity within the bibliographies and reading lists of the field. I am underlining this pattern because not only does it exemplify a bias within the field that should be corrected from an ethical and equity-based perspective, but it also has significant material implications for the capacity of the discipline to reflect and anticipate trends in contemporary fan cultures. To cite an example, a few years ago, when the K-Drama *Squid Game* (2021) was taking the world by storm, I was in conversation with a noted scholar of the field who was surprised by the global popularity of South Korean media products. To me this was quite a concerning gap of knowledge as the Hallyu wave is far from recent and has extremely crucial lessons for all fan scholars on broad-ranging issues from fan tourism to the integration of fanfiction platforms like Wattpad into corporate branding (Khan 2021; Hur and Kim 2020). But such a knowledge gap is perhaps an inevitable product of the siloing of fan studies focus areas that I have been discussing so far.

My first provocation therefore argues that it is vital that fandom scholars understand the interconnectedness of the global mediascape that fans inhabit and increase their knowledge of platforms outside of those that have been perhaps over-surveyed in existing scholarship. I will demonstrate this through an examination of how complex geopolitical issues had an impact on fan organizations such as the Organization of Transformative Works (OTW) located in the Global North. My second provocation focuses on the need for existing models of fan identity that address intra-fandom conflict such as anti-fandom studies to seriously account for evolving patterns of fan communities deflecting structural critique of issues such as systemic racism by framing such work as efforts to censor and police fanwork by "fandom antis." Finally, my third provocation argues that all fan communities today are interfacing explicitly with deeply entrenched, globalized, and networked social formations amplifying fascist politics including white supremacy, racism, gender-essentialism, xenophobia, religious fundamentalism, enthnonationalism, and neocolonialism amongst many others. While fandom scholars are surely aware of these issues, their study of them continues to set up binaries between "progressive" and "reactionary" fandoms, thus missing how a larger cultural shift to the right is expressing itself through social justice rhetoric. I examine this through the global circulation and framing of the US television show *Sense 8* (2015–18) and the Tamil language film *RRR* (2022). Each case study offers concrete steps that fan scholars can take to decenter the Global North and whiteness from their own choice of methodology. This includes diversifying their data sets, questioning assumptions of inherent political progressiveness about certain fan spaces, and digging further into narratives that posit that discussions about systemic racism in fandom are equivalent to censorship. It must be said here that these are all recommendations that have already been made multiple times by critical fan scholars (Johnson 2019; Pande 2020a). The challenge remains, as ever, for fandom studies as a field to take them seriously.

(Dis)connected Networks

My first provocation addresses the question of how researchers choose to frame their work with regards to mediascapes that are both increasingly networked and fragmented at the same time. The transmission of media texts across borders and languages has always been a site of fandom activity through scanlations, fan-subs, and other types of media sharing, but the advent of transnational streaming platforms has introduced both increased accessibility and corporate control. In terms of fan activity, the mainstreaming of fandom means that there is greater knowledge of and participation in fandom activities previously assumed to be subcultural, such as the creation of fanwork such as fanfiction. At the same time, there has been a decline of fandom-specific hosting sites for fanwork, leading to the rise of centralized sites such as the Archive of Our Own (AO3) and Wattpad. At the same time, there are less shared communitarian norms around fanfiction's production, hosting, dissemination, and monetization. While there has always been conflict in fanfiction communities, the operations of algorithmically driven social media platforms mean that these points of rupture have greater visibility in contemporary fan cultures. In such a mediascape, researchers must also have greater awareness of not just their chosen fan communities, but how participants are interacting with broader fandom debates and discussions. As these are often dispersed across multiple platforms, researchers also must be aware of silos of discussion and dominant framings of contentious issues, often generated and sustained by algorithms that incentivize conflict. The lack of broader context and acceptance of certain established truisms with regard to fandom operations can result in scholarship scrambling to catch up to important developments or controversies, or worse, ending up mischaracterizing them in our work.

To give one illustration, much of established fan studies research has focused on fan platforms popular in anglophone fandoms, from mailing lists to sites such as Livejournal and Dreamwidth, and more recently Tumblr and Twitter (now regrettably known as X), along with dedicated fanwork-hosting platforms such as the AO3 which is run by the Organization of Transformative Works (OTW). In the case of the latter, the fan-run and fan-led site has long been perceived as outside of corporate interests and as a hospitable environment for fans from diverse backgrounds (Fiesler 2019). This has meant that it has received less critical commentary than hosting platforms such as Wattpad or Kindle Worlds. Simultaneously, knowledge of sites that host fanwork which are popular with non-anglophone fans such as Weibo are seen as relevant only to scholars working on those particular fandoms. However, in contemporary fan cultures it is vital to be attentive to ways in which conversations and conflicts around fanwork content play out across assumed transnational boundaries as these are extremely permeable.

An example of how research boundaries based primarily on language use or geographical location do not stand up to scrutiny is the AO3 itself. There has been a long history of differential language use within fandom communities even on the assumed "Western" platforms. The AO3 now allows posting of fanwork in over 70 languages but has had to make repeated revisions to its sorting and tagging systems as the original "default" language was English (Archive of Our Own 2019) which has become increasingly unwieldy. While the AO3 has long been the main site used for research on English language fanwork (primarily fanfiction) produced in various fandoms, the politics of its own infrastructure and decision-making with regards to issues of language use, hosted content, and targeted harassment has been given less attention. As mentioned previously, the AO3 being run by fans has historically shielded it from critical enquiry but between 2020 and 2023, several non-white volunteers, on whose labor, specifically in translation and tag wrangling, the site depends, have brought up patterns of racism they have faced within the organization (dhobikikutti 2023a, 2023b).

These patterns concern amongst other things, decisions that had the potential to impact volunteers from mainland China, such as adding language options (specifically Cantonese and Tai-gi) which could be politically sensitive topics without due consultation with said volunteers and also responding to their concerns around the matter with dismissal (dhobikikutti 2023c). To expand briefly, language use is a politically sensitive matter in mainland China and individuals have faced consequences for any activity that is deemed to be significant in that regard (Davidson 2023; Shen 2022). Another issue identified involved the AO3 operating and then shutting down an account on Weibo, allegedly without sufficient information and consultation with volunteers (end-otw-racism 2023). While it is not within the scope of this chapter to discuss all the intricacies of the incident, I argue that it exemplifies why fan scholars who choose to work on fanfiction today need to be aware of issues rooted in transnational and transcultural geopolitics, language use, and platform policy as those can have significant and unanticipated ramifications for their research. More generally, it also points to how fans and fandoms historically seen to be separate entities, are interfacing in multifaceted ways. This is perhaps most obvious in fandoms marked as transcultural such as K-pop, but, as I hope the brief example I have given above has proven, assuming that scholarship on these dynamics is not relevant to fan studies as a discipline decreases its ability to be at the forefront of analyzing significant cultural shifts.

Fandom Killjoys and the Undermining of Anti-racism Efforts

My second provocation builds on the first and addresses the dynamics of conflict mentioned therein more closely. I am particularly interested in the figure of the fandom "anti" which now plays a significant role in online fandom discourse. This figure differs from what has so far been conceptualized by scholars working on anti-fandom, who have largely located their studies in specific fandoms and their anti-objects (Click 2019; Burkhardt, Trott, and Monaghan 2022). Unlike an anti-fan of a particular object, the generic term anti designates an individual who is seen to fundamentally oppose fandom pleasure in general, and more specifically wishes to police and censor the production of fanworks, attempting to impose their definition of appropriateness on popular character pairings, or ships, in various media texts. The anti is also seen to be aggressive and prone to personal harassment of fanwork creators and unable to distinguish between fiction and reality and their arguments are always seen to be in bad faith (Romano 2023).

A disturbing aspect of the mobilization of this figure is the increasing identification of anti-racist critique as part of what is perceived as anti behavior. In my most recent work (Pande 2024), I argue that this is a dangerous mischaracterization as it seeks to deflect from and delegitimize a larger historical critical tradition in fan spaces as anti-racist critique in fandom has been documented for as long as fandom spaces have existed. Further, the individuals examining those issues, for the most part, are longtime participants, well aware of fandom etiquette and mores around fanwork production and reception. Indeed, in most cases, these fans are also engaged in the production of fanwork of various kinds, including those dealing with taboo erotic themes. This is also reflected in the sample of fans that I have interviewed for my larger project on the issue.

The rise in combativeness in fandom spaces over the last ten years has been noted by multiple scholars, including Morimoto's (2015) conceptualization of fandom as a series of "contact zones," Mel Stanfill's (2020) examination of "reactionary fandom," and Renee Barnes' (2022) analysis of Facebook discourse. This is also in line with broader trends in internet spaces with polarization being the new norm. As already addressed, conflicts over characterization, shipping practices, and fanwork itself are also not new, as thoroughly documented (Bothe 2014; Brennan 2014; Freund 2010). Other scholarship in the area has also found that the term anti is applied extremely broadly, frequently including critical fans who are highlighting the operations of systemic issues in fandom such as racism, sexism, ableism, homophobia, transphobia, etc. (Editor 2022).

The animating focus of my research so far has been to make visible the role of race and racial identity in anglophone online media fandom as well as within the discipline of fan studies itself (Pande 2018a, 2020b). I have also discussed the effects of institutional whiteness on fan studies methodologies and publication processes (Pande 2021b). One of my primary arguments remains that issues of race/ism, particularly around Black characters, interrupt broadly held assumptions about media fandom spaces as uniformly politically progressive, offering a special refuge to fans from marginalized identities. It was in the context of these arguments that I formulated the figure of the fandom killjoy (Pande 2018a: 13), based on Sarah Ahmed's (2010) discussion of the feminist killjoy. This was conceptualized as a position that critical fans of color were often forced into when discussing racism in fan spaces. At the time, I did not place the fandom killjoy within the domain of anti-fandom studies as the fans I was discussing certainly did not identify as being against any media text or other fan object.

However, with an increase in polarization in fandom spaces, I now must note that what was a theoretical construct is being increasingly concretized, and further weaponized, by fandom discourses that seek to other and undermine fans who are vocal about ideas of race and racism within them. That is, fans vocal about systemic racism are routinely suspected to be actively seeking to police fandom pleasure as their primary goal. This is part of a perceptible rise in polarization in fandom spaces around issues of racist fanwork, micro- and macro-aggressions against vocal fans of color (especially Black fans) who identify problems in fandom spaces, and a concerted push to undermine any critiques of the same which seek to highlight the workings of systemic racism, rather than individual issues by "bad" actors (Stitch 2020). This is a vital aspect of contemporary fan cultures, once again reflected across assumed transnational and transcultural boundaries that fan scholars need to be informed about in order to understand how discussions around race/ism are being weaponized in different ways.

This also brings me to my third provocation, which concerns the importance of understanding that the shift in global geopolitics towards rightwing majoritarianism is also being negotiated in fan cultures and communities, including those communities which have been historically assumed to be hostile to such political positioning. This is also because of the ways in which majoritarian communities globally are leveraging the language of progressive movements in the Global North to legitimize their actions. While these may seem like issues that are not directly pertinent to fan scholars, I hope to show that, in actuality, researchers of these communities are often in front row seats, as it were, to the operations of these rightwing dynamics as they are very evident in fandom.

Shifting Meanings

My previous work (Pande 2018a) has held up the hope for solidarity and coalition-building around the category of "fans of color" in fandom spaces, pointing to a longer legacy of similar work led by critical fans around events such as RaceFail '09 (Klink 2010). I continue to believe in the power and vital importance of such coalition-building but want to reiterate that identifying and dismantling structural white supremacy is extremely difficult work and requires sustained effort. It does not begin or end with the personal identity of individuals. The power of whiteness operates in many ways including the co-option of marginalized voices and identities. Further, it is vital to understand the increasing role of majoritarian political ideologies (often rooted in ethno-nationalism) in the global mediascape. Fan communities being transnational and transcultural have always been and continue to be profoundly influenced by these dynamics.

Fandom spaces and communities have been demonstrably proven to be powerful arenas for civic participation ranging from pushing for changes in specific media properties, to broader socio-political mobilization. While initially optimistic about the progressive potential of such activity, recent scholarship has also taken into account the reactionary elements in these spaces. This is an extremely important step. For instance, to take up Mel Stanfill's (2020) work in more detail, they list a set of "jarring questions" in the introduction of a special issue on "Reactionary Fandom" which is a good summation of the concerns of this branch of scholarship. They ask, "What can we understand about reactionary politics by examining them through the lens of fandom? Should Gamergate be understood as the beginning of the alt-right? Do models of gift economies in fan fiction help us understand the production and circulation of conspiracy theories on YouTube? Can sexism be understood as fanon? Is white supremacy a fandom?" (Stanfill 2020: 2). These are all extremely interesting provocations and the special issue's scope includes a case study of fanfiction-based fandom by Anastasia Salter (2020). This also connects to Poe Johnson's (2019) earlier perceptive questioning of fanworks' troubled relationship with the Black body. However, taken together with other work in the same area, there continues to be a noticeable skew towards either using the tools of fandom studies to examine explicitly white supremacist organizations like the MAGA movement or QAnon in the US, or interrogating fandoms with observably reactionary elements in the majority such as Gamergate or sports fandoms (Johnson 2020; Lobinger et al. 2020; Miller 2020; Reinhard et al. 2021). I am not trying to minimize the importance of this work but rather underline that it's equally vital for scholars to understand more covert forms of white supremacy and other forms of majoritarianism operating in fandom spaces assumed to be resistant to such ideas.

I argue that while the question of white supremacy *as a fandom* is one that has been taken up by many scholars, the presence of white supremacist structures in progressive media fandom is now well evidenced but less examined. Indeed, I would go further to state that the backlash against anti-racist efforts in these spaces, by branding them as censorship and policing of fannish pleasure, is actually gaining ground because it is couched in the language of social justice. These are extremely complex issues and the need for scholars to be aware of these global power dynamics has never been more urgent. To expand on an example, many fandom scholars and commentators saw the mobilization of K-pop fandoms around the 2020 BLM protests in the US as a potentially politically transformative act. However, a more detailed analysis has shown those fandoms to be as marked by anti-Blackness as any others (Chaudhry 2020; Omolade 2021). To put this in another way, we cannot come to broad conclusions about the politics of any space, even one with a majority of individuals from marginalized identities, without sustained engagement and granular analysis.

This also extends to fandom spaces engaged in the consumption and creation of queer content, which has often functioned as a kind of shorthand for scholars, almost automatically designating those participants as having a larger progressive politics. However, in a world where queerwashing and homonationalism (Puar 2007) are extremely powerful forces, shaping everything from foreign policy to media texts, to fan reactions, we need a more robust and critical theoretical approach. To give an example relevant to my current geopolitical location, the fandom of the US television series *Sense 8* (Netflix, 2015–18), created and directed by the Wachowski siblings, had all the markers of a queer and racially diverse space which might have been expected to result in a politically progressive fan community. However, the series itself had some extremely disturbing narrative threads, including one centered on India which reinforced dominant Hindu nationalist beliefs. These same beliefs, now very much the mainstream, have pushed the country further and further into authoritarianism. The storyline in the show itself did not generate much debate or protest within the fandom, precisely because it was framed within a queer utopic universalist frame which made locale-specific critique difficult to explain or sustain.

Today, any effort to critique Hindu nationalism locally or internationally is framed (erroneously) as colonialist and racist. The larger co-optation of postcolonial and decolonial theorization by ethnonationalist movements has not remained in the domain of politics but rather, is very much part of discourses in contemporary fandom communities. This pattern was also visible in the narrative around the global success of *RRR* (2022), a Telugu-language Indian film directed by S. S. Rajamouli and set during India's independence struggle. While the overt narrative is anti-colonialist, the film also has significant amounts of Hindutva messaging which was largely lost on North American audiences who were more focused on the over-the-top action sequences and usage of songs within the film. While these elements are far from unique in South Indian film traditions, as Rajmouli himself pointed out, the role of social media was key in building hype for *RRR* as offering a unique moviegoing experience to viewers new to the genre (Abrams 2023). While there were efforts to critique the film for its leveraging of religious and caste markers, these remained limited in their impact as fan narratives remained celebratory of the success of an Indian film in the US market, which has been previously disdainful of such productions. The success of the film on the awards circuit – it won an Oscar and a Golden Globe for Best Song and got nods for best non-English film from several other organizations – was also seen as a triumph by Hindutva leaders such Indian Prime Minister Narendra Modi. The narratives around *RRR* are important for fan scholars to understand because they underline the necessity of locating the complex power relations of media texts in multiple contexts. *RRR* could be rightfully hailed as an example of South Indian cinema getting global recognition for the genre, thus aiding South Asian representation at US award shows and by extension opening new opportunities for underrepresented filmmakers and actors. However, at the same time, its implications vis-à-vis the larger Hindutva project of erasing India's diverse cultural and social history for a Hindu-centric narrative, also being executed via large scale changes to school and college syllabi amongst other measures, cannot be ignored (Wire Staff 2021). This is also relevant in light of the rise of Hindutva organizations aiming to influence politics in the US itself (Masih 2021).

The point I wish to make through these provocations is that while transnational fandom spaces (which is all of fandom) continue to function as points of connection and enjoyment for fans from marginalized backgrounds, scholars must push beyond single-lens understandings of political and social affiliations in a rapidly evolving global mediascape. Fan studies must move beyond a shallow perception of intersectionality merely as a politics of citation or representation into the conditions it enables and the contexts it functions within. My aim in this chapter was to question pervasive assumptions that continue to structure fandom studies methodologies. I did this by pointing out the need for fandom scholars to cultivate broader knowledge of geopolitical events outside of their core interests, to be aware of the ongoing weaponization of fandom identity politics in intra-fandom conflicts, and to urge the critical examination of the use of social justice structures in the fan positioning of certain texts from the Global South. I have previously strongly advocated for scholars to "decolonize" fan studies methodologies by taking seriously the institutional whiteness embedded in the discipline, including aspects like what it deems to be essential scholarship, appropriate methodologies, and ethical standards amongst many other structural issues (Pande 2018b, 2020a, 2021c, 2021b). I continue to believe that this is vital, but also acknowledge that such calls must contend with the reality of "decolonization" either remaining a buzzword, employed to pay lip service to claims of academic openness to debate and inclusion while institutions work to push out and silence dissenting voices (Dhillon 2021), or worse, it being branded as part of a "genocidal" project by vastly powerful individuals like Elon Musk (Gopal 2023). In my view, global fan cultures will only become more fraught as political polarization continues to escalate. It is therefore of immediate importance that fan scholars broaden their horizons so that they are better prepared to produce accurate and ethical scholarship in increasingly troubled times.

References

Abrams, S. (2023) "The Man Behind India's Controversial Global Blockbuster 'RRR'", *The New Yorker*, 16 February.
Ahmed, S. (2010) "Feminist Killjoys (And Other Willful Subjects)", *Polyphonic Feminisms: Acting in Concert*, Vol. 8 No. 3.
Barnes, R. (2022) *Fandom and Polarization in Online Political Discussion: From Pop Culture to Politics*, Palgrave Macmillan, Basingstoke.
Bothe, G. (2014) "'If Fandom Jumped Off a Bridge, It Would Be Onto a Ship': An Examination of Conflict That Occurs Though Shipping in Fandom", presented at the Australia and New Zealand Cultural Association Annual Conference, Melbourne.
Brennan, J. (2014) "'Fandom is Full of Pearl Clutching Old Ladies': Nonnies in the Online Slash Closet", *International Journal of Cultural Studies*, Vol. 17 No. 4, pp. 363–380, doi: 10.1177/1367877913496200
Burkhardt, E., Trott, V. and Monaghan, W. (2022) "'#Bughead Is Endgame': Civic Meaning-Making in Riverdale Anti-Fandom and Shipping Practices on Tumblr", *Television & New Media*, SAGE Publications, Vol. 23 No. 6, pp. 646–662, doi: 10.1177/15274764211022804
Chaudhry, A. (2020) "Black K-Pop Fans Continue to Face Racism Online", *The Verge*, 24 July, available at: www.theverge.com/2020/7/24/21335831/kpop-racism-fans-black-lives-matter-harassment (accessed 31 May 2023).
Click, M. A. (2019) *Dislike, Hate, and Anti-fandom in the Digital Age*. New York, New York University Press.
Davidson, H. (2023) "Hong Kong: Cantonese Language Group Shuts Down after Targeting by National Security Police", *The Guardian*, 29 August.

Dhillon, S. (2021) "An Immanent Critique of Decolonization Discourse", *Philosophical Inquiry in Education*, Canadian Philosophy of Education Society, Vol. 28 No. 3, pp. 251–258, doi: 10.7202/1085079ar

dhobikikutti. (2023a) "Racism within the OTW", 29 July, available at: https://dhobikikutti.dreamwidth.org/135655.html (accessed 25 February 2024).

dhobikikutti. (2023b) "Letter to the 2023 Board of Directors of the Organization for Transformative Works", 13 June, available at: https://dhobikikutti.dreamwidth.org/134130.html (accessed 25 February 2024).

dhobikikutti. (2023c) "Demand for Suspension of OTW Board Member", 26 July, available at: https://dhobikikutti.dreamwidth.org/135023.html (accessed 25 February 2024).

Editor, T. (2022) "What is an Anti? Exploring a Key Term and Contemporary Debates", *Transformative Works and Cultures*, Vol. 37, doi: 10.3983/twc.2022.2277

Fiesler, C. (2019) "Why Archive of Our Own's Surprise Hugo Nomination Is Such a Big Deal", *Slate*, 9 April.

Freund, K. (2010) "I'm glad We Got Burned, Think of All the Things We Learned": Fandom Conflict and Context in Counteragent's" Still Alive", *Transformative Works and Cultures*, Vol. 4.

Gopal, P. (2023) "Is Decolonization 'Genocide'? Let's See.", Medium, 22 November, available at: https://zen-catgirl.medium.com/is-decolonization-genocide-lets-see-de91184cb8af (accessed 25 February 2024).

Hur, J. and Kim, T. (2020) "Understanding Contraflow Pop-Culture Tourism: The Case of Transnational Fandom of South Korean Pop-Culture and the 'Hallyu' Tourism", *Journal of Tourism Insights*, Vol. 10 No. 1, doi: 10.9707/2328-0824.1101

Johnson, P. (2019) "Transformative Racism: The Black Body in Fan Works", *Transformative Works and Cultures*, Vol. 29, doi: 10.3983/twc.2019.1669

Johnson, P. (2020) "Playing with Lynching: Fandom Violence and the Black Athletic Body", in *Television & New Media*, Sage Publications Sage CA, Los Angeles, CA, Vol. 21 No. 2, pp. 169–183.

Khan, A. (2021) "HYBE comments on fans' concerns regarding adult fan fictions on Wattpad", 6 November, available at: www.sportskeeda.com/pop-culture/news-hybe-comments-fans-concerns-regarding-adult-fan-fictions-wattpad (accessed 15 August 2023).

Klink, F. (2010) "RaceFail: Race and the Fantastic", *MIT Comparative Media Studies/Writing*, 17 May, available at: http://cmsw.mit.edu/racefail-race-and-the-fantastic/ (accessed 20 July 2016).

Lobinger, K., Krämer, B., Venema, R., and Benecchi, E. (2020) "Pepe–Just a Funny Frog? A Visual Meme Caught Between Innocent Humor, Far-Right Ideology, and Fandom", *Perspectives on Populism and the Media: Avenues for Research*, Nomos Verlag, Vol. 7, p. 333.

Masih, N. (2021) "Under Fire from Hindu Nationalist Groups, U.S.-Based Scholars of South Asia Worry About Academic Freedom", *Washington Post*, 2 October.

Miller, L. (2020) "'Wolfenstein II' and MAGA as Fandom", *Transformative Works and Cultures*, Vol. 32.

Morimoto, L. (2015) "Fandom in/as Contact Zone", *The Fan Meta Reader*, 28 May, available at: https://thefanmetareader.org/2015/05/28/fandom-inas-contact-zone-by-tea-and-liminality/ (accessed 25 August 2016).

Omolade, T. (2021) "When Black K-Pop Fans Are Terrorized Online, Who Listens?", *Refinery29*, 21 March, available at: www.refinery29.com/en-us/2021/03/10180347/black-k-pop-fans-doxxed-harassed-cyber-bullying (accessed 31 May 2023).

Pande, R. (2018a) *Squee from The Margins: Fandom and Race*, University of Iowa Press, Iowa City.

Pande, R. (2018b) "'Who Do You Mean by "Fan"?' Decolonizing Media Fandom Identity", in Booth, P. (Ed.), *A Companion to Fandom and Fan Studies*, Wiley-Blackwell, Oxford, pp. 417–434.

Pande, R. (2020a) "How (not) to Talk About Race: A Critique of Methodological Practices in Fan Studies", *Transformative Works and Cultures*, Vol. 33, doi: 10.3983/twc.2020.1737

Pande, R. (Ed.) (2020b) *Fandom, Now in Color: A Collection of Voices*, University of Iowa Press, Iowa City.

Pande, R. (2021a) "Global Fandom: Rukmini Pande (India) – Pop Junctions", *Pop Junctions: Henry Jenkins*, 12 October, available at: http://henryjenkins.org/blog/2021/9/12/global-fandom-rukmini-pande-india (accessed 26 January 2024).

Pande, R. (2021b) "Naming Whiteness: Interrogating Fan Studies Methodologies", in Booth, P. and Williams, R. (Eds.), *A Fan Studies Primer*, University of Iowa Press, Iowa City.

Pande, R. (2021c) "Framing Fandom History: The Effects of Whiteness on Memorialization Rukmini Pande / O.P. Jindal Global University – Flow", *Flow: A Critical Forum and Media and Culture*, 16 October, available at: www.flowjournal.org/2021/11/framing-fandom-history/ (accessed 5 June 2022).

Pande, R. (2024) "'Get Out of Here You Anti': Historizing the Operation of Structural Racism in Media Fandom", *Feminist Media Histories*, Vol. 10 No. 1, pp. 107–130, doi: 10.1525/fmh.2024.10.1.107

Puar, J. K. (2007) *Terrorist Assemblages: Homonationalism in Queer Times*, Duke University Press, Durham.

Reinhard, C. D., Stanley, D., and Howell, L. (2021) "Fans of Q: The Stakes of QAnon's Functioning as Political Fandom", in *American Behavioral Scientist*, SAGE Publications Inc, p. 00027642211042294, doi: 10.1177/00027642211042294

Romano, A. (2023) "Puritanism took over online fandom – and then came for the rest of the internet", *Vox*, 23 May.

Salter, A. (2020) "#RelationshipGoals? Suicide Squad and Fandom's Love of 'Problematic' Men", *Television & New Media*, SAGE Publications, Vol. 21 No. 2, pp. 135–150, doi: 10.1177/1527476419879916

Shen, X. (2022) "TikTok Sibling App in China Cuts Off Influencers Speaking in Cantonese", *South China Morning Post*, 5 October.

Stanfill, M. (2020) "Introduction: The Reactionary in the Fan and the Fan in the Reactionary", *Television & New Media*, Sage Publications Sage CA: Los Angeles, CA, Vol. 21 No. 2, pp. 123–134.

Stanfill, M. (2020) "Special Issue: Reactionary Fandom", *Television & New Media*, Sage Publications, Vol. 21 No. 2, pp. 123–217.

Stitch. (2020) "Anti What, Exactly?", *Stitch's Media Mix*, 11 April, available at: https://stitchmediamix.com/2020/04/11/anti-what-exactly/ (accessed 31 May 2023).

Wire Staff. (2021) "UGC's New Draft History Syllabus Plays Up Mythology, Faces Allegations of Saffronisation", The Wire, 23 March, available at: https://thewire.in/education/ugcs-new-draft-history-syllabus-plays-up-mythology-faces-allegations-of-saffronisation (accessed 20 August 2023).

3
(MEDIA) FANDOM IS NOT A NOUN

Katherine E. Morrissey

The phrases "media fandom" and "fandom" can be found scattered across the pages of fan studies scholarship. Fandom and media fandom are terms used to describe both a community and a range of physical and virtual spaces associated with this community – fan conventions, mailing lists, and social media platforms. In *Enterprising Women* (1992) Camille Bacon-Smith talks of a "road to fandom" and explains that the word, fandom, represents community (1992: 7). In *Textual Poachers* (1992) Henry Jenkins introduces media fandom as an "identifiable grouping of enthusiasts" and a "recognizable subculture" (1992: 1). Fans share histories of "finding fandom," talk about being "in" or "out" of a fandom, or joke about being "from fandom." These constructions are common among scholars and fans. The problem is, a fixed form of media fandom, media fandom as a singular community or a knowable space, no longer exists.

This chapter problematizes the use of terms like fandom and media fandom as singular nouns. I approach this issue three ways: first, by outlining media fandom's historic use as a label for physical/virtual spaces associated with transformative fan practices.[1] Second, by tracing media fans' migration from offline to online platforms like LiveJournal and Archive of Our Own. Finally, by building on Rukmini Pande's (2018) concept of "fandom algorithms," I argue that constructing media fandom as a noun has become an algorithm for bias within fan and scholarly networks.

Today, media fandom no longer exists as a discretely identifiable community. Today, the idea of fandom as a single culture/space is an illusion, one that can be problematically manipulated. Currently, media fandom exists as a broad range of global practices, interests, individuals, networks, and norms. This shift from a knowable community towards dispersed networks was facilitated by digital technologies, the changing economics of media industries, and broad cultural shifts associated with media convergence. These global technological, industrial, and cultural changes require a rethinking in fan scholarship and methods. We need to interrogate our use of these terms to understand their limitations today. Reconceptualizing fandom as a verb or set of practices helps fan scholars begin distinguishing between the media fandom of the past and the many dispersed fan networks and practices existing today.

The Emergence of the *Term* Media Fandom

Media fan histories have been documented in limited ways. Bacon-Smith's *Enterprising Women* (1992) and *Science Fiction Culture* (2000), Joan Verba's *Boldly Writing* (1996), Francesca Coppa's "A Brief History of Media Fandom" (2006), and Anne Jamison's *Fic* (2013) all offer glimpses of American, Western, and/or English-language media fan histories. Edited by Mark McLelland et al., the anthology *Boys Love Manga and Beyond* (2015) gives us a peek at media fan histories in Japan. More recently, Jungmin Kwon provides a history of South Korean fans in *Straight Korean Female Fans and Their Gay Fantasies* (2019).

In English-language publications, most of the "history" of media fandom is centered around American/Western fan networks and has been focused on specific subsets of media fans. With this issue in mind, I want to maintain a distinction between histories of media fans (plural) and the idea of *a* history of media fandom or fanfiction (singular). We need to be careful of conflating the history of the term "media fandom" with all the various networks and practices described as media fandom today. To do this, we need to understand how the term media fandom initially emerged.

Until the 1960s, networks of American/Western science fiction fans were relatively small.[2] Their focus was primarily on *written* science fiction and less on film or other *media*. The popularity of media like *Star Trek* brought new fans and interests into the existing network. This, in turn, led to tensions between traditional and incoming fans. In 1972, a group of *Star Trek* fans "tired of being ignored and/or patronized at the regular science fiction conventions" organized the first Star Trek Lives! convention in New York ('STAR TREK LIVES --- AGAIN!!!' 1973). Cons like these, coupled with *Star Trek* fanzines and fanclubs, meant that *Star Trek* fans had their own gathering points and communication networks. These networks overlapped heavily with already established networks of science fiction fans. However, they also allowed parallel networks and practices to emerge. One of these practices was fanfiction.

Fanfiction began to appear in English-language *Star Trek* fanzines in the 1960s (Jamison 2013). While fanfiction pre-dates *Star Trek*, it took off among *Star Trek* fanzines. Early fanfiction was controversial. The stories were not always romantic or sexual, but a notable amount of early fanfiction was. *Star Trek* fanfiction also seemed to be reorienting the focal points of science fiction. Action and conflict were "located around issues of emotion and trust and sex" and male characters were "feminized to access a greater demonstration of feeling" (Bacon-Smith 2000: 113). Some argue that the science fiction elements were secondary or unnecessary for these fans, at least in comparison to the focus on interpersonal relationships (Verba 1996: 24–25). Fans were showing a particular interest in a certain "buddy dynamic" present in the original media (Verba 1996; Coppa 2006). Fanfiction exploring this dynamic could feature either platonic or sexual relationships. However, a growing number of fans were interested in homoerotic content.

By the late 1970s and early 1980s, *Star Wars* films, *Starsky and Hutch*, and *The Man from U.N.C.L.E.* were popular with many existing *Star Trek* fans. By 1976, fanzines "with stories based on more than one television show or movie became known as 'media' fanzines" (Verba 1996: 34). These stories offered the same buddy dynamic to which many *Star Trek* fans seemed to respond. Coppa argues this dynamic is what "distinguishes media fandom from Star Trek fandom" (2006: 46). This is also when the term "media fandom" emerges. The growing interest in a range of media (beyond *Star Trek* or sci-fi), the increased conservatism of the 1980s, and a continued need for adults-only spaces, meant "media fans" carved out their own communication networks and gathering spaces. This furthered the sense that media fandom was its own space, one that was fanfiction friendly and often (not always) open to male/male fanfiction.

Keep in mind, this is not the only place these types of fan interests and practices were emerging during this period. The first "Comic Market" (also known as Comiket) was held in Japan in 1975 (Welker 2015: 53). "[I]nitially billed a 'manga fanzine fair,'" Comiket has become "synonymous with the buying and selling of *dōjinshi* (coterie magazines)... variously including original and parodic manga and prose fiction, as well as criticism about manga, anime, and, eventually, video games" (Welker 2015: 54). In the 1970s and 1980s, Comiket was an important distribution point for early homoerotic *doujinshi*. Some of these were fan works and others original fiction. Comiket played an important role in the development of fan, amateur, and commercial *yaoi*/Boys Love (BL) media in Japan (Welker 2015). By the late 1980s, homoerotic manga and *doujinshi* were making their way into South Korea, leading to the emergence of fanfiction there (Kwon 2019: 43). Only, in South Korea, this fanfiction focused "primarily on imagined homoerotic relationships between male idol stars," something that was still more taboo among English-language fan networks at the time (Kwon 2019: 40). In Japan, South Korea, and English-speaking countries, fan works and practices have their own distinct contexts and traits. However, all of these histories (and many others) feed into the networks and practices associated with media fans today.

While today's fan networks are global in reach and origin, only some of this global history has been published by or made accessible to English-language fan scholars. In the 1980s and 1990s, several important works of English-language fan scholarship were published in the United States. Patricia Frazier Lamb and Diana L. Veith published an early article on Kirk/Spock fic in 1986. An early article from Jenkins was published in 1988, with Constance Penley and Bacon-Smith following in 1991 and 1992. These works are often associated with the emergence of fan studies in the West and introduced many academics to transformative fan practices. This research is also generally focused on the networks of fans associated with the early *Star Trek* and media fan networks I discussed earlier.

It's understandable that Western/English-speaking scholars would be more familiar with Western/English-language-speaking fans. However, we need to be careful not to mistake these particular histories of fans for *a* history of media fandom or of fan practices. In doing so, we risk reinforcing the idea that a) media fandom is a knowable community/space located primarily in the United States/Western countries and b) that this network is the origin of transformative fan practices.

Fandom Goes Digital

In 1992, Bacon-Smith conceptualized fandom as a social organization with multiple layers. There was a broad "interest group" or "fandom," followed by increasingly smaller and intimate subsections of that group, ending with smaller circles of close friends (1992: 22–31). By the 2000s, these social structures were increasingly dependent on the internet. Initially, much of this activity happened on smaller mailing lists, Usenet, websites, and fan archives. These fan archives and mailing lists often extended and reinforced offline interest groups. Unlike contemporary social media platforms, these tools were also generally more closed and self-contained. Rhiannon Bury argues that "the design and architecture of listservs, newsgroups and discussion forums plays an important role in enabling the kind of in-depth, sustained interactivity required for community formation and maintenance" (2016: 7). At the time, fans used these technologies to construct meaningful *online* communities for themselves (Baym 2000; Bury 2005).

The introduction of LiveJournal in 1999 was a key turning point. By 2003, the platform was a hub for media fans (Bury 2016: 7). LiveJournal's design accommodated the layers of fandom Bacon-Smith identified in 1992. At top level, the interface connected users with larger networks of fans via tags on profiles, platform-level search features, publicly available posts, and community accounts where groups of users could share information. Underneath this were layers of smaller and more personal connections. LiveJournal offered privacy filters on posts, allowing for more intimate conversations. LiveJournal also offered reading lists, filtering a user's feed and allowing for even smaller user circles. Additionally, in the early 2000s, many pre-internet structures associated with media fandom still existed. This allowed existing offline structures to be reinforced, pre-existing social ties to be extended, and new social ties to be formed.

LiveJournal's interface helped make fan social networks more tangible. It "created a new culture of visibility" and "allowed easier entry into fandom" (Busse and Hellekson 2006: 14). Looking at a user or community profile indicated how people were connected and gave a sense of the overall network's size. Previously, fans had been sorted into different mailing lists or Usenet groups. LiveJournal, as an early social networking site, made these silos more porous. For both new and old fans, this allowed for an important moment of visibility and provided the sense that media fans were centralizing on a particular platform.

LiveJournal was an early social networking platform which offered a particular set of affordances at a time when there were few competitors. It was popular at a specific moment for fans, internet technologies, and fan studies. These factors form a larger context which helped reify a sense of a "fandom" and "media fandom" and associated them with a specific platform. As such, these terms and spatial understandings of fandom continued to thrive at a time when, in reality, fans and fan practices were increasingly digitized and diffused.

LiveJournal enabled fans and fan practices in two contradictory ways. The platform helped many networks of fans connect and become visible to one another. When accounts were mass deleted and the relationship between fans and the platform soured in 2007, fans organized efforts like "Fandom Counts" to collectively count themselves, positioning fandom as a large and organized block of users (McCullagh 2007). All of this, combined with the techno-optimism of the early 2000s and the preexisting structures of media fans, afforded collaboration and organization. The idea for the fanfiction archive Archive of Our Own (AO3) began as a LiveJournal post (Astolat 2007a). Three days later, planning for the Organization for Transformative Works (OTW) (and AO3) was launched via a LiveJournal community (Astolat 2007b). Media fans leveraged the affordances offered by LiveJournal (and other early Web 2.0 tools) to organize and develop lasting structures like the OTW. However, if we consider how tools like LiveJournal also helped disperse fan networks and practices, it's clear LiveJournal was an important point for the widespread dissemination of media fan practices and the larger disintegration of *a* media fandom.

Fandom as Discourse

In *Enterprising Women* (1992), Bacon-Smith describes media fandom as a "community" with many layers of interests and sub-interests (1992: 7–43). In *Textual Poachers* (1992),

Jenkins describes a "weekend-only world" fans collaboratively create and move into on weekends (1992: 280). This idea of media fandom as a community, a culture, and a particular grouping of fans has continued forward in more recent fan studies research. Summarizing research on fan communities from 1992 forward, Louisa Stein argues this research "points to fandom as a space for predominantly female audience communities and for queer identification" (2015: 11). In *Exploiting Fandom* (2019), Mel Stanfill interrogates the construction of the word "fan" while reassuring readers that fandom clearly remains "a culture" (2019: 6). In 2022, Coppa refers to media fandom as "a creative community organized around genre television and movies" (2022: 2). In my own writing, I have also defaulted to the singular, claiming that "the suffix '–dom' [in fandom]... signals a broader and shared declaration of affection, a group status, and a space in which one fan's interests are shared with others" (Morrissey 2017: 353). I want to close by thinking about this term, fandom, as a signal. I want to consider how terms like fandom and media fandom are, in and of themselves, enculturating and discursive moves.

One way that fans affirm their networks and practices is by labeling themselves a fandom. As scholars, we know this. Bacon-Smith explains fandom as a "conceptual space" and "a state of being" (1992: 3). Jenkins calls fandom "a discursive logic that knits together interests across textual and generic boundaries" (1992: 40). Kristina Busse and Karen Hellekson describe the "specific terminology used in media fandom" explaining that the "exclusionary nature of the discourse enculturates newbies and cements the online community" (2006: 9, 12).

Framing fandom as a vibrant culture (or counterculture) gives fan scholars an object of study. Part of Jenkins' project in *Textual Poachers* was "to make the case for fandom as having... coherence and stability" (1992: 3). Jenkins does this because he wants scholars to take fans and fan practices seriously. English-language fan studies scholars continually return to the singular language used in these earlier publications. We do it, in part, to echo a terminology used by fans. However, we are also aware of the potential problems this construction poses. Fan scholars often add caveats to the concept of a singular or unified fandom. For example, Jenkins explains that media fandom circa 1992 is "amorphous but still identifiable" (1992: 1). Busse and Hellekson caution that fandom circa 2006 is "not cohesive" and warn "[i]t is impossible... perhaps even dangerous to speak of a single fandom" (2006: 6). Another strategy is to define more specific fan networks. For example, in "A History of Media Fandom," Coppa frames "U.S. media fandom" as "something distinct from, but related to, science fiction, comics, anime/manga/yaoi, music, soap opera, and literary fandoms" (Coppa 2006: 42). Or, similarly, Alexis Lothian, Kristina Busse, and Robin Anne Reid construct "online slash fandom" as "a particular demographic group: fans who tend to consciously identify with media fandom's roots as developed in the 1970s and 1980s" (2007: 105–106).

In articles on fans, we frequently vacillate between fandom as a singular or a plural entity. For example, in Casey Fiesler and Brianna Dym's "Moving Across Lands" (2020), the writing switches between uses of "fandom," as a singular entity, and the term "fandom communities" (2020). Or, like Lothian et al., we try to acknowledge that fans can participate "without feeling that they belong to any particular community," but then that these fans "remain self-aware about **the** history and context of their practices" (2007: 105–106, emphasis mine).

Our use of fandom shifts between singular space/history and multiple communities/histories, as well as place(s) and practice(s). With so much fan scholarship anecdotal and self-reported by "acafans," discussion of "fandom" is subjective and contextual. For example, Coppa may draw a distinction between American media fandom and "science fiction, comics, anime/manga/yaoi, music, soap opera, and literary fandoms" (2006: 42). However, many media fans would see no distinction between these things. For many, anime/manga/yaoi, music, etc. were the media that introduced them to American media fan networks and practices. This is just one example of how challenging it is to maintain the concept of *a* media fandom or to try and describe one fandom history, place, or community.

Part of the difficulty here is that media fandom can be experienced as *a* space or *a* community. In the twentieth century, fandom may have been a "weekend only world," but it was a world that manifested in physical gatherings – area fan clubs, regional fan conventions, sub-sections of other conventions, etc. It also manifested materially in zines, slideshows, VHS tapes, etc. Media fandom was, literally, a word-of-mouth network with its own material and discursive culture. In the twenty-first century, fan networks are deeply dependent on internet technologies. However, many material manifestations of fandom still exist. Cons like Shore Leave, Escapade, and Dragon Con are still being organized each year, along with San Diego Comic Con or Japan's Comiket. Many contemporary fans still associate fandom with the idea of a community and a subculture of like-minded individuals. However, even prior to the internet, media fandom was *always* a loosely defined and amorphous community. It was also, at its core, a term that described sets of fan interests and practices as much as it described any kind of established group or subculture. Once fans and fan practices moved online, this loosely defined community became more amorphous than ever.

The concept of fandom, as a noun, has become what Rukmini Pande (2018) calls a "fandom algorithm." For Pande, fandom algorithms are structures of thinking which "order the workings of media fandom, both in terms of communitarian etiquettes and technical strategies that involve fannish digital infrastructure" (2018: 116). Pande argues that concepts like intertextuality and subversion circulate among fans and fan scholars, allowing "the core liberal nature of media fandom spaces to operate unquestioningly" (2018: 116).

In our current moment, terms like fandom and media fandom are functioning as fandom algorithms. Pande touches on this problem, observing that when transcultural/national fans and practices are discussed, "these are invariably located as outside 'the fandom'" (2018: 6). This means, "when 'the fandom' or fangirls are discussed, the referents of these terms remain US- or UK-centric popular media texts and white, cisgender, middle class women" (Pande 2018: 6). While this exclusion may be unintentional, this is precisely what occurs when we use phrases like "media fandom" in our research and only parenthetically acknowledge that we are actually discussing a limited slice of media fans and practices.

Fan scholars have formed feedback loops, affirming the idea that fandom is a knowable culture or community. In continually using fandom, singular, to discuss and historicize one segment of media fans, we risk promoting the idea that all of "fandom" has the same singular, traceable history back to Western, English-language, American media-dominated, *Star Trek*/science fiction fan networks. In reality, fans and fan practices are now (and have always been) global, with complicated international histories and influences. We need to be wary of this slippage between the idea of media fandom as a specific network of fans with a particular history and culture and media fandom as a broad range of fan interests and fan practices. This slippage turns these terms into a kind of problematic shorthand where their meaning remains ambiguous and where particular sets of fans are identified as "fandom" far more than others.

The structures associated with the Organization of Transformative Works provide us with examples of how this media fandom algorithm works. As I explained earlier, the 2007 call for volunteers on LiveJournal led to the creation of AO3, academic journals like *Transformative Works and Cultures*, and projects like Fanlore and Open Doors. These projects are dedicated to archiving fan works and histories. These structures all function as ways to organize fans, archive fan histories, and make fan networks more visible to the world.

The existence of OTW and the story of building AO3 have become a kind of triumphant fannish folklore. "Fans" wanted to own their own servers and now they do. In 2023, AO3 was ranked as the #103 most visited website in the world (archiveofourown.org n.d.). In 2024, the archive had roughly 6.7 million users and hosted roughly 12.5 million fan works in multiple languages (Home n.d.). There are many things to celebrate about these achievements. However, we also need to unpack the idea of "fans" or "fandom" owning those servers. Given AO3's prominence, we need to think about how it and its parent organization operate symbolically as manifestations of *a* media fandom and contribute to the slippage between broad and narrow understandings of fandom.

Archives "help a community, especially a subcultural group such as a media fandom, to define and locate itself" (De Kosnik 2016: 95). Abigail De Kosnik finds that early fan archives created centralized spaces for fans to connect with one another. These were important because, "[i]n such a centralized system, the culture of an online community can be easily found, clearly identified, and quickly learned by every member of that community" (De Kosnik 2016: 95). As LiveJournal use increased and many fans left mailing lists behind, this led to a period of decentralization in the early-to-mid-2000s (De Kosnik 2016). We could see the formation of AO3 as a shift back to centralization. However, given the size, scope, and mission of OTW, AO3 is not going to supply community or centralization in the ways fan archives did in the past.

The OTW's mission statement says: "The Organization for Transformative Works (OTW) is a nonprofit organization established by fans to serve the interests of fans by providing access to and preserving the history of fanworks and fan culture in its **myriad forms**" (What We Believe n.d., emphasis mine). Reading this, the organization's mission seems to go beyond any one fan community or culture, and beyond the scope of fandom/media fandom as defined by earlier fans and fan scholars. However, there's also an important contradiction or tension built into the Organization's mission. The second part of the Organization's mission statement reads:

> The OTW represents a practice of transformative fanwork historically rooted in a **primarily female culture.** The OTW will preserve the record of **that history** as we pursue our mission while encouraging new and non-mainstream expressions of cultural identity within fandom. (What We Believe n.d., emphasis mine)

Herein lies a problem. If we understand "that history" and "primarily female" fan culture as one rooted in the American/Western science fiction, *Star Trek*, and media fanzines of the 1970s, 80s, and 90s, then this constitutes just one part of AO3's vast international user base. Part of the organization's mission may be to serve "fan culture in its myriad forms," but, at its core, the project was built by a network of roughly 70 fans, many (if not all) aligned with more Western media and slash-focused fan-networks (Coppa 2022: 164). So, which history is being alluded to in this mission? Is it rooted in media fandom, in *one* sense of the term? Or, does this encompass the myriad of global fan histories and practices AO3 exists to serve?

Depending on how we deploy them, terms like fandom and media fandom can operate as a kind of reification. We take an amorphous concept like "fandom" and deploy the term as if it can still represent a knowable group or culture. Fans and fan practices are diffused across a myriad of platforms. Even on the same platform, clusters of individual users and interests may never come into contact with one another. Now, more than ever, we need to problematize the notion of a single centralized fandom or media fandom. Fan scholars need to think carefully about the language we use to discuss fans.

One way to do this is to begin pushing back against the fandom algorithm. We need to stop relying so heavily on the term *fandom*. One important step is to talk about *fan networks* rather than fandom. For example, I would argue that AO3 was not made by fandom. It was made by a particular network of fans. I would also argue that AO3 was not made for fandom. It was made in a way that tries to serve many different networks of fans simultaneously, while also inevitably privileging some more than others. "Fandom," "media fandom," or more specific groupings like "Harry Potter fandom," do not exist in today's digitally mediated world. Instead, there are many different networks of fans which share these interests in varying, sometimes intersecting, ways. Conceptualizing fans in networks, rather than fandoms, helps us account for the complicated ways that social media and other technological tools do and do not connect contemporary fans to one another. Changing our language helps interrupt the algorithm and complicate our default assumptions.

It is not possible for fan scholars to fully comprehend all of "fandom," if such a thing exists today. However, it is possible to try and focus on specific networks and sets of users. Or, to explore links and overlaps across different fan networks. In research and in peer review, we need to problematize terms like fandom, community, and culture, and insist on contextualization. This language is a shorthand and it is easily misused. For example, Jamison's *Fic* is a phenomenally valuable resource on some fan writing practices, but it is not, as the back cover proclaims, an "exploration of the history and culture of fanwriting" (2013). Instead, it is a detailed history of specific forms of fanwriting. *Fic* is a detailed but partial history on fanwriting, focused on specific networks of (primarily) Western/English-language fans. Contextualizing our terminology helps us clarify which specific clusters of fans and fan practices we are referring to without, simultaneously, erasing variation. Contextualization and specificity also help to make all the omitted and unexplored fan histories a little bit more visible. This includes contextualizing the platforms fans are using, how these platforms connect users to one another, and how they connect users to content. All of these details inform the construction of fan networks today.

From the beginning, media fandom has been used as both a verb and a noun. What if we think, instead, of what it means "to fan" or of fandom as a field of activity? What happens when we approach "fan" as a verb and an active practice? To fan something can make it cool or hot, it strengthens or weakens an existing energy source. Activities and people can fan out from many points, moving beyond, complicating, or extending them. All these actions connect with broader processes of cultural engagement, production, and negotiation, as well as individual and collective meaning-making.

For fans, these points of contact may be experienced as communities. This understanding derives, in part, from a time when it was common for fans to literally join a club, pay dues, and where membership served as a marker of your status as a fan. Today, terms like fan community or fan culture are used more loosely. Rather than paying dues, contemporary fans express their fandom through user interests on their Facebook profile or by reblogging a picture on Tumblr. Digital technologies and social media have made fan engagement a more casual act. This looseness should not invalidate the sense of community many fans experience. However, it speaks to a need for researchers to interrogate how fans are activating these terms. All these communities are inflected with their own priorities, politics, and pleasures, as well as the limits and affordances of the technologies they are using to communicate. The values and codes of conduct embraced within these networks reflect different technologies and concerns. As fan practices disseminate globally and fans appear on numerous digital platforms, at what point is "fandom" still a known space or a definable community? And, given that reality, what do terms like fandom and media fandom afford, or disafford, fans and fan scholars?

Notes

1 Transformative fan practices include creating fanfiction, fanvideos, art, etc.
2 Scholars and fans will often use shorthand and call this "science fiction." However, depending on the context, fantasy may be implicitly included.

References

archiveofourown.org (n.d.) *Similarweb*, www.similarweb.com/website/archiveofourown.org/, accessed 22 June 2023.
Astolat (2007a) 'An Archive of One's Own', *astolat's livejournal*, https://astolat.livejournal.com/150556.html, accessed 19 June 2022.
Astolat (2007b) 'First Call for Volunteers', The Organization for Transformative Works, https://otw-news.livejournal.com/820.html, accessed 23 October 2023.
Bacon-Smith, C. (1992) *Enterprising Women: Television Fandom and the Creation of Popular Myth*, University of Pennsylvania Press, Philadelphia.
Bacon-Smith, C. (2000) *Science Fiction Culture*, University of Pennsylvania Press, Philadelphia.
Baym, N.K. (2000) *Tune in, Log on: Soaps, Fandom, and Online Community*, Sage Publications, Thousand Oaks, CA.
Bury, R. (2005) *Cyberspaces of Their Own: Female Fandoms Online*, Peter Lang, New York.
Bury, R. (2016) 'Technology, Fandom and Community in the Second Media Age', Convergence: The International Journal of Research into New Media Technologies, 23: 627–42, doi:10.1177/1354856516648084
Busse, K. and K. Hellekson (2006) 'Introduction: Work in Progress', in K. Busse and K. Hellekson (eds) *Fan Fiction and Fan Communities in the Age of the Internet*, McFarland & Company, Inc., Jefferson.
Coppa, F. (2006) 'A Brief History of Media Fandom', in K. Busse and K. Hellekson (eds) *Fan Fiction and Fan Communities in the Age of the Internet*, McFarland & Company, Inc., Jefferson.
Coppa, F. (2022) *Vidding: A History*, University of Michigan Press, doi:10.3998/mpub.10069132
De Kosnik, A. (2016) *Rogue Archives: Digital Cultural Memory and Media Fandom*, doi:10.7551/mitpress/10248.001.0001

Fiesler, C. and B. Dym (2020) 'Moving Across Lands: Online Platform Migration in Fandom Communities', *Proceedings of the ACM on Human-Computer Interaction*, 4, Issue CSCW1, Article No. 42, pp. 1–25. doi:10.1145/3392847

Home (n.d.) *Archive of Our Own*, https://archiveofourown.org/, accessed 4 February 2024.

Jamison, A. (2013) *Fic: Why Fanfiction Is Taking Over the World*, Smart Pop, Dallas, TX.

Jenkins, H. (1988) 'Star Trek Rerun, Reread, Rewritten: Fan Writing as Textual Poaching', *Critical Studies in Mass Communication*, 5(2): 85–107.

Jenkins, H. (1991) 'Star Trek Reread, Rerun, Rewritten: Fan Writing as Textual Poaching', in C. Penley, E. Lyons, L. Spigel, and J. Bergstrom (eds) *Close Encounters: Film, Feminism, and Science Fiction*, University of Minnesota Press, Minneapolis.

Jenkins, H. (1992) *Textual Poachers: Television Fans and Participatory Culture*, Routledge, New York.

Kwon, J. (2019) *Straight Korean Female Fans and Their Gay Fantasies*, University of Iowa Press, Iowa City, https://muse.jhu.edu/pub/165/monograph/book/64359, accessed 30 January 2024.

Lamb, P.F. and D.L. Veith (1986) 'Romantic Myth, Transcendence and Star Trek Zines', in D. Palumbo (ed) *Erotic Universe: Sexuality and Fantastic Literature*, Greenwood Press, Westport, CT.

Lothian, A., K. Busse and R.A. Reid (2007) '"Yearning void and infinite potential": online slash fandom as queer female space', *English Language Notes*, 45(2): 103–111.

McCullagh, Declan (2007) "LiveJournal Apologizes for Mass Deletion." CNET. 1 June 2007, www.cnet.com/culture/livejournal-apologizes-for-mass-deletion/

McLelland, M., K. Nagaike, K. Suganuma and J. Welker (eds) (2015) *Boys Love Manga and Beyond: History, Culture, and Community in Japan*, 1st ed., University Press of Mississippi, Jackson.

Morrissey, K.E. (2017) 'Gender and Fandom: From Spectators to Social Audiences', in K.L. Hole, D. Jelača, E.A. Kaplan, and P. Petro (eds) *The Routledge Companion to Cinema and Gender*, Routledge, New York.

Pande, R. (2018) *Squee from the Margins: Fandom and Race*, 1st ed., University of Iowa Press, Iowa City.

Penley, C. (1991) 'Brownian Motion: Women, Tactics, and Technology', in C. Penley and A. Ross (eds) *Technoculture*, University of Minnesota Press, Minneapolis, https://ezproxy.rit.edu/login?url=http://site.ebrary.com/lib/rit/Doc?id=10159361

Stanfill, M. (2019) *Exploiting Fandom: How the Media Industry Seeks to Manipulate Fans*, University of Iowa Press, Iowa City.

'STAR TREK LIVES --- AGAIN!!!' (1973) *STAR-BORNE*, 1(5): 1.

Stein, L.E. (2015) *Millennial Fandom: Television Audiences in the Transmedia Age*, 1st ed., University of Iowa Press, Chicago.

Verba, J.M. (1996) *Boldly Writing: A Trekker Fan & Zine History, 1967–1987*, FTL Publications, Minnetonka, MN.

Welker, J. (2015) 'A Brief History of Shōnen'ai, Yaoi and Boys Love', in M. McLelland, K. Nagaike, K. Suganuma, and J. Welker (eds) *Boys Love Manga and Beyond*, University Press of Mississippi, United States.

'What We Believe' (n.d.) *Organization for Transformative Works*, www.transformativeworks.org/what_we_believe/, accessed 19 June 2022.

4
AFTER POACHING AND NEGOTIATED READINGS

Towards the Real-time Emergence (and the Temporary Pauses) of Fans' Co-decoding

Matt Hills

It would be fair to say that Stuart Hall's "encoding-decoding" model (2005, originally 1980) has been one of the most influential approaches to audience interpretation. Yet this way of classifying audience responses was sidelined in foundational fan studies, with Henry Jenkins' *Textual Poachers* (1992) offering a critique of its relevance to fandom. I want to revisit encoding-decoding, suggesting that we need to rethink it for a world where fannish engagement with beloved texts is rarely only about an individualized fan-text encounter. Instead, fan decodings are contextualized *by other fans' readings* in the real-time of social media updating.

This will partly build on my contribution to the previous edition of *The Routledge Companion to Media Fandom*, where I first set out a need to address what I termed fannish "co-decoding" (Hills 2018). Going beyond this, I will argue that it is important to integrate reworkings of encoding-decoding with the rise of fan studies' analysis of parasocial relationships (PSRs; Hills 2016). Linking revisionist analysis of encoding-decoding to debates on contemporary "platformized" fandom (Morris 2018) experienced as intensely parasocial will enable me to demonstrate how fans' co-decoding can be understood as "multisocial" in terms of how fans engage with one another at the same time as desiring and/or projecting relationships with celebrities (Yin 2021).

The key issue is the extent to which fandom's migration onto a range of platforms has reconfigured media fandom from an individualized initial experience of a fan object which then enters communal evaluations into a fan experience in which individual/personal decodings have to be self-consciously protected from the readings of other fans constantly circulating on social media. The term "ante-fandom" has been used to theorize fan-text relations which precede the social media whorl of co-decoding (Hills 2019), as well as being used to define how fans can attempt to retreat, and shield their readings, from the rival interpretations of other fans (Fazel and Geddes 2022). As such, I will conclude by briefly exploring the way in which a kind of ante-fandom is deployed by fans to regulate pauses in their "time engagements" with beloved fan objects (Bourdaa 2022), temporarily

DOI: 10.4324/9781003373025-6

blocking out the social media "noise" of fellow fans' readings, and momentarily suspending the entire eco-system of fan blogs, podcasts, tweets, YouTubers, and so on. First, though, I want to return to Hall's encoding-decoding model, and its sometimes uneasy place in fan studies.

When Fans Weren't Simply Decoders: From "Poaching" to Negotiation and Co-decoding

Henry Jenkins' (1992) applications of textual "poaching," taken from Michel de Certeau, made a point of distinguishing this from Stuart Hall's encoding-decoding model, arguing that it was too rigid, and too polemically classificatory, to make sense of the fluidity and contradictoriness of fan readings:

> Hall's model of dominant, negotiated, and oppositional readings tends to imply that each reader has a stable position from which to make sense of a text rather than having access to multiple sets of discursive competencies by virtue of more complex and contradictory place within the social formation. Hall's model… suggests that popular meanings are fixed and classifiable, while de Certeau's "poaching" model emphasizes the process of making meaning and the fluidity of popular interpretation. (Jenkins 1992: 34)

Rather than fan responses being easily categorizable as dominant (according with dominant ideologies and meaning-making), negotiated (partially challenging dominant ideology but not fully breaking with it), or oppositional (strongly resisting dominant ideologies encoded in a text's preferred meaning or reading), Jenkins argued for a messier sense of fan readings. By stressing the "process" of fan interpretations it became possible to analyze how each fan-reader was "continuously re-evaluating his or her relationship to the fiction and reconstructing its meanings according to more immediate interests" (1992: 35). And by emphasizing the "fluidity" of fan reading, Jenkins was interested in how the same fan could "shift between… progressive and reactionary modes of thinking in the course of a single conversation" (1992: 36). Indeed, such a complication of clear-cut politicized readings, where people were not always "resistant," and resistance wasn't necessarily progressive (Jenkins 1992: 35), might seem at odds with the strongly divided cultural politics of latter-day fandom (Driessen, Jones, and Litherland 2024). But it was rooted in Jenkins' focus on "the particularities of specific instances of critical reception, cultural appropriation, and popular pleasure," on which side he placed a notion of "poaching" and selective fan appropriation, as opposed to "the abstractions of theory" (1992: 36), on which side Jenkins placed Stuart Hall's encoding-decoding with its categories of dominant, negotiated, and oppositional reading.

However, some years later Jenkins would revise his opposition to encoding-decoding, perhaps no longer feeling that it was so crucial to displace Hall's schema with his own commitments to de Certeau and fannish "poaching." Tackling the issue of race and representation, Jenkins argued that fans of color engaged in "negotiated readings" akin to those identified by Hall (Jenkins 2018a: 384 and 2018b: 14; see also an updated version of Jenkins 2018a in this volume). Specifically, where fans enact "racebending" in their fanfic and fanart, rewriting characters that are denotatively or implicitly white in the source text/

canon as characters of color, Jenkins argues this "represents a particularly vivid example of such negotiations, preserving aspects of the original characters fans have found pleasurable, while generating alternative representations" (2018a: 388). More broadly, fandom can be viewed as "[e]mbodying Hall's concept of reading as negotiation... often motivated by a complex balance between fascination and frustration" (Jenkins 2018b: 16). Despite returning to Hall, Jenkins retains the focus on process and fluidity which had underpinned his initial critiques of encoding-decoding: "Understanding fandom... as a form of negotiation suggests... an ongoing process of negotiation with changing meanings that reflect changing times, rather than fixed positions" (Jenkins 2018b: 16). This makes a similar point to Jonathan Gray's likewise revisionist use of Hall's encoding-decoding, this time in a study of audiences for *The Simpsons*, where Gray refers to "redecoding" (2006: 34). Gray also argues that we need more work on how audiences interpret the same media text differently over time:

> I propose... that we talk not of encoding/decoding, but of encoding/redecoding... Both reading and the text are a continual journey *through*, a continuance of motion, and while there might be determinate moments, there are always potentially more determinate moments to come. (Gray 2006: 34)

Gray even poses the question, "which *people* are more or less likely to redecode[?]" (2006: 35), to which we might respond that media fans are known for practices of re-watching, both soon after a new TV episode has aired, and years later as part of the desire to re-experience a beloved fan object.

But Hall's encoding-decoding model, even if worthy of revisitation, remains marked by significant lacunae when applied to fandom. It assumes that meanings are negotiated between a TV text and an individual viewer in the audience, or as Jenkins puts it, "Hall... describes negotiation primarily as occurring within the head of the individual audience member" (2018a: 388). By contrast, fandom involves "a more collective dimension – groups of people negotiate meanings together, thus empowering them to make stronger claims on texts that matter to the group" (2018a: 388). Applied without alteration to fandom, Hall's negotiation could make sense of "headcanon" as personally negotiated textual meanings, but would have little purchase on "fanon" as a communally agreed-upon reading of the source text (Jenkins 2018a: 392). In order to contest the individualization of reading, or the mental interiority attributed to it, we "need to think about negotiation differently – not in terms of how an individual negotiates their relationship with a text but rather how community members negotiate interpretations... among each other" (Jenkins 2018b: 16).

And yet perhaps this corrective doesn't go far enough. When contemporary fans encounter rival interpretations on Twitter/X, or on YouTube, they do so in a context where there is no singular fan "community" but rather a collision between fractious segments of fan meaning-making. Establishing a form of "silosociality" (Tiidenberg, Hendry, and Abidin 2021: 52) where only like-minded fan readers form part of one's social media feed or timeline is extremely difficult, and liable to require constant monitoring and "call-outs, virtue-signalling, and normative performances of the 'right way' of being in order to protect or maintain the experience" (Tiidenberg, Hendry, and Abidin 2021: 56). Platformized fans are thus likely to encounter unexpected and rival fannish readings that are algorithmically circulated to them, being exposed to a variety of contentious fan interpretations without even pursuing them, as fan cultural capital (i.e., performed fan knowledge) is caught up in algorithmic mediation (Van Es 2017: 138).

Fans will also encounter other fans' interpretations in real-time and via a constructed liveness or platform-driven "compulsory continuous connectedness" (Lupinacci 2020: 3), where not to participate in this social-mediation carries the anxiety of missing out on "eventful" content (Hills 2018: 20). Whereas fan cultural capital – or fan status/knowledge – used to center on knowledge of the fan object (Hills 2002), it could be argued that contemporary fan cultural capital centers not only on this kind of knowledge, but also on the "time engagement" (Bourdaa 2022) required to stay up-to-date with the fan "discourse" unfolding at the present moment, now, on Twitter/X (or on one's preferred platform). Such fan status is not just about the temporality of years spent invested in a fan object, but crucially about the rolling temporality of constructed "liveness" as fans reflexively monitor how their peers, and how other sections of fandom, are reacting to new texts and paratexts such as press releases, previews and reviews.

This scenario, of reconfigured fan cultural capital which stresses "continuous connectedness" as much as years of fandom history, means thinking differently about negotiation once more – addressing ongoing and real-time processes of co-decoding which make negotiation more, even, than a process working "at multiple levels… [including] amongst and against other fans" (Jenkins 2018a: 392). Negotiation has become the drumbeat, the insistent pulse, of platformized fan experience, with the permeability of fan community – its openness to rival interpretations, reactionary/progressive fan-others, and algorithmically-circulated factions – making it far more difficult to sustain any naturalized or secured sense of belonging to a fandom. In such a context, fan identity starts to feel like a questioned form of "conditional belonging" (Yodovich 2022: 94) or a precarious sense of "differential belonging" (Hannell 2024: 108) for feminist fans, and perhaps also for reactionary anti-feminist fans, aware of the disdain felt for them by progressive sections of fandom (Hills 2021), though it should be noted that self-declared feminist fans are the focus of important empirical work from both Neta Yodovich (2022) and Briony Hannell (2024). Paul Booth and Craig Owen Jones suggest that despite disagreements within a fandom, there could still be a "convivial evaluation" (2020 23) of canonical texts whereby fans at least agree on the "worthwhileness" of paying attention to their shared fan object (2020: 22). But such conviviality seems optimistic in the face of multiple types of anti-fan dislike and/or hatred (Gray 2021).

Fan studies needs to recontextualize processes of negotiation between fans as part of a real-time, platformized fan experience, one where negotiations of meaning between fan and text become increasingly contested, qualified or over-written by fans' continuous connectedness and engagement with Twitter/X "discourse," say. But if the individual fan-text relation is called into question through such a scenario, then what might this mean for that strand of fan studies' work which has emphasized individualized fan engagements in the form of parasocial relationships (PSRs)? I will turn to the issue of how fans' co-decoding potentially impacts on PSRs in the next section, arguing that a revisionist approach to "negotiated" fan readings means recognizing that contemporary parasocial interactions involve more fan-fan relationality than has previously been suggested. I will then conclude by considering two definitions of "ante-fandom" (Hills 2019; Fazel and Geddes 2022) as a response to the pressures of contemporary fandom's co-decoding and multisocial relations between fans.

When Fans Weren't Only Parasocial: From "PSRs" to Multisocial Fandom and the Pauses of Ante-fandom

Historically, analyzing fandom in terms of parasocial relations (Horton and Wohl 1956) has raised the specter of pathologizing fandom, as David Giles has noted, since parasocial relationships and fandom have been "frequently associated with social dysfunction in both academia and mainstream media" (Giles 2023: 44). This is partly because parasocial relations – non-reciprocal intimacy between audiences and media figures – have been viewed as inadequately social, or as a compensation for a lack of "real" social interactions. However, as Giles remarks, viewing fandom as strongly parasocial is awkward for a number of reasons. Firstly, fandom "does not necessarily attach itself to an individual media figure" (Giles 2023: 44) given its frequent focus on media texts/characters. Secondly, it is also a "communal activity… associated… with social interaction" between fans, rather than being articulated with an absence or loss of sociality (2023: 45). And thirdly,

> the parasocial criterion of nonreciprocity has always been problematic. Unlike other media users, fans have formal channels that provide them, up to a certain point, with access to media figures. For certain types of fan, conventions… have always allowed longer and more meaningful interaction with the media figures (fan objects) themselves. (Giles 2023: 45)

This is clearly also intensified by fans' interactions with media figures via social media. However, despite parasocial relationships' scholarly history as a pathologized/pathologizing term, and despite the possibility of a problematic fit between the concept and media fandom, there has been a turn towards the normalizing of fan parasociality, especially as experienced through social media platforms. This has played out in academic work on the intensities of "stanning" (Malik and Haidar 2023); on Lady Gaga fans (Click, Lee, and Holladay 2013); Taylor Swift fans (Nisbett and Schartel Dunn 2021; Zafina and Sinha 2024); and via analyses of K-pop and BTS fandom as parasocial (Chang et al. 2023; Alisya et al. 2023).

This normalizing of platformized fandom-as-parasocial has tended *to isolate out (and assume) a singular, heightened fan-celebrity relationship*, however, consequently downplaying the role of co-decoding (and fans' awareness of an array of other fan voices and readings online). Like Hall's original encoding-decoding model of the 1970s/80s, parasociality was initially theorized in the 1950s when individualized audience-text relations and readings could be largely taken for granted. By marked contrast, today's social media audiences encounter an insistent paratextual frame of other audiences' readings and feelings. Such discursive multiplicity tends to appear in work on parasocial relations as a bug rather than a feature. Thus, when Xu et al. hypothesize that followers of micro-celebrities might experience greater perceived intimacy with these figures as opposed to mass-mediated celebrities (2023: 372), and are surprised to find that their data doesn't support this assumption, they "suggest that micro-celebrity culture is characterized by abundance, meaning that one user can follow numerous micro-celebrities instead of devoting their intimate attachment only to one performer" (2023: 380). But this is only worthy of an addendum when a focused singularity to the audience-celebrity relationship has been *a priori* posited or isolated out.

To the contrary, emergent work on fans' "multisocial" rather than strictly parasocial relations (Hills 2016) has sought to restore the co-decoding complexity of current social media fandom. As Yiyi Yin points out: "Facilitated by algorithms and digital technologies,

...fandom has become a 'networked network' ...in which various fan-related participants... [are] complexly tangled" (2021: 461). Yin summarizes this development:

> the relationship between fan and fan object is not only played by the engagement in communication between celebrity and fans but is also realized and performed through interactions among fans themselves. ...The emergence of digital media further reinforces... multi-social interactions in celebrity fandom, as it facilitates... increasingly intimate fan-celebrity interactions and fan-fan communicative events. (2021: 463)

Yin empirically studied four fandoms – Japanese anime-comics-games (ACG); idol fandom; esports fandom; and Anglo-American fandom – on the Chinese social media platform Sina Weibo between 2017 and 2020 (2021: 465), adding 20 semi-structured interviews with fans and fan celebrities (i.e., fannish micro-celebrities known within a fandom). Her analysis demonstrates that "idol fan logic" (2021: 466), where fans support their favored Idol and defend them from attacks from rival fan factions, has encroached on ACG fandom, traditionally a space of individualized consumption of texts/characters (2021: 465). Yin observes that

> [t]he change of ACG fandom today seems to echo the idol fan tradition. As interviewees such as Zack, Sarna, and Seven all reported, ACG fans started to fight with others online to 'protect the character's honor' or to complain that the authors mistreated the characters. (2021: 466)

Such "protective fan practices," common in relation to celebrities, have become relevant for fan objects "no matter virtual or real" (i.e., for media texts/characters and celebrities) (Yin 2021: 471). This shift in fandom's "emotional style" (Yin 2021: 471) results in fans of anime-comics-games' texts and characters anticipating that their favored fan objects might be trolled or attacked online, hence focusing on how to counter such attacks.

The result is an "invasion of ACG fandom by... celebrity fan culture" (Yin 2021: 465) involving a reflexive focus on the "prominent roles of fan networks" (2021: 470) across social media. Fans identify powerfully with their fan object at the same time as splitting other fans into what effectively constitute opposed teams or groupings. Fan defenses of their object are common in Western "stanning" (Malik and Haidar 2023), and as these logics blur out into media fandoms more generally, fans of texts start to resemble sports fans in the "allegiance" stage of fan psychology (Wann and James 2019: 33, 42). Such fans identify so strongly with "their" team that if the fan object is perceived as under threat then fans will likewise feel threatened and will "engage in outgroup **blasting** (or derogation) as a means of repairing damage to their identity" (Wann and James 2019: 137). As Yin says, multisocial interactions become central to such processes: how fans react to and engage with an array of other(ed) fan voices and interpretations on social media works to embody the "abstract relationship between fan and fan object" (Yin 2021: 470). It thus becomes impossible to separate out any parasocial fan relationship from how this attachment is enacted through multisocial (i.e., fan-fan) co-decodings. And such co-decodings are likely to be split into those that are "with" and those that are "against" a given media fan's allegiance (however this is perceived in terms of progressive/reactionary cultural politics and fan identity).

If platformized media fans are increasingly engaged in multisocial practices of for/against co-decoding in relation to other fan readings – practices which support parasocial connections – then we might wonder what cultural spaces (and times) remain sheltered from these social media performances of fannish allegiance. Fans' first encounters with new episodes of beloved texts seem to be prioritized as spaces that should be set apart, symbolically and experientially, from multisocial struggles over co-decoding. To give two examples, here is Matthew Toffolo, fan co-host of the *Doctor Who* podcast "Review of Death," explaining how he watched the 2023 *Doctor Who* Christmas Special. This is followed by two co-hosts, Steven and Sarah of another *Who* fan podcast "Radio Free Skaro," discussing their first-time viewing routines:

Matthew: No-one in our household liked it; it was, like, me, Annie and Johnny all sat on the sofa watching the telly, and we were just a bit stony-faced throughout the whole thing. We went straight on to Twitter, as everybody does, to see what everyone else thought. And obviously everyone loved it, and there was high praise across the board… [W]e were in a bit of a daze really, because we kind of felt like 'wow, are we missing something, why do we feel like the only three people on planet Earth that thought this was a bit … crap' ("Review of Death," December 28, 2023).

Sarah: I like to have a routine for my first viewing… I need to be uninterrupted, phone's on 'do not disturb' "…, leave me alone, I'm having my Church time…

Steven: …I'm like you, Sarah, *airplane mode*, it's just, like, it's off, everything is off when it comes to watching *Doctor Who* for me ("Radio Free Skaro," May 5, 2024).

And in response to the regular RFS team planning to livestream their YouTube review of new *Doctor Who* episodes, Sarah remarks:

It's always interesting to go back and hear reviews fresh when they haven't had a chance to – …'calcifies' is the wrong word… received fan wisdom starts to affect everybody's judgements, that sort of thing. ("Radio Free Skaro," May 5, 2024)

There's a repeated sense of defending first-watching as an enclave for the fan-self, consciously divided from "what everyone else thought" or from "received fan wisdom." Other(ed) fan responses on social media are felt to subsequently weigh on the individual fan, hemming in or qualifying later decodings. There is an apparent desire for co-decoding to be temporarily suspended, in favor of a moment of personal, quietened fan experience, away from the communal online chatter of co-decoding and the conflictual for/against performances of allegiance.

This *before-ness*, "being sat on the sofa watching" with partners and family, smartphones switched to "airplane mode," could be considered a form of *ante-fandom*. It isn't a projected autobiographical block of time in childhood before one joined socially-organized fandom, which is how I've previously used the term (Hills 2019). At first glance it appears closer to Valerie Fazel and Louise Geddes' coinage of "ante-fandom," which they define very differently as "a defensive strategy designed to keep out anything that might contaminate the fan object and, by extension, the attached fan" (2022: 173). But they go on to characterize this as a highly problematic "stasis," acting as "a strategy of fan control" (2021: 175) in which fans refuse to engage with alternative fan voices and refuse to learn about progressive challenges to "their" beloved text, conservatively embracing "classist, sexist, or racist strategies to prohibit the intrusion of external voices" (2022: 176). By contrast, the ante-fandom of these *Doctor Who* podcasters is not at all marked by such reactionary cultural politics, and seems more concerned with enacting a pure "pause in the processes of fandom" (Fazel and Geddes 2022: 173), especially social media allegiance and co-decoding, without any wish to restrict or avoid progressive challenges to the fan object. This particular incarnation of ante-fandom pursues a specific "time engagement" with the fan object (Bourdaa 2022). It is one where the routinized social-media-world of fannish co-decoding can be momentarily toggled off ("airplane mode"), but only in full recognition of the communal fact that any such break from multisocial fandom cannot be sustained. Of course, this is doubly true for fan podcasters, who need to monitor "received fan wisdom" and all the "divisive positionalities" (Fazel and Geddes 2022: 175) operating across the fandom that they create content for.

To conclude, I've argued that current fan studies needs to pay attention not just to fans as poachers/negotiators of meaning, but rather to the co-decoding processes of social media fandom. In this context, fans are constantly aware of alternative fan interpretations (and cultural politics). Their sense of any singular fan community is rendered permeable and unstable due to the algorithmic circulation of varied fan readings and the difficulty of maintaining a social media presence comprised only of like-minded fan peers (Tiidenberg, Hendry, and Abidin 2021: 56). Fans have little choice other than to contrast, in real-time, their own interpretations and feelings about their fan object to rival decodings, especially those which take on the symbolic weight of "received fan wisdom." As Yin has demonstrated, this results in a sports-fan-like mentality and "emotional style" (2021: 471) of protective fan practices through which platformized media fandom performs for/against allegiance to fan objects in its co-decoding (i.e., having to anticipate or counter rival decodings from other(ed) fans). As I then suggested, this means that normalized accounts of fan-celebrity parasocial relations (Giles 2023) need to focus on the multisocial nature of fan-fan relationships and co-decodings online that sustain parasocial attachments (Hills 2016). Such parasociality is less an isolated-out, individualized or singular fan-celebrity relationship than an intensity supported by fans' co-decodings and, again, performed allegiances involving fan-fan interactions. Lastly, I considered the concept of ante-fandom, repurposing this *contra* Hills (2019) and Fazel and Geddes (2022) to highlight how fans seek temporary pauses from the pressures of "continuous connectedness" (Lupinacci 2020) and associated processes of co-decoding. Although Henry Jenkins' (1992) work criticized Hall's encoding-decoding model, revisiting it by connecting fandom to "negotiation" (Jenkins 2018a, 2018b), in each case Jenkins stressed processes of fandom (1992: 34; 2018b: 16). And as I've argued, the real-time emergence of fannish co-decoding – plus the desire to pause it through a kind of "airplane mode" of fan reading – likewise show that today's *processes of fan interpretation*, both on and off social media, continue to require careful unpacking.

References

Alisya, Vidya, Nurhayati, Sharfina and Boer, Rino Febrianno (2023) 'Study of Parasocial Interaction Between Bangtan Boys (BTS) and ARMY in Indonesia: The Meaning of One-Way Closeness Between Fans and Idols' in *Injurity: Interdisciplinary Journal and Humanity* 2(5): 401–414.

Booth, Paul and Jones, Craig Owen (2020) *Watching Doctor Who: Fan Reception and Evaluation* Bloomsbury Academic, New York.

Bourdaa, Mélanie (2022) 'The Fandom Is a Welcoming Place Unless I Know More Than You: Generations, Mentorship, and Super-Fans' in Bridget Kies and Megan Connor (eds) *Fandom, The Next Generation* University of Iowa Press, Iowa City: pp. 172–180.

Chang, Ho-Chun Herbert, Pham, Becky and Ferrara, Emilio (2023) 'Parasocial diffusion: K-pop fandoms help drive COVID-19 public health messaging on social media' in *Online Social Networks and Media* 37–38: 1–10.

Click, Melissa A., Lee, Hyunji and Holly Willson, Holladay (2013) 'Making Monsters: Lady Gaga, Fan Identification, and Social Media' in *Popular Music and Society* 36(3): 360–379.

Driessen, Simone, Jones, Bethan and Litherland, Benjamin (2024) 'From Fan Citizenship to "Fanspiracies": Politics and Participatory Cultures in Times of Crisis?' in *Convergence*, Online First: 1–9.

Fazel, Valerie M. and Geddes, Louise (2022) *The Shakespeare Multiverse: Fandom as Literary Praxis* Routledge, New York.

Giles, David (2023) 'Defining Parasocial Relationship Experiences' in Rebecca Tukachinsky Forster (ed) *The Oxford Handbook of Parasocial Experiences* Oxford University Press, Oxford: pp. 33–50.

Gray, Jonathan (2006) *Watching with The Simpsons: Television, Parody and Intertextuality* Routledge, New York.

Gray, Jonathan (2021) *Dislike-Minded: Media, Audiences, and the Dynamics of Taste* New York University Press, New York.

Hall, Stuart (2005; originally 1980) 'Encoding/Decoding' in Stuart Hall, Dorothy Hobson, Andrew Lowe and Paul Willis (eds) *Culture, Media, Language* Routledge, London: pp. 117–127.

Hannell, Briony (2024) *Feminist Fandom: Media Fandom, Digital Feminisms, and Tumblr* Bloomsbury Academic, New York.

Hills, Matt (2002) *Fan Cultures* Routledge, London.

Hills, Matt (2016) 'From Para-Social to Multisocial Interaction: Theorising Material/Digital Fandom and Celebrity' in P. David Marshall and Sean Redmond (eds) *A Companion to Celebrity* Wiley Blackwell, Malden: pp. 463–482.

Hills, Matt (2018) 'Always-On Fandom, Waiting and Bingeing: Psychoanalysis as an Engagement with Fans' "Infra-Ordinary" Experiences' in Melissa A. Click and Suzanne Scott (eds) *The Routledge Companion to Media Fandom* Routledge, New York: pp. 18–26.

Hills, Matt (2019) 'Anti-Fandom Meets Ante-Fandom: *Doctor Who* Fans' Textual Dislike and "Idiorrhythmic" Fan Experiences' in Melissa A. Click (ed) *Anti-Fandom: Dislike and Hate in the Digital Age* New York University Press, New York: pp. 102–122.

Hills, Matt (2021) 'Toxic YouTubers "Hated" by *Doctor Who*? Animating Multiphrenic Incarnations of Not My Doctor Anti-Fandom' in *Literatura Ludowa: Journal of Folklore and Popular Culture* 65(2): 69–82.

Horton, Donald and Wohl, R. Richard (1956) 'Mass Communication and Para-Social Interaction: Observations on Intimacy at a Distance' in *Psychiatry* 19: 215–229.

Jenkins, Henry (1992) *Textual Poachers: Television Fans & Participatory Culture* Routledge, New York.

Jenkins, Henry (2018a) 'Negotiating Fandom: The Politics of Racebending' in Melissa A. Click and Suzanne Scott (eds) *The Routledge Companion to Media Fandom* Routledge, New York: pp. 383–394.

Jenkins, Henry (2018b) 'Fandom, Negotiation, and Participatory Culture' in Paul Booth (ed) *A Companion to Media Fandom and Fan Studies* Wiley Blackwell, Oxford: pp. 13–26.

Lupinacci, Ludmilla (2021) '"Absentmindedly Scrolling through Nothing": Liveness and Compulsory Continuous Connectedness in Social Media' in *Media, Culture & Society*, 43(2): 273–290. https://doi.org/10.1177/0163443720939454.

Malik, Zunera and Haidar, Sham (2023) 'Online Community Development through Social Interaction — K-Pop Stan Twitter as a Community of Practice' in *Interactive Learning Environments* 31(2): 733–751.

Morris, Jeremy Wade (2018) 'Platform Fandom' in Melissa A. Click and Suzanne Scott (eds) *The Routledge Companion to Media Fandom* Routledge, New York: pp. 356–364.

Nisbett, Gwendelyn and Schartel Dunn, Stephanie (2021) 'Reputation Matters: Parasocial Attachment, Narrative Engagement, and the 2018 Taylor Swift Political Endorsement' in *Atlantic Journal of Communication* 29(1): 26–38.

Tiidenberg, Katrin, Hendry, Natalie Ann and Abidin, Crystal (2021) *Tumblr* Polity Press, Cambridge.
Van Es, Karin (2017) *The Future of Live* Polity Press, Cambridge.
Wann, Daniel L. and James, Jeffrey D. (2019) *Sports Fans: The Psychology and Social Impact of Fandom – Second Edition* Routledge, New York.
Xu, Yang, Vanden Abeele, Mariek, Hou, Mingyi and Antheunis, Marjolijn (2023) 'Do Parasocial Relationships with Micro- and Mainstream Celebrities Differ? An Empirical Study Testing Four Attributes of the Parasocial Relationship' in *Celebrity Studies* 14(3): 366–386.
Yin, Yiyi (2021) '"My Baby Should Feel No Wronged!": Digital Fandoms and Emotional Capitalism in China' in *Global Media and China* 6(4): 460–475.
Yodovich, Neta (2022) *Women Negotiating Feminism and Science Fiction Fandom: The Case of the "Good" Fan* Springer, Cham.
Zafina, Nadzira and Sinha, Annapurna (2024) 'Celebrity-Fan Relationship: Studying Taylor Swift and Indonesian Swifties' Parasocial Relationships on Social Media' in *Media Asia*, Online First: 1–15.

5

SURVEYING FANDOM

The Ethics, Design, and Use of Surveys in Fan Studies

Lucy Bennett

The use of surveys within fan studies is an important methodological tool which fosters the ability of a multitude of voices and articulations from fans to be gathered and analyzed. The development of the internet and online survey software has also heightened the use of surveys by researchers, with specific groups, networks, and communities being seemingly more easily accessed and studied through utilizing this method. However, as this chapter will argue, although surveys offer many advantages for the study of fans, they raise new, and magnify old, critical issues surrounding ethics, and can pose challenging questions and limitations surrounding how to design and distribute for rich engagement, response, and representation of the fan community under study. Thus, this chapter will reflect on the use of this method within fan studies, outlining my own experiences and offering suggestions on the design and use of surveys within this field. As there are few comprehensive or specific works on survey use as a method in fan research, this chapter will provide an analytic and useful guide for fan studies scholars intending to use surveys in their scholarship.

Surveys as a Fan Studies Method

The use of surveys within research on fans in particular has been key since the inception of the fan studies field, with this method being used to "describe the behaviours, attitudes, and beliefs" (Deacon and Keightley 2014: 303) of these groups of individuals and give an insight into different fan cultures, importantly bringing a "fannish voice into scholarship on fans" (Booth and Kelly 2013: 131). There has been a wealth of studies that successfully draw upon surveys as a basis for their rich empirical research data (for example, Yodavich 2023; Oh and Kim 2023; Williams 2015; Kington 2015; Gray and Mittell 2007; Deller 2015; Halbert 2009; Włodarczyk and Tyminska 2015). Although interviews and ethnography have also been, and remain currently, important methods used within fan studies, surveys have notably flourished in recent times, particularly due to the development and ease of online surveys and their distribution via social networks. They can be used as a singular tool of analysis, or combined with other methods, such as interviews, ethnography, and focus groups. Although there is much scholarship on survey ethics, design, and use in general research (for example, Deacon et al. 2007; Dillman, Smyth, and Melani 2014; Fowler 1995 and 2014; Sudman and Bradburn 1982) there have previously been no specific guides surrounding their use within fan studies.

In this landscape, I argue that there are three main elements offered by surveys which resonate quite strongly with fandom research: (1) surveys can be both quantitative *and* qualitative, thereby allowing for statistical data, yet also longer, individually written responses; (2) they can be circulated online to potentially reach large quantities of individuals; and (3) they allow for researchers to tap somewhat directly into the *voices, articulations, and performances* of some fans – a point I will return to later. I now want to move on to consider in turn three pressing and critical areas of survey research within fan studies that I believe should be considered by all scholars engaging in this method: (1) ethics, (2) survey design, and (3) distribution, representation, and sampling.

Ethics

Adherence to clearly communicated ethics should be a central consideration of fan studies research in general (Whiteman 2012) regardless of method used, and should consequently be a keystone element of survey research. Online research in particular should correspond to the ethical decision-making guidelines suggested by the Association for Internet Researchers (Franzke et al. 2020) and also receive ethical clearance from the department that the researcher studies within (such as through the Institutional Review Board, or Ethics Committee), if they are affiliated to a university, especially if including responses from those under 18 years of age. In terms of ethical clearance, different universities may have different ethical requirements that must be adhered to in order to proceed.

However, it is not always the case that ethical guidelines are considered and I have viewed many academic surveys online that give no information to participants, but just list the questions. In this sense, *every survey should begin with a statement clearly stating who you are, where you are from, the purposes of the research and how the responses will be used, how long it should take to complete, and, importantly, if anonymity will be granted to respondents*. Anonymity is a particularly important and key consideration when conducting fan studies research, especially for some fans engaged in producing transformative work that may encounter considerable impact on their personal and professional lives if their identity is revealed:

> Although many fans believe that they ought not hide and that fictional (homo)erotic fantasies ought not be shameful, most are well aware that exposing fannish activities in real-world situations can be a difficult situation for some fans; it may negatively affect their family or work life.
>
> (Busse and Hellekson 2012: 41)

With this in mind, I recommend that the opening statement be constructed along the lines as follows, which was used for my most recent survey research, on Kate Bush fandom (Bennett 2017):

> My name is Dr Lucy Bennett and I'm a media researcher at the school of Journalism, Media and Cultural Studies, Cardiff University, Wales, UK. I have been researching

music fan culture for a number of years – you can find more information about me and my work here: www.cardiff.ac.uk/jomec/contactsandpeople/researchstaff/bennett-lucy.html.

I am a Kate Bush fan and am currently conducting a study concerning audience experience of the absence of smartphones and cameras during Kate Bush's 2014 London live show residency "Before the Dawn". I would very much welcome and value your contribution to my survey if you attended any of these concerts.

The sole purpose of this survey is to inform academic research on music fandom and the results will only be used for scholarly publication or presentation. Any quotations or information obtained via this survey will be reported anonymously, with no attribution to any specific individuals.

The survey should take you 15–20 minutes to complete, your participation is voluntary and you do not have to answer any question that you do not want to. You may withdraw from the research at any time, and for any reason.

At the end of the survey, you have the option of providing your email address if you wish to make yourself available for follow-up questions or interviews surrounding this study, but you may complete this survey without any self-identification. As mentioned, all answers to this survey will be treated in confidence and no identifiable information will be used in the publishing and writing up of the research.

If you have any questions about this survey, its procedures, or your participation, please contact: Bennettlucyk@gmail.com

Ultimately, this opening statement is of crucial importance in treating with respect the fans being sought as respondents and allowing them to make more informed judgements about their participation in the survey. Following this, informed consent should be obtained from all participants, and this can be achieved by the inclusion of a tick box that states, "I give my consent that my answers will be anonymous but the responses I give to this questionnaire may be used in academic publications." Another example of how a survey can be explained to potential participants can be found on The World Hobbit Project website (https://worldhobbit.wordpress.com/), an international audience study of the Hobbit trilogy that was led by Professors Martin Barker, Matt Hills, and Ernest Mathijs and was comprised of researchers from 46 countries worldwide. The survey appeared in a multitude of different languages in order to reach a rich a sample as possible. All researchers with their contact details were listed on the "About" page of their website, grouped by language and country.

How the survey may impact upon respondents if the questions being asked are of a private, sensitive, or possibly triggering nature should also be considered. As McKeown and Weed suggest, "if we ask questions that introduce stress or anxiety, then we also have an obligation to assist those who are affected by these questions" (2004: 67). In response to this prospect, Natasha Whiteman concludes that "the issue then is how these obligations are worked through by the researcher and how this informs their subsequent actions" (2012: 14). Therefore, the researcher should always provide a contact email, in case a participant needs to discuss their contributions and their impact at any point.

Survey Design

Once the main topic of focus for the survey is decided upon, the next step is to select its hosting site. There are a variety of different free survey websites available, such as Survey Expression, Survey Monkey, and Google Forms. All have different options on offer, with some having restrictions that require payment. However, I would recommend that the basic necessities for the platform selected comprise the following:

1. The limit of questions you can include should not be too restricted – the architecture of the platform you have chosen should not dictate the design and breadth of the survey;
2. Email updates when a survey is filled in can be received, if required;
3. Utilities such as graphs and diagrams can be automatically made from answers to survey questions;
4. Answers to each survey question should be able to be collated into one document, for easier analysis; and
5. There should be a reliability in the storing of data so that nothing is lost.

Surveys can begin (or end) with questions centered on demographic information, such as "what gender do you most identify with?" (providing options of "male," "female," "non-binary," "rather not say," and "other"), age (giving different age range options, such as 0–18 (a range which may require special consent, since the university may not want you to include minors), 19–29, 30–44, 45–65, older than 66), country of residence (possibly dividing by continent), and race/ethnicity. This is important information that is vital to know about the fans that are responding to the survey, since it may have implications on the findings of the research, such as impacting the results, if the sample is skewed in one way. Some researchers also like to ask about occupation, and other fan-related information, such as "how long have you been a fan?" Following these opening questions, the main body of the questionnaire can then focus on the area of research enquiry. For example, the survey I conducted in 2015 exploring experiences of Kate Bush fans surrounding the absence of technology at the Before the Dawn concerts was comprised of the following questions:

1. Before the concerts took place, Kate Bush issued the following request to fans attending the shows: "It would mean a great deal to me if you would please refrain from taking photos or filming during the shows. I very much want to have contact with you as an audience, not with iphones, ipads or cameras... it would allow us to all share in the experience together" (Katebush.com, 2014). What were your thoughts upon reading Kate's request?
2. How closely during the show did you follow Kate's request to refrain from using iPhones, iPads or cameras? Were you ever tempted to break this request?
3. In what ways, if any, did your experience of attending a Before the Dawn concert feel different without technology?
4. Do you usually use your smartphone and/or camera during live music concerts? If so, please describe how you have done this and why. If not, please also describe why.
5. In your experience, how did other audience members respond to Kate's request? Did anyone visibly break these rules, and if so, how did others respond?

6. Did the absence of technology improve your engagement with the concert in any way? If so, please explain why/why not.
7. How do you feel that use of technology (such as smartphones and cameras) is changing the concert experience for fans, if at all?
8. Reflecting back on Before the Dawn, do you miss in any way fan-produced videos and photos of the shows? Please explain why or why not.
9. Do you have any other comments about your Before the Dawn concert experience that you have not addressed in this survey?
   Thank you for your time in completing this survey. If you have any questions, please contact Bennettlucyk@gmail.com. Would you be interested in helping further through taking part in follow-up interviews or questions? If so, please fill in your email address below, which will not be used beyond this purpose and will not be used to identify your responses. If you would rather not be contacted, please simply click Submit. Thank you!

As evident, all of these questions were open-ended and qualitative in nature. This was because I wanted to specifically tap into the articulations and experiences of fans at the Kate Bush concerts, and multiple choice statistical questions, although useful in other regards, were not suitable for this particular survey other than for demographical information.

Multiple choice questions are most commonly included with answers listed on a Likert scale, or with groupings respondents can select from. If a survey does include these for some of the main questions, I recommend including a box option that says "other" or "none of these" and allows fans to write in their responses that may not be included in the answer options. However, relying on these multiple choice questions alone in fan research "creates the danger that the answer given reflects the bias of the survey as much as, if not more than, the thoughts of respondents" (Ruddock 2001: 56). Reflecting back on a survey of Lady Gaga fans I conducted in 2012, I relied too heavily on multiple choice for a handful of questions, which, although beneficial and revealing, somewhat restricted the breadth of responses. The design of surveys can be "difficult, since researchers need to ensure that the form of the questionnaire does not influence the answers given" (Ruddock 2001: 55). To this end, I would argue that surveys in fan research (especially if not being combined with any other research method such as interviews or focus groups) are most fruitful when they are composed of a mix of multiple choice and open-ended questions, allowing for both structured and unstructured answers from respondents. Open-ended questions that allow fans to set the terms, rather than imposed rigidity from the researcher, can sometimes be very beneficial. However, with qualitative questions, care should be taken that they do not simply produce "yes" or "no" answers, but instead provoke and encourage more expanded responses. This can be achieved by adding a prompt for respondents to give more information surrounding their answers, such as "please explain why or why not."

An example of successful survey design can be found within the questionnaire for *The Lord of the Rings* international project, which received almost 25,000 responses. This was designed for audiences, so not *just* fans, but included very useful questions such as: "Can you sum up your response to the film in your own words?" and "What were the main reasons why you wanted to see it? Please give up to three" (see appendix of Barker and

Mathijs 2012 for the full questionnaire). Asking respondents to submit specific words like this can be very fruitful in order to ascertain patterns and surprises.

It is good practice to close with a question that asks participants: "Do you have any other comments about [insert research topic here] that you have not addressed in this survey?" This allows for observations outside the constructed questions to be addressed and captured – in my experience, this can be a valuable addition to a survey since it can raise points previously not considered or anticipated by the researcher.

Distribution, Representation, and Sampling

A critical area within the use of surveys surrounding fandom ignites questions of representation, which is already a problematic area in terms of fans often being portrayed in a singular manner that does not represent the prism-like nature of fandom (Bennett and Booth 2016). When distributing the survey and connecting with fans to solicit participation, then, care should be taken to be as respectful as possible. Although fans can be very welcoming of researchers, others can likewise be suspicious, especially if the researcher is an "outsider" to the fan community. This could be due to possible misrepresentations of fan cultures and communities in the past, or their information being used in a manner not intended by the participant. One option for assuring fans of reliability and authenticity as a researcher would be to contact site administrators (if indeed, it is a specific network or community under study) for their support and approval before reaching out to fans and posting the survey.

The widespread use of online surveys, as I mentioned earlier in this chapter, has resulted in a vista where predominantly online fans who have taken the time to respond are reached. Thus, the sample and voices of fans represented by these surveys can sometimes be somewhat limited and self-selecting, giving scant room or visibility to those who do not participate in online networks or spaces, such as those on the margins who do not engage as strongly, or those of an older age who may not use technology. Those who have different conceptions of what the term "fan" means may also not be well represented in the survey – some individuals who may not describe, or perceive of themselves as fans, but may engage in fannish activity may not feel impetus to respond and will thereby not be represented: "any profile of the 'typical fan' is necessarily going to be incomplete and to favour certain characteristics" (Rebaza 2009: 150). Surveys authored in one language can also exclude those who do not speak the language, thus not including a rich variety of international perspectives. In this light, there should be an acknowledgment from the researcher (and in the method section of the research output) that the survey does not claim to represent all fans, but rather, those who responded to the survey. As others have pointed out, online surveys can be problematic in providing information on broader groups (Evans and Mathur 2005; Hastall and Sukalla 2014). Thus, scholars should be careful in their wording of the claims that the survey results can make towards fandom in general, using caveats such as "this study shows that *for these fans...*," and importantly refraining from generalizations and assumptions.

However, this prospect of the gaps in representation does raise an additional question: can you, or should you try to, ever reach or represent *everyone*?

Perhaps one way of achieving more inclusivity in surveys is by creating a stronger dialogue with the fans they are aimed at. Christine Schreyer (2015) discovered, with her experiences in conducting a survey of Na'vi speaking *Avatar* fans and their online practices, that fans displayed a welcoming interest in her project, enabling it to be more representative of the community. When she posted the survey they "provided suggestions on how to make sure all of their members' voices could accurately be heard," such as adjusting the age limit for the survey, and translating it for free into eight other languages for non-English speaking fans (Schreyer 2015). This response from fans allowed the survey to be more encompassing and inclusive, thereby allowing both researcher and fans to benefit from this collaborative process. In this sense, perhaps more dialogue between fans and scholars within the research process may be fruitful and result in a richer, more expansive set of data. Piloting a survey before its full launch could also be useful in this regard, as experienced by Candie Syphrit Kington, who piloted her convention fandom survey with a group of ten fans to pinpoint "any issues with accessibility, technological compatibility, or question biases and to determine whether any questions should be removed from the study" (2015: 213).

Reaching as widespread a fan audience as possible was my own concern when conducting a survey of Lady Gaga fans surrounding their political and activist participation (Bennett 2014), especially since I was an "outsider" to the fandom. I posted survey invitations in her official and non-official forums, but it can also be very valuable to share surveys across wider networks on social media, as friends may share it further, with it potentially and importantly reaching those who may reside and participate outside the boundaries of the online fan communities. The Kate Bush survey I conducted most notably benefitted from this, since a number of friends and colleagues who were at the concerts completed it, offering explicitly more complicated and different responses than those who were reached through the Kate Bush forums and news channels. This raises an interesting problem of surveys in fan studies – surveys that attempt to reach the breadth of a specific fan culture should endeavor to expose themselves to as wide a network as possible, beyond the bounded groupings of fan communities and networks, since those who may view themselves as fans, yet reside on the fringes of these groups and do not regularly participate, may otherwise be rendered silent.

Analyzing Data

Another critical element of survey research is how to analyze the potentially huge wealth of responses that are garnered. Once I have the data from a survey I focus on individual questions and examine the responses for clear key themes and patterns that occur within answers. For one publication I tend to focus on two to three questions from the survey exclusively, making each of these a distinct section within the main body of the paper. In this sense, one survey could result in the authoring of multiple articles/chapters, as long as they raise sufficiently different themes or threads of analysis. Overall, the analysis should communicate an argument that contributes something new to scholarship – and this is usually based on the specific themes and patterns that are evident within fan responses to the survey.

One advantage of online survey tools is that they can very often offer statistical analysis of the data, grouping them into percentages, graphs, and pie charts, and collate written responses to open-ended questions. Comprehensive analysis of statistical responses would be impossible to cover in this chapter, but in terms of the qualitative responses, analyzing them can be done through coding software, such as NVivo (a qualitative data analysis software package), or by exporting them to Excel. Alternatively they can be coded through SPSS (a statistical software package owned by IBM), with each response within each question being assigned a category depending on its content and placed into it (a method I used for the analysis of the Kate Bush fan survey – exploring the answers in Excel and also having a statistical basis for them in SPSS, a process that is particularly useful as you can map and number the frequency and range of themes that occur).

Another option is to read through all responses and observe notable and key themes that unveil themselves within the responses. However, if there is an extremely high volume of respondents, it could be difficult to determine patterns across hundreds of responses, and those that appear only a handful of times could otherwise be overlooked.

However, when analyzing and writing up the data, attention should also be paid to nuances in the responses, focusing not just on the majority of themes, but also the *outliers and contradictions*, in order to work towards achieving a more rounded picture of the fan culture under study. *I strongly recommend that researchers be open to surprise.* Do not simply look to validate ideas that you may already have about a particular fan culture or community, but be open to being wrong about any assumptions/knowledge you may have formed at the outset, and welcome surprise. Likewise, the reporting of the responses should refrain from mentioning "fans think," "fans tend to" and so on, as there is a danger there of presenting all fan respondents to the survey as one homogenous entity when that is likely not the case. This could be relieved by stating that *some* fans respond in certain ways, and also by giving specific percentage information surrounding these answers.

Conclusion

As I have shown and argued, surveys remain a keystone method for fan studies research in that the voices and articulations of fans can be grasped, forming the basis of rich empirical data that is invaluable when discussing fandom. The ease of creating and circulating online surveys can be somewhat deceptive, since, as I have shown, there are key critical questions surrounding ethics, design, analysis, representation, and inclusion that fan studies scholars should give strong consideration to when designing and distributing surveys. In this sense, I recommend that surveys be circulated not only within the confines of specific fan communities, but also outside, across wider social networks.

Future research could investigate fan and audience experiences towards completion of surveys, in terms of their experience as research participants (such as any gaps they felt were evident in questions) and their responses surrounding the eventual published research. Recounting of these experiences could be especially fruitful for researchers of fans to gain more insight into the research processes from those under study, and importantly re-center and bring to the fore the voices of fans and audiences within considerations of method in fandom research.

Acknowledgements

The author would like to thank Paul Booth and Kristina Busse for their very valuable comments on a draft of this chapter.

References

Barker, M. and Mathijs, E. (2012) "Researching World Audiences: The Experience of a Complex Methodology," *Participations*, 9 (2), pp. 664–698.

Bennett, L. (2014) "'If We Stick Together We Can Do Anything': Lady Gaga Fans in Philanthropy and Activism through Social Media," *Celebrity Studies*, 5 (1–2), pp. 138–152.

Bennett, L. (2017) "Resisting Technology in Music Fandom: Nostalgia, Authenticity and Kate Bush's 'Before the Dawn'," in J. Gray, C. Sandvoss and C. Lee Harrington (eds.), *Fandom: Identities and Communities in a Mediated World* (new revised edition), New York: New York University Press, pp. 127–142.

Bennett, L. and Booth, P. (2016) *Seeing Fans: Representation of Fandom in Media and Popular Culture*, London: Bloomsbury.

Booth, P. and Kelly, P. (2013) "The Changing Faces of Doctor Who Fandom: New Fans, New Technologies, Old Practices?," *Participations*, 10 (1), pp. 56–72.

Busse, K. and Hellekson, K. (2012) "Identity, Ethics and Fan Privacy," in K. Larsen and L. Zubernis (eds.), *Fan Culture: Theory/Practice*, Newcastle upon Tyne, UK: Cambridge Scholars Publishing, pp. 38–56.

Deacon, D. and Keightley, E. (2014) "Quantitative Audience Research: Embracing the Poor Relation," in V. Nightingale (ed.), *The Handbook of Media Audiences*, Oxford: Wiley, pp. 302–319.

Deacon, D., Pickering, M., Golding, P., and Murdock, G. (2007) *Researching Communications: A Practical Guide to Methods in Media and Cultural Analysis* (2nd edition), London: Arnold Publishing.

Deller, R. (2015) "Simblr Famous and SimSecret Infamous: Performance, Community Norms, and Shaming among Fans of The Sims," *Transformative Works and Cultures*, 18. http://dx.doi.org/10.3983/twc.2015.0615

Dillman, D., Smyth, J., and Melani, L. (2014) *Internet, Phone, Mail, and Mixed-Mode Surveys: The Tailored Design Method* (4th edition), New Jersey: Wiley.

Evans, J. R. and Mathur, A. (2005) "The Value of Online Surveys," *Internet Research*, 15 (2), pp. 195–219.

Franzke, A. S., Bechmann, A., Zimmer, M., Ess, C., and the Association of Internet Researchers (2020) Internet Research: Ethical Guidelines 3.0. Available at: https://aoir.org/reports/ethics3.pdf

Fowler, F. (1995) *Improving Survey Questions: Design and Evaluation*, London: Sage.

Fowler, F. (2014) *Survey Research Methods* (5th edition), London: Sage.

Gray, J. and Mittell, J. (2007) "Speculation on Spoilers: Lost Fandom, Narrative Consumption and Rethinking Textuality," *Participations*, 4 (1). Available at: www.participations.org/Volume%204/Issue%201/4_01_graymittell.htm

Halbert, D. J. (2009) "The Labor of Creativity: Women's Work, Quilting, and the Uncommodified Life," Transformative Works and Cultures, 3. http://dx.doi.org/10.3983/twc.2009.0041

Hastall, M. R. and Sukalla, F. (2014) "Digging the Web: Promises and Challenges of Using Web 2.0 Tools for Audience Research," in G. Patriarche et al. (eds.), *Audience Research Methdologies: Between Innovation and Consolidation*, London: Routledge, pp. 177–195.

Kington, C. S. (2015) "Con Culture: A Survey of Fans and Fandom," *The Journal of Fandom Studies*, 3 (2), pp. 211–228.

Mckeown, R. E. and Weed, L. (2004) "Ethical Choices in Survey Research," *Social & Preventative Medicine*, 49 (1), pp. 67–68.

Oh, I. and Kim, K. (2023) "Gendered Melancholia as Cultural Branding: Fandom Participation in the K-Pop Community," *Asia Pacific Business Review*, 29 (5), pp. 1300–1323.

Rebaza, C. (2009) "The Problematic Definition of 'Fan': A Survey of Fannish Involvement in the Buffyverse," in Kirby-Diaz, M. (ed.), *Buffy and Angel Conquer the Internet: Essays on Online Fandom*, London: McFarland, pp. 147–171.

Ruddock, A. (2001) *Understanding Audiences: Theory and Method*, London: Sage.

Schreyer, C. (2015) "The Digital Fandom of Na'vi Speakers," *Transformative Works and Cultures*, 18. http://dx.doi.org/10.3983/twc.2015.0610

Sudman, S. and Bradburn, N. (1982) *Asking Questions: A Practical Guide to Questionnaire Design*, San Francisco: Jossey-Bass Publishers.

Whiteman, N. (2012) *Undoing Ethics: Rethinking Practice in Online Research*, London: Springer.

Williams, R. (2015) *Post-Object Fandom: Television, Identity and Self-Narrative*, London: Bloomsbury.

Włodarczyk, A. and Tyminska, M. (2015) "Cultural Differences: Polish Fandom of Welcome to Night Vale," *Transformative Works and Cultures*, 19. http://dx.doi.org/10.3983/twc.2015.0591

Yodavich, N. (2023) "How Long is Life-Long? Evaluating and Measuring Time Through Life-Long/Long-Term Fandom," *The Journal of Fandom Studies*, 11 (2–3), pp. 189–204.

6
FANDOM AND DISABILITY
Expanding Theoretical Perspectives to Fan Studies

Divya Garg

Fan studies has frequently presumed and focused on the white, Western, and abled fan, despite the engagement of fans with diverse cultural locations, abilities, and differences in both offline and digital fan spaces. The understanding of the term "fan" itself mobilizes a key question of ability, yet disability is typically considered an ontological category separate from mainstream theorizations of fan practices. Fan communities are conceived as safe spaces and support groups (Dandrow 2016), evoking discourses of mental health and psychosocial therapy. Additionally, in seeing fan work as a way for marginalized fans to perform and seek representation and participation, the work of disabled fans or those involving disabled characters is clearly important yet missed. Indeed, fandom is seen to have a high percentage of disabled and neurodiverse participants and stories that involve a range of physical, emotional, and mental sensitivities, and fans appreciate digital platforms such as Archive of Our Own for their use of safety mechanisms including trigger warnings and content tags (Coppa 2014). These factors contribute to making fandom a valuable site of disability representation and engagement, attesting to the existence of mechanisms that address issues of inclusivity and access in fandom spaces, as well as suggesting a significant representation of individuals with disabilities in fandom. This chapter explores how a disability lens to fandom offers unique potential in realizing its value and how it can facilitate a revisiting and revisioning of research objectives, methods, and theoretical frameworks in fandom scholarship.

Despite this promising interest in fandom for studies of disability and health, fan research centering these subjects and identity positions remains relatively scarce, and little attention has been given to the intersections of disability and race, in particular. To date, the only comprehensive fan research on disability is a special volume of the *Canadian Journal for Disability Studies* (2019) edited by Bridget Liang and Catherine de Montrouge. This significant edition examines how "disability manifests itself in fannish spaces" (Liang and de Montrouge 2019: 5). The essays in the collection explore themes such as representations of mental illness and the relationship between fan authors and their texts (Rogers 2019), disability stereotypes and tropes within fan texts (Newman-Stille 2019), ways of reading fanfiction from a disability perspective (Clemons 2019), and framing certain fan practices in an "activism of care" (Leetal 2019). The authors of this volume suggest multiple possibilities of using a disability lens to engage with fandom and demonstrate a critical need to develop and explore further avenues for disability in fandom.

Recent work on the decolonization of fan studies has involved increasing attention to questions of race (Woo 2017; Stanfill 2018; Pande 2018). As part of this decolonizing impetus, I am interested in diversifying the subject of media fandom and its project(s) of inquiry through the important yet often invisible category of ability. Fan identities, practices, and pleasures, as well as conceptions and experiences of disability vary for diverse fans globally. Even fan descriptors such as "geek" and "nerd" are rooted in specific Anglo-American contexts and traditions (of gender expression and social and cultural capital, among other aspects). I briefly identify some ways fan studies and disability studies can speak to each other in mutually generative ways, keeping in mind the transcultural nature of global fan communities and deploying a decolonial approach to disability.

Decolonizing Disability: The Role of (Racialized) Ability in "Fan" Conceptualizations

A decolonial approach provides a valuable way of using the intersections of disability and race to study the material and ideological investments in hegemonic systems of ability that structure unequal fan relations. Decolonial scholars have argued that historically disability and race relations problematize the "other," that is, disabled bodies rather than systems of ability (Dirth and Adams 2019) and non-white status rather than whiteness (Guess 2006). Moreover, as Artiles argues, white people are centered when defining concepts like ability and disability, leading to the otherization of non-white people (2013: 341). In the context of fan studies, Rukmini Pande (2018) notes that the analysis of race should not be reserved to non-white subjects alone, urging scholars to consider whiteness itself as a racialized identity. Similarly, a decolonial approach can involve utilizing disability "as an epistemic and epistemological standpoint for reconsideration of under-theorized and taken-for-granted notions of ability" (Dirth and Adams 2019: 262). This shifts the gaze "from a disability pre-occupied minoritization towards ableist normativity, and concentrates on what the study of disability tells us about the production, operation and continuation of [ability]" (Campbell 2012: 215).

Non-white race and disability form two critical systems whose mutual displacement from centers of power reveals how systems of ability are sustained. Decolonial scholars argue that considering the intersections of race and disability can "denaturalize ability by illuminating its material and ideological investments" (Dirth and Adams 2019: 207). Decolonial strategies reveal, for instance, how the material affluence needed for social and economic resources that enable certain experiences of independence and freedom for disabled people, is "a product of historical and ongoing violence that (re)produces material disablement in its wake" (Dirth and Adams 2019: 273). Hence, an analysis of the politics of exclusion which is readily associated with minority subjects is necessary to critically explore the intersections of race and disability by looking at fans – both non-disabled and those with disabilities – beyond the Global North.

The question of ability is mobilized in the conceptualization of the identity (as well as practice) of being a "fan." Definitions of who qualifies as a fan have varied throughout the history of fan studies. Although media consumption practices today would qualify almost anyone as a fan in terms of self-identification, degrees of affective engagement and creative participation still complicate scholarly understandings of the term. Borrowing from its origin associations with religious zealotry, some scholars see fans as devoted audiences closer to cultists and enthusiasts (Abercrombie and Longhurst 1998). More recent scholars, however, have included anyone who loves a show and follows it regularly, and who may participate in common and communal forms of fan practices (Gray et al. 2017). Still others distinguish between a "fan" and a "follower," where participating in creative labor would qualify one as a fan (Coppa 2014), as opposed to the latter regular affective consumer who would merely be a follower (Jenkins and Tulloch 1995). The growing digitalization of fan cultures facilitated by historical developments in technologies is also responsible for this multiplicity in participation forms and formats (Sandvoss 2005), which has also changed the dimensions of who gets to be a fan.

Limiting the study of fans to networked individuals who consciously perform resistive work or certain kinds of participatory activity can discount certain populations, fans, and traditions, especially non-Anglo-American ones (Gray et al. 2017). It might also exclude those whose participation in particular fields – online and offline – is affected by disabilities and/or health or social conditions that may restrict the potential for communal activity. The digital medium is seen as a space that reduces barriers of communication and participation, but that does not make it necessarily democratic. As Ellcessor (2017) demonstrates, technological features and digital fan spaces have not empowered all fans equally, and many fan platforms, including Tumblr, can be inaccessible. Conceptions of fans as participatory may then not fully account for those who are restricted from participating in specific ways (e.g., chatting or commenting) owing to the frequency of exclusionary experiences that can adversely impact their health. In my forthcoming monograph involving self-identified Marvel fans, non-white fans and fans with disabilities (and particularly mental illness) emerged as especially vulnerable to experiences of hostility and reported more frequent self-censorship and "lurking" behavior as a preemptive response to prevent toxic encounters (Garg 2022). Lurking activities such as invisibly following and "liking" certain content nevertheless indicate participation in fandom, predicated as it may be upon physical/emotional and technological affordances. In the first edition of this volume, Click and Scott discussed the delimitations to fans and fan practices by raising the question of the lurker, "who 'lurks' in online discussions, following fan sites or celebrities on social media without engaging with them directly" (2017: 1–2). Perhaps a more useful way of thinking about fan cultures can be through focusing on "engagement" whether it be in the form of creation, consumption, or in-between, rather than focusing solely on fan creators and their works.

Linking Disability Studies with Fan Studies

Both fan studies and disability studies have relatively recent pasts and share ethical concerns regarding the entry of academic interest in subjects and issues of marginal status. The most prominent model in disability studies is what is termed the social model of disability, which is the foundational approach in the emergence of the discipline. While the medical discourse locates disability in the individual with a clear split between the body and the mind (McDougall 2006), the social model sees disability as a social phenomenon. Disability activism in the 1970s in the UK led to the development of social theories of disability that challenged reductive understandings of disability as something to be pitied or cured. The Union of the Physically Impaired Against Segregation (UPIAS), a group of disabled people inspired by Marxism, differentiated between impairment, defined as "lacking part or all of a limb, or having a defective limb, organ or mechanism of the body," and disability, which they perceived as the social discrimination, restrictions, and exclusion caused by societal structuring that does not account for people's impairments (UPIAS 1976: 3–4). This social understanding of disability led to the development of the social model that emphasizes the inadequacy of an ableist society that creates disability (Oliver 2013), but which can also, if addressed, prevent or redress disability. The social model that places disability in social institutions rather than in individuals allows us to subvert and resist forms of disablement that institutions – including the media and the academy – create and perpetuate. Though predicated upon a disability/impairment binary and erasure of the body that later disability theorists challenged (Hughes and Patterson 1997), the social model is an important tool for thinking about disability for imagining inclusive fandom futures. In the following subsections, I draw attention to some prominent work in disability studies and highlight their connections as well as potential contributions to expanding fan research and its approaches/inquiries.

Cripping Media Fandom's "Queer Female Space": Feminist Disability Studies and Crip Theory

The relationship between feminism and disability studies is central to the site of media fandom. A significant majority of fan writers are women, and several fanworks engage with the depiction of sexual desire, particularly through the queering of cisgender men. Intersectional models of queer and disability frameworks are particularly helpful in studying fan narratives given the framing of media fandom, especially slash fandom, as "queer female space" (Lothian et al. 2007), which not only involves queer women but centers queer desire. Women fans are pathologized through a gendered disability discourse. Fangirls are described using terms such as "hysterical," "rabid," and "obsessive," in ways that male fans and associated fan practices are not (Hampton 2016: 229). This pathological construction of the fan(girl) relies on negative associations of affect, which is also prevalent in persisting ableist constructions of the "mind" within disability studies. As Donaldson and Prendergast (2011) argue, psychiatry and culture are concerned with regulating and monitoring emotion: both excess emotion and a lack of it is pathologized. In this regard, fan studies' revaluation of affect through framing emotion as a positive and fundamental aspect of fannish identity (Sandvoss 2005) can be a critical tool in reclaiming emotion in disability studies and demonstrating how their intersections can be mutually generative.

A second area of marginality that connects the two disciplines and their primary constituents is that of sexuality. The persistent discomfort with and disregard of female sexuality as well as non-normative sexualities is evidenced from the lack of safe spaces for sexual consumption of women (Coppa 2009) and the desexualization of people with disabilities (Rembis 2010). Queer disability studies explore questions of disability and sexuality, addressing, among others issues, "the cultural contradiction that lesbian is a sexual identity while disabled women are considered asexual" (Tremain 1996: 15). Fan work is a prolific site of erotic engagement with a variety of sexual practices, kinks, and stimulants. Fan narratives can thus help respond to disability scholars' call for rethinking ideas of sexual ability and normativity. Disability studies scholar Tom Shakespeare, for instance, raises several pertinent questions that resonate with fanfiction's role as a sexual archive that challenges heteronormative ways of conceptualizing sex and sexual practices: "Why should men be dominant? Why should sex revolve around penetration? Why should sex only involve two people? Why can't disabled people be assisted to have sex by third parties? What is normal sex?" (2000: 163). Media fandom frequently visualizes such experiences and it is this preoccupation with sex; the charge of pornography, particularly when associated with women, that contributes to its denigration as perverse, extreme, and marginal in mainstream culture and imagination (Later 2018). However, it is important to note that even in doing so fandom often perpetuates other hegemonic ideas of sexual roles and performances through its overrepresentation of conventionally attractive cisgender white men who are often able-bodied or whose disability does not affect their sexual performance (Garg 2018). When centering queerness, it is therefore essential to acknowledge and examine what kinds of queer bodies are privileged in media fandom.

Recent work in the field of disability studies has taken a *crip* turn that partly involves important parallels between queer theory and disability studies. Robert McRuer (2006) articulates the similarity of queer and disabled identities in terms of their shared medicalized history and marginalization, as well as their resistive potential to normative systems of ability, gender, and sexuality. Challenging assumptions of a heteronormative and ableist society, crip theory seeks to *crip* able-bodiedness the way queer theory *queers* heteronormativity. Using Adrienne Rich's (1980) concept of compulsory heterosexuality, McRuer argues that "the system of compulsory able-bodiedness, which in a sense produces disability, is thoroughly interwoven with the system of compulsory heterosexuality that produces queerness" (2006: 2). Hence, true able-bodiedness can never be achieved. This has led to the coinage of the term "temporarily able-bodied" for non-disabled people as disability is something that everyone eventually experiences due to age or illness. Although crip theory's implications of everyone being "queer/disabled" can posit the danger of imagining disability as a metaphor and undermining the struggles of those critically or severely disabled, McRuer resists such implications, arguing that:

> – there are *moments* when we are all queer/disabled, and that *those disabled/queer moments are desirable*. In particular, a crip theory of composition argues for the desirability and extension of those moments when we are all queer/disabled, since it is those moments that provide us with a means of speaking back to straight composition in all its guises. (2006: 157, emphasis in original)

Queerness and disability are experienced by everyone, in moments, and crip theory seeks resistance to compulsory regimes of being through the desirability and extension of these moments.

Conceptions of disability through such moments where fans occupy marginal positions hold resistive potential. While slash has the potential to become crip (Newman-Stille 2019), it often fails to do so because of the use of disability as a cultural tool to make the male protagonist vulnerable and facilitate romantic intimacy. In the case of sexual dynamics, this is often achieved through a feminization of the disabled character in a male same-sex coupling, particularly in hurt/comfort narratives where the hurt is facilitated through temporarily disabling a character who is comforted by the non-disabled penetrating partner. Such depictions and the use of disability as a plot device or "narrative prothesis" (Mitchell and Snyder 2013) can reproduce reductive stereotypes of disability (and sexuality). However, focusing on these moments through McRuer's (2006) articulation of queer/disabled resistance as a means of speaking back to compulsory able-bodied heterosexuality can also help us interrogate the norms that treat disability simultaneously as ubiquitous *and* exceptional. This can serve as a bridge to question the taken-for-granted fixedness of ability/able-bodiedness.

What's Minority Status Got to Do with It? Mental Disabilities, Neurodivergence, and the Discourse of Marginality

The interdependence of physical and mental health is crucial to the way we think about disability and ability. Mental health studies have shared a contested relationship with/in the field of disability studies, in part due to the problems in situating mental illness as purely impairment or purely a social construct, which can lead to an obfuscation of the neurological causes of some forms of mental illness (Graby 2015). The distinction between able-bodiedness and able-mindedness needs to be further interrogated. Alison Kafer defines able-mindedness as "a way of capturing the normalizing practices, assumptions, and exclusions that cannot easily be described as directed (exclusively) to *physical* functioning or appearance" (2013: 184), which helps accommodate mental disability in a broader disability formulation. Furthermore, Price's use of the "bodymind" acknowledges that "mental and physical processes not only affect each other but also give rise to each other" (2015: 269). These imbrications are most clearly prevalent in sociological discourses of disability.

Sociological approaches to mental illness stress the dependent relationship between mental health conditions and social problems. Building upon socio-political analyses from Foucault's (1977) thesis of how power operates through psychiatric institutions to maintain dominant social norms, such theorizations signal the vested interests of psychiatric systems and pharmaceutical companies in "treating" mental illness and controlling "deviant" populations. This is useful in understanding the relationship of disadvantaged or minority positions with mental disorders and/or illnesses. Scholars have traced the historical association of women's emotions and behaviors with psychiatric labels such as hysteria and borderline personality disorder (Morris 2018). Another example is the inclusion of homosexuality as a medical illness until the third version of the Diagnostic and Statistical Manual of Mental Disorders (DSM) (Drescher 2015). Indeed, homosexuality continues to be considered as a mental disorder in many countries even today. Moreover, racial and ethnic minorities have been subject to the power-laden systems of psychiatric discourse. Suman Fernando (2010) demonstrates how categories of mental illness such as schizophrenia have been used to pathologize and politicize minority groups. The history of the eugenics project in Europe is a highly racialized one where both disability and non-white race were deemed undesirable characteristics (Mitchell and Snyder 2003). And significantly, colonialism has impacted both the construction of idealized normativity (Grech 2015) as well as contributed to greater (physical and psychological) disablement in postcolonial nations (Fanon 2008).

The neurodiversity movement may also provide a way to connect the mental health system survivors' movement and disabled people's movements (Graby 2015). Aligning people with conditions positioned somewhere between the categories of "disability/impairment" and "illness" such as autism spectrum disorders, learning difficulties, and behavioral differences, the neurodiversity movement acknowledges the diversity of neurotypes, and critiques medicalized normalization drives much like the major theories in critical disability studies and mental health studies. A neurodiversity framework further seeks to reclaim medicalized notions of impairment to re-value them as positive and can enable the inclusion of both "those who identify their mental distress as purely biochemical, and those who regard it as purely 'socially reactive'" (2015: 238). Neurodivergence is also a commonly used term in fan discourse.

Representations of neuroatypicality as well as (certain) mental disabilities and illnesses are abundant in many popular media fandoms. *Doctor Who* and *Sherlock* studies have noted the presence of coding main characters on the autism spectrum and the practice of reading them as such in fanfiction (Manning 2015; Poore 2017). As a study on the representation of autism in *Harry Potter* fanfiction (Lugo et al. 2017) indicates, fan platforms can function as inclusive spaces incorporating alternative forms of representation and a space to negotiate the meaning of a particular disability/difference by drawing upon the experiences of therapists, family members, and individuals on the autism spectrum. In Marvel fanfiction, there is particular focus on mental disabilities such as post-traumatic disorder, identity disorders, and anxiety and depression, among others. Indeed, in dominant global media fandoms, disability is most clearly and frequently represented in terms of mental health issues rather than physical disabilities. However, these representations can be reductive or problematic, displaying what McRuer (2018) terms a "politics of austerity." In Marvel fandom, for instance, physical disabilities often form part of the "overcoming" storyline where a disability is "fixed" or "cured" through scientific technology or magic, thus reproducing negative connotations of disability. This necessitates engaging with the question of disability representation in fandom in a more meaningful and nuanced way.

Representing and Engaging with Dis/ability: The Cultural Model and a Praxis of Decolonization

While popular culture representations today try to replace negative stereotypes with positive ones through an increasing public awareness and fan activist agendas to enable representational diversity, they frequently depict disability and illness inadequately in a capitalist regime. In framing resistance as representational diversity, they participate in "the neoliberal commodification of difference as a resource for corporate profit" (Fawaz 2018: 31). While fan work, created and disseminated non-commercially through a gift economy (Turk 2014) challenges the logic of capital and provides multiple forms and narratives of representation that may provide grounds for resistance, it can still contribute to the dehumanization of fans with disabilities or further disablement. In fannish terms, gifting is based on "giving, receiving, and reciprocating" (Turk 2014: 1.1), but this does not prevent fandom from perpetuating disability myths and limitations in its own realm as discussed above. However, this reciprocal nature of fan economies and the collaborative nature of content creation therein does enable more informed approaches through the possibilities for interaction between non-disabled fans and fans with disabilities.

Digital platforms including media fandom can function as a significant space for representation of marginalized identities and one which can potentially subvert an austerity politics. Conversations around mental illness and distress, propagated through social media posts and comment threads, memes, and blog entries are increasingly turning from the casual dismissal of ableist language towards those distinguishing experiences of individuals suffering from such problems, the socio-political roots and consequences of mental illness, and the need to address ableism on a structural level. In much fanfiction across English-language global media fandoms, fans extensively engage with these issues and stress the importance of therapy and other mental health services. Although it has limitations and problems, the significant discourse on mental health in fandom can offer valuable insights and inform contemporary understandings of disability and health.

Drawing attention to this cultural role of disability, Snyder and Mitchell's (2006) cultural model frames disability as beyond the discriminatory encounters encapsulated by the social model. They use disability not only as a cultural site of oppression but also as a source of previously suppressed cultural agency. Experiential forms of disability including personal narratives and performance art are seen as positive alternative locations against the institutionalization of disability that produces research on disabled people. To this end, fan narratives can serve a crucial function of performing identity work using their lived experiences of disablement, recovery, and healing through the appropriation of shared cultural texts. However, despite the emphasis on lived experiences, the cultural model in its present context lacks empirical instances of globalized disability and geopolitical difference, much like earlier models of disability (Barker and Murray 2010). Neither fandom practice nor disability operates in a space outside of racialization and coloniality, therefore it is important to frame a politics that can address this.

A decolonial approach to both fandom and disability can assist in conceptualizing frameworks to address these limitations. As Grech (2015) observes, disability is disproportionally present in southern spaces, yet there remains a dearth of disability perspectives from the Global South. Given the transcultural nature of global media fandoms (Chin and Morimoto 2013), fan communities provide a generative space for inclusive and intersectional studies of disability, not least through the perspectives of those beyond the Global North. By including an analysis of racially and culturally diverse fans' experiences and moments of disability, greater attention can be paid to how ability and capacity are predicated upon other markers of identity and historical legacies of colonialism. The transcultural nature of modern media fandom provides a valuable pathway to interrogating global experiences, ideas, and understandings of ability/disability. In addition, disability need not only be studied through negative framings or analogies of othering but also as a productive site of both representation and experience. This can involve multiple approaches, including but not limited to, exploring the shared struggles and joys of fans with disabilities, representational work around disability, tracing the racialized contours of disability engagement, and interrogating hegemonic systems of ability and normativity.

Conclusion

Locating a gap regarding intersectional perspectives on disability in fandom, I link fan studies with disability studies to signal how their intersections provide a meaningful route to explore understandings and experiences of disability in media fandom. Foundational conceptualizations of fans, and fan practices and communities, utilize key mobilizations of ability and speak to discourses of disability and health. Tracing the connections between these two fields alongside questions of marginality, I conceptualize media fandom as a generative site of cultural representations and transcultural encounters with dis/ability and argue that a decolonial approach to both fan studies and disability studies can potentially serve as a practical response to the discursive demands of inclusive disability theories and utilize the creative and political potential of disability.

References

Abercrombie, N., & Longhurst, B. (1998). *Audiences: A sociological theory of performance and imagination*. London: Sage.

Artiles, A. J. (2013). Untangling the racialization of disabilities: An intersectionality critique across disability models. *Du Bois Review: Social Science Research on Race*, 10(2), 329–347.

Barker, C., & Murray, S. (2010). Disabling postcolonialism: Global disability cultures and democratic criticism. *Journal of Literary and Cultural Disability Studies*, 4(3), 219–236.

Campbell, F. K. (2012). Stalking ableism: Using disability to expose 'abled' narcissism. In D. Goodley, B. Hughes, & L. Davis (Eds.), *Disability and social theory: New approaches and directions* (pp. 212–230). Basingstoke, UK: Palgrave Macmillan.

Chin, B., & Morimoto, L. (2013). Towards a theory of transcultural fandom. *Participations*, 10(1), 92–108.

Clemons, A. (2019). Enabling/disabling: Fanfiction and disability discourse. *Canadian Journal of Disability Studies*, 7(3), 247–278.

Click, M. A., & Scott, S. (Eds.). (2017). *The Routledge companion to media fandom*. Routledge.

Coppa, F. (2009). A fannish taxonomy of hotness. *Cinema Journal*, 48(4), 107–113.

Coppa, F. (2014). Fuck yeah, fandom is beautiful. *The Journal of Fandom Studies*, 2(1), 73–82.

Dandrow, C. (2016). Fandom as a fortress: The gendered safe spaces of online fanfiction communities. *Media Report to Women*, 44(1), 6–23.

Dirth, T. P., & Adams, G. A. (2019). Decolonial theory and disability studies: On the modernity/coloniality of ability. *Journal of Social and Political Psychology*, 7(1), 260–289.

Donaldson, E. J., & Prendergast, C. (2011). Introduction: Disability and emotion: "There's No Crying in Disability Studies!". *Journal of Literary & Cultural Disability Studies*, 5(2), 129–135.

Drescher, J. (2015). Out of DSM: Depathologizing homosexuality. *Behavioral Sciences*, 5(4), 565–575.

Ellcessor, E. (2017). Accessing fan cultures: Disability, digital media, and dreamwidth. In M. Click & S. Scott (Eds.), *The Routledge companion to media fandom* (pp. 202–211). New York: Routledge.

Fanon, F. (2008). *Black skin, white masks*. New York, NY: Grove Press.

Fawaz, R. (2018). Legions of superheroes: Diversity, multiplicity, and collective action against genocide in the superhero comic book. *Social Text*, 36(4), 21–55.

Fernando, S. (2010). *Mental health, race and culture*. London: Bloomsbury Publishing.

Foucault, M. (1977). *Discipline and punish: The birth of the prison*. New York: Pantheon Books.

Garg, D. (2018). (Un)sanctioned bodies: The state-sexuality-disability nexus in *Captain America* slash fan fiction. In A. Spacey (Ed.), *The darker side of slash fan fiction: Essays on power, consent and the body* (pp. 76–96). Jefferson, NC: McFarland.

Garg, D. (2022). *Fandom and dis/ability: Imagining a politics of inclusivity through Marvel global media fandom*. RMIT University [PhD dissertation].

Graby, S. (2015). Neurodiversity: bridging the gap between the disabled people's movement and the mental health system survivors' movement?. In H. Spandler, et al. (Eds.), *Madness, distress and the politics of disablement*. Bristol; online edn, Policy Press Scholarship Online, 21 Jan. 2016, https://doi.org/10.1332/policypress/9781447314578.003.0017, accessed 4 Nov. 2024.

Gray, J., Sandvoss, C., & Harrington, L. (2017). Introduction: Why study fans? In J. Gray, C. Sandvoss, & L. Harrington (Eds.), *Fandom: Identities and communities in a mediated world* (pp. 1–16). New York: New York University Press.

Grech, S. (2015). Decolonising eurocentric disability studies: Why colonialism matters in the disability and Global South debate. *Social Identities*, 21(1), 6–21.

Guess, T. J. (2006). The social construction of whiteness: Racism by intent, racism by consequence. *Critical Sociology*, 32(4), 649–673.

Hampton, D. (2016). Slashy rotten pervs: Transnational media representation of Sherlock slash fans and the politics of pathologization. In L. Bennett & P. Booth (Eds.), *Seeing fans: Representations of fandom in media and popular culture* (pp. 229–238). New York: Bloomsbury.

Hemmann, K. (Ed.). (2020). Link is not silent: Queer disability positivity in fan readings of *The Legend of Zelda: Breath of the wild*. In *Manga cultures and the female gaze*. East Asian Popular Culture. Palgrave Macmillan, Cham. https://doi.org/10.1007/978-3-030-18095-9_6

Hughes, B., & Paterson, K. (1997). The social model of disability and the disappearing body: Towards a sociology of impairment. *Disability and Society, 12*(3), 325–340.

Jenkins, H., & Tulloch, J. (1995). *Science fiction audiences: Watching Star Trek and Doctor Who*. New York: Routledge.

Kafer, A. (2013). *Feminist, queer, crip*. Bloomington, IN: Indiana University Press.

Later, N. (2018). The monstrous narratives of transformative fandom. *Participations, 15*(2), 329–342.

Leetal, D. (2019). Those crazy fangirls on the Internet: Activism of care, disability and fan fiction. *Canadian Journal of Disability Studies, 8*(2), 45–72.

Liang, B., & Duchastel, C. M. (2019). An editorial of sorts. *Canadian Journal of Disability Studies, 8*(2), 1–9.

Lothian, A., Busse, K., & Reid, R. A. (2007). "Yearning Void and Infinite Potential": Online slash fandom as queer female space. *English Language Notes, 45*(2), 103.

Lugo, N., Melon, M. E., & Castillo, N. C. (2017). The representation of autism in the narratives of fanfiction.net: Affinity spaces as an opportunity for the negotiation of meaning. *Palabra Clave, 20*(4), 948–978.

Manning, L. (2015). Negotiating doctor who: Neurodiversity and fandom. In *Media, Margins and Popular Culture* (pp. 153–165). London: Palgrave Macmillan.

McDougall, K. (2006). 'Ag shame' and superheroes: Stereotypes and the signfication of disability. In B. Watermeyer, L. Swartz, T. Lorenzo, M. Schneider, & M. Priestly (Eds.), *Disability and social change: A South African agenda* (pp. 387–400). Cape Town: HSRC Press.

McRuer, R. (2006). *Crip theory: Cultural signs of queerness and disability*. New York: New York University Press.

McRuer, R. (2018). *Crip times. Disability, globalisation, and resistance*. New York: New York University Press.

Mitchell, D., & Snyder, S. (2003). The eugenic Atlantic: Race, disability, and the making of an international eugenic science, 1800–1945. *Disability & Society, 18*(7), 843–864.

Mitchell, D., & Snyder, S. (2013). Narrative prosthesis. *The Disability Studies Reader, 4*, 222–235.

Morris, B. (2018). *Borderline women: Sexual difference, abjection and liminal spaces*. University of West Georgia [Doctoral dissertation].

Newman-Stille, D. (2019). From slash fan fiction to crip fan fiction: What role does disability have in fandom? *Canadian Journal of Disability Studies, 8*(2), 73–95.

Oliver, M. (2013). The social model of disability: thirty years on. *Disability & Society, 28*(7), 1024–1026. https://doi.org/10.1080/09687599.2013.818773

Pande, R. (2018). *Squee from the margins: Fandom and race*. Iowa City: University of Iowa Press.

Poore, B. (2017). *Sherlock Holmes from screen to stage*. London: Palgrave Macmillan.

Price, M. (2014). The bodymind problem and the possibilities of pain. *Hypatia: A Journal of Feminist Philosophy, 30*(1), 268–264.

Rembis, M. A. (2010). Beyond the binary: Rethinking the social model of disabled sexuality. *Sexuality and Disability, 28*(1), 51–60.

Rich, A. (1980). Compulsory heterosexuality and lesbian existence. *Signs: Journal of Women in Culture and Society, 5*(3), 631–660.

Richardson, N. (2010). *Transgressive bodies: Representations in film and popular culture*. London: Routledge.

Rogers, J. (2019). Authentic representation and author identity: Exploring mental illness in *The Hobbit* fanfiction. *Canadian Journal of Disability Studies, 7*(3), 127–146.

Sandvoss, C. (2005). *Fans: The mirror of consumption*. Malden, MA: Polity Press.

Shakespeare, T. (2000). Disabled sexuality: Toward rights and recognition. *Sexuality and Disability, 18*(3), 159–166.

Snyder, S. L., & Mitchell, D. T. (2006). *The cultural locations of disability*. Chicago and London: University of Chicago Press.

Stanfill, M. (2018). The unbearable whiteness of fandom and fan studies. In P. Booth (Ed.), *A companion to media fandom and fan studies* (pp. 401–416). Hoboken, NJ: John Wiley and Sons.

Thomson, R. G. (2005). Feminist disability studies. *Signs, 30*(2), 1557–1587.

Titchkosky, T. (2000). Disability studies: The old and the new. *Canadian Journal of Sociology and Anthropology, 25*(2), 197–224.

Tremain, S. (1996). *Pushing the limits: Disabled dykes produce culture*. Toronto, Canada: Women's Press.
Turk, T. (2014). Fan work: Labor, worth, and participation in fandom's gift economy. *Transformative Works and Cultures, 15*, 113–118.
UPIAS. (1976). *Fundamental principles of disability*. London: Union of the Physically Impaired Against Segregation.
Woo, B. (2017). Whiteness and media fandom. In M. Click & S. Scott (Eds.), *The Routledge companion to media fandom*. New York: Routledge.

7
TRANSNATIONAL MEDIA FAN STUDIES

Lori Morimoto

Introduction

The terms 'fandom', 'fan', and even 'fan studies' appear to be, at first glance, self-evident. But considered in the context of both fan cultures and scholarship outside the English language-centered West, we begin to see the assumptions that underlie them. Whether we are talking about Japanese fans of manga and anime (somewhat codified itself, both given the diversity of Japanese fan practices and objects, as well as non-Western fandoms generally), the Korean Wave, Nigerian fans of Bollywood films, and so on, scholarship of 'transnational media fans' is often confined to the periphery by virtue of its seeming irrelevance to the work of fan studies proper. It might be argued that such practices and cultures actually were peripheral to English language, Western fandoms of the past, part of an analog era in which transnational media distribution and circulation were firmly under the control of media corporations, and fandoms around the world seldom mixed. Yet, in disregarding even these bygone fan cultures, we demonstrate a somewhat alarming lack of interest in a comparative approach to fan studies; one that, in turn, reifies the foundational concepts of fan studies—transformative works, gift economy, affirmational fandom, among others—to reflect little more than our own English language habitus.

Today, in an era of intensifying cultural convergence, when fans from around the world congregate and commingle in the online spaces of Internet fandom, fan studies can no longer afford to overlook fan cultures as they play out globally. Particularly when, as I discuss later in the chapter, international markets such as mainland China are something of a golden ring for Anglo-American media industries, targeted through affective appeals to those fans as much as (if not more than) those of Western fandoms, our better understanding of fans and fandoms depends on incorporating research of transnational fandoms in our own English language scholarship.

DOI: 10.4324/9781003373025-9

Fan Studies in Transnational Context: An Overview

As an American growing up in the then-British colony of Hong Kong in the 1970s and 80s, my access to Hollywood films was largely unimpeded by distance or distribution. Popular movies might have screened in Hong Kong long after they had trickled down to second-run theaters in the US, but they were still the same movies, and my fannish investment in them was akin to that of other American fans. What set my fandom—and that of non-American fans of Hollywood media—apart was its material and cultural contexts, characterized by different (and often uneven) access to extra-filmic movie paratexts, as well as local cultures of film consumption and fandom. Thus, where US fans of *Star Wars* (1977) lined up outside mall theaters to watch and rewatch the film, I first saw it from the dress circle (balcony) of a small Chinese theater that sold sweet popcorn and chicken feet at the concessions counter. While American fans in the US consumed information about *Star Wars* through such entertainment magazines as *Starlog*, *Rolling Stone*, *People*, and *Time*, I clipped movie stills from Japanese movie magazines such as *Screen* and *Roadshow* to paste in Chinese embroidered photo albums. Such activities are the minutiae of film fandom; but the fact remains that the frustration entailed in not being able to read the Japanese movie magazines I bought in Hong Kong resulted in my learning the language, which led me to Japan, which led me eventually back to Hong Kong and its movies, and so on in an intensifying, if idiosyncratic, circuit of borderless, globalized fandom. Indeed, from the days when my movie fandom was constrained and shaped by local iterations of a transnational phenomenon, to the present and my active, primarily online, participation in fandoms with real-time global reach, this circuit is emblematic of the ways scholarship of transnational media fandoms has evolved over the past three decades.

We might locate the beginnings of transnational media fan studies in disciplines that themselves grappled with transnational media consumption in varying ways. Coming out of then-young cultural studies, Ien Ang's 1985 study of Dutch viewers of the American television show *Dallas*, in many ways set the terms of transnational media fan scholarship, not only in its concern with how viewers' specific cultural contexts inflected their interpretations of foreign media, but especially in its exploration of how the show's unavoidable *Americanness* played out in a decidedly non-American milieu. Ang's work brought together the sociopolitical concerns of British cultural studies (Hall 1980; Morley 1980) and the interpretative focus of feminist film and television criticism (Mulvey 1975; Brunsdon 1981; Modleski 1982) in such a way that it became one of the foundational texts of ethnographic research of media globalization (Gillespie 1995; Mankekar 1999; Kraidy 1999). In turn, *Watching Dallas* contributed to a then-growing body of work on women's media consumption that, among other things, set the stage for Henry Jenkins's (1992) *Textual Poachers*.

Within 'mainstream' fan studies, Jenkins's work—together with that of Constance Penley (1992) and Camille Bacon-Smith (1992)—was central in establishing not only fandom generally, but women's media fan cultures in particular, as worthy of sustained scholarly engagement. Throughout the 1990s, fan studies flourished alongside cultural studies in complementary scholarship that strategically emphasized the oppositional, anti-hegemonic cultural work of fannish engagement. As Internet usage became more globally widespread, and heretofore geographically limited fandoms began to meet and commingle in such online spaces as Yahoo! Groups and LiveJournal, this anti-hegemonic bent carried over into the discussion of converging transnational fandoms. Drawing from then-emerging debates on how non-Japanese anime fans understood Japan (if at all), Jenkins proposed the idea of "pop cosmopolitanism" (2004: 117) as a way of thinking about cross-border media fandoms that, at their most progressive, might offer "an escape from parochialism and isolationism, the beginnings of a global perspective, and the awareness of alternative vantage points" (Ibid.: 130). Jenkins was careful to note that "pop cosmopolitanism walks a thin line between dilettantism and connoisseurship, between orientalist fantasies and a desire to honestly connect and understand an alien culture" (Ibid.: 127); nonetheless, it falls on the side of the centrifugal possibilities of transnational fandoms, aligning—however ambivalently—with the anti-hegemonic "first wave" (Gray et al. 2007: 1) of fan studies. Such scholarship is characterized by a strategic shift in discussions of fans from both academic and journalistic discourses of ridicule and even pathologization, to work that foregrounds the "creative, thoughtful, and productive" (Ibid: 3) activities that fans engage in. At the same time, such work has been criticized for unwittingly refiguring the "moral dualism" (Hills 2002: 8) of good (not-fans) and bad (fans) into one of good (resistant) fans and bad (complicit) fans, a binary that was echoed in responses to Jenkins's theory of pop cosmopolitanism.

Fan studies coalesced in tandem with not only cultural studies, but also research of media globalization, particularly where they overlap in the discussion of intensified spatio-temporal circulation of media and the rise of multinational media corporations. By the end of the 1990s, one key concern of media globalization research was the ability of such corporations to effectively create a homogenous global culture distinguished by one-way flows from first to third world nations, the erosion of indigenous cultures in favor of a universal culture of mass consumption, and the consolidation of power into the hands of the few (McChesney & Herman 1998; Miyoshi 1998). Such critique reflected a cyclical concern over converging global media distribution and consumption, with antecedents in the concerns of nearly a decade earlier about the center-to-periphery flow of media and culture, collectively termed 'cultural imperialism'. The alarm it engendered was countered by critics who argued for the need to attend to lived experiences of media globalization (Hannerz 1989; Tomlinson 1991), embodied in this second wave in calls for 'hybridity' (Bhabha 1994; Nederveen Pieterse 1994; Clifford 1997) as one means of thinking outside of the dualism of "homogenization versus hetereogenization" (Robertson 1995: 27). Within transnational media fan studies, these concerns echoed the transition from the first to second wave of fan studies as they played out in the moral dualism of resistance, characterized by Jenkins's pop cosmopolitanism, and complicity, advanced by Koichi Iwabuchi's sustained and influential (Chua & Iwabuchi 2008; Jung 2011; Lee 2014; Kim 2014) critique of transnational fandoms as implicated in, however unintentionally, economic and even political strategizing (2010; 2015).

In a theoretical sense, we might say that this moral dualism hinges on two divergent understandings of Benedict Anderson's (1991 [1983]) thesis of 'imagined communities', emerging in primarily Internet-centered media fandoms, that "exist as an idea grounded in a necessary mental abstraction; the impression of affective connections with people and places we rarely if ever meet or visit" (Ruddock 2007: 80). In its more political iteration, the community imagined by state and corporate actors is one in which diversity and differences are discounted in the interests of securing their cultural and political–economic hegemony. Within the transnational circulation and consumption of media, such imagined communities become a means by which nations may successfully 'brand' culture for overseas export (Kim 2008: 4). Here, the seemingly innocuous nature of popular media acts as a Trojan horse of sorts, masking the assumptions and elisions on which the homogeneity of the imagined community depends. Through their deployment of 'soft power,' these players render fans complicit in attempts to fix their representational legitimacy at the global level, which in turn has the effect of strengthening that same legitimacy domestically (Iwabuchi 2010). At the same time, 'imagined communities' as used by media fan studies scholars equally describes fannish communities "defined through affinities rather than localities" (Jenkins 2006: 137), and constituted "through common patterns of reading and appropriation" (Sandvoss 2005: 92) that "bypass the nation-state on both the local and global level" (Ibid.: 55). It is in this ability of fandoms to forge transnational alliances of affect that exceed hegemonic state definitions of the 'national' that its counter-nationalist potential is located; and here we are returned to the stalemated moral dualism of "semiotic guerrillas [and] capitalist dupes" (Pearson 2010: 92).

Inasmuch as it spans both the inception and maturation of mainstream media fan studies, the moral dualism that has characterized transnational fan studies closely reflects not only the 'first wave' of fan studies, with its emphasis on the ways that fan cultures may circumvent, or even subvert, institutional power, but also 'second wave' concerns with fans "as agents of maintaining social and cultural systems of classification" and fandoms as "embedded in the existing economic, social, and cultural status quo" (Gray et al. 2007: 6). This affinity with the first two waves of mainstream fan studies in turn foregrounds what has been missing from this conversation; namely a 'third wave' concern with "the individual motivations, enjoyment, and pleasures of fans" (Ibid.)—in particular, how the "neat socio-political critique of trans/national fandom is fundamentally haunted by the 'messy' world of affect" (Chin & Morimoto 2013: 97). By way of shifting the focus of transnational fan studies to actual fan activities and understandings, recent work (Annett 2011, 2014; Chin & Morimoto 2013) argues that any nuanced discussion of the fandoms that grow up around transnationally circulating media must account for how and why such media circulates outside its own industrial or national context. While taking into account corporate and even government strategies for overseas distribution of media, such research explores the idiosyncratic meanings and "transfandom" (Hills 2015) associations fans bring to bear on their consumption of media. At the same time, this research expands the scope of transnational media fan studies to encompass border-crossing fan practices under the aegis of trans*cultural* fan studies, drawing attention to the diversity and differences inherent in even the most seemingly homogenous fan communities.

This recent emphasis in transnational fan studies on intersections of affect and media objects gives us a way of talking about the real-world implications of fandom and, in particular, fan labor outside of the generally oppositional framework used in both English language fan studies and fandoms themselves. To paraphrase Nele Noppe (2015: 232), scholarship of non-Anglo-American fan cultures enables us not only to understand what media fan cultures around the world look like, but also to reimagine the unquestioned truisms of English language media fan studies. Alternative transnational perspectives on the divisive issue of the monetization of fanworks (Noppe 2015) and intensified blurring between fans and media producers (Bird 2011)—two key concerns of present-day fan studies—enable us to challenge the terms and frameworks through which we define 'fans' and 'fandom'. Particularly in the case of (seemingly) familiar fan objects, this transnational perspective serves to denaturalize what we know to be true.

By way of illustrating how a transnational perspective might inflect and even alter our understanding of media fandoms, and the objects around which they form, the remainder of this chapter will look at the television series *Sherlock* (2010–present) and its titular lead, Benedict Cumberbatch, through the lens of his East Asian transnational fans and the media producers who would capitalize on them. *Sherlock* and, in particular, the '*Sherlock* fandom,' have been the subject of an exponentially growing amount of fan studies research in the six years since its debut on BBC1. Yet, the *Sherlock* fandom of English-language fan studies has been, to date, overwhelmingly comprised of women in the English language, transformative works-centered online fan spaces of Tumblr, Twitter, LiveJournal, and Dreamwidth; which is to say, it reflects exactly that normative fandom of English language media fan studies that a transnational fan studies seeks to complicate. Further, as a key export of BBC Worldwide, the show appears at first glance to be fully implicated the British soft power machine—something that in fact is belied by both its production contexts and the myriad ways that *Sherlock*, and its Britishness, are (re)configured by distributors and fans alike along more culturally recognizable lines.

Transnational *Sherlock* (Fandom)

Among my online acquaintances is a woman who has seen the January 2016 special episode of *Sherlock*, "The Abominable Bride," some 6 times in the theater, and Benedict Cumberbatch's *Hamlet* both live in London and upwards of 11 times in movie theaters over a 7-month period. Her dedication is hardly unusual in the context of celebrity fandom; what is noteworthy is her unusual access to these productions relative to Anglo-American *Sherlock* fans. Until late 2016, theatrical screenings of the National Theatre (NT) Live's *Hamlet* had a limited run of just a few days in October 2015 in the US, primarily in select theaters that had pre-existing arrangements with NT Live; similarly, "The Abominable Bride" screened in theaters for only a handful of days at the beginning of 2016 both in the United States and the United Kingdom. Yet in Hong Kong, where this woman resides, *Hamlet* has enjoyed at least three encore runs following the first in December 2015, while— as a peripheral part of that Chinese audience so coveted by US and UK media producers alike—Hong Kong was also given access to a subtitled theatrical screening of "The Abominable Bride" on the day of its UK broadcast, grossing over US$1.6 million through early March 2016 (all box office figures are from boxofficemojo.com).

Parenthetically, "The Abominable Bride" grossed US$24 million in mainland Chinese theaters over the same period, while South Korea, its second-biggest overseas market, saw a more modest, albeit respectable, US$8 million box-office return. In Japan, where subtitled theatrical screenings of the episode did not begin until mid-February, some fans had unprecedented access to in-theater sales of a plethora of *Sherlock*-related paraphernalia (ranging from the usual printed pamphlets to umbrellas, stickers, and framed stills of the show's characters) unavailable to theatergoers in other countries, entirely congruent with Japanese theatrical paraphernalia sales generally. Moreover, certain urban Japanese fans have also enjoyed access to a variety of *Sherlock* goods in temporary shops set up in department stores, co-sponsored by AXN Mystery (which broadcasts reruns of the series), the BBC, Hartswood Films, and host department stores, in conjunction with the British Embassy in Japan.

Which is to say, East Asian fans have had a degree of *official* access to things *Sherlock* that exceeds that of American and British audiences alike, begging the question of who, exactly, comprises the 'Sherlock fandom' and what its activities actually look like. Within English--language fan studies research, the 'Sherlock fandom' typically is figured as female and Anglo-American, heavily skewing towards fans that produce and consume transformative works. Where non-Western fans are acknowledged, they dot the periphery; yet clearly Sherlock fandom neither begins nor ends here, and particularly not for the show's overseas distributors. When Ang was writing in the 1980s about Dutch viewers and fans of Dallas, overseas audiences often were considered ancillary markets, and historically they have been treated as such in media fan studies scholarship. But with the ever-increasing profitability of overseas markets driving localized transnational media marketing along specifically fan cultural lines, English language media fan studies' current understanding of 'fans' and 'fandom' as *de facto* Anglo-American communities of shared interest seems unable to adequately account for what is an increasingly diverse fandom playing field (Morimoto & Chin, 2017). Television today is "multiple spaces or levels of television production, flow, and reception, corresponding to multiple levels of culture and identity" (Straubhaar 2007: 1), and fandoms of even shared media objects worldwide reflect this multiplicity in ways that belie the normative fans and fandoms of English language fan studies scholarship.

At the same time, localized fan marketing—and the ways it is consumed outside those localities—subverts conceptions of soft power as always benefiting only the country of media origin. This is perhaps nowhere better exemplified than in Benedict Cumberbatch's summer 2013 Japan junket to promote *Star Trek into Darkness* (STID) (J. J. Abrams, 2013). Preceded by another STID junket in December 2012, Cumberbatch's summer trip was the culmination of some seven months' worth of promotional activity on the part of both Paramount Japan and the Japanese mass media, eager to capitalize on his theretofore unrecognized appeal to the mostly female fans who greeted him at Narita International Airport on his earlier December junket. As in other countries, the Japanese mass media is forever in search of the next big thing, having had particular success since the late 1980s with nation-based 'booms' centered on attractive, foreign male stars. Thus, when some 500 fans arrived at the airport to greet Cumberbatch on his first trip, women's and movie magazine editors jumped on the chance to parlay his nascent popularity into something more lucrative. In the seven months between December 2012 and July 2013, Cumberbatch graced the covers of over 15 Japanese magazines; and by the March release of the May 2013 issue of *Screen* magazine, his appeal was being described in terms of his 'Britishness' alongside that of such actors as Ben Whishaw, Eddie Redmayne, and Robert Pattinson, effectively sparking a new (and second, the first occurring in the late 1980s) British boy boom that continues as of this writing.

How, then, do we understand the 'Britishness' of both *Sherlock* and Benedict Cumberbatch? Research of the intersection of soft power and fans warns that,

> as fans' appreciation of cultural and media products from abroad cannot be neatly separable from their broader perception of the products' country of origin, such fandom may be associated with fans' discovery and recognition of cultural appeal of the producing countries and may become a key concern of the countries, nation branding projects.
>
> (Lee 2014: 195)

The sheer amount of fan-culturally localized exposure *Sherlock* enjoys in Japan (as well as throughout East Asia) through the combined efforts of its production companies, local distributors, and even the British government is unequivocal proof that the show is seen as a cog in the British soft power apparatus. Yet, who benefits from this soft power is less clear: certainly, the United Kingdom in the form of tourism and exports, however modestly (Japan accounts for a generally consistent ~1% of tourism [VisitBritain 2016: n. p.] and 1.4% of exports [OEC 2016: n. p.]), but also the Japanese media industries that capitalize on the ancillary economic activity of the nation-based boom. Indeed, insofar as it resonates with other global fan cultures of a given media object, marketing targeted at one transnational market may have the paradoxical effect of garnering goodwill towards the target (rather than/in addition to the producing) country in other markets. For example, the television trailers for *Sherlock* series one and two created by South Korean satellite broadcaster OCN, uploaded to YouTube by local fans, created a delighted uproar within some segments of the online *Sherlock* fan community for foregrounding a romantic relationship between Cumberbatch's Sherlock Holmes and Martin Freeman's John Watson. That this romance has been repeatedly refuted by the show's producers, yet is the subject of myriad fanworks and fandom discussion globally, endeared the promos—and their South Korean producers—to fans inured to (British) producer-side rejection.

Cumberbatch's July 2013 STID junket similarly confounded nationally discrete conceptions of soft power when, as part of marketing tactics intended to appeal specifically to Cumberbatch's women fans in Japan, he was outfitted in a Japanese summer kimono (*yukata*) for a television interview and appearance in the *Screen* magazine-sponsored "King of Magazines" event held at Tokyo's Ritz Carlton Hotel. This was, in fact, entirely congruent with *Screen*'s history of dressing Western stars in Japanese *yukata* (or, more infrequently, kimono) for their readers, of a part with localized Japanese promotional activities. But when official photographs of a Sherlock-coiffed Cumberbatch in *yukata* were released online by *Screen*, they quickly became the basis of what was dubbed "yukata!Batch" art produced by *Sherlock* and Cumberbatch fans in places as diverse as France, Thailand, Taiwan, and China. Notably, regardless of fans' country of origin, much of this art was produced in something of an anime or manga style, which might be understood as reflecting the success of Japan's own anime-centered soft power activities. However, for many of these fans, while anime had influenced their art style, that style remained wholly their own. As one American fan artist observed of her own work, "Yeah, it definitely has Japanese influence [but] as I got older I just couldn't connect to it anymore But that had less to do with the art style itself and more with [anime] stories" (Reapersun 2016: n. p.). What we see here is one way that a nation-based object becomes unmoored from its origins, and this at a time when governments globally are invested in the promotion of 'national' popular culture under the aegis of well-funded soft power initiatives. It reflects the increasingly uncontainable, border-confounding nature of both the nation as producer of cultural content and fandoms themselves. In the same way we have historically spoken of 'Japanese' or 'British' or 'American' fans as definable by geography and culture, fan studies scholars also tend to speak of 'anime fans', '*Sherlock* fans,' and 'Benedict Cumberbatch fans' as if they, too, are definable by that one object of interest. What a transnational and transfandom approach to the complicated intersections of nation, fan cultural object, and fans brings to fan studies conversations is a greater awareness of the extent to which such discrete categorization is in fact antithetical to the ways that fandoms emerge and evolve, both globally and locally (Morimoto 2014: 8).

From Transnational to Transcultural Fan Studies

Historically, border-crossing fandoms have been conceptualized primarily through a transnational lens. Yet, as cultural intersections, and even clashes, in the "contact zones" (Pratt 1991: 34) of online fandoms increasingly make visible the heterogeneity of fan communities, we have begun to shift our attention from the strictly transnational to a more transcultural approach to fan studies. In a way that is perhaps emblematic of the current muddled media moment, there is no clear line neatly dividing the transnational from the transcultural; if anything, the necessarily transcultural orientation of transnational fan studies inextricably links one to the other. Equally, in its focus on the differences and disjunctures that arise in the meeting of cultures—fan or otherwise—transcultural fan studies equips us to recognize them within seemingly normative, homogenous fan communities. Cultures of race, sexuality, disability, class, and so on are, in a transcultural fan studies framework, analogous to those geographical, political, economic, and social differences that may distinguish one national (or even regional) culture from another. Not newcomers to online fandom, such fans (whose own subjectivities—like my own—may be varied and even contradictory) have simply become increasingly visible through fans' online migration to the relatively non-hierarchical, rhizomatic social media spaces of Twitter, Tumblr, Weibo, and so on.

Today, research of transcultural fandoms increasingly proliferates in the pages of academic journals and anthologies, as well as in conferences globally. Yet, as the above *Sherlock* case study demonstrates, in keeping global fandoms on the margins of mainstream fan studies, we risk an incomplete understanding of the complexity of 'fandom' as it exists today. As a frequent participant in transcultural fan studies panels and workshops, I've witnessed first-hand the way a conference room clears out when the next group of presentations doesn't fall under recognizable categories of fandom, fan practices, or fan objects. But in an age of intensifying media convergence, when fans around the world hailing from cultures of nationality, language, race, ethnicity, gender, and so on, co-mingle in widely accessible fan spaces and bring with them their own culturally generalizable, yet broadly idiosyncratic, understandings of fandom and media, can we in media fan studies afford to overlook the perspectives such fans bring with them?

References

Anderson, B. (1991) *Imagined Communities: Reflections on the Origin and Spread of Nationalism*, London: Verso.
Ang, I. (1985) *Watching Dallas: Soap Opera and the Melodramatic Imagination*, London: Methuen.
Annett, S. (2011) "Imagining Transcultural Fandom: Animation and Global Media Communities," *Transcultural Studies* 2, pp. 164–188.
Annett, S. (2014) *Anime Fan Communities: Transcultural Flows and Frictions*, New York: Palgrave Macmillan.
Bacon-Smith, C. (1992) *Enterprising Women: Television Fandom and the Creation of Popular Myth*, Philadelphia, PA: University of Pennsylvania Press.
Bhabha, H. (1994) *The Location of Culture*, London: Routledge.
Bird, S. E. (2011) "Are We All Producers Now?" *Cultural Studies* 25.4–5, pp. 502–516.

Brunsdon, C. (1981) "'Crossroads' Notes on Soap Opera," *Screen* 22.4, pp. 32–37.
Chin, B. & Morimoto, L. (2013) "Towards a Theory of Transcultural Fandom," *Participations* 10.1, pp. 92–108.
Chua B. H. & Iwabuchi, K. (eds.) (2008) *East Asian Pop Culture*, Hong Kong: Hong Kong University Press.
Clifford, J. (1997) *Routes: Travel and Translation in the Late Twentieth Century*, Cambridge, MA: Harvard University Press.
Gillespie, M. (1995) *Television, Ethnicity and Cultural Change*, Oxon: Routledge.
Gray, J., Sandvoss, C. & Harrington, C.L. (2007) "Introduction: Why Study Fans?" in *Fandom: Identities and Communities in a Mediated World*, New York: New York University, pp. 1–16.
Hall, S. (1980) "Encoding/Decoding," S. Hall, D. Hobson, A. Lowe, and P. Willis (eds.), *Culture, Media, Language: Working Papers in Cultural Studies, 197279*, London: Hutchinson, pp. 128–138.
Hannerz, U. (1989) "Notes on the Global Ecumene," *Public Culture* 1.2, pp. 66–75.
Herman, E. & McChesney, R. (1998) *The Global Media: The Missionaries of Global Capitalism*, London: Cassell.
Hills, M. (2002) *Fan Cultures*, London: Routledge.
Hills, M. (2015) "Interview: Fandom as an Object and the Objects of Fandom," *MATRIZes* 9.1, pp. 147–162.
Iwabuchi, K. (2010) "Undoing Inter-national Fandom in the Age of Brand Nationalism," *Mechademia* 5, pp. 87–96.
Iwabuchi, K. (2015) *Resilient Borders and Cultural Diversity: Internationalism, Brand Nationalism, and Multiculturalism in Japan*, Lanham: Lexington Books.
Jenkins, H. (1992) *Textual Poachers: Television Fans and Participatory Culture*, New York: Routledge.
Jenkins, H. (2004) "Pop Cosmopolitanism: Mapping Cultural Flows in an Age of Media Convergence," M. Suarez-Orozco and D. Qin-Hilliard (eds.), *Globalization: Culture and Education in the New Millennium*, Berkeley, CA: University of California Press, pp. 114–140.
Jenkins, H. (2006) *Fans, Bloggers, and Gamers: Exploring Participatory Culture*, New York: New York University Press.
Jung, S. (2011) *Korean Masculinities and Transnational Consumption*, Hong Kong: Hong Kong University Press.
Kim, J. (ed.) (2014) *Reading Asian Television Drama: Crossing Borders and Breaking Boundaries*, London: I. B.Taurus.
Kraidy, M. (1999) "The Global, the Local, and the Hybrid: A Native Ethnography of Glocalization," *Critical Studies in Mass Communication* 16.4, pp. 456–476.
Lee, H. K. (2014) "Transnational Cultural Fandom," L. Duits, K. Zwaan, and S. Reijnders (eds.), *The Ashgate Research Companion to Fan Cultures*, Farnham: Ashgate Publishing, pp. 195–208.
Lin, M. (2014) *The Transnational Flow of BBC Sherlock: Investigating the Role of Chinese Fans in the Success of BBC Sherlock in Mainland China*, M. A.Thesis, University of Warwick.
Mankekar, P. (1999) *Screening Culture, Viewing Politics: An Ethnography of Television Womanhood, and Nation in Postcolonial India*, Durham, NC: Duke University Press.
Miyoshi, M. (1998) "'Globalization,' Culture, and the University," F. Jameson and M. Miyoshi (eds.), *The Cultures of Globalization*, Durham, NC: Duke University Press, pp. 247–272.
Modleski, T. (1982) *Loving with a Vengeance: Mass-Produced Fantasies for Women*, New York: Routledge.
Morimoto, L. (2014) "Yukata!batch Goes Global: Japanese Entertainment Booms in the Age of Social Media," *ACA/PCA Southwest Conference*, Feb. 22.
Morimoto, L. & Chin, B. (2017) "Reimainging the Imagined Community: Online Media Fandom in the Age of Global Convergence," J. Gray, C. Sandvoss, and C.L. Harrington (eds.), *Fandom: Identities and Communities in a Mediated World*, Second Edition, New York: New York University Press, pp. 174–188.
Morley, D. (1980) *The 'Nationwide' Audience: Structure and Decoding*, London: BFI.
Mulvey, L. (1975) "Visual Pleasure and Narrative Cinema," *Screen* 16.3, pp. 6–18.
Nederveen Pieterse, J. (1994) "Globalization as Hybridization," *International Sociology* 9.2, pp. 161–184.

Noppe, N. (2015) "Mechanisms of Control in Online Fanwork Sales: A Comparison of Kindle Worlds and Dlsite.com" *Participations* 12.2, pp. 218–237.
Pearson, R. (2010) "Fandom in the Digital Era," *Popular Communication* 8.1, pp. 84–95.
Penley, C. (1992) "Feminism, Psychoanalysis, and the Study of Popular Culture," in L. Grossberg, C. Nelson, and P. Treichler (eds.), *Cultural Studies*, New York: Routledge, pp. 479–500.
Pratt, M. L. (1991) "Arts of the Contact Zone," *Profession* 1991, pp. 33–40.
OEC (2016) "United Kingdom (GBR) Exports, Imports, and Trade Partners," Cambridge, MA: MIT Media Lab.
Reapersun (2016) Personal Correspondence, January 26.
Robertson, R. (1995) "Glocalization: Time-space and Homogeneity-heterogeneity," M. Featherstone, S. Lash, and R. Robertson (eds.), *Global Modernities*, London: Sage Publications, pp. 25–44.
Ruddock, A. (2007) *Investigating Audiences*, Los Angeles: Sage Publishing.
Sandvoss, C. (2005) *Fans: The Mirror of Consumption*, Cambridge: Polity.
Straubhaar, J. (2007) *World Television: From Global to Local*, London: Sage Publishing.
Tomlinson, J. (1991) *Cultural Imperialism: A Critical Introduction*, London: Routledge.
VisitBritain (2016) *Nation, Region & County Data*, London: VisitBritain Headquarters.

8
WHEN PLATFORMS FALL
Scraping and Interpreting Fandom Data in Tumultuous Times

Anastasia Salter and Bridget Blodgett

Our collective understanding of fandom frequently relies upon conversations across platforms: looking back, scholars have continually trusted the accessibility of fandom discourse on platforms ranging from early web spaces such as FanFiction.net, Geocities, and LiveJournal through to more current spaces including Tumblr, Archive of Our Own, and the platform formerly known as Twitter. These platforms serve many roles for fandom: they are spaces to commune and argue, as well as archives and repositories of transformative works and history. And yet some of those platforms have already been lost, whether through closure (in the case of the neighborhoods of Geocities, one of the original homes for personal websites) or platform mismanagement (as with the now notorious decision of Tumblr to remove all content deemed "Not Safe For Work"). While efforts to preserve these platforms and their history, namely the critical interventions of Jason Scott's Archive Team and the Internet Archive, are ongoing, the reality is that the web is changing more rapidly than collective scholarly and archival efforts can intervene: as we write this chapter in 2024 we have already witnessed shifts that will dramatically impact the potential for fandom research on many platforms going forward. Given these tumultuous times and the increasingly contested positioning of data access, fandom scholars looking to understand the history of digital fandom spaces and production must be prepared to work differently. In this chapter, we first position the opportunities and value of large-scale platform-driven research, contextualizing the platforms of significance and the types of fandom research most commonly conducted through data scraping. Next, we contextualize the imminent challenges to that work, ranging from shifts in platform management and expectations of data cost to the interventions of machine learning models on data norms. Finally, we speculate on the future of fandom data and its impact on our work.

Fan Platforms, Fan Data

Data scraping's allure is as a means of preservation and discovery: it enables us to work at scale, and in doing so draws upon a broader set of texts than our own close reading can allow us to access. In the digital humanities, this method is termed "distant reading," as

DOI: 10.4324/9781003373025-10

it makes visible patterns that might not be immediately recognizable across related work (Underwood 2017). In the overlapping study of fandom and social media platforms, data scraping has emerged as a dominant method in socially oriented scholarly disciplines. Data scraping allows scholars to collect social events as they emerge and trace the development of community discourse and place it within the larger socio-political sphere of that community and the web at large. With the changing nature of social media, scholars often feel extreme time pressure to capture information about a fandom community while it exists, as can be best demonstrated through the losses that the Twitter communities faced in 2022, and the Tumblr, LiveJournal, and FanFiction.net communities faced previously. As capitalist pressures mount to make fandom spaces profitable and friendly to marketers, scholars will often find themselves in the ethical pinch between attempting to collect their own data in the deluge of incoming information for developing events and the external pressure to act as archivists to secure and document existing fan information before it disappears to a content ban, financial collapse, or copyright fight which causes it to disappear forever.

Abigail de Kosnik points to the value of "rogue archives" (2016) for preserving, curating, and sustaining fandom: from wikis to Archive of Our Own's (AO3) incredible fanfiction repository, these projects are inescapably important to those of us studying media fandom. Many such rogue archives have sprung up throughout the 2010s and 2020s as a means of capturing a snapshot of the early web. Notable examples include the archiving of Geocities by The Internet Archive and One Terabyte of Kilobyte Age, MySpace Music and AOL Hometown by restorativland, and archives of Issuu, Reddit, and Telegram by the Archive Team (Ogden 2021). These archives are often gathered in the short period between the announcement of a site's closure and the date it finally shutters or in the panic caused by stability issues, policy changes, and company sales, as in the case of attempts at archiving fanfiction.net (wiki.archiveteam.org 2022) and Twitter in 2022. Such archives are incomplete but critical for the history of fandom: one example of time-critical data scraping in the service of fandom and broader digital cultural history is Archive Team's efforts to save the "Not Safe for Work" content of Tumblr following a change in moderation policy (Ogden 2021).

AO3 exemplifies the possibilities of the rogue archive and has been held up as an exemplar of feminist Human-Computer Interaction (HCI) (Fiesler, Morrison, and Bruckman 2016): notably, this structure emerged out of a need for a platform not subject to shifting values external to that of the fan community itself (Lothian 2012). The emergent tagging practices remain a compelling case study for information studies (Price and Robinson 2021). At the same time, Mel Stanfill and Alexis Lothian (2021: 1.4) have criticized the limitations of the "maximal inclusivity" in terms of the platform's practices with regards to who truly owns the servers, and who is welcome, particularly as "racial justice is not currently part of fanfiction's digital infrastructure." Lindgren Leavenworth (2016: 60) notes that some of the value of these archives is in the paratextual and peritextual elements, which allow us access to the conversation as "sites of transactions of meaning." The persistence of identity through AO3 may not directly mimic the more real-name driven expectations of platforms such as Facebook, but it does allow for identifiable continuity, and thus has become an important space for examining author-reader relationships and the dynamics of fandom. However, the persistence of the archive can also allow for engagement with orphaned and abandoned works, prescribing importance and intention to texts an author no longer claims.

Questions of ownership and persistence (often in spite of authorial or creator intention) make navigating our access to this type of data, and its possibilities for understanding fan community, ethically challenging: as Fiesler, Beard, and Keegan (2020: 188) note, it is often possible to collect data in ways that violate a platform's Terms of Service, and often such policies are "ambiguous, inconsistent, and lack context," leaving scholars frequently making their own ethical and technological determinations. Such ethical questions are even more difficult when working with fan-maintained and moderated spaces. While many traditional archives have funding and time to select and curate their approaches and audiences, fandom's rogue archives often work on minimal funding and technology or under extreme time pressures. However, for many rogue archivists, these pressures are worth the struggle. The work of these archivists is representative of the investment of fan labor into communities and practices not necessarily intended for, or even anticipating, the scholarly gaze: when we look to such archives as objects of study, we risk co-opting, trivializing, or misinterpreting such fan labor in ways that can be harmful. The Association of Internet Researchers (AoIR)'s ethical guidelines (franzke et al. 2020) have emerged as an exemplar for how we can navigate those risks and think about what informed consent might reasonably mean in the context of data-driven projects, as different communities have their own perception of how public their work might be.

Lin et al. (2020) expand on the many ways that ethical complications arise during the practice of digital archiving and research. They argue that in many ways, existing ethical guidelines for research in North America are unprepared to properly assess the ethical considerations of digital research. The authors identified three different types of analyses that can be completed on a digital archive: 1) content-based retrieval, 2) large-scale distant reading, and 3) user re-identification. Using their example of a GeoCities archive, they demonstrate that two of these forms of research have already been produced and the third is technically feasible although not yet produced. Drawing from ethical frameworks put forward by digital historians for oral history and the AoIR Principles for Internet Research, Lin et al. (2020) expand existing ethical research guidelines to include context and scale as values to be assessed before a research project can ethically move forward. Both of these values attempt to understand the authors' expectations of privacy and scale of the work to be conducted. There are additional considerations for archives that are being created around still-active communities as well. As Hegarty (2023) establishes, the process of creating archives also constructs a type of digital imaginaries within the minds of the authors, the audience, and the archivists. This viewpoint attempts to account for: the cultural significance of the work archived, contextual understanding of the use of the archive, prominence of the institution archiving, and temporality. All four of these aspects shape subjects' responses to the archive's development and continued existence. Hegarty (2023) demonstrates that an institution with as much cultural heft as the National Library of Australia can make an author whose work is being archived feel proud, overwhelmed, and with enough time, possibly embarrassed. But for other institutions, the Internet Archive for example, the viewed cultural weight can cause authors to devalue their inclusion and as a result how they will continue to create materials to be archived.

A meta-study of publications using Reddit warned: "while Reddit has become an important data source for researchers, there are serious questions regarding the degree to which this prominence matches users' expectations for their data. Many subreddits position themselves as small communities rather than public fora, setting up a potential mismatch between institutional review boards' interpretation of Reddit as a public space and users' understandings of the communities they are participating in" (Proferes et al. 2021). Indeed, many research review boards themselves differentiate between information that was obtained from truly public websites and those which require a user to log in before supplying them with access to the contents. Although both are considered exempt under many interpretations of the Belmont Report's guidelines, Metcalf and Crawford (2016) argue that there are secondary considerations for big data sets, including archives, that may need to be better integrated into ethical guidelines in the near future. As the authors state:

> It [big data] moves ethical inquiry away from traditional harms such as physical pain or a shortened lifespan to less tangible concepts such as information privacy impact and data discrimination. It may involve the traditional concept of a human subject as an individual, or it may affect a much wider distributed grouping or classification of people. It fundamentally changes our understanding of research data to be (at least in theory) infinitely connectable, indefinitely repurposable, continuously updatable and easily removed from the context of collection. (Metcalf and Crawford 2016: Introduction para. 5)

Previously, data collected about human subjects or produced by human subjects would have a limited life span within a research study, and therefore limited secondary uses. The modern archival approach to these works results in data sets that have unset lifespans and many potential secondary uses outside of their original purpose.

APIs and Access

Much of this data collection and archive formation is due to the general availability of free and low-cost tools on the web. The term "data scraping" captures a method that enables us to study the web at scale: "As a technique of online data extraction, scraping seems of special interest to us because it is an important part of what makes digital social research practically possible" (Marres and Weltevrede 2013: 2). The authors establish that a significant value to social scientists in data scraping as a tool is its ability to collect not only the text but the metatextual content on a page, including formatting, images, pre-established connections through linking, and other ways that the creators of the data imposed their own classification and meaning (Marres and Weltevrede 2013). Basic software for data scraping can easily be set up to run on a personal computer, web server, or occasionally, a digital drive. This availability makes the creation of impromptu archives and collections very available to those with limited resources and technological knowledge. However, just collecting data is only the first step in the process of creating a digital archive and many rogue archives have, in the past, failed to consider the longer technological, financial, and maintenance needs for a true archive. In 2021, the Organization for Transformative Works (OTW) collected $804,701.68 in revenue, mostly from donations (Organization for Transformative Works 2021). Of this budget, 78.2% cumulatively went to their archiving projects, Archive of Our Own, Open Doors, Transformative Works and Culture, and Fanlore (Organization for Transformative Works 2021). The bulk of these expenditures are on server hosting, maintenance, and expansion, although recent projects have also included improving the search functionality and general site security (Organization for

Transformative Works 2021; Heleen 2022). OTW represents an outstanding public archive but also shows the considerable costs associated with developing these technologies and making them available at scale. For smaller rogue archives, the initial impulse to capture may be noble but the longer planning is often lacking, leading to archives meant to capture fandom history often failing themselves, still leading to loss.

In other contexts, fandom and scholars are being restricted from access to our collective data, leaving its persistence and study in the hands of those who can afford to pay. Regardless of the power of the tools available for data scraping, the data also needs to be accessible to potential archivists. The application programming interface (API) of a platform dictates how outside software may access the data contained on a website or platform. The simplest form of management comes in the format of a robots.txt file hosted on the website or platform's page that dictates to any potential scrapers how and what may be accessed. In the last five years, API restrictions have risen in the wake of public scrutiny following Facebook's 2018 Cambridge Analytica scandal: as Mancosu and Vegetti (2020) note in their examination of the ethics and legalities of scraping Facebook data following the changes, this primarily raises questions about the tension between what is feasible and what is permissible per the platform's terms. Other websites have limited their API access as a means to find additional opportunities for monetization, such as Reddit, or reduce server load and increase brand control, like Twitter (Shakir 2023; Riggins 2023). Twitter makes for an excellent case study in the technological restrictions that scholars often face when trying to collect web archives. For scholars making use of Twitter as a data source, collecting all relevant tweets made within a time period was often a dream proposal. Twitter's API restricted requests to the service, limiting how many tweets could be retrieved each hour. For anyone studying a popular or widely emergent issue, this limitation often falls well below their needs. While "firehose" or total backend access was available to some, the method for obtaining such access was difficult, expensive, and often seemed arbitrary. For a while, the US Library of Congress proposed the total archiving of Twitter messages from 2006 forward on their own servers and allowing researchers access, but the proposed project never had wide reach due to its difficulty and was ultimately rescoped (Bruns 2018). Such projects are possible only through the willingness of the original sites to make such access available to outside parties at all. And that willingness has been shown to be dictated by economic and social forces outside of the control of potential archivists.

Certain types of content are already omitted from API-based scholarship and fan studies work, and ultimately difficult to study at scale: ephemeral content, such as SnapChat or Instagram stories, is intentionally designed to be forgotten – it thus raises additional ethical questions (Bainotti, Caliandro, and Gandini 2020). There are also concerns that researchers and potential archivists may not be capturing what is important but simply what is available. The API wars are a defining moment for scholarship that relies upon publicly available data. Reddit and Twitter have historically been some of the most relied-upon platforms for the study of fandom, not necessarily because they are the dominant spaces where the conversation unfolds, but because of their ease of study. Changes to Reddit API access (Grantham-Phillips 2023) threaten the viability of this work moving forward.

Meanwhile, many platforms with refined tools for access are shifting to pricing models that are unsustainable for most researchers in fandom. When Blodgett and Salter (2013) collected data about #1ReasonWhy using the TAGS software, the limit for tweets pulled was 1,500 every hour, the maximum at the time unless one had unlimited access. The cost of accessing an API like that of the platform formerly known as Twitter is, as of May 2024, only available at commercial rates for an equal number of logins and tweets sampled (Porter 2023). As Fiesler (2023) establishes on her TikTok account, the grant required to fund such access in a modern university establishment would need to exceed $800,000 without accounting for any other costs for the research. Official communication on the availability of academic pricing has been limited thus far and the resulting changes are likely to reflect the availability of NSF and NIH funding to support this type of study in other fields (Developers 2023). Rate limiting is becoming a more and more common practice, which in turn limits any researcher interested in studying at scale: machine learning has provided the excuse (Mollman 2023).

One of the most telling cultural shifts driving API changes is the growing realization that publicly available data is fueling the AI revolution: from Reddit to Archive of Our Own, platform stakeholders are starting to recognize the value that has been extracted from their work. In a now-notorious example, an AI model's recognition of sex acts particular to Omegaverse fanfiction revealed the placement of such fanfiction in the training data set (Eveleth 2023). The use of machine learning (ML) or artificial intelligence (AI) models, exemplified by OpenAI's ChatGPT and DALL-E or Midjourney's self-titled software, are secondary uses by parties not originally considered in the development of online archives. These models make use of large data sets to train the software's statistical models and open sets of cultural text and image produced and stored in archives and web platforms, seemingly available for free, which was a boon to their development and refinement.

While AO3 doesn't have an API to alter in response to that usage, they are changing their policies and have enabled rate-limiting. The AO3 moderators have asked that the platform be removed from the Common Crawl data set powering ChatGPT in the future and have tried to block other future scraping of that kind; however, they note that they don't want to block everything: "we don't have a policy against responsible data collection – such as those done by academic researchers, fans backing up works to Wayback Machine or Google's search indexing" (Archive of Our Own 2023). All works remain downloadable through external scripts and traditional means, keeping this archive a critical place for future work (Archive of Our Own n.d.).

Distant Reads of Fan Data Futures

While a user may be pleased to have their work included in what they consider a cultural touchstone of their fan community, they often did not agree to that use by outside parties to shape the development of software to create works similar to their own. In early 2023 a class action lawsuit was filed by several artists who felt their inclusion in the Laion-5B database of images used to train several image generation models and scrapped from public internet servers, such as DeviantArt, was a violation of their copyrights (Chayka 2023). These artists allege a violation against uncredited and uncompensated derivative works, while the defense claims that their scraping and collection of the works should be considered fair use under both the educational and transformative clauses (Chayka 2023). This case is one of a growing number of such cases raised in the last two years which will likely set legal precedent for how such items will be handled in the future. Many of the fanworks on sites like Archive of Our Own and DeviantArt are able to exist due to the transformation clauses in US copyright law (and similar legal standards worldwide) and there currently isn't a clear legal distinction between transformative works created by humans and based upon copyrighted media properties and those made by computer software with a human's prompt. Ethical questions regarding fandom data, and internet research more broadly, have apparently been bypassed entirely in the training of such models – while this might change going forward, it is not surprising that suspicion of data scraping is on the rise in the wake of such violations.

Additionally, AI generation and the large data sets that act as training grounds for them often rely on separating the data from the context within which it was created and existed. For some readers the phrase, "cerulean orbs" will mean nothing but for others it presents a visceral emotional response related to its contextual use within certain fandom cultures and time periods (Fanlore n.d.). Similarly, while many have enjoyed remixes of Jane Austen's *Pride and Prejudice*, AI generated versions may capture some of the numerically relevant commonalities of the piece but will likely leave behind niche but intense references, phrases, and touchstones of cultural cachet. Indeed, the approach to AI-generated fanworks highlights a long-standing epistemological conflict within modern society. As Leurs (2017) points out:

> Often, number-crunching positivist 'discovery' is propagated as superior to small-scale, in-depth research, and this ideology commonly reflects cultural attributes of white, middle-class, masculine, able-bodied, heteronormative domination and Western-centric military-industrial imperialism. Feminist, critical race, de- and post-colonial and activist researchers have firmly put on the agenda the politics of knowledge production: knowledge is partial, situated and contextual, and power flows along intersectional axes of difference. (Leurs 2017: 150)

Fan studies research incorporating data scraping and related methods for viewing community at scale offers opportunities to make interventions in the conversation and can particularly draw our attention to the darker side of fandom discourse on social media. Continuing this work will be critical, but only more difficult, as increased platform regulation in the wake of machine learning's data appropriation continues.

Currently, data scraping and AI generation have significantly changed the future for fandom studies on multiple levels. It is hard to speculate what the future for fans, fanworks, and fandom studies will bring during an era of such volatility and uncertainty. New legal precedents will be set by cases that are currently making their way through the courts, or that will be entered soon. Fans are increasingly renegotiating their relationship to media, fanworks, and culture as more are becoming aware of social issues and their integration and impact on fandom. Scholars are also re-evaluating their use of large data sets and the ethical implications of not only collection but potential secondary uses that far out-scope both their own and their subjects' understandings.

References

Archive of Our Own. (2023). *AI and Data Scraping on the Archive*. Available at: https://archiveofourown.org/admin_posts/25888 [Accessed 31 Jul. 2023].

Archive of Our Own. (n.d.). *Downloading Fanworks FAQ*. Available at: https://archiveofourown.org/faq/downloading-fanworks?language_id=en [Accessed 31 Jul. 2023].

Bainotti, L., Caliandro, A., and Gandini, A. (2020). From archive cultures to ephemeral content, and back: Studying Instagram stories with digital methods. *New Media & Society*, 23(12), pp. 3656–3676. https://doi.org/10.1177/1461444820960071

Blodgett, B. M., and Salter, A. (2013). Hearing "Lady Game Creators" Tweet: #1ReasonWhy, Women and Online Discourse in the Game Development Community. AoIR Selected Papers of Internet Research, 3. Retrieved from https://spir.aoir.org/ojs/index.php/spir/article/view/8633

Bruns, A. (2018). *The Library of Congress Twitter Archive: A Failure of Historic Proportions.* Available at: https://medium.com/dmrc-at-large/the-library-of-congress-twitter-archive-a-failure-of-historic-proportions-6dc1c3bc9e2c

Chayka, K. (2023). Is A.I. Art Stealing from Artists? The New Yorker. 10 Feb. Available at: www.newyorker.com/culture/infinite-scroll/is-ai-art-stealing-from-artists

De Kosnik, A. (2016). *Rogue archives: Digital cultural memory and media fandom.* Cambridge, MA: The MIT Press.

Developers. (2023). [Twitter]. 29 Mar. Available at: https://twitter.com/XDevelopers/status/1641222788911624192

Eveleth, R. (2023). The fanfic sex trope that caught a plundering AI red-handed. Wired. 15 May. Available at: www.wired.com/story/fanfiction-omegaverse-sex-trope-artificial-intelligence-knotting/

Fanlore. (n.d.). *Cerulean Orbs – Fanlore.* Available at: https://fanlore.org/wiki/Cerulean_Orbs [Accessed 31 Jul. 2023].

Fiesler, C. (2023). Replying to @snarfelle Twitter API cost Reveal! 11 Mar. Available at: www.tiktok.com/@professorcasey/video/7209443544266935598

Fiesler, C., Beard, N., and Keegan, B. C. (2020). No robots, spiders, or scrapers: Legal and ethical regulation of data collection methods in social media terms of service. *Proceedings of the International AAAI Conference on Web and Social Media*, 14(1), pp. 187–196. https://doi.org/10.1609/icwsm.v14i1.7290

Fiesler, C., Morrison, S., and Bruckman, A. S. (2016). An Archive of Their Own: A Case Study of Feminist HCI and Values in Design. In Proceedings of the 2016 CHI Conference on Human Factors in Computing Systems (CHI '16). Association for Computing Machinery, New York, NY, USA, 2574–2585. https://doi.org/10.1145/2858036.2858409

Franzke, A.S., Bechmann, A., Zimmer, M., Ess, C., and the Association of Internet Researchers. (2020). Internet Research: Ethical Guidelines 3.0. Available at: https://aoir.org/reports/ethics3.pdf

Grantham-Phillips, W. (2023). *The Reddit Lackout, Explained: Why Thousands of Subreddits a Reprotesting Third-Party App Charges.* Available at: www.kark.com/news/tech-news/ap-technology/the-reddit-blackout-explained-why-thousands-of-subreddits-are-protesting-third-party-app-charges/ [Accessed 31 Jul. 2023].

Hegarty, K. (2023). Imagining permanence on the web: Tracing the meanings of long-termpreservation among the subjects of web archives. *New Media & Society*, 0(0). https://doi.org/10.1177/14614448231187031

Heleen. (2022). OTW Finance: 2022 Budget. *Organization for Transformative Works.* Available at: www.transformativeworks.org/otw-finance-2022-budget/

Leurs, K. (2017). Feminist data studies: Using digital methods for ethical, reflexive and situatedsocio-cultural research. *Feminist Review*, 115(1), pp. 130–154. doi: https://doi.org/10.1057/s41305-017-0043-1

Lin, J., Milligan, I., Oard, D.W., Ruest, N., and Shilton, K. (2020). We Could, but Should We? In: Conference on Human Information Interaction and Retrieval. *CHIIR '20: Conferenceon Human Information Interaction and Retrieval.* https://doi.org/10.1145/3343413.3377980

Lindgren Leavenworth, M. (2016). Paratextual navigation as a research method: Fan fiction archives and reader instructions. In: G. Griffin and M. Hayler (eds.), *Research methods for reading digital data in the digital humanities.* Edinburgh, Scotland: Edinburgh University Press, pp. 51–71.

Lothian, A. (2012). Archival anarchies: Online fandom, subcultural conservation, and the transformative work of digital ephemera. *International Journal of Cultural Studies*, 16(6), pp. 541–556. https://doi.org/10.1177/1367877912459132

Mancosu, M. and Vegetti, F. (2020). What you can scrape and what is right to scrape: A proposal for a tool to collect public Facebook data. Social Media + Society, 6(3). https://doi.org/10.1177/2056305120940703

Marres, N. and Weltevrede, E. (2013). Scraping the social? *Journal of Cultural Economy*, 6(3), pp. 313–335. https://doi.org/10.1080/17530350.2013.772070

Metcalf, J. and Crawford, K. (2016). Where are human subjects in Big Data research? The emerging ethics divide. *Big Data & Society*, 3(1). https://doi.org/10.1177/2053951716650211

Mollman, S. (2023). Twitter users get error messages as Elon Musk outlines new limits, blames A.I. data scraping: 'Rate limit exceeded'. *Fortune*. 1 Jul. Available at: https://fortune.com/2023/07/01/twitter-error-messages-technical-problems-elon-musk-rate-limit-exceeded/

Ogden, J. (2021). 'Everything on the internet can be saved': Archive Team, Tumblr and the cultural significance of web archiving. *Internet Histories*, 6(1–2), pp. 113–132. https://doi.org/10.1080/24701475.2021.1985835

Organization for Transformative Works. (2021). *OTW Finance: 2021 Budget*. Available at: www.transformativeworks.org/otw-finance-2021-budget/ [Accessed 31 Jul. 2023].

Porter, J. (2023). Twitter announces new API pricing, posing a challenge for small developers. *The Verge*. 30 Mar. Available at: www.theverge.com/2023/3/30/23662832/twitter-api-tiers-free-bot-novelty-accounts-basic-enterprice-monthly-price

Price, L. and Robinson, L. (2021). Tag analysis as a tool for investigating information behaviour: Comparing fan-tagging on Tumblr, archive of our own and etsy. *Journal of Documentation*, 77(2), pp. 320–358. https://doi.org/10.1108/jd-05-2020-0089

Proferes, N., Jones, N., Gilbert, S., Fiesler, C., and Zimmer, M. (2021). Studying reddit: A systematic overview of disciplines, approaches, methods, and ethics. Social Media + Society, 7(2), p. 205630512110190. https://doi.org/10.1177/20563051211019004

Riggins, J. (2023). What we can learn from Twitter's outages. *The New Stack*. Available at: https://thenewstack.io/what-we-can-learn-from-twitters-outages/ [Accessed 31 Jul. 2023].

Shakir, U. (2023). Reddit's upcoming API changes will make AI companies pony up. *The Verge*. 18 Apr. Available at: www.theverge.com/2023/4/18/23688463/reddit-developer-api-terms-change-monetization-ai

Stanfill, M. and Lothian, A. (2021). An archive of whose own? White feminism and racial justice in fan fiction's digital infrastructure. *Transformative Works and Cultures*, 36. https://doi.org/10.3983/twc.2021.2119

Underwood, T. (2017). A genealogy of distant reading. Digital Humanities Quarterly, 011(2). Available at: www.digitalhumanities.org/dhq/vol/11/2/000317/000317.html

wiki.archiveteam.org. (2022). *FanFiction.net – Archiveteam*. Available at: https://wiki.archiveteam.org/index.php/FanFiction.net [Accessed 31 Jul. 2023].

9
ARCHAEOLOGIES OF FANDOM
Using Historical Methods to Explore Fan Cultures of the Past

Kathy Fuller-Seeley

Active media fandom is so widely assumed to be a contemporary phenomenon that students look at me quizzically when, in teaching reception studies research methods, I broach the subject of studying historical audiences and past fandoms. They ask how can we analyze fans and the relationships that they formed, decades ago, with film, radio, television, or other media objects, if we cannot directly observe or interview enthusiastic viewers? Some scholars approach the research exclusively through a theoretical lens of film spectatorship, teasing out fans' fervor from the media objects themselves. While cultural theories always play a major role in analyzing and extrapolating from the evidence we can uncover, that is not the only avenue for the study of past fandoms.

This chapter will explore how scholars have been locating fragments of past fan practices, applying the methods of what Daniel Cavicchi terms "historical anthropology" (2009). Although the conclusions gained from such research will always remain partial, what we learn can be both valuable and fascinating. The study of historical fandoms is necessary for us to understand that affinity relationships have long roots, and that few practices are truly new. Scholars in a variety of fields loosely connected to contemporary fan studies, from literary studies and the history of the book, to music studies, to cultural and social history and gender studies, have been exploring historical examples of the relationships between the most ardent audience members and the media they were passionate about, and historical celebrities' interactions with their admirers. This chapter will use as a case study the early twentieth century origins of the movie fan, trace the ways that scholars in history and cinema studies have analyzed fan cultures and historical movie audiences of the silent film era, and then provide suggestions for a variety of ways in which evidence of historical film fan practices can be found and evaluated.

Past Fandoms

One of the most striking differences between fan cultures of the past and present is their scope – the ability of fans today to create and participate with others in interactive communities, collecting media objects and ephemera, making fanart, sharing fanfiction, and having the ability to easily discuss their interests with others online; this has enabled the study of contemporary fandom to mushroom. Without convention gatherings and digital platforms for sharing their passions and products, without the ease with which fans today can make their own sophisticated media objects – could there have been real fan cultures in the past? The rise of mass-produced and mass-distributed media itself was a core necessity to enable fan culture to form (Cavicchi 2009).

In formative studies published in the 1980s, scholars began to dig deep into archives to find early examples of enthusiastic audiences' relationships with celebrities, texts, and media objects. Braudy (1986) located the origins of celebrity culture in the celebration of leaders of the classical world, like Alexander the Great, and intellectuals of the Renaissance era like Erasmus, and then the spread of fame through the spread of mass-produced images and news made possible by the printing press. Darnton (1986) and Davidson (1989) sparked the field of the history of reading in the eighteenth and nineteenth centuries in Europe and the US, which intertwined the development of technologies and industries of book publishing with attention to individuals' documentation of their reading practices. Fans in the past flocked to see famous authors, joined book clubs, created scrapbooks, and engaged in dialogues with their favorites via fan letters. Historians of opera and classical music, who study prominent singers and composers, and those who research novelists, poets, and playwrights in the eighteenth and nineteenth centuries, have unearthed evidence of, among other fandom moments, the addictions of avid music fans to the attendance of live concerts in the 1850s, and promoter P.T. Barnum's creation of a publicity frenzy around superstar vocalist Jenny Lind (Cavicchi 2011), fan correspondence with Elizabeth Barrett Browning (Eisner 2007), and the expansion of General Lew Wallace's blockbuster novel *Ben Hur* into widely-shared cultural events (Ryan 2016). The affinity of female theatergoers for the players in hometown stock companies (Fuller 2002), and the cultivation of support for local sports teams from the league's managers and team owners (Dewberry 2003) are other examples of proto-fandom microhistories. Archeological approaches can be applied to many other historical moments, to search for historical audiences and fan cultures of the past.

Fans and Audiences in the Writing of American Film History

Evidence of the emergence of an informal, loosely connected, nationwide movie fan culture in the first two decades of the twentieth century, especially in the United States, home of the largest population of early moviegoers (Butsch 2000), has been a byproduct of scholarship in the last 30 years into the cultural history of cinema and its audiences. The earliest chroniclers of motion picture history focused on inventors, technological developments, prominent early directors and studio heads, aesthetic developments in film style, and star personae. Audiences originally entered into this history through distanced observation, through the concerns of social critics, who were nonplussed at the enthusiasm of the urban immigrant audiences who flocked to makeshift nickelodeons in working class areas of major cities. Early twentieth century observers expressed concerns about these moviegoers – they gathered as an impressionable mass audience, vulnerable to the persuasive impact of the films they watched. Women and children were prominent in the nickel theater audiences, and they stood out more to critics because many nineteenth 1century entertainments had been marketed exclusively for men. Social critics worried about protecting children and women from indecent films and lewd behavior in theaters, and sought, along with church leaders and local police and civil officials, to regulate the theaters and censor the films (Fronc 2017). Rarely did social critics actually ask audiences why they enjoyed movie shows. While urban immigrant audiences received the most attention from social critics and the motion picture trade press, enthusiastic viewers also were drawn to movie shows in small towns and rural areas (Waller 1995; Fuller 1996). As film exhibition matured into an accepted commercial endeavor across the nation, with purpose-built theaters, steady local connections, and wide audience attraction, cinema audiences were considered inactive, passive viewers absorbing media messages, although critics remained concerned for vulnerable child viewers.

The techniques of crafting history "from the bottom up" by social and cultural historians in the 1980s brought nickelodeon audiences back to scholars' attention. Rosenzweig (1985) and Peiss (1986) investigated the impact of the new cheap commercial entertainments of the 1900s on urban immigrant workers, who fought for expanded leisure time. Analyzing the pull of consumer culture to muffle more widespread labor movement activity and militant class consciousness, these authors persuasively argued that urban immigrant workers, especially young women, made these cheap nickel theaters their own vital centers of community. They and other historians have used social critics' dour reports to tease out evidence of the audiences' pleasure in the films, the early performers, and the social connections forged in small spaces of leisure carved out in overstuffed ghettos especially available for women, girls, and children.

Hansen (1991) combined feminist film spectatorship theory with cultural theory to chart the importance of films and nickelodeons in the incorporation of female audiences into an expanded public sphere. She explored how middle-class female audiences could bring their knowledge of classic literature like *Uncle Tom's Cabin* and biblical stories to form a greater appreciation of early tableaux films, to the appeal of Edison's Teddy Bear films to draw women into consumer culture, and later, the commodification of female sexual desire in the stardom of Rudolph Valentino. deCordova (2001) linked early movie fans' interest in "Picture Personalities" like Mary Pickford, Charlie Chaplin, and Douglas Fairbanks to a changing cultural order. Stamp (2000) analyzed popular culture depictions of the urban working-class female movie fan in fiction, art, and film, as well as the central place of vulnerable women in sociological discourse and film censorship concerns. Film historians have continued to connect films of the nickelodeon and transitional period of silent film to the fannish devotion and emotional pleasure female audiences gained from genres like serial films and female-centered melodramas. Anselmo (2015, 2023) has brought a material culture approach to her research into silent film female fandom, as she examines primary source artifacts such as fans' scrapbooks of favorite stars, diaries of films they've seen, fan works of art and poetry, and other records of their moviegoing practices. Her work connects to that of historians of reading like Sicherman (2010), who has studied the reading and collecting habits of nineteenth century middle class young women, and to investigations of historians of gender such as Schrum (2004), who has sought to chart the rise of adolescent culture in the 1930s and 1940s through both representations of young women in the media and girls' own personal diaries, scrapbooks, and school yearbooks, and Reagin (2021), who connects Western novels, media fandom, and tourism to historical recreations and gender identity. These items both intensely personal and shared by their communities helped their owner/creators form a sense of teenaged identity and placed them firmly within growing consumer and movie fan cultures.

Social scientists' concerns about the possible deleterious effects of film on its audiences led to their creation of several massive research investigations in the late 1920s, such as the projects known as the Payne Fund Studies. Jowett, Jarvie, and Fuller (1996) located some of the primary source evidence gathered for the studies as well as archived correspondence between the researchers as they discussed the evolution of their projects. While Payne Fund-associated scholars, and the bulk of their studies, dismissively characterized their young movie-going subjects as vulnerable to the strong influence of motion pictures and in need of protection from Hollywood influence, some of the original materials, such as autoethnographic essays collected for Blumer's volume (1932), read against the grain, revealing young audience members exhibiting anecdotal evidence of fannish behaviors. Girls and boys imitated their favorite movie stars, invented games that drew on popular film genres, collected photos and articles about actors from the fan magazines, habitually attended local movie theaters with friends who shared their passion for films, copied the fashions, make up and quirky behaviors of beloved stars, and discussed the latest movies between classes at school.

Historical examinations of film exhibition and local movie-going practices have also contributed to the study of cinema audiences and past fans. While documenting the circuits through which distribution and exhibition of films contributed to the building of an American film industry, Gomery (1992), Waller (2001), Allen (2007), and Fuller (2008) have encouraged researchers to think about the roles of place and space, cultural and economic geography of a town's amusement district in determining the impact of theaters on their communities, the active roles of theater managers in attracting audiences and catering to viewers' needs. Klenotic (2011) has brought the tools of social geographic analysis through mapping to analyze the impact of theater location on moviegoing practices. Moore (2008) and Abel (2015, 2021) have examined the ways in which public discourse about films, theaters, and fan culture circulated through local newspapers. Research in all these historical areas continues to expand as cinema scholars further explore the connections between film texts, the production, distribution, and exhibition arms of the film industry, and reception by audience members in a variety of cultural contexts.

Methods for Researching Historical American Movie Fans and Audiences

Training in research methods associated with social and cultural history has shaped my own quest to understand movie fans in historical settings, as I search for contextualization of past film and media production and consumption practices. While analyzing specific film texts provides one form of information to understand what kinds of meaning fans in the past took from them, I enjoy starting my research from the other end, examining the peripheral contexts of moviegoing practices and fan affinities. My searches locate the scraps left behind by individuals and their intermediary interpreters, and fragments among the records of institutions that were concerned about those who attended the movies. In examining the materials I locate, I try to understand patterns of difference that factors such as social class, gender and age, race and ethnicity, wealth and poverty, education level and religious faith, and geographic/regional location meant to the experience of being a movie fan.

First to discuss are the most personal items of individual movie fandom evidence. During years of digging around museum, university, and private archives, antique shops, and eBay listings, I have been fortunate enough to unearth fan scrapbooks and diaries, letters and postcards, and creative works produced by movie fans. I have also located ephemeral items produced by film studios and third-party trinket-makers, which reached fans' hands as souvenirs given out at movie theaters, or as dime store merchandise, and I work to build historical contexts around them, looking for patterns and links to the time and place of their creation, the ways these items represent the movies and their audiences, and the range of possible meanings they created for the fans who collected them. Oral histories of movie fans from the silent era, or contemporary interviews, are very difficult to find; a few exist in journalistic accounts or surveys taken by social service agencies in the 1910s and 1920s. One rare cache of memories of moviegoing in Northern New England in the 1920s and 1930s is found in surveys and oral histories gathered from senior citizens in Maine and New Hampshire as part of Northeast Historic Films' Going to the Movies project in the 1990s. These accounts have been made available for online viewing, along with other primary source documents of fan and film exhibition history, on the NHF website.

Scrapbooks were one of the most popular ways in which fans in the first four decades of the twentieth century collected and creatively explored their interests in early movie stars and films. They can still be found in antique stores and on eBay. Among the ones in my collection are a school composition book filled with pictures of silent cowboy stars and male movie actors, assembled by a young boy, which demonstrates that fandom was not exclusively a feminine pursuit; another that focuses on the 1916 film *Intolerance* and its performers, detailing a fan's approach to a film that scholars usually don't consider as popular cinema; and a Mary Pickford scrapbook compiled over at least 20 years by a dedicated fan, who layered fan magazine and newspaper clips over the years on top of each other, creating a multi-faceted portrait of the fan's evolving relationship with her favorite star. Scrapbooks pull together articles, photos, and brightly colored cover portraits that moviegoers clipped from the fan magazines, combined with newspaper clippings and theater programs; they might be annotated by the scrapbook maker with lists of favorite performers, drawings, and embellishments. Additional sources that might reveal how a fan expressed her or his special interests can be found in material such as personal diaries, letters and postcards sent to family and friends, and comments written in school yearbooks.

Industrially produced ephemera linked to the movies which were given out to fans had been produced from the earliest days of film exhibition. A fascinating array of inexpensively produced souvenirs, advertising tie-ins, and other ephemera were distributed to fans by film studios, movie theaters, fan magazines, consumer product advertisers, and third-party companies. Photos, postcards, toys, spoons, buttons, and badges – giveaway items attracted viewers to theaters, promoted particular serial film titles, studios, and stars, and transformed a fan's fascination with the movies into concrete material objects to possess and collect, from cigarette cards, felt pennants, silver-plate spoons with portraits of stars on the handles, playing cards, candy boxes, scarves, pillow covers, postcards, cardboard fans, celluloid broaches, school notebooks with Alice Joyce or William S. Hart on the covers, Charlie Chaplin figurines, to chromolithograph yard-long prints of Mary Pickford or Marguerite Clark, to hang on the wall. These fragments of paratextual evidence produced by the film industry (and allied trinket manufacturers) helped to spread the ideas of film stardom and fan culture among the moviegoing public.

Cultural Intermediaries as Fan History Resources

The majority of evidence of early movie fan practices comes from locating materials produced by cultural intermediaries – in the reports of theater managers, issues of fan magazines, discussions of audiences in film industry trade publications, and references to fans found in the reports of investigative groups and institutions concerned about the well-being of people who frequented movie theaters (Stewart 2005, Hallet 2013, Bowers and Fuller 2013). Theater executives, film critics, business people, writers, and investigators reported on fan activity. Some found it was in their interests to cater to fan desires, while others sought to manage, contain, or limit those desires. Audience intermediary sources can range from the reports of movie theater managers and newspaper and fan magazine columnists, to material culture studies of advertising and marketing ephemera, to geographical, cultural, and architectural studies of the theaters and the place of movie theaters in local communities, to the reports of sociologists and social workers.

Movie theater managers and other film exhibitors were key audience intermediaries in the study of their local patrons, as it was important to the exhibitors' livelihoods to attract and satisfy their local clientele, through film booking choices, building environments, advertising and public relations, theater service, and safety measures. Pleasing their local audiences, and adapting to their changing tastes, was top priority for exhibitors. Fannie Cook, half of the itinerant traveling exhibitors Cook and Harris High Class Moving Picture Company, received a letter from a host at an opera house in rural Vermont in 1906 who was nonplussed at the quick spread of movie fandom when she related that a young man who had seen the Cook program expressed a wish that he could watch movie shows every night (Fuller 1996). Film exhibitors in the stationary nickelodeons and later neighborhood movie theaters promoted fan activities among their patrons, providing publicity materials about current films and players, holding contests and finding other ways to keep their patrons engaged with Hollywood culture.

Local theater managers learned about upcoming films, and shared information about their patrons in the film industry trade press. While entertainment industry publications geared to producers and actors (like *Variety* or the *New York Clipper*) addressed audience issues in a perfunctory way, journals that included theater managers and film exhibitors among their correspondents discussed audiences frequently. *Moving Picture World, Exhibitors Trade Review*, and other publications, available online through the Media History Digital Library, provide details about recurring tensions and negotiations between fans and the businesspeople who wanted their admission money. *Motion Picture Herald* from the late 1910s until the mid-1940s provided small-town exhibitors with a forum, the "What the Picture Did for Me" department, in which individual exhibitors like Gladys McArdle of the Owl Theater in the 800-person village of Lebanon, Kansas, discussed localized examples of fan behaviors and audience reception of current film releases. The reports and comments she and her fellow theater managers submitted offer a fascinating glimpse into the workings of small-town movie fan culture (Fuller 2008).

While some newspapers like the *New York Times* gave film little coverage in the silent era, most publications in small towns and medium-sized cities offered their readers a wide variety of information about local promotion and reception of films and stars, and detailed the relationships between theater managers and the communities they served. In Cooperstown, NY, the editor of the weekly paper also owned the nickelodeon, and so he printed a great deal of commentary linking his local audiences to the Manhattan-based industry. Upstate New York newspapers have been digitized for online searching, as have a growing number of other newspapers through genealogical research websites. Local film critics and Hollywood correspondents for some of the larger newspapers became intriguing intermediary links between fans and film culture. Mayme Ober Peake, Hollywood correspondent for the *Boston Globe* from 1926 to 1940, is one example of a journalist who explored connections between fans in New England and their interests in Hollywood.

If Klinger (2006) argues that fan cultures grow with the ability to collect, own, and repeatedly view media objects, then fan magazines and the ephemera that moviegoers collected were the closest fans in the old days could get to the material film object or their favorite picture personalities. *Motion Picture Story Magazine* (*MPSM*) begun in 1911 and *Photoplay* in 1912 provide an invaluable intermediary source for studying fan culture. As the number of stationary nickel theaters spread after 1905, thousands of film enthusiasts scattered across cities and small towns, some interested in the techniques of production and projection, others intrigued by films' narratives and content, and those entranced by the "picture personalities" who appeared on screen, looked for ways to increase their knowledge. They eagerly read the first special-interest film magazines and even the movie industry trade journals, and started submitting questions and inquiries about film casts and plots to the editors; these enthusiastic audience members helped transform some of those publications into fan magazines.

Examining the ways in which the editorial and reader-submission content of *MPSM* changed over its first years of publication is a testimony to the influence and desires of its readers to know more and different information than the publishers originally intended. *MPSM* began as something akin to the journal collections of short stories that were so popular in the early twentieth century (Fuller 1996). Establishment of *MPSM*'s Answer Man column gave fans individual and collective voices – as correspondents asked for information about films, producing companies, and players, the magazine grew and the Answer Man's column expanded to dozens of pages of correspondence. *MPSM* and its rival *Photoplay* began to include fanart, poetry, and testimonials to their favorites. Almost like a movie fan internet website that included discussion fora, blogs, and tweets, *MPSM* readers had unprecedented ability to read each others' questions, involve the Answer Man in dialogue, promote their favorites and their pleasures. The fan magazines enabled vicarious participation in movie fan culture from hundreds of thousands of readers and served, in their earliest years, as a collective space of inquiry, discussion, and outlet for the creativity of fan poetry and art. After about 1916 and Hollywood's rise to dominance in the American film industry, concentrating on feature-length films and nationally-known stars, the fan magazines incorporated a much smaller amount of direct input from their readers, and marginalized representations of male fans, but they generated a great deal of information with which fans could expand their knowledge and interests. *MPSM* and *Photoplay* were joined by dozens of other magazines in the silent era, and many of them are now available to read through the Media History Digital Library, and through other websites. Recent scholarship by McDonald and Lanckman (2019, 2020) encourages historians to delve further into the communities created within fan magazine readership. McCracken (2018) and Patterson (2020) extend the history of fandoms in broadcasting history.

Conclusion

While searching through the industry publications digitized at mediahistoryproject.org, I uncovered a new fragment contributing to the origins and spread of movie fan culture. I found that Kent Webster, reporter for the trade journal *Nickelodeon*, while visiting the Essanay studio's production of "Take Me Out to the Ballgame" (adapted from the popular vaudeville song), then filming on location at the White Sox stadium in Chicago, remarked: "I am not only a film fan, but… also a dyed in the wool baseball bug as well" (1910: 62). This is one of the earliest published references to movie fans that I have yet located, and Webster's linkage of what we think of as feminine movie fandom with masculine affinities for baseball is fascinating.

As we undertake further research into historical audiences made possible by searching through the increasing numbers of digitized journals and fan magazines and by investigating new collections of source materials being unearthed from basements and archives, I join Daniel Cavicchi (2014: 70) in his call for participating in a "Fan History Initiative." Researchers in fan studies should work together with scholars in other fields to expand the fascinating enquiries that are being done across the disciplines to study the complexities of historical fandom, so that we can better understand the continuities and differences between past audience behaviors, those that are so intriguing today.

Starting in on the adventure of excavating evidence from more than 100 years ago about fannish practices is a challenge, and the results will always remain partial and speculative. But our understanding of past film viewers' relationships with the movie actors, films, and movie culture that so engaged them will be much more enhanced when we do it. The more we can make links to ongoing behaviors and desires, we will find that the opera fans of the 1820s, theater fans of the 1880s, baseball fans of the 1900s, and movie fans of the 1910s and 1920s were a lot like the passionate media fans of today. We will gain a more nuanced understanding of the interactions between past media, past audiences, and the culture that those viewers created for themselves.

References

Abel, R. (2015) *Menus for Movieland: Newspapers and the Emergence of American Film Culture, 1913–1916*, Berkeley: University of California Press.
Abel, R., ed. (2021) *Movie Mavens: US Newspaper Women Take on the Movies, 1914–1923*, Champaign, Illinois: University of Illinois Press.
Allen, R., et al. (2007) *Going to the Show: Mapping Moviegoing in North Carolina*, University of North Carolina Library. http://docsouth.unc.edu/gtts/
Anselmo-Sequeira, D. (2023) *A Queer Way of Feeling: Girl Fans and Personal Archives of Early Hollywood*, Berkeley: University of California Press.
Anselmo-Sequeira, D. (2015) "Screen-Struck: The Invention of the Movie Girl Fan," *Cinema Journal*, 55 (1), pp. 1–28.
Blumer, H. (1932) *Movies and Conduct*, New York: Macmillan.
Bowers, D. and Fuller-Seeley, K. (2013) *One Thousand Nights at the Movies: An Illustrated History of Motion Pictures 1895–1915*, Atlanta: Whitman Publishing.
Braudy, L. (1986) *The Frenzy of Renown: Fame and Its History*, Oxford: Oxford University Press.
Butsch, R. (2000) *The Making of American Audiences: From Stage to Television, 1750–1990*, Cambridge: Cambridge University Press.
Cavicchi, D. (2007) "Loving Music: Listeners, Entertainments, and the Origins of Music Fandom in Nineteenth-Century America," in Gray, J.A., Sandvoss, C. and Harrington, C.L. (eds.) *Fandom: Identities and Communities in a Mediated World*, New York: NYU Press, pp. 235–249.

Cavicchi, D. (2009) "History and Fan Studies: A Conversation between Barbara Ryan and Daniel Cavicchi (Part One)," *Confessions of an Aca-Fan*, 20, pp. 85–102. http://henryjenkins.org/2009/03/a_conversation_between_barbara.html

Cavicchi, D. (2011) *Listening and Longing: Music Lovers in the Age of Barnum*, Middletown: Wesleyan University Press.

Cavicchi, D. (2014) "Fandom before 'Fan': Shaping the History of Enthusiastic Audiences," *Reception: Texts, Readers, Audiences, History*, 6, pp. 52–72.

Darnton, R. (1986) "First Steps toward a History of Reading," *Australian Journal of French Studies*, 23 (1), pp. 5–30.

Davidson, C. (1989) *Reading in America: Literature & Social History*, Baltimore: Johns Hopkins University Press.

deCordova, R. (2001) *Picture Personalities: The Emergence of the Star System in America*, Champaign: University of Illinois Press.

Dewberry, E. (2003) "Jake Wells, Commercial Entertainment Entrepreneur of the South: A Study of His Career in Richmond, Virginia, 1894–1927," MA thesis, Virginia Commonwealth University.

Eisner, E. (2007) "Elizabeth Barrett Browning and the Energies of Fandom," *Victorian Review*, 33 (2), pp. 85–102.

Fronc, J. (2017) *Monitoring the Movies: The Fight over Film Censorship in Early Twentieth-Century Urban America*, Austin: University of Texas Press.

Fuller, K. (1996, 2001) *At the Picture Show: Small-Town Audiences and the Creation of Movie Fan Culture*, Washington, DC: Smithsonian Institution Press, rpt. Charlottesville, University of Virginia Press.

Fuller-Seeley, K. (2002) *Celebrate Richmond Theater*, Richmond: Dietz Press.

Fuller-Seeley, K., ed. (2008) *Hollywood in the Neighborhood: Historical Case Studies of Local Moviegoing*, Berkeley: University of California Press.

Gomery, D. (1992) *Shared Pleasures: A History of Movie Presentation in the United States*, Madison: University of Wisconsin Press.

Hallett, H. (2013) *Go West, Young Women!: The Rise of Early Hollywood*, Berkeley: University of California Press.

Hansen, M. (1991) *Babel and Babylon: Spectatorship in American Silent Film*, Cambridge: Harvard University Press.

Jowett, G., Jarvie, I., and Fuller, K. (1996) *Children and the Movies: Media Influence and the Payne Fund Controversy*, Cambridge: Cambridge University Press.

Klenotic, J. (2011) "Putting New Cinema on the Map: Using GIS to Explore the Spatiality of Cinema," in Maltby, R., Bilteryest, D. and Meers, P. (eds.) *Explorations in New Cinema History: Approaches and Case Studies*, New York: John Wiley & Sons, pp. 58–84.

Klinger, B. (2006) *Beyond the Multiplex: Cinema, New Technologies, and the Home*, Berkeley: University of California Press.

Lanckman, L. (2020) "Fans, Community and Conflict in the Pages of *Picture Play*, 1920–38," *Transformative Works and Cultures* 33.

McCracken, A. (2018) "A History of Fandom in Broadcasting," in Aniko Bodroghkozy (ed.) *A Companion to the History of American Broadcasting*, Hoboken, NJ: Wiley, pp. 413–442.

McDonald, T. and Lanckman, L. eds. (2019) *Star Attractions: Twentieth-Century Movie Magazines and Global Fandom*, Iowa City: University of Iowa Press.

Media History Digital Library (n.d.) www.Mediahistoryproject.org.

Moore, P. (2008) *Now Playing: Early Moviegoing and the Regulation of Fun*, Albany: State University of New York Press.

Northeast Historic Film (n.d.) Bucksport, Maine. http://oldfilm.org/content/exhibits

Orgeron, M. (2009) "'You Are Invited to Participate': Interactive Fandom in the Age of the Movie Magazine," *Journal of Film and Video*, 61 (3), pp. 3–23.

Patterson, E. (2020) "Capturing Flow: The Growth of the Old-Time-Radio Collecting Culture in the United States during the 1970s," *JCMS: Journal of Cinema and Media Studies*, 59 (3), pp. 46–68.

Peiss, K. (1986) *Cheap Amusements: Working Women and Leisure in New York City, 1880–1920*, Philadelphia: Temple University Press.

Reagin, N. (2021) *Re-Living the American Frontier: Western Fandoms, Reenactment, and Historical Hobbyists in Germany and America Since 1900*, Iowa City: University of Iowa Press.

Rosenzwig, R. (1985) *Eight Hours for What We Will: Workers and Leisure in an Industrial City, 1870–1920*, Cambridge: Cambridge University Press.
Ryan, B. ed. (2016) *Bigger Than Ben-Hur: The Book, Its Adaptations, and Their Audiences*, Syracuse: Syracuse University Press.
Schrum, K. (2004) *Some Wore Bobby Sox: The Emergence of Teenage Girls' Culture, 1920–1945*, New York: Palgrave Macmillan.
Sicherman, B. (2010) *Well Read Lives: How Books Inspired a Generation of American Women*, Chapel Hill: University of North Carolina Press.
Stamp, S. (2000) *Movie-Struck Girls: Women and Motion Picture Culture after The Nickelodeon*, Princeton: Princeton University Press.
Stewart, J. (2005) *Migrating to the Movies: Cinema and Black Urban Modernity*, Berkeley: University of California Press.
Waller, G. (1995) *Main Street Amusements: Movies and Commercial Entertainment in a Southern City, 1896-1930*, Washington, DC: Smithsonian Institution Press.
Waller, G. ed. (2001) *Movie Going in America: A Sourcebook in the History of Film Exhibition*, New York: Wiley-Blackwell.
Webster, K. (1910) "Little Stories of Great Films," *Nickelodeon*, August 1, pp. 61–62. http://archive.org/stream/nickelodeon04elec#page/60/mode/2up

10
CONVERSATION ON STUDYING "TOXIC" FANS

Kishonna L. Gray, CarrieLynn D. Reinhard, and Adrienne Shaw

Recent publications on anti-fandom (Click 2019) and special issues on toxic fan practices (Proctor and Kies 2018) and on reactionary fandom (Stanfill 2020), highlight fan scholars' interest in studying polarization and hate in fan communities, and what these affects and practices – regardless of the labels we use to describe them – tell us about fandom and the culture at large. To share their expertise conducting research on practices and populations we might call "toxic," we asked Kishonna L. Gray, CarrieLynn Reinhard, and Adrienne Shaw to talk together about methods and ethics, and ultimately to provide guidance in this area of research. Kishonna L. Gray is an interdisciplinary, intersectional, digital media scholar whose areas of research include identity, performance and online environments, embodied deviance, cultural production, video games, and Black Cyberfeminism. She is the author of *Race, Gender, & Deviance in Xbox Live* (Routledge, 2014), which situates video games within a hegemonic framework deploying whiteness and masculinity as the norm to examine the nature of social interactions within Xbox Live, which are often riddled with deviant behavior, including but not limited to racism and sexism. CarrieLynn Reinhard is author, co-editor, and co-author of various articles, books, and book chapters, including research on the community around the far-right American political conspiracy theory QAnon, and the book *Fractured Fandoms: Contentious Communication in Fan Communities* (Lexington, 2018), which observes the problems or fractures that occur within and between fandoms as fans and fan communities experience differences in interpretation, opinion, expectation, and behavior regarding the object at the center of their fandom. Adrienne Shaw's research and teaching focus on video games and gaming culture, LGBTQ video game history, representations of marginalized groups in media, and cultural production. She has written about her first-hand experience of GamerGate and is the author of *Gaming at the Edge: Sexuality and Gender at the Margins of Gamer Culture* (University of Minnesota Press, 2015), which builds on feminist, queer, and postcolonial theories of identity to make sense of how representation in video games comes to matter, particularly for women, people of color, and LGBT people who are often brutalized in forums and in public channels in online play. Together, these scholars discuss how they conceptualize toxicity in fan cultures; methods, challenges, and best practices for conducting research about toxic practices and communities; and advice for scholars embarking on this work with "toxic" research subjects.

DEFINING TOXICITY

Why do we need to be mindful of the particular practices and identity performances of "toxic" fans? What can they tell us about fandom and/or culture at large?

Adrienne Shaw: I study areas of popular culture where inevitably there will be some toxicity. For me, that is very different from starting from the place of trying to understand people who are doing toxic things. I cannot do my research without running into toxicity.

CarrieLynn Reinhard: I actually think that is a good place to start. I don't like thinking of them as toxic, either, because I try very hard when I am looking at QAnon or other folks to not dehumanize them. Rather, I try to see them as people struggling like we all are to cope with life and to make sense of life. That idea of "toxic" is very subjective. It is based on how you see it. That being said, though, there are definitely segments of any fandom that I would be more concerned engaging with as a researcher, and how to do that while not losing yourself is something I have had to wrestle with.

Kishonna Gray: For me, I would like to see how maybe we collectively think about what a "toxic" fan is, because I know, especially with my earlier work, looking at the online communities of console gaming – PlayStation and Xbox in particular – the toxic folks would have been people like us because we deviated from the norm of what is expected in some of those spaces. We were deviant because we were calling out the norms to be sexist, racist, and homophobic that the platforms had accepted. The comments all lump under trash talk: that is the norm, the modus operandi, the core operating system in a lot of these spaces. I was having to frame women of color as the deviant actors in the space, because they were trying to do interventions by saying, "hey, stop being toxic, stop being mean, can we all just play?" We were like the outsiders invading this Boys Club, this boy space. I think it's really important that we think about that and even define what we mean when we say toxic fans. You know they would not call themselves toxic, right? I don't often use the word toxic in my work. But I understand the utility of it and why we use it.

Adrienne Shaw: The struggle when Shira Chess and I (2015) were writing about our experiences with GamerGate was distinguishing between the people who were actually angry, and the people who were just trying to get people riled up. Those are two different articulations of the same thing. Hatespeech has the same effect on the people who hear it, but it's very hard to study people who are just shit talking and don't mean it. I think the toxicness, for me, is the people who are trying to manipulate others into acting a certain way. Which is why I don't think people who are not supposed to be in the space are people I would frame as toxic. It's the people who are trying to make the space inhospitable to other people, whether that is academia, an industry, or a fanbase that I see as toxic.

CarrieLynn Reinhard: True, because what we consider to be a toxic fan doesn't necessarily equate to conservative or progressive, right or left, or anything like that. You can definitely have individuals who espouse much more progressive ideas and ideologies, but they are still doing that same type of gatekeeping and policing the boundaries. From the context of that specific space, that is a toxic behavior to engage in.

Kishonna Gray: For the concept of toxic fans, I stopped studying them right before GamerGate happened, right after my dissertation work. I was doing this project where I was basically in the spaces that people would later call "alt-right." For the most part, most actors were just provocative. They were just trying to trigger folks, to just get a rise out of them, and I remember asking a few of them: "Hey, why did you use those words? Why did you say that?" They were like: "I'm not really racist. I'm not sexist. It's just a word to say. I'm just trying to be cool. We're all using it." I was fascinated by that. It was not like the deep recesses where folks get radicalized and are going to buy guns and shoot something. I don't think that those kinds of folks were on that path. I think there's a different kind of pathway and recruiting for those kinds of people.

But I had a moment where I asked myself, why am I here? Why do I care about these stories? There is already a huge body of literature on why people are sexist and racist. We have bodies of literature on this topic, and this is just another space where we can say racism and sexism are happening. I didn't think there was anything new to be found in that space. Then I started to ask myself the question: What are we missing? Whose stories do we not have? What perspectives do we not have? This was also around the time the LGBTQ Game Archive was coming out that Adrienne was working on telling queer stories.

So I changed gears; let me just tell Black stories in here, forget about that other stuff. That is where I started to plant the seeds for *Intersectional Tech* (Gray 2020), so I could just really focus on, in spite of all this stuff happening, why are folks still in the space. I think that has been so much more generative; what Adrienne and I are doing, adding to those stories instead of just focusing on the toxicity.

But if I had stayed in those alt-right spaces – I left in 2013 – I felt the rumblings. I knew this was going to happen. I could tell they were feeling like they were being pushed out. They were feeling like they had to make space for these women, for all this new diversity. These dudes were mad, and I didn't want to be the punching bag for when they blew up. Let me just get out of here, before I felt compelled to have to say or do something. We all felt compelled to have to say something in that moment, but we didn't want to spend too much time and energy on that, because that's not what drew us to the space in the first place. We will talk about it because we can, but this is not what makes up gaming cultures, and this is not the story we want our legacies to be.

ENGAGING TOXICITY

Is it important to delineate who is or is not a "fan" in these instances of protest and harassment? How can we determine whose actions are being driven by (anti-)fannish affect or merely a desire to provoke a response?

CarrieLynn Reinhard: We already know the history of fans not wanting to talk to academics because they don't want to engage with the possibility of being critiqued and judged. You add on these additional layers to it as well when it comes to all the culture wars that are going on, the sides that people have chosen, and that becomes another issue of how do we talk to anyone, then, if they're not willing to be honest and open and reflective – that they are just engaging in performative outrage.

Adrienne Shaw: One of the things that I try to get my students to think about is that toxic doesn't have to be the default behavior. It doesn't have to be what the internet is. Obviously, people are going to be assholes on the internet, as they are in physical spaces. But I try to get my students to think about a specific platform that encourages that behavior, and what would make it better. What about the site encourages that behavior, and the counter to that: how do we design spaces that promote more prosocial behavior?

Thinking about the toxicity not as a feature of the person, but as a behavior that gets promoted, is something that I think about a lot. With online gaming, what about those spaces makes it fun to say racist things? What makes it fun to be homophobic? I play women's ice hockey, and a lot of people I play with are also on coed teams where the men are terrible to each other. We play the exact same sports, but in different ways. Nobody in our women's league (or at least very few) would consider the kind of trash talking that happens in the exact same equivalent skill-level of adult, recreational hockey in majority men's spaces.

So, what is it about the space? What is it about the culture that promotes that kind of activity? That becomes a more interesting question than whether or not somebody means it. That helps us get away from the question of whether that person is intentionally being hateful or are they just trying to provoke a response out of people.

CarrieLynn Reinhard: I take a sensemaking perspective where I try to understand the individual's perspective, but to understand their perspective not just on themselves but on the platform, on a mesolevel analysis of the community and the culture, but also the macrolevel and thinking about the society and social values, and all of these structures that their agency is acting within and against. At the same time, I also need to pair that with an interdisciplinary approach that is doing the analysis of the platforms; doing social network analysis, looking at the sociology of the community and the culture, and looking at the political economics of the person's platforms and living circumstances.

Because I love the idea that we should have platforms encourage prosocial behaviors, even though what is defined as prosocial is probably going to change from time to time and from culture to culture. At the same time, if they aren't having that education before they even get to the platforms, or regularly having such behavior consistently cultivated, then actual prosocial behavior may just be existing within the space and may not transcend and transverse with them as they move throughout life.

Kishonna Gray: How would you start? To me that sounds really big. There's a lot of lofty goals there, but I am thinking tangibly. Where do we start with that? Because in my mind, it sounds like your focus is on fixing these bad actors while they are still doing harm. A place to start is where the platforms are taking a stance and saying they are not going to accept or tolerate this kind of behavior. Platforms have done that significantly in their terms of service and code of conduct. They are banning people; they have tiers of things. They have multiple ways to get at this problem.

I think we have to figure out a way to make the platforms feel responsible for the experiences of all their users. They need to feel responsible for the bad actors harming their vulnerable populations. Like kids; kids are being harmed. Kids are growing up listening to some of that. All of our research is cool, but if we cannot make that problem make sense to the industry – if we are not translating that into something actionable, then what are we even doing with all this stuff?

CarrieLynn Reinhard: I don't see this as fixing people, because I come from the psychology perspective that says you can never fix someone. They have to fix themselves. One of my goals is to try to understand people's stories, how they make sense of what they are doing, what they see going on. Maybe with particular individuals I can shine a light back on them, I can hold up a mirror so that they can see the reflection. Maybe they can think about what they are doing. Yes, it's probably not always going to happen. It probably will not happen a lot. But I cannot force them to change. They have to want to change.

My bigger goal, though, is to address it from the education level: to go to the educators, K-12, go to the parents and say, "Hey, this is what is going on. This is how these things are happening and what the effects are." Forewarned is forearmed. I recognize the fact that we need to be teaching these types of literacy skills for empathy, social literacy, and communication, to foster the prosocial type of offline and online behavior.

And for once and for all, we have to stop thinking that a person who is online is going to be completely different from how they are offline, because that just is not the case. Yes, the spaces may afford them to act out in ways that they cannot in person. But to say that they are just acting that way because they are online – if anyone still believes that, then we really have to dispel that myth, and I don't think we have dispelled it enough yet.

Adrienne Shaw: I think it's a hard myth to dispel, because trolling is a beloved part of internet history. I had a conversation with students last semester who grew up on a version of the internet where they kind of loved hearing people say all this ridiculous stuff about others. They would also say this ridiculous stuff, and then they grew out of it. We are all terrible when we are teenagers and do a lot of things we probably should not have.

I feel like we don't necessarily take seriously enough that so much of this is being done by 13- to 18-year-olds who will then (hopefully) become better people if given the right support system. But the space that they have set up stays there in a way that it persists more than earlier teen culture did. The chatrooms I was in as a teenager didn't get archived the way Reddit posts are (at least until the platform or users decide to remove them). This (semi-) permanent content allows for people to feel that this is how people are here; because if you go back through the message threads, that is what everybody's saying, even if all of those people have moved on to do other things.

Trying to understand why people are doing these things is actually really helpful and important. McKernan, Rossini, and Stromer-Galley (2023) did a study that demonstrates something that I already felt knowing people who are conspiracy theorists. They are not just "nut cases" who pull random things off the internet and believe it, as is the common caricature. They are very serious people pulling together different sources of information and coming to their own conclusion. People who are analytical in a way that is unique and intuitive to them. They don't trust institutions. And I am not going to tell them that they should trust institutions unquestioningly. But I do think they should believe in scientific studies, even if science cannot answer everything. Both of these things exist simultaneously: science is deeply problematic in many ways, but also climate change and Covid-19 are real. I think the struggle is trying to get at that nuance.

Kishonna Gray: If we want to call out people who are being toxic, some of that is just stuff in the world. How do we get rid of sexism? How do we get rid of racism? Our doing it in fandom is not the only entry point. I think we all know that. But then it becomes this bigger question of what are we doing if we cannot fix it? Are we studying it just to understand it better? If we cannot fix people, they will go find somewhere else to be terrible. They will learn that they are not allowed to say racist things in public, so they will go find other people they can say it to. They will learn that the platform prevents them from doing certain things, so they will go create another space.

I also don't want to ignore the power of bots, either. Bots do harm. The assumption is that we care about real people, but what we know from things like GamerGate is that it was a lot of bots. Think about the misinformation, fake news campaigns. It was a lot of bots, but they did a lot of real harm. I think, methodologically, a person is behind a username, or a screen name, or a bot. Sure, that might matter, but I just want to make sure that we acknowledge that those bots do real harm, regardless of if it's a real person behind the content.

Adrienne Shaw: Bots are actors in these massive hate campaigns. They are actors in disinformation campaigns. The idea that bots are part of toxic communities is something that I hadn't actually thought about until just now. As researchers, we discuss whether it matters if they "mean it" when people say hateful things online because the effect of it's the same, and I think that same logic can apply to bots. It doesn't matter that it's not a real human actor. It's saying these things, and that has an effect. I don't know that we have yet found a way, research-wise, to include bots as part of the research subjects, not just as things to be accounted for.

CarrieLynn Reinhard: Right, because somebody is still making the bots.

Adrienne Shaw: And somebody is following the bots, and the bots are doing things on their own once they are out there.

Kishonna Gray: I want to make sure that we also don't assume a certain thing about what bots are. I think we're assuming bots are these toxic actors. But, especially in Twitch, people enable bots for protection, to filter out things. So remember, like, these AI tools can also be used to protect us and communities, too.

RESEARCHING TOXICITY

What are some methodological approaches, best practices, or particular challenges when it comes to studying "toxic" research subjects?

CarrieLynn Reinhard: For the study that I just did – and I had to seek a renewal of the IRB because I didn't think we received enough conservative voices – part of what I saw happening was how hard it was to recruit. I had a lot of people who were conservatives, who were just telling others not to trust our study, that this is just someone trying to do phishing and identity theft, a lot of pushback. At one point, I just went to YouTube where

I did searches with conservative keywords; I just went into the comments and asked people to do the study. Our response numbers went up from around 300 to 600.

But when I reviewed everything that we collected, there was so much repetition and fake email accounts – there was definitely a lot of spamming going on. I don't know how much it was that someone had created a bot or sock puppets, and they were just trying to spam and manipulate the results. But I do know some people used a generative AI to complete the self-interview. So we had to remove all of that, and it cut the sample size in half. Now I am trying to figure out how to find more authentic voices. But that is hard, too, especially in this area. I wonder how much of this is due to just the increased politicization of academics and academic research, so that people want to spam research to undermine a potential conclusion that might benefit one group politically versus another group.

Research is constantly fraught with this idea about getting authentic responses. But, how can you trust anything that a person tells you? They may not remember or don't want to tell you for some reason. I don't think that problem is necessarily any different today. It may be just manifesting in different ways than we would have seen in the past, with bots, trolls, and spamming.

Adrienne Shaw: I wonder if it's a difference in scale. Because, if you do a survey pre-internet, there was always a chance of getting a bunch of people filling it out who are not really taking it seriously. But if you put it online, open to everybody, then it's easier for more people and bots to flood it with information. The scale is part of what bots produce. It's not necessarily the good or the bad of them. It is the mass quantity of them.

Kishonna Gray: Especially when we started doing internet research, people always asked us, how do you know that is who they are? If we allowed those conversations to distract us from what was important and significant, we wouldn't have made all these beautiful strides in internet research. So some of the best practices have come from people in internet research involving the commitments to communities and to protecting folks. If people aren't who they say they are, that doesn't mean that what we do is insignificant, because we know that there are folks who are experiencing these things, and we do the research for them to shed light on what is happening in these online spaces.

Dealing with bots fits within these methodological challenges, especially as we are training students while we are also learning. For platform studies, we need to think about the infrastructure and the affordances of these spaces. So I also want to think about bots as existing because of these platforms. Platforms enabled their creation. We need to bring in such infrastructure.

Adrienne Shaw: Anybody who studies the internet is going to have to think about how to incorporate the non-human. We have to start accounting for these as part of the community, not as noise to sort through. However, it can be frustrating when non-internet researchers don't realize that internet research has been around for over two decades. I've had a lot of students outside of media studies come to me and say I am doing this internet-based project, I have to go through the IRB, and I don't know how to approach the ethics. So I send them the Association of Internet Researchers guidelines (Franzke et al. 2020), and then they share that with their advisor who says they had no idea those guidelines existed.

I think good internet research follows best practices of any research. But it also recognizes the norms of internet spaces. For example, in web-based forums, the expectation is that it is a semi-private space. Even if a person has a public Twitter account, they do not necessarily think they are talking to the public when they are online, unless they are really famous and get thousands of retweets.

CarrieLynn Reinhard: For me, best practices are collaborative, being mindful of interdisciplinary, transdisciplinary, multi-methodology – and not assuming that you have the one right way to study something, because there's no such thing. Each research method has its benefits and drawbacks, its affordances and constraints, and you need to be mindful of all of this when it comes to designing a research study.

Whenever I do a reception/audience/fan study, my goal is to get underneath all of these differences, because, yes, we have people who are acting in ways that are toxic, whether from the right or the left. But with my goal and the methodology I use, I try to understand what is driving all of that toxicity. So, taking a step back to before they get to those points where they are expressing those types of attitudes, what was happening before? What's happening around it? What's happening during it? How do they see what is going on?

It is interesting, because the Sense-Making Methodology (SMM), when I was learning it, my mentor, Brenda Dervin, liked to equate it with Carl Rogers' humanistic approach to therapy, and that idea of talk therapy: how sometimes what people need is the ability to talk things out to understand how things are connected. Pretty abductive based. My goal with SMM is to give people the space to talk and be heard without judgement from me. That is my approach with whatever method I use. With this politics, religion, and fandom project, it starts as a questionnaire, all close-ended, and then it uses SMM for self-interviews, similar to my fractured fandom work (Reinhard 2018). The idea is to allow people a structured space to investigate their own experiences and behaviors within it. I am hoping to give people that space to tell me how they see these things connecting to each other without my framing what they do as toxic.

Adrienne Shaw: I do think that there's a power in that. The trouble with getting people to realize that people are not different online than they are offline, is also realizing that what we see online is not everything. During the height of GamerGate, after my 2014 book had just come out, I had a Twitter alert for when people mentioned my name. I remember at one point, somebody said something very terrible about me. I clicked over to his Twitter profile, and the tweet exactly before that was the person being really excited for the next *Doctor Who* episode. It took every bit of my will to not respond with: "I'm also excited. Can we talk about *Doctor Who* instead of my book you didn't read?"

CarrieLynn Reinhard: Getting to understand what leads people somewhere, rather than trying to convince them, is the best goal of my research. Some people in the social sciences may just want to push a button and make people be better. Like just have electrodes so when people do bad things, we just zap them. But we shouldn't do that. Instead, can we understand what leads people down that path, and then find the points of intervention before that, or find a way to bring them back.

MINDFUL RESEARCH

How do you set boundaries to protect your mental and physical health? What advice do you have for scholars who are interested in pursuing this kind of research?

Adrienne Shaw: The compulsion to have to say something is interesting. I just want to be upfront: GamerGate happened when I was going up for my third-year review, and I had to do this deep dive of my name on the internet. I started finding people who were very mad, and reading my CV in a very scary voice on YouTube. I was like: what is happening? There was a lot of pressure to write about it, talk about it, engage with it because I was being targeted. But it became clear that most of that anger was the result of willful misunderstanding of my work, and it felt not worth it to correct people intentionally mischaracterizing my arguments.

Kishonna Gray: What is the scale at which we can operate? And, where are we at the end of the day? What are our goals and our intentions? What do we hope to accomplish? For me as an academic, I realize I don't have the power to change much. I realized that a lot of the power that we have, really, is in the classroom. We have heard that several times in this conversation. That is really one of the reasons why we became educators. We cannot change the world, but maybe we can influence these few lives here in this classroom. Are we okay with that? When I think about scale, I guess I just settle on reducing harm, making sure the platforms could just reduce harm, just to protect folks in the meantime.

Because I have shifted away from focusing on fans, individually and collectively, and I focus a lot more on the platforms, I realized we want to improve the conditions and spaces for people. So I have settled on a reduced harm model. I got really interested in technical tools like Intel's Bleep. People who are trying to do voice-based moderation. Rather than asking, can the person be "fixed" or "improved?" I think that is the longer, more impossible task, and so in the immediate, borrowing from bystander interventions, I just want people to be safe. We can fix the bad behavior later. I have settled on how to create and reward spaces that support prosocial behaviors.

CarrieLynn Reinhard: To address your question about what impact academics can have, I have two suggestions. One is networking among academics, so that we recognize that no one person among us has to try to do all of it, because that leads to burnout. But I also wish we had more social sciences, or at least digital humanities, public intellectuals and public scholars who could talk about these things on a larger scale. To essentially be the mouthpiece for that network of academics and the research those academics are doing.

Adrienne Shaw: It is a terrible metaphor, but what about death by a 1,000 paper cuts? Can we repurpose that to not be about microaggressions, but like microliberation, microrevelation moments? When I wrote my book (Shaw 2014), I was a nobody for the game industry and assumed they would never care what I have to say. Now I have evidence that people have taken what I said in my book and put it into practice. It was not a sudden change. It cannot be a magic change, but it's a long-term change. So, we need to recognize that we get to choose what we research. We're very lucky to get to choose what kind of research we do. You should pick something you get energy out of doing, over those things drain you.

Kishonna Gray: I want to highlight that. We can get carried away by the moment, and we want to study online gaming and make sense of it because we're invested in gaming and those communities. But that concern doesn't have to carry your research trajectory. I'm really glad that you, Adrienne, contributed in beautiful ways in those kinds of moments, because we needed those voices. But I only have one piece on GamerGate, and I decided I didn't want to do more, because there are so many other kinds of questions to ask. So I want to make sure that students, future researchers, don't feel that just because something is trending that it should dictate their research trajectory.

Whenever I teach methods, I always talk about what kinds of questions move you, and rarely are they about the trend. I remember a student interested in a phenomenon trending that then passed, and they thought they could not study it. Academics can study a thing that happened 50 years ago, and it still matters. So I also want students, especially this new generation who are interested in internet research, to remember that they are not journalists. They are not supposed to write that hot piece about the thing that is happening. Do a blog or a podcast for that.

CarrieLynn Reinhard: Especially when we look at fan studies, a lot of times we see people doing research on something that they love, something that they are a fan of, because partly it's to try to help legitimize that thing that they are a fan of. Thus, in some way, they want to legitimize themselves as well. But that comes down to that idea of personal significance. What you are studying should not just be something important to you. Maybe sometimes you should not be studying what you are a fan of to have that distance to get the clarity, insight, and reflection. And you cannot think that just because you are studying something you are making it important. You are just studying it, and what other people do with your study is out of your control. And, yes, that does suck. It's one of my biggest challenges looking at politics as a fandom, because I really don't want to give the next would-be dictator the playbook for how to activate fans to do toxic things. But I'm also not saying that when I study you, I'm doing it because I agree with or respect you. I'm just studying you. I'm just trying to provide insight into this thing.

Adrienne Shaw: We have to remember sometimes that distance is necessary when it comes to being a researcher.

References

Chess, S., & Shaw, A. (2015). A conspiracy of fishes, or, how we learned to stop worrying about GamerGate and embrace hegemonic masculinity. *Journal of Broadcasting and Electronic Media*, 59(1), 208–220.

Click, M. A. (2019). *Anti-fandom: Dislike and hate in the digital age*. New York: New York University Press.

Franzke, A. S., Bechmann, A., Zimmer, M., Ess, C., & the Association of Internet Researchers (2020). Internet research: Ethical guidelines 3.0. https://aoir.org/reports/ethics3.pdf

Gray, K. (2020). *Intersectional tech: Black users in digital gaming*. Baton Rouge: Louisiana State University Press.

Gray, K. (2014). *Race, gender, & deviance in Xbox live: Theoretical perspectives from the virtual margins*. New York: Routledge.

McKernan, B., Rossini, P., & Stromer-Galley, J. (2023). Echo chambers, cognitive thinking styles, and mistrust? Examining the roles information sources and information processing play in conspiracist ideation. *International Journal of Communication*, 17, 1102–1125. https://ijoc.org/index.php/ijoc/article/view/19244/4041

Proctor, W., & Kies, B. (2018). Toxic fan practices [Themed Section]. *Participations: Journal of Audience and Reception Studies*, 15(1), 127–142.

Reinhard, C. D. (2018). *Fractured fandoms: Contentious communication in fan communities*. Lanham, MD: Lexington Books.

Shaw, A. (2014). *Gaming at the edge: Sexuality and gender and the margins of gamer culture*. Minneapolis: University of Minnesota Press.

Stanfill, M. (Ed.). (2020). Reactionary fandom [Special Issue]. *Television & New Media*, 21(2), 123–134.

PART II

Fan Practices and Platforms

A large body of work within fan studies has and continues to focus on the transformative textual practices of fans, from writing fanfiction to the creation of fanart and fanvids. Fan scholars have also increasingly turned their attention to how emergent technologies and the affordances of specific digital platforms shape and are shaped by fan practices. As we noted in the introduction to this collection, there are myriad books and articles (and, indeed, entire academic journals) devoted to the study of fans' production and communal circulation of transformative works. Accordingly, this section focuses on fan practices that have received comparatively less attention by fan scholars, such as the emergent practice of "shifting," or the role that language and national context plays in fanfiction. Likewise, discussions of technologies and platforms in this section offer both timely case studies and historical context to help us better understand fan culture's dialogic and, at times, contested, relationship with platform affordances.

Three chapters from the first edition have been reprinted for this new edition. These include Louisa Ellen Stein's consideration of the development of distinct "fan aesthetics" on Tumblr, ranging from tagging styles to gifsets, Derek Kompare's discussion of the archival impulse within fan communities and how fans function as curators, and Henry Jenkins' exploration of "racebending" (the practice of changing the race or ethnicity of a pre-existing character) as an interventionist form of negotiated reading by fans of color. Several other chapters from the first edition have been revised and updated. Rhiannon Bury's "Where the Fans Are: Rethinking Fan Studies and Participatory Culture," revisits Bury's call to view fandom as a "participatory continuum" and interrogates fan studies' longstanding focus on community. Building on her expansive and impactful work on fan tourism and theme parks since the publication of the first edition of this collection, Rebecca Williams' "Fan Tourism and Pilgrimage: Revisited" explores the immersive pleasures of these spaces, as well as the tensions between commercialization and the "authentic" experiences these fan sites produce. In "Accessing Platformed Fandoms: Disability and Digital Fan Practices," Elizabeth Ellcessor updates their exploration of how disabled fans navigate and build community through a discussion of emergent digital platforms like Mastodon and TikTok. Finally, Francesca Coppa, Alexis Lothian, and Tisha Turk have revisited their roundtable conversation focused on intersections of vidding and identity, making some minor updates to their consideration of the political nature of vidding's critique of media representations, as well as the place of vidding within broader digital remix cultures.

This section also includes four new chapters for the second edition, each exploring global and emergent perspectives on fan practices and platforms. First, Clarice Greco engages the role that language and cultural specificity plays in transcultural fanfiction. Performing a qualitative analysis of fanfiction posted to Brazil: Spirit Fanfic and Stories, Greco explores how authors navigate language barriers between and integrate references to Brazilian culture. Next, Claire Whitley and Katharine Perrotta explore the emergent fan practice of "shifting," or a process where fans claim to "shift realities" into the fictional world of their media fan object. Emerging on TikTok in 2020, Whitley and Perrotta argue that shifting creates a distinct fan community and practice in which "evidence" and the policing of experience becomes a fan practice and mode of content creation in and of itself. Agnieszka Urbanczyk discusses the Americanization of fan practices by focusing on how early media fandom in Poland presents a distinct break from these norms, and how this has shifted as millennials gained more access to global digital publics. Finally, Quiyan Guo analyzes how Chinese fans utilize different digital platforms for specific purposes, focusing on the distinct discursive uses and migratory patterns of celebrity fans on Weibo, WeChat, and Douban. Collectively, the chapters in this "Fan Practices and Platforms" section call on readers to interrogate the interplay between the two.

Further Reading

Alper, M. (2021) "Critical media access studies: Deconstructing power, visibility, and marginality in mediated space," *International Journal of Communication* 15, 840–861. https://ijoc.org/index.php/ijoc/article/view/15274/3353

Andrejevic, M. (2008) "Watching television without pity: The productivity of online fans," *Television and New Media* 9(1), 24–46.

Bacon-Smith, C. (1992) *Enterprising women: Television fandom and the creation of popular myth*, Philadelphia, PA: University of Pennsylvania Press.

Bennett, L. (2014) "Tracing textual poachers: Reflections on the development of fan studies and digital fandom," *Journal of Fandom Studies* 2(1), 5–20.

Black, R. (2006) "Language, culture, and identity in online fanfiction," *E–Learning* 3(2), 170–184.

Bury, R. (2018) *Television 2.0: Viewer and fan engagement with digital TV*, New York: Peter Lang Publishing.

Bury, R. (2021a) "'A small Christmas for me': A study of binge-watching and fan engagement on Reddit," in M. Jenner (ed.), *Binge-watching and contemporary television studies* (pp. 40–58), Edinburgh: University of Edinburgh Press.

Busse, K. (2017) *Framing fan fiction: Literary and social practices in fan fiction communities*, Iowa City: University of Iowa Press.

Cho, A. (2015) "Queer Reverb," in K. Hillis, S. Paasonen and M. Petite (eds.) *Networked affect* (pp. 43–57), Cambridge: Massachusetts Institute of Technology.

Coppa, F. (2017) *The fanfiction reader: Folk tales for the digital age*, Ann Arbor: University of Michigan Press.

Coppa, F. (2022) *Vidding: A history*, Ann Arbor: University of Michigan Press.

Couldry, N. (2007) "On the set of *the Sopranos*: "Inside" a fan's construction of nearness," in J. Gray, C. Sandvoss and C. L. Harrington (eds.) *Fandom: Identities and communities in a mediated world* (pp. 139–48), New York: New York University Press.

De Kosnik, A. (2016) *Rogue archives: Digital cultural memory and media fandom*, Cambridge, MA: MIT Press.

Dym, B., & Fiesler, C. (2018) "Generations, migrations, and the future of fandom's private spaces," *Transformative Works & Cultures* 28.

Edwards, A. (2023) *Before fanfiction: Recovering the literary history of American media fandom*, Baton Rouge: LSU Press.

Fathallah, J. (2022) "'Being a fangirl of a serial killer is not ok': Gatekeeping Reddit's true crime community," *New Media & Society* 26(10), 5638–5657.

Fathallah, J. (2017) *Fanfiction and the author*, Amsterdam: Amsterdam University Press.

Geraghty, L. (2014) *Cult collectors: Nostalgia, fandom and collecting popular culture*, New York: Routledge.

Gillespie, T. (2010) "The politics of 'platforms'," *New Media & Society* 12(3), 347–364.

Guo, Q. (2022) "How do fans purposively create information to promote a celebrity? An analysis of fans' information practices and literacy improvement," *Library & Information Science Research* 44(3), 101170.

Hellekson, K. (2009) "A fannish field of value: Online fan gift culture," *Cinema Journal* 48(4), 113–118.

Hellekson, K., & Kristina B. (eds.) (2006) *Fan fiction and fan communities in the age of the Internet*, Jefferson City, NC: McFarland.

Hills, M. (2014) "From Dalek half balls to daft punk helmets: Mimetic fandom and the crafting of replicas," *Transformative Works and Cultures* (16). http://dx.doi.org/10.3983/twc.2014.0531

Hyde, L. (2007) *The gift: Creativity and the artist in the modern world*, New York, NY: Vintage.

King, C. (1993) "His truth goes marching on: Elvis Presley and the pilgrimage to graceland," in I. Reader & T. Walter (eds.) *Pilgrimage in popular culture* (pp. 92–104), London: Macmillan.

Kustritz, A. (2015) "Transnationalism, localization, and translation in European fandom: Fan studies as global media and audience studies," *Transformative Works and Cultures*, 19.

Kucharska, J., Sterczewski, P., Schweiger B., Płaszewska, J., & Janik, J. (2015) "Finding Poland: Negotiating the local and the global in the construction of semiperipheral identity in Polish science fiction and fantasy fandom," *Transformative Works and Cultures*, 19. Retrieved July 17, 2023 from https://journal.transformativeworks.org/index.php/twc/article/view/592/491

Jenkins, H. (1992) *Textual poachers: Television fans and participatory culture*, New York: Routledge.

Jenkins, H., Ford, S., & Green, J. (2013) *Spreadable media: Creating value and meaning in a networked culture*, New York: New York University Press.

Jørgensen, T., & Reichenberger, I. (2023) "Breaking bad behaviour: Understanding negative film tourist behaviour through moral disengagement," *Current Issues in Tourism*, 26(7), 1183–1198. https://doi.org/10.1080/13683500.2022.2051447

McCracken, A., Cho, A., Stein, L., & Neill, I. (eds.) (2020) *A tumblr book: Platforms and cultures*, Ann Arbor: University of Michigan Press.

Okamoto, T. (2015) "Otaku tourism and the Anime Pilgrimage phenomenon in Japan," *Japan Forum* 27(1), 12–36. https://doi.org/10.1080/09555803.2014.962565

Pande, R. (2018) *Squee from the margins: Fandom and race*, Iowa City: University of Iowa Press.

Phillips, W., & Milner, R. M. (2017) *The ambivalent Internet: Mischief, oddity, and antagonism online*, Cambridge: Polity Press.

Yin, Y. (2020) "An emergent algorithmic culture: The data-ization of online fandom in China," *International Journal of Cultural Studies*, 23(4), 475–492.

Zhang, Q., & Negus, K. (2020) "East Asian pop music idol production and the emergence of data fandom in China," *International Journal of Cultural Studies* 23(4), 493–511.

Zhang, W. (2016) *The internet and new social formation in China: Fandom publics in the making*, New York: Routledge.

Zulli, D., & Zulli, D. J. (2022) "Extending the Internet meme: Conceptualizing technological mimesis and imitation publics on the TikTok platform," *New Media & Society* 24(8), 1872–1890. https://doi.org/10.1177/1461444820983603

11
WHERE THE FANS ARE
Rethinking Fan Studies and Participatory Culture

Rhiannon Bury

Over thirty years have passed since Henry Jenkins (1992) published *Textual Poachers* and introduced the concept of participatory culture. This now seminal work was an inspiration to many "acafans" including myself and was without question key to the establishment of fan (or fandom) studies. The result is a sizeable body of literature across a range of social science and humanities disciplines, including three journals dedicated to the area of study. Constituting participatory culture as a legitimate object of study, however, has had the unfortunate effect of constituting only certain types of fans and fan practices as legitimate subjects of study. The focus on a very specific understanding of participation has served to operationalize, even if unintentionally, a binary between those fans who interact with other fans and are involved in "community" and those who are not. In this chapter, I set out to deconstruct the participatory/non-participatory binary and unpack what constitutes participation, community, and fandom. To this end I move away from placing fans in one category or the other, constructing instead a continuum of participatory practice based on one's level of involvement with other fans. I then cast a spotlight on those fans who only engage in those practices with little or limited involvement with others – the lower and middle ranges of the participatory continuum. Based on findings from my Television 2.0 project (Bury 2017) and preliminary findings from a discourse analysis I conducted on a fan forum on Reddit in October 2023, I contend that the increased visibility and accessibility of fandom afforded by social media platforms has not led to increased involvement in fan communities.

Are We There Yet? Towards a Participatory Continuum

Gray, Sandvoss, and Harrington state that the "first wave" of fan studies, which spanned the early to mid-1990s, can be characterized by the phrase "fandom is beautiful" (2007: 1). Its overarching aim was to claim devalued practices and behaviors, particularly those associated with the gendered stereotypes of the obsessive, socially-inept male fan and the overwrought, deluded female fan (Bury 2005). This early work sets out to establish a clear link between affective relations with media texts, participation, and community. In her ethnography of female *Star Trek* fans, Bacon-Smith makes the case that those fans with a deep enough investment will desire connection with other fans and "take their first true steps along the road to fandom before they have ever heard of the word or the *community* it represents" (1992: 7, emphasis mine). Jenkins (1992) outlines a series of activities undertaken by the committed viewer already on that road, including reading as many secondary texts before and after viewing. Such texts "provide the information needed to participate fully in the critical debates *of the fan community*" (57–58, emphasis mine). The practice of textual poaching involves the reworking of the storylines in ways which both extend and challenge "canon" through cultural production – works of art, fiction, music, and videos. For Jenkins a desire for connection is at the heart of this creative participatory culture; creative works are produced to be shared with other fans, creating what Paul Booth (2010) will later describe as a gift economy of fandom.

It is not my intention in this chapter to rain on the "fandom is beautiful" parade. I have done so in the past in a case study of *textual gamekeeping* (Bury 2008), and there is a growing body of scholarship on anti-fandom, fandom wars, and toxic fandom, the latter of which includes discussions of racism and homophobia among fans (see Click 2019; Jones 2015; Reinhard 2018). Instead, I take issue with this framing of fandom as a particular set of practices and their imbrication with particular sets of communal relations. Doing so creates a hierarchy of legitimacy in which fans who are not directly engaged in this version of participatory culture are measured up against those who are and found to be lacking. More specifically I question the persistent assumption that fans devoted to a text are on a journey to a destination that is community. In a later work, after most fan communities and sites of fan activity and fan communities had migrated online, Jenkins suggests that the increased visibility and accessibility afforded by digital technologies means that even more committed viewers will seize the opportunity to become participatory fans:

> Certainly, there are still people who only watch the show, but more and more of them are sneaking a peek at what they are saying about the show on *Television Without Pity*, and once you are there, why not post a few comments. It's a slippery slope from there. (2007: 361)

The slippery slope metaphor functions in a similar way to that of the road/journey but I note it is also a logical fallacy even when used to indicate a positive rather than negative outcome (e.g., drinking alcohol leads to alcoholism).

Jenkins' (2007) claim about fandom being the future has been challenged by other media and internet scholars, who contend only a minority of fans can be considered participatory (see Bird 2011; Burgess 2011). The problem is not just a lack of empirical evidence to support either side of the debate: both positions rely on this same narrow understanding of participation and participatory culture, the effect of which is to mark out the parameters of fan studies. I share Sandvoss' position that,

> what has formed as a field of academic study of 'fandom' does not necessarily include all fans and their activities, but focuses on specific social and cultural interactions, institutions and communities that have formed through the close interaction of committed groups of fans in a subcultural context. (2005: 5)

In order to reimagine a field that is less exclusive, we need to start with a critical examination of the key concepts used in the field and define them clearly. In the context of this discussion, I use "fandom" and "participatory culture" interchangeably, although I note that fandom can also be used more narrowly in reference to a specific text (e.g., *X-Files* fandom). Sandvoss suggests redefining fandom as "the regular, emotionally-involved consumption of a given popular narrative or text" (2005: 8). I agree with Sandvoss that fans who only view a favorite media text and talk about it with family or friends – view-only fans – are legitimate subjects of study. Given their lack of visibility online, such research requires qualitative methods such as surveys, interviews, and/or focus groups. The exclusion question for my TV 2.0 survey asked respondents to self-identify as a fan based on a definition that required that they had watched at least one series with regularity in the previous 12 months. Perhaps not surprisingly, 89% identified as fans (Bury 2017).

That said I contend that this reconceptualization bends the stick too far in the other direction, decoupling fandom from participatory culture and the opportunities it affords to directly interact and establish relations with other fans not based on established social or familial relations, whether on the convention floor, on an online forum, or on social media. To cover off both viewing and participation, I use the term engagement. Jenkins, Ford, and Green take issue with the term due to its use by the media industries: "engagement-based models see the audience as a collective of active agents whose labor may generate alternative forms of market value" (2013: 116). This may be true, but I feel that the term can be fruitfully redeployed from being a buzzword to a *bridgeword* (Bury 2021b).

As for fandom as participatory culture, its meaning does need to broaden but in a different way, namely, by loosening its close ties to community. The meaning of the latter has been so taken for granted in fan studies that the noun operates as a synonym for the name of a specific online or social media site (e.g., "alt.tv.x-files" in one sentence and "the community" in another). This choice made sense in the early internet era, where bulletin boards, listservs, and even Usenet newsgroups were small enough in scale to build and maintain a set of shared interactional and exchange practices among members with a shared passion for a particular media text. As I found in my study of the David Duchovny Estrogen Brigades (Bury 2005), participation levels varied but the size of the listservs were limited and their architecture allowed for extended discussion, which in turn created opportunities to develop a sense of belonging as well as close connections and even lifelong friendships with other members. With the exponential growth of discussion boards and rhizomatic blogging technology in the 2000s and then social media platforms built on algorithmic architecture ten years later, we cannot assume that the relationship between participation and community making has remained the same.

As a first step to rethinking that relationship, I propose that participation be understood as a *continuum* of practice, comprising a series of activities that I have organized based on the degree of involvement with other fans. Clustered at one end of the continuum are practices related to information seeking: browsing secondary web sources, reviews by professional critics, etc. Next are passive expressions of commitment by liking/following feeds related to favorite series on Facebook and the platform formerly known as Twitter. The next cluster involves seeking out the reactions, views, and critical analysis of other fans on websites and social media. Further along the continuum would be sharing feelings of anticipation, and/or reactions, observations, and criticisms post viewing on these online public forums. Finally at the far end of the continuum are the hallmark practices associated with cultural production and community making. (While I have only included activities specific to online fandom, I recognize that collecting through purchase of media content and merchandise or attending conventions are also examples of fannish practice.)

Slip Sliding Away?

The Television 2.0 project was designed, in part, to study shifting patterns of fan engagement at a time (2011–12) when streaming and downloading technologies were becoming more accessible. The survey (n=671) asked a series of questions about participation with the notion of a continuum in mind. When asked how often they visited any type of online site, including social network sites, discussion forums, and social media platforms in relation to the series of which they were fans, 41% reported doing so frequently, 26% sometimes, 22% occasionally, and 12% answered never. Almost half (47%) had "liked" a post about a series on Facebook (just under 10% did not have Facebook accounts), but only 11% had posted a comment on a Facebook page dedicated to a favorite series. Only one third of the respondents reported using Twitter for fan-related activities. When asked specifically about online discussion forums, 37% reported having visited at least one, although less than half of those who had participated in discussions. As for creative production, one quarter had read fanfic and 13% had written it and shared with others online. The gap between "consumption" and "production" of fanvids was even more striking: whereas 31% had viewed at least one fanvid, only 3% had produced at least one and shared with others online (6% were unfamiliar with fanfic and vids respectively).

Turning to the interview data (n=72), all participants reported seeking information online. A number mentioned doing Google searches which led them to sources from news or entertainment industry sites. Some specified going directly to Wikipedia and IMDB. These searches were mostly related to enriching their connection to the text. Annika, for example, noted that she "will just get curious about one of the characters or the setting or any sort of detail like that and decide to go look it up." Several participants confirmed that they would conduct these searches on a mobile device while viewing to enhance their viewing experience. Will gave a different reason for seeking information: to keep up with a series in which he was losing interest in watching but did not want to give up on entirely.

Facebook and to a lesser extent Twitter were mentioned as sources of information. Their customized newsfeeds are "push oriented," serving to transform "pull-oriented" browser-based information-seeking practices into information receiving and aggregation. Tasha estimated that more than half of her Facebook feed was related to favorite shows. Similarly, Douglas relied on Twitter for most of his series-based information, noting that when he saw a link to an interesting secondary text embedded in a tweet from someone he followed, he would click on it.

A number of the TV 2.0 participants expressed interest in seeking out reviews and recaps after viewing, not just from newspaper or magazine-based critics but from dedicated sites such as Hitflix (2008–2021), Television Without Pity (TWoP 1998–2014), as well as the AV Club (2005-present). Camden stated that he liked "reading the different perspectives. There are probably 5 or 6 that I will read." Such information seeking is linked to practices of critical interpretation and reflection. It was Jenkins (1992) who first challenged the notion that fans are too emotionally attached to their "objects" of affection to be critical. On the contrary, many fans are heavily invested in *bourgeois aesthetics* (Bourdieu 1993), a set of discourses which emphasize the quality of the writing, acting, and production of media texts (Bury 2005).

While a few of the participants flatly stated that they were not interested in the opinions and reactions of other fans, some were regular visitors to comment sections of sites such as the AV Club and the discussion forums under the auspices of TWoP. For Margene, the latter site was her "go to" site for all the shows she was watching where she could "check out real time responses and things like that." Phillipe noted that when he watched a new series he went online "to see what people said about it. Is it good?" The implication is that after reading the responses of others, one's interpretation may change accordingly. Suzie noted that going on a discussion forum for *Lost* helped her pick up on things that she had missed while viewing. A few participants mentioned following Twitter hashtags of live tweets during broadcast of a show they were watching.

The majority of these participants, however, did not share their own responses, primarily because they felt that they had nothing further to contribute. Camden described himself as a "perennial lurker... . I didn't really feel like I had anything to say in the comments or in response to other people's comments." Farah and Margene both stated that they felt awkward and uncomfortable engaging in discussion with large groups of people they didn't know. A few did add the odd comment on occasion. After noticing some "egregious editing" on an episode of a reality chef competition show, Max "went to a site and looked and was absolutely sure that somebody else noticed it too and commented and then I commented on it. ...But usually it's me looking to see what other people have to say." To sum up, I found no evidence of a "slippery slope" from occasional posting to regular, sustained interaction with other fans.

Another reason given for not participating on these forums was established personal networks:

> I will [talk about TV] face-to-face: at work, at school with friends but it's not the thing I will do online... . I may sometimes if I am amazed or if I am really touched by something, communicate it on Facebook and then if some people respond I will respond to them. But that's as far as I will go (Phillipe).

Watching and talking about the show with family and friends was considered fulfilling enough. Tasha noted that although she was mainly a lurker, she did participate in forums dedicated to shows that her husband and friends did not watch.

Taken together these findings demonstrate that the majority of participants were active in participatory culture as defined in the previous section but engaged in practices clustered at the lower- and the mid-ranges of the continuum – the middle of the road was the end of the road for them. In the next section, I will discuss data from my recent Reddit study that suggests that direct engagement with other fans is not necessarily associated with building and maintaining communal relations.

The Middle of the Road

Reddit, founded in 2005, is often described as a social media site but is better thought of as a hybrid communications technology: discussion boards with content sharing and aggregator functionality. In some ways it is a logical gathering space for fans who want to talk about television, or just read about what other fans had to say, in the post-discussion board era. Recent statistics indicate that almost three-quarters of Redditors visit for entertainment (Dean 2023). Although far smaller than r/computer or r/gaming, the subreddit, r/television is still sizable, with almost 17 million subscribers as of January 2024. As was the case with TWoP, there are subreddits dedicated to every television series broadcast/streamed in the English-language markets. Although moderators generally set up a discussion "hub" for a new series/season and pin it at the top of the subreddit, any Redditor can add their own post for others to upvote/downvote and comment on. Thus, fan discussion is less centralized than on the older discussion forums.

While traditional fan communities are traditionally associated with female fans and their practices (Bury 2005; Hellekson and Busse 2006; Jenkins 1992), Reddit has been characterized as a "manosphere" of incels and Red Pillers who are hostile to women; indeed the platform, along with 4Chan, played a prominent role in Gamergate (Ging 2019). At the very least it has what Adrianne Massanari describes as a "geek sensibility" (2015: 28). Yet like traditional fandom, connection with others is central to Reddit's identity, with many members seeing themselves as part of the Reddit community, as family even (e.g., "Thanks fam!"). Until 2023, Reddit even had its own form of gift economy with Reddit Awards and Reddit Gold. In recent years, a few fan studies scholars have recognized Reddit's potential as a fannish space (see Fathallah 2022; Hills 2019; Lynch 2022; Pearson 2018).

In 2019 I conducted a study on binge-watching practices, which involved reviewing the discussion hubs of eight subreddits dedicated to Netflix original series. To get a sense of how many Redditors had binge-watched each series, I recorded Reddit's counts for the number of posts at 24 hours and then at 2, 3, and 7 days, up until two weeks had passed since release. The level of engagement varied depending on the popularity of the series: under 500 comments for *Russian Doll* (Season 1) to almost 25,000 for *Stranger Things* (Season 3) at the 14-day mark (Bury 2021a). Although I did not do a close analysis of the comments that were not directly related to binge-watching, I saw anecdotal evidence of practices typical of the older discussion forums such as reaction sharing, collective anticipation, speculation, interpretation, and criticism.

In 2022, I returned to Reddit to examine fan engagement more closely and to get a sense of whether it was associated with community building. I decided to look at the Netflix series, *The Fall of the House of Usher* (henceforth referred to as FHU), created by Mike Flanigan and released on October 12, 2023. Although there were two small subreddits dedicated to the series, with 12,000 and 10,000 subscribers respectively, I chose to examine the dedicated discussion hub set up at r/HauntingofHillHouse, Flanigan's 2018 mini-series produced for Netflix, which has 70,000 subscribers. The 332 comments posted to this hub in the first two weeks after release were a mix of shorter reaction-style and longer review-style posts. Some Redditors provided impressions of the series as a whole, sometimes in the context of adaptation from Poe's original stories or in terms of how FHU ranked against other series in the horror genre, particularly those produced by Flanigan. A number of posters compared it to HBO's *Succession* as a multi-generational family business drama. Others focused on particular storylines, scenes, characters, music/sound, and the actors, including identification (e.g., a few had not recognized Mark Hamill in the role of Arthur Pym until they went on Reddit). A few talked about bingeing all eight episodes in one sitting within one to three days after release. One Redditor was on a third rewatch.

To get a sense of how much direct interaction among the posters was taking place – the basis of community making, I counted up all the original comments. By this I mean those which were posted as "standalone" comments and not as a reply to another comment made on the hub. Since these posters are not technically OP (original poster in Reddit parlance, who in this context would be the moderator who set up the hub), I will refer to them as "OC" (original commenter). I found it striking that of the 69 original comments, almost half (31) received no replies. The latter were generally the newest comments, made

10–14 days after release. The lack of response might be explained by the amount of time that had passed, the immediate post-release binge-watchers having already commented and left the forum. Moreover, Redditors who had just finished viewing after a couple of weeks may not even have seen the earlier comments, especially the ones that did not receive a high number of upvotes; the default algorithm sorts comments by "best" based on the number of upvotes. Thus, the early bird binge-watching fan does indeed get the interactional worm.

Turning to the remaining 38 original comments, I will treat them as exchanges since at least one other fan has replied. The majority of these exchanges (n=28) were short with less than ten replies; only three had over 20 replies. Looking more closely at these exchanges, I noted some turn taking. For example, OC1 posted background information about one of Poe's stories and traced out the parallels to a main character's action. Another Redditor opened their reply with "Ah, great recall of the original story," to which OC1 responded, "Thanks, your recall is pretty impressive as well haha" before providing further details on the story, including a quote and a link. The final turn was as follows: "That quote was in my email sig file for several years… ☺." This is the type of polite, affirming exchange that I considered to be part of community making on the female-only listservs I studied over 30 years ago. I also came across a couple of vitriolic exchanges more typically associated with Reddit and geek masculinity. After OC2 made a parallel of the deaths of the Usher children to the seven deadly sins, there was some debate at which point another Redditor stated, "I wouldn't say you 'realized it,' I would say you read it somewhere on the internet after you watched it and just regurgitated it on Reddit shortly after." OC2's response, "Nope. Girlfriend and I noticed and discussed it before ever looking up anything online," was followed by a dismissive "Suuuuure." At this point another Redditor intervened to call out the rudeness of OC2: "Jeez why are you so miserable? Some people can have an observation that feels novel to them."

Based on my review of the time stamps of the posts in this sample, however, few of the exchanges involved *synchronous* turn taking as per the data samples above or did not actually involve turn taking at all. The following pattern was the norm, not the exception: three days after release OC3 commented on the performance of actor Bruce Greenwood and the reshoots that were done. Two days later another Redditor asked for clarification. Two days after that, a different fan explained that the role was recast. One day later, four other Redditors added comments about the success of the recasting and their dislike of the original actor. A full week later, OC3 returned to add a final comment. In another example, OC4 stated, "This may sound weird but I love Carl Lumbly's face. He looks like he's carved out of stone." There were five replies, all of which expressed appreciation for the actor. The first was posted two days later, the second five days later, the next six days later, the fifth a whole week after the fourth reply and the last three days after that. OC3 does not reply to any. Although both these exchanges *read* like a conversation, they are a series of discrete posts.

A final finding worth noting is that the bulk of the exchanges were themselves discrete, in that there was almost no overlap of participants; five Redditors including the "miserable" OC2 participated in two unrelated exchanges, and three contributed to three or more. A lack of sustained, extended interaction among regular participants does not necessarily make a sense of community impossible but it certainly does not foster it. I would suggest that Page's (2012) notion of *ambient affiliation* made in relation to live tweeting may also be an accurate description of fan relations on Reddit. She argues that what appears to be conversational may in fact be "para-social simulations of conversationality" (184); in other words, people talking at each other rather than to each other.

Conclusion

As I hope I have demonstrated, fandom remains an important cultural formation that is worthy of scholarly analysis. To be meaningful in the era of digital TV, it needs to be redefined in a way that recognizes participation as a continuum of practice. This continuum acknowledges that fans are participatory even if they do not engage directly with other fans they do not already know through "real life" networks. Others who do wish to share reactions and criticisms may enjoy exchanges but may not have any desire for community. As such, the continuum serves to unhitch participation from the community making wagon. It behooves fan studies scholars to pay more attention to the types of fans I have discussed above, those who only engage in practices at the "less-involved" end and middle ranges of the continuum. To cite Melissa Click, "there is much to be learned from studying fans who do not fit traditional descriptions" (2007: 301). As for next steps, we need to learn more about the nature of engagement among fans on social media and content sharing platforms. Are Reddit television forums primarily made up of binge-watchers who pop in to make an original comment and/or reply to a couple of other comments and then move on to the next series? Is there a core albeit small community of fans who engage regularly with one forum or across forums? Answering these types of questions needs to be part of the future of fan studies.

References

Bacon-Smith, C. (1992) *Enterprising women: Television fandom and the creation of popular myth*, Philadelphia, PA: University of Pennsylvania Press.
Bird, S. E. (2011) "Are we all producers now?," *Cultural Studies*, 25(4–5), 502–516.
Booth, P. (2010) *Digital fandom: New media studies*, New York: Peter Lang.
Bourdieu, P. (1993) *The field of cultural production: Essays on art and literature*, New York: Columbia University Press.
Burgess, J. (2011) "User-created content and everyday cultural practice: Lessons from YouTube," in J. Bennett & N. Strange (eds.) *Television as digital media*, Durham, NC: Duke University Press.
Bury, R. (2005) *Cyberspaces of their own: Female fandoms online*, New York: Peter Lang.
Bury, R. (2008) "Setting David Fisher straight: Homophobia and heterosexism in 'six feet under' online fan culture," *Critical Studies in Television* 3(2), 59–79.
Bury, R. (2017) *Television 2.0: Viewer and fan engagement with digital TV*, New York: Peter Lang.
Bury, R. (2021a) "'A small Christmas for me': A study of binge-watching and fan engagement on Reddit," in M. Jenner (ed.) *Binge-watching and contemporary television studies* (pp. 40–58), Edinburgh: University of Edinburgh Press.
Bury, R. (2021b) "Mend the gap: Engagement with digital television," *Participations: Journal of Audience and Reception Studies*, 18(1), 230–243. Retrieved from www.participations.org/
Click, M. A. (2007) "Untidy: Fan response to the soiling of Martha Stewart's spotless image," in J. Gray, C. Sandvoss & C. L. Harrington (eds.) *Fandom: Identities and communities in a mediated world*, New York: New York University Press.
Click, M. A. (ed.) (2019) *Anti-fandom: Dislike and hate in the digital age*, New York: New York University Press.
Dean, B. (2023, March) "Reddit user and growth stats," Retrieved October 29, 2023, from https://backlinko.com/reddit-users#reddit-gender-demographics
Fathallah, J. (2022) "'Being a fangirl of a serial killer is not ok': Gatekeeping Reddit's true crime community," *New Media & Society*. Advance online publication. doi: 10.1177/14614448221138768

Ging, D. (2019) "Alphas, betas, and incels: Theorizing the masculinities of the manosphere," *Men and Masculinities*, 22(4), 638–657. doi: 10.1177/1097184X17706401

Gray, J., Sandvoss, C., & Harrington, C. L. (eds.) (2007) *Fandom: Identities and communities in a mediated world*, New York: New York University Press.

Hellekson, K., & Busse, K. (eds.) (2006) *Fan fiction and fan communities in the age of the Internet: New essays*, Jefferson, NC: McFarland & Co.

Hills, M. (2019) "*Black Mirror* as a Netflix original: Program brand 'overflow' and the multidiscursive forms of tranatlantic TV fandom," in M. Hills, M. Hilmes & R. Pearson (eds.) *Transatlantic television drama: Industries, programs & fans* (pp. 213–238), Oxford: Oxford University Press.

Jenkins, H. (1992) *Textual poachers: Television fans & participatory culture*, New York: Routledge.

Jenkins, H. (2007) "Afterword: The future of fandom," in J. Gray, C. Sandvoss & C. L. Harrington (eds.) *Fandom: Identities and communities in a mediated world*, New York: New York University Press.

Jenkins, H., Ford, S., & Green, J. (2013) *Spreadable media: Creating value and meaning in a networked culture*, New York: New York University Press.

Jones, B. (2015) "My Little Pony, tolerance is magic: Gender policing and Brony anti-fandom," *Journal of Popular Television* 3(1), 119–125. doi: 10.1386/jptv.3.1.119_1

Lynch, K. S. (2022) "Fans as transcultural gatekeepers: The hierarchy of BTS' Anglophone Reddit fandom and the digital East-West media flow," *New Media & Society*, 24(1), 105–121. doi: 10.1177/146144482096210

Massanari, A. L. (2015) *Participatory culture, community, and play: Learning from Reddit*, New York: Peter Lang.

Page, R. (2012) "The linguistics of self-branding and micro-celebrity in Twitter: The role of hashtags," *Discourse & Communication* 6(2), 181–201. doi: 10.1177/1750481312437441

Pearson, R. (2018) "You're Sherlock Holmes, wear the damn hat!: Character identity in a transfiction," in P. Brembilla & I. A. De Pascalis (eds.) *Reading contemporary serial television universes: A narrative ecosystem framework* (pp. 144–165), New York: Routledge.

Rheingold, H. (1993) *The virtual community: Homesteading on the electronic frontier*, Reading, MA: Addison-Wesley Publishing Co.

Reinhard, C. D. (2018) *Fractured fandoms: Contenious communication in fan communities*, New York; London: Lexington Books.

Sandvoss, C. (2005) *Fans: The mirror of consumption*, Cambridge, UK: Polity Press.

12
FAN CURATORS AND THE GATEWAYS INTO FANDOM

Derek Kompare

Fan studies, as an academic field, has greatly increased our understanding of how fans relate to media texts and fandoms, from a long, rich emphasis on fanfic and other transformative fanworks and communities, to more recent attention to fannish collecting, building, and tourism. However, it has not devoted as much attention to how fans discover and are initiated into these texts and fandoms in the first place. This is particularly odd since discovery and self-awareness narratives are a long-established part of fan autobiography and lore (Hills 2002: 65–89). Telling stories of how you encountered your first David Bowie song, episode of *Doctor Who*, or Harry Potter book is part of how you establish your fan credentials and reveal the moment when interest became passion. Such narratives are still a typical form of self-revelation in online fan spaces and convention hotel bars.

At that point of discovery, you then, presumably, sought more texts and information about your new fannish object. This always requires consultation with other fans, who, directly or indirectly, help guide you into the depths of the fandom. Initiation practices like this, converting the first-time viewer, reader, or listener into a hungry fan, have always been a part of organized fandoms. These practices can take many forms, but generally include *encyclopedic media* (e.g. discographies, episode guides, universe indexes, and the like), that have routinely been a part of fandoms for decades, and are particularly prevalent today (e.g. in the many wikis maintained by active fans); *suggested canon* (e.g. which albums to listen to next), which critically guide the new fan further into the fandom (i.e. their second, third, and beyond episodes); and *fan gatherings*, which could be physical (ranging from small meetups to large conventions), but have also always been active at a distance: over mail, phone, and online. Regardless of how it happens, this "gateway" phase is constant across different media forms and fandoms. Whether the fandom is centered on analyzing Beach Boys recording session logs, documenting twenty-fourth-century galactic politics, developing "head canons" of alternative Hogwarts histories, or rapidly conversing through SuperWhoLock GIFs and memes, all fans at some point have to be initiated into their fandom.

The key figures in this initiation are *fan curators*: more established fans (usually, though not always, older) with deeper knowledge of, and access to, the fandom and its texts. This role could be taken on by an individual, several individuals, or a collective (as with a fan club or online space), but the key thing is that *curators organize their expertise in service of bringing new people into the fandom,* or at least their particular corner of it. While these established fans may be part of long-established fandoms, they may also bring their fannish curatorial skills to new, emergent fan texts (e.g. a new TV series), which may foster its rapid coalescence into an "established" fandom. These acts of curation expose the new fan to further information about their new obsession, shaping their attitudes and interests for a long time. Just as a curated museum exhibit affects ways in which visitors understand the objects displayed, curated fan experiences shape how fans understand and engage with a text and fandom that is new to them.

Cornel Sandvoss describes the fan object as having a "field of gravity constituted through a multiplicity of textual elements; it is by definition intertextual and formed between and across texts" (Sandvoss 2014: 55). Similarly, Jonathan Gray describes paratexts—the promotional and referential materials that transport media texts and fan objects across the culture—as "the very stuff upon which much popular interpretation is based" (Gray 2010: 26). Curated encounters with fan texts and paratexts help constitute Sandvoss' "field of gravity," not only through their production, distribution, and consumption, but also in the interpersonal communication and relationships fostered by these exchanges. They transform solitary experiences with texts into community participation, and readers, listeners, or viewers into fans.

Although they share some similarities, fan curation is distinct from commercial marketing and advertising. Marketing strategies, such as televised promos, print and online advertising, and giveaways and special offers, aim to convert fan interest into fan economic consumption. They may lead the fan deeper into the text and its official offshoots, but not as much into the *fandom* (with the exception of corporate-authorized spaces, such as a message board hosted on a comics publisher's website). Granted, in most cases, as in the purchase of a novel, album, DVD box set, or movie ticket, or the viewing of a TV show through a licensed distributor, fan consumption of officially released material is an inevitable part of most fandoms. Moreover, as Gray describes, marketing paratexts, such as movie trailers, inevitably bleed over into fannish consumption. The studios' massive promotional spectacles (usually hyping upcoming science fiction (SF), fantasy, or superhero films) staged each July at the San Diego Comic-Con are particularly prominent examples of curated texts that attempt to circumscribe the boundaries of authorized consumption. However, fandoms typically quickly respond with their own accounts of these events, adding fannish layers of curation to the corporate original paratext, such as when fans devote entire blog posts or podcast episodes to decoding a two-minute trailer for an upcoming *Star Wars* film. Thus, while commercial promotion is certainly an expected aspect of fan experience, it is only a thin outer layer of fan curation.

Every fandom has its own codes, rituals, and media. However, throughout the history of fandom, we can still identify some major common practices, all tied to the availability of particular media forms and formats, that have brought fans into contact with fannish works and with actual fans. The key common factor here is *access*: fandom thrives when its objects and knowledge are actively reproduced and circulated. While this may sound obvious and easy, in an era when fandom (and media culture) predominantly resides online, and the tools of production and reproduction are relatively accessible, it still requires fans (individually or collectively) to produce, reproduce, curate, and distribute those materials. Without that labor, there would be no fandom.

The most basic form of curation is *suggested canon*: simply *suggesting, loaning, copying, or gifting* additional material to interested fans. This canon is likely not "official," but is based instead on the *curator's perceptions* of fannish texts, and their relationship to their fandom. That is, the curator provides *their version* of the key information needed to best "get into" (for example) Marvel Comics continuity. Before the prevalence of digital media, and streaming services in particular, curators typically provided physical copies of zines, books, records, videotapes, CDs, or DVDs to new fans, or might make physical copies for them (copying a CD to a cassette tape, for example). In the age of Google, Netflix, Amazon, Spotify, and the like, much of this sort of curation has been ceded to algorithms which immediately suggest related material available on their service, providing you with links to *The Outer Limits* or *Night Gallery* after you watch an episode of *The Twilight Zone*, for example. But the catalogs of licensed and even unlicensed digital distributors are far from complete; plenty of unmigrated material exists only in physical formats or in the halfway house of offline digital files. Moreover, even robust streaming platforms can't fully predict where a person's interests may lead them. For access to different fannish textual combinations, and particularly to offline materials, active human curation and connection are still necessary. In addition, even while on-demand online media has rapidly become our default expectation, there is also potentially an attraction to fan objects *as objects* (Geraghty 2014). In seeking recommendations, fans might seek not only access to texts, but acquisition of particular physical iterations of it, such as a first-edition novel, or a special edition Blu-ray. Thoughtful fan curators go beyond the easily available to point new fans to particular versions, collections, or creators.

Encyclopedic media are curated descriptions of a fandom's objects, and generally take the form of discographies (of records), filmographies (of films), episode guides (of television shows), and similar indexes. These are arguably the most common form of curated fan media, the perspectives that fans research, write, discuss, and argue about. They come in myriad forms, from bare-bones factual overviews, such as the "airdates, titles, and credits" approach of television guide site epguides.com, to passionately evaluative top-ten lists found all over blogs and YouTube, to lengthy published exegeses (e.g. Elizabeth Sandifer's multi-volume *TARDIS Eruditorum* series, 2012–15, exploring eras of *Doctor Who*). As much of fandom is not only "reading" but "rereading," such guides and retrospectives are an ongoing genre in many fandoms, where subsequent fan perspectives and access to materials keep curated accounts perpetually in flux. As Lincoln Geraghty states, "fans are always reassessing and re-evaluating media texts from the past; they bring them into the present and reconstitute them as part of contemporary fan culture." (Geraghty 2014: 2–3). Curated fan assessments of a 1967 *Star Trek* episode might be very different if written in 1973, 1989, 1997, or 2011. Moreover, as fandoms diversify in terms of gender, sexuality, race, and ethnicity, and younger fans review older texts, new curated guides to the same original materials offer up valuable new perspectives. The *Geek Girl Chronicles* anthology series from Mad Norwegian Press offers feminist fan critiques of many popular programs and forms, including *Doctor Who*, comics, and the works of Joss Whedon. Similarly, the Feminist Frequency YouTube channel produces ranges of short videos that explore gendered tropes in video games, figures from feminist history, and reviews of current films, television, and games. Even while new analyses and overviews are published, older guides might still be available and sought, providing an intriguing history of shifting fan perspectives and encyclopedic perspectives.

Curation requires connection. *Gatherings*, both online and physically, bring fans and their materials together, and offer new fans in particular the opportunity to learn much more about their fandom. Physical gatherings, such as fan club meetings or conventions, have long been a crucial aspect of many fandoms, and, somewhat counter-intuitively, have only increased in prevalence, frequency, and size in the online area. At conventions, fans see and hear about their fandom in person, get their hands on its material, and, most importantly, meet other fans. Convention panels might feature prominent participants from the texts themselves (in the form of actors, writers, and other production personnel), or from the fandom (in the form of more established "expert" fans). Similarly, convention dealers' rooms typically include vendors selling popular and rare material associated with the text and its fandom, and fan groups (such as cosplayers or game players) seeking to connect with new fans. Online, curators can help socialize fans into the customs and manners of particular forums or platforms (such as LiveJournal and Tumblr), and can facilitate connections and participation.

A Brief History of Fan Curation

Space does not permit a deep dive into the history of fan curation (and a comprehensive scope would certainly be impossible). However, we can still broadly trace its development, primarily through the media technologies available to and used by fans over the past century. These technologies are all significant, in distinctive ways, in shaping the ways in which curators can present texts and other information to new fans. Despite constant technological change, no form goes away completely—print newsletters and broadcast television, for example, are still, as of this writing, viable, if marginal media forms—but each of their technological affordances, and the cultures and economies that sustain them, shape not only how fan texts are curated, but how fandoms function as well. A fandom is still a fandom whether it circulates in a quarterly print newsletter or a constantly updating Tumblr tag nearly a century later. But the way in which each form functions has had a profound impact on how fandoms operate and inculcate new fans.

Print newsletters and fanzines are perhaps the most venerable form of curation, dating back at least as far as the 1920s (Coppa 2006). The origin story of organized fandom in most Western cultures is of young, overwhelmingly white, educated middle-class men writing science fiction for print publications like Hugo Gernsback's *Amazing Stories*, which would then publish letters from fans (including their contact information) and help publicize fan gatherings and other publications. Fans thus had a few widely distributed publications, and curators (i.e., editors), that they consulted to discover new authors, genres, or debates, and meet other fans.

Over the next few decades, in the middle of the twentieth century, as the periodical market grew, contracted, and grew again, this form of commercially mediated fan engagement would extend to other fannish genres and forms, most notably comic books and popular music. In addition, the first amateur "fanzines" started: fan-produced publications, with relatively tiny print runs, in which fans generated and shared their own canons, knowledge, and creations outside mainstream media economics, and connected more directly with other fans. Fanzines (aka "zines") might include commentary and reviews (of novels, recordings, films, TV episodes, etc. depending on the fandom), but also correspondence (as letters columns, or "lettercols") and original creative work. *Xero* (1960–63), created by Dick Lupoff, Pat Lupoff, and Bhob Stewart, was an influential example from this era, publishing fan-produced analysis, fiction, poetry, and art. Media fandom, centered primarily on TV shows like *Star Trek* and *The Man From UNCLE*, began to coalesce in the 1960s and 1970s largely through early zines like *Spockanalia* (1967–70). New fans would typically encounter these fan-produced and narrowly distributed publications only through more experienced fans that they already knew (or, in rare cases, the occasional independent retailer), who would curate this next step into fandom. The relatively cozy physical spaces of fandom in this era—living rooms, libraries, bookstores, record stores, and the handful of nascent fan conventions—were also crucial in connecting fans to each other and to burgeoning bodies of fan knowledge and canon.

In the 1970s, new, relatively inexpensive media-copying technology became available, in the forms of the photocopier and audio and video cassette recorder (VCR). Each greatly impacted the range and speed of organized fandom, as they allowed fan objects to be much more easily disseminated. They were particularly impactful in the 1980s and 1990s, as they became even more accessible alongside the facilitating technologies of the personal computer and internet. This was the "Gutenberg Press" moment for fandom. These devices revolutionized the ability of fans to reproduce and distribute both original fanworks and the media texts themselves, and their importance to the history of fandom cannot be overstated. Black and white fanzines with text and illustrations could be prepared in word processing and desktop publishing (DTP) software and run off relatively cheaply, particularly if the editor had access to professional copy machines. Accordingly, zines spread into many genres and subgenres of fiction, non-fiction, poetry, and art across a widening range of fannish franchises and objects. In addition, fueled by the efficiencies of DTP software, the length of individual zine issues often expanded, with some fanfic anthologies running into hundreds of spiral-bound pages. Meanwhile, fans also recorded and dubbed (i.e. copied) albums, films, and TV episodes on audio and videocassettes, building up tape libraries, and trading tapes with other fans. As with print copying, tape copying facilitated the expansion of material to new fans at a time when distribution might otherwise be limited. Prior to the 1980s rapid expansion of home video, access to most films and TV shows was limited to the broadcast and cable TV schedule. If you weren't at home to watch it (or tape it, if you were an early VCR adopter), you missed it. Even during the heyday of the video rental store in the 1990s, while the catalog of available films to rent continually increased, TV shows were relatively sparse on VHS. Moreover, the fan-produced video work inspired by these shows (fan music videos and original productions in the form of "fan films"), was only available in fan distribution circuits. The sharing and copying of curated tape dubs of this otherwise unavailable material allowed fans to screen, review, and collect it, and was instrumental in bringing many fans into their fandoms.

An important component of these technologies was the human connections they fostered. These new technologies of production and reproduction were now relatively accessible, but they were not necessarily cheap; few people had direct access to photocopiers or multiple dubbing VCRs. But fandom leveraged the abilities of the people who had access to these technologies, who organized themselves into networks of curators. Zine editors helped gather fan authors into large anthologies that would foster the development of subgenres and themes, and would often help other editors with their zine distribution. For example, from the US Midwest, famed zine distributors, Bill and Ann Hupe, functioned as a major "zine hub" for many years in the 1980s and 1990s, connecting editors with readers across many fandoms, and, at their peak, globally distributing dozens of fanfic zines across several media fandoms, including *Blake's 7* (BBC 1978–81), *Doctor Who* (BBC 1963–89; 2005–), *Star Trek* (NBC 1966–69; Syndicated 1987–99; UPN 1995–2005), *Quantum Leap* (NBC 1989–93), and *Robin of Sherwood* (ITV 1984–86).

Other curators functioned as "tape hubs" for film and TV fans, and obtained additional audio and video equipment, at their own expense, to facilitate dubbing multiple copies of sought-after recordings for fans who did not have access to them otherwise, usually only for the cost of postage and a blank videotape. Tape hubs were most often run (from their own homes) by individual fans who were also usually active in their local fan circles, planning and staffing conventions, editing fanzines, and/or running fan clubs. Their impact was felt well beyond their local community, as they sent their tapes across the country and even around the world. In the 1980s, hubs in North America, Australia, New Zealand, and the United Kingdom helped bolster and connect global *Doctor Who* fandom. UK fans would send off-air recordings of new episodes airing there to North America or Australia, in exchange for older episodes, which were airing in those countries but *not* in the United Kingdom. Since the UK tapes would be recorded in PAL video, which was incompatible with the North American NTSC television system, resourceful US and Canadian fans would either invest in PAL VCRs and TVs and shoot the screen with an NTSC video camera (to produce flickering "camera copies"), or, much more expensively at the time, get the PAL tapes digitally converted to NTSC. The result was a diffuse network of contacts distributing increasingly fuzzy multi-generation VHS dubs to fans in three continents, building up exposure to otherwise unavailable episodes at a pace that the licensed distributors could never match. Linked together by contact information in print fanzines, early online fan networks, and/or personal contact, just a handful of such fan curators were the original sources of countless tape dubs. As fans produced more and more work on video (in the form of music videos, original films, and compilations of ephemera) these hubs increased their connection and activity. In the late 1980s, Phoenix-based fan, Lee Whiteside, operated a tape hub, facilitated local conventions, and was an active pioneer in early online SF forums on CompuServe, and on his own Magrathea BBS (later sftv.org, which no longer updates), which maintained news and information for many SF and fantasy texts and fandoms. Similarly, in the late 1990s and early 2000s, from Minnesota, Kathryn Sullivan was one of many fans who facilitated the North American video dubbing and distribution of fan-made VHS reconstructions of dozens of 1960s *Doctor Who* episodes, which were missing from the BBC archives (produced by a few different fan collectives, mostly in the UK, using audio and scant still images).

In the 1990s and 2000s, the internet added new levels of depth and speed to fan curation. Fans produced and posted lengthy bibliographies, discographies, episode guides, and analyses, and made them available to the broad and growing public of the internet, rather than only through "snail mail" to fans in the know. USENET forums (mostly clustered in the rec.arts domain; e.g. "rec.arts.anime") facilitated the global discussion and connection of online fans, and were particularly active in the mid to late 1990s, when "amateur" fans and "professional" writers often bumped up against each other in these spaces. At the turn of the century, potential fans could type "buffy the vampire slayer" in nascent search engines like Google and Yahoo, and easily be led to dozens of fan sites. Fanfic and fanart moved online, and new platforms, most significantly LiveJournal (1999–), became not only centralized hubs for online discussion, but also fostered new forms and practices of fandom, like real-time viewing commentary threads and GIF art. Again, the facilitating of copying is key, as online sites enabled long threaded discussions (replicating dozens, hundreds, and in some cases, thousands of individual messages), and the easy copying and pasting of text, links, and images. Tumblr, which debuted in 2007, offered an even more image-centered platform, and quickly became a major hub for fandoms centered on the production and sharing of memes and gifsets. Fan-designed and maintained fanfic archives, most notably archiveofourown.org, which also began in 2007, became key sites for organizing and providing online access to millions of fanfic stories, from tens of thousands of specific fandoms.

At the same time, the processing speed of computers and the internet itself (through broadband connection) facilitated the distribution of more complex media as audio and video files. As Jeremy Wade Morris details, the explosion of "pirated" music distribution in the form of MP3 files is the most famous and influential example from this era (Morris 2015). But by the mid-2000s, television episodes and films were also readily available online in USENET "binaries" forums or through peer-to-peer (P2P) sites and software (most notably BitTorrent). As with the other aspects of fandom that moved online, this could also be a curated space, with particular users, uploading collectives, and file-sharing sites offering "high quality" and complete collections of particular TV or film series. As Abigail De Kosnik has analyzed, deeply secretive file-sharing hubs, for example, thrived in the internet underground as a repository of long deleted and otherwise unavailable cult films, and required ostensible members to prove their "cult film" bona fides before granting access (De Kosnik 2014). Even as much mainstream and cult music, film, and television has become more prevalent in the legitimate commercial market (through DVD, Blu-ray, download, and streaming), these sites persist not only because they offer content for free, but also because they may still offer material that has yet to be officially released. The fan-sourced collective attempt to generate a definitive "despecialized" high definition (HD) version of the original *Star Wars* (1977), returning it to its pre-CGI, pre-"Special Edition" tinkering, and completely without the cooperation of rightsholders Lucasfilm or Disney, is perhaps the most prominent and telling example of digital era fan curation. It not only leads to knowledge about the fan object; it produces a new, highly curated, and desired fan object (Eveleth 2014).

Suggestions for Further Research

This brief exploration of fan curation hopefully points the way toward further research. A better understanding of how new fans are socialized into fandom, how new fannish objects are brought into existing fandoms, and how curation practices shift over time (not only due to technology, but to changing relationships between fans and objects), would help deepen our understanding of the relationships between people and media more broadly, and particularly illuminate eras of fan history which are difficult to document. A comparative history of encyclopedic fan media, for example, particularly of long-running fandoms, would trace how fan canons were formed, disseminated, and challenged. A rare example of this work is the 1997 *Doctor Who* fanzine anthology *Licence Denied*, which presents essays from successive generations of UK fans who debate and often reject earlier fan "received wisdom" about certain aspects or eras of the series (Cornell 1997). While not an academic study, it still provides an intriguing model of fandom in dialogue with its history at a particular moment.

In addition, as Matt Hills' work on fans as subcultural celebrities argues, it's important to understand how particular individual fans may function within particular fandoms (Hills 2003). Fan curators have always been people and groups of stature within their fandoms, and have influential roles as gatekeepers. Accordingly, the identities of these fans (particularly in terms of gender and race) may shape how they keep those gates, which fans get to pass through, and how the fandom is mapped out for those new fans. The same fan objects have had radically different fandoms diverge along these lines of identity. An admittedly broad caricature of *Star Trek* fandom, for example, shows that for some, predominantly female, fans, *Star Trek* is a series about interpersonal and interspecies relationships in trying circumstances, while for other, predominantly male fans, *Star Trek* is a series about the adventure of human space exploration and advanced technology. A better understanding of the role and history of fan curation—the point at which fans become fans—would help trace how fan objects are socialized not only into particular fandoms, but into broader social identities.

References

Coppa, F. (2006) "A Brief History of Media Fandom," in K. Hellekson and K. Busse (eds.), *Fan Fiction and Fan Communities in the Age of the Internet*, Jefferson City, NC: McFarland.

Cornell, P. (ed.) (1997) *Licence Denied: Rumblings from the Doctor Who Underground*, London: Virgin.

De Kosnik, A. (2014) "Exploitation Film Fandom and Piracy: A Case Study of a Private Torrent Tracker," Society for Cinema and Media Studies Conference, 21 March, Seattle.

Eveleth, Rose R. (2014) "The *Star Wars* George Lucas Doesn't Want You To See," *The Atlantic*, August 27, n.p., www.theatlantic.com/technology/archive/2014/08/the-star-wars-george-lucas-doesnt-want-you-to-see/379184/.

Geraghty, L. (2014) *Cult Collectors: Nostalgia, Fandom and Collecting Popular Culture*, New York: Routledge.

Gray, J. (2010) *Show Sold Separately: Promos, Spoilers, and other Media Paratexts*, New York: NYU Press.

Hills, M. (2002) *Fan Cultures*, New York: Routledge.

Hills, M. (2006) "Not Just Another Powerless Elite? When Media Fans Become Subcultural Celebrities," in S. Holmes and S. Redmond (eds.), *Framing Celebrity: New Directions in Celebrity Culture*, New York: Routledge, pp. 101–18.

Morris, J. W. (2015) *Selling Digital Music, Formatting Culture*, Berkeley: University of California Press.

Sandvoss, C. (2014) "The Death of the Reader? Literary Theory and the Study of Texts in Popular Culture," in K. Hellekson and K. Busse (eds.), *The Fan Fiction Studies Reader*, Iowa City, IA: University of Iowa Press, pp. 61–74.

13
THE ROLES OF LANGUAGE IN TRANSCULTURAL FANFICTION

Clarice Greco

This chapter addresses transcultural fandom through analysis of fanfiction that situates international celebrities or fictional characters within Brazilian culture. It focuses on crossover fanfiction set in Brazil through a qualitative content analysis of 34 fanfictions. Through these stories, I aim to observe how fanfiction writers use characters from foreign countries as a tool for showing a perspective on the writer's own country. More closely, I intend to show how language and the ability to communicate are set as an important cultural trait that outlines a sort of canon in transcultural fanfics in Brazil, since it appears as an element that cannot or should not be changed without explanation. Language also appears as a *communicative resource* (Lopes 2011) to point out cultural differences and as a tool to show the authors' cosmopolitanism or *poly-competence* (Morin 2003).

The stories were collected from one of the leading fanfic platforms in Brazil, *Spirit Fanfic and Stories*. The platform, known as Spirit, is a place for self-publication of books, fanfics, or original stories, and claims to have gathered over one million stories in 2023. The search was carried out using the tag "Brasil," with 1,900 results from May to June 2023. After collection, I focused on the synopses to narrow down the pool of stories, selecting fanfics in which a celebrity or foreign character came to visit Brazil and experienced the local culture. Stories about footballers from the Brazilian national team, stories about Brazilians who went abroad, or even some fanfics with characters named "Brazil" were eliminated. From the synopses, 34 fanfics fit the scope, totalling 98 chapters and almost 200,000 words that were fully read for the analysis. The fanfictions are written in Brazilian Portuguese, meaning that the authors are from Brazil and thus are a native's look at Brazilian culture. In general, the analyzed stories show the authors' points of view about Brazil, or their fantasies about presenting their country to their idols, instead of showing interest in learning from the celebrity's cultural background. In other words, they use pop culture as a *communicative resource* (Lopes 2011) for reflections or points of discussion about national culture.

Findings show different possibilities and depths of cultural exchange, ranging from brief mentions of Brazilian cultural items to elements from other cultures through the main character of the fanfic, such as food, nature, and language. Overall, language was the most prominent cultural trait and appeared to be a valuable item in the fanfics that confront two cultures or nations. That is, even if written in Portuguese, it was very common to find mentions of idiomatic challenges (such as misunderstood conversations due to language barriers), expressions in foreign languages (usually English or the idol's native tongue), or even explanations about how the celebrities or characters were capable of communication in Brazil. It was almost like language was treated as a sacred element of culture that represents the celebrity's identity and roots. And if the canon in Real Person's Fic (RPF) includes the cultural universe of the real person (Thomas 2014), thus the mention of language in said fanfics works as a component of the canon. Sometimes, language was almost the canon itself. This is why this chapter reflects upon language as a cultural trace that marks transcultural fanfics.

Transcultural Fanfics

In this chapter, I use the term "transcultural fanfics"[1] to describe stories written by fans in which the narrative incorporates national elements from two or more cultures. Under the large possibilities of transcultural fanfiction, my focus is on the importance of language as a cultural trait that receives attention from the authors in stories about foreign celebrities or characters that come to Brazil. Although the stories are written by Brazilians for Brazilians, they lean towards a transcultural practice when they acknowledge cultural differences and use cultural traits to outline the canon. This brings light to the importance of studying fanfiction as an element of transcultural fandom and as a source of transcultural manifestation. By looking at how the fanfics work the language barrier in the cultural interactions they create, I attempt to understand in which ways cross-border consumption of cultural products may form a space of *multiculturality, interculturality,* and *transculturality* (Silveira 2008). If we apply this reflection to fandoms, *multiculturalism* would happen when fans of many countries and cultures coexist but do not engage in social interaction, such as the fanfic repository in which each author posts their story. *Interculturality* amongst fans would require interaction and cultural exchanges – for example, fans who watch and comment on foreign products or a community that brings together fans from different countries and cultures interacting with each other. The *transcultural* aspect would incorporate extra cultural or cross-cultural elements to recreate and re-elaborate cultural knowledge, affection, and social bonds.

Because intercultural import-export dynamics effect the construction and reconstruction of cultures, Morimoto (2017: 283) states that "any nuanced discussion of the fandoms that grow around transnationally circulating media must account for how and why such media circulate outside their own industrial or national context." However, it is worth mentioning the perspective of the Global South since the circulation of media products, as Jenkins (2004) points out about the idea of *pop cosmopolitanism,* involves power relations and the economic and political strategies of multinational corporations. Because we are talking about fanfictions written in Portuguese, the national culture has probably no relevant circulation outside Brazil to be exported as soft power. What we find is the opposite: Brazilians bringing slices of foreign culture to circulate among other Brazilians.

This means that a Brazilian fan can have cosmopolitan consumption. Even without having left their country, they can look into the cultural products that they consume, learn the language (whether English, Japanese, or Korean), understand the laws – such as the difficulty suffered by gay couples in Boy Love (BL) or Girls Love (GL) dramas because they know that homosexual marriage was prohibited until 2024 in Thailand – and start to admire and desire cultural behaviours that are different from those of their country (but not free *from* criticism, such as the perception of gender stereotypes). In the case of the cosmopolitan fan, they also become *poly-competent* (Morin 2003) as they gather information about other cultures, capable of a hybrid look even though they maintain their nationality as predominant. As Black (2006) pointed out, popular culture and technology converge in fanfic platforms to provide a context in which fans can develop a transcultural identity, discursively constructed through the different cultural perspectives and literacies brought by fans from across the globe. This can be seen in Brazilian fanfics about international celebrities when fans make an effort to mention cultural elements from their idols' countries, showing their *poly-competence* through fanfic writing.

For Fiorin (2009), the idea of a nation is condensed into a kind of national soul, which brings together symbolic elements in which inhabitants can recognise themselves, such as history, heroes, language, monuments, folklore, landscapes, anthems, flags, cuisine, and typical flora and fauna. The author also notes that national culture is based on self-description and is always partial. This is also how fanfics are configured: because Brazilians write about their own country, they present a self-description of national culture. All fanfics analyzed in this chapter bring in national elements: some mention the city where the celebrity arrives, typical foods (the chocolate sweet *brigadeiro* and the street food *coxinha* being the most common), beaches, legends, and music. They act like "textual commemorators" (Hills 2014) by writing fanfics that contribute to the fandom's collective memory or to national celebration.

In the analyzed fanfics, transculturality usually appears in a very superficial way. Occasionally, there are mentions of cultural products, names of songs, or characters from the canonical universe with which the story deals. In these cases, language has almost no narrative function, like the fanfic *Garraduendes (BTS)* that mentions that Jimil (BTS) teaches Korean in an online language school. Korea is also mentioned in the fanfic *Uncertain Destiny (BTS – K-pop)*, when Jungkook comes to Brazil for an exchange program and a colleague asks about his country of origin. However, the stories do not use the space to learn or teach about Korean culture or any other culture. This suggests that, despite wanting to place the idol in an intercultural context, there is little actual interest in his culture of origin. Even if transculturality was not prominent in the fanfictions, Jamison (2017) states that when we look at fanfiction as a collection of narratives, instead of isolated stories, we can see that the lines cross and create patterns – if not in the stories, at least in the reader's mind. In the data collected, I found that language was the most prominent cultural element used to punctuate the canon.

Language as "Canon"

Fanfics are inspired by the canonical universe of the original story. In celebrity fanfictions, or "Real Person Fic" (RPF), the sense of an agreed canon is problematic (Thomas 2014). For this type of fanfic, the canon implies not the original setting of a narrative, but the cultural universe of the real person and therefore is closely related to nationality. The same applies to fictional characters. Pugh notes that fanfic writers can set their stories in many timelines or directions, "but they must ultimately work with a particular set of people, who have to behave and speak like themselves in every situation" (2005: 67). In the transcultural fanfictions analyzed in this chapter, the way fic writers portrayed how celebrities speak came to attention as the most visible marker of cultural specificity.

One aspect that deserves special attention is the language barrier. Spoken language – with its slang, accents, and dialects – is one of the constituent pillars of national identity (Hall 2000; Riley 2007; Fiorin 2009). In fanfics, this was the cultural trait most used as a marker of crossing borders in the imagined universes of fan narratives. At least 16 fanfics pointed out language difficulties or mentioned that the character visiting Brazil spoke another language. Before parsing some examples, it is worth mentioning that language can be observed at different levels. Riley (2007) points out three types of results or competencies that speakers or learners of a language should demonstrate. The first is *linguistic competence,* a term coined by Chomsky (1965) to designate the ability of a speaker to produce or recognise specific phrases in a language based on an "ideal native speaker." The second would be *communicative competence,* used by Hymes (1972) to include the ability to adapt speech to the situation and social context in the language process. In turn, *sociocultural competence* (Celce-Murcia1995) refers to the individual's practical knowledge of the language, the social context, and the culture of which one speaks. In the analyzed fanfics, it was possible to observe examples of all three forms of competence.

Some fanfics do not position the linguistic issue as an obstacle or difficulty; they just point out a language difference. For example, the fanfic *Oh, Brasil!* (*Lucas NCT*) differentiates, in italics, the conversations written in Portuguese to indicate when celebrities are speaking in their native language. The author writes in the description of her text that the idea for the story was inspired by the song "Morena Tropicana" by Brazilian musician Alceu Valença that mentions many fruits from the northeast of Brazil to describe the beauty of a woman. After this brief introduction, she explains that the lines from the conversation between the Chinese family members are italicized: "I decided to put this way to indicate that they are speaking Chinese, ok?" It is not possible to state the intention of the author when she calls their language "Chinese," instead of Mandarin or Cantonese and it is possible that she does not know the name of the languages they speak in China. Either way, the decision suggests that the author is more interested in fantasizing about the Brazilian song than engaging with the idol's culture of origin.

In two fanfics, the authors rely on the fictional universe to explain the characters' communication in Brazil. In *Winchester Brothers* (*Supernatural*), the brothers decide to go to Brazil, but one of them says "we don't even speak Portuguese" to which the other one replies that he will talk to Rowena (a character from the show who is a very powerful witch), because "She must have one of those spells to solve this." A similar strategy is used by the author of the fic *Profeta no Brasil* (*Doctor Who*). In the story, the character "Amy" sees many fanfics about *Doctor Who* and the narrator explains: "even if the language of the stories is Brazilian Portuguese, in TARDIS there are no language barriers, so as an immediate translation from the machine, Amy understands each word of the material." TARDIS is the time machine and spacecraft that Doctor Who uses in the show. In these cases, the fanfic authors use resources from the canonical universe to justify the acquisition of the Portuguese language by the characters, thus being able to start the narrative without further punctuating the idiomatic difference. These cases also reveal the author's concern not to ignore linguistic boundaries. Therefore, we can see the authors' commitment to maintaining fidelity to the characters' original language, as if simply placing them as Portuguese speakers would corrupt the canon.

Black (2006) has written about language and identity in fanfictions, basing her argument on Gee's notion of discourse (with a lower-case d) as the language in use, and Discourse (with a capital D) as the communication tools that encompass semiotic, material, and expressive resources that form the cultural identity of a community. This perspective can be seen in fanfics in which language differences are not only a cultural marker, but also a barrier to communication. In these cases, language appears as *linguistic competence* (Chomsky 1965), related to discourse (or lower-case d, as in Black 2006). That is, language is mentioned in situations of difficulties with grammar or when explaining the language learning process. One example is in the fic *Oh, Brasil! (Lucas NCT)*, when a Brazilian girl talks to Lucas (a rapper from Hong Kong) in Portuguese and he replies that he doesn't understand the language, leading both to start a conversation in English. At another point of the story, Lucas mentally thanks his father for enrolling him in English classes, thus allowing him to meet the girl with whom he falls in love. In this case, linguistic competence is related to grammar and to the understanding of the language.

Another example of linguistic competence in fanfics appears in the story *EXO no Brasil (EXO)* in which members of the K-pop group EXO come to Rio de Janeiro during Carnival. In at least three pieces of dialogue the fanfic author mentions difficulties with language or with communication, such as when one of the boys from EXO asks what is the typical Brazilian truck that plays during Carnival, called *Trio Elétrico*. The dialogue goes: "What is this?" "I think is a... 'Trio Elétrico' – Kyungsoo said, trying to pronounce the last word with a little difficulty." Later in the same fic, a popular singer in Brazil (Wesley Safadão) is playing and begins to speak to the boys and ask their names: "They were a bit confused but ended up supposing by 'nome' that he wanted to know their names." In another moment the author recounts that Sehun shouted that he loves Rio but commits a grammar mistake. "'Eu AMAR o Rio!!!' Sehun shouted with his broken Portuguese, dancing." This story is particularly interesting because the author presents, through language, other Brazilian cultural symbols, such as Trio Elétrico or Wesley Safadão, playing with *interculturality* and *transculturality* (Silveira 2008).

These types of mentions of language barrier issues were surprisingly common in fanfics: for example, in *Uncertain Destiny (BTS)*, Jungkook comes to Brazil for an exchange programme and mispronounces some words because he is still learning Portuguese. Likewise, characters from *Tokyo Revenge* in the fic *A Christmas out of Location (Tokyo Revenge)* explain that they studied Portuguese because they had always wanted to go to Brazil, since they were part of a gang when they were young and they heard that Brazil had many "cool gangs." What is noticeable is the authors' concern with maintaining some degree of verisimilitude towards the characters' original language, as if simply placing them as Portuguese speakers could corrupt the canon. One interesting aspect is that the commitment to explaining language acquisition could be seen both in Real Person Fanfics and in character fics. Therefore, the idea of "corrupting the canon" would possibly operate differently in each context. For RPF, for example, placing South Korean idols such as Jungkook (BTS) or Kyungsoo (EXO) suddenly speaking a different language could give the impression of an "unreal" event, since it deals with a more concrete idea of reality, and thus it requires a more "respectful" approach to the celebrities' origin. On the other hand, when authors explain why/how characters such as Sirius Black or Doctor Who can speak

Portuguese, it may lean towards a magical rationale, through which the lack of explanation would become narratively incoherent.

In any case, language appears as an almost sacred element, which cannot be changed without a plausible explanation in the plot. The notion of sacred related to religion and/or patriotism is understood by Durkheim (2000) as the expression of a collective conscience, or a collective force rooted in the history of tribes or societies and therefore constitutive of the group identity. In other words, the rites, beliefs, and values of a community are sacred for being a representation of the society itself (Carey 1992). In this sense, language could be seen here as a collective force that represents the celebrity and/or the canon's identity and thus becomes sacred.

However, there are occasions when communication barriers are more related to *communicative competence* (Hymes 1972). An example would be the fanfic *Playing with Feelings* (*Yuri on Ice*) in which Yuri starts selling bananas at the farmers' market and begins to learn Portuguese. However, he needs help understanding a customer who speaks using neutral pronouns (*banane, elu*, etc.). In Portuguese grammar (taught in schools), nouns are feminine or masculine; no neutral pronoun exists. In spoken language, however, some groups currently claim the use of neutral pronouns as a form of social gender inclusion, even though such words do not exist in the formal dictionary. By joking about that, the author plays with the difficulty of a language learner in understanding details of the spoken "world," beyond the books, in addition to inserting a progressive and socio-political factor in the story. Yuri's difficulty in understanding permeates not only the idiomatic issue (*linguistic competence*) but also *communicative competence*, as it deals with the ability to adapt speech to the situation and social context (Hymes 1972).

Finally, two examples of *sociocultural competence* (Celce-Murcia 1995) appear in the story *A Christmas outside Location* (*Tokyo Revengers*) when Brazilian women laugh at Baji (a character from the Mangá) because he thinks that tangerines are the same as oranges. At another point, a Brazilian woman claims that "prawns are the cockroaches of the sea," and Seishu, who has already eaten his food, is mocked by his friends:

At the end of lunch:

- Do you know that prawns are the cockroaches of the sea? – the Brazilian with short hair says out of nowhere.

Seishu, who had eaten all of his food, becomes serious.

- I didn't know that.

The new trio, composed of Mikey, Haruko, and Atsuko, starts to hit the table, laughing so hard.

The story jokes about the fact that prawns need to be correctly cleaned for consumption. In the ocean, they would be "dirty" animals, like cockroaches. On both occasions, the Brazilian and Japanese characters in the fic make fun of the cultural lack of knowledge about prawns or oranges. It is not just a linguistic issue but one of familiarity with elements of local cuisine. The example implies that it is not enough to know how to speak the language, the communication can still be imperfect because of the *sociocultural competence* (Celse-Murcia 1995).

Foreign Language as Reinforcement of Cultural Differences

Although the fanfics I analyzed are written in Portuguese, some stories use sentences or expressions in a foreign language to highlight the cultural contrast. In an excerpt from the story *Prophet in Brazil (Doctor Who)*, the character "Doctor Who" comes to the country to look for fanfics about him and is offered coffee by one of the authors he meets. Most of the original dialogue is written in Portuguese, but the last sentence is in English, to emphasize that the Brazilian author spoke the language of the character. The translation of the dialogue goes as follows, with the italics indicating the part that was originally written in English: "Do you want something? I like the coffee from here, I think you'll like it. In Brazil, coffee is like British tea, only much better." The author takes her cup of coffee that was on the table and drinks all the liquid that was left – "*A damn fine cup of coffee.*" In the excerpt, there is a cross between the presentation of an element of national culture (Fiorin 2009) and the maintenance of interculturality (Silveira 2008) presented by the fanfic, which tensions typical Brazilian beverages (coffee) against English tea, including the use of foreign language. Moreover, she uses the English language to end the conversation, as if trying to strengthen the contrast between the cultural differences. It is interesting that the Brazilian character is the one to speak an English sentence. This line carries a sense of inclusion since the native Portuguese speaker is trying to communicate with the English character in his original language. However, it could also point to sarcasm, as she continues to speak Portuguese knowing that the Doctor can understand her. It is also significant that she uses slang in the sentence– "damn fine" – moving from a mere *linguistic competence* to a *communicative competence*. Again, language appears as an allusion to *Doctor Who*'s canonic universe, which is easier to identify in fictional fanfics. Thus, the use of the character's original tongue to reference the fictional canon can be useful to confirm language as a trope for transcultural analysis that can be also applied in Real Person Fic.

Another example appears in the fic *Uncertain Destiny (BTS – K-pop)* when Jungkook, who is studying in Brazil, drops the bottle of a colleague in class and says "Mianamnida. Mianamnida. Mianamnida" ("I'm sorry" in Korean three times) and the narrator explains that "From the desperate sequence and the way he said it, I concluded that it was an apology." Again, the use of the original language is more than just an ornament to the story. It reveals the desire of the author to show the author's (even limited) knowledge of the Korean language. It is important to mention that this is not always a positive approach to language differences. In the same fic, moments later Jungkook says "Gomapseumnida" ("thank you" in Korean), to which the colleague responds "arigatō" ("thank you" in Japanese), leaning towards a comedic or even pejorative approach on cultural differences for mistaking (even if on purpose) his nationality. This example shows language error as a lack of knowledge or interest about the other's culture that albeit used for humor can also lead to stereotype and prejudice (Lippman 2008). The same happens in fanfics that introduce foreigners thinking Brazilians speak Spanish, as I present further. In general, the above examples show the use of language to reinforce cultural differences and to display the writers' *poly-competence* (Morin 2003) about the celebrities' or characters' canonical/cultural universe. More than that, it is a *communicative resource* (Lopes 2011) to highlight the cultural contrast.

In five fanfics, language was used to point out common stereotypes of foreigners about Brazil, such as thinking that locals speak Spanish, not Portuguese. As already mentioned, this chapter analyzes Brazilian perspectives over their own culture, using the look of a foreign idol to show their own look to their country. The common mistake made by foreigners about the language that we speak in Brazil appeared as a trace of cultural contrast. For example, this misconception occurs in the fic *Come to Brazil (Attack on Titan)*, when the character Jean listens to a few Brazilians chatting in Los Angeles (before coming to Brazil) and says to them:

- You know, something made me curious. Where are you from?
- Oh, yeah. We are Brazilians.
- Brazilians? What language do you speak there? Spanish?
- No – she answers with a quiet laugh – We speak Portuguese.
- Portuguese? Like in Portugal?
- Sort of. The language is similar, they are our colonizers after all, but there are variations – She said taking her order and handing me mine.
- Really? Like what?
- For example, in each region certain words have a totally different meaning. We can know where a person is from just by the way she speaks. – She says finishing her drink.
- Really? Doesn't that cause prejudice?
- It depends. Some stupid people do that, but in general we like this language variation. It makes the country more unique.

In the dialogue, the girl not only informs Jean about the language spoken in Brazil but explains about colonization and about the language variations one can find between different states. The example shows an approach to language that leads to a dialogue about cultural specificities.

Nonetheless, some exchanges are less friendly and informative, leading towards a rude approach to the Portuguese-Spanish confusion. For example, in the fic *Brave New World (Supernatural)* a Brazilian woman welcomes the Winchester brothers and warns them: "First, it is important that, under no circumstances, are you one of those foreigners who think that Brazilians speak Spanish." In this case the tone is slightly impolite and reveals a complaint about foreigners who do not know that Portuguese is spoken in Brazil, suggesting that the fanfic author considers this language mistake to be offensive. This relates to Lippmann's (2008) notion of stereotypes that can become prejudice due to their negative charge. The narratives that address the issue point to a common stereotype that foreigners have about Brazil, but this is also a stereotype of Brazilians about foreigners. These examples of transcultural fanfics show how cultural confrontations can point to stereotypes and prejudices, whereas it can also make us reflect about how cultural exchanges often begin with stereotypical understandings that need to be corrected.

Conclusion

Through fanfics, fans can generate intersections between the national identity and cultural elements of their idol or object of worship. Using foreign characters visiting Brazil sets up a tool to show the author's perspective on their own culture – especially language barriers, one of the most prominent elements in the analyzed stories. These barriers operate in different ways, from characters learning words in Portuguese and committing pronunciation mistakes (markers of a *linguistic competence* according to Chomsky 1965) to their misunderstanding the context of communication in informal conversations (regarding a *communicative competence* as used by Hymes 1972) or even by being confused for not knowing elements of Brazilian culture such as fruits or carnival artifacts (lacking *sociocultural competence* as defended by Celce-Murcia 1995). Language issues were also mentioned when fanfic authors explained how and why characters or celebrities learned Portuguese or when the foreign character thinks Brazilians speak Spanish. All these approaches to the language barrier in fanfictions can be looked at as a trope, or as a potential marker of cultural differences. It is important not only to look at language as an issue in transcultural fanfictions but also to consider the different ways language barriers are addressed since they can give us clues about how cultures are perceived and portrayed.

Overall, language appears as an almost sacred element, which cannot be changed without a plausible explanation in the plot. It was possible to notice at least three main roles of language: as a reference to the canon, as a *communicative resource* (Lopes 2011) to reinforce cultural contrast, and as demonstration of the authors' cosmopolitanism or *polycompetence* (Morin 2003). It was also possible to observe an intent to disseminate elements of the idol's culture or cultural product, contributing to intercultural and even transcultural narratives, as they bring together characteristics of Brazilian and foreign national identities.

References

Black, R. (2006). "Language, Culture, and Identity in Online Fanfiction". *E–Learning*, v. 3, n. 2, pp. 170–184. DOI: 10.2304/elea.2006.3.2.170
Carey, J. (1992). *Communication as Culture. Essays on Media and Society*. [1975]. London: Routledge.
Celce-Murcia, M., et al. (1995). "Communicative Competence: A Pedagogically Motivated Model with Content Specifications". *Issues in Applied Linguistics*, v. 6, n. 2, pp. 5–35.
Chin, B. and Morimoto, L. H. (2013). "Towards a Theory of Transcultural Fandom". *Participations*, v. 10, pp. 92–108.
Durkheim, É. (2000). *As Formas Elementares da Vida Religiosa – O Sistema Totêmico na Austrália*. [1912]. São Paulo: Martins Fontes, p. 536.
Hymes, D. (1972). "On Communicative Competence". In: J. Pride & J. Holmes (eds.) *Sociolinguistics*. 1. Harmondsworth: Penguin Books, pp. 269–293.
Chomsky, N. (1965). *Aspects of the Theory of Syntax*. Cambridge, MIT Press, p. 296.
Fiorin, J. L. (2009). "A construção da identidade nacional brasileira". *Bakhtiniana* (São Paulo), v. 1, n. 1, pp. 115–126.
Hall, S. (2000). *A Identidade Cultural na Pós-modernidade*. Rio de Janeiro: DP&A, p. 102.
Hills, M. (2014, Apr). "Doctor Who's Textual Commemorators: Fandom, Collective Memory and the Self-Commodification of Fanfac". *Journal of Fandom Studies*, v. 2, n. 1, pp. 31–51.
Jamison, A. (2017). *Por que a fanfiction está dominando o mundo*. São Paulo: Rocco.
Jenkins, H. (2004). "Pop Cosmopolitanism: Mapping Cultural Flows in an Age of Media Convergence". In: M. M. Suárez-Orozco & D. B. Qin-Hilliard (eds.) *Globalization: Culture and Education in the New Millennium*. Berkeley, CA: University of California Press, pp. 114–140.
Lippmann, W. (2008). *Opinião Pública*. Rio de Janeiro, RJ: Editora Vozes.
de Lopes, M. I. V. (2011). "Telenovela como recurso comunicativo". *MATRIZes*, 3(1), pp. 21–47.
Morimoto, L. (2017). "Transnational Media Fan Studies". In: M. A. Click & S. Scott (eds.) *The Routledge Companion to Media Fandom*. London: Routledge, pp. 280–288.
Morin, E. (2003[1921]). *A cabeça bem-feita*: repensar a reforma, reformar o pensamento. Translation: Eloá Jacobina. – 8a ed. Rio de Janeiro: Bertrand Brasil, p. 128.
Pugh, S. (2005). *The Democratic Genre: Fan Fiction in a Literary Context*. Bridgend: Seren, p. 282.
Riley, P. (2007). *Language, Culture and Identity*: An Ethnolinguistic Perspective. London: Continuum, p. 265.

Silveira, E. P. D. (2008). "Multiculturalismo versus interculturalismo". *Desenvolvimento em Questão*. v. 6, n. 12, pp. 63–86.

Thomas, B. (2014). "Fans Behaving Badly? Real Person Fic and the Blurring of the Boundaries between the Public and the Private". In: B. Thomas & J. Round (eds.) *Real Lives, Celebrity Stories: Narratives of Ordinary and Extraordinary*. New York: Bloomsburry, p. 225.

Acknowledgements

I thank Graciele Carnevale for her help with data collection.

This research was supported by a grant from São Paulo Research Foundation (FAPESP) – 2022/1400-6.

14

FAN TOURISM AND PILGRIMAGE

Revisited

Rebecca Williams

Following the airing of the final season of the HBO television series *Succession* in May 2023, dedicated fans were seen taking photos of themselves in New York's Battery Park. Sitting on a specific park bench and photographed from behind whilst staring out over the Hudson River, these fans sought to imitate the final shot of the show in which lead character Kendall Roy (played by Jeremy Strong) contemplates his future after losing his opportunity to take over his family's media company (Macias 2023). Although information on the locations used for homes, restaurants, and bars throughout the series is easily available online, the fact that fans felt inspired to re-enact this specific moment from the finale indicates the important connection that they feel to places related to their objects of fandom. Media fans often have strong emotional interests in finding and visiting sites related to their favorite films, TV shows, or celebrities since "fan-text affective relationships cannot be separated from spatial concerns and categories" (Hills 2002: 145). This chapter discusses the importance of fan tourism to our understandings of fans practices and experiences, considering how affective ties to specific places offer fans the "opportunity to relocate in place a profound sense of belonging which has otherwise shifted into the textual space of media consumption" (Sandvoss 2005: 64). Studies of space and place within fan studies have explored a range of practices related to important locations and sites associated with different texts and icons, allowing us to understand how fans' relationships with beloved objects are not just dependent on interpreting or discussing favorite texts (such as films or TV shows) or collecting merchandise. Engaging in acts of tourism can offer fans opportunities to learn more about fan objects, immerse themselves in fictional worlds, and make connections with others who share their interests.

This chapter focuses on what Matt Hills refers to as "cult geographies" which he defines as the "*diegetic and pro-filmic spaces (and 'real' spaces associated with cult icons) which cult fans take as the basis for material, touristic practices*" (2002: 144, emphasis in original). First, the chapter outlines the key practices associated with fan tourism and the pleasures that these offer to fans. The chapter discusses practices such as taking photographs at key sites, recreating important moments or scenes, and tracking down locations as part of the broader quest for acquiring and sharing fannish knowledge that fans often engage in. Fan tourism offers the opportunity for a range of practices since it can be "a form of performance, a form of participatory fan culture in which fans are able to appropriate the text and, when necessary, to enact their own counter-narratives in opposition to those provided by the site curators" (Larsen 2015: 40). The chapter also introduces one of the most common ways in which fan visits to important places has been approached within fan studies by outlining the idea of "fan pilgrimage." This concept perceives fans as occupying a liminal space which is outside of everyday life, offering opportunities for "performances, fantasies and rituals of transformation" at sites which allow for "imagining and enacting forms of social intimacy other than those constrained by the everyday" (Erzen 2011: 12).

Throughout, the chapter explores how tensions between commercialization and "authentic" experience at fan sites can challenge how fan tourism has been understood as well as complicating the practices that fans engage in in these spaces. Furthermore, the increase in a wider cultural and touristic interest in media places is considered to evaluate how sharing of spaces with non-fans, or antagonistic visitors or locals, can impact upon the experience of fan tourism or pilgrimage. Finally, the chapter briefly plots a course for future research by considering how we might differently explore fan attachments and practices when it is specific places themselves that are the object of fandom (e.g., theme parks, restaurants), what may happen when important fan places cease to exist, and how issues of sustainability and ethical consumption are essential in developing work on fan tourism in the future.

Fan Tourism, Knowledge, and Commodification

Fans often engage in practices of research and collecting information in relation to their tourism, seeking to archive information, photographs, and maps of important places and often trying to track down more obscure locations. Thus, much as fans often seek knowledge of other kinds about fan objects (for example, learning as much as possible about actors or writers from a favorite TV series), they can also engage in these kinds of practice when looking for film or TV locations. For example, in his discussion of Vancouver, Canada as a destination for fans of the television series *The X-Files*, Matt Hills notes the lack of a

> direct attempt on the part of organised tourism to 'cash in' upon the distinction which has been generated for Vancouver by the international success of *The X-Files*. Scouting for *X-Files* locations remains an 'underground' activity in the sense that one cannot simply join a guided tour. (2002: 147)

Hills argues that the need to obtain insider information about filming locations means that "the experience is not thoroughly commodified, packaged and offered up to be bought, but has to be (skillfully) worked at via the discovery of hidden information" (2002: 148). Thus fans' "underlying fantasies can operate in an unrestricted or loosely characteristic way, rather than being rigidly imposed" (Hills 2002: 149) by organized and commercialized spaces. Fans are thus more able to interpret these spaces according to their own fan interests since they are not being forced to experience them in a prescribed way. For example, fans on an organized tour must visit sites in the order that they are taken to by a tour guide and are often limited in the time they can spend at each site. In contrast, a fan who has sought out locations for themselves can visit in whatever order they choose, spend as much time as they want at each place, and have more freedom in terms of how they behave at these sites. It has thus often been assumed that fans will prefer to visit non-commodified places which are not owned and operated by media companies rather than officially endorsed experiences because these are seen as more authentic and to allow the fan more control over how they interpret a place and the practices they engage in there.

However, this "commodification versus 'authentic experience'" argument is an uneasy binary (Hills 2002: 153) since fans themselves may run tours for profit and some sites actively re-play "themes and realities" relevant to certain fan cultures, such as Graceland's reiteration of the heavily commodified life of its celebrity owner Elvis Presley (Hills 2002: 153). Fans may also visit a range of different places during visits including highly commodified spaces as well as less commercial ones. For example, in her discussion of *Twilight* fan tourism in the American town of Forks, Washington, Tanya Erzen (2011) describes how fans joined an organized "Dazzled by Twilight" tour which visited sites such as Forks City Hall, the Cullens' house, and La Push at a Quileute reservation but, unhappy with its lack of a visit to a meadow used in the first *Twilight* movie, sought it out for themselves (2011: 22–24). Even within official spaces, fans may engage in a range of practices and be free to varying extents to behave in different ways. For example, *Star Wars* fans within the Galaxy's Edge-themed lands in Disneyland and Walt Disney World find ways to subvert Disney's rules that forbid the wearing of costumes or engaging in lightsaber fights in the parks (Williams 2020: 247). We must therefore continue to understand fan tourism as a practice riven with conflicts and contradictions as fans negotiate both highly commercialized and non-commodified spaces and form their own views on the apparent "authenticity"' of these various experiences.

When fans seek out locations for themselves outside of pre-arranged or commercialized opportunities (such as organized location tours or official museums), they must often work hard to find more obscure locations that may be difficult to identify. Even when they track these down and visit them, they may find these sites to be "thoroughly banal" (Hills 2002: 149) such as the "back-street alleyway, a university building, a shopping precinct escalator" (2002: 149) of *The X-Files* locations discussed by Hills. Fans must thus engage in imaginative work to make the place significant, to remember how it looked on-screen, and to make it meaningful for them. As Kim notes, "screen tourists consciously plunge themselves in/between representation and reality and form unique memories of a specific time and space" (2010: 71) often through acts such as photographing themselves recreating iconic moments or scenes. Fans may also find that they are accorded prestige and levels of "subcultural capital" (Thornton 1995) by other fans when they identify and visit more obscure locations, allowing some fans to gain the pleasure of recognition from fellow fans. Fan tourists thus take part in a range of behaviors which may involve different sites and places, moving across a complex continuum of cultural value and distinction.

Fan Emotion, Memorial Practices, and Authenticity

Once they get to visit important sites, fans can engage in a range of different practices. Many of these help fans feel a closer connection to a text since places can function as an "imaginary action-space" where fans experience the "possibility of imagining, for a moment, that [they] are characters exploring the narrative space" (Couldry 2007: 143). For example, fans often take photographs of themselves at these locations to remember their visits and to record their presence in the space of the text or icon. Fans of fictional texts often recreate iconic poses or stand in specific places to take photographs which replicate key moments from their favorite fan objects. This can be seen, for example, at the *Harry Potter* photo opportunity at Platform 9¾ at Kings Cross train station in London. Fans queue at this official and commercially operated space to have a photo taken of themselves pushing a train trolley through the wall of the Platform, wearing a scarf from the appropriate House from the fictional wizarding school of Hogwarts. Here, fans can insert themselves into an iconic moment from the *Harry Potter* text and potentially relive their own memories of reading the books or viewing the films for the first time because these practices allow fans to

> attach an emotional bond or link between themselves and… locations and to recall what they were touched by during the previous viewing experiences and its meanings. They do this by expressing a desire for feeling the same sense and emotion at the actual filming locations. (Kim 2010: 71)

Those engaged in fan tourism can also interact with important places by making their mark on that space. For example, fans may write messages on walls or furniture, engaging in "vernacular memorial practices" (Alderman 2002: 29). Such practice is common at sites such as the walls of Graceland, the walls outside Abbey Road Studios where The Beatles' famously recorded their music, or the park benches in Viretta Park, near the site of Nirvana singer Kurt Cobain's death in Seattle. Fans may simply inscribe their name and the date, or leave longer messages such as poems, messages of adoration of the fan object, or declarations about the importance of the fan object and space to them. However, such messages may not always be positive; they may challenge dominant narratives of a fan pilgrimage site or constitute silly or offensive messages left by non-fans, anti-fans, or more general tourists. The practice of leaving messages at sites such as Graceland shows how fans can engage in acts of authorship, making visible the "articulation of multiple, sometimes competing discourses about [such sites]" which are "made socially important and meaningful to visitors" (Alderman 2002: 28). Similarly, Craig Norris (2013) discusses messages left in a visitor book for the anime text *Kiki's Delivery Service* at a bakery in Tasmania. Based on these fan messages, Norris argues that fan tourism can offer a transformative journey which participants often draw on to express their "own narratives, experiences, or ideas" (2013: paragraph 1.2). However, such experiences can be threatened; in Norris' study this largely resulted from the inability of the real location to live up to the imagined one, offering a dirty and noisy working bakery rather than the "authentic" place that fans imagined (2013: paragraph 10.6).

Despite the difficulty in defining what authenticity means, the tension between authentic and inauthentic places and experiences is one that is often negotiated by fan tourists. For example, one *Twilight* fan on the "Dazzled by Twilight" tour discussed by Tanya Erzen expressed disappointment when a piano in the location used as the Cullen house wasn't the exact type of instrument played by the character of Edward Cullen (Erzen 2011: 15) and that the house that Bella Swan lived in "appears drab and ordinary" in comparison to her imagination (2011: 16) Fans also make distinctions between different officially-operated spaces, as Larsen's (2015) discussion of Warner Brothers-owned *Harry Potter* properties makes clear. In addition to privileging certain types of location over others (e.g., those that are more difficult to find, those that are not included on official tours), fans judge the authenticity of places based on "physical differences, an atmosphere that takes one out of the [fictional world], or moral concerns around commercial exploitation" (Norris 2013: paragraph 10.18). When places fail to live up to fans' expectations, they can cause a "negative aura" (Couldry 2007) and threaten the affective and emotional links that fans form to such spaces and practices they can engage in at these sites.

Fan Tourism, Community, and Communitas

Fans also engage in practices of community-building and sharing with others regarding their tourist experiences. This can take place before and after visits as fans share information about locations or photographs with others. For example, fans of the TV series *Sherlock* have contributed to the website *Sherlockology* which details different filming locations. Some of these are well-known and promoted by the BBC, and by the locations themselves, but others are more obscure and require intimate local knowledge or for fans themselves to undertake detective work to seek them out. This knowledge exchange among fan communities is another way in which fan tourism builds on and extends existing fan practices since fans can connect with others by sharing their experiences online after their visits, engaging in knowledge acquisition and circulation.

However, fans can also engage in communal practices whilst present at specific sites, sharing their experience with others within the same spaces. Studies have often understood the links between fan tourism and community through the concept of pilgrimage, viewing fan journeys to places as invested with almost religious importance. In her discussion of *Twilight* Tanya Erzen describes fan tourists as "*Twilight* pilgrims" (2011: 11), how fans "trekked to Forks like supplicants to a holy site" (2011: 13), and the books' importance as "sacred texts" (2011: 15). Similarly, fan visits to sites associated with objects as varied as *Harry Potter* (Larsen 2015), *Star Trek* conventions (Porter 1999), Elvis Presley's home Graceland (Alderman 2002; King 1993), and anime (Okamoto 2015) have been discussed as forms of pilgrimage. During the pilgrimage participants occupy a so-called "liminal space" where they are outside of the normal routines of everyday life and where "social relations are 'simplif[ied] and homogenize[d]'" (Porter 1999: 248). These "moments of liminality are also moments of play, when we are released from the constraints of everyday norms, customs, and boundaries, temporarily free to 'act' outside of those norms" (Larsen 2015: 39). This means that all fans at a specific important place can be seen as equal and as able to connect with one another through a concept called "communitas," described as "a mode of communal fellowship which the pilgrim cannot attain within the social structural bounds of everyday life" (Porter 1999: 252). In these moments, fans' ordinary markers of identity such as age, class, or gender cease to be important and connection with other fans depends only on a shared feeling of solidarity. When fans share moments at important spaces with fellow fans, they have been seen to be participating in practices of communitas and sharing a sense of belonging with others who share the same interests. In these moments, fan tourists "simultaneously produce and perform their own individualized text and interpretive community within which individuals can feel unique yet part of a larger congregation" (Aden et al. 1995: 377).

However, fans may often find themselves sharing spaces with non-fans who do not share the deep affective or emotional links that they have to that place because it is becoming more common for non-fans to visit places associated with the media. This is related to an increase in official place-branding tactics which link locations to popular media texts to increase tourism such as Dubrovnik, Croatia, and Belfast, Northern Ireland's associations with the HBO television series *Game of Thrones* or Cardiff, Wales' links with *Doctor Who*. This may challenge the concepts of pilgrimage and communitas since not everyone at a site has the same purpose or interest, meaning that fans are ever-increasingly having to traverse such spaces with non-fans or "anti-fans" (Gray 2003), a development which can yield its own challenges. For example, fans on a *Game of Thrones* walking tour in Dubrovnik will likely be undertaking the experience with more general tourists with a more casual interest in the series. Fans may thus feel unable to engage in specific fan practices such as taking photographs which recreate key moments from a text, or approaching other people at sites that are shared with non-fans. This lack of communitas may thus threaten fan practices, limiting fans' experiences and their freedom to express their fandom in specific ways. Furthermore, some places may not only be shared with non-fans but with those who actively oppose or dislike such sites and what they signify. For example, fan visitors to the memorial to deceased *Torchwood* character Ianto Jones in Cardiff Bay, Wales must share the space with residents of the city for whom "the memorial may offer a complex duality, functioning as both a site of media significance and as a more ordinary place that one passes on the way to work or when enjoying an evening out" as well as "non-viewers,... [who view the space as] an interesting anomaly, as a point of bemusement or even vitriol and outrage" (Williams and McElroy 2016: 205) since this fan-space memorializes a gay character.

This can limit opportunities for fans to experience forms of communitas and connection with other fans at these sites since other people may not share the fans' attachment and may even respond to fan visitors with hostility. Equally, some places may be doubly coded as tourist and media sites, operating as different locations for different fans. For example, Lee notes that the village of Lacock, England visited on a *Harry Potter* tour "can simultaneously exist as a heritage site, Meryton (from the BBC production of *Pride and Prejudice*), [and] Godric's Hollow and Hogwarts" causing "[f]rissons between the diverse cartographies" (2012: 62). Locations thus become multi-coded, and fans may operate their own distinctions regarding which version of the story, and therefore which locations, are the most privileged and worth visiting. The necessity of sharing "sacred" spaces with non-fans – or competing fans of other texts or versions of a text – can reduce the opportunities for fans to engage in the practices of community and bonding that some fans seek at such sites.

Fan Tourism, Identity, and Self-narratives

Considering fan tourism also offers opportunities to consider how fan practices around self-identity and narrative are performed differently in a spatial context. Fans often link themselves closely with favorite fan objects and discuss the importance of these to their sense of self (see Williams 2015) and visiting important places can allow fans to feel closer to beloved texts or icons. However, some people may not be fans of an object *until* they visited a specific site, and some visitors may "pass as" a fan by performing or adopting the characteristics of the fandom associated with a space (see Geraghty 2015). Mark Duffett questions how much can a place guide us to have an emotional response? Does that response occur because of what it is, what it represents to us, how it has been arranged, or a combination? Can places *do things* to those who visit them? Or is the experience entirely down to what mental expectations visitors bring along? (2013: 231)

It is thus useful to consider what places can do to visitors who may not bring media or fan-specific imaginative expectations with them and yet may respond strongly to a particular place. What aspects of that spatial experience are these individuals responding to? What confluence of affective, emotional, and experiential elements may cause them to become fans of that site and its associated texts or cult icons? Further investigation of how fandom emerges from engagement with specific mediated or fan-specific spaces allows us to begin to answer some of the questions posed by Duffett and, again, to broaden our understandings of the complex relationships between fans, texts/objects, and places. There is also much to learn from examining those who are fans of specific places *themselves* such as theme parks (Williams 2020) or restaurants or bars (Geraghty 2014) who engage in practices like those of fans engaging in fan tourism of media texts and icons. In these cases, "Unlike some ordinary tourism, where mediation comes between the material place and its travelling audience, in fan tourism the media text is always the *first* point that guides fan-tourists' interpretations and valorises those places for them" (Duffett 2013: 227).

It is also worth considering what happens when beloved places disappear and how fans respond when these are no longer available to visit. Fan studies has focused on the process of "becoming-a-fan" (Hills 2002: 6) whilst responses to the ends of fan objects or one's fandom have been less well explored (Williams 2015). However, the loss of spaces is common in a landscape of urban regeneration and change in which buildings and sites may be demolished, rebuilt, or moved (Lee 2014). A future avenue for fan scholars is to pay attention to how fans react to such changes and the impact these can have on their emotional and affective investments in important places. Examining how fans respond to the loss of important locations allows us to explore the discourses that fans deploy in these instances and the impact upon the practices that they engage in. If, indeed, "in fandom… place remains a fundamental point of reference" (Sandvoss 2005: 66), it is also crucial for fan studies scholars to consider the consequences and reactions when those places cease to be accessible for fans.

The Covid-19 global pandemic offered some opportunities for exploring fan reactions to being unable to visit favorite places, highlighting how many turned to online digital spaces to recreate the experiences of "being there." For example, fans of the Disney theme parks created home videos, with home-made versions of favorite rides such as the Haunted Mansion or Jungle Cruise (Schweizer 2021), whilst others visited the parks virtually through on-ride videos on YouTube (Moulton 2020). Moreover, however, the pandemic opened avenues for discussion around the difficulties in traveling to favorite fan places in the face of ongoing global instabilities. As work on fandom turns towards wider consideration of ethical consumption and sustainability (Wood et al. 2020), there are questions to be asked about how global fan travel can be justifiable given deep concerns over climate change and the environmental impacts on heavily trafficked locations (Cohen 2005; Hua et al. 2021). There can also be consequences when media tourism has adverse effects on perceptions of a location (Pratt 2015), and when tourists exhibit unwelcome fan behaviors (Jørgensen and Reichenberger 2023). Considering the broad spectrum of fan practices and activities linked to travel, future work on fan tourism and pilgrimage will need to consider ethical fan tourism including environmental issues, the ethics of traveling to countries or sites where people from certain cultural and social backgrounds are not welcomed, the impact on local areas and populations, and issues of access and equality.

Conclusion

As with many fan practices, there are a range of tensions inherent in fan tourism. Physical locations "constitute sites of appropriation of popular culture as well as sites of interaction between and among fans" but, paradoxically, "often amount to the crudest display of commercialism, commodification and to a society based on an economy of signs, simulation and spectacle" (Sandvoss 2005: 53). This tension between commercialization and the lived experiences and practices of fans sits alongside other debates around the "authenticity" of experiences, how fans can engage in certain practices at meaningful sites in the face of broadening "film-induced tourism" (Beeton 2005) which attracts a mix of travelers and tourists, and the impact of the loss of important fan places in a fast-changing media and geographic environment. It is clear, however, that tourism remains a key element of fan practice, allowing fans to forge and maintain connections with imagined worlds, engage in face-to-face interaction and experience a sense of communitas with other fans, and construct self-narratives that link their fandom with their own identities and important places and spaces. As fan studies moves forward, studies of fan tourism must continue to complicate and challenge our ideas of who fan tourists are, the places they visit, and the fan practices they engage in before, during and after their visits to these sites. In particular, the implications of climate change and increasing awareness of ethical consumption and sustainability will be increasingly crucial to understanding fan tourism in the future.

References

Aden, R.C., R.L. Rahoi, and C.S. Beck (1995) "Dramas are Born on Places Like This: The Process of Interpretive Community Formation at the *Field of Dreams* Site," *Communication Quarterly*, 43(4): 368–403. https://doi.org/10.1080/14790530903522630

Alderman, D. (2002) "Writing on the Graceland Wall: On the Importance of Authorship in Pilgrimage Landscapes," *Tourism Recreation Research*, 27(2): 27–35. https://doi.org/10.1080/02508281.2002.11081217

Beeton, S. (2005) *Film-Induced Tourism*, Clevendon, Buffalo, and Toronto: Channel View Publications.

Cohen, E. (2005) "The Beach of 'The Beach'? The Politics of Environmental Damage in Thailand," *Tourism Recreation Research*, 30(1): 1–19. https://doi.org/10.1080/02508281.2005.11081229

Couldry, N. (2007) "On the Set of *The Sopranos*: "Inside" a Fan's Construction of Nearness," in J. Gray, C. Sandvoss and C. L Harrington (eds.) *Fandom: Identities and Communities in a Mediated World*, New York: New York University Press, pp. 139–148.

Duffett, M. (2013) *Understanding Fandom: An Introduction to the Study of Media Fan Culture*, London and New York: Continuum.

Erzen, T. (2011) "The Vampire Capital of the World: Commerce and Enchantment in Forks, Washington," in M. Parke and N. Wilson (eds.) *Theorizing Twilight: Critical Essays on What's At Stake in a Post-Vampire World*, Jefferson, NC: McFarland, pp. 11–24.

Geraghty, L. (2014) "It's Not All About the Music: Online Fan Communities and Collecting Hard Rock Café Pins," *Transformative Works and Cultures*, 16. http://dx.doi.org/10.3983/twc.2014.0492

Geraghty, L. (2015) "Passing Through: Identity, History and the Importance of Pilgrimage in Fan Studies," *Keynote Presented at* Fan Studies Network Conference, University of East Anglia, June 2015.

Gray, J. (2003) "New Audiences, New Textualities: Anti-Fans and Non-Fans," *International Journal of Cultural Studies*, 6(1): 64–81. https://doi.org/10.1177/1367877903006001004

Hills, M. (2002) *Fan Cultures*, London: Routledge.

Hills, M. (2014) "Returning to 'Becoming-A-Fan' Stories: Theorising Transformational Objects and the Emergence/Extension of Fandom," in L. Duits, K. Zwaan and S. Reijnders (eds.) *The Ashgate Research Companion to Fan Cultures*, Surrey: Ashgate Publishing, pp. 9–21.

Hua, Y., C. Jittithavorn, T.J. Lee, and X. Chen. (2021) "Contribution of TV Dramas and Movies in Strengthening Sustainable Tourism," *Sustainability*, 13(22): 1–14. https://doi.org/10.3390/su132212804

Jørgensen, T. and I. Reichenberger. (2023) "Breaking Bad Behaviour: Understanding Negative Film Tourist Behaviour Through Moral Disengagement," *Current Issues in Tourism*, 26(7): 1183–1198. https://doi.org/10.1080/13683500.2022.2051447

Kim, S. (2010) "Extraordinary Experience: Re-Enacting and Photographing at Screen Tourism Locations," *Tourism and Hospitality Planning & Development*, 7(1): 59–75. https://doi.org/10.1080/14790530903522630

King, C. (1993) "His Truth Goes Marching On: Elvis Presley and the Pilgrimage to Graceland," in I. Reader and T. Walter (eds.) *Pilgrimage in Popular Culture*, London: Macmillan, pp. 92–104.

Larsen, K. (2015) "(Re)claiming Harry Potter Fan Pilgrimage Sites," in L.S. Brenner (ed.) *Playing Harry Potter: Essays and Interviews on Fandom and Performance*, Jefferson, NC: McFarland, pp. 38–54.

Lee, C. (2012) "Have Magic, Will Travel: Tourism and Harry Potter's United (Magical) Kingdom," *Tourist Studies*, 12(1): 52–69. https://doi.org/10.1177/1468797612438438

Lee, C. (2014) "'Welcome to London': Spectral Spaces in Sherlock Holmes's Metropolis," *Cultural Studies Review*, 20(2): 172–195. https://doi.org/10.5130/csr.v20i2.3195

Macias, T.J. (2023) "'Succession' Fans are Recreating an Iconic Kendall Roy Scene After HBO Show's Finale," *Miami Herald*, 30 May 2023. www.miamiherald.com/news/nation-world/national/article275918696.html

Moulton, C. (2020) "'Welcome (Or Stay At?) Home': Theme Parks and COVID-19," *In Media Res*, 22 September 2020. http://mediacommons.org/imr/content/welcome-or-stay-home%E2%80%9D-theme-parks-and-covid-19

Norris, C. (2013) "A Japanese Media Pilgrimage to a Tasmanian Bakery," *Transformative Works and Cultures*, 14. http://dx.doi.org/10.3983/twc.2013.0470

Okamoto, T. (2015) "Otaku Tourism and the Anime Pilgrimage Phenomenon in Japan," *Japan Forum*, 27(1): 12–36. https://doi.org/10.1080/09555803.2014.962565

Porter, J.E. (1999) "To Boldly Go: *Star Trek* Convention Attendance as Pilgrimage," in J.E. Porter and D.L. McLaren (eds.) *Star Trek and Sacred Ground: Explorations of Star Trek, Religion, and American Culture*, Albany: SUNY Press, pp. 245–270.

Pratt, S. (2015) "The Borat Effect: Film-Induced Tourism Gone Wrong," *Tourism Economics*, 21(5): 977–993. https://doi.org/10.5367/te.2014.0394

Sandvoss, C. (2005) *Fans: The Mirror of Consumption*, Cambridge: Polity Press.

Schweizer, B. (2021) "Playing Make-Believe with #homemadeDisney Pandemic Ride Videos," *Eludamos: Journal for Computer Game Culture*, 12(1): 199–218. https://doi.org/10.7557/23.6368

Thornton, S. (1995) *Club Cultures*, London: Routledge.

Williams, R. (2015) *Post-Object Fandom: Television, Identity and Self*-Narrative, London: Bloomsbury.

Williams, R. (2020) *Theme Park Fandom*, Amsterdam: Amsterdam University Press.

Williams, R. and R. McElroy (2016) "Omnisexuality and the City: Exploring National and Sexual Identity in BBC Wales' *Torchwood*," in H. Osborne (ed.) *Queer Wales: The History, Culture and Politics of Queer Life in Wales*, Lampeter: University of Wales Press, pp. 195–208.

Wood, R., B. Litherland, and E. Reed. (2020) "Girls Being Rey: Ethical Cultural Consumption, Families and Popular Feminism," *Cultural Studies*, 34(4): 546–566. https://doi.org/10.1080/09502386.2019.1656759

15
NEGOTIATING FANDOM
The Politics of Racebending

Henry Jenkins

Growing up, the discovery of Harry Potter was nothing short of a revelation. It revolutionized the way I thought about the world, humanity, and myself. And like many young girls at the time, I found myself relating quite a lot to the series' most prominent female character.

Alanna Bennett (2015)

In this much-circulated 2015 *Buzzfeed* article, Alanna Bennett traces her evolving relationship with Hermione Granger, speaking for many who identify with characters not designed for their consumption. Writes Bennett:

> As a biracial girl growing up in a very white city, I found myself especially attaching to the allegory of *Harry Potter*'s blood politics. In middle school, when I was confronting that there were people out there who'd call me "n****r," I thought back to Hermione being called "mudblood" and harassed by teacher and students alike.

Bennett traces many twists and turns as she struggled to maintain her identification with Hermione:

> I related to her deeply, but like with so much of what I watched and read, I couldn't *see* myself in Hermione. There was a gap, and even for a kid as obsessed with pop culture as I was it was one that existed between me and most of the things I was reading and watching.

In this chapter, I will explore that "gap" and how fans (do or do not) work across it. I've long argued that fan cultural production was born from a mixture of fascination and frustration (Jenkins 1992). Fans engage closely with texts because they are fascinated; they continue to rework them because they are frustrated with some aspect of the original. Yes, fans poach. They take what they want from texts they did not create. And fans resist; they often rewrite stories so that things come out differently. But, fans also engage with the text on terms not of their own choosing, and this process looks very much like what cultural studies calls "negotiation."

Audience researchers are often accused of making the issue of representation go away by collapsing it into the possibilities of reception, but a model based on negotiation stresses the importance of struggles over representation. Fandom studies often fluctuates between two poles—the fan as all-consuming and the fan as all-resisting. The field's growing interest in anti-fans unwittingly positions the fan as its exact opposite; if the anti-fan hates, the fan adores. The oft-cited distinction between the transformational fan and the affirmational fan has a similar effect, dividing the field into two diametrically opposed poles, rather than imagining diverse fan activities occupying the space between. Negotiation represents a middle position between adoration and resistance.

Bennett's self-reflections cited at the beginning of this chapter suggests the urgency of thinking more deeply about the negotiation that all readers, viewers, and listeners perform within a still largely segregated media landscape—especially fans of color who are struggling with issues of inclusion and representation within popular media. Rebecca Wanzo (2015) notes that treating race as peripheral to the field meant that early fan researchers (myself among them) turned our backs on the strong strands of research about race that ran through the Birmingham School tradition that informed our perspectives and, also, we were disconnected from important work by scholars of color being published alongside our early books, often in related fields such as sports or music. Wanzo asks the provocative question:

> If we privilege African Americans in the story we tell about fans in the United States, how might that change our understanding of what a fan is, our understanding of how they are producers as well as consumers, or the role identity can play in the importance of identifying as a fan?
>
> (n.p.)

From the point of view of Black fans, she suggests, these experiences look and feel differently. "African American fans make hypervisible the ways in which fandom is expected or demanded of some socially disadvantaged groups as a show of economic force and ideological combat" (n.p.). I focus on the ways fans of color use various forms of racebending to advocate for alternative representations at a time when America is once again working through conflicts concerning racial and ethnic diversity. While Wanzo reminds us that there are particular histories and concerns impacting the Black community that require overdue attention, my shift from Wanzo's "African American fans" to "fans of color" is conscious since fans of diverse races and ethnicities all struggle over—and in many cases, within fandom, are making common cause together around—issues of identification and representation. Intersections between these different identities and interests shape the particular examples being considered. As such, I am writing—as a senior white male scholar—in dialogue with fans, bloggers, and scholars of color who have already made important contributions to our understanding of these issues. Those of us who write from positions of privilege have an obligation to incorporate these perspectives into our teaching and our scholarship.

Stuart Hall and Negotiation

To understand the particular circumstances through which fans of color negotiate with pop culture characters, we may need to revisit some classic work in British cultural studies. Stuart Hall's 1973 essay "Encoding, Decoding" (Hall, 1980) sought an integrated model of the communication process, one which considered production, circulation, use, and reproduction. Today, the "encoding" process (production, circulation) remains mostly in the domain of production studies, while what Hall calls "use" (reception) and "reproduction" (how audiences respond once they "decode" a text)—and, in more recent work (Jenkins, Ford, and Green, 2013), grassroots circulation—constitutes fandom or audience studies. Drawing inspiration from Gramscian Marxism, Hall describes the ways that social and semiotic codes (often, unexamined assumptions) inform choices about what content to produce, circulate, consume, and reproduce. Hall (1981) rejects, on the one hand, the idea that the people are simply dupes of a powerful media industry and, on the other, what he describes as the "heroic alternative," a "whole, authentic, autonomous" popular culture outside "cultural power and domination." Rather, Hall writes: "Popular culture is one of the sites where this struggle for and against a culture of the powerful is engaged: it is also the stake to be won or lost in that struggle" (518).

Hall (1980) discusses how differently situated consumers relate differently to mass media messages. Some read them fully within the terms of dominant ideology; others resist or reject them outright—often not bothering to engage with the text at all; but many will negotiate, taking texts apart, and taking part in them in equal measure because such works are imperfectly aligned with their experiences:

> Decoding within the negotiated position contains a mixture of adaptive and oppositional elements: it acknowledges the legitimacy of the hegemonic definitions to make the grand significations (abstract), while, at a more restricted, situational (situated) level, it makes its own ground rules—it operates with exceptions to the rule.
> (Hall, 1980, 102)

Audiences have agency, but they do not have autonomy; various forms of power shape what meanings they can assert. These readers, viewers, and listeners embrace textual elements they recognize and value, but they also encounter problematic aspects that produce a discomfort that has to be addressed before they can claim ownership over these representations. Each of us is positioned somewhat differently in relation to dominant representations, negotiating different identities and identifications within ourselves (as Hall, 1992b notes), but those of us whose gender, class, racial, and sexual identities fall within dominant groups find it easiest to forge identifications with mass media texts; we are the recipients the producers anticipated. Meanwhile, other audience members must transform these texts into better vehicles for their fantasies.

The most active fans are often "surplus audiences," unintended recipients of media texts produced for others—female consumers of male-centered action genres, adult consumers of young adult texts, or minority consumers of mainstream media (Jenkins, Ford, and Green, 2013, 129–132). Hall's initial focus was issues of class, but Hall (1992a) recounts how feminist dissent within cultural studies forced him to reconsider the place of gender and inspired him to write more directly about his own identity as a Black man. In "What is This 'Black' in Black Popular Culture?", Hall (1992b) focuses on the implications of this encoding/decoding model for understanding race. While acknowledging the "contradictory" and often "deformed, incorporated, and unauthentic" forms popular culture takes in its representations of Black identity, Hall also sees something there worth negotiating for: "Black popular culture has enabled the surfacing, inside the mixed and contradictory modes even of some mainstream popular culture, of elements of a discourse that is different—other forms of life, other traditions of representation" (470).

Representation matters, Hall tells us, because it shapes the language through which Black people understand their own lives and through which others understand who they are—not because popular culture offers realistic representation of lived experience but because popular culture is "profoundly mythic a theater of popular desires, a theater of popular fantasies" (Hall, 1992b, 474). This focus on fantasy and myth makes Hall's discussion especially valuable for understanding fandom. Fantasies about magic or superpowers are ultimately myths about power—who possesses it, who is entitled to it, and who deploys it towards what ends, and on whose behalf. Struggles over how race operates in fantastical genres are essential when you consider how important these stories are for younger audiences still mapping their place in the social order (Thomas, 2019). People of color have historically been excluded from representation within these genres or they have been treated as various versions of the monstrous "other" but new, imperfect, and often problematic representations are starting to emerge where characters of color are at least sometimes allowed to be wizards, stormtroopers, or superheroes. Hall's work remains foundational for our analysis of the process by which fans of color work through their responses to these shifts—dealing with differing degrees of inclusion, marginalization, and misrepresentation, and yet also pleasure, recognition, and empowerment.

"Not-me": Authenticity and Legitimacy

> In *Harry Potter and the Sorcerer's Stone*, Hermione is introduced with a description of her bushy brown hair and her large teeth. There's nothing there to indicate she didn't look just like me, yet I always pictured a white face under that bushy head. I always pictured her not-me.
>
> (Bennett, 2015)

J. K. Rowling's text leaves open—but does not actively assert—the possibility that Hermione *might be* "non-white," but Bennett already knows she is not. Whiteness is unmarked in our culture (Dyer, 1997; Morrison, 1993; Phalen, 1993), so any character who is not otherwise specified gets read as white. And, sometimes, characters of color still get read as white by white audiences. For instance, white fans protested Rue's blackness in the *Hunger Games* films, even though the books *explicitly* described her race (Williams 2015). Rue *was canonically* Black, but they had not *seen* her as such. Rowling's references to "mud-blood" in the Harry Potter books provide an allegory for contemporary race relations, but readers only recognize those connections if they want to see them. Allegory works through connotation and implication, not through denotation (that is, through explicit statement). And, as D. A. Miller (1990) writes in relation to characters who may, or may not, be queer, "Defined in contrast to the immediate self-evidence ... of denotation, connotation will always manifest a certain semiotic insufficiency ... Connotation enjoys, or suffers from, an abiding deniability" (123–124). Fans, thus, debate whether when Rowling (1999) described Hermione as "very brown," (46) was this a marker of her race or an indication that she's been spending too much time in the sun? Quick to defend her caucasian-ness, other fans located a passage where Rowling (1999) describes Hermione as turning "white" with fear (293), though, again, fans debate whether this passage precludes other racial backgrounds (Spicy Winter, 2016). That said, whatever possibilities for diversity Rowling left open on the level of connotation are quickly foreclosed by denotative factors such as the book's cover art and illustration or the film's casting decisions, reasserting Hermione's whiteness.

Textual determinations still matter; the denotative cannot be ignored, even in fandom, which has so often declared the death of the author and the autonomy of the reader. Consider two different responses posted after Bennett's online essay:

> I always figured that unless a book specifies exactly what a character is, then you can interpret the character however you want. It's art. It's different to everyone.
> * * * * * *
> I love that in the books her race is never actualy [sic] mentioned, so any interpretation is valid! maybe I'll draw a Latina one next; D

Within this gap, fans are *free to imagine* characters as having any race they want—as long as their race is not specified. And, yet, American and British fans at least live within a culture where whiteness is assumed (Pande, 2018; Pande, 2020). Fans can and often do explicitly choose to rework or ignore some core aspect of a beloved story, but they know that not everyone will appreciate their interventions; the canonical still exerts a strong pull on the community's consensus, even if the fan can negotiate, at least temporarily, a localized "exception to the rules. "Their alternative reading remains precarious. Bennett (2015) writes:

> I'd dress up in Hogwarts uniforms for Halloween but avoid going overtly as Hermione because I knew I could never get my hair like Emma Watson's My hair was a whole different kind of frizzy. I loved her so much, but it took me a long time to accept that I could never *be* her.

In *Writing Superheroes*, Anne Haas Dyson (1997) describes how textual meanings get reinscribed in the context of school yard play. Some children have the "ticket" (or privilege) to perform their favorite characters without being questioned, whereas children of color often have to struggle for the right to play characters that are white in the original, often forced to play subordinate or marginalized roles—again and again reminded of their unequal status. While some fans of color deploy cosplay to enact alternative conceptions of popular characters, claims about "authenticity"—who is entitled to embody particular characters—are disputed within the cosplay community as well, perhaps legitimately in the case of white fans performing other racialized identities (given the history of blackface, yellowface, redface, etc.) but also more problematically when they exclude fans of color from playing the heroes (Miller, 2015; Cumberbatch, 2013). And such mechanisms also operate along other dimensions such as gender, sexuality, age, size, and disability, with the effect that many people find themselves doubly or multiply excluded from playing particular roles. Such mechanisms also operate within fandom to determine who gets to speak as a fan and thus who gets to tap the sense of moral ownership (or, described in more negative terms, entitlement) that have empowered fans historically (Condis, 2014; Stanfill, 2011). Bennett (2015) describes the impact of such bruising encounters:

> As I grew up I stopped comparing myself as much to Hollywood actors and tried to train myself out of seeing white as the default for fictional characters. Call it maturation, call it learning to love myself, call it education; whatever it was, I started looking at my media and my stories through a more critical lens—and as someone learning to feel more comfortable speaking up when not enough of those stories are representing me.

Given these circumstances, fandom is always already political for fans of color, even as many white fans steadfastly defend fandom as a play space, "free from politics." The ideal of fandom as a "safe space" reflects various forms of white privilege (Pande, 2019), seeing whiteness as neutral or apolitical, whereas other racial categories always represent the "threat" of "special interests," which can be accommodated only when people "make an issue of it."

Fandom as a Counterpublic

Subsequent writers have been more attentive to the ways the concept of negotiation applies to the experiences of women or people of color as they encounter popular representations. In her 1988 essay, "Pleasurable Negotiations," Christine Gledhill stresses the tension between dominant representations and "the differential social and cultural constitution of readers or viewers—by class, gender, race, age, personal history, and so on" (70–71). For Gledhill, mass media texts often speak *about* women or people of color, but rarely speak *to* them and even more rarely speak for them, given how few people of color or women control production decisions within the media industries. At such moments, the outcomes of negotiation are "variable and unpredictable" (71).

Jacqueline Bobo (1995) provided one of the first detailed ethnographic accounts of Black women as negotiating readers of popular media, using focus groups to tease out responses to *The Color Purple* as a book and a film adaptation. She described how a repeated history of having to work through negative representations shaped these women's interpretive practices:

> A black audience, through a history of theatre-going and film-watching, knows that at some point an expression of the exotic primitive is going to be offered to us We understand that mainstream media has never rendered our segment of the population faithfully Out of habit, as readers of mainstream texts, we have learnt to ferret out the beneficial and put up blinders against the rest.
>
> (Bobo, 1995, 101)

Hall (1981) describes negotiation primarily as occurring within the head of the individual audience member, whereas Bobo stresses a more collective dimension—groups of people negotiate meanings together, thus empowering them to make stronger claims on texts that matter to the group. As such, networked fandom constitutes a "counterpublic," as variously described by Nancy Fraser (1990) in relation to women, or Michael Warner (2005) in relation to queer people coming together to forge opinions outside of the view of more dominant groups.

Bennett (2015) describes how involvement within fandom changed her relationship to Hermione:

> "Racebent" characters have long been making appearances on sites like Tumblr, but they've been picking up heat recently. One of the most popular and frequent, at least on my dash? Hermione Granger as a woman of color, most often Black. For the first time, I was seeing Hermione's subtext brought out into text.

Fans do not simply "use" texts but they also "reproduce"—or, more accurately, "reproduce"— them. Fan-made texts are not best understood as interpretations; they do not simply document what these stories mean to fans. They also model alternatives fans might like to see but often know they will never receive from the producers. Such cultural productions constitute material forms of textual negotiation; much greater power resides in the audience's hands when fan production enters the picture, freed from the burden of canonicity. Fan fiction operates within shared social norms, determining which forms of textual rewriting are apt to be widely accepted and which are going to be more contested; changing the sexual orientation of a character has a long fannish history, whereas changing racial identities pushes much further against the grain. And fandom norms often dictate which ships are preferred, further marginalizing forms of fan production that seek to transform our understandings of race. Given all of this, racebending represents a particularly vivid example of such negotiations, preserving aspects of the original characters fans have found pleasurable, while generating alternative representations.

Racebending as Encoding

Within fandom, racebending initially referred to discriminatory production decisions. Racebending.com (n.d.) uses the term to refer to:

> situations where a media content creator (movie studio, publisher, etc.) has changed the race or ethnicity of a character. This is a longstanding Hollywood practice that has been historically used to discriminate against people of color. More often than not, this practice has a resultant discriminatory impact on an underrepresented cultural community and actors from that community (reinforcement of glass ceilings, loss of opportunity, etc.)

This group coalesced around fan opposition to the casting decisions for a big screen adaptation of the popular animated series, *Avatar: The Last Airbender*. Lori Kido Lopez (2011) sums up the key issues:

> Despite the fact that the television show seemed to have appropriated cultural practices, architecture, religious iconography, costumes, calligraphy, and other aesthetic elements from East Asian and Inuit cultures, four white actors had been cast in the lead roles. Many fans became irate, demanding that the roles go to Asian actors because they had always imagined that the characters were racially Asian. (1)

Working through their existing networks and in partnership with more traditional advocacy groups, these fan activists educated the public about Hollywood's "white-casting" practices. Within fandom, much of their appeal was grounded in notions of "authenticity" and supported by a powerful consensus that "Aang [the protagonist] Ain't White."

This appeal is problematic. As Lopez notes, the campaign depended on an essentialized conception of what it meant to be Asian, one defined around pre-existing stereotypes and cultural references, which could reinforce orientalist fantasies. Further, similar arguments about protecting the authenticity of existing characters have been mounted by mostly white fans against Marvel's efforts to diversify its superhero characters (McWilliams 2013). When, for example, Michael B. Jordan was cast as Johnny Storm in *Fantastic Four*, the news media reported on white backlash accusing Hollywood of making "politically correct" decisions to "racebend" characters that had historically been white (Berlatsky, 2014). Here are a few characteristic responses from angered white fans:

> Why do they keep casting black people in roles that were made and written in the comics as white people NOWHERE in Fantastic Fours (sic) history has any of them EVER been black… the comic geeks (sic) like myself that know the true history of comic series' are up in arms over the discrepancies in these movies.
> (As quoted in, Warren 2014)

> (N)ot trying to sound racist here, but seriously, directors, Stop trying to change a superheroes (sic) race … Stick with the way they are in the comic books.
> (As quoted in, Warren 2014)

In this case, white fans speak from a privileged position precisely because they are making claims that are canonically and denotatively supported, where-as fans of color, fighting to change dominant representations, are forced to argue against such authenticity claims (except under rare circumstances). Absent from these news reports were those fans arguing that the producers were not going far enough, because they cast a white actress as Johnny's sister: "I am sad that, when Fox had a perfect opportunity to cast two people of color in their movie instead of just a token one, they decided to not go with it" (comment in response to Bricken 2014). Similar fan feuds have surrounded Black stormtroopers in *Star Wars:The Force Awakens* (Garcia 2015) and, even more ironically, around the all-Black cast in a television staging of the historically all-Black *The Wiz (Hello Beautiful Staff* 2015). Comics blogger Zina (2015) identifies the hidden assumptions behind such efforts:

> They constantly talk about how the white versions of the character being racebent is the one from their childhood, never once thinking that maybe people of color would like to be represented for a second … They couch their dislike in coded language and long-winded essays about how it's "disrespectful" to the original comic creators to give people of color representation … Never mind that these racebent roles don't often last and that they're not always guaranteed to be permanent.

The news media's focus on narratives of white backlash serves the interests of media producers, who often depict themselves as needing to go slow in developing more diverse representations for fear that they may alienate their consumer base.

Racebending as Re-Production

When Bennett (2015) refers to "racebending," she deploys a different definition—illustrating her piece with examples of fan art explicitly depicting a Black or mixed-race Hermione. In recent years, this sort of racebending has become a more widespread genre of fan cultural production. For example, the Tumblr site "Fuck Yeah, Racebending" assembles examples of "fan casting," collages and photo manipulations reimagining popular films and television series with more diverse casts. Such practices open alternative spaces for identification and also represent an explicit critique of Hollywood's casting practices, flagging minority performers who could have played such parts if they were not so undervalued and underemployed. There has been a long-standing meme in Harry Potter fandom re-imagining Harry as a South-Asian "desi." As one fan explains:

> All the blood status in the hp universe is a metaphor for racism but you know what's boring? Metaphors for racism that only involve white people ... If James Potter's family was desi and Lily Evans's was white, that would enhance Harry's feelings of otherness while growing up with the Dursleys.
>
> (halfdesiqueen, 2015)

Another fan artist, Vondell Swain (2014), imagines Harry with a Black father:

> James' skin color, hair texture, etc to my knowledge has never been specified and that means to me that even a reader who strictly contains themselves within the bounds of canon is free to imagine him as any number of ethnicities ... It reflects my desire to contribute to young people of color feeling empowered by popular fiction and not othered by it. It reflects my desire not to let blockbuster casting directors dictate what you may or may not imagine the characters that populate your fiction to be.

In both cases, these fans are taking advantage of denotative gaps to justify their own creative choices—negotiating room within the canon to imagine more diverse representations.

Not all fans of color agree that racebending existing characters is the best way to change the kinds of racial identities found within popular fictions. As one fan responded to Bennett's post:

> The reason why it's wrong is because ethnicity is a part of who you are, and changing it wouldn't be true to the character ... To have diversity in fiction we must CREATE diversity in fiction not change it!
>
> (comment in response to, Bennett 2015)

Bivouac (2014), an Asian-American blogger, reacted to another project that race-bends Disney characters, often in problematic ways:

> If you change someone's race, you'll need to change their entire story, too. You'll need to change the way people interact with the character, you'll need to change the character's culture, change their values, their identities and maybe their personality.

Fan fiction offers one way to more deeply reconsider how race matters for these characters. An Archive of Our Own hosted a "racebending revenge" story competition in 2010 in response to the struggles around *Last Airbender*:

> Re-write one or more white characters in the fandom(s) of your choice as chromatic/non-white/PoC, in a story of at least 500 words, with some acknowledgment of how the racial difference would make a difference to the story being told. [...] We want to know how a man called Sherlock Holmes in Victorian England would function if his skin was the colour of soot, or what Latino Dean and Sam Winchester would do to convince people to trust them, and if Buffy the Vampire Slayer can be Asian and still save the world (a lot).
>
> (dark_adminstrator 2010)

Such projects (DeKosnik, 2016) are not without their dangers, especially insofar as fan artists and writers embrace essentialized and stereotypical representations and as these types of projects invite participants who may be ignorant of the cultural and historical contexts from which such identity markers emerge:

> Alright, so you're going to turn Ariel brown and have her wear henna and a bindi but do you know the significance of these things? … It's easy enough to write a newly-recast character of colour like a white person if you don't know what you're doing, and it's even easier to recast a character as a POC, complete with whatever you as a white person/outsider think that race and culture should look and sound like, without realising the significance of that "aesthetic".
>
> (Bivouac, 2014)

Bennett's post sparked extensive debates about the appropriateness of racebending, helping us to map other fault-lines:

> Art is the creative expression of the author. It is their rightful intellectual property because it stems from individuality, not the audience. If the reader can't enjoy it for what it is, then simply don't bother changing it.
>
> (Comment in response to Bennett, 2015)

✳✳✳✳✳✳✳✳✳✳✳✳✳✳✳✳✳✳✳✳✳✳

> As far as I'm concerned, headcanon whatever you want. Just as long as you're not forcing others to accept your headcanon.
>
> (Comment in response to Bennett, 2015)

Both illustrate how implicit, yet widely shared, rules of interpretation inhibit, but do not fully restrict, fan interpretations. In the first case, the reader accepts constraints to protect authorial authority, whereas, in the second, a more tolerant attitude exists as long as a negotiated reading is not "forced" on others. But we are back in the space of "semiotic insufficiency": the phrase "headcanon" implies a gap between what the text "says" (denotation, canon) and what is in the "heads" of individual fans (connotation, interpretation). However, a consensus amongst larger numbers of fans can gain greater rhetorical force, becoming "fanon," and, thus, accepted as a shared term within debates about representation. Just as fans agree that "Aang ain't white," more and more also accept that Hermione might not be, either.

Final thoughts

Hall (1980) talks about a negotiated reading position, implying some fixity, whereas Gledhill (1988) understands negotiation as a process characterized by "flux, discontinuities, digressions rather than fixed positions" (73). As Bennett's account of her own evolving relationship with Hermione illustrates, readers have different relationships with texts, characters, producers, and other fans over time. Readers move through cycles of proximity and distance, enchantment and disenchantment, engagement and critique; they work through contradictions, repudiate negative elements, and embrace potentials. I am often asked why fans struggle so hard to make certain texts work for them rather than walk away, yet this is to understand fans simply as rejecting textual meanings, rather than seeing fandom as emerging from a strong affection for, among other factors, particular characters, even as those fans are often disappointed with how those characters get represented—again, both fascination *and* frustration. Furthermore, as we have seen, negotiation works at multiple levels: within the head of the individual fan, amongst and against other fans, and between fans and producers. The explicit discussions of interpretation and re-production within fandom render these various processes of negotiation more conscious and visible. Acts of meaning-making pave the way for new forms of cultural production.

The alternative representations that emerge from fan re-imaginings often remain within a closed community and thus are not necessarily accessible to the public at large. Yet, sometimes, these negotiated meanings help shape future iterations of the same franchise—one of the ways that fandom can play a progressive role in the struggle for a more diverse and inclusive popular culture. Shortly before Christmas 2015, the cast was announced for the West End stage production of *Harry Potter and the Cursed Child*, J. K. Rowling's continuation of her popular series. The production cast a Black actress, Noma Dumezweni, as the adult Hermione. Defending the casting choice in the face of the typical white backlash, Rowling tweeted: "Canon: brown eyes, frizzy hair and very clever. White skin was never specified. Rowling loves black Hermione" (Riviera, 2015).

Had she read Bennett's post? Was she responding to the general trend to racebend the *Harry Potter* characters? Is this simply another example of Rowling's ongoing process of "retconning" (or retrospectively rewriting her characters[1]) to reflect what she wishes she had written? We may never know, but the ability of such fan negotiations to move via social media into greater public visibility means that they do have the potential to impact both creative decisions and larger public responses to those decisions. As Bennett (2015) explains as she wraps up her own essay:

> Hermione Granger will always be an icon, no matter what color her skin. At least if I have anything to say about it. The least we could do is provide her with more room to be that icon. Maybe along the way more people will be able to see themselves reflected back at them.[2]

Notes

1. This text was written and first published prior to the news of J.K. Rowlings advocacy for what has widely been read as an "anti-trans" perspective.
2. I am grateful for helpful feedback I have received from Diana Lee, Joan Miller, Roxanne Samer, Abigail DeKosnik, Mel Stanfill, Rukmini Pande, and Patrick Johnson, each of whom is, through their own work, challenging our understandings of race, gender/sexuality, and fan identity.

References

Bennett, Alanna (2015), "What a 'Racebent' Hermione Granger Really Represents," *Buzzfeed*, February 1, www.buzzfeed.com/alannabennett/what-a-racebent-hermione-granger-really-represen-d2yp.
Berlatsky, Noah (2014), "The Incoherent Backlashes to Black Actors Playing 'White' Superheroes," *The Atlantic*, February 20, www.theatlantic.com/entertainment/archive/2014/02/the-incoherent-backlashes-to-black-actors-playing-white-superheroes/283979/.
Bivouac (2014),"On Racebending: We Are More Than Just a Twist," *Medium*, December 31, https://medium.com/@BIVOUAC/on-racebending-we-are-more-than-a-twist-ae11689265d3.
Bobo, Jacqueline (1995), *Black Women as Cultural Readers*, New York: Columbia University Press.
Bricken, Rob (2014),"This May Be the New Fantastic Four," *io9.com*, February 20, http://io9.com/this-may-be-the-new-fantastic-four-1526858787.
Condis, Megan (2014), "No Homosexuals in *Star Wars*? BioWare, 'Gamer' Identity, and the Politics of Privilege in a Convergence Culture," *Convergence: The International Journal of Research into New Media Technologies* 21(2): 198–212.
Cumberbatch, Chaka (2013), "I'm a Black Cosplayer and Some People Hate It," xoJane, February 4, www.xojane.com/issues/mad-back-cosplayer-chaka-cumberbatch.
dark_administrator (2010), "The Racebending Revenge Ficathon," *Dreamwidth*, June 4, http://dark-agenda.dreamwidth.org/7371.html.
De Kosnik, Abigail (2016), *Rogue Archives: Digital Cultural Memory and Media Fandom*, Cambridge: MIT Press.
Dyer, Richard (1997), *White: Essays on Race and Culture*, New York: Routledge.
Dyson, Anne Haas (1997), *Writing Superheroes: Contemporary Childhood, Popular Culture, and Classroom Literacy*, New York: Teachers College Press.
Fraser, Nancy (1990), "Rethinking the Public Sphere: A Contribution to the Critique of Actually Existing Democracy," *Social Text* 25/26: 56–80.
Garcia, Antero (2015), "#BoycottStarWarsVII, Racism and Classroom Responsibility," *DML Central*, October 22, http://dmlcentral.net/boycottstarwarsvii-racism-and-classroom-responsibility/.
Gledhill, Christine (1988), "Pleasurable Negotiations," in E. Deidre Pribram (ed.), *Female Spectators: Looking at Film and Television* (London: Verso), 64–89.
halfdesiqueen (2015), "Anonymous Asked: Can You Explain Why Many People Think Harry Potter Is Desi? Not Hating Just Curious! That's so Lovely!!" *3 am Headcanons Are the Best Headcannons*, August 8, http://harry-potter-headcanon.tumblr.com/post/126179755754/can-you-explain-why-many-people-think-harry-potter.
Hall, Stuart (1973; 1980), "Encoding/Decoding," in Stuart Hall et al. (eds.), *Culture, Media, Language*, London: Hutchinson, 134–148.
Hall, Stuart (1981; republished 2008),"Notes on Deconstructing 'The Popular'," in John Storey (ed.), *Cultural Theory and Popular Culture: A Reader*, New York: Routledge, 508–518.
Hall, Stuart (1992a), "Cultural Studies and Its Theoretical Legacies," in Kuan-Hsing Chen and David Morley (eds.), *Stuart Hall: Critical Dialogues in Cultural Studies*, London: Routledge, 1996 262–274.
Hall, Stuart (1992b),"What is This 'Black' in Black Popular Culture?" in Michele Wallace and Gina Dent (eds.), *Black Popular Culture: A Project*, Seattle, WA: Bay Press, 21–33.
Hello Beautiful Staff (2015),"Confused White People Are Shocked The Wiz Has an All Black Cast," *Newsone*, http://newsone.com/3281350/confused-white-people-are-shocked-the-wiz-has-an-all-black-cast/.
Jenkins, Henry (1992), *Textual Poachers: Television Fans and Participatory Culture*, New York: Routledge.
Jenkins, Henry, Sam Ford, and Joshua Green (2013), *Spreadable Media: Creating Meaning and Value in a Networked Culture*, New York: New York University Press.
Lopez, Lori Kido (2011),"Fan Activists and the Politics of Race in The Last Airbender," *International Journal of Cultural Studies* 15(5): 431–445.
McWilliams, Ora C. (2013), "Who Is Afraid of a Black Spider(-Man)?" in Matthew Costello (ed.), "Appropriating, Interpreting, and Transforming Comic Books" special issue, *Transformative*

Works and Cultures 13, http://journal.transformativeworks.org/index.php/twc/article/view/455/355.

Miller, D. A. (1990), "Anal Rope," *Representations* 32(Fall): 114–133.

Miller, Joan (2015), "Raceplay: Cross-Racial Pop-Culture as Political Activism," *Academia. edu*, www.academia.edu/10338896/Raceplay_Cross-racial_pop-culture_cosplay_as_political_activism.

Morrison, Toni (1993), *Playing in the Dark; Whiteness and the Literary Imagination*, New York: Vintage.

Phalen, Peggy (1993), *Unmarked: The Politics of Performance*, New York: Routledge.

Racebending.com (n.d.), "What Is 'Racebending'?," www.racebending.com/v4/about/what-is-race bending/.

Riviera, Natalie (2015), "J. K. Rowling's Response to a Black Hermoine Is Perfect," *Popsugar*, December 22, www.popsugar.com/celebrity/JK-Rowling-Responds-Black-Hermione-39499803.

Rowling, J. K. (1999), *Harry Potter and the Prisoner of Azkaban*, London: Bloomsbury.

Stanfill, Mel (2011), "Doing Fandom, (Mis)doing Whiteness: Heteronormativity, Racialization, and the Discursive Construction of Fandom," in Robin Anne Reid and Sarah Gatson (eds.), "Race and Ethnicity in Fandom," special issue, *Transformative Works and Cultures* 8, http://journal.transformativeworks.org/index.php/twc/article/view/256/243.

Swain, Vondell (2014), untitled Tumblr post, http://vondellswain.tumblr.com/post/78532381055/its vondell-my-hp-headcanons-all-have-and.

Wanzo, Rebecca (2015), "African American Acafandom and Other Strangers: New Genealogies of Fan Studies," *Transformative Works and Cultures* 20, http://journal.transformativeworks.org/index.php/twc/article/view/699/538.

Warner, Michael (2005), *Publics and Counterpublics*, New York: Zone Books.

Warren, Ken "Kwik" (2014), "Comic Book Geeks in Uproar over Black Human Torch; Won't Be Long Before Megyn Kelly Chimes in," *Daily Kos*, February 20, www.dailykos.com/story/2014/02/20/1279001/-Comic-Book-Geeks-in-Uproar-Over-Black-Human-Torch-Won-t-Be-Long-Before-Megyn-Kelly-Chimes-In.

Williams, Stereo (2015), "Amandla Stenberg Understands Appropriation Better Than You," *The Daily Beast*, April 17, www.thedailybeast.com/articles/2015/04/17/amandla-stenberg-understands-appropriation-better-than-you.html.

Zina (2015), "Dear Comic Fans: We Get It. You are Racist and Racebending Scares You," *Stitch's Media Mix*, August 7, https://stitchmediamix.wordpress.com/2015/08/07/dear-comic-fans-we-get-it-youre-racist-and-racebending-scares-you/.

16

SHIFTING, *HARRY POTTER*, AND TIKTOK FAN PRACTICES

Claire Whitley and Katharine Perrotta

In April of 2021, TikTok account @livshifts111 posted a video claiming they had just returned from seven months studying at Hogwarts, the fictional wizarding school for children in J.K. Rowling's *Harry Potter* book series. This video was not the first of its kind: a similar video posted in 2020 by a different TikTok user, @marleyswaffordd, depicted a crying young person with the caption: "its 4:00 AM, i just woke up from a shift of 8 months at hogwarts. i want to go back, let me leave." These users, and many like them, were some of the first on TikTok to articulate and popularize what would come to be known as "Reality Shifting" or "Shifting", in which a person's consciousness is believed to shift from their Current Reality (CR) to a different or "Desired Reality" (DR). Although the practice of Shifting does not inherently lend itself to one particular social media platform (and is claimed to have existed as a practice long before the advent of social media [Stgviez 2023]), it has risen to substantial prominence on TikTok. While the online practices of media fandoms have been extensively studied, the recent emergence of TikTok as one of the most prominent social media platforms of the 2020s offers further opportunities for scholarly analysis on online fan practices. The purpose of this chapter, therefore, is to introduce the practice of Shifting and its associations with fandom to the academic context, and to offer a preliminary approach to studying ShiftTok as a fan community.

The Unique Sociality of TikTok

Communal sociality on TikTok emphasizes "creative interaction… over discursive interaction" (Zulli and Zulli 2022: 1873). This emphasis, coupled with the increased viewer engagement resulting from a creator's use of trending audios and formats, ensures that mimesis is positioned as "the basis of sociality on the site" (Zulli and Zulli 2022: 1873). As a fan community based on TikTok, ShiftTok therefore foregrounds mimesis as an integral part of its functionality. This is observed most clearly in Shifters' frequent employment of the "Use This Sound" feature, which "allows users to use, remix, and transform the audio from other videos" and which Ariadna Matamoros Fernández argues "is TikTok's central build-in technical feature for memetic engagement" (2022: 2).

The intersection of these TikTok practices with the development of the community around Shifting has had significant ramifications for the way this community understands and engages with moral permissibility. This chapter therefore presents and examines the phenomenon of ShiftTok and its use of TikTok as a space for community, surveillance, and moral arbitration. ShiftTok's prominence is evidenced by its high viewership: at the time of writing, the hashtag #shifttok had 5.7 billion views. As a popular online fan practice, ShiftTok offers unique insight into a distinct kind of fan engagement which relies on communally enforced codes of morality and an eschewing of the anonymity often associated with these online spaces. Also important to note about the unique structure of ShiftTok as a community is that it is not unified around a particular object: Shifters are first and foremost fans of the act of Shifting itself, while the texts they aspire to Shift to are varied and numerous. While ShiftTok as a fan-built entity therefore intersects with several fandoms, this work will focus primarily on the section of the Shifting community which centers around the *Wizarding World* franchise, and specifically, the *Harry Potter* book and film series.

This focus on *Harry Potter* is first and foremost because of the extensive work already done on its fandom (Brown 2011; Martens 2019; Seymour 2018). With academic (and popular) understanding of and familiarity with *Harry Potter* – both as an object and as a site particularly suited for online fan discourses and engagement (Martens 2019) – already established, this work can focus on how this object intersects with the practice of Shifting and ShiftTok. The intersection of *Harry Potter* fandom and ShiftTok also developed organically through ShiftTok's rise to prominence occurring at the same time as #DracoTok, a fandom reappraisal of *Harry Potter* character Draco Malfoy, which took place in April of 2020.

An Introduction to Shifting

To understand Shifting as both a fan practice and a community of fans, it is important to first understand what Shifting *is*. Common verbiage within the Shifting community dictates that the process of Shifting entails sending one's consciousness into a different Desired Reality. The types of DRs shifters believe themselves to inhabit are vast and varied: they may range from popular works of fiction such as *Harry Potter* and *Star Wars* to realities in which the Shifter is famous, dating a celebrity, or simply a different age. Most Shifting focuses on a relationship between a Shifter and a character or celebrity – a common motivational question exchanged between Shifters is "who are you shifting for?" Shifters may also be encouraged to Shift to "rewire old traumas" (Christine and C 2022) through the ability their DR gives them to redeem or "fix" undesirable elements or events that have occurred in their Current Realities.

The idea that the details of a DR can contribute to the real-life mental wellbeing of a Shifter mirrors early theories of fan pathologies. As Joli Jensen argues, popular and academic identification of fans as "obsessive" or "fanatical" (1992: 18) has pathologized fan behavior as deviant. Fans, Jensen argues, are perceived to be at risk of isolation, destructive behaviors, and deviancy because of their alleged inability to remain rationally detached from their preferred object. As a result, it follows that they are unable to "distinguish the real from the imaginary" (1992: 18) and are therefore susceptible to fanatical behaviors which destroy their social, mental, or even physical wellbeing. By contrast, ShiftTok's communal approach to Shifting as a healing or reparative practice – one which apparently allows for the creation of safe and meaningful relationships and a reprieve from trauma acquired in the real world – reframes this pathologization. ShiftTok's focus on the reparative nature of the blurring of real and imaginary, which was once a key site for the pathologization of the fan as isolated and deviant, is further indication of its significance as an emergent fan practice.

The popularity of ShiftTok has instigated an array of content creation, encompassing guides for hopeful Shifters, "explainer" videos, and even podcasts. In one such podcast, *Get Shifty*, popular ShiftTok Shifters @sectumsempress and @cshitposts2 describe shifting as follows: "Reality Shifting is the practice of becoming aware of deeper layers of consciousness that you previously thought unreachable… it feels like a real, physical experience" (Christine and C 2022). ShiftTok content creation also extends to the production and distribution of community symbols – the most popular of which depicts two circles stacked on top of each other with a vertical line through both shapes. These symbols are generally used to discreetly identify fellow Shifters. For most ShiftTokers, the process of Shifting is made possible by the existence of multiple realities and involves a person's consciousness moving from their CR to an alternative reality.

Shifting also involves rigid processes which facilitate effective and fulfilling Shifting experiences. One such process is "scripting," described on r/shiftingrealities as "how you decide what your desired reality (the place you're shifting to) is going to be like… Basically anything you want to change about this reality can go in your script" (PopKitsune 2021). This, the element of fan labor most like fanfiction, provides a scaffolding to set the parameters of a DR. Shifters will write, in varying levels of detail, the story they wish to experience when Shifting, similar to self-insert fanfiction. It is common for Shifters to script both aesthetic and physiological changes to their body, ranging anywhere from giving themselves freckles to the ability to avoid death.

The practice of Shifting itself often involves induction methods utilized by Shifters to travel to their Desired Reality. These are referred to as "methods" and commonly include a mixture of meditation and positive affirmations such as "I have Shifted to my Desired Reality." Some Shifters will listen to "subliminals" when they Shift, YouTube videos that include a mixture of ambient sounds, music, affirmations, and sometimes lines of dialogue from the films which they are attempting to Shift to. Somer et al. hypothesize that the process Shifters describe is similar to self-hypnosis, dissociation, lucid dreaming, or maladaptive daydreaming (2021). Though we cannot definitively argue whether this Reality Shifting is happening, we can understand this community as being held together by their dedication to Shifting as a *real* phenomenon.

In addition to the tools ostensibly designed to build a robust and immersive Shifting experience, there are also many rules which a Shifter must follow to align with the moral codes of the Shifting community. This morality usually mirrors contemporary discourses around identity politics, sexuality, and interpersonal power dynamics, and therefore these Shifting rules are commonly agreed upon and arbitrated by the collective. For example, it is widely considered taboo to script sexual assault into a DR, primarily because this is viewed as amoral "trauma porn." There are also moral guidelines which align with contemporary age-gap discourse. For example, if a Shifter is over 18 or legally an adult, it's expected that they age up the fictional characters they will engage with in their DR to avoid what is seen as sexual misconduct. As a result, many adult *Harry Potter* fans Shift to a universe in which Hogwarts is a university. The extent to which these rules are determined and policed by the Shifting community at large is a central consideration of this chapter's analysis of ShiftTok as a community.

Community

Belonging to the Shifting community is unique in that it implies at least two allegiances – one to the text the fan wants to Shift to, and one to the practice and theory of Shifting itself. This is further complicated by the practice of Shifting to a Desired Reality in which the Shifter is famous, or simply a different age. These realities are not pre-established in fiction, and instead function as a kind of wish fulfilment universe for the Shifter. So, while a love of *Harry Potter* may have been what Henry Jenkins describes as a "point of entry into a broader fan community" (2013: 40) of Shifting, it is important to recognize Shifting and ShiftTok as a fully formed fan practice within itself, independent of a specific media text.

One way that ShiftTokers cultivate community is through a framework of fan curation as outlined by Derek Kompare: fan curators are "more established fans… with deeper knowledge of, and access to, the fandom and its texts… The key thing is that curators organize their expertise in service of bringing new people into the fandom" (2017: 107). In the context of ShiftTok and the Shifting community more broadly, these fan curators perform a key role in inducting new Shifters, providing advice to less experienced Shifters around the details and nuances of different methods, and compiling vast amounts of information into one place to form "one-stop shops" for hopeful Shifters. In short, fan curators operate as arbiters of the internal communal discourses that permeate ShiftTok.

These curators obtain the "more established" moniker for one key reason: they have ostensibly actually Shifted, and most have done so multiple times. This achievement is highly desirable, and doubly so because it has proven to be elusive for many Shifters, with many expressing frustration at their inability to Shift despite months (or in some cases, years) of trying. Many seek motivation from others, bemoan how "sure" they were that they would finally be successful, or track their attempts through recording the length of time they have been attempting to Shift or the number of "methods" they have tried during the process (see Figure 16.1).

Figure 16.1 A selection of TikTok videos which establish the elusivity of successful Shifting.

Fan curators in the Shifting community therefore act as guides and motivators for these unsuccessful Shifters, answering questions about what worked for them and speaking with authority as someone who has undergone the experience. This also allows them to offer insights into the experiences Shifters may hope to have themselves, or give feedback on what may be useful to script beforehand. As leaders or authorities, these curators may also share their favorite subliminal materials or their Shifting routines. They may also compile "encyclopedic media" (Kompare 2017: 109) in the form of detailed subreddits, which can include Frequently Asked Questions, scripting templates or master lists of Shifting methods. Frequently Asked Questions in particular are often utilized to further emphasise "appropriate" Shifting behavior, and include answers to questions like "Do I have to drink a lot of water to shift? How much water do I need?" and "Is shifting to experience love / a specific relationship immoral and against free will?" (r/shiftingrealities, 2021) This encyclopedic media even extends to the discovery and circulation of allegedly secret CIA documents which are argued within the community to prove the legitimacy of Shifting and a governmental awareness of its power (r/shiftingrealities 2021). Another instance of this fan curation can be seen in the development and popularity of the *Get Shifty* podcast, which details Shifting experiences and "hot takes" about the shifting community.

Surveillance and Monitoring Morality on ShiftTok

The intensive gatekeeping that occurs on ShiftTok has significantly characterized the community and reflects contemporary online culture more broadly. Because the processes of Shifting are so personal and intangible, and yet so highly regulated, a pattern of peer monitoring and surveillance has become an immutable characteristic of this community. This permeates every element of the Shifting experience: peer surveillance ensures "misinformation" is not spread about the Shifting community and its methods, and "red flags" (@shiftingwithkarms 2022) are identified and signify to others that a ShiftToker may be lying about their experience. Most significantly, rigid codes of morality, particularly around sexuality, are imposed and upheld by this network of surveillance. This policing and surveillance are described by Melissa Gregg as a form of affective fan labor that is often present in fan communities existing within Web 2.0 (2009).

One such example of this policing comes from the account of prominent ShiftToker @lenarblack (2021). In their video, @lenarblack has "stitched" (a term for what is essentially a video "reply" to an earlier post) a video wherein another creator describes her experience with Shifting. However, @lenarblack states that this experience does not align with their view of Shifting as a concept and therefore unequivocally indicates their dishonesty to "the entire Shifting community." "I don't want to start drama, but I want to bring attention to some of the things that she's done," @lenarblack says. "Namely, lying about Shifting." @lenarblack then goes on to detail the original poster's transgressions against the community – most significantly, accusing them of lying about Shifting. When commenting on the original poster's claims about the difficulties of the physical experience of Shifting, @lenarblack declares that "This would be really sad, if it had actually ever happened to you. This is not physically possible, and it's not how Shifting works." Moreover, @lenarblack also accuses the original poster of engaging in behavior in their DR that is tantamount to sexual misconduct because of the poster's recounting of an incident in which they accidentally administered a love potion to a *Harry Potter* character. In response to this, @lenarblack condemns these actions as "basically non-consensual."

This post by @lenarblack offers a microcosmic insight into the practices of surveillance and moral arbitration utilized by those in the ShiftTok community to secure and maintain the legitimacy of their activities. Despite discourses of "individual Shifting journeys," the rules which Shifters must adhere to are stringently followed in practice and associated with a morality that mirrors contemporary discourses around consent and sexual autonomy. Moreover, the style of this video aligns with forms of content specific to TikTok as a platform. Through the platform's "stitch" feature, ShiftTokers can create videos which serve the dual purpose of gatekeeping and content creation, aligning with the platform's prioritisation of "creative interaction" over "discursive interaction" (Zulli and Zulli 2022: 1873). By using the stitch function, ShiftTokers engage in discourse within the functionality and design affordances of TikTok as an app – creating their own content instead of simply engaging in off-app or in-comment discourse. In this way, new artefacts are consistently being created which dictate the acceptability and permissibility of Shifting practices.

Producing and Performing Evidence

In addition to the surveillance and gatekeeping that occurs (particularly in instances of undesirable behavior), ShiftTokers also engage with each other and build community through the dissemination of video content that serves as evidence of their Shift. This production and distribution of evidence may manifest through the typical TikTok story-time, but much more commonly, through the performance of interactions and exchanges the Shifter has experienced within their DR. This kind of evidence – which is a performance of an already-embodied experience occurring within a fan-constructed fictive universe – forms the basis of many of the community-building and maintenance practices found throughout ShiftTok. This material is therefore ostensibly a performance intended to offer insight into what these characters and situations "are really like" while allowing creators to talk through and unpack the very real and tangible impact these experiences have on them. This practice is therefore both performative and confessional, with ShiftTokers taking the position all at once of established "fan curator" (Kompare 2017) and innovative traverser of a brand-new knowledge community (Jenkins 2013: 20).

To understand the different styles of material that Shifters create to evidentiate their Shift, a simple taxonomy of video formats is helpful. While Shifting content is also produced on Reddit and YouTube, ShiftTok content is uniquely governed by the specific sociality of the platform itself. Zulli and Zulli describe TikTok as a unique platform which creates community via transformation and replication of popular TikTok formats or "sounds," observing that "imitation and replication are digitally and socially encouraged by the TikTok platform, positioning mimesis as the basis of sociality on the site" (Zulli and Zulli 2022: 1873). It is important, therefore, when discussing Shifting content, to consider the content formats that are consistently used by ShiftTokers and are subsequently transformed and replicated by them.

Though somewhat reductive of the myriad styles of TikTok and ShiftTok content, evidence on ShiftTok tends to be created in two main formats: Vlog Style and Theater Style. Vlog Style draws on the informal YouTube genre in which a creator may sit down in front of the camera and speak casually about an event. On ShiftTok, Vlog Style functions in much the same way – Shifters will sit, often in their home, and position the camera at eyeline and in portrait mode. Shifters will then engage in "story time" in which they will recount an event which happened in their DR, using minimal or no editing to evoke the feeling of a continuous and casual encounter. This style prioritizes intimacy and relatability, recalling the affordances and style of a FaceTime call. In this way, Vlog Style is used within ShiftTok to reinforce notions of community and authenticity, while also positioning particular creators as "authorities."

Prominent ShiftTok creator @cshitposts often evidences their Shifts using Vlog Style. In a TikTok posted on the May 21, 2023, captioned "it's been a while, here's what you missed! #shiftingstories #shifting realities #shifttok," they update their audience on the most recent events of their DR: "It's been a really long time, so here's what's been happening in my DRs. I am currently on sabbatical from being a professor at Hogwarts" (@cshitposts, 2023). The ShiftToker has set up their phone at eye-level and is recording in what appears to be their home, denoted by a couch and a small cameo from their cat at certain points within the video. Their speech here is a direct-to-camera address, their language is casual and friendly, echoing the style of "story-time" vloggers like IJustine or Casey Neistat. Moreover, background music choices within Vlog Style content have also been adapted from YouTube, commonly using royalty-free instrumental music being played at a low volume to allow for clarity of speech.

While Vlog Style prioritizes the recounting of a Shifting experience, the format of Theater Style emphasizes the embodied re-creation and re-living of a Shifting event. Theater Style – which we are proposing as an umbrella term to encompass most other forms of evidentiary content – breaks down into three distinct categories, wherein the Shifter uses their videos to embody the characters from within their DR, and as a result, provides evidence of the legitimacy of their experience. The first category of evidence identifiable under Theater Style resembles a theatrical play in which the Shifter will use both their voice and their body to read dialogue and perform events which have occurred in their DR. Popular ShiftTokers such as @sectumsempress use this format to produce evidence of their Shifts. When reproducing this format, ShiftTokers will frame themselves in a mid to wide shot, using the app's standard portrait framing. They will then use the principles of continuity editing (eye-line matches, the 180-degree rule, etc.) to create visual consistency between two or more characters. ShiftTokers will also use different costumes and acting styles to provide an embodied performance of their Shifting experience. Interestingly, these costumes are not meant to *represent* different characters, but are instead used to visually differentiate between characters on screen. For example, when performing the role of Mad Eye Moody, @sectumsempress (2022) does not dress up in cosplay, but instead simply changes their shirt. Shifters are therefore able to maintain a semblance of *self* while expressing the characters that are present within their DR (Figure 16.2).

The second category of Theater Style evidence sees the Shifter mime, rather than speak, the dialogue that has apparently already occurred within their DR, while a popular TikTok sound (usually an instrumental or otherwise unobtrusive soundtrack) plays overtop. Captions will then be used to express the dialogue that has been experienced within the Shifter's DR. ShiftTokers therefore use this format to evidence their Shifting experience, while also maintaining a level of congruence with TikTok's most popular audios. This category is similar to the previous in that ShiftTokers will use the same principles of continuity editing to create visual consistency across different characters; however, it is not common

Shifting, Harry Potter, *and TikTok Fan Practices*

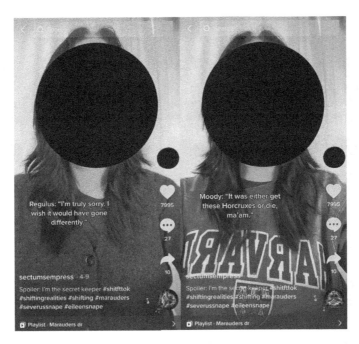

Figure 16.2 Stills from a TikTok video which demonstrate the creator using changes in casual clothing to signify different characters.

for ShiftTokers to change costumes in between characters, nor is it common for them to change their style of acting (Figure 16.3).

The final type of evidentiary content often produced in Theater Style – and the most similar to the mimetic style of TikTok as a medium – uses viral TikTok sounds to express a mood or theme that is common within the Shifter's DR. As established, TikTok as a platform is designed to encourage sociality through mimetic engagement (Matamoros-Fernandez 2023; Zulli and Zulli 2022), so the ways in which Shifters approach TikTok's "Use this Sound" feature is not unique to ShiftTok. The universality of this mimetic engagement, however, does mean that it is foundational to how Shifters engage with their community and further prove their familiarity with Shifting practices. For example, a Shifter will mime along to a viral sound, wherein two people are having a conversation. The Shifter will then use captions that slightly re-write or alter the dialogue in the given sound, all while maintaining the mood of the viral clip. The Shifter will then label themselves as a character from within their DR, distinguishing between characters by using simple shot-reverse-shot editing techniques and eye-line matches.

While Shifters do not claim that the conversation within the TikTok sound happened verbatim within their DR, the video is used to express the kind of relationships or themes that the sound evokes, once again using popular TikTok audios to create content which creates a congruence between ShiftTok and TikTok's broader viral formats. In one such example, popular ShiftToker @starkortmall777 (2022) uses a viral TikTok sound attributed to YouTubers Arcana Craniacs labelled "OMGGG" (which includes the dialogue "It's behind you," "What?," "Look," "Oh my God") to express the relationship between her and some

Figure 16.3 Stills from a TikTok video which demonstrate the use of continuity editing (shot-reverse-shot, eyeline match) to distinguish between characters.

minor characters from *Harry Potter* – Blaise Zabini, Gregory Goyle, and Lavender Brown. This sound, which went viral in 2022 with 69,500 videos, was used outside of ShiftTok too, effectively aligning shifting content with the platform-specific mimesis of TikTok.

The common utilization of Theater Style for the performance and provision of evidence on ShiftTok raises the issue of the fan body and its unique function on ShiftTok as a fan space. Francesca Coppa's analysis of the "body" in fanfiction offers a framework with which to approach this subject. Coppa's argument that the body in fanfiction functions much the same as a body in a dramatic performance does (that is, that the body is "the carrier of symbolic action" [2014: 229]) – aligns with how ShiftTokers both experience Shifting and provide proof of that Shifting. Following a "successful" Shift, the preferred mode of evidence delivery for prominent ShiftTokers is this Theater Style acting out – frequently apparently verbatim – of various DR experiences. As established, a ShiftToker's representation of characters through Theater Style demonstrations serves to offer their followers "insight" into their experience, but also as further "proof" of the authenticity of their familiarity with the fictive world. Coppa's theories on the function and position of the body in fanfiction, therefore, are useful as a framework for how we may approach the intersection of fandom and the practice of Shifting.

Analyzing Shifting as an emergent fan practice, and ShiftTok as the result of this practice, offers substantial insight into the changing nature of online fan communities. ShiftTok's reliance on fan-driven content creation by virtue of its platform on TikTok has resulted in a communal culture that emphasizes the sharing of knowledge and "authentic' experiences. What remains to be seen, however, is whether the self-imposed policing and gatekeeping so rigidly enforced by the Shifting community ensures its continued function, or if it is this very policing which renders this particular type of fan practice unsustainable.

References

Brown, S. (2011) "Harry Potter and the Fandom Menace," in B. Cova, R.V. Kozinets & A. Shankar (eds.) *Consumer Tribes*, London: Routledge, pp. 177–191.

Coppa, F. (2014) "Writing Bodies in Space: Media Fan Fiction as Theatrical Performance," in K. Hellekson & K. Busse (eds.) *The Fan Fiction Studies Reader*, Iowa: University of Iowa Press, pp. 218–237.

Gregg, M. (2009) "Learning to (Love) Labour: Production Cultures and the Affective Turn," *Communication and Critical/Cultural Studies*, 6(2), pp. 209–215.

Jenkins, H. (2013) *Textual Poachers: Television Fans and Participatory Culture*, Oxfordshire: Taylor & Francis.

Jensen, J. (1992) "Fandom as Pathology: The Consequences of Characterization," in L.A. Lewis (ed.) *The Adoring Audience Fan Culture and Popular Media*, London: Routledge, pp. 9–30.

Kompare, D. (2017) "Fan Curators and the Gateways into Fandom," in M.A. Click & S. Scott (eds.) *The Routledge Companion to Media Fandom*, New York: Routledge, pp. 107–113.

Martens, M. (2019) *The Forever Fandom of Harry Potter: Balancing Fan Agency and Corporate Control*, Cambridge: Cambridge University Press.

Matamoros-Fernández, A. (2023) "Taking Humor Seriously on TikTok," *Social Media + Society*, 9(1), pp. 1–4. https://doi.org/10.1177/20563051231157609

Seymour, J. (2018) "Racebending and Prosumer Fanart Practices in Harry Potter Fandom," in P. Booth (ed.) *A Companion to Media Fandom and Fan Studies*, Oxford: Wiley Blackwell, pp. 333–349.

Somer, E.C., E. Catelan, and R.F. Sofer-Dudek (2021) "Reality Shifting: Psychological Features of an Emergent Online Daydreaming Culture," *Current Psychology*, 42, pp. 11415–11427. https://doi.org/10.1007/s12144-021-02439-3

Zulli, D. and D.J. Zulli (2022) "Extending the Internet Meme: Conceptualizing Technological Mimesis and Imitation Publics on the TikTok platform," *New Media & Society*, 24(8), pp. 1872–1890. https://doi.org/10.1177/1461444820983603

Primary Sources

AutoModerator (2021) "'START HERE' [Online Forum Post]," *Reddit r/shiftingrealities*. Available at www.reddit.com/r/shiftingrealities/comments/mn86d1/start_here/ (Accessed 30 July 2023).

Christine and C. "[Get Shifty Podcast]. Get Shifty Ep 1: What is Reality Shifting?." Available at www.youtube.com/watch?v=irc6XFozNlA&t=908s&ab_channel=GetShiftyPodcast (Accessed 13 January 2022).

PopKitsune (2021) "'New to Shifting? Here's Some Common Questions and Misconceptions!' [online forum post]," *Reddit r/shiftingrealities*. Available at www.reddit.com/r/shiftingrealities/comments/m8sxz4/new_to_shifting_heres_some_common_questions_and/ (Accessed 30 July 2023).

Stgviez (2023) "'Shifting in Ancient Times, Short Examples' [online forum post]," *Reddit r/shiftingrealities*. Available at www.reddit.com/r/shiftingrealities/comments/12oumbt/shifting_in_ancient_times_short_examples/ (Accessed 2 August 2023).

@cshitposts (2023 May 21). Available at www.tiktok.com/@cshitposts/video/7235299611940834603?_t=8ediYlwd4rQ&_r=1 (Accessed 7 August 2023).

@lenarblack (2021). Available at www.tiktok.com/@lenarblack?lang=en (Accessed 22 June 2022).

@livshifts111 (2021 April 6). Available at www.tiktok.com/@livshifts111?lang=en (Accessed 22 June 2022).

@marleyswaffordd (2020). Available at www.tiktok.com/@mjsoh33/video/6870039580406549766 (Accessed 7 August 2023).

@sectumsempress (2022 April 21). Available at www.tiktok.com/@sectumsempress?lang=en (Accessed 22 June 2022).

@shiftingwithkarms (2022 January 27). Available at www.tiktok.com/@shiftwithkarms/video/ 7057667544622189830?q=shift%20tok%20red%20flags&t=1691409419989 (Accessed 7 August 2023).
@starkortmall777 (2022 February 19). Available at www.tiktok.com/@starkortmall777/video/7066 140506283265326?_r=1&_t=8ediZrcFrwg (Accessed 7 August 2023).

Images

@minimalfoyy (2022 August 8). Available at www.tiktok.com/@mimimalfoyy/video/712916877637 7158918?_r=1&_t=8edjHGFdtRg (Accessed 7 August 2023)
@starkortmall777 (2023 June 22). Available at www.tiktok.com/@starkortmall777/video/72472441 86750061866 (Accessed 7 August 2023)
@sectumsempress (2022 April 21). Available at www.tiktok.com/@sectumsempress?lang=en (Accessed 22 June 2022).
@starkortmall777 (2022 April 26). Available at www.tiktok.com/@starkortmall777/video/70906659 06237459754?_t=8edjhyrXwXQ&_r=1 (Accessed 7 August 2023).
@strangershania111 (2023 February 20). Available at www.tiktok.com/@strangershania111/video/ 7202046933685325102?_r=1&_t=8edjEzXAsrw (Accessed 7 August 2023).

17
TUMBLR FAN AESTHETICS

Louisa Ellen Stein

As fan communities move from one digital platform to another, the tenor of fan communication and creativity changes. Fans choose particular platforms because they seem to better fit the needs of a fan community or the evolving foci of the larger multifannish culture. At the same time, fan aesthetic traditions evolve in response to the affordances and limitations of the particular platforms in use at a given moment (Stein and Busse 2009). Each interface used by fans develops and maintains its own community norms, expectations, and limits of code and culture. In some cases, fans will use a given interface in a way consistent with its officially stated intent. In other instances, fans use interfaces in unintended, negotiative, and even resistant ways. This chapter focuses on fans' negotiative use of the visual microblogging site Tumblr, with special attention to the emerging aesthetic traditions that have evolved out of the friction between fan and interface.

In the last decade, Tumblr has emerged as a dominant growth space for fan activity and authorship. Fans use Tumblr in tandem with other sites, including Dreamwidth, Archive of Our Own, Twitter, YouTube, 8Tracks, DeviantArt, and many others. Within this multiplatform context, Tumblr highlights an aesthetic of abundant multiplicity and multidirectional flow. Perhaps this emphasis on abundance is most clearly seen in Tumblr's "infinite scrolling," where you can continuously scroll through posts made by other Tumblrs you "follow," or through posts made with a specific hashtag. Where Tumblr can feel opaque and confusing to newcomers, at the same time its various design elements—most especially infinite scrolling—convey a sensation of limitlessness; no need to click on an arrow or the word "next." Just keep scrolling and the Tumblr posts keep coming.

History

For the sake of context, let us look for a moment at the interface that immediately preceded Tumblr as fandom's home base, and that persists in various forms alongside Tumblr: LiveJournal (LJ). LJ was founded in 1999 as a journaling system intended to keep young adult friends in touch. Although not initially created with fandom in mind as a userbase, by the early 2000s, LJ seemed the place to be for fan communities (Moellenberndt 2013).

But things were soon to change. In May of 2007, what became known to fans as "Strikethrough" shook many fans' trust in LJ. Prompted by a conservative, religious special interest group called "Warriors," LJ deleted (indicated by their names being struck through) a range of fannish journals that included erotic fan fiction, on the grounds that their "interests lists" included topics related to pornography (Hellekson 2015: 130; Larsen and Zubernis 2013: 20). Widespread concern in LJ fan communities led many to sign up for accounts on other journaling sites based on the LJ code (as LJ was open source and thus facilitated many copies), including DeadJournal, InsaneJournal, and JournalFen.

And yet no mass exodus from LJ occurred, at least not all at once or in an organized fashion. In 2007 the core of fannish discussion still centered in LJ, but fans on LJ were now discussing how they could better control their own creative communities online. Fans created the LJ community "fanarchive" in 2007 to plan what would eventually become the fan-designed, owned, and run archive, An Archive of Our Own (A03), supported by not-for-profit Organization for Transformative Works (also founded in 2007). Alongside the development of A03, fans founded and developed the journaling site Dreamwidth (DW) in 2009, a fan-friendly rework (or fork) of the LJ code.

Enter Tumblr

It was in this era of transition for fandom's social media usage, with various fan-created social media projects in the works but not yet available, that Tumblr entered the picture. David Karp founded the microblogging site in 2007. Tumblr evolved alongside Dreamwidth, A03, and Twitter (as well as Pinterest, Instagram, DeviantArt, etc.) as digital platforms used by fandom to together form a cross-platform fandom footprint. Tumblr was bought by Yahoo in 2013 for $1.1 billion, but despite fan concerns over the implications of the buyout, Tumblr still remained (and remains) a significant home to fan communities.

From the start, some key elements of Tumblr appeared to align well with fannish concerns. From its initial entry in 2007, Tumblr offered users the ability to share visual images, still and moving, combined with limited text, in what seemed like a fresh aesthetic, although in truth it had evolved from prior platforms Projectionst and Anarchia (Alfonso). With its unfamiliar and somewhat opaque-to-outsiders interface, Tumblr felt less policed in comparison with fans' perception of LJ after Strikethrough. Tumblr's seeming illegibility to outsiders, while a deterrent for some fans, also functioned as part of its appeal. Like LJ, users navigated Tumblr via hyperlinked interests, but Tumblr's user-driven tagging practice seemed more excessive and disorganized, sometimes even put to expressive rather than organizational purposes (e.g. a hashtag might read #ilovethisshowsomuch). Tumblr seemed to offer a coded public, in which individual authorship was subsumed into the collective, and within which transgressive meanings could hide in plain sight.

Tumblr's reblogging logic, in which a user could easily "reblog" any post they find onto their own dashboard, with or without the addition of notes, resonated with fan practices of return, recirculation, and transformative reworking. Posts on Tumblr could be reposted tens of thousands of times, giving them the weight of community-held beliefs or community-hailed icons. This recirculation and reworking of cultural meaning meshed with fandom's valuing of transformative reworking and repeating of tropes and beloved images. Tumblr's particular brand of reblogging also resonated with fandom's emphasis on a multiplicity of interpretations and affective returns to beloved media objects. Moreover, retumbling suggested a copyright stance that embraced the collective creative repurposing of already existing media, a core value for much of fandom (Rodrigo). Indeed, Tumblr's emphasis on collective authorship yielded a sense of power in multiplicity, including the power to evade cultural policing.

Tumblr's approach to microblogging encouraged visual textual conversation and thus a sense of community based on the synthesis of text and visual imagery. Its particular deployment of "endless" or "infinite" scrolling led to a sense of plentitude that felt simultaneously niche and mainstream, in an era where fandom uncomfortably straddled these two cultural positions (Scott 2011). On Tumblr, you could endlessly explore the community you yourself curated, or you could follow a particular fannish interest through all of its (often seemingly limitless) iterations. In addition, Tumblr's deployment of hashtags facilitated visibility for multiple intersecting fan communities including fans of color, trans fans, queer fans, younger fans, older fans, and fans of little known media sources (Cho, Dame, Pande, Fink and Miller, Warner).

Other key elements of the Tumblr interface also mapped organically onto the practices of fan culture, for some at least. Tumblr's "dashboard"—which compiles the posts of the various Tumblr-blogs a user follows—for some created a balance between individual control and community context. For others, Tumblr's dashboard confused the relationship between individual and community to a troubling degree; I will examine this perspective shortly. The Queue, where a Tumblr user could arrange images and text to automatically post even if they themselves were not online, accommodated the diverse life patterns and geographical locations of fans in increasingly transcultural fan communities, allowing for a continuous dialogue that seems based in real time yet traversed time zone differences (Morimoto and Chin 2013). The introduction of an official mobile app in 2009 allowed fans to integrate Tumblr into their increasingly mobile-based engagement, in a continuous flow including work hours and overnight. Within this seeming infinite flow that (again, seemingly) transcends geographic boundaries, hashtags connected those focused on particular topics or particular dimensions of particular topics. Even hashtags on Tumblr conveyed a sense of fannish multiplicity, as fans began to include extensive hashtags on a post, with hashtags sometimes dwarfing the content of the post, or even composing the content of the post itself.

And yet at the same time, many fans found the Tumblr interface opaque and alienating. As more fans and fan communities seemed to make a primary home on Tumblr, some complained that it was hard to see the dividing line between self and community in the context of the dashboard, which combines both. One fan wrote:

> For me, Tumblr has reversed the notion of "my space" vs "your space." We don't encounter/respond to posts on the blog where they originated. Instead, other people's posts appear on our dashboards, where posts may feel like an intrusion into our space. I think we respond to Tumblr posts differently than on DW/LJ where we were mindful of posts being on so-and-so's blog, where you had to go to their blog, their space, to comment and participate, as a guest.

In part, as a result of this blurring of self and other, individual and collective, it was difficult for some to identify where conversations were taking place. Although Tumblr offered appeal in its visual spectacle, its sense of plentitude, and its coded opacity to outsiders, at the same time it provided limited and limiting tools for conversations among users. As another fan put it:

> the main issue I have with Tumblr: you can't really have a good conversation there. It's inherent in the site itself; I would go so far as to say the site is purposefully designed to discourage conversation, given its lack of a workable messaging system and the limitations on replying to posts. Tumblr is designed to be a broadcast medium, not

a community platform. Of course, people being people, they've found ways to build community anyway, but we have to fight the system to do it.

Where LJ and its various clones offered threaded comment trees, the Tumblr interface deployed what seemed to be more blunt instruments. You could reblog, you could reblog with a note, or you could post an "ask" on someone's Tumblr, which they could repost and respond to. The "fan mail" tool (disabled in 2015) offered the chance to send a message to the authors of the Tumblogs you followed. "Fan mail" cast Tumblr readers as "fans" of one another, thus suggesting an equally unequal playing field structured on parasocial celebrity/fan relationships as opposed to more decentralized fan community networks. The "fan mail" conceit encouraged a multiplicity of one-to-many communications rather than a congregation of individuals dialoguing together. Fan mail was eventually replaced with Instant Messaging, which removed the overt celebrity/fan reference but still encouraged one to many and one-on-one dialogue rather than a multivocal conversation. While substantive conversations do happen on Tumblr, they happen out of fan negotiation with the limits of the interface. Fans have found many creative ways to enable dialogic or communal conversation on Tumblr: they use particular tags to build sub communities, they invite "asks" explicitly in posts to their followers, they use tags for conversation, they post screen captures of followers' "likes" or reblog "fanmail" to thank them in notes or tags. For some, these tactics create a sense of intimate and perhaps subversive community, bound in part by its hidden legibility. For others, these tactics remain opaque and alienating. In sum, Tumblr felt (and continues to feel) inclusive to some and exclusive to others.

This brings us to 2016—the time of writing this chapter: although many (often older/long time) fans still express discomfort with Tumblr, Tumblr is arguably the dominant fan space. Aesthetic forms and language have evolved on Tumblr that have taken fandom in new directions. For the remainder of this chapter, I examine three emerging and intertwined aesthetic traditions on Tumblr—the hashtag, the gifset, and the multiauthored, iterative post. Fans use hashtags not only for organization but also to create poetry, analysis, conversation, and even fiction. Fan artists on Tumblr use the gifset to offer character study, thematic commentary, visual analysis, intertextual connections, worldbuilding, storytelling, and satiric humor (Booth 2015: 30–31). Hashtags and gifsets come together to perform the multifaceted process of fan engagement and authorship in self reflexive posts that circulate across fandoms.

Hashtag Creativity

Given Tumblr's seemingly poor tools for organization and archiving, one might expect fans on Tumblr to use tags primarily to organize and archive, functioning as hyperlinks connecting related material. However, this is very much not the case. On Tumblr, many fans use hashtags in what often seems like purposefully illogical and incoherent ways (Busse 2017). When Tumblr fans do use hashtags to organize and police, they don't do so only by sorting via categorical labels (fandom, character, pairing, etc.) but also as a way of hailing and limiting audiences, tagging with fandom specific or even user-specific hashtags that only a select few would even know how to search. Thus, tags become an attempt to carve out a private-in-public for fandom on Tumblr (Lange 2008; Stein 2015).

Hashtags have also become a mode of expression in their own right. Yes, each tag functions as a hyperlink that sorts and connects, albeit only if used multiple times to tag different posts. Even orphan tags always have the potential to link to another: they imagine a multitude of posts that share that tag, even if the multitude remains forever imagined. Together tag clusters exist in meaning-making sets that signify precisely in their collective excess, their inability to be contained within interface norms or information organization systems. This is most obvious with hashtag sets composed of idiosyncratic tags that likely lead only to accidental paths of links, as in the following set of tags that accompanies hand-drawn art of characters Tracer and Widowmaker from the videogame Overwatch:

> #widowtracer #i think a part of amelie wants so desperately to break lena #because lena is pure and sunshine and everything good in this messed up world #their attraction to each other is born from this curiosity of the otherside #in essence amelie walks in a dark tunnel and lena is her lightsource so she's dawn to it #but if you've lived in the dark for so long how can you not hate the sunlight? #meta in the tags!!!! #otp: scoped in on you and wont look away #my art (see Figure 17.1).

This tag set combines more straightforward categorizational tags (#widowtracer, the name for the pairing) with more personal tags (#my art), and with extended interpretive tags that perform their lack of categorization (#i think a part of amelie wants so desperately to break lena). It also includes a self-reflexive tag that both categorizes and celebrates the poster's use of tags: #metainthetags!!!.

Figure 17.1 Example of fan art image and accompanying poetic tag.

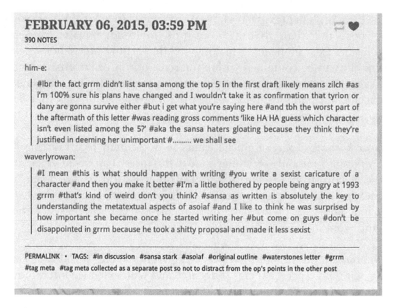

Figure 17.2 Tumblr tags can simultaneously occupy both the center and margins of a post.

Fans also put clusters of hashtags in the text of a post's note (Figure 17.2), adding additional notes in the note section. These tags no longer remain in the margin of the post but instead fully take over the content as interpretation, analysis, performance, and art.

The associative collectivity of tagging is also present in posts with less obvious intent to use hashtags as a resistive aesthetic. That is, tagging functions as a cultural mode and formal aesthetic, whether intended by their author or not. Take for example this post that accompanies audio streaming of the song "Wait For It" (from the fan favorite musical *Hamilton*), with hashtags that include more straightforward categorizational tags #hamilton and #wait for it, and more affective/effusive #we we so excited and #we so excited (a reference to the song "Friday" by Rebecca Black). The "we so excited" hashtags (hyper)link to a multifandom (and beyond fandom) mêlée of excitement regarding a range of topics from Mary Poppins to Star Wars to Taylor Swift (Figure 17.3).

Thus, transformation happens on Tumblr both in the duplication/replication/reiteration of posts and in the affective, analytic, interpretive acts of the accompanying hashtags. Indeed, even the categorization work of tags function as transformative acts of analysis and recontextualization.

GIFs and Sparkly Queer Tumblr Feels

The GIF (which stands for Graphical Interface Format) originated in 1987, and at the time its 256 colors and looping images offered a technological advance. However, this same format of 256 colors and looping images now persists as a form unto itself, in some ways an artifact of past technological history that has been repurposed in recent years to serve the interests of remix culture and fandom (Buck 2012). Katherine Brown argues that animated GIFs inherently invite or even necessitate engagement. Drawing on Lawrence

Figure 17.3 Fannish tagging recontextualizes and thus transforms media objects such as this audio from the musical *Hamilton*.

Lessig's notion of remix culture, Brown posits that "the very nature of the GIF does not allow for a complete referent, as it is cropped from a larger piece of film and the size limitations require a short loop of ten to fifteen frames and a limited 256-color palette. Due to these limitations, and its inherent obsolete technology, reaction GIFs … encourage … a read write interaction" in which "the user not only consumes the image but also changes its context and the way it is read …" (Brown 2012: 9).

We can understand the predominance of GIFs on Tumblr as a natural development given the centrality of images to the version of blogging the Tumblr interface offers. As Fernando Alfonso III notes, Tumblr's early marketing branded itself as a home for artists. Tumblr's evolution as fandom's choice interface (at least for a significant and visible segment of the fan community) resonates with aspects of its original branding and cultural uses beyond fandom. In an essay on queer culture on Tumblr, Alex Cho speaks of a similar affinity between the concerns and needs of the queer community and Tumblr as an interface. Cho writes: "Tumblr felt different from the 1990s era web 1.0 blogs. Instead of literal testimonials and narrative storytelling, it appeared that Tumblr users favored communication through image, mostly without attribution or caption; they relied less on text and more on the imagery, assemblage, intensity, and aesthetic… It seemed, from the moment I was in that space, that Tumblr traded in affect" (Cho 2015: 44).

Fandom too trades in affect—not surprisingly, as there is much overlap between queer communities and fan communities—indeed many understand fan communities as queer communities in the broadest sense. Elsewhere I have called this emphasis on affect in fandom "feels culture," drawing on the common fandom invocation of the Internet meme "right in the feels," which has evolved within fandom multifold (all the feels …) (Stein 2015: 158–161; Kohnen this volume).

Cho understands queer Tumblr's emphasis on affect as a form of resistance to traditional notions of the subject. Cho writes: "An analysis vis-à-vis affect adopts a resistance to the neatness of the 'subject'… in favor of an understanding of interlocking forces and fields of intensity" (Cho 2015: 45). We can link this "resistance to the neatness of the 'subject'" to concerns that have been pervasive in fandom for decades, specifically fandom's resistance to traditional author/audience relations (Busse 2013). Fannish reworking of authorship surfaces in Tumblr through the exuberant reblogging and processes of additive collective authorship, where a post created by one out of material created by others (often by commercial media industries) is reposted by many others, who add comments, hashtags, and layers of additional material in acts of collective transformative authorship. Thus, this collective authorship helps contribute to fans perception of Tumblr's safe opaqueness; one fan's perspective does not seem to stand alone but is supported by potentially hundreds and thousands of likes. Fandom on Tumblr celebrates the possibilities of collective readings, collective critiques, collective creativity, and a collective affect.

Affect reverberates (to use Cho's term) in Tumblr not only because of the platform's emphasis on imagery and feeling, but precisely because of the blurring of self and other that seem to mark Tumblr as distinct from LJ/Dreamwidth models, and for that matter on other concurrent interfaces including AO3 and Dreamwidth. Cho suggests that this blurring of tidy divides between self and other present in Tumblr's interface logic can itself be understood as queer; he argues that we can read queer to be a "relational stance" of "shared marginal relationship to dominant power …," a "palpable, subterranean rhythm that … runs through much of the Tumblr landscape" (Cho 2015: 46; Lothian, Busse, and Reid 2007). Thus, collective fannish affect as cultivated, fostered, and curated on Tumblr can arguably be understood as a queer mode of cultural engagement (Zacharias and Arthur 2008; McCracken 2013).

The exuberance and excess of fannish effect on Tumblr can also be understood as articulating a new mode of feminism. Usha Zacharias and Jane Arthur write that evolving social media networks like LJ and Tumblr "may not be particularly empowering, or particularly liberating to women as subjects of feminism," and yet they "create a space for new idioms of intimacy, flashpoints, and emoticons; perhaps one that suggests a reinvented girlhood" (Zacharias and Arthur 2008: 197) Mary Celeste Kearney describes what she terms the "the sparklefication" of and by girls as simultaneous a self-reflexive "masquerade" and an affective experience (Kearney 2015: 267). Akin to Cho, Kearney argues that we might understand the sparklification of girls in contemporary digital culture as a "potentially resistant force," that may "contribut(e) … to the subversion of patriarchy and post-feminism …" (2015: 270). Thus, as Tumblr fandom's often quite sparkly affective visual displays highlight excessive, boundary-blurring affect and the celebration of the spectacle of luminosity, we might hail this evolving mode of fan engagement as both feminist and queer.

One of my personal favorite images is this GIF of *Supernatural*'s angel Castiel. In this moving image GIF (which I've attempted to convey here through three images in Figures 17.4–17.5) a dark image conveys only a vague silhouette, but then an illuminating flash of lightning zig-zags across the image, revealing the angel Castiel, with his now-iconic (to fandom at least) trench coat, wings, and all. This GIF post plays with and depends upon the processes of iterative in process revelation, repetition, and luminosity that define Tumblr fandom's affective aesthetic mode.

Multimodal Self-Reflexivity on Tumblr

Although GIFs are themselves already creative acts of remix, fans on Tumblr commonly take this function further by combining individual GIFs into gifsets. Fans curate collections of GIFs that together create new meanings through cumulation or collision. Gifsets function similarly to fan remix videos by creating meaning out of combination, juxtaposition, and

Tumblr Fan Aesthetics

Figure 17.4 Dynamic gifsets such as this embody Tumblr's affective multimodal aesthetic.

Figure 17.5 Dynamic gifsets such as this embody Tumblr's affective multimodal aesthetic.

collision. Through image combination, gifsets offer particular character studies, highlight repeated imagery in a given series, recast series, often to insist upon greater diversity in representation. Gifsets also create crossovers across media texts, draw parallels to articulate tropes in media representation and media culture, represent fandom and social media, and offer self-reflexive commentary on the very processes of fandom

The aesthetic modes of the gifset and hashtag-set weave together into the collective authorship of the self-reflexive, multiauthored Tumblr post. Syntheses of gifsets and hashtags, reiterated and transformed in reblogs with notes and textual and visual additions, together form collective commentary on the experience of fandom, or of digital citizenship more broadly. These ongoing articulations of collective self-analysis emerge out of the

Figure 17.6 Dynamic gifsets such as this embody Tumblr's affective multimodal aesthetic.

negotiation between fan communities, individual artists, and the Tumblr interface more broadly. Moreover, this fan self-reflexivity incorporates the Tumblr interface's multiplicity and potential for discord, while trading on the affective language and aesthetics of fandom. Self-reflexive posts unfold via text, image, link, gifset, audio clip, and hashtag. Analyses of fans by fans evolve in a constant reiterative flow, created by multiple authors. By combining GIFs and hashtags, sometimes accented with additional text and images, fans analyze their own participation, their fan experience, and their own cultural import.

Fans build upon posts with multiple images to create over time a mosaic of fan experience that transcends particular fandoms. For example, a post entitled, "Coming into a fandom late" depicts various experiences in which an individual fan may feel somehow out of sync with the larger context of fandom. This post uses the protocol of "what should we call me" posts, a format that also originated on Tumblr, in which an animated GIF is appropriated and decontextualized to represent a recognizable experience (Brown 2012: 6). However here the experiences represented are for the most part of fannish dissonance and the images used are from a range of fandom favored texts, for example "coming into a fandom early and watching it become a clusterfuck," "being in a dormant fandom that suddenly comes alive again after a new movie," and "being in a fandom and not even knowing there's a war going on," with each example added by a new author and illustrated by images from *Supernatural*, Disney, and *Spiderman* respectively. This post has accumulated 475,138 notes and continues to grow as people reblog it with new additions of universally recognizable feelings of marginality within fandom.

Tumblr fans also use hashtags and gifsets to address an individual fan's relationship with Tumblr as a corporation and as an interface. The former we can see in a gifset post that casts *Hannibal*'s Will as the author of the post (who in turn serves as a stand in for *Hannibal* fandom), and Tumblr the corporation as his boss, Jack, with Will pretending to be fine with Tumblr/Jack's choices but instead telling himself "I need to stop tumblin' altogether," while Jack as Tumblr says "I'm the Big T, U'll come back." This gifset aptly captures the ambivalent power relationship between fandom (or an individual fan) and the corporate interface on which it depends, with a fan feeling alienated enough to strongly consider leaving the interface, while the interface/corporate interest seems to care little for the individual fan or fandom.

The power of the Tumblr interface is also a formative theme in a genre of self-reflexive Tumblr posts known as "my dash did a thing." This genre of Tumblr posts indeed reaches beyond fandom and in as much demonstrates how fannish celebration of collective ethos has come to inform Tumblr culture more broadly. In these posts, Tumblr users take a screen capture of their dashboard to share the seemingly meaningful yet random juxtaposition of two posts on their dashboard that seem to speak to one another. For example, one post tagged with "my dash did a thing," shows a post that reads "3 words every girl wants to hear," followed by a post that reads "could be gayer." This post finds its humor in the way the Tumblr interface seems here to know and support the queer female space (or queer female desire) that makes itself visible on Tumblr, and moreover that rejects more traditional notions of femininity, where the expected/stereotypical three words every girl wants to hear would be "I love you."

"My Dash Did a Thing" entries emphasize how Tumblr posts speak together in multi-layered conversation, sometimes harmonious, sometimes discordant, whether intentionally in conversation or not. This conversation merges text and image, imagined hyperlink and actual hyperlink, individual and collective, self and other, in ways that can be both limiting and generative, productive, and unsettling.

In the context of Tumblr's infinite flow (although not necessarily determined by it), fandom's evolving authorship through gifsets and hashtags represents a new affective mode of cultural conversation, one that rejects heteronorms, the control of narrative structure, singular authorial ownership, and the boundaries between public and private and appropriate and inappropriate emotion. Of course, there are meaningful exceptions to this: fans who request that their work not be reblogged without attribution, fans who lock down their Tumblr's entirely when they realize unintended audiences have found them, and those who do not feel their opinions are welcome in the Tumblr sphere. It's not that fandom on Tumblr is truly infinite, inclusive queer affect as community, but rather that it represents itself as such.

References

Alfonso III, Fernando. (2013) "The Real Origins of Tumblr." *The Daily Dot*, May 23.
Booth, Paul (2015) *Playing Fans: Negotiating Fandom and Media in the Digital Age*. Iowa City, IA: University of Iowa Press, pp. 30–33.
Brown, Katherine. (2012) "'Everyday I'm Tumblin': Performing Online Identity through Reaction GIFs." MA Thesis, The School of the Art Institute of Chicago.
Buck, Stephanie. (2012) "The History of the GIF." http://mashable.com/2012/12/14/GIFs-2012/#QGkr33vvsaqa
Busse, Kristina. (2013) "The Return of the Author: Ethos and Identity Politics," in Jonathan Gray and Derek Johnson (eds.) *Companion to Media Authorship*. Oxford: Blackwell, pp. 48–68.
Busse, Kristina. (2017). "Fictional Consents and the Ethical Enjoyment of Dark Desires," in *Framing Fan Fiction: Literary and Social Practices in Fan Communities*. Iowa City, IA: University of Iowa, pp. 197–217.
Cho, Alexander. (2015) "Queer Reverb," in Ken Hillis, Susana Paasonen, and Michael Petite (eds.) *Networked Affect*. Cambridge, MA: Massachusetts Institute of Technology, 44.
Dame, Avery. (2016) "Making a Name for Yourself: Tagging as Transgender Ontological Practice on Tumblr." *Critical Studies in Media Communication* 33: 23–37. http://dx.doi.org/10.1080/15295036.2015.1130846
Fink, Marty and Quinn Miller. (2014) "Trans Media Moments: Tumblr, 2011–2013," *Television & New Media* 2014, 15(7): 611–626.

Hellekson, Karen. (2015) "Making Use of: The GIF, Commerce, and Fans." *Cinema Journal* 54(3): Spring.

Lange, P. G. (2008) "Publicly private and Privately Public: Social Networking on Youtube." *Journal of Computer-Mediated Communication* 13: 361–380.

Larsen, Katherine and Lynn Zubernis. (2012) *Fandom at the Crossroads*. Newcast-Upon-Tyne: Cambridge Scholars Publishing, 2011.

Lothian, Alexis, Kristina Busse, and Robin Anne Reid. (2007) "'Yearning Void and Infinite Potential': Online Slash Fandom as Queer Female Space." *English Language Notes* 45(2): Fall/Winter.

Kearney, Mary Celeste. (2015) "Sparkle: Luminosity and Post-Girl Power Media," *Continuum* 29(2): 263–273, DOI:10.1080/10304312.2015.1022945, 270.

Keller, Jessalynn. (2016) *Girls' Feminist Blogging in a Postfeminist Age*. London: Routledge.

McCracken, Allison. (2013) "From LGBT to GSM: Gender and Sexual Identity among LeakyCon's Queer Youth." *Antenna* August 6, 2013. http://blog.commarts.wisc.edu/2013/08/06/from-lgbt-to-gsm-gender-and-sexual-identity-among-leakycons-queer-youth-leakycon-portland/

Moellenberndt, Christine. (2013) *LiveJournal Loyalty and Melodrama: Stakeholder Relations in Web 2.0*. UMI 1541543.

Morimoto, Lori and Bertha Chin. "Towards a Theory of Transcultural Fandom" *Participations* 10(1): May 2013.

Pande, Rukmini. (2016) "Squee from the Margins: Racial/Cultural/Ethnic Identity in Global Media Fandom," in Lucy Bennett and Paul Booth, *Seeing Fans*. New York: Bloomsbury, pp. 209–220.

Rodrigo, Rochelle. (2014) "Remixing the Concept of Author, or Not." http://mediacommons.futureofthebook.org/question/how-has-reblogging-and-reblogging-culture-sites-tumblr-and-twitter-complicated-notion-aut-2

Russo, Julie Levin. (2010) "Indiscrete Media: Television/Digital Convergence and Economies of Online Lesbian Fan Communities." Dissertation, Brown University, pp. 223–243.

Scott, Suzanne. (2011) "Revenge of the Fanboy: Convergence Culture and the Politics of Incorporation." Dissertation, University of Southern California.

Stein, Louisa. (2015) *Millennial Fandom*. Iowa City, IA: University of Iowa Press.

Stein, Louisa and Kristina Busse. (2009) *Limit Play*. Popular Communication 7: 192–207, 2009.

Warner, Kristen J. (2015) "ABC's *Scandal* and Black Women's Fandom," in Elana Levine (ed.) *Cupcakes, Pinterest, and Ladyporn*. Champaign, IL: University of Illinois Press.

Zacharias, Usha and Jane Arthurs. (2008) "The New Architectures of Intimacy? Social Networking Sites and Genders." *Feminist Media Studies* 8(2): 197.

18
ACCESSING PLATFORMED FANDOMS
Disability and Digital Fan Practices

Elizabeth Ellcessor

Where is digital fandom? From Discord and TikTok to Amino, Webtoons, or An Archive of Our Own, there are more (and more varied) digital spaces for fans to find one another, communicate, and produce and circulate creative works than ever before. Baym describes the wide variety of fan spaces online as indicative of "a new form of online social organization in which members move amongst a complex ecosystem of sites, building connections amongst themselves and their sites as they do" (2007). However, each of these digital platforms offers its own affordances and constraints, communicating ideology through its shaping of what is possible, what is desirable, and what is discouraged or excluded (Shaw 2017; Stanfill 2015). As Louisa Stein points out, "with every new media platform, we see fanfiction being shaped by the technical affordances" (Geraghty et al. 2022: 6), as are fan communities and interactions. Platform choice can be essential for international fans seeking low-bandwidth platforms or platforms with support for non-Western languages. And for disabled fans, the structure and (in)accessibility of various platforms can limit their networked participation in fan communities and practices.

While there has been increasing attention to disability within fan studies, much of this work has emphasized physical accessibility (Hanna 2022; Morimoto 2019) and representations of disability in fan works (Clemons 2019; Raw 2019). All of this work is crucial given that "fandom has a high percentage of disabled participants, and is concerned with issues of accessibility (both digital and meatspace) and positive disability representation in a way that is still not mainstream" (Coppa 2014: 78). Yet, the accessibility of fandom in digital spaces has rarely been the focus of scholarship. This represents a lack of overlap between fan studies, critical media access studies (Alper 2021), and platform studies (Gillespie 2018; Van Dijck 2013).

In this chapter, I consider how disabled fans negotiate and create access to varied platforms. Fan communities have long been hotbeds of accessibility innovation and cultural accessibility – setting norms, teaching skills, and going beyond technocentric definitions (Ellcessor 2016). These efforts are crucial forms of bottom-up, innovative "crip technoscience" (Hamraie and Fritsch 2019) and offer strategies for increasing and implementing accessibility at both technological and cultural levels. Much as fans have remixed and expanded upon texts, they have worked around, co-constructed, and hacked digital platforms, often going well beyond mainstream forms of disability representation and access. My analysis considers both top-down technological and corporate features and ground-up innovations designed to enhance access. The former is grounded in platforms' public documentation and interface designs, while the latter is informed by public user conversations and interviews with select innovators in fan accessibility. What follows are snapshots of select platforms at the current moment.

Platforms, Affordances, and Interfaces: Twitter and Mastodon

Maria Alberto has argued that fan studies and platform studies could be mutually helpful theoretical approaches (2020). However, she is correct to note that there are two bodies of work often referred to as "platform studies," one focused firmly on questions of technological architecture and the other focused on questions of policy, governance, and sociotechnical impact. My use of "platform" in this chapter relies primarily on the second body of work but also considers platform architecture in order to assess actual implementation of accessibility features.

In the previous edition of this collection, I offered a historical discursive interface analysis of various websites used by fans, highlighting how inaccessibility limited the utility of these sites and marginalized disabled fans (2018). This could be described as a platform study, but Jeremy Wade Morris's chapter in that volume more directly addressed platforms, arguing that even as fans utilize platforms, "platforms simultaneously mediate that fandom" (2018: 358), routinely privileging forms of user and fan behavior that can be surveilled, policed, and channeled into refining the platform in the interests of owners rather than fans.

Such tracking, datafication, and refinement in the interest of profit is common across digital platforms used by fan communities. Twitter (now X), for instance, was a widely used platform for the fan practice of "live-tweeting" alongside television programs (Barker 2022; Warner 2015). Fans participated in conversation via hashtags, which the platform promoted to push this content to others, further driving levels of activity on the platform at particular times, such as during the infamous "Red Wedding" episode of *Game of Thrones* (Forcier 2017). This increased activity, driven by fans, increased participation and ad recall on the site (Twitter Marketing 2017) and in turn bolstered the public perceptions of Twitter's value and centrality.

The affordances of Twitter – posts and threads, replies and hashtags, multimedia formats such as reaction gifs and memes – enabled vibrant conversations and drove user participation. Yet, while Twitter as a platform facilitated and encouraged this kind of fan activity, its technological architecture retained numerous barriers to participation by disabled fans. Reaction gifs, for instance, may trigger some seizure-related conditions or may be meaningless to users with vision impairments when presented without an accompanying textual description. Drawing on "critical media access studies" to interrogate both "access to media and communication technologies" and "access to human communication enabled by media" (Alper 2021: 843), an accessibility-focused platform analysis of Twitter could consider first, the accessibility of Twitter's user-generated content to disabled audiences and, second, the accessibility of the platform itself to disabled would-be content creators.

Historically, Twitter featured barriers for both creators and users. The posting interface was inaccessible to blind users due to a lack of form labeling in early years, resulting in the creation of alternatives. EasyChirp, for instance, used the Twitter API to create a separate accessible interface that enabled blind users and anyone else reliant upon screenreader and alternative input devices to create and post messages (Ellcessor 2016). For users, the lack of alternative text for images or gifs and the lack of video description posed an ongoing challenge.

While Twitter's accessibility features changed over time, with some significant improvements – such as the ability to add alt text via the "advanced options" of the posting interface in 2016 – the platform regularly made missteps. For instance, in 2020, the release of the "voice tweet" feature was criticized for its inaccessibility to d/Deaf users. In the ensuing coverage, it emerged that Twitter had never had any employees dedicated to accessibility. Developer Andrew Hayward stated that he and other "volunteers behind accessibility at Twitter" were "frustrated and disappointed" (Coldewey 2020) by voice tweets. While accessibility work has often relied upon "evangelism" and voluntarism by particularly motivated staff who may officially hold other positions (Ellcessor 2014; Kennedy 2011), the fact that a prominent social media platform had relied entirely on uncompensated labor for its accessibility revealed a blithe inattention to these issues and an implicit devaluation of disabled audiences.

Following this gaffe, Hayward was promoted to head of an official accessibility team, with a staff of ten people (Knibbs 2022). The team worked to provide live captioning for conversations on Twitter Spaces, and added visible "badges" to images that had alt text to aid users who relied upon this feature and draw nondisabled users' attention to it by making it less hidden. Yet, this success was short-lived. After the purchase of Twitter (rebranded as "X") by Elon Musk in 2022, the entire accessibility team was laid off (Knibbs 2022). Without such a team in place, X went on to make changes that decreased accessibility, such as the removal of headlines from links shared through the platform; without headlines, screenreaders cannot express the meaning of a given link (Métraux 2023). Whether accessibility was deliberately or accidentally reduced, these changes reflect a return to or even an intensification of the marginalization of disabled people – and disabled fans – using Twitter/X.

Since Musk's purchase of Twitter/X, many users have attempted to find other platforms for text-based conversation, such as Threads (tied to Instagram accounts), BlueSky (founded by Twitter founder Jack Dorsey), or Mastodon. In fact, in the two weeks after Musk's purchase, Mastodon reported an influx of over one million new users (He et al. 2023). Mastodon works quite differently from other social media platforms; it is an open-source "fediverse," a federated platform for interacting across multiple independent instances (servers), each of which has its own management, rules, focus, and community culture. Accounts are created on specific servers, allowing groups (like fan communities) to set up their own servers and attendant technical rules and expectations for social interaction. As with past migrations in communities of transformative fans, the migration of fan communities from Twitter/X is partial and ongoing, likely driven by a "push" in the form of "design changes, policy changes, technical problems" (Fiesler and Dym 2020: 42;9). For disabled fans and those invested in accessibility, the degradation of accessibility at Twitter acts as one such push towards alternative spaces.

While there is variation across the fediverse, Mastodon has built "all the important foundations" for accessibility into its interface (Eggert 2022). Many popular Mastodon servers not only allow alt text but include reminders to enter it when uploading an image (see Figure 18.1). Like Twitter in recent years, many Mastodon servers add ALT badges to designate images that contain alt text, and automated text detection can provide context for undescribed images in some cases. While Mastodon has no formal accessibility team, due to its open source nature, the developers nonetheless seem to be prioritizing accessibility as a component of broader user interface and experience development as evidenced by the inclusion of accessibility concerns in system issue reports and updates ("Mastodon Project" 2023).

Beyond technical features, however, the culture of Mastodon has had a distinct impact on the accessibility of the platform. The system prompts are not the only reminder regarding alt text. Soft pushes for accessibility include the use of hashtags to ask for others to add alt text, decisions to only share content that contains alt text, and reminders from other users if alt text is forgotten. Fedi.Tips, a Mastodon account sharing tips for navigating the platform, regularly explains the benefits of accessible content for both audiences and creators (Fedi.Tips 2023).

This "really strong ethos of accessibility" (Thompson 2023) is crucial to making user-generated content accessible, and is precisely what many fan communities have pushed for on Twitter, Facebook, Instagram, and Tumblr. It is a form of cultural accessibility, demonstrating that access is a shared value within a community and a matter of mutual responsibility, not merely legal compliance or technological automation. Similarly, many Mastodon instances incorporate content warnings as an option when creating a post, bringing a common online practice in fan and activist communities into the very interface. Content warnings, which indicate content that may be triggering, have long been considered an accessibility feature within disability communities (Ellcessor 2016; Stanfill and Lothian 2021). Once again, this technological feature is supported by a shared cultural

Figure 18.1 Screenshots as the author prepares to post a screen capture from the 2023 *Dr. Who* episode "The Giggle," which featured a character (and actress) who uses a wheelchair. The three screenshots show Mastodon's prompts, the writing of alt text, and the ALT badge on the final post.

value: "it is considered extremely poor form in the fediverse to force your followers to look at content they might not want to see" (Navarro 2022).

The nuances of Mastodon's platform culture, however, can be a challenge to new users and communities. Tech journalist Erin Kissane conducted an informal survey on BlueSky about why people did not move to Mastodon, and found that the most common response involved "feeling unwelcome, being scolded, and getting lectured" (2023), including getting pushback related to content warnings. Anecdotally, people experienced similar frustrations regarding reminders from others about accessibility and alt text, as it felt like the imposition of another unstated rule. Conflicts between the expectations of various instances could also create tension. Mastodon instances and users are still grappling with how to welcome new users while preserving important elements of a culture that has prioritized accessibility.

For disabled fans, Mastodon might offer a useful combination of accessibility and conversational affordances that allow for the intentional creation of community expectations and norms, particularly on dedicated instances. However, the decentralized nature of Mastodon may also pose a challenge to the kind of reach and influence that fan communities exerted on Twitter; many have noted that discoverability on Mastodon is challenging, and that navigation through hashtags works well only once you have identified the exact hashtags you wish to find. This may result in more insular communities, or less opportunity for newcomers to find and join a fandom compared to more centralized platforms, such as Twitter.

Cultural Accessibility and Community Norms: Tumblr and TikTok

The cultural expectations around accessibility on Mastodon are a useful example of how any evaluation of platform accessibility must go beyond the technological or policy details to consider conditions of use and user cultures. Often, such ground-up activism – in the forms of tips, reminders, and call-outs – has been central to how disabled internet users and fans have *created* accessibility and enabled their own conditions for participation. For instance, in my previous research on Tumblr, it became clear that disabled users were developing and sharing workarounds designed to create accessibility in the face of technological systems that worked against these goals (2016). In the 2010s, Tumblr did not use alt text tags for images, and asked users to write "captions" for images; captions and alt text do not serve the same function for screenreaders. The Tumblr page "Fuck Yeah, Accessibility" shared techniques for uploading images in a "text" (HTML-based) window, adding alt tags manually.

Despite the platform's inaccessibility, many disabled users celebrated Tumblr as "the most accessible site… in terms of things like trigger warnings and image descriptions" (Ellcessor 2016). Trigger warnings – not generally an officially mandated accessibility feature – and image descriptions created by working around platform defaults both represent important forms of cultural accessibility, those "coalitional, collaborative, and participatory types of media technologies, content, regulation, and use" (Ellcessor 2016: 180) that create accessibility and increase disabled users' comfort and inclusion in online spaces. That content warnings have now been both culturally and technologically implemented on platforms like Mastodon represents an important mainstreaming of these features and an expanded understanding of accessibility that prioritizes the ease and satisfaction of participation.

Tumblr has not only fostered culturally accessible practices, but has been host to large numbers of fans, often progressive-minded fans who have shared content highlighting and decrying racism, sexism, heteronormativity, and ableism. Alison McCracken describes Tumblr as "central to fannish passions and creative production among youth, especially girls, people of color, and LGBTQ-identified fans" (McCracken 2017: 151) who are bound together by affective investments and experience Tumblr as a space for media literacy, identity formation, and political awakening. Tumblr has been home to sprawling fan communities around media texts such as Harry Potter, *Glee*, and Taylor Swift, among others, and has fostered creative practices aimed at challenging or correcting stereotypical or limited forms of media representation. Melanie Kohnen thus calls Tumblr a pedagogical platform, in which users employ fannish practices to educate one another about media representations, industries, diversity, and digital technology (2018).

Similar forms of informal pedagogy and identity formation seem to characterize use of TikTok, which is now one of the most-used social media platforms among young users (Massarat 2022). Like Tumblr, TikTok is a social media platform reliant nearly entirely on the creation, remixing, and circulation of user-generated content. Unlike Tumblr, TikTok is a video-centric platform, driven not by follows or hashtags but by the algorithmic cultivation of a "for you page" (FYP) that uses previous user activity to suggest new content. Fan communities are using TikTok to create and share commentary, fannish creations such as cosplay, and more. The centrality of video to TikTok means that this sharing is more closely connected to fans' faces and voices than were more historically pseudonymous platform creations.

The combination of the algorithmic opacity, centrality of real bodies and identities, and slow adoption of accessibility features on TikTok (Simpson et al. 2023) means that TikTok is potentially an ambiguous platform for disabled fans. TikTok has been criticized for seeming to intentionally suppress content by fat, non-white, unattractive, and visibly disabled creators by deprioritizing them via the algorithm, a process known as "shadowbanning" (Rauchberg 2022). Shadowbanned users can create content, but will find their reach to be routinely limited, as few people will see their videos through the FYP. Furthermore, TikTok has been criticized for inaccessible platform features, such as a lack of closed captioning in early years (Simpson et al. 2023). Much like Tumblr, TikTok seems to be a platform that does not prioritize technological accessibility, but nonetheless hosts active and culturally accessible communities, including active and transformative fandoms.

Given this tension between the affordances and cultures of TikTok, it is unsurprising that disability communities are once again negotiating issues of accessibility and advocating for workarounds and institutional change. Simpson et al., in their study of neurodivergent TikTok creators, found that for these individuals, accessibility "is derived from community norms that are negotiated through social interactions" (Simpson et al. 2023: 57:3). Neurodivergent TikTok creators described hacks of the default platform infrastructure, such as prerecording response videos using alternative software rather than using the built-in "live" feature. As both viewers and creators, they prioritized captions (often going beyond TikTok's automated features) and built norms around asking for captions, similar to what we see around alt text on Mastodon.

Such norms are built through the processes of sharing, commenting, and building connections, as seen in many corners of disability and fan TikTok, where users once again treat the platform as a space for education and identity formation around critical media and political literacies (Geraghty et al. 2022; Rauchberg 2022). To an extent, users on TikTok are once again co-creating the platforms that they want to use by adding, hacking, and extending the possibilities of use. Perhaps, then, it is no surprise that there are several niche platforms built by and/or for fans that attempt to alleviate the tensions found on mainstream platforms by centering fan cultures and norms around mutual responsibility and inclusion.

Building Technological Accessibility: Dreamwidth, Pillowfort and An Archive of Our Own

There is not only a great deal of similarity between fan communities and open source development communities (Winter et al. 2021), but there can be significant overlap in these groups, both often characterized as parts of "geek culture" (Woo 2018). Many fans, including disabled fans, have high-level technical skills related to digital media creation, front- and back-end development, and dynamic coding languages. Thus, when considering the significant effort that we see fans and disabled users putting into making mainstream platforms technologically and culturally accessible, it makes sense that some groups have turned towards developing bespoke platforms that reflect their cultures, values, and priorities.

One such platform is Dreamwidth, a "social networking, content management, and personal publishing platform" ("About Dreamwidth Studios" n.d.) that is based on open source LiveJournal software. Dreamwidth displays both technological and cultural accessibility through its "Diversity Statement," its code and volunteer developer community (which has included disabled women focused on ensuring accessibility), and its provision of resources for more accessible online and fan cultures (Ellcessor 2017).

More recently, Pillowfort has emerged as an alternative social media platform. Currently in open beta testing, Pillowfort was founded in 2017 as an alternative to other blogging platforms, such as LiveJournal or Tumblr, and it has been particularly popular for fan communities and LGBTQ users as well as among creators of adult sexual content, many of whom were pushed off of Tumblr in 2018 (Liao 2018). While Pillowfort offers several desirable features for fans, such as management of audiences and content warnings, its work on accessibility lags behind. Pillowfort's FAQ describes accessibility as important and claims that the platform is "taking steps" towards meeting the accessibility guidelines ("Frequently Asked Questions" n.d.), but a recent update indicates ongoing problems with alt text implementation and lists accessibility improvements as a future goal ("Staff: Known Issues and Prospective Features" n.d.). While browsing the community demonstrates the same kind of accessibility tips, requests, and reminders seen elsewhere, there does not appear to be the same degree of success seen in other niche platforms' accessibility efforts.

The best-known example of a fan-created platform is, of course, An Archive of Our Own (AO3). Built to archive fan works and history, and prioritizing user anonymity, AO3 has since become central to shaping how fans think about questions of genre and audience through its tagging options (Geraghty et al. 2022; Lothian 2013). In terms of its technological structure, AO3 "is built on open-source archiving software designed and built by and for fans" ("Archive FAQs" n.d.), and maintained by volunteers, accessibility for fans and volunteers with disabilities appears to be of secondary concern. The FAQ states that

AO3 attempts "to keep the Archive compatible with the current releases of commonly used desktop browsers, e-readers, screen readers, and the default browsers of most iOS, Android, and Windows mobile devices." This implicitly addresses only text accessibility, not the accessibility of multimedia features. At the level of interface design, there are several publicly available user-developed skins that provide the style sheets to create a "dark mode" or facilitate use by low-vision users. Such options require users to do a degree of research and technological implementation on their end to access these accessibility features. While there is a volunteer team dedicated to "Accessibility, Design and Technology," it should be noted that this team's current focus is development of an open-source software package to support AO3; in other words, it appears to be the primary team dedicated to software development, of which accessibility is a part without being a dedicated focus.

The efforts towards accessibility on these niche platforms do not, as a whole, appear significantly stronger than those found in mainstream social media and blogging platforms. This speaks to a larger deprioritization of accessibility in many technological workforces, where accessibility is often addressed through volunteer labor and is rarely formally part of required curriculums or onboarding. While volunteers involved in the development of fan platforms may have an interest in accessibility, they may similarly be undertrained, busy, and focused on other things. And while disabled fans and users often do know how to make things more accessible for themselves, they understandably may resent being called upon to volunteer their own labor or go through cumbersome processes in the interest of access.

Conclusion

This chapter has provided only brief accessibility-focused evaluations of several contemporary platforms used by fan communities; there are many other platforms that could be similarly explored, and there is undoubtedly detail about the platforms discussed here that has been left out. More in-depth analysis of specific platforms, their policies and affordances, and the practices of disabled and nondisabled fans in the pursuit of access can – and should – be a part of fan studies scholarship.

As fandoms expand and splinter across websites, social media sites, apps, and other digital platforms, it becomes increasingly important to acknowledge how specific platform affordances and constraints – including those tied to accessibility – can shape fandoms in various ways that may make a space more or less inclusive. Fan communities do not merely use platforms, they are platformed – raised up or given voice (Gillespie 2010) – to varying degrees based upon what a given platform makes possible or encourages. Simultaneously, understanding fans and platforms means looking beyond policies and technological features to consider use. When fans push back on platform design, as in the case of various experiments, workarounds, and collaborative practices of accessibility, they apply transformative logics similar to those seen in other fan creations, taking what is valuable and building upon it to move towards a desired world in which access is possible, pleasurable, and a priority.

References

"About Dreamwidth Studios," n.d. *Dreamwidth*. Available at: www.dreamwidth.org/about (accessed 5.13.16).

Alberto, M., 2020. "Fan users and platform studies." *Transformative Works and Cultures* 33.

Alper, M., 2021. "Critical media access studies: Deconstructing power, visibility, and marginality in mediated space." *International Journal of Communication* 15, 840–861.

"Archive FAQs," n.d. *Archive of Our Own.* Available at: http://archiveofourown.org/faq?language_id=en (accessed 5.13.16).

Barker, C., 2022. *Social TV: Multiscreen Content and Ephemeral Culture.* Jackson, MS: University Press of Mississippi.

Baym, N., 2007. "The new shape of online community: The example of Swedish independent music fandom." *First Monday* 12.

Clemons, A., 2019. "Enabling/disabling: Fanfiction and disability discourse." *Canadian Journal of Disability Studies* 8, 247–278.

Coldewey, D., 2020. "Somehow, Twitter does not have a team dedicated to accessibility." *TechCrunch.*

Coppa, F., 2014. "Fuck yeah, fandom is beautiful." *The Journal of Fandom Studies* 2, 73–82.

Eggert, E., 2022. Accessibility in the Fediverse (and Mastodon). Available at: https://yatil.net/blog/accessibility-in-the-fediverse-and-mastodon (accessed 12.4.23).

Ellcessor, E., 2017. "Accessing fan cultures." In: Click, M.A., Scott, S. (Eds.), *The Routledge Companion to Media Fandom.* New York, NY: Routledge, pp. 202–211.

Ellcessor, E., 2016. *Restricted Access: Media, Disability, and the Politics of Participation.* New York, NY: New York University Press.

Ellcessor, E., 2014. "<ALT="Textbooks">: Web accessibility myths as negotiated industrial lore." *Critical Studies in Media Communication* 31, 448–463.

Fedi.Tips (@feditips@mstdn.social), 2023. "Just a reminder, please do add alt text descriptions to your images, videos and audio clips." *Mastodon.*

Fiesler, C., Dym, B., 2020. "Moving Across Lands: Online Platform Migration in Fandom Communities." *Proceedings of the ACM on Human-Computer Interaction* 4, 1–25.

Forcier, E., 2017. "Re(a)d wedding: A case study exploring everyday information behaviors of the transmedia fan." *Proceedings of the Association for Information Science and Technology* 54, 93–101.

"Frequently Asked Questions," n.d. *Pillowfort.* Available at: www.pillowfort.social/FrequentlyAskedQs (accessed 12.8.23).

Geraghty, L., Chin, B., Morimoto, L., Jones, B., Busse, K., Coppa, F., Santos, K.M., Stein, L.E., 2022. "Roundtable: The past, present and future of fan fiction. *Humanities* 11, 2–11.

Gillespie, T., 2018. *Custodians of the Internet: Platforms, Content Moderation, and the Hidden Decisions That Shape Social Media.* New Haven, CT: Yale University Press.

Gillespie, T., 2010. "The politics of 'platforms'." *New Media & Society* 12, 347–364.

Hamraie, A., Fritsch, K., 2019. "Crip technoscience manifesto." *Catalyst: Feminism, Theory, Technoscience* 5, 1–33.

Hanna, E., 2022. "The limits of comic-con's exclusivity." *Transformative Works and Cultures* 38.

He, J., Zia, H.B., Castro, I., Raman, A., Sastry, N., Tyson, G., 2023. "Flocking to Mastodon: Tracking the Great Twitter Migration." In: *Proceedings of the 2023 ACM on Internet Measurement Conference, IMC '23.* pp. 111–123.

Kennedy, H., 2011. *Net Work: Ethics and Values in Web Design.* New York, NY: Palgrave Macmillan.

Kissane, E., 2023. "Mastodon is easy and fun except when it isn't." Available at: https://erinkissane.com/mastodon-is-easy-and-fun-except-when-it-isnt (accessed 12.4.23).

Knibbs, K., 2022. "Twitter's layoffs are a blow to accessibility." *Wired.*

Kohnen, M.E.S., 2018. "Tumblr Pedagogies." In: Booth, P. (Ed.), *A Companion to Media Fandom and Fan Studies.* Hoboken, NJ: John Wiley & Sons, Ltd, pp. 349–367.

Liao, S., 2018. "Tumblr will ban all adult content starting December 17th." *The Verge.*

Lothian, A., 2013. "Archival anarchies: Online fandom, subcultural conservation, and the transformative work of digital ephemera." *International Journal of Cultural Studies* 16, 541–556.

Massarat, E.A.V., R. Gelles-Watnick, Navid, 2022. "Teens, social media and technology." *Pew Research Center.*

Mastodon Project, 2023. GitHub. Available at: https://github.com/mastodon (accessed 12.9.23).

McCracken, A., 2017. "Tumblr youth subcultures and media engagement." *Cinema Journal* 57, 151–161.

Métraux, J., 2023. "'X' axed headlines. That sucks for accessibility." *Mother Jones.*

Morimoto, L., 2019. "Physical disability in/and transcultural fandom: Conversations with my spouse." *The Journal of Fandom Studies* 7, 73–78.

Morris, J.W., 2017. "Platform fandom." In: Click, M.A., Scott, S. (Eds.), *The Routledge Companion to Media Fandom*. New York, NY: Routledge, pp. 356–364.

Navarro, D., 2022. "Notes from a data witch – Everything I know about Mastodon." Available at: https://blog.djnavarro.net/posts/2022-11-03_what-i-know-about-mastodon/ (accessed 12.4.23).

Rauchberg, J.S., 2022. "#Shadowbanned: Queer, trans, and disabled creator responses to algorithmic oppression on TikTok." In: Pain, P. (Ed.), *LGBTQ Digital Cultures*. New York, NY: Routledge, pp. 196–209.

Raw, A.E., 2019. "Normalizing disability: Tagging and disability identity construction through marvel cinematic universe fanfiction." *Canadian Journal of Disability Studies* 8, 185–200.

Shaw, A., 2017. "Encoding and decoding affordances: Stuart Hall and interactive media technologies." *Media, Culture & Society* 39, 592–602.

Simpson, E., Dalal, S., Semaan, B., 2023. " 'Hey, can you add captions?': The critical infrastructuring practices of neurodiverse people on TikTok." *Proceedings of the ACM on Human-Computer Interaction* 7: 57, 1–57:27.

"Staff: Known Issues and Prospective Features," n.d. *Pillowfort*. Available at: www.pillowfort.social/posts/19 (accessed 12.8.23).

Stanfill, M., 2015. "The interface as discourse: The production of norms through web design". *New Media Society* 17, 1059–1074.

Stanfill, M., Lothian, A., 2021. "An archive of whose own?" *Transformative Works and Cultures* 36.

Thompson, C., 2023. "The literary style of alt-text." Medium. Available at: https://clivethompson.medium.com/the-literary-style-of-alt-text-9f1595cd8f0c (accessed 12.4.23).

Twitter Marketing, 2017. "New research: Twitter TV fans tune in live to their favorite shows." Twitter. Available at: https://marketing.twitter.com/en/insights/new-research-twitter-tv-fans-tune-in-live-to-their-favorite-shows (accessed 12.4.23).

Van Dijck, J., 2013. *The Culture of Connectivity: A Critical History of Social Media*. Oxford: Oxford University Press.

Warner, K., 2015. "ABC's scandal and black women's fandom." In: Levine, E. (Ed.), *Cupcakes, Pinterest, and Ladyporn: Feminized Popular Culture in the Early Twenty-First Century*. Urbana, IL: University of Illinois Press, pp. 32–50.

Winter, R., Salter, A., Stanfill, M., 2021. "Communities of making: Exploring parallels between fandom and open source." *First Monday*.

Woo, B., 2018. *Getting a Life: The Social Worlds of Geek Culture*. Montreal, Canada: McGill-Queen's Press – MQUP.

19
A TALE OF TWO COMMUNITIES

The Polish Fandom, the Fandom in Poland, and the Internet's Influence on Fan Identities

Agnieszka Urbańczyk

Introduction

In 2005, Krzysztof Bortel published a piece that was supposed to introduce the readers of Poland's most important science fiction and fantasy (SF&F) magazine to the alien notion of media fandom and its practices: cosplay, fanfiction, even slash. The closing paragraph stated: "In Poland, media fandom has not developed as of yet" (Bortel 2005: 8), despite the fact that I and my Polish classmates had already been participating in all the practices Bortel listed for some time.

In 2019, a friend of mine, an avid fanfiction reader, claimed that there were no fanboys in Poland. What she actually meant, I can only assume, was that she had never met a male fan participating in the same practices she did. Every day, she would see the most popular magazine of SF&F fans in the newsstands, and yet she did not consider its audience fannish. The goal of this paper, therefore, is not only to describe fans in Poland, but to discuss the parallel existence of *two* communities in the same country, and the reasons why they tend to forget about each other. While one of these – the SF&F fandom – has been discussed by scholars at length, the transformative media fandom in Poland tends to be analyzed as merely a part of a larger, international formation when, in fact, the situation is much more complex. This case study can be considered an investigation into both Eastern European fan communities consciously adopting Western practices, and into broader cultural changes brought about by the internet. Fan communities in Poland, and the ways they differ from the American ones show that globalization is neither linear nor all-encompassing, but we should also be wary of narratives that downplay its role.

Inclusion of voices that do not come from the center might help fan studies break with two contradictory but quite popular assumptions: that of American modes of fandom being the universal default, and that of specific countries' fan cultures being monolithic. In Poland, the popularization of the internet, and the access to anglophone media and resources have

DOI: 10.4324/9781003373025-22

played a pivotal role in the emergence of a community whose practices and identities, while still shaped by local context, are far removed from the modes of fandom established by Poles whose fan engagement preceded internet access. As I demonstrate, these different fandoms coexist within the geographical confines of the same country. Throughout this chapter, I outline the main problems fan studies faces when discussing communities in non-Western countries, I briefly describe the Polish SF&F fandom and the ways in which it has been mimicking its American curative counterpart, and I proceed to give an account of the emergence of the – mostly ignored by scholars – transformative media fandom in my country.

Globalization and Transnational Communities

Jenkins, Ford, and Green (2013) describe today's media as allowing for texts to be spread among different places and in different formats, manipulated, and accessed from anywhere. Fan communities, no longer depending solely on local infrastructures, would appear to be one of the clearest examples of said spreadability's power, and it is true that people from different countries may participate in a larger, transnational fandom. Jenkins (2006: 155), noting the emergence of "pop cosmopolitanism," observed that some fans seek "to escape the gravitational pull of their local communities to enter a broader sphere of cultural experience."

The notion of cosmopolitanism, however, not unlike globalization, can easily be used to gloss over the inequalities in both access and attention. The flow of culture, after all, is highly asymmetrical, with a "stronger flow from center to periphery than vice versa" (Hannerz 1996: 60). While there are some cases of non-English language productions becoming popular worldwide, the vast majority of texts succeeding abroad originate in the US and UK (Kustritz 2015: ¶2.2; Pande 2018: 61). It is no wonder that they become the default when scholars consider possible objects of fandom, and it is also not surprising that the practices surrounding said objects are presumed to be the same as in English-speaking communities. Pande (2018: 5) points out: "when 'the fandom' or fangirls are discussed, the referents of these terms remain US- or UK-centric popular media texts and white, cisgender, middle-class women located in the United States or the United Kingdom." While Pande focuses on race and its invisibility in fandom and the scholarship surrounding it, I would argue that her diagnoses apply to geographical location and nationality as well, especially given that English is the default language used in larger fandom spaces. Online, everyone is American until proven otherwise.

There indeed is a risk of local, non-Western fan communities, and practices and identities specific to them, being ignored by English-language research, sometimes because of the language barrier, sometimes because the objects of fandom seem obscure to anglophone academia (Pande 2018: 6). Despite the progressing Americanization of the internet, different local productions still exist and compete with the American ones for attention in their countries, even if they rarely have a chance to be noticed by the international audience. This entails the existence of fandoms formed around texts that are not recognized globally. Even in the case of English-language media, the modes of their consumption vary, given that accessibility differs depending on the region, and many practices still require being denizens of the center. Fans from peripheral and semi-peripheral countries who have enough time and money at their disposal to participate in the same practices Americans do, are still not the target audience of Western shows (Siuda 2012: 159). The differences in cultural context and accessibility cause vast dissimilarities between fan communities, and even fandoms of *American* franchises have their own, local traditions.

It is, however, easy to go to the extremes when trying to describe local fandoms and their specificity, ignoring the existence of others in the same country. In the case of Poland, the SF&F fandom is not completely underresearched, and there are numerous papers on it written not only in Polish but in English as well. One monograph on Polish fans (Siuda 2012) even argues that it is impossible to form transnational fandoms, given how varying traditions, languages, and experiences of the audiences from different countries inform their identity, reception, and practices, making them nothing like communities across the border or the American default.

Adopting Pieterse's (2009) notion, Kucharska et al. (2015: ¶2.3) propose to discuss Poland as a semiperiphery, "a place of mediating activities between core and peripheral regions and areas in which institutional features are in some ways intermediate between those forms found in core and periphery." Consequently, they describe Polish SF&F fandom as semiperipheral, negotiating between cultural autonomy and global trends. It is difficult to disagree with that assessment, and it complements Siuda's (2012: 232–236) observations that the local Polish community, being uninterested in romance fanfiction and unfamiliar with slash, is different from what most of the scholarship on anglophone fans describes. Nevertheless, SF&F fandom is not the *only* fandom in my country.

Even though at times they overlap, there are at least two separate fan communities in Poland. Most of the research focuses on one of them, the aforementioned SF&F fandom whose establishment precedes the popularization of the internet, and which indeed has been shaped by the local context. The second one – a younger, Americanized media fandom whose emergence was facilitated by the spread of internet access – is rarely discussed by scholars interested in fan practices of Poles, to the point where its existence is ignored. This may be partially caused by the fact that it is difficult to call it a community in its own right, since it rarely functions as one. The more adequate description of it would be "fans who happen to be Poles, engaging in typical media fandom behaviors online." Thus, I propose to differentiate between the *Polish fandom* and *fandom that happens to be in Poland*. To do so, however, I need to take a look at their respective histories. The division between these two in many ways mirrors the division between the older, curative SF fandom, and the younger, more feminized and LGBTQ-friendly transformative media fandom in the US. It is, however, impossible to discuss the development of Polish communities as simply parallel to the American ones.

Polish Fandom

As Justyna Deszcz-Tryhubczak and Agata Zarzycka (2013) point out, in Poland, the emergence of fandom was delayed by several decades. That deferment is noticeable even in comparison to the Soviet Union, where the first fan clubs appeared in the 1950s and 1960s (Nowakowski 2017: 87), while the first structures in Poland sprang into existence in 1975 and 1976. Ogólnopolski Klub Miłośników Fantastyki i Science Fiction, the first centralized Polish fan organization, survived only for a couple of years, and was quickly succeeded by Polskie Stowarzyszenie Miłośników Fantastyki, responsible for the influential *Fantastyka* magazine, introduced in 1982 and still in print (since 1990, as *Nowa Fantastyka*). Albeit *Fantastyka* was a commercial magazine, it was pivotal to Polish fandom's development.

Similar to numerous smaller local club zines (*Kwazar, Pulsar, Feniks*, among others), *Fantastyka* was focused on literature. The articles published in the magazine included classic Polish works on speculative genres, and more recent Western essays. The main function of the magazine, however, just like in case of zines, was to present the audience with pieces of Polish speculative fiction, translations of Western ones, and information about Western movies and TV series. Illustrations were most often instances of original art, and there was no place for – and no notion of – fanfiction.

The contents of Polish zines and fandom-adjacent magazines of the 1980s differed profoundly from their anglophone counterparts of that time, which offered a *surplus*: materials supplementary to source texts. Siuda (2014: 199–202) points out that the key factor in the case of Eastern European fan practices was scarcity: that of rationed paper and ink, and, more importantly, of media. The access to many aspects of Western culture was not restricted, but genre fiction, movies, TV series, and comics – typical components of geek culture – were frowned upon and considered capitalist propaganda. It was the familiarity with *pop* culture that was considered a valuable cultural capital among both dissidents and general audiences, while the act of its consumption was perceived as taking a stance against communist Poland's government (Siuda 2014: 204).

Albeit I find it difficult to agree with the notion of Polish fandom activity being completely subversive, given that it required approval of – and resources from – the government, Big Name Fans of the era are still celebrated as champions of democracy and members of the anti-communist opposition. As a result, Polish fandom tends to be conservative (Janik et al. 2013). The predominantly anti-communist speculative fiction in Poland has quickly become intertwined with conservatism (Krawczyk 2022: 90–126), or, later on, libertarianism (Kołodziejczak 2000: 23), and that situation is changing very slowly. What the fall of the regime in 1989 changed was not the political stance of the community, but the accessibility of literary and media texts.

Given the initial restricted access to Western objects of fandom, the Polish community has developed its own canon of cult texts (a mixture of Western and Soviet literature with fewer examples of cinema and virtually no TV), which remains different from the international geek canon to this day. Given that few people owned a VHS, it was easier to distribute literature zines than movies or, especially, TV series. Even though in the 1990s many Western works have entered the fandom's orbit, the canon established in the 1970s and 1980s had already been there, and the differences this caused prevail to this day. For example, while *Star Wars*' status in Poland is similar to the one in the US, *Star Trek* is less popular than *Babylon 5* or the *Battlestar Galactica* remake. Cult classics such as *Forbidden Planet* or *Zardoz* are marginalized, and their place has been taken by Eastern Bloc SF cinema and literature. Even in the case of tabletop role-playing games, *Dungeons&Dragons* is overlooked in favor of *Warhammer* (the first system to be translated into Polish), *Call of Cthulhu*, or the fairly obscure *Earthdawn*.

The Polish fandom originating in the 1970s is predominantly male (Krawczyk 2022: 75; Janik et al. 2013; Kucharska et al. 2015). Despite how vastly this community differs from the contemporary English-speaking (and also male-dominated) curative fandom, it is surprisingly similar to the American fandom of the 1930s and 1940s, and there are reasons for that. The aforementioned lack of access to media caused the community to focus on older literature, and while some more recent pieces were translated and published in parts in zines, underground distribution of video proved difficult, limiting Poles' field of interest to types of texts that, in the USA, had been objects of fandom decades earlier. Kochanowicz (2016: 260), noting how scarcity shaped both communities, points out that "the motivation to create zines was very similar to one that drove the production of American amateur magazines of 1930s."

I would argue that the community described as proof of local traditions prevailing was actually doing everything in its power to be similar to the American SF fandom, even if Poles' vision of it was highly outdated. Both zines and officially distributed fandom-adjacent press contained not only information about Polish conventions and clubs, but also meticulous accounts of Poles who attended events abroad. One of the early issues of *Fantastyka* included a piece that detailed Western fan activities, explaining the words "fan," "fanzine," and "fandom" (Staniewski 1985: 65). Notably, none of the media fandom practices were mentioned, and the image of SF fandom emerging from that piece was outdated as well. In 2001, one of the fan journalists, while discussing *Galaxy Quest*, a movie universally recognized as a love letter to Trekkies, described it as a cruel mockery of fan culture, since fans were shown wearing uniforms of a fictional crew, learning alien languages, and memorizing worthless trivia (Grzegorzak 2001: 57–58). All of these activities, stereotypical of Western fanboys, were still so alien to Polish audiences that their portrayal was considered insulting.

In a couple of years, however, there would emerge another community, one that would quickly become familiar with contemporary American fan practices and would rarely interact with the already established Polish fandom.

Fandom That Happens to Be in Poland[1]

There have been case studies of specific Polish fanworks (Perzyńska 2015) and genre phenomena (Kobus 2019), and numerous Polish papers and monographs refer to Polish media fans when discussing media fandom in general. Still, to my knowledge, neither the emergence of this community, nor its status as situated in Poland have been discussed at length. It is not an oversight; the engagement and practices of Polish media fans have not been analyzed as a phenomenon separate from the anglophone international media fandom *because* Polish media fandom does not exist as – and does not consider itself – a separate entity.

In the early 2000s, the use of the internet in Poland became widespread thanks to a much cheaper provider. In the years preceding its introduction, the internet was considered either a necessity for intellectual workers, or a luxury, and in both cases, perceived as a domain of adult and fairly affluent people (Jutkiewicz 2016: 35). Still, it was not used solely in a professional capacity, and since the 1990s, mailing lists and message boards were gradually becoming important parts of the Polish SF&F fandom infrastructure. The sudden spike in accessibility of the internet meant that preadolescents and adolescents, interested in similar objects of fandom but lacking any knowledge of online etiquette, started to enter already established communities. The new users were, often unintentionally, causing disruption, and were quickly dubbed trolls. They either changed their behavior and adapted to the norms and expectations of the elders, or left to seek out their peers and create their own communities.

It is that second eventuality that facilitated the birth of media fandom in Poland. Among the behaviors deemed unacceptable on Polish message boards, there were consecutive posts about one's love for a character, discussions about emotions they evoked, and – later on – posting fanfic, especially non-heteronormative romance or self-insert stories about brilliant, pretty young women (in many cases, both the authors and their audiences were unfamiliar with terms "slash" or "Mary Sue"). It did not help the newcomers' cases that they were younger than the core userbase and interested in other kinds of media as well. TV dramas, cartoons, manga, anime, and young adult literature, suddenly available in Poland, while very appealing to the new generation, were often perceived as infantile by the older one.

To add insult to injury, users interested in such childish pursuits were often *girls*. Similarly to American women watching *Star Trek* and forming media fandom in 1960s (Coppa 2006), Polish teenage fangirls of 2000s – perceived as overtly emotional and focused on media less sophisticated than works that used to be celebrated by fans – were often met with distaste. They formed separate sets of norms and behaviors, which came to be almost identical with these of their American counterparts. Even though *Star Trek* has never been important to Polish fan culture, *Harry Potter*, manga, and anime played the same role, serving as the change's catalysts. None of them, however, were as important as the medium that made accessing these texts and forming communities around them possible: the internet.

Millennials, unwelcome in SF&F fandom spaces established by adults, created their own message boards dedicated to objects of fandom, and started using blogging platforms. Soon, Polish sites intended for personal blogging (i.e., blog.onet.pl, mylog.pl) were hosting tens of thousands of blogs written by Hogwarts students and *Naruto* characters. Given that in 2000s' Poland, blogging was considered a feminine activity, the gender composition of fanfic community started to resemble the American one, while teenage boys tended to migrate to the older fandom, gradually adopting its norms.

Girls and others drawn to this tools of fandom, logging onto their blogs around 2004, were suddenly encountering fictional characters' diaries on a mass scale. Soon, stories written in third person followed. People running blogs of this kind often started out unaware of what their narratives were called, but the community was quickly learning about the existence of fanfic and Western genre categorizations. By 2005, there were already blogs dedicated to evaluation of others' stories, and by 2006, terms such as "Mary Sue" (or *Maria Zuzanna*), "beta-reading," and ship-related abbreviations had entered the evaluators' and writers' vocabularies.

A lot of said knowledge did not come directly from the English-speaking internet. Most teenagers attending elementary and middle school, despite being the first generation of Poles to learn English instead of Russian, did not know the language well enough to consider reading in English anything but a chore. The key facilitator of the exchange of information between the anglophone and Polish-speaking media fandoms, and the main cause for media fandom in Poland becoming so similar to the American one, was *Mirriel*.

Mirriel, established in 2004 as a "literary message board," has always been a strange place – a community of mostly adult and mostly female fans who at times participated in the Polish SF&F fandom, but decided to carve out a space for themselves and their writing. Albeit they were often publishing original stories, they encouraged writing fanfiction, including slash. One could have expected *Mirriel* to mediate between the emerging millennial media fandom and the older Polish community, but what it actually did was bridge the gap between the teenage fangirls and the anglophone fanfic community.

Every *Mirriel* user was subjected to rigorous vetting processes before being allowed to enter some sections, and the key criterion was maturity (judged by the content of the posts, spelling, and linguistic prowess). Fics were expected to undergo a beta reading, and mistakes, tired clichés and out-of-character behaviors, were pointed out in the comments. Given that some of the users were recognized professional writers, the community was highly hierarchized (Kulesza-Gulczyńska 2015: 117). Millennials quickly formed a love-hate relationship with it, feeling both drawn to *Mirriel*, and unwelcome there, often too afraid of criticism to post anything, lurking, reading the older users' fics and discussions instead. It was *Mirriel* that introduced Poles to basic fanfic terminology and foreign stories. A chunk of the message board was dedicated to translations of popular English-language fics, and there were separate threads explaining the process of receiving an author's permission to translate fanworks from various platforms.

As the teenage audience of *Mirriel* was gaining a better understanding of Western fanfiction tropes and subgenres, they were simultaneously acquiring better knowledge of English at school. Soon, it was no longer necessary to wait for fic translators to catch up with the updates, and young media fans entered platforms such as FanFiction.Net, DeviantArt, and LiveJournal (replaced by AO3, Tumblr, and Wattpad within the next decade). Gradually, international repositories and microblogging platforms became more popular than Polish services.

Siuda (2012: 204–220), claiming that Poles did not participate in practices like writing slash, based his argument on male-dominated message boards popular among members of the SF&F fandom, and was looking for data in all the wrong places. Prompted by the outrage among Polish LiveJournal users who encountered his papers, he did include in his monograph's final chapter a discussion on the Polish LJ fan community (Siuda 2012: 232–236), noting: "while physically they are placed in front of computer screens in Poland, they do not belong to the local fan community" (Siuda 2012: 236). Nevertheless, LJ was the only platform he took notice of, failing to mention fanfiction and art repositories, as if never looking at the statistics there.

There are tens of thousands of stories translated into or originally written in Polish, published in anglophone repositories and categorized according to American norms. Poles post fanvids on YouTube and share their fanart on Tumblr, X, and Instagram. Millennials – and, later on, Gen Z – have adopted fan practices and terminology they encountered in English-speaking spaces. Nowadays, writing or discussing the object of fandom in Polish is incidental – and as one's English improves, they switch to fandom's lingua franca. Oftentimes, Poles come across other Poles, and have no way of knowing it. As one of the Polish fangirls Siuda quotes in the last part of his monograph points out, "people don't go around asking every Anglophone person they meet where do they actually live" (Siuda 2012: 236). Similarly, Prassolova (2007), when describing Russian media fandom, noted:

> Those Russian-language artists who create something of interest prefer to participate in English-language communities for want of greater audience and appreciation: they may speak Russian or be physically located in Russia, but in reality they do not belong to this particular national fandom.

Polish media fans rarely seek out each other, given that using English gives them a much better shot at recognition. Kustritz (2015: ¶3.1) rightly notes that when researching or attending fan spaces, especially online ones, there is a risk of "assuming that because conversations there take place in English, the participants all come from Anglophone countries," which causes elision of the actual diversity of the communities. Nationality in fandom, not unlike race (Pande 2018), is often invisible.

Nowadays, there are some Polish-speaking communities within media fandom, but they are formed almost exclusively on international platforms and apps like Facebook, Tumblr, or Discord. While they use the Polish language, their online practices are almost identical with those of anglophone fans. From the very beginning, media fans in Poland not only have had few ties to the community established during the communist era, but have been interacting with each other via the internet, and (with the exception of manga and anime community) rarely at conventions. The situation is gradually changing, and since around 2010, there have been many events attracting representatives of different types of fandom. Still, attending these is not considered a crucial media fan behavior – or even an important one, compared to running a Tumblr blog, participating in social media outrages, and posting stories on AO3 or Wattpad.

It is impossible to call that large group of Polish fans engaging in transformative practices a *Polish* fandom. It has very little to do with local traditions, its fan loyalties lie elsewhere, and its practices are the transformative "default mode" established in the US long ago. They might have grown up in Poland, but as fans, they have grown up *online*, and they do not experience any pressing need to form a community based on nationality, considered far less important than other factors (e.g., mental health, disabilities, gender, or sexuality).

That, of course, is not to say that there are no differences between fans in Poland and those in other countries. As Tymińska and Włodarczyk (2015: ¶7.7) note, media fans, especially Tumblr users, "tend to perceive themselves as the most tolerant and open-minded of people – equality in general, as well as LGBTQ rights, are well known and supported," and Polish users are no different. Włodarczyk and Tymińska, however, rightly point out that issues such as racial or ethnic minorities' rights often go unnoticed because the exposure to people of other races and/or ethnicities varies depending on one's location. Indeed, fans from Poland – an almost monoethnic country since World War II – rarely focus on issues alien to their own everyday experiences. Instead, they are mostly concerned with LGBTQ rights, which have been under attack in Poland for some time.

Globalization is not a linear process that would envelop chosen fields and leave them absolutely identical across the continents, and thus, the experiences of media fans living in Poland differ from ones of people from other countries. Unlike the communities which have emerged before the popularization of internet access, however, they do not consider historical and national factors important to their identity, and rarely seek out each other on these bases.

Conclusions

The proliferation of fanworks posted on international platforms in languages other than English, and the sheer number of fandom platform users from non-English speaking countries suggest that the discussed phenomenon is hardly specific to Poland, but, more likely, typical of semi-peripheral online fan culture. For instance, Prassolova's (2007) account of Russian *Harry Potter* fandom's introduction to fanfic tropes and terminology is extremely similar to the one I presented here. Analogically, some Czech fans do not consider themselves a part of Czech fandom but members of the international community (Jansová 2021). Cuntz-Leng and Meintzinger (2015: ¶4.2) hypothesize that "German fan fiction writers of a certain age and education tend to migrate to English-speaking areas of fan culture," while young Swedes' involvement in fandom is an important factor in their acquisition of the English language (Olin-Scheller and Sundqvist 2015: ¶4.1).

As I attempted to demonstrate throughout this chapter, it is impossible to discuss Polish fans as homogenous. Just like in case of the anglophone communities, there is an obvious split between the curative community originating from the male-dominated SF fandom, and the transformative media fandom. I would suggest that this division, however, runs even deeper, since in the case of Poland, it is juxtaposed with issues such as generation, internet access, and, most importantly, national identity – one that, oddly enough, matters very little to media fans in my country.

Further investigation into development of media fandoms and their practices in peripheral and semiperipheral countries, especially if it were to take into account the existence of other (and perhaps older) local structures and their traditions, could not only change the way media fandom is being discussed, but also give us more insight into the internet's influence on local languages, practices, and identities. It is, however, crucial to remember while conducting research that there might be numerous fan communities in the same territory. Approaching solely one of them will not necessarily lead to the others.

Note

1 Since the emergence of this community is underresearched, in this section, I am leaning heavily on my own experience as an obnoxious teenage fangirl in 2000s' Poland, and on numerous discussions with Poles who entered fandom spaces around the same time. For ethical reasons, I refrain from citing specific blogs and message boards, with the exception of *Mirriel*, which has already been discussed in papers (e.g., Kulesza-Gulczyńska 2015).

References

Bortel, K. (2005). Medialni barbarzyńcy. *Nowa Fantastyka*, 9, pp. 6–8.
Coppa, F. (2006). A Brief History of Media Fandom. In K. Busse, K. Hellekson (eds.), *Fan Fiction and Fan Communities in the Age of the Internet*. Jefferson, NC: McFarland, pp. 41–59.
Cuntz-Leng, V. and Meintzinger, J. (2015). A Brief History of Fan Fiction in Germany. *Transformative Works and Cultures*, 19.
Deszcz-Tryhubczak, J. and Zarzycka, A. (2013). *Paritcipatory Poland: An Introduction*. http://henryjenkins.org/blog/2013/11/participatory-poland-part-one-participatory-poland-an-introduction.html [accessed 17 July 2023].
Grzegorzak, A. (2001). Huzia na fanów. *Nowa Fantastyka*, 6, pp. 57–58.
Hannerz, U. (1996). *Transnational Connections: Culture, People, Places*. New York: Routledge.
Janik, J., Kucharska, J., Majkowski, T. Z., Płaszewska, J., Schweiger B., Sterczewski P., and Gąsienica-Daniel, P. (2013). *Participatory Poland (Part Five): You Forgot Poland: Exploratory Qualitative Study of Polish SF and Fantasy Fandom*. http://henryjenkins.org/blog/2013/12/participatory-poland-part-five-you-forgot-poland-exploratory-qualitative-study-of-polish-sf-and-fantasy-fandom.html [accessed 17 July 2023].
Jansová, I. (2021). *Global Fandom: Iveta Jansová (Czechia)* [online]. http://henryjenkins.org/blog/2021/9/6/global-fandom-iveta-jansov-czech-republic [accessed 17 July 2023].
Jenkins, H. (2006). *Fans, Bloggers, and Gamers: Exploring Participatory Culture*. New York: New York University Press.
Jenkins, H., Ford, S., and Green, J. (2013). *Spreadable Media: Creating Value and Meaning in a Networked Culture*. New York: NYU Press.
Jutkiewicz, M. (2016). Internauci w oczach mediów. *Autoportret*, 1(52), pp. 32–39.

Kobus, A. (2019). Opowiadanie *yaoi*. Hybrydowe gatunki w polskiej twórczości fanowskiej. In D. Brzostek, A. Kobus, K. Marak, and M. Markocki (eds.), *Chińskie bajki: Fandom mangi i anime w Polsce*. Toruń: Wydawnictwo Uniwersytetu Mikołaja Kopernika, pp. 157–180.

Kochanowicz, R. (2016). "Kwazar", "Fantom", "Czerwony Karzeł", "Inne Planety". Kilka uwag krytycznych o nietypowej sytuacji fantastycznych fanzinów w kulturze polskiej. *Poznańskie Studia Polonistyczne. Seria Literacka*, 28, pp. 249–269.

Kołodziejczak, T. (2000). Naprawdę, jaki jesteś, nie wie nikt.... *Magia i Miecz*, 2, pp. 23–24.

Krawczyk, S. (2022). *Gust i prestiż: O przemianach polskiego świata fantastyki*. Warszawa: Scholar.

Kucharska, J., Sterczewski, P., Schweiger B., Płaszewska, J., and Janik, J. (2015). Finding Poland: Negotiating the Local and the Global in the Construction of Semiperipheral Identity in Polish Science Fiction and Fantasy Fandom. *Transformative Works and Cultures*, 19. https://journal.transformativeworks.org/index.php/twc/article/view/592/491 [accessed 17 July 2023].

Kulesza-Gulczyńska, B. (2015). O dwuznaczności słowa *canon*. *Casus* Forum Literackiego Mirriel. *Miscellanea Anthropologica et Sociologica*, 16(2), pp. 112–126.

Kustritz, A. (2015). Transnationalism, Localization, and Translation in European Fandom: Fan Studies as Global Media and Audience Studies. *Transformative Works and Cultures*, 19.

Nowakowski, A. (2017). *Fanzin SF. Artyści – wydawcy – Fandom*. Poznań: Instytut Kultury Popularnej.

Olin-Scheller, C., and Sundqvist, P. (2015). A Connected Country: Sweden – Fertile Ground for Digital Fandoms. *Transformative Works and Cultures*, 19.

Pande, R. (2018). *Squee from the Margins: Fandom and Race*. Iowa City: University of Iowa Press.

Perzyńska, A. (2015). Literackie zabawy w środowiskach fanowskich: Studium przypadku. *Teksty Drugie*, 3, pp. 246–260.

Pieterse, J. N. (2009). *Globalization and Culture: Global Mélange*. Plymouth: Rowman & Littlefield.

Prassolova, K. (2007). 'Oh, Those Russians!': The (Not So) Mysterious Ways of Russian-language Harry Potter Fandom (Part Two). http://henryjenkins.org/blog/2007/07/oh_those_russians_the_not_so_m_1.html [accessed 17 July 2023].

Scott, S. (2019). *Fake Geek Girls. Fandom, Gender and the Convergence Culture Industry*. New York: New York University Press.

Siuda, P. (2012). *Kultury prosumpcji: O niemożności powstania globalnych i ponadpaństwowych społeczności fanów*. Warszawa: ASPRA-JR.

Siuda, P. (2014). In Pursuit of Pop Culture. Reception of Pop Culture in the People's Republic of Poland as Opposition to the Political System – Example of the Science Fiction Fandom. *European Journal of Cultural Studies*, 17(2), pp. 187–208.

Stanfill, M. (2019). *Exploiting Fandom. How the Media Industry Seeks to Manipulate Fans*. Iowa City: University of Iowa Press.

Staniewski, P. (1985). Fanowie – Fanziny – Fandom. *Fantastyka*, 11, p. 65.

Tymińska, M., and Włodarczyk, A. (2015). Cultural Differences: Polish Fandom of *Welcome to Night Vale*. *Transformative Works and Cultures*, 19. https://journal.transformativeworks.org/index.php/twc/article/view/591/490 [accessed 17 July 2023].

20
NAVIGATING ONLINE ECOSYSTEMS

Chinese Celebrity Fans' Participation across Social Media Platforms

Qiuyan Guo

As fans participate and develop communities across various websites, digital servers, social media, etc. (Bennet 2014; Jenkins et al. 2015), they increasingly explore beyond the boundaries of individual platforms, negotiating the diverse features offered by a combination of platforms that cater to their fandom preferences and needs. However, the evolution of multi-platform fandom practices has received little scholarly attention, with researchers focusing primarily on the choices fans make regarding individual platforms: either engaging with or acquiescing to one platform's features or migrating completely to another platform (Leiser 2018; Fiesler and Dym 2020). For instance, scholars have presented how fans assert self-policing rules to negotiate Tumblr's lack of administration (Stein 2018) or promote celebrities to the public as prompted by Weibo's algorithm (Guo 2022; Yin 2020). When facing irreconcilable challenges on a platform such as an unfavorable interface design, a fan community may switch their primary engagement to another platform (e.g., AO3; Price and Robinson 2021). Yet, overlapping platform usage during such migrations is viewed as temporary since fans intend to eventually abandon the original platform (Fiesler and Dym 2020).

Nevertheless, it is also crucial to analyze contemporary fans' evolving practice of expanding fan participation beyond individual online spaces to explore how fans utilize a combination of platforms. This expanded online engagement is illustrated in this chapter by contemporary Chinese celebrity fans who, in order to connect with various particular audiences, develop distinct modes of fan discourse across social media platforms. Examining this fan participation can help scholars understand fans' increasingly nuanced attitudes, awareness, and decision-making processes as they explore additional platforms and collectively develop insights about themselves and their communities. As Chinese celebrity fans' multi-platform engagement flourishes, their online communities are a productive site to examine how contemporary fans more generally conduct fandom activities across combinations of social media platforms.

This chapter presents a case study exploring the practices of representative celebrity fan groups of two Chinese musical actors, Yunlong Zheng and Ayanga. Rising to fame together in the 2018 reality show *SuperVocal*, Ayanga and Yunlong have attracted over one million fans on Weibo, many of whom are also highly active on two other popular Chinese platforms, WeChat and Douban. This study suggests that fans often seek to interact with common netizens (internet users who are not celebrity fans), senior and/or trusted fans in their communities, and fans of other celebrities; these interactions cannot be satisfied on any single platform. As fans encounter difficulties practicing such diverse discursive modes on single platforms, they increasingly recognize their preferences and, in turn, expand their online engagement to multiple platforms. Without abandoning familiar online spaces, fans mindfully build and learn to navigate a multi-platform ecosystem comprising, collectively, a variety of desirable platform features.

Exploring a Combination of Chinese Social Media Platforms

Fandom centered on Ayanga and Yunlong started in early 2019. While some fans exclusively like one of the two actors, others are spurred by Ayanga and Yunlong's long-standing friendship and enjoy pairing them as an intimate "couple," or CP (Guo 2023), thus forming three communities: Ayanga-exclusive fans, Yunlong-exclusive fans, and CP fans who enjoy the Ayanga/Yunlong "couple." Fans in these communities have engaged in abundant celebrity promotion, analysis of celebrity performance, and online fighting across Weibo, WeChat, and Douban, making these fan groups a suitable site for such research. Based on observation of online fan practices and semi-structured interviews with 20 individual fans (conducted from June 2021 to May 2022), this section examines in detail how Chinese celebrity fans interact with different audiences on each platform and how they negotiate platform features accordingly.

Weibo

As Weibo is the foremost social media platform favored by the Chinese entertainment industry for promoting celebrities toward the public, it often serves as the primary space where common netizens first discover and become fans of a celebrity, and where fans establish and cultivate their communities (Guo 2022; Yin 2020). Launched by *Sina Corporation* in 2009 and sharing similarities with Twitter, Weibo allows fans to (re)post, comment, "like," search, and follow other users while staying anonymous about their name, age, gender, and/or profession. (Re)posts and comments may contain texts, images, (hash)tags, links, and @s; whereas posts can have a maximum of 2,000 textual characters and 18 images, reposts and comments are restricted to 140 characters and a single image. One unique function on Weibo is the "supertopic," which, while remaining accessible to the public, enables users to construct interest-based community circles separate from the main Weibo space. Fans often request Weibo administrators to form supertopics for particular celebrities; once these supertopics are approved by the site, fans themselves may then establish multiple sections within a supertopic (e.g., posts, videos, photos, fanworks, etc.) and invite fellow fans to join. Meanwhile, the open accessibility of these supertopics, as well as general celebrity publicity, lead common netizens on Weibo to be quite familiar with any fan activities happening in these spaces.

Weibo was the initial space for Ayanga and Yunlong fans to form their communities. In 2019, three main supertopics were created for Ayanga, Yunlong, and their CP, respectively, in accordance with Weibo's rules as early fans posted their affections for the actors and connected with each other. Within these supertopics, fans frequently write fanfiction (either for an exclusive actor or the CP), collect and share the actors' show photos, analyze the actors' skills using their performance videos, and express their love and enthusiasm while directly @-ing the actors. Beyond these primarily in-community discussions, fans also seek to promote Ayanga and/or Yunlong toward the public, which is encouraged both by the industry and by Weibo's algorithm (Guo 2022; Zhang and Negus 2020). One primary way such advertising works is by generating more "traffic data," a term that references the entirety of (re)posts, comments, and hashtags related to a particular celebrity on Weibo (Yin 2020). In this sense, many Ayanga and Yunlong fans create massive (re)posts to publicize the actor(s)' handsomeness, singing/performing skills, new albums, etc. with related photos and hashtags. Along with these promotions, which flourished after the 2019 establishment of supertopics, each of the three fan communities grew rapidly, reaching populations of over 300,000 by 2021, as millions of fan posts were created across Weibo.

However, as reported by many interview participants, although Weibo allows fans to discover Ayanga and Yunlong, connect with like-minded fans, and promote the actor(s) toward common netizens, the public accessibility offered by this platform also brings limitations to their practices. Facing public audiences, fans must constantly consider how their promotions and their communities are perceived by the public, while restricting activities that demand greater privacy. For example, in recent years, fans grew increasingly frustrated with how common netizens ridiculed fan efforts to advertise their celebrities. Beginning around 2020, instead of accepting or ignoring fans' promotional activities as they had in the past, many people became irritated by excessive posts "bragging" about celebrity achievements and diligence, which they deemed "trivial," condemning fans for "ridiculously worshiping" celebrities. One Ayanga fan explained their frustration with this perspective:

> I feel this attitude change is mainly because of the pandemic... since the economic situation is not good, many people have to struggle with reduced incomes and naturally become crankier online, especially when they see promotions of celebrities they don't care about. I get this, but we also didn't do anything wrong in supporting Ayanga... it's so annoying to see all that ridicule, but this shouldn't stop Ayanga from being publicized...

As this statement shows, although many fans were often understanding of the attitude change among common netizens, they still faced difficulties promoting Ayanga and/or Yunlong on Weibo due to such rejection and criticism. Nevertheless, while many senior fans seek to develop solutions for this situation, they find themselves unable to collectively devise new promotional strategies on Weibo. The fear is that even their discussions about how to make posts more interesting or trustworthy are publicly accessible, open to discovery by common netizens, which could potentially invite additional ridicule. In fans' minds, these conversations require more private settings that can be accessed only by trustworthy senior fans.

Further, most fans are frustrated that some of their in-community interactions on Weibo are also criticized by the public, not only undermining their promotional efforts but further tarnishing the reputation of their communities. This happens most typically when fans from the three communities – Ayanga-exclusive, Yunlong-exclusive, and CP fans – engage in heated arguments on Weibo, thus "annoying" common netizens (Lin 2021). The actors' frequent collaborations since 2019 inevitably prompted continuing cross-community encounters wherein fans considered some posts in opposing supertopics "unacceptable," especially regarding the comparison between the two actors and depictions of their intimacy. For example, posts suggesting that Ayanga has better singing skills and Yunlong is more proficient in acting might stimulate argument among fans of the three communities. Similarly, when CP fans interpreted Ayanga and Yunlong's dynamic in an interview as "intimate," it irritated Ayanga-exclusive fans who perceived the actors as enemies, who believed Yunlong's every move "stabbed Ayanga in the back." Because such "unacceptable" content often results in fierce cross-community flame wars and invites criticism from the public, many fans are hesitant about what they should post on Weibo. One CP fan shared during an interview:

> I hate fighting with Ayanga- or Yunlong-exclusive fans because it can show other people [common netizens] that fans of the two actors are all crazy; I don't want to give people a bad impression of Ayanga and Yunlong… I think to avoid having conflicts, many fans have to stop making comparisons between them or sharing analysis of their intimacy on Weibo…

This statement presents the typical perception among fans that they should avoid fighting in front of common netizens on Weibo by exercising caution in making certain comparisons or analyses. Some interview participants further suggested that expanding platform censorship on posts that include "unhealthy" sexual content (Chen et al. 2023) also dissuaded CP fans from including erotic descriptions in their analyses of or creation of fanworks about the actors' intimacy. Nevertheless, since fans still desire to make comparisons between the actors or imagine their intimacy, they seek to have these discussions between only trusted fans in more private spaces.

In general, due to the open accessibility of supertopics, Ayanga and Yunlong fans are frustrated with how their practices are perceived by common netizens on Weibo, leading them to decide that certain conversations should be conducted not on Weibo but on more private platforms facing only selected audiences. However, since fans still need Weibo to attract new fans and publicize the actor(s), they often view the platform's limitations not as reasons to resent Weibo entirely but as unfortunate difficulties to be solved. Thus, many fans continue with their "publicly appropriate" activities on Weibo while seeking other platforms that allow more private discussions between senior/trusted fans.

WeChat

Since 2020, group chat channels on WeChat have become the primary platform where fans of Ayanga and Yunlong host more private discussions for only senior or trusted fans who have been in the fandom for a relatively long time (e.g., over six months). First released in 2011, WeChat is a multipurpose application developed by *Tencent* company and used by over one billion Chinese people in everyday life. Similar to WhatsApp, WeChat's primary social media function allows fans to privately share "sensitive" messages or content that may be "irritating" to others. For example, a fan can first create a new WeChat group channel and then share that channel ID or QR code in their Weibo supertopic to invite other senior or trusted fans to join. Fans often keep WeChat group populations relatively small, often under 100 people, to maintain a close and manageable circle. Early members of a group tend to establish specific rules (e.g., no attacking each other, no ad-posting) and give channel creators the authority to remove individuals who violate those rules. Since WeChat is also fans' most frequently used application for everyday socializing with people outside the fandom realm, talking with each other in these groups appears to be much easier for fans than sending direct messages on Weibo.

These private, fan-managed WeChat channels are helpful for fans to accomplish their intended goals of discussing topics that they do not want to share publicly on Weibo, especially regarding their promotional strategies and deeper comparisons/analyses of Ayanga and Yunlong. For example, many fans use WeChat groups as a space to collectively review Weibo's algorithm to figure out how (re)posts, comments, and hashtags are showcased and calculated into the platform's data framework, seeking to exploit these rules to increase the visibility of their publicizing posts about the actor(s). They also strategize approaches to make fan advertisements on Weibo appear trustworthy and less "annoying," such as fans composing their own recommendational sentences rather than using similar, formulaic language. Meanwhile, knowing their audiences are relatively "mature" and loyal fans, group members often express more honest judgements of Ayanga and/or Yunlong's "real" singing and acting skills, such as how Ayanga needs to perform less like a "robot" or how Yunlong should practice more to not sing "off-tune." CP fans in particular analyze when Ayanga and Yunlong started a real-life romantic relationship and share erotic fan art/fiction without facing outsider judgement or censorship. Although fans are often uncertain about the efficiency of their strategies or the accuracy of their analyses, WeChat still gives them the chance to release emotional discontent by discussing difficulties, complaining about common netizens or Weibo censorship, and "trashing" extreme fans who "always want to fight."

Through these more private discussions, many fans tend to form much closer relationships with fans in their WeChat group than with those on Weibo. One CP fan commented in an interview:

> Although we never met in person, some group members are really my friends now. We talk about Ayanga and Yunlong all the time, and I can even tell them about my personal stuff… it's definitely different from what it's like on Weibo.

This statement shows that WeChat has provided fans a private environment where, by conducting intentional fandom activities, they gradually develop deeper friendships and build ongoing fandom discussions. On this basis, fans gradually set more specific criteria for whom to invite into their groups, such as those in similar age groups or those holding similar expectations for Ayanga and/or Yunlong. These expectations may also collectively change over time, as more fans bring in their own fandom perspectives and experiences. Fans who are more experienced participating in online platforms may regard joining a WeChat group as a direct opportunity to find more like-minded friends. As one interview participant said: "When I don't get along with someone in a group, I would create a new channel and ask a few friends from that group to join… a smaller group would be more fun, and it's kind of my goal now." In general, unlike Weibo that mainly serves as a "posting" space toward common netizens, private discussions in front of trusted audiences lead to WeChat groups becoming comparable to fans' pre-internet offline gathering places that often help fans further connect with each other on both fantasied and personal levels (e.g., Jenkins 1992; Lamerichs 2018).

While fans enjoy WeChat's private group channels, this has not led to their rejection of other platforms; instead, many Ayanga and/or Yunlong fans began learning how to navigate various online spaces for different types of fan discourse: publicly interacting with common netizens and privately interacting with senior/trusted fans. Most interview participants reported that, after using WeChat to discuss how to better publicize the actor(s) on Weibo, they become more active in creating promotional posts while employing their new "strategies." Even though such efforts may have yet to change the attitudes of common netizens, fans do exhibit more confidence and a greater sense of righteousness when facing ridicule for publicizing their actor(s). For instance, groups often request all members to maintain confidentiality, particularly prohibiting fans from screenshotting their conversations and subsequently posting them on Weibo. While fans still publicly invite new group members who meet specific criteria, they have become more vigilant in identifying and deterring "undercover fans" (e.g., an exclusive fan who aims to gain access to private discussions among CP fans). While these self-regulations are employed on the relatively private WeChat platform, they are comparable to how fans assert self-policing or gatekeeping rules on Tumblr and AO3 (Leiser 2018; Price and Robinson 2021).

On the basis of accumulating in-group discussions, fans often arrive at the conclusion that they should broaden their information sources to more effectively improve their strategies and analyses. This may include learning from more experienced celebrity fan communities and retrieving more "insider" information on how the industry judges fan practices. This realization serves as a catalyst for them to explore additional platforms to interact with fans of other celebrities.

Douban

Launched in 2005, *Douban.com* is one of the oldest social network sites in China (Zhang 2016). While this platform has long attracted users to discuss various aspects of their social lives (e.g., books, sports, cooking, movies, etc.), in recent years it has particularly invited celebrity fans to create posts and review celebrity performances. Numerous groups have also been created centering on these various interests; based on the popularity of the topic, groups can be either formed by Douban administrators or requested by enthusiasts. In the form of a discussion forum, textual or visual posts and comments are created that align with the central interests of each group. Celebrities, in particular, are customarily and constantly discussed in a number of related Douban groups. For instance, Ayanga and Yunlong are frequently mentioned not only in the groups created specifically for each actor and the CP but also in the groups for musicals, reality shows, and those that discuss Chinese celebrities and entertainment news in general. The audiences that Ayanga and Yunlong fans interact with in these groups are thus often fans of other celebrities as well as experts who are familiar with the Chinese entertainment industry.

Unlike Weibo supertopics or WeChat groups, which protect fans' offline information while emphasizing their specific fan identities, Douban groups are operated in a more anonymous manner that deemphasizes both aspects. As Douban allows users to create duplicate ID names, the majority of celebrity fans choose to use the default name "momo" along with the same indistinguishable profile picture, which is also set as a default by the platform. It thus becomes difficult to search for and locate the previous posts of a specific "momo," thereby preventing others from directly recognizing their fandom opinions and identities. In this sense, fans often assume the identity of "a common netizen" on Douban when praising celebrities in discussions, aiming to conceal their "true" fandom identities. This is because, while audiences in Douban groups are mostly celebrity fans rather than common netizens, most fans still seek to distance their Douban speeches from their beloved celebrities and their fan communities to avoid affecting the reputations of those parties in any possible way. This heightened level of anonymity results in more intense debates and freer sharing of information, even though the truthfulness of these opinions and information may be questionable.

These features have led many Ayanga and/or Yunlong fans to consider Douban a suitable platform for interacting with other celebrity fans and acquiring experiences and new information. In one instance, fans received a list of keywords that is shared by other celebrity fans on Douban, which, when incorporated into promotional posts on Weibo, can automatically increase the visibility of these posts and help them appear in search results for Ayanga and/or Yunlong. Fans may also learn from Douban about how to better evaluate a celebrity's singing or acting skills and how to judge if two celebrities truly have an intimate relationship. As one Ayanga-exclusive fan shared, "I really didn't know how to analyze his [Ayanga's] singing in a professional way... after reading more people judging different singers on Douban, I got a clearer idea and shared that with others [fellow Ayanga fans]." Some fans further make posts to express their support of Ayanga and Yunlong in front of other celebrity fans while pretending to be common netizens and worrying less about repercussions for the actor(s) and their communities.

In this sense, Douban has become a supplementary yet indispensable platform for fans to systematically interact with other celebrity fans outside their own fan communities. Compared to Weibo and WeChat where fans conduct their main fandom activities, Douban functions as an information channel for fans to better practice what they engage in on the other two platforms. Douban's anonymity appears to be fans' primary motivator: not only does the platform facilitate a heated flow of information, but it also allows celebrity fans to share experiences and express beliefs in a seemingly more trustworthy manner (pretending to be a "common netizen"). Some fans also seek to employ this approach on Weibo in front of real common netizens, trying to minimize their fan identities when praising the actor(s). Nevertheless, fans have yet to succeed, as previous posts and account connections are quite easy to locate on Weibo; how to solve this issue is still one of the main topics discussed by some fans in their WeChat groups.

Learning to Navigate a Multi-platform Online Ecosystem

These practices by Ayanga and Yunlong fans demonstrate the emerging navigation of multiple online platforms among celebrity fans. Negotiating with platform affordances and functions, fans develop different modes of discourse on each individual platform as they face different audiences – common netizens (Weibo), senior/trusted fans (WeChat), and other celebrity fans (Douban). When facing limitations on one platform, fans move beyond the binary choice previously presented in scholarship of either abandoning or adapting to this platform (Fiesler and Dym 2020; Yin and Xie 2021), instead maintaining their familiarized spaces while seeking particular solutions elsewhere. Ayanga and Yunlong fans have also occasionally explored additional platforms that offer similar features, as each of the existing three main platforms is sufficient for only a portion of their communal needs. For example, CP fans often seek out other sites that can both host their erotic fanfiction and reach broader audiences who are interested in fan creations. In 2021, some CP fans even tried to launch their own platform for exchanging fanworks and confidential information, accessible only through a CP fan identity verification questionnaire.

Engaging with multiple platforms both helps fans to recognize the functions that they truly value in each particular platform and facilitates their learning more about fan culture and the online environment (Guo 2022). As Chinese celebrity fans especially need to interact with different audiences – common netizens and fans themselves at least (Guo 2022; Yin 2020) – spanning their activities across expansive online spaces appears to be a necessary act. Experiences on these platforms and encounters with different audiences in turn also foster a rich exchange of practices, choices, and values among different fan communities, enabling them to learn from one another and gain insight into contemporary Chinese fan culture. Fans also develop comprehensive understandings of the patterns governing platform rules and regulations, and they acquire practical knowledge for making requests to different platforms. These experiences greatly contribute to fans' understandings of the contemporary online environment as a whole; in particular, the interactions between fans and other parties enable fans to enhance their abilities to seek, analyze, and create information (Guo 2022). Ultimately, such evolving understandings and information literacy further empower fans to transcend the limitations of specific platforms and adeptly navigate a multi-platform ecosystem while safeguarding their established territories.

As Chinese celebrity fans continuously develop new modes of discourse and demand to be satisfied by different platforms, they serve as a typical example that showcases how online fan practices are evolving worldwide. Many fans in the West also appear to be moving away from singular platform usage to a more encompassing combination, signaling how fandom practices are currently evolving on a larger scale. For instance, fans of Marvel movies may create and (re)post their fan art/fiction on both Tumblr and AO3 while discussing new character depictions on Twitter. In this sense, many fans may no longer confine their fandoms to a single circle (e.g., Jenkins et al. 2015) but rather expand their activities across the internet. Contemporary fans appear to cultivate increasingly specific awareness of different audiences and nuanced attitudes toward various platform features, which affects the corresponding decision-making processes undergone as they explore additional platforms and maintain their familiar spaces. This development further reveals fans' growing proficiency in navigating not only single-platform functionality but also a complex multi-platform ecosystem that collectively provides ideal online features.

References

Baym, N.K. (2000) *Tune In, Log On: Soaps, Fandom and Online Community*, London: Sage.
Bennett, L. (2014) "Tracing textual poachers: Reflections on the development of fan studies and digital fandom," *The Journal of Fandom Studies*, 2(1), pp. 5–20.
Busse K. and K. Hellekson (2006) "Introduction," in K. Busse and K. Hellekson (eds.) *Fan Fiction and Fan Communities in the Age of the Internet*, Jefferson: McFarland & Company.

Chang, Y. (2014) *Research on the Identity Construction of Korean Pop Music's Fandom Groups on the Weibo Platform: Exemplified by G-Dragon (Kwon Ji-Yong)*, Uppsala University. www.diva-portal.org/smash/get/diva2:725402/FULLTEXT01.pdf

Chen, X., J. Xie, Z. Wang, B. Shen, and Z. Zhou (2023) "How we express ourselves freely: Censorship, self-censorship, and anti-censorship on a Chinese social media," in *International Conference on Information*, Cham: Springer Nature Switzerland, pp. 93–108.

De Kosnik, A., L. El Ghaoui, V. Cuntz-Leng, A. Godbehere, A. Horbinski, A. Hutz, R. Pastel, and V. Pham (2015) "Watching, creating, and archiving: Observations on the quantity and temporality of fannish productivity in online fan fiction archives," *Convergence*, 21(1), pp. 145–164.

Fiesler, C. and B. Dym (2020) "Moving across lands: Online platform migration in fandom communities," *Proceedings of the ACM on Human-Computer Interaction* 4 (CSCW1), pp. 1–25.

Guo, Q. (2022) "How do fans purposely create information to promote a celebrity? An analysis of fans' information practices and literacy improvement," *Library & Information Science Research*, 44(3), p. 101170.

Guo, Q. (2023) "Fiction and reality entangled: Chinese 'coupling' (CP) fans pairing male celebrities for pleasure, comfort, and responsibility," *Celebrity Studies*, 14(4), pp. 485–503.

Jenkins, H. (1992) *Textual Poachers*, London: Routledge.

Jenkins, H., M. Ito, and D. Boyd (2015) *Participatory Culture in a Networked Era: A Conversation on Youth, Learning, Commerce, and Politics*, Cambridge: Polity.

Lamerichs, N. (2018) *Productive Fandom*, Amsterdam: Amsterdam University Press.

Lange, P. G. (2008) "Publicly private and privately public: Social networking on Youtube," *Journal of Computer-Mediated Communication*, 13, pp. 361–380.

Leiser, S. (2018) "Throne of fans: Examining the roles of feminism, platform and community in an online fandom," *Electronic Theses and Dissertations*, 1448. University of Denver. https://digitalcommons.du.edu/cgi/viewcontent.cgi?article=2448&context=etd

Lin, X. (2021) "One year since 227: Reporting, Collapsing, Involution, idol, and fans' 996," Weixin. https://mp.weixin.qq.com/s/U_J-vIlAMwBnEeskeAEJtA

Mittell, J. (2012) "Wikis and participatory fandom," in Aaron Delwich and Jennifer Jacos Henderson (eds.) *The Participatory Cultures Handbook*, London: Routledge, pp. 35–42.

Price, L. (2019) "Fandom, folksonomies and creativity: The case of the Archive of Our Own," in D. Haynes and J. Vernau (eds.) *The Human Position in an Artificial World: Creativity, Ethics and AI in Knowledge Organization*, Würzburg: Ergon, pp. 11–37.

Price, L. and L. Robinson (2021) "Tag analysis as a tool for investigating information behavior: Comparing fan-tagging on Tumblr, archive of our own and etsy," *Journal of Documentation*, 77(2), pp. 320–358.

Stein, L. (2018) "Tumblr fan aesthetics," in Melissa Click and Suzanne Scott (eds.) *The Routledge Companion to Media Fandom*, New York: Routledge, pp. 86–97.

Yin, Y. (2020) "An emergent algorithmic culture: The data-ization of online fandom in China," *International Journal of Cultural Studies*, 23(4), pp. 475–492.

Yin, Y. and Z. Xie (2021) "Playing platformized language games: Social media logic and the mutation of participatory cultures in Chinese online fandom," *New Media & Society*, 26(2), pp. 619–641.

Zhang, W. (2016) *The Internet and New Social Formation in China: Fandom Publics in the Making (Media, Culture and Social Change in Asia)*, New York: Routledge.

Zhang, Q. and K. Negus (2020) "East Asian pop music idol production and the emergence of data fandom in China," *International Journal of Cultural Studies*, 23(4), pp. 493–511.

21
VIDDING AND IDENTITY
A Conversation

Francesca Coppa, Alexis Lothian, and Tisha Turk

> Vidding has been widely discussed as a distinctly "feminine," or potentially "feminist," fan practice. Does the historic emphasis on gender in analyses of both vids and vidding communities potentially obscure other marginalized fans or fan identities?

Francesca Coppa: I think vidding connects importantly to the invisible history of women in film, or maybe I should call it the history of invisible women in film, or maybe even the deposed women of film, because there were many women involved in early film when it wasn't so prestigious or profitable (Mary Pickford, Lois Weber, Anita Loos), even as there is a strong ongoing tradition of female film editors (Margaret Booth, Verna Fields, Thelma Schoonmaker, Sally Menke, etc.). But these women worked in the dark, and their contributions are often seen as secondary to the male directors for whom they worked.

Vidding is a part of female film history in that it is the story of women re-cutting popular culture to make it more attractive to them, or to emphasize a different narrative or emotional strand of the story; vidding in that way is a perfect example of the Kuleshov effect, where to change the sequence of images is to change our emotional reaction to them. Marcia Lucas was able to get Steven Spielberg to film additional scenes for *Raiders of The Lost Ark:* the original cut of the film left Marion Ravenwood on an island full of melted Nazis. Spielberg quickly gathered his lead actors to film a quick emotional resolution. The rest of us don't have that sort of power, but women vidders can re-edit film footage and, by setting the new montage to music, create emotions that weren't in the original, or turn subtext into text. Taste seems to be gendered in this regard: women seem to care about relationships and emotional resolutions more than men do.

As to your question of whether the emphasis on gender obscures other marginalized fans or fan identities, I'd say that a) it is women overwhelmingly who vid and b) "women" is a pretty big category which encompasses any number of other identities. Women vid from different places starting with the classic fannish dilemma of "be him or have him" but which include many different ways of being queer and any number of kinks, sexual and otherwise (I think of vids like The Clucking Belles' "Hot Hot Hot" with its focus on BDSM, and thingswithwings' vid "We Go Together" which is about urination as kink). While vidding, like the media itself, has struggled with issues of racial representation there are many vidding fandoms – *Scandal, Community, The Wire* come immediately to my mind – and fannish BSOs (John Boyega, Gina Torres, Lucy Liu, Anthony Mackie) who are instigating conversation, and maybe even some change, in this area.

Alexis Lothian: The points that Francesca has made, both here and in her published work, about the feminized labor of editing and the histories of women in film, are incredibly important. But it still feels like not quite the right question to me to ask whether vidding is feminine or feminist. Vidding is a form, an artistic practice, a way of making meaning; it can be used in a feminist way, or not. "What kinds of feminist practice and politics does vidding facilitate?" is a crucial question for me.

I think that vidding is a useful form for exploring and expressing feminist politics, feminist practices, because it works by reframing: by taking what is already in the world, already crafted, already seemingly replete with its meanings and significances, and using it as raw material to say something new. Vids invite viewers to look again at what has been familiar, and that's also often what feminism asks people to do. And there's a reason why "transformative" is a phrase that's used equally often in social justice and fan culture contexts – because both people who are trying to change the world and people who are invested in the fannish kinds of creativity, of which vidding is one example, are invested on some level in the proliferation of possibilities, in the malleability of things that often feel as if they're set in stone. That could be capitalism or it could be the gruesome death of one's favorite character.

A way to frame this question that I find useful, is to ask to what extent transformative works are invested in transformative possibilities of social justice. And I think it's very clear that on the level of content they are not – even fan works that we would joyfully hail as feminist are often problematic on a million other levels. This gets to the second part of the question. Rebecca Wanzo's 2015 article "African American Acafandom and Other Strangers," makes the case that the very basis of fan studies has structurally excluded Black fan practices. Our histories and analyses of vidding only rarely mention race, and we have to acknowledge that this is because they have been dominated by whiteness. If we want to reckon with the relationships between transformative fan works and political transformations – which I think is what we have to do to answer the question about whether vidding is feminist – we have to also ask how vidding is racialized and how the subcultural history and present in which we are all embedded has been effectively segregated from racialized forms of remix culture.

Tisha Turk: Yeah, vidding has traditionally been really white – in a lot of different ways and for a lot of different reasons. Francesca's written about the history of vidding as grounded in *Star Trek* specifically and science fiction more generally, and science fiction on television (TV) has tended, especially outside the *Star Trek* franchise, to be pretty white, so in terms of raw materials vidders in that genre have been at something of a disadvantage. But the whiteness of vidding can't just be attributed to racial representation in the casts of shows with big fandoms; it also has to do with what vidders choose to do with those shows. Anecdotally, as I think about where I see characters of color in vids, it's often in character studies or as part of an ensemble. It's much rarer to see a character of color – let alone *two* characters of color – in a relationship vid. That matters. Relationship vids are both one of the most common kinds of vids and the first kind of vid that a lot of people watch or make. So, in that sense, vidding participates in a larger tendency of media fandom: white fans tend to "ship" white pairings, whether canonical or non-canonical.

Many vidders in the 1980s and 1990s and even beyond had white tastes in music as well: show tunes, soft rock, folk music. In the early 2000s, when vidders like Luminosity and sisabet started using hip-hop in vids, a lot of long-time vidwatchers were startled and even put off by those vids; they didn't like this music, they didn't know how to listen to it. That's changed, to some degree, but it's part of the legacy of the form. Whose cultures, tastes, and interests have been welcomed, or even acknowledged, in vidding spaces?

Like Alexis, I'm more interested in vidding as a *creative* practice and fandom as a place for people to claim creative identities. For some scholars – especially, maybe, scholars trained in media studies – it's easy to see vidders primarily as audience members reacting to a media text. But when I look at vidders, I see *creators*, artists – we just happen to be using bits of other people's video to make our art. And even though some vid fans watch vids in an undifferentiated way – not keeping track of who made things, or conflating vidders whose work is really different – there are plenty of other fans who have favorite vidders just like they have favorite shows. That's part of the feminist potential of vidding, for me: it expands the range of artistic practices available for women and girls to claim.

Alexis Lothian: In my own practice, the idea of fandom as connected to a text has slipped away; my own participation in fan communities for a long time has revolved around vidding as a form and feminist science fiction as a politics, with processes and people rather than a particular text in common. But I definitely think that everything I have been saying in this discussion is predicated on that idea of vidder as creative identity and vidding as art form. Which is not to say that all vidders have to see themselves as artists, there are many vidding networks and communities creating vids from many perspectives and with many goals, and none of us could possibly speak for all of them. For me, the main reason to argue for vidding as artistic identity is to make the point that vids are contributions to culture that individuals work hard to create – they're not some kind of anonymous emanation of the footage or song that they use, even though they might seem to come from nowhere when people discover them on random YouTube searches. And the more people get their hands on the tools and understand what it means to produce work in this art form the more people are able to recognize what it takes to create something beautiful, something complex, something cohesive in the form of a vid.

Francesca Coppa: Our own little corner of vidding aside, it's been delightful to see these enormous vidding subcultures develop on YouTube. "Collabs" and "MEPs" – that is, multi-editor projects – seem to be a contemporary reinvention of the old vidding collectives of the VHS era, where women came together to make work and share tools. Vidding is giving young women a sense of artistic identity as video artists: you can now be a vidder because you create and edit video, the way you can see yourself as a dancer because you dance. It's put the tools (and the interesting problems) into people's hands early on.

> Many of the most widely circulated or "visible" vids, at least within studies
> of fanvids, are those that overtly engage or critique media representations.
> What does the prominence of these vids say about vidding's potential as
> a political project, particularly in an era in which there is scrutiny around
> the (lack of) diversity of media representations? Are there any dangers in
> canonizing these examples within fan studies?

Francesca Coppa: A lot of the most visible vids (those that have been written about in critical journals or part of academic or legal presentations) were chosen to help us articulate a case for fair use, and I'd say that it's not that they were more political than most vids but that they were more *comprehensibly* political than most vids; that is to say, even people who didn't care about pop culture, or media, or women, or sexuality could see that these vids had a message. So, for example, Tisha and I, as part of the Organization for Transformative Works (OTW), submitted a number of vids to tri-annual hearings at the Library of Congress first to get and then to renew the Digital Millennium Copyright Act (DMCA) exemption for vidders and other noncommercial remixers. Our opponents tended not to see the message of the vids – or, no, it's more accurate to say that our opponents' lawyers were paid a lot of money to misunderstand the vids we submitted. So, for example, twice we submitted James Bond vids to the DMCA hearings, and twice our opponents tried to argue that these vids were "merely" restatements of the basic Bond franchise, insisting that they were blind to any feminist critique in them – but Bond is seriously low-hanging fruit when it comes to feminist critique, no? We submitted the most overtly critical sort of vids we could find and they *still* claimed not to understand them – but at least the Librarian's panel could see it. So, we weren't going to submit complex emotional vids that shifted a text's genre and points of emotional identification – i.e., the ones we love that make us cry. The lawyers from the MPAA (Motion Picture Association of America) and RIAA (Recording Industry Association of America) weren't going to cry with us over the death of Spock. But most vids – actually I'll go further and say all successful vids (not all art is good but we usually don't penalize art for that) – have a message to the extent to which they significantly alter the narrative of the original, but it's hard to explain the meaning of vid readings if the audience isn't already familiar with the underlying text; it's like making people read literary criticism for a book they haven't read. And I think that vids do important grassroots intellectual work with these readings even when they're not actively performing a particular identity beyond "media fan" – it's still protected speech and valuable artmaking.

Tisha Turk: Vids do, by their very nature, alter the original narratives they're based on. Narratives are complicated structures that we experience holistically, but breaking them down into parts is useful for understanding how they work – or, in the case of vidding, how they can be made to do different work. From a narrative theory point of view, a narrative has two parts: the story (what happens) and what narratologists call the discourse (how the story gets told). Vids can (and often do) change the story, but even if they leave the story basically intact, they change how the story gets told. One of the key elements of narrative discourse is narration: who's telling this story, and how are they telling it? If you're looking at a written text, this means asking questions like: Is the narration first person or third person? Is the narrator omniscient or limited? The central character or a peripheral character? But TV and film typically aren't narrated with words; the story gets told by the camera and the soundtrack: What shots, for how long, in what order? What sounds, what music? So, when vidders recut and re-sequence clips, and when they set those clips to different music, the narrative is changed even if the key elements of the story stay the same. And realistically, the story *doesn't* stay completely the same, because condensing it and setting it to new music and timing clips in relation to lyrics and music emphasizes some details and downplays others. Vidders make choices – consciously or not – about what's essential or interesting in a narrative and what can be discarded or manipulated or re-deployed to do something totally different. This is why I'm so interested in the way that song choice can shape not only a vidwatcher's experience but also the vidder's creative process ("Transformation" 2015).

But I would also like us to talk about how the academic uptake of vids that are explicitly critical and analytical reproduces a blind spot in fan studies and cultural criticism, and even some feminist criticism, which is *female pleasure*. Most vids are relationship vids and character studies that exist to give fellow fans ALL THE FEELS together in women-oriented spaces. It's absolutely true that those vids aren't as useful as Explicit Thesis Statement vids when we're building a case about fair use; Francesca's right that the MPAA lawyers aren't going to cry with us over the death of Spock. But lawyers aren't the only people who are nervous about female pleasure – especially pleasure that has to do with women being desiring subjects, or, even scarier, women gathering in groups (in person or online) to celebrate being desiring subjects together. I don't think we've neglected this element of vidding (or fandom) completely; Francesca's certainly written about it. But it does get downplayed, and its political implications get downplayed, because it's not the overt politics of righteous indignation so much as the everyday politics of self-determination.

Francesca Coppa: Amen. A-MEN. But it's a difficult case to make. Our culture is still so hostile to female pleasure – in fact, I'd argue that in many ways it's more hostile to female pleasure than ever. That's one of the things at stake in the idea that fandom is a waste of time – women's time isn't supposed to be theirs! You should be working for money, tending to the kids or your parents, your house is a mess. And there's a puritanical case from the left as well: you should be working for social justice, actively articulating for change all the time – but that's work, too, as well as an excuse: "Well, yes, I did spend all that time making that vid – but it was for The Cause." Women aren't allowed to do things for themselves: there needs to be some social benefit. If women take artistic time, pleasure time, they're not doing enough for others.

There's also the fact that pleasure is hard to communicate: it is so much harder as a critic to write about things that touch you emotionally rather than cerebrally. To say: that moment makes me cry because I am being touched on multiple emotional levels: *grabs your arm*: Because Spock has turned around and is looking at Jim and we are just praying that he will remember their decades-long intimacy and partnership. And Kirk has sacrificed *so much* to save Spock's life – his only son has just been killed, like something out of Greek tragedy – and will Spock even remember him? And the music is swelling, the singer is keening softly, whispering like the voice in our heads, "please remember me, please remember me," and the timing is exquisite and the vidder has cut away a bunch of nonsense dialogue so that there's a kind of breathless silence before Spock ventures, hesitantly, almost stammering: "Jim?" And then Kirk's face breaks into a beatific smile and he says, simply, "Yes," – and that yes echoes through all time, a moment of catharsis and recognition. (And that's just about 12 seconds of Killa's vid "Dante's Prayer" – there are another

4 minutes and 28 other seconds to explicate!) Or maybe you're watching Talitha's vid "Problem," where the drum-thumping, guitar-whining chorus is a chant: "That girl is a *goddamned problem*," except the footage you're watching is from *Captain America: The Winter Soldier*, and the "girl" in question seems to be brainwashed assassin Bucky Barnes. How to explain the pleasure of thinking of the character in those terms? How to explain that it's not a parody or a joke to call him "that girl" – can you imagine a world in which calling someone a girl is not an insult? Where it's a sign of recognition and acceptance? Where the pleasure of the vid is in the intuitive and internal mapping out of the ways in which *that girl*, Bucky Barnes, is a goddamned problem? Because being female is the normal and default state of all humanity? This is my artworld.

Tisha Turk: Pleasure really is hard to talk about, because it's so personal and idiosyncratic – hard to communicate, absolutely, and potentially hard even to understand if it's not shared. I've seen "Problem," and it doesn't bring me the same pleasure it does Francesca, because I am just not that interested in Bucky Barnes. I have been in fandom long enough that when I watch it I can say "Yes, I know people who will be utterly delighted by this vid," and I can appreciate the ways in which it's clever and well-made, but Bucky's not my guy. It's easy to turn that around and say, well, Francesca *only* likes the vid because Bucky's her guy, but of course that's not correct – there's a lot more going on, as her comments above suggest! And I think we can safely say that plenty of fans who have gone through all the available vids about a character or pairing we adore have found a vid or two that made us think "Okay, I *love* this character, but this vid is just not doing it for me;" the subject matter alone isn't enough! But articulating and explaining what else goes into producing pleasure – yeah, that's hard.

Alexis Lothian: The issue of pleasure is everything. I come from queer studies and so I am used to thinking about pleasure as politics, the politics of pleasure; I think of Juana Maria Rodriguez's 2014 book *Sexual Futures*, in which she writes about gesture, and dance, and fantasy as queer Latina femme political subjectivities, and about José Muñoz's work on performance as world making. Being embodied with others in a transformative experience of queer pleasure. And it's by no means a straightforward analogy but that happens when we experience vids together, we give that to each other – I remember my first overwhelming emotional experience watching a vid ("Superstar" by here's luck), which was at the 2008 DIY Conference at USC, where I was taken completely unawares, shocked into a feeling of recognition, communication, overwhelming embodiment where a few moments earlier I had been nodding along in unperturbed intellectual admiration. It's no exaggeration to say that moment changed my life, and I would have told you that I knew what vidding was before it; but I actually didn't, because I hadn't experienced it fully.

I continue to desperately love writing about vids because there's something about straining to verbalize the excitement, the power, that I feel when the sound/image swells together to produce a moment of realization that contains paragraphs and paragraphs. The process of seeking for and finding those words somehow for me is a regeneration – it has many of the high points of making a vid myself but without the more painstaking and difficult parts. Yet, the vids that I have written about most have in fact often been the critical vids; I get very emotional about critique, apparently.

There's something specific about the way that critique gets done in vid form that is different from a lot of the more overt remix critique that is out there. I make vids to think my way through critical arguments I'm working on about visual texts, but the relationship between the vid and the argument is never one to one. It's different from what gets put out under the sign of political remix video, or examples like Dylan Marron's "Every Word Spoken By a Person of Color…" videos. For one thing, there is the depth to which you have to become one with the footage and music in order to make a vid. You aren't just scouring for clips that demonstrate a problem; you are crafting a narrative, and that demands a high level of complexity and depth even when the argument you are making is a serious indictment of the footage you are working with.

Tisha Turk: That's true, and I think it goes to the heart of a much larger cultural issue, which is that criticism and enthusiasm are frequently assumed to be opposite ends of a continuum, a line – whereas I think what fandom demonstrates is that it's not a line, it's a grid. You can love something a whole lot – or, okay, *love* doesn't quite capture the ambivalent complexities here, but you can be *super invested in a text* and still want to criticize it, call it out, and mutilate it. They're independent variables. Henry Jenkins (2013) was writing about this way back in *Textual Poachers*: you can sit too close *and* still have critical distance. And, on the flip side, even when you're vidding a text that you really want to skewer, you have to be invested enough to rip the clips, fight with the software, etc. If you didn't care, you'd walk away – you'd just stop watching the show, or maybe you'd rant to your friends; you wouldn't put in all that *work*.

Actually – maybe "love" is exactly the right word for ambivalent investment when we're talking about a community of women: there is not much in this world, and certainly not a lot in our pop culture landscape, that women get to love unambivalently.

How has vidding been excluded from broader remix culture discourses?

Francesca Coppa: I would argue that vidding has not been excluded from the broader remix culture discourses, but only because we forced our way in. The long-standing, tightly knit community of vidders was able to mobilize quickly to petition for a DMCA exemption and do other advocacy work on behalf of the entire remix community. Vidders had connections to academia and law (and were part of the founding of the OTW) that have allowed them/us to advocate for vidding as an art form in museums and to try to educate social media providers about fair use and fair dealing. YouTube's practices are arguably affecting the practice of the art itself: young vidders are making choices (length of clip, speed of music) affected by the pragmatics of the sorting algorithm and what will trigger a take-down rather than by their own best artistic judgment or vision. I discuss this algorithmic effect on vidding in the last chapter of my book, *Vidding: A History* (2022).

Tisha Turk: I think vidding *has* been excluded, though. We've made some successful interventions: the DIY conference, the DMCA hearings. But because remix got so hot so fast, and there were so many people writing about it from so many disciplines and backgrounds, there are books and articles and exhibits out there where we *didn't* show up in time to advocate and intervene. Where is vidding in Burgess and Green's book on YouTube? Spoiler alert: it's only in Henry Jenkins's afterword.

Francesca Coppa: This is true, it's gestured at but only that in things like *The Oxford Handbook of New Audiovisual Aesthetics*, and even more interestingly, vidding is mostly absent from work on music video itself – when fan music video is more popular now than commercial music video.

Tisha Turk: Well, more popular in the aggregate, at least. But that's part of the point of fandom, of course: many, many people creating many, many things; grassroots creativity happening all the time rather than the record industry praying that one super-popular artist's new album drop will save their numbers for the year.

Alexis Lothian: I now find myself in the odd position of both teaching vidding to students who are primed to see it as central to remix history while also having to explain how specific and marginal its practices actually are. Vidding is both visible and invisible. Everyone watches fan-made music videos and edits on YouTube and TikTok, but how many viewers think much about the labor and the art and the craft involved? There are multiple creative communities sharing tips and practices, but more people who are watching and shuffling past quickly to the next video. To take vidding seriously as a way of engaging with media, of making meaning, of creating art, requires a way of relating to online video that is counterintuitive to most of us now, that goes against the speeded-up temporality of internet time.

Any particular thoughts on queer vidding communities, fans, and practices?

Alexis Lothian: Vidding is a queer kind of pleasure, for sure, taking media and remaking it in the ways that bring us joy. But the answer to this question really depends on how we define "Vidding": fan remix video writ large, or the specific community of vidders that came to be within a specific sub-subculture of what we call media fandom? Because the latter is full of queer people and queerness but it isn't necessarily defined by them. Clearly slash, which was a huge part of the vidding world that the three of us inhabit, is all about same-sex eroticism, but slash fandom and LGBTQ history have intersected and failed to intersect in some fascinating ways; Kristina Busse and I wrote an essay on this for the 2017 *Routledge Companion to Media, Sex and Sexuality*, where we focused on m/m slash, and *Transformative Works and Cultures* published a special issue on femslash in 2017 that discussed these issues with regard to f/f.

In addition to the self-defined media fandom networks, there are gay and lesbian and queer spaces where people are making vids from a perspective where the identification and politics of participants is a bigger part of the network/community's self-understanding than it is in self-identified vidding subculture. For example, there is a distinctive history of vidding among queer remix artists – Dayna McLeod's work comes to mind, as well as the 1991 video "Meeting Two Queens" by the Chilean filmmaker, Cecilia Barriga, which we could accurately describe as a 14-minute multifandom femslash VCR vid featuring Marlene Dietrich and Greta Garbo, but which circulated in queer art and film circuits under different terms. Barriga's video is made more legible through vidding than it is through art film, I think, because it's so clearly a pleasure-centered project; Barriga basically invented vidding as a queer art practice, without (I assume) knowing that a whole community already existed around it. That's evidence for what I was saying about transformative works and transformative politics earlier.

Are there particular frameworks that you find especially useful or productive for studying vids, as opposed to other forms of transformative textual production?

Tisha Turk: I think that one thing the three of us share is an interest in *vidding* as well as vids: practices, processes, and change over time in addition to artifacts. We're all trying to illuminate the phenomenon of vidding as a practice, not just individual vids.

Francesca Coppa: Definitely as a practice, and as a pleasure practice, but one of the things that the historical approach – and my close readings! – mean to me is a case for vidding as an art practiced by named artists, and not as a generalized craft/practice even though fandom certainly is that as well. Vidding has great importance as an artistic practice that gives pleasure and a voice to all women who vid, but I have and will hold individual vids up as examples of cinematic art. I curated a segment on vidding for *Spectacle: The Music Video*, which went all around the world, including to The Museum of The Moving Image. And an enormous Mashup exhibition opened in Vancouver in early 2016. I would put a vid like Lim's "Flow" up against any piece of work in the show – which includes Andy Warhol, Barbara Kruger, you name it. If you can understand what you're seeing – which is my job, as a critic: to theorize, contextualize, to make new art visible – you will see that "Flow" is a work of genius. So, it's not for me an either/or choice between vidding as practice and vidding as art – even high art – any more than there should be a conflict between writing as practice, and a criticism that selects certain examples of that practice as outstanding. I want to see names like Kandy Fong, Lim, Bironic, Obsessive24 in the same line of artists as Dara Birnbaum and Jean-Luc Godard, as they are in the Vancouver show. And Luminosity and Killa had vids in the Museum of the Moving Image next to work by Spike Jonze and Michel Gondrey. Being a critic is a kind of public responsibility to stand up and direct attention to artistic work I think is good and values that I wish to see promulgated.

Tisha Turk: For sure – it's a both/and for me, not an either/or, which is part of why I find the ecology metaphor valuable. I'm interested in exactly that both-ness, because exposure to lots and lots and lots of vids is part of how fandom has created a culture of readers who can make sense of a vid as complicated as "Flow," when so many people – not only lawyers, but even other fans who aren't into vidding – are frankly terrible at reading vids. It's a very specific set of skills, though it certainly overlaps with other fannish and new media literacy skills as well as just basic attention to detail.

Alexis Lothian: I definitely share the focus on vidding as a process. It's important to me not just to look at what vidders create but also to think about the relationship to culture that you develop when media stops being a finished product and becomes material that you can use; even the vids that are least recognized as "good" are still building that kind of engagement. It's important to me when I teach vidding to show my students what that feels like; for myself, that process of critical synthesis and creative reinterpretation runs parallel to the intellectual work of creating scholarship and often feeds it.

I also am invested in understanding vidding as art, though when we want to name vidders as artists, we have to attend closely to what that erases as much as what it makes possible. After all, the art museum and its prestige are not neutral. Even as I feel the excitement about "our" people ascending to them, I am very wary of what gets left out in that transition.

Vids

The Clucking Belles (2005) "A Fannish Taxonomy of Hotness," aka "Hot Hot Hot."
here's luck (2003) "Superstar."
Killa (2001) "Dante's Prayer."
Lierdumoa (2008) "How Much Is That Geisha In The Window."
Lim (2013) "Flow."
Luminosity (2002) "Southwest Voodoo."
Luminosity (2007) "Vogue.
Luminosity and sisabet (2007) "Women's Work." sisabet (2004) "Two Words."
Talitha78 (2014) "Problem."
thingswithwings (2009) "We Go Together."

References

Burgess, J. and Green, J. (2009) *YouTube: Online Video and Participatory Culture*, Cambridge, UK: Polity Press.
Busse, K. and Lothian, A. (2017) "A History of Slash Sexualities: Debating Queer Sex, Gay Politics, and Media Fan Cultures," in F. Attwood, D. Egan, B. McNair, and C. Smith (eds.) *The Routledge Companion to Media, Sex and Sexuality*, London: Routledge.
Coppa, F. (2008) "Women, Star Trek, and the Early Development of Fannish Vidding," *Transformative Works and Cultures*, 1. http://dx.doi.org/10.3983/twc.2008.0044
Coppa, F. (2016) "Vidding: The Art of Flow," in Daina Augaitis, Bruce Grenville, and Stephanie Rebick (eds.) *MashUp: The Birth of Modern Culture, Vancouver Art Gallery Exhibition Catalogue*, London: Black Dog Press, pp. 150–153.
Coppa, F. (2022) *Vidding: A History*. Ann Arbor: University of Michigan Press. www.fulcrum.org/concern/monographs/hq37vq792
Jenkins, H. (2009) "What Happened Before YouTube," in J. Burgess and J. Green (eds.) *YouTube: Online Video and Participatory Culture*, Cambridge, UK: Polity Press, pp. 109–125.
Jenkins, H. (2013) *Textual Poachers: Television Fans and Participatory Culture*, updated 20th anniversary edition, New York: Routledge.
Lothian, A. (2015) "A Different Kind of Love Song: Vidding Fandom's Undercommons," *Cinema Journal* 53: 138–145.
Muñoz, J. (1999) *Disidentifications: Queers of Color and the Performance of Politics*, Minneapolis, MN: University of Minnesota Press.
Rodriguez, J. M. (2014) *Sexual Futures, Queer Gestures, and Other Latina Longings*, New York: New York University Press.
Turk, T. (2015) "Transformation in a New Key: Music in Vids and Vidding," *Music, Sound, and the Moving Image* 9(2): 163–176. https://doi.org/10.3828/msmi.2015.11
Turk, T. and Johnson, J. (2012) "Toward an Ecology of Vidding," *Transformative Works and Cultures*, 9. http://dx.doi.org/10.3983/twc.2012.0326
Wanzo, R. (2015) "African American Acafandom and Other Strangers: New Genealogies of Fan Studies," *Transformative Works and Cultures*, 20. http://dx.doi.org/10.3983/twc.2015.0699

PART III

Identities

Concerns about media texts' representational practices have been at the center of fan studies since early texts like Camille Bacon-Smith's *Enterprising Women* and Henry Jenkins' *Textual Poachers* explored how the fan works produced within women's and queer fan cultures pushed back on and rewrote mainstream media texts whose portrayals of women and LGBTQ people were limited, at best. Harrington and Bielby's *Soap Fans*, alongside Janice Radway's *Reading the Romance*, also drew attention to fan communities that have organized around historically devalued feminine media forms. While one of fan studies' strengths is its enduring focus on women's and queer fan cultures, this section focuses on a range of identities that we feel ought to be more fully represented in fan studies. As fan studies scholars, we must be willing to foreground and scrutinize the intersectional forces at play in the questions we ask in our work, and push past our comfort zones of familiar assumptions, questions, texts, and communities, to explore crucial questions about race, ethnicity, and local and global cultures through fandom. To this end, alongside chapters on gender and sexuality, this section contains scholarship on race, ethnicity, nationality, and age. The chapters in this section are intended to set agendas in these areas, present strong models, and offer a glimpse of a more complex fan studies.

This section includes three essays that are reprinted from the first edition. Benjamin Woo describes the dearth of discussions about race in fan studies as a "yawning void" and usefully criticizes fan studies scholars' reluctance to focus on race in our work. Arguing that race and racialization should be at the core of fan studies, alongside and intersecting with other identity categories, Woo considers the empirical question of the whiteness of fan communities, the ideological construction of media fans as a category that excludes non-white fans, and the efforts of fan communities to make white privilege visible. C. Lee Harrington and Denise D. Bielby use their contribution to this collection to shine a light on one of the richest, yet largely undertheorized, topics within fan studies: namely, how fans and fandom are shaped by age and aging. Because many fans have longstanding relationships with their objects of fandom, Harrington and Bielby suggest the need for us to not only consider how age impacts the fan experience, both individually and collectively, but to develop a greater understanding of how we relate to media over our life course. A conversation among Bertha

DOI: 10.4324/9781003373025-25

Chin, Aswin Punathambekar, and Sangita Shresthova explores the promises and challenges of transcultural scholarship, including necessary methods and competencies, the kinds of knowledge that transcultural scholarship offers fan studies, and the directions for future work. The challenges of language, immersion, and citational practices figure prominently in their discussion.

Three additional chapters have been revised and updated for this second edition. Julie Levin Russo opens this section by tracing the history, intentions, and impact of femslash (creative fanworks that romantically pair female characters and use the / symbol to indicate the coupling); Russo traces femslash's influences, and argues that despite its underrepresentation in remix culture, femslash's contributions as a resistant and queer practice make it vital to fan studies. Jillian M. Baez calls for fan studies scholars to focus on Latinx fan communities, arguing that these communities are understudied. Through an exploration of scholarship on Latinx music fandom and *telenovela* fandom, Baez demonstrates that an increased focus on the Latinx fans would offer useful opportunities to explore questions of language, borderlands, nation, and hybridity. Elizabeth Affuso examines MAC's, Benefit's, Colourpop's, and Covergirl's campaigns to sell fan-branded cosmetics, and demonstrates that while the practices signal both the mainstreaming of fan culture and a move toward more gender inclusive fan practices, appeals to women through beauty products ultimately reinforce the gendered divide in fan cultures.

This section contains five new chapters. Erika Chung explores how women of color fans navigate and participate in comics fandom by drawing on the multiplicities of their identities and lived experiences to inform and shape their fan identity and participation; love of reading and reflection as a fan practice figure prominently in the ways the fans Chung interviewed rendered racial and gendered gatekeeping ineffective and incorporated comics into multiple areas of their lives. Highlighting the complex relationships and unique power dynamics nested within non-Western transnational and transcultural fandoms, Celeste Oon investigates internal fragmentation between domestic (Korean) fans and international (non-Korean) fans of K-pop. Oon argues that the attitudes, knowledges, and behaviors that structure this fragmentation produce racist, xenophobic, classist, and nationalist sentiment, which further drives the groups apart. Dimitra Laurence Larochelle's chapter focuses on fans of Turkish soap operas in Greece, exploring how Greek fans negotiate long-standing negative stereotypes about Turks. Noting how transcultural studies often overlook the ways real-world events shape fan practices and perceptions of media content, Larochelle's case study reveals the intricate dynamics of cultural exchange and diplomatic relations between neighboring countries. The absence of trans and nonbinary gender in fan studies is at the heart of Olivia Johnston Riley's chapter, in which they examine podfic – fanfiction read aloud, recorded, and shared online. Riley asserts that podfic extends fans' gendered possibilities, inviting them to reimagine the affordances of their lived gender worlds, and also allows fan scholars to begin to untangle fan studies' complicity in various marginalizations and reimagine what contributions a more equitably queer fan studies can offer. Thomas Baudinette's chapter examines the role that fantasy plays in fans' everyday consumption of Boys Love, suggesting that this transcultural fandom is grounded in "queer affects" that challenge societal heteronormativity. He argues that Boys Love fandom in Asia provides scholars an opportunity to reconsider questions relating to queerbaiting, recentering fan studies' discussions of the role of affective affordances as a site for producing novel understandings of queer media's political potentials.

For Further Reading

Affuso, E. and Scott, S. (eds.) (2023) *Sartorial Fandom: Fashion, Beauty Culture, and Identity*. Ann Arbor, MI: University of Michigan Press.

Báez, J.M. (2020) "Latinx Audiences as Mosaic." In: L.K. Lopez (ed.) *Race and Media: Critical Approaches*. New York: New York University Press, pp. 218–229.

Busse, K. and Hellekson, K. (2014) *The Fan Fiction Studies Reader*. Iowa City: University of Iowa Press.

Duggan, J. (2023) "Trans Fans and Fan Fiction: A Literature Review." *Transformative Works and Cultures*, 39. https://doi.org/10.3983/twc.2023.2309

Duggan, J. and Dahl, A. (2019) "Fan Translations of *SKAM*: Challenging Anglo Linguistic and Popular Cultural Hegemony in a Transnational Fandom." *Scandinavian Studies in Language*, 10(2), pp. 6–29.

Ellis, K. and Kent, M. (eds.) (2016) *Disability and Social Media*. New York, NY: Routledge.

(2012, March 15) "Fan/Remix Video: A Special Issue." In: Coppa, F. and J. L. Russo (eds.) *Transformative Works and Cultures*, 9. http://journal.transformativeworks.org/index.php/twc/issue/view/10

Hannell, B. (2020) "Fan Studies and/as Feminist Methodology." *Transformative Works and Cultures*, 33. https://doi.org/10.3983/twc.2020.1689

Jeffries, L. (2011) "The Revolution Will Be Soooo Cute: YouTube 'Hauls' and the Voice of Young Female Consumers." *Studies in Popular Culture*, 33(2), pp. 59–75.

Larochelle, D. L. (2023) "Transnational Soap Operas and Viewing Practices in the Digital Age: The Greek Fandom of Turkish Dramas." *International Communication Gazette*, 85(3–4), pp. 233–249.

Larochelle, D. L. (2019) "Brad Pitt Halal" and the Hybrid Woman: Gender Representations and Religion through Turkish Soap Operas." *ESSACHESS*, 12(2(24)), pp. 61–78.

Leetal, D. (2022) "Revisiting Gender Theory in Fan Fiction: Bringing Nonbinary Genders into the World." *Transformative Works and Cultures*, 38. https://doi.org/10.3983/twc.2022.2081

Lynch, K. S. (2022) "Fans as Transcultural Gatekeepers: The Hierarchy of BTS' Anglophone Reddit Fandom and the Digital East-West Media Flow." *New Media & Society*, 24(1), pp. 105–121.

Mountfort, P., Peirson-Smith, A., and Geczy, A. (eds.) (2019) *Planet Cosplay: Costume Play, Identity, and Global Fandom*. Bristol, UK: Intellect Books.

Ng, E. and Russo, J. L. (eds.) (2017) "Queer Female Fandom" special issue. *Transformative Works and Cultures*, 24. Available at: <http://journal.transformativeworks.org>

Paredez, D. (2009) *Selenidad: Selena, Latinos, and the Performance of Memory*. Durham & London: Duke University Press.

Scott, S. (2017) "#Wheresrey?: Toys, Spoilers, and the Gender Politics of Franchise Paratexts." *Critical Studies in Media Communication*. https://doi.org/10.1080/15295036.2017.1286023

Stanfill, M. (2019) *Exploiting Fandom: How the Media Industry Seeks to Manipulate Fans*. Iowa City: University of Iowa Press.

Williams, R. (2020) *Theme-Park Fandom: Spatial Transmedia, Materiality and Participatory Cultures*. Amsterdam, The Netherlands: University of Amsterdam Press.

Wilson, A.E. (2021) Not Just Superhero Stories. In: Woo, B. and J. Stoll (eds.) *The Comics World. Comic Books, Graphic Novels, and Their Publics*. Jackson: University Press of Mississippi, pp. 195–207.

22
THE INVISIBLE BAG OF HOLDING
Whiteness and Media Fandom

Benjamin Woo

There is a yawning void in fandom studies where a serious, on-going conversation about race ought to be. Generally progressive folks, fan scholars agree on the importance of engaging questions of race and racialization but we have been somewhat weak on the follow through. As a result, race remains a marked absence in the literature, indicated more by apologies and lampshading than by sustained research or reflection. For instance, within sentences of critiquing Pierre Bourdieu's failure to foreground gender and race in his analyses of cultural consumption, John Fiske (1992: 32) writes, "I regret being unable to devote the attention to race which it deserves, but I have not found studies of non-white fandom." More recently, Gray, Harrington and Sandvoss (2007: 16) flag race as an obvious "omission" from their edited collection, along with "comic book fans, telenovela fans, or teen fandom," seemingly equating the diversity of persons with a diversity of texts. Again and again, race's significance is affirmed in the abstract while its salience in any concrete instance is deferred. As Henry Jenkins (2014: 97) puts it, fan studies "has been 'colour blind' in all the worst senses of the term." Where race does appear, it is often in response to conflicts *about* race within fan communities. That work is important, but race is not only relevant when it becomes a "problem." The racial status quo also demands explanation. As Rebecca Wanzo (2015: ¶1.4) has pointedly suggested, a consideration of how "an investment in whiteness may be foundational to some groups of fans" is long overdue.

For the purposes of this chapter, I shall treat race as a set of categories that are ultimately independent of the biological or physical differences in which we typically imagine them to consist. Rather, when we identify people (including ourselves) as belonging to some racial group, we are engaging in a socially situated classifying practice.[1] As Kenneth Huynh and I (2015) have argued elsewhere, however, slippage may occur between categories, such that people often end up trading in what Peter S. Li (2001: 77–78) calls "racial subtext, that is, the hiding of racial signification in a benign discourse." When done purposefully, as in political campaigning, this is called a "dog whistle," but it does not require intent or design. Such slippage becomes particularly likely when some categories routinely go unnamed and unmarked:

> Not to speak about race, gender, class, sexuality—or being pressured not to speak—in a fandom space ends up creating the image of a "generic" or "normalized" fan. Such a fan identity is not free of race, class, gender, or sexuality but rather is assumed to be the default.
>
> (Gatson and Reid 2011: ¶4.1)

To put it crudely, we say one thing ("fans"), but people may hear and understand another ("white people"). Thus, I want to take the "color blindness" of fandom and fan studies as my point of departure in this chapter. First, I shall summarize what we know about the racial composition of fan communities. Are they really as white as we imagine? This is an *empirical* question. Second, I shall discuss the discursive work that has constructed "media fans" as a category, largely to the exclusion of people of color. These are matters of *ideology*. Finally, I shall briefly address some ways that white privilege is being made visible within contemporary fan discourse, with a particular focus on popular cultural criticism. These efforts seek to make the status quo *unbearable*.

Empirical Whiteness

Most fan research emerges out of humanistic and qualitative traditions of inquiry. It is unsurprising, then, that their accounts of who participates in fan communities are anecdotal and impressionistic. In his seminal *Textual Poachers*, for example, Jenkins (1992: 1) asserts that media fans are "largely female, largely white, [and] largely middle class"—indeed, that is one of the very first things he tells us about fans. However, it is difficult for the reader to evaluate this assertion, as intuitively correct as it may seem: How were the variables defined? What does "largely" mean—a preponderance, simple majority, or supermajority? Is there variance among fandoms, such that some communities are whiter than others? While I believe in the depth and richness of qualitative methods, they are unable to answer the basically quantitative question, *how white is fandom?* with satisfactory precision.

A handful of recent studies have provided more concrete, if still provisional, data concerning the racial composition of fan communities. Each addresses itself to a slice of fan activity, rather than fandom as a whole. They are further limited by the fact that race, as a social construct, is extremely context dependent. Racial categories don't travel well; even within the same society, asking someone's race in terms of ancestry and identity can produce very different results. But, taken together, these studies are suggestive of what fan communities look like today. For a series of studies on the psychology of "geeks," McCain, Gentile, and Campbell (2015) constructed seven samples, largely via Amazon's Mechanical Turk platform. For some, they specifically sought participants with high levels of geek culture engagement, while others used a more "generic" posting in order to attract a "variety of geek engagement levels" (7). While racial identity was not a variable in their analysis, the proportion of participants self-reporting their race as white in the former set varied between 67% and 88%; in the latter, between 71% and 86% (6). Kington's (2015) online survey of convention-goers produced more extreme results: nine in ten survey respondents identified as white, though she notes that conventions located in urban centers like Toronto and Detroit were more diverse (215). These findings in the peer-reviewed literature seem to be corroborated by projects originating in fandom. Although many "fan demography" projects undertaken by members neglect race and ethnicity, a survey of 10,000 users of the fan fiction portal Archive of Our Own (AO3) found that 77% of users were white.

Unsurprisingly, representation of almost every minority racial/ethnic group increased in the youngest age cohort compared to the oldest (Lulu 2013, 2015).

Attempting to explain her findings, Kington (2015: 226) observes that "convention attendance necessitates at least a comfortable income level" and speculates that "the predominance of conventions in the United States leads to the majority of attendees being … Caucasian." Like claims that fandom is white because it attracts middle-class and relatively well-educated participants, this sounds reasonable at first but does not hold up to scrutiny. Notably, the United States is not that white, either: based on American Community Survey estimates, slightly less than two-thirds of the US population report themselves as non-Hispanic whites (United States Census Bureau 2016). It is true that many fan activities, including travelling to geographically distant conventions, involve some expenditure, and that economic class is racialized. However, various strategies for "gleaning" access to media goods are available, including public libraries, lending and trading with peers, and using file-sharing networks, and the rise of an extensive network of regional conventions may also reduce economic barriers to participation for some. Simple geographic or economic explanations are not sufficient to explain the apparent underrepresentation of people of color in fan communities.

The evidence is limited, but it seems to corroborate the anecdotal impression that media fans are "largely" white. Depending on who you ask—and how—media fans are slightly to substantially whiter than the population at large. Yet, somewhere between 10% and 33% of fans, according to these sources, belong to visible-minority groups, and you'd never know it from reading many accounts of fan communities. Minority voices and experiences don't make up 10%—and certainly not one-third—of fan studies.

Ideological Whiteness

Research suggests that fandom is somewhat whiter than the population at large, but it is not as though people of color do not develop deep, meaningful engagements with cultural goods. Why do we not hear more about them? The observed whiteness of media fandom is neither natural nor neutral. In this section, I take much of my inspiration from Mel Stanfill (2011), who argues that fandom has been constructed across various fictional and factual media so as to erase actually existing diversity in place of a normative discourse of fan identity, one which presumes whiteness (among other things). In focusing on media representations of fans, however, Stanfill arguably doesn't go far enough. Fans and fan scholars also participate in "doing" the whiteness of media fandom, even when we know better. A series of discursive moves and slippages have acted, first, to marginalize discussions of race from fandom studies and, second, to justify this marginalization by defining "fandom" (and the questions that are interesting to ask about it) in ways that tend to foreground and, indeed, privilege white fans.

Studies of media fandom grew out of a tradition of feminist audience studies that pushed back against the dismissal of women audiences and their tastes by male critics, especially those within the modernist tradition (Huyssen 1986). These scholars raised important questions about the complexity of media use in everyday life, particularly in the lived experience of women. In the transition from examining traditional "women's genres" (e.g. Radway 1984; Ang 1985) to studying women's engagement with conventionally masculinized genres like science fiction (e.g. Bacon-Smith 1992; Jenkins 1992), fan fiction—and slash fiction, in particular—became a signature motif. The apparently counterintuitive presence of women in fan communities demanded explanation, and their creative and transformative practices of reading and writing offered clear examples of audiences acting outside the manifest intentions of media producers. Studies of female media fans helped build the case for the "active" or "resistive" audience paradigm. However, this project and these particular examples obviously sensitized researchers to questions of gender and sexuality, which became much more salient to the emerging field than race (or class, ability, age, or nationality/geography, for that matter)—hence, Fiske's difficulty even locating studies of visible-minority fans. That is to say, one reason race has been marginal is because gender and sexuality have been the center of attention.[2]

In addition, the migration of fan activity to online platforms has profoundly shaped the field's self-conception. Digital forums and fan-fiction repositories make the hard work of locating media fans to study easier, but they also make some research questions easier to pursue than others. For example, the blog *Fan Fiction Statistics* (active between 2010 and 2011) analyzed a range of topics with reference to fanfiction.net, providing a data-driven examination of one facet of contemporary online fan practices. However, the scope of these analyses was limited by the metadata available. Some users choose to disclose their gender (though the site's profiles do not specifically invite them to do so and most don't) so, with some effort, tentative inferences can be made about the gender identities of site users (Sendlor 2011), but the project did not attempt to mine for evidence of racial diversity. However, the project was able to track site traffic and the popularity of various story categories in exhaustive detail, reinforcing the impression that the diversity of fan objects and ships is more important or interesting than racial diversity.

Of course, a great deal of fan activity has always been mediated by technologies that enable "disembodied" discourse (from the letter column, fanzine, and amateur press association to the bulletin board, the Internet Relay Chat channel or discussion forum) and, thus, tend to reinforce the Cartesian split between mind and body. Ron Eglash (2002) has noted that this dualism is itself racialized, but the conventional association of fans and their objects with intellect and imagination deemphasizes the embodied dimensions of subjectivity in general. However, just because our words can circulate independently of our physical bodies does not imply that they are free of racial significations, as Mary Bucholtz's (2001) observations about the use of "Superstandard English" by a clique of self-described nerdy girls in a multiracial high school attest. Bucholtz argues that the girls' preference for superstandard forms—that is, "hypercorrect" usages formulated in distinction from African American Vernacular English (AAVE)—marked them as white, in contrast not only with their African American peers but also "cool" white youth who freely borrowed features of AAVE in their ordinary speech. In other words, in their pronunciation and word choice, they sounded whiter than white. Bucholtz's identification of Superstandard English as a racially marked register has consequences for fan studies. For example, Rhiannon Bury (2005) emphasizes the role of linguistic capital as a component of identity performance in the communities of *X-Files* and *Due South* fans she studied (though, this was not uniform across online fandoms; 109–10); on this view, however, their investment in correct usage not only indexed their "middle class-ness" (31, 108) but is also tied up in a performed whiteness. To the extent that these communities are constituted through language, they are also constituted through a mode of discourse that carries a racial subtext.

Finally, there is the question of who researchers will recognize and count as "fans" in the first place. In a bibliographic essay introducing fan studies, Jenkins (2012, "Introduction") notes a terminological instability at the center of the field:

> Fans might be broadly defined as individuals who maintain a passionate connection to popular media, assert their identity through their engagement with and mastery over its contents, and experience social affiliation around shared tastes and preferences ... In a narrower sense, fandom sometimes refers to a shared cultural space that emerged from science fiction fandom in the early 20th century, which was reshaped by *Star Trek* fans in the 1960s and which has since expanded to incorporate forms of cultural production mostly by women around genre entertainment.

He glosses this as "a split between those who focus on individual fans and those who study a larger community," but it also speaks to how the examples typically discussed by scholars in the field draw the circle of "fandom" as a cultural space much tighter than it needs to be. In addition to being white, middle-class, cisgendered, male, and heterosexual, the "default fanboy" described by Gatson and Reid (2012: 4.1) also possesses "an overlay of geek or nerd identity, identities that are simultaneously embedded in emphasized whiteness, and increasingly certain kinds of class privilege, often displayed by access to higher education, particularly in scientific and technical fields." Indeed, Kristina Busse (2013) suggests that the stereotyped figure of the nerd/geek (usually, but not uniformly, white men; Eglash 2002) is one of the main ways that media articulate discourses about fans. At the same time, many of the key cultural texts for fan studies, such as the *Star Trek* franchise, are conventionally considered "geeky." While the mainly female communities that populate the literature often have to push against the image (and reality) of "fanboys," letting the former stand in for fans as such equally distorts the picture of fandom. Even if fans of science fiction, comics, games and "cult" media, fan fiction writers and fan artists, and the people who attend conventions are "largely white," it doesn't mean that fandom in the broader sense of a "passionate connection to popular media" is largely restricted to white people. As Wanzo (2015) persuasively argues, fan studies would look very different if it fully embraced fans of sports, music, and mainstream rather than cult media, communities where there are rich traditions of engagement by fans, scholars, and fan-scholars of color and which would be included in any ordinary-language understanding of the phrase "media fan." Research on sports fans, for instance, often addresses race and whiteness, but these studies are frequently excluded from the field by virtue of the "narrower sense" of media fandom (Wanzo 2015: ¶1.4). Indeed, the emergent nomenclature of *fandom* studies, rather than the older *fan* studies, could be read as formalizing these implicit exclusions. For example, while the aims and scope of Intellect's *Journal of Fandom Studies* invites contributions about fans of "popular media," including sports, the sample cover illustrating the page features an apparently Caucasian hand making the "live long and prosper" Vulcan salute, once again linking fandom, geek culture, and white audiences (*Journal of Fandom Studies* 2015).

These factors work together to erase or at least bracket race and ethnicity in fan studies discourse, and all this takes place within the context of a media system that chronically underrepresents people of color and treats white people's experiences as universal to human beings as such. Thus, as Jenkins (2014: 98) argues, the problem is much more complex and insidious than the good intentions of fans and fan scholars can address alone:

Even if fandom were as welcoming of cultural diversity as it has sometimes perceived itself to be, there would be many forms of exclusions and marginalizations based on the racialization of taste that would determine who came to conventions or which texts became incorporated into fandom's canons.

That is to say, whiteness has been baked into the way that fans and fan scholars conceptualize the field. The persistent "difficulty" scholars have in finding non-white fans suggests we cannot simply "add minorities and stir" to correct these imbalances. Rather, we must learn to see differently.

Unbearable Whiteness

The constructed category of *media fans* is not only demographically but also ideologically white, and these two factors are not unrelated. It is of course part of the definition of ideology that its workings are mostly invisible to those caught up in it. To those situated outside this discursive formation, however, the whiteness of popular media and its fandoms is a reality that constantly impinges on their everyday, lived experience. In reading, for example, tweets and articles associated with the recent social-media campaign to cast an Asian American actor as the lead in Marvel/Netflix's *Iron Fist* (a role that eventually went to the white English actor, Finn Jones), the sense of exhaustion at the anticipated rehearsal of much-critiqued Orientalist tropes is palpable. While fan scholars have often neglected questions of race (despite noble intentions), "fans have been more advanced ... in trying to address these issues" by making the presumptive whiteness of fandom visible and, therefore, a problem that must be dealt with (Jenkins 2014: 99).

At the same time, however, it is also clear that other fans wish discussions of race would go away. If race talk typically only happens in the presence of conflict about race, then the last few years have given us plenty of opportunities to talk. Controversies about racial diversity and inclusion have swept across a number of fan communities, including science-fiction and fantasy literature (e.g. RaceFail '09 and the Sad Puppies/Rabid Puppies voting blocs at the 2015 Hugo Awards), games (e.g. GamerGate's #NotYourShield campaign), comics (e.g. the introduction of Miles Morales as Spider-Man and the casting of people of color in film adaptations), film (e.g. the "racebending" critique of Shyamalan's *Last Airbender* and #OscarsSoWhite), and television (e.g. debate over "Caught Between Earth and Sky," a real-person slash fiction set in Haiti after the 2010 earthquake, which was critiqued for both explicit and implicit racism). This is hardly an exhaustive list.[3]

These are complex cases, resulting from a range of contingent and local factors that extend well beyond individual racial animus. They probably also say something about the changing ecosystem of popular cultural criticism and the mainstreaming of feminist and anti-racist critiques in some online publishing platforms. But I would argue that they are, first and foremost, examples of "classification struggle"—i.e., the effort to impose a definition of the field on the field (Bourdieu 2010: 481)—as much as the politics of representation. That is to say, however important it is for individuals to encounter racially diverse experiences and lifeworlds depicted in popular media, the more fundamental stakes at play are whether fan communities are spaces for people with racialized bodies and identities, whether the definition of *fan* can stretch beyond the ideological limitations discussed above.

Somewhat ironically, efforts to claw back relatively small victories that women and people of color have achieved with respect to representation have problematized the "default fanboy" identity more than ever, particularly to people outside of various fan communities. Yet, the outcomes of such struggles are never guaranteed. And, while I suspect the vast majority of fan studies scholars would side with efforts to increase inclusivity, we might also ask if our field has contributed to or emboldened reactionary sentiment by depicting fandoms as (mostly) white spaces for so long.

Conclusion

In this chapter, I have argued that fan studies must center race and racialization as core "sensitizing concepts" (Blumer 1954), not in place of, but alongside and intersecting with sex, gender, class, ability, and geography. As apologetic fan scholars have demonstrated, though, this is easier said than done. Accounting for race presents at least two significant challenges: first, it needs to expand beyond the framework of crisis and conflict; second, it cannot be seen as a matter only of concern to racialized scholars. As Wanzo (2015) and Jenkins (2014) both suggest, critical attention to whiteness is a necessary, if not entirely sufficient, way of addressing both of these challenges.

In focusing on whiteness, my goal has not been to paralyze emerging researchers in this field. I identify as a person of color, and I too have had the uncomfortable realization that only white people were responding to a call for participants—and I rationalized making do with this unrepresentative sample as a "pragmatic" decision. I don't have easy answers to these problems, but before closing I want to briefly offer two suggestions on what foregrounding whiteness might look like in practice. First, don't bracket race and ethnicity away. Ask about people's racial identifications. If the population you are studying really is mostly white, so be it, but this needs to be a fact, not an untested assumption. In any case, a majority white community doesn't mean race is irrelevant, either to minority or majority racial groups. Second, be aware of how race unconsciously shapes how you see the world. As Bourdieu might say, "objectify the objectifier"—that is, account for your own position as an observer and the ways that position shapes how you are defining your object of study. Why have you chosen the particular community or practice you are studying, and what are the implications for race (and gender, and sexuality, and ability, and so on) of that choice? We can never be neutral, but we don't have to be ignorant of the consequences of our actions.

Peggy McIntosh (2016: 74) famously taught us that white privilege is like a knapsack of "special provisions, assurances, tools, maps, guides, codebooks, passports, visas, clothes, compass, emergency gear, and blank checks" that lies so lightly on white people's shoulders they forget they're carrying it. That is, privilege is so unremarkable to its holders that it becomes invisible. The whiteness of fan communities is typically presented as a simple, unremarkable fact about media fandom. Despite foregrounding "a utopian understanding of fans in science fiction communities as being antiracist and progressive" (Wanzo 2015: ¶1.4), benign discourses of media fandom often contain a racial subtext related to the presumed whiteness of the people it describes. Whiteness is an unmarked and frequently unremarked-upon predicate of the category *fan*—at least in its "narrower sense." Studies of non-white fans almost always explicitly racialize their subjects, for instance, while hardly anyone would describe *Textual Poachers* as a study of "white fans," even though Jenkins (1992: 1) explicitly identifies the community as such. It is the privilege of white fans and fan scholars to ignore or relegate race to a parenthetical comment or footnote. Like the Bag of Holding—a kind of magical "knapsack" in Dungeons & Dragons and other fantasy games—white privilege is much bigger than it appears from the outside. We have to become aware of how the weight of history, of white supremacy, impinges upon our taken-forgranted assumptions about media fans. We have to feel its burden on our shoulders before we can ever set it down.

Notes

1 I am drawing on the Membership Categorization Analysis (MCA) approach to identity here. See Hester and Eglin (1997).
2 This is not to imply that sex/gender and race/ethnicity are necessarily competing frameworks, only that fan scholars have heretofore tended to focus on one while neglecting the other. The emergence of intersectionality as a key political and epistemic virtue—one whose articulation we owe to the Black feminist tradition—makes this obvious and suggests a way forward (Crenshaw 1989).
3 The Organization for Transformative Works' *fanlore* wiki has an entry on Race and Fandom that summarizes fans' anti-racist critiques of cultural works as well as these race-related "imbroglios" in fandom: http://fanlore.org/wiki/Race_And_Fandom.

References

Ang, I. (1985) *Watching Dallas: Soap Opera and the Melodramatic Imagination*, New York: Methuen.
Bacon-Smith, C. (1992) *Enterprising Women: Television Fandom and the Creation of Popular Myth*, Philadelphia, PA: University of Pennsylvania Press.
Blumer, H. (1954) "What is Wrong with Social Theory?" *American Sociological Review*, 19(1), pp. 3–10.
Bourdieu, P. (2010) *Distinction: A Social Critique of the Judgement of Taste*, Basingstoke, UK: Routledge.
Bucholtz, M. (2001) "The Whiteness of Nerds: Superstandard English and Racial Markedness," *Journal of Linguistic Anthropology*, 11(1), pp. 84–100.
Bury, R. (2005) *Cyberspaces of Their Own: Female Fandoms Online*, New York: Peter Lang.
Busse, K. (2013) "Geek Hierarchies, Boundary Policing, and the Gendering of the Good Fan," *Participations: Journal of Audience & Reception Studies*, 10(1), pp. 73–91.
Crenshaw, K. (1989) "Demarginalizing the Intersection of Race and Sex: A Black Feminist Critique of Antidiscrimination Doctrine, Feminist Theory and Antiracist Politics," *University of Chicago Legal Forum*, 1989, pp. 139–168.
Eglash, R. (2002) "Race, Sex, and Nerds: From Black Geeks to Asian American Hipsters," *Social Text*, 20(2), pp. 49–64.
Fiske, J. (1992) "The Cultural Economy of Fandom," in L. A. Lewis (ed.), *The Adoring Audience: Fan Culture and Popular Media*, London: Routledge, pp. 30–49.
Gatson, S. N. and Reid, R. A. (2011) "Race and Ethnicity in Fandom," *Transformative Works and Cultures*, 8, doi:10.3983/twc.2012.0392.
Gray, J., Sandvoss, C. and Harrington, C. L. (2007) "Introduction: Why Study Fans?" in J. Gray, C. Sandvoss, and C. L. Harrington (eds.), *Fandom: Identities and Communities in a Mediated World*, New York: New York University Press, pp. 1–16.
Hester, S. and Eglin, P. (eds.) (1997) *Culture in Action: Studies in Membership Categorization Analysis*, Washington, DC: International Institute for Ethnomethodology and Conversation Analysis & University Press of America.
Huynh, K. and Woo, B. (2015) "'Asian Fail': Chinese Canadian Men Talk About Race, Masculinity, and the Nerd Stereotype," *Social Identities*, 20(4–5), pp. 363–378.
Huyssen, A. (1986) "Mass Culture as Woman: Modernism's Other," in *After the Great Divide: Modernism, Mass Culture and Postmodernism*, Basingstoke, UK: Macmillan, pp. 44–62.
Jenkins, H. (1992) *Textual Poachers: Television Fans & Participatory Culture*, New York: Routledge.
Jenkins, H. (2012) "Fan Studies," *Oxford Bibliographies in Cinema and Media Studies*, doi:10.1093/OBO/9780199791286-0027.
Jenkins, H. (2014) "Fandom Studies as I See It," *The Journal of Fandom Studies*, 2(2), pp. 89–109.

Journal of Fandom Studies (2015) "About," http://journaloffandomstudies.com/about/ (Accessed 2 March 2016).

Kington, C. S. (2015) "Con Culture: A Survey of Fans and Fandom," *The Journal of Fandom Studies*, 3(2), pp. 211–228.

Li, P. S. (2001) "The Racial Subtext in Canada's Immigration Discourse," *Journal of International Migration and Integration / Revue de l'integration et de la migration internationale*, 2(1), pp. 77–97.

Lulu (2013) "Ethnicity," *The Slow Dance of the Infinite Stars*, blog, [online] Available from: http://centrumlumina.tumblr.com/post/62895154828/ethnicity (Accessed 19 February 2016).

Lulu (2015) "The Changing Face of Fandom," *The Slow Dance of the Infinite Stars*, blog, [online] Available from: http://centrumlumina.tumblr.com/post/110625302514/the-changing-face-of-fandom-although-people-come (Accessed 19 February 2016).

McCain, J., Gentile, B., and Campbell, W. K. (2015) "A Psychological Exploration of Engagement in Geek Culture," *PLoS ONE*, 10(11), e0142200.

McIntosh, P. (2016) "White Privilege: Unpacking the Invisible Knapsack," in M. L. Andersen and P. H. Collins (eds.), *Race, Class, and Gender: An Anthology*, 9th edition, Boston, MA: Cengage Learning, pp. 74–78.

Radway, J. (1984) *Reading the Romance: Women, Patriarchy, and Popular Literature*, Chapel Hill, NC: The University of North Carolina Press.

Sendlor, C. (2011) "Fan Fiction Demographics in 2010: Age, Sex, Country," *Fan Fiction Statistics: Fan Fiction Statistics, Numerics and Unique Research about FanFiction.Net by FFN Research*, blog, [online] Available from: http://ffnresearch.blogspot.com/2011/03/fan-fiction-demographics-in-2010-age.html (Accessed 16 March 2016).

Stanfill, M. (2011) "Doing Fandom, (Mis)Doing Whiteness: Heteronormativity, Racialization, and the Discursive Construction of Fandom," *Transformative Works and Cultures*, 8, doi:10.3983/twc.2011.0256.

United States Census Bureau "2010–2014 American Community Survey 5-Year Estimates, Table DP05," Available from: factfinder.census.gov (Accessed February 19, 2016).

Wanzo, R. (2015) "African American Acafandom and Other Strangers: New Genealogies of Fan Studies," *Transformative Works and Cultures*, 20, doi:10.3983/twc.2015.0699.

23
THE QUEER POLITICS OF FEMSLASH

Julie Levin Russo

"Slash" is a term deriving from the convention, since the 1970s, of using the / symbol to designate a relationship between two characters, as in the iconic Kirk/Spock. Metonymically, it came to denote creative fan works featuring same-sex couples – meaning, in most cases, male/male (M/M) pairings. As the unmarked term, slash can be simultaneously general and particular, while pointing to female/female (F/F) pairings specifically requires a variant: femslash (also styled as femmeslash or girlslash). As this hierarchy might suggest, F/F remains underrepresented in scholarly research, and arguably in fandom itself (in comparison to M/M and also to het [heterosexual] and gen [general] fiction and art).

Femslash fans often frame their experience in this way, as was the case at the "Where's the F/F?" panel at Wiscon (Madison WI, May 2015). The conversation took as a jumping off point detailed statistics, compiled by destinationtoast, on fanfiction posted at Archive of Our Own (AO3), the most important non-profit fan archive. The proportion of F/F on AO3 has plateaued since 2016 at 8–9% (destinationtoast 2021), versus around 50% for M/M, the largest relationship category (2019). Of course, it's possible that AO3 isn't the site of femslashers' most active participation – destinationtoast notes (2016) that popular archives FanFiction.net and Wattpad (not to mention social network platform Tumblr) are impossible to profile as accurately because they have no femslash category, and authors use a wide variety of tags to identify content. Presuming that femslash does lag behind other genres, the head start slash and het have gotten since the 1970s is one possible explanation (femslash certainly wasn't unheard of in pre-Web media fandoms, but it was comparatively rare), as is the dearth of significant female relationships in popular media (this deficit has been gradually decreasing). Participants at the Wiscon panel also cited internalized or systemic sexism as a potential barrier, and the LGBTQ tradition of separatism or "safe space" as a factor that may make femslash less visible.

Whatever the demographic realities, I resist the narrative of scarcity as a framework for understanding femslash. It is the foundation of a vibrant online community that deserves to be considered on its own terms. That said, this chapter does situate femslash in relation to claims, in the tradition of fan studies scholarship, about how creative fandom in general (and male slash in particular) is resistant or queer. Linking these two values together is not an accident: "queer" is sometimes an umbrella term roughly synonymous with LGBT (a noun), but its widespread theoretical sense reserves it for resistance to sexual or gender norms (a verb). Queer world-making challenges – but also, to put it positively, offers alternatives to – dominant ideas about identity, sex, and relationships. As such, the same-sex focus of either slash or femslash does not alone make it queer, but nor should we assume that queerness is the only significant mode of resistance. Moreover, queer as an intersectional concept is inextricable from decolonial struggles along axes of race, class, disability, and so on, a perspective necessary to any assessment of the radical potential of fandom and increasingly forceful in fan studies scholarship.

The notion of resistance or subversion has been such a touchstone in academic accounts of slash that it's worthwhile to review how this construct originated and developed, as I will do later in this chapter, to ground an analysis of the particular politics of femslash. Even if we're past the point of marveling at "normal female interest in men bonking" (Green et al. 1998), the speculative, non-normative aspect of women imagining and realizing an erotics – for themselves and each other – through male characters remains a defining characteristic of slash as scholarly object. A defining characteristic of femslash fandom, by contrast, is the presumed synchronicity between its participants (primarily queer women) and its content (queer relationships between women). So, from a fan studies vantage point, femslash may have seemed unremarkable. My intent here is to intervene in this tacit dismissal by foregrounding the more direct forms of resistance that today's femslash communities engage in: critical and activist responses to the mainstream media industry. But in the end, I will argue that we can see a facet of something subversively queer in femslash, too.

The Femslash Collective

In the 1990s, fan discussion and participation was largely siloed by fandom due to its dependence on specifically themed mailing lists and sites. With the rise of social blogging platform LiveJournal as a home base for media fan cultures, beginning around 2001, an environment with more permeable boundaries between fandoms (and between fan activity and other domains of life) developed, laying the groundwork for femslash to become a unifying investment that transcends any particular show or couple. To cite one landmark: femslash_today was founded on December 1, 2005, and a collaborative team posted lists of femslash fan works and other links of interest to this LiveJournal community almost daily through 2013. Femslash fans are also known to flock collectively from fandom to fandom, particularly around media that manifest lesbian relationships through strong subtextual or explicit portrayals.

The femslash sensibility also has effects with wider implications: fans can and do mobilize collectively around issues of queer female representation, celebrating favorite examples and publicly condemning missteps – a dynamic animated by a feeling of shared identity. The demographics of AO3's fan community are increasingly queer and trans/nonbinary overall, with recent surveys showing up to 81% LGBTQ+ (centreoftheselights 2024) and up to 40% non-cisgender (Rouse and Stanfill 2023a) users. However, qualitative scholarship (Hanmer 2014; Ng 2008; Pande and Moitra 2017), formal and informal surveys (Rouse and Stanfill 2023b), community self-definition, and my own observations suggest that an unusually close correspondence between femslash fandom and participants who identify as lesbian, bisexual, and/or queer women has been consistent over time. Notably, alternative terms like "sapphic" are gaining in popularity because, by avoiding derivation from "female," they are more inclusive of fans and characters with transmasculine and nonbinary identities who are part of F/F communities. In their 1998 chapter in *Theorizing Fandom*, Green,

Jenkins, and Jenkins offer one of the earliest chronicles of fans' discussions about "female slash;" writers in their APAs (a kind of collaborative zine exchange) wrestled with the queer politics of male slash and its exclusion of women, but some reported that they prefer male slash precisely because they enjoy "[w]riting (and reading) about things we can't experience directly" (Green, Jenkins, and Jenkins 1998: 18). Femslash fans certainly don't write and read only about characters who are a perfect match to our identities, and we certainly explore situations and acts in fantasy that we wouldn't in real life, but I believe many are drawn to femslash precisely to delve into things that we *can* experience directly – sexually, romantically, or politically.

This variance from male slash perhaps contributes to the dearth of research on femslash from the core of fan studies. There has been some scholarship on fan communities surrounding lesbian media – such as Candace Moore's (2009) ethnography of *The L Word* viewing parties and Maria San Filippo's (2015) framing of AfterEllen.com as a site of vernacular media criticism – and through the mid-2010s a few scholars had considered femslash directly (not merely as an aside in articles on male slash), particularly in relation to *Xena: Warrior Princess* (Gwenllian Jones 2000a, 2000b, 2002; Hamming 2001; Hanmer 2003, 2014) and other major fandoms (Isaksson 2009, 2010 [on *Buffy the Vampire Slayer*]; Jones 2013 [on *The X-Files*]; Kapurch 2015 [on Disney]). This body of work tends to foreground fanfiction as an axis that connects us with either fans' community structures or fans' engagement with media texts (or both). Today, research on femslash is gaining momentum, and the contested relationship between fans and commercial television creators is a newer avenue of inquiry. Elena Maris (2016) looks back at online encounters with *Xena* writers, arguing that "fans capitalized on… [the early Web's] upset of social boundaries between producers and audiences, to significantly influence the show's narrative arc" (124). By contrast, Eve Ng (2017) models the current debate over "queerbaiting" as "the outcome of increased paratextual discourse about LGBT content at a specific moment of queer contextuality" (para 2.8) – that is, as a collision between expectations set by producers (often via unstructured outlets like Twitter) and expectations brought by fans (via their understanding of the media landscape). The multiplication and fragmentation of film and television audiences means that the industry appeals to queer fans as it hasn't before, and queer fans have a corresponding capacity to impact and referee the industry via social media. To understand why femslash fandom's power to mobilize in this way hasn't captured more scholarly attention until recently, we need to trace the disciplinary phylogeny of slash back to a previous evolution of audience studies that emphasized marginality from a subcultural and feminist perspective.

Is Resistance Futile?

British cultural studies advanced the idea that audiences (particularly working class, female, youth, or minority audiences who were commonly seen as unsophisticated) are active in their consumption, interpreting and negotiating media texts in complex and surprising ways. The year 1992 saw the publication of two formative ethnographies of creative media fans built on the concept that marginalized subcultures are able to resist the dominant culture through their practices of meaning making: Camille Bacon-Smith's *Enterprising Women* and Henry Jenkins's *Textual Poachers*. Each devoted a chapter of their book to M/M slash and, while less oriented to systemic critiques of domination than their British or European counterparts, each claimed that it is a site of resistance to social norms. Both authors describe fandom as an empowering, supportive subculture for (mainly white, straight, middle-class) women, and suggest that it fulfills the role of earlier folk cultures or myths in the era of commercial media. This framing is characteristic of subcultural models from the 1970s and 1980s, which tended to highlight ideological agency by stressing cultural marginality.

In feminist frameworks, it is the disjuncture between female creators as subjects and male lovers as objects, and the reversal of patriarchal hierarchies and exploration of queer possibilities this entails, that invests slash with its revolutionary potential. The premise that M/M slash is exceptional (that women eroticizing gay male sex is something to marvel at) and that this uniqueness indicates a site of feminist intervention was often recapitulated in subsequent generations of scholarship on slash. If fans are active readers who interpret television shows in diverse and unpredictable ways according to their own imperatives, we can say the same for acafans (scholar-fans in the field) with respect to our objects of study. If the defining fantasy of slash is that characters of the same gender are in love, I would propose that the defining fantasy of research on slash is that it is a form of grassroots resistance. With the advent of the Web in the second half of the 1990s, it became possible to argue that creative fans could radically transform what cultural production means by subverting the mass media's social and economic systems. But techno-utopias (even feminist ones) began to tarnish in the new millennium with the increasing commercialization of digital and online platforms, until as academics we were almost embarrassed to acknowledge the effusive optimism these new technologies had inspired. Weighty critiques of the blind spots of this enthusiasm demanded an accounting also, including the elision of raced, economic, national, and gendered dynamics that were less than liberatory.

Accordingly, we must be wary of the limitations of framing the predominantly white, middle class, and Western iteration of media fandom as subversive – not to mention the limitations of ignoring fans who are not white, middle class, and Western. In her well warranted indictment of fan studies, Rebecca Wanzo (2015) explains how scholars' attachment to "a utopian understanding of fans in science fiction communities as being antiracist and progressive" can lead us to overlook the ways that "some fans of speculative works depend on the centrality of whiteness or masculinity to take pleasure in the text" (para. 1.4). This invisible privileging is baked into the persistent focus on gender in the fan studies literature over its first two decades, although the progressiveness of fandom has become less romanticized over time. It is now much more common to see scholars acknowledge the prevalence of racism in fan communities as a counterpoint to positive aspects of its queerness (in relation to femslash, see Marks 2023; Navar-Gill and Stanfill 2018; Pande and Moitra 2017), following from a longer vernacular tradition of what Lothian and Stanfill (2021) have called "fans of color critique" that indicts fandom's "structural whiteness." Rukmini Pande (2018) likewise points out that "media fandom spaces, theorized as inclusive and liberating, are not immune to hierarchies structured by privilege," and here fan studies "lags behind actual fan practice where these debates have never been more energetically pursued" (210). For Pande, the degree to which American media and American fans are dominant in anglophone fandom, the postcolonial complexities of this dominance, and how national contexts shape fans' understanding of race, still need to be interrogated.

The utopian rhetoric around slash fandom was also necessarily tempered as fandom became less oppositional and more essential to commercial media. If digital technologies initially seemed to fulfill the radical promise of fan subcultures by realizing their community networks and creative production on a grander scale, it was also digital technologies that shifted the attention of the entertainment industries toward fan practices. In their introduction to the anthology *Fandom*, Gray, Sandvoss, and Harrington (2007) point out that the first wave of scholarship ("fandom is beautiful") relied on revaluing – without reassessing – the culturally marginal status of fans (3). In the decade since, however, "the fan as a specialized yet dedicated consumer has become a centerpiece of media industries' marketing strategies" (Gray et al. 2007: 4), which renders the model of fandom as resistance suspect. But Busse and Gray (2011) worry that "a fan studies that follows industry-sanctioned fans too closely may lose much of its critical edge" (439). Their chapter echoes other feminist work of this period in urging an attention to *which* fans and fan activities are legitimized in the commodification process (and its study), and which may actually be left more marginal and vulnerable (Stanfill 2013).

Industry studies and critical race studies, then, are two approaches that challenge the utopian discourse of the first waves (pre- and post-digital) of slash scholarship, and yet neither framework encourages us to toss out the notion of resistance wholesale. As fan studies cycled through increasingly complex debates about fandom as subversive, queerness emerged as a motif that continues to hold space for optimism and idealism. While I point to some problematic assumptions and oversights that manifest in the celebration of slash as queer, I don't want to suggest that there is no value or truth to this construction – indeed, it is one on which I often rely. It is fair to say, though, that in terms of the formative tension in queer theory and politics around an understanding that is oppositional (aimed at subverting norms) versus identity-based (aimed at becoming normal), the most prevalent analyses of slash have rested almost exclusively on the former. As a representation of this tendency as it persisted into the internet era, I cite several articles here that deploy this device in their central argument. While the theme has been more widespread than these examples, it is deservedly on the wane, and yet this 2000s scholarship held significant sway over the trajectory of the field. Falzone, for one, builds on David Halperin's definition of queer as "whatever is at odds with the normal, the legitimate, the dominant" (2005: 249) to claim, rather symptomatically, that "K/S is queer precisely because it is not about homosexuality" (251). This turn explicitly puts the two poles of queerness at odds, and positions not necessarily queer-identified women writing about not necessarily queer-identified men as *more* queer than people who are queer.

Reid (2009), for her part, formulates nuanced critiques of such trends in previous slash scholarship, yet also chooses to "emphasize queer practices rather than queer as a gender identity: my discussion in this paper makes no claim about the sexuality of the writers of the two fics, nor about the sexuality of the readers" (472). As Jung (2004) chronicles, fans themselves began to question the politics of this pervasive association of slash communities with queerness despite their general lack of engagement with " 'real'... gay culture" (para. 26). In an article that incorporates the voices of fans from a dedicated online discussion, Lothian, Busse, and Reid (2007) attempt to address this divergence head on by considering fan communities as queer spaces. Their work highlights the erotic dimension of connections forged between women through a shared language of desire and often through sexually explicit fan works, irrespective of how they identify. This represents a unique and subtle approach to the subversive problematic, but it is still the "queer potential" of fandom that they frame as significant. This research exemplifies a well-developed thread in fan studies, which could be summed up by Dhaenens, Van Bauwel, and Biltereyst's (2008) thesis that "[t]he concept of resistance is at the core of queer theory" (337) and "slash fiction and queer readings seem to be practices within the realms of this potential resistance" (344). I hope that this lens brings into focus some of the persistent acafantasies that have shaped an understanding of male slash as a queer phenomenon: namely, that it is in fluid, unsettled, discontinuous relations of sexuality and gender that the greatest queerness lies.

A final challenge to emerge countering the utopian interpretation of slash is the idea that, even within creative fan communities where the identity of characters seems untethered to the identity of readers and writers, identity counts. Busse and Lothian (2018) claim that women who slash have been self-consciously engaged with real-world LGBT politics since the 1990s, and Lucy Neville's (2018) research showed that three-quarters of women surveyed believed that their involvement with slash impacted their awareness of social issues around sexuality and over two-thirds "felt that what they read and/or wrote had some sort of political angle" (390). On a more individual level, Jennifer Duggan (2023) looks at the "trans turn" in fan studies, citing her own ethnographic research suggesting that for some, slash may be less about women exploring an opposite gender as "gender identity development" toward (for two different interviewees) a genderqueer or transmasculine identity (para. 2.10). These claims point to the interface between slash and lived realities of queerness.

However, Mel Stanfill (2024) cites persistent critiques of how slash may be characterized by "fetishization or exploitation [that] ultimately rests on treating eroticism between men as entirely separable from the lived experience of queer men" (75). Indeed, Joseph Brennan (2014) has written about his own experience with homophobic backlash, and James Joshua Coleman (2019) applies the lens of cultural appropriation to slash. Moreover, Stanfill (2024) has seen in fandom "outright homophobia from slashers toward femslashers," relying on the legitimacy of "slash shipping of men... to shield people from consequences for homophobia enacted against actual queer people" (75–76). I would position this as a cautionary tale for fan studies as well, which has largely dismissed femslash as a queer female practice in favor of male slash (acknowledging here that slash is increasingly practiced by queer people too). I'm not asking that we discard the subversively queer elements of male slash, but I am arguing that this shouldn't be (and increasingly isn't) the sole axis of slash's validity or scholarly interest. It's time to look more broadly at the range of ways creative fandom is animated in positive and negative ways by queerness defined as a socially contextualized identity.

Assimilation/Transformation

If we look at slash as queer resistance only in terms of anti-normativity, we will miss a pivotal intersection between fan cultures and the evolution of the entertainment industry. Femslash communities, while a minority segment of creative media fandom, have been leaders in positioning themselves as a critical counterpublic within an investment in shifting the dominant terms of representation. This stance was an organic outgrowth of fan activity precisely because of the privileged correspondence between being queer women and transforming queer female characters, which animates an imperative to see oneself reflected onscreen. Since the early days of online femslash, as Maris (2016) observed within *Xena* fandom, the themes of fans' transformative works of fiction and art have been tied to an activist engagement with entertainment media. In a special issue on Fan Activism, Brough and Shresthova (2012) assert in their overview that fan activism has often been discussed in terms of "fans lobbying for a content-related outcome, such as a program staying on the air" (para. 2.2), whereas the essays therein deal more with "fandom as a resource or springboard for civic and political action" (para. 2.4). Somewhere in between, perhaps, lies advocacy around "the representation of racial or sexual minorities" (para. 2.2), the latter of which is one of the most characteristic concerns of femslash communities.

One common motif here is a reflexive awareness of femslash in relation to fan culture and media culture. To agitate for their interests as lovers of queer women, fans have collectively developed both brash guerilla tactics (like flooding tabloid polls and rapid-response Twitter storms) and sophisticated forms of critique, which increasingly generate enough impact to gain mainstream attention. Most notably, in the spring of 2016, a sizable percentage of the queer female characters on television were killed off (Waggoner 2018), culminating in the dramatic murder of rival commander Lexa on *The 100* (The CW, 2014–2020) just after she consummates her romance with the heroine, Clarke. In response, enraged fans leveled criticism and demands not just at the show's writers and producers, but at the representational system that puts lesbian and bisexual women perpetually in the crosshairs (lesbian media and culture website Autostraddle began an archive of these casualties at the time, and as of 2023 the count was at 235 [Riese 2023]). Through collective action on social media (ranging along a continuum from chaotic emotional declarations to highly organized and strategic interventions), devotees of the "Clexa" relationship parlayed their sense of injury and betrayal into Twitter trending topics; a broader LGBT Fans Deserve Better campaign, including a "Lexa Pledge" that got some traction with industry personnel; and donations ultimately totaling over $100,000 to The Trevor Project (Waggoner 2018), a suicide prevention organization for LGBT+ youth. This outcry also led to articles condemning the "Bury Your Gays" trope in major cultural news outlets. Many journalists emphasized fans' direct interaction with *The 100* showrunner, Jason Rothenberg, and producer/writer, Javier Grillo-Marxuach, and, in a broader sense, the industry's growing responsibility to understand and respect queer fans' expectations.

This watershed came at the convergence of changes in culture, entertainment, technology, and fandom, as observed by Navar-Gill and Stanfill (2018), that coalesced in femslash fans' "sense of a right to be heard" (87). Indeed, Elizabeth Bridges (2018) writes that "queer fandom proved to be, in this case, a force to be reckoned with and should serve as a wake-up call for series creators" (129). Identity politics, deeply felt, was constitutive of both the discourse and its forcefulness, as in representative tweets wherein "fans made themselves part of the issue by using the pronoun we/our and thus identifying themselves as lesbians, justifying their right to be mad and vocal on this issue" (Bourdaa 2018: 391). It is true that male slashers have made similar interventions, and attention to and investment in media representation is increasingly prevalent in slash fandom (perhaps corresponding to an increasing proportion of queer participants). Still, the fusion that femslash presumes between fans and characters in terms of sexual and gender identities – its primary difference from the ways male slash has been defined – affords it a powerful platform for literal campaigns of resistance to the heteronormative structures and ideologies that overdetermine narrative (and not just business) choices.

It is important to recognize that this activist configuration has its problems and is no more pure than any fan formation. Navar-Gill and Stanfill (2018) compare #LexaDeservedBetter and related hashtags to #BlackLGBTDeserveToBe in response to the murder of Black lesbian Poussey on *Orange Is the New Black* (Netflix, 2013–2019) a few months later, pointing out that there was minimal solidarity from Lexa's white fanbase for this cause. Stanfill (2024) further cautions that framing fan interventions around personal identification may not only fail to foster, but actively hamper an intersectional approach: "the tendency of the Lexa and Clexa fandom to think only about their own marginalization at the expense of others" predisposed them to "ignoring the show's flagrant racism in the way it depicted characters of color" (98). Queer as it manifests here takes the shape of identity politics, and it brings with it the idea that gender and sexuality are essential categories of being, that they can be transparently visible as essential categories in the media, and that identity and visibility are profoundly linked for individuals and for society. Queer theory has a stake in troubling these assumptions because of the hierarchies and ideologies they leave undisturbed – the unified subject, the monogamous couple, binary gender, whiteness, capitalist aspirations, to name a few. We need the oppositional mode of queerness, but if we're interested in resistance and what it means to fans, the politics of visibility is a popular phenomenon that we should not discount. Moreover, if we infer that femslash equates only to an identity-based call for and investment in portrayals of queer women, we might overlook an important dimension of these transformative communities that is not reducible to a politics of visibility.

That is, even if femslash communities have repeatedly talked back to mass media in these terms, demanding explicitly lesbian characters and relationships onscreen across the decades, they are still engaged in slashing – a creative intervention in these characters and relationships before and beyond their explicit visibility. In earlier years, femslashers' Xena/Gabrielle "über" (alternate universe) fanfiction "demonstrate[d] how easily fans are able to wrest away control of the characters and their fictional lives from the television text" (Gwenllian Jones 2000b: 14) and their Buffy/Faith BDSM erotica "transgress[ed] stereotypical ideas about female desire and sexual behaviour" (Isaksson 2010: 9). More recently, Emily Coccia (2022) finds in femslash fic "the possibility of reimagining what bodily pleasures and eroticism could look like untethered from heteronormative sexual scripts" (para. 8.1) and Rachel Marks (2023) points to two subtextual pairings (each featuring two women of color) that garnered a following in *Legends of Tomorrow* (The CW, 2016–2022) fandom, despite its dominance by an onscreen F/F couple. The perversely queer characteristics that have been celebrated in slash have always been, and continue to be, present in femslash production. It's undoubtedly true that the politics of visibility is a conservative and homonormative logic (Stanfill 2024: 78), yet placing canon (official) and fanon (subtextual) couples on one cathected continuum doesn't seem to have troubled femslashers (Russo 2013). In a discussion on this topic at TGIF/F, the first multi-fandom femslash fan convention (Los Angeles, February 2016), participants expressed a complex understanding of textual/sexual indeterminacy, identifying examples of canon "grey areas" that included transitions from subtext to main text, different levels of onscreen consummation, supplementary information from transmedia tie-ins or paratexts, and conflicting forms of "evidence" for characters' sexuality. Although we cared about visibility and legitimacy for queer women in mainstream and independent media, we also celebrated the unique pleasures of subtext and the transformative possibilities it offers.

To me, the capacity to interrogate the boundaries of a text and to analyze and critique the systems of power that determine who gets to draw those boundaries, whose gaze is legitimate, and whose representation is visible, is the most important sense in which femslash is queer. This interrogation is possible with the intensity that is typical here because of the coupling of socially circumscribed identity and transformative online practices. At this node, the two meanings of queer – queer as noun and queer as verb, what femslashers are and what femslashers do – can intersect, in ways they can't when we define slash's queerness in terms of a divergence between the genders and sexualities of fans and characters. We need to situate fans' forms of resistance in historical, technological, and industrial context to better understand how femslash fandom's activities loop the production of new texts into the process of mass culture consumption, and in so doing generate distinct queer interventions.

Acknowledgements

My deepest thanks to Mel Stanfill for offering feedback toward both the original and revised versions of this chapter.

References

Bacon-Smith, C. (1992) *Enterprising Women: Television Fandom and the Creation of Popular Myth*, Philadelphia, PA: University of Pennsylvania Press.

Bourdaa, M. (2018) "'May We Meet Again': Social Bonds, Activities, and Identities in the #Clexa Fandom," in P. Booth (ed.) *A Companion to Media Fandom and Fan Studies*, Hoboken, NJ: John Wiley & Sons, pp. 385–399.

Brennan, J. (2014) "'Fandom Is Full of Pearl Clutching Old Ladies': Nonnies in the Online Slash Closet," *International Journal of Cultural Studies*, 17(4), pp. 363–380.

Bridges, E. (2018) "A Genealogy of Queerbaiting: Legal Codes, Production Codes, 'Bury Your Gays' and 'The 100 Mess,'" *Journal of Fandom Studies*, 6(2), pp. 115–132.

Brough, M. and Shresthova, S. (2012) "Fandom Meets Activism: Rethinking Civic and Political Participation," *Transformative Works and Cultures*, 10.

Busse, K. and Gray, J. (2011) "Fan Cultures and Fan Communities," in V. Nightingale (ed.) *The Handbook of Media Audiences*, New York: Wiley-Blackwell, pp. 425–443.

Busse, K. and Lothian, A. (2018) "A History of Slash Sexualities: Debating Queer Sex, Gay Politics, and Media Fan Cultures," in C. Smith, F. Attwood, and B. McNair (ed.) *The Routledge Companion to Media, Sex and Sexuality*, New York: Routledge.

Centreofthelights. (2024) "Survey Results: Demographics," *Archive of Our Own*, 23 February. Available at: https://archiveofourown.org/works/54011047/chapters/137376028 [Accessed 7 April 2024].

Coccia, E. (2022) "Femslash Fan Fiction's Expansive Erotic Imaginary," *Transformative Works and Cultures*, 38.

Coleman, J. J. (2019) "Writing with Impunity in a Space of Their Own: On Cultural Appropriation, Imaginative Play, and a New Ethics of Slash in Harry Potter Fan Fiction," *Jeunesse: Young People, Texts, Cultures*, 11(1), pp. 84–111.

Destinationtoast. (2016) "[Fandom Stats] F/F Stats (Femslash February 2016)," *Archive of Our Own*, 17 February. Available at: https://archiveofourown.org/works/6045463 [Accessed 7 April 2024].

Destinationtoast. (2019) "[Fandom Stats] Shipping on Wattpad vs. AO3 and FFN," *Archive of Our Own*, 5 May. Available at: https://archiveofourown.org/works/18721183 [Accessed 7 April 2024].

Destinationtoast. (2021) "[Fandom Stats] F/F Stats (February 2021)," *Archive of Our Own*, 28 February. Available at: https://archiveofourown.org/works/29747142 [Accessed 7 April 2024].

Dhaenens, F., Biltereyst, D., and Van Bauwel, S. (2008) "Slashing the Fiction of Queer Theory: Slash Fiction, Queer Reading, and Transgressing the Boundaries of Screen Studies, Representations, and Audiences," *Journal of Communication Inquiry*, 32(4), pp. 335–347.

Duggan, J. (2023) "Trans Fans and Fan Fiction: A Literature Review," *Transformative Works and Cultures*, 39.

Falzone, P. J. (2005) "The Final Frontier Is Queer: Aberrancy, Archetype and Audience Generated Folklore in K/S Slashfiction," *Western Folklore*, 64(3/4), pp. 243–261.

Gray, J., Harrington, C. L., and Sandvoss, C. (2007) "Introduction: Why Study Fans?" in *Fandom: Identities and Communities in a Mediated World*, New York: NYU Press.

Green, S., Jenkins, C., and Jenkins, H. (1998) "'Normal Female Interest in Men Bonking': Selections from The Terra Nostra Underground and Strange Bedfellows," in C. Harris and A. Alexander (ed.) *Theorizing Fandom: Fans, Culture, and Identity*, Cresskill, NJ: Hampton Press.

Gwenllian Jones, S. (2000a) "Histories, Fictions, and *Xena: Warrior Princess*," *Television & New Media*, 1, pp. 403–418.

Gwenllian Jones, S. (2000b) "Starring Lucy Lawless?" *Continuum: Journal of Media and Cultural Studies*, 14(1), pp. 9–22.

Gwenllian Jones, S. (2002) "The Sex Lives of Cult Television Characters," *Screen*, 43(1), pp. 79–90.

Hamming, J. (2001) "Whatever Turns You On: Becoming-Lesbian and the Production of Desire in the Xenaverse," *Gender's* 34. Available at: https://web.archive.org/web/20140730011739/www.genders.org/g34/g34_hamming.html [Accessed 7 April 2024].

Hanmer, R. (2003) "Lesbian Subtext Talk: Experiences of the Internet Chat," *International Journal of Sociology & Social Policy*, 23(1/2), pp. 80–106.

Hanmer, R. (2014) "'Xenasubtexttalk': The Impact on the Lesbian Fan Community Through its Online Reading and Writing of Lesbian Fan Fiction in Relation to the Television Series *Xena Warrior Princess*," *Feminist Media Studies*, 4(14), pp. 608–622.

Isaksson, M. (2009) "Buffy/Faith Adult Femslash: Queer Porn with a Plot," *Slayage*, 7(4). Available at: http://whedonstudies.tv/volume-71.html [Accessed 7 April 2024].

Isaksson, M. (2010) "The Erotics of Pain: BDSM Femslash Fan Fiction," in J. Fernandez (ed.) *Making Sense of Pain: Critical and Interdisciplinary Perspectives* [e-book], Inter-Disciplinary Press, pp. 203–210.

Jenkins, H. (1992) *Textual Poachers: Television Fans & Participatory Culture*, New York: Taylor & Francis.

Jones, B. (2013) "Mulder/Scully versus the G-Woman and the Fowl One," in A. Jamison (ed.) *Fic: Why Fanfiction Is Taking Over the World*, Dallas: Smart Pop, pp. 122–129.

Jung, S. (2004) "Queering Popular Culture: Female Spectators and the Appeal of Writing Slash Fan Fiction," *Gender Queeries*, 8. Available at: http://genderforum.org/gender-queeries-issue-8-2004/ [Accessed 7 April 2024].

Kapurch, K. (2015) "Rapunzel Loves Merida: Melodramatic Expressions of Lesbian Girlhood and Teen Romance in *Tangled*, *Brave*, and Femslash," *Journal of Lesbian Studies*, 19(4), pp. 436–445.

Lothian, A., Busse, K., and Reid, R. A. (2007) "'Yearning Void and Infinite Potential': Online Slash Fandom as Queer Female Space," *English Language Notes*, 45(2), pp. 103–111.

Maris, E. (2016) "Hacking Xena: Technological Innovation and Queer Influence in the Production of Mainstream Television," *Critical Studies in Media Communication*, 33(1), pp. 123–137.

Marks, R. (2023) "Fan Perspectives of Queer Representation in *DC's Legends of Tomorrow* on Tumblr and AO3," *Transformative Works and Cultures*, 40.

Moore, C. (2009) "Liminal Places and Spaces: Public/Private Considerations," in M. Banks, J. Caldwell, and V. Mayer (eds.) *Production Studies: Cultural Studies of Media Industries*, New York: Routledge.

Navar-Gill, A. and Stanfill, M. (2018) "'We Shouldn't Have to Trend to Make You Listen': Queer Fan Hashtag Campaigns as Production Interventions," *Journal of Film and Video*, 70(3), pp. 85–100.

Neville, L. (2018) "'The Tent's Big Enough for Everyone': Online Slash Fiction as a Site for Activism and Change," *Gender, Place and Culture*, 25(3), pp. 384–398.

Ng Eve. (2008) "Reading the Romance of Fan Cultural Production: Music Videos of a Television Lesbian Couple," *Popular Communication*, 6(2), pp. 103–121.

Ng Eve. (2017) "Between Text, Paratext, and Context: Queerbaiting and the Contemporary Media Landscape," *Transformative Works and Cultures*, 24.

Pande, R. (2018) "Squee from the Margins: Racial/Cultural/Ethnic Identity in Global Media Fandom," in L. Bennett and P. Booth (eds.) *Seeing Fans: Representations of Fandom in Media and Popular Culture*, London: Bloomsbury.

Pande, M. and Moitra, S. (2017) "'Yes, the Evil Queen is Latina!': Racial Dynamics of Online Femslash Fandoms," *Transformative Works and Cultures*, 24.

Reid, R. A. (2009) "Thrusts in the Dark: Slashers' Queer Practices," *Extrapolation*, 50(3), pp. 463–483.
Riese. (2023) "All 235 Dead Lesbian and Bisexual Characters On TV, And How They Died," *Autostraddle*, 27 February. Available at: www.autostraddle.com/all-65-dead-lesbian-and-bisexual-characters-on-tv-and-how-they-died-312315/ [Accessed 7 April 2024].
Rouse, L. and Stanfill, M. (2023a) "Fan Demographics on Archive of Our Own," *Flow*, [online] 22 February. Available at: www.flowjournal.org/2023/02/fan-demographics-on-ao3/ [Accessed 7 April 2024].
Rouse, L. and Stanfill, M. (2023b) "Mapping Tumblr Through Fannish Homophiles," *AoIR Selected Papers of Internet Research*.
Russo, J. L. (2013) "Queer Female Fandom Online," in C. Carter, L. Steiner, and L. McLaughlin (eds.) *The Routledge Companion to Media and Gender*, New York: Routledge, pp. 450–460.
San Filippo, M. (2015) "Before and After AfterEllen: Online Queer Cinephile Communities as Critical Counterpublics," in M. Frey and C. Sayad (eds.) *Film Criticism in the Digital Age*, New Brunswick, NJ: Rutgers University Press, pp. 117–136.
Stanfill, M. (2013) "'They're Losers, but I Know Better': Intra-Fandom Stereotyping and the Normalization of the Fan Subject," *Critical Studies in Media Communication*, 30(2), pp. 117–134.
Stanfill, M. (2024) *Fandom Is Ugly: Networked Harassment in Participatory Culture*, New York: NYU Press.
Waggoner, E. B. (2018) "Bury Your Gays and Social Media Fan Response: Television, LGBTQ Representation, and Communitarian Ethics," *Journal of Homosexuality*, 65(13), pp. 1877–1891.
Wanzo, R. (2015) "African American Acafandom and Other Strangers: New Genealogies of Fan Studies," *Transformative Works and Cultures*, 20.

24
IDENTITY, POSITIONALITY, AND COMICS FANDOM
Women of Color Fans

Erika Chung

The success of *Ms. Marvel* in 2014 brought attention to racial and gender diversity in comics. The new protagonist reflected an intersectional positionality which better reflected the reader demographic Marvel Comics was trying to attract (Kashtan 2020). Originally a short-lived series published in 1977, the 2014 *Ms. Marvel* series revival featured a new character. Kamala Khan, a Muslim teen from a Pakistani immigrant family, was introduced to take over the mantel from Carol Danvers, also known now as Captain Marvel. The character and narrative of *Ms. Marvel* complicate assumptions about superheroes. Kamala's gender, race, and religion are incorporated into her narrative and experience as an American teenager, Muslim, and superhero. The inclusion and engagement with her family, friends, mosque, school, and neighborhood provide a rich context that rooted her to multiple parts of her identity and life. This resonated deeply with me because as a Chinese-Canadian woman from a Hong Kong immigrant family, it was heartwarming to read a comic that featured a character who shared similar experiences of growing up in two cultures.

Ms. Marvel was part of the Marvel NOW! branding initiative from Marvel Comics, which focused on featuring more female character leads and efforts to diversify its cast of characters (McMillan 2013; Griffin and Van den Bulck 2022). This initiative drew attention to marginalized creators and fans, such as women of color (WOC), in comics. However, the attention and visibility on racialized female fans in comics fandom only indicates recent mainstream recognition. WOC fans have always been part of comics fandom, regardless of invisibility. As Kristen J. Warner noted in her study on fan labor behind the Iris West Defense Squad, "…Black female fandom continues to thrive in spite of the ways their spaces are relegated to the background. In fact, part of what may strengthen these pluralist communities is the fact that they are left alone to create their own safe spaces for interaction and creative labor" (Warner 2017: 256). In other words, despite being ignored, Black women have always been a part of fan culture and have created spaces that support them and their fan interests and practices.

Despite the field's attention to highly visible fan communities and practices, this chapter demonstrates how WOC comics fans navigate and participate in comics fandom in ways that are not always visible. Gatekeeping on the basis of sexism and racism remains in fandom. Despite this, my research demonstrates how WOC fans' participation in comics fandom is interconnected with interests rooted in other aspects of life, for instance, interests in art and literature, and in professional and family lives, contribute to WOC fans' approaches and experiences in fandom. This interconnected foundation is reflected in how WOC fans navigate and negotiate their participation in fandom. Women of color are not segmenting, or isolating, any part of themselves as comic fans. They draw on the multiplicities of their identities and lived experiences to inform and shape their fan identity and participation. This chapter highlights how being a comic book fan does not need to be qualified or characterized solely on the basis of mainstream visibility. Instead, WOC comic fans demonstrate how being a comics fan can be personal and meaningful for the self, therefore decentering whiteness and masculinity. After all, a key characteristic of fandom is how it promotes emotional and intellectual stimulation (Yodovich 2022). This chapter draws on 14 semi-structured ethnographic interviews with self-identified WOC comics fans in order to center their experiences and perspective on comics fandom.

Gatekeeping in Comics Fandom: Sexism and Racism

Fans are known for their deep positive emotional bonds to their favorite media products and their open expression of those feelings (Duffett 2013). Comics fans, in particular, are also known for their intense affective relationships that can evolve into a sense of obligation to protect the fandom, medium, and industry (Pustz 2000). This sense of obligation to defend comics in its entirety results in gatekeeping based on race and gender. Comics fandoms are known to be white and masculine, partly because the comics industry in North America has reinforced this by centering narratives that reflect white men. According to Shawna Kidman (2019: 138), since the late 1950s, the comics industry in the US has been cultivating, "…a narrow but highly engaged consumer base of privileged adult males." She goes on to describe this demographic as, "…typically educated, wealthy, urban, white and male…" (Kidman 2019: 138) and seen as valuable to advertisers. This laid a foundation and contributed to how women and racialized fans, especially racialized female fans, were marginalized in comics, both off and on the page. The comics industry, and popular culture, still market towards white male fans and audiences (Cocca 2016; De Dauw 2021), and primarily see female fans through a gendered perspective (Scott 2019).

Beyond the comics industry, comics fandom also gatekeeps. In general, gatekeeping is the process of crafting and filtering information or characteristics that not only shape people's perspectives on reality (Shoemaker and Vos 2009), but that are also deemed valid and valuable within a specific community. In this case, gatekeeping is used to determine what kinds of behavior, understanding, and participation qualify someone a fan or non-fan (Yodovich 2022). Gatekeeping is rooted in people's positionality, as related to their gender, race, class, and all that is interconnected and relational to their social location, which influences what people do or do not have access to (Martin and Van Gunten 2002; Misawa 2010). Gendering in fandom is one form of gatekeeping used to differentiate between "real and fake fans." For instance, Suzanne Scott (2013) notes how female comic book readers and fans are contained and compartmentalized via genres. Genres like indie or romance comics are gendered as feminine because either that is where many female writers and artists work, or the titles produced are not counted as part of the main series canon (Scott 2013). This limits the scope and visibility of female fans.

In regards to race, it is either erased or ignored in fandom. Otherwise, race and racism in comics are met with hostility and/or tension. One expression of this dynamic is how fandom treats non-white characters (Pande 2018). While the popularity of *Spider-Man: Into the Spider-Verse* (2018), and its sequel *Spider-Man: Across the Spider-Verse* (2023), now indicate acceptance of Miles Morales, just over a decade ago the fandom was not as open to the idea of a Black Spider-Man. As noted by Albert Fu (2015: 278) in his examination of the language fans used online in reaction to the possibility of actor Donald Glover being cast as Spider-Man, "In both fiction and non-fiction, race plays a role in whether or not people believe someone is qualified for a job or belongs in a position." Fu's study highlighted how online fans used language to pre-empt critiques of racism in their insistence of keeping Spider-Man white. This highlights how hegemonic ideologies are constituted and reconstituted within fandom. In other words, race is a factor in gatekeeping comics fandom and marginalizes those who are not white and/or male. Therefore, the intersection of race and gender in comics fandom as a form of gatekeeping results in the reconstitution of hegemonic structures of power and exclusion that is also located in society and culture. Comics fandom is a conflicting space for racialized female fans. The intersection of race and gender in comics fandom highlights how fandom is not be experienced equally by all – escapism in fandom is not a one size fits all (STITCH 2021; STITCH 2022).

Intersectionality of Race and Gender in Comics Fandom

Fan studies and comics studies recognize the need for research on race and racism (Woo 2017; Guynes and Lund 2020; Pande 2020; De Dauw 2021; Stanfill and Lothian 2021). As Rebecca Wanzo (2015: 1.6) notes, "…race is still frequently treated as an add-on or as something that should be addressed somewhere later…" within these fields. To address this, this chapter draws on an intersectional perspective on racialized female comic book fans and their experiences with comics and the fandom. Intersectionality recognizes the interconnected dynamics of social locations and power structures, like race, gender, class, sexuality, and disability, that are interdependent of one another in forming systems of oppression and marginalization. Intersectionality generates insight into where systemic issues are located and how they operate in tandem with each other (Carbado et al. 2013). Kimberlé Crenshaw (1991: 1283) notes how an intersectional analysis recognizes, "…how racial and sexual subordination are mutually reinforcing… ." One of intersectionality's purposes is to form counter-hegemonic and transformative knowledge that offers space to build non-oppressive coalitions between various social justice-oriented movements that can collaborate and form solidarity (Bilge 2013). Intersectionality provides context to how WOC fans navigate their positionalities as racialized women in a space that does not center them. Therefore, their forms of engagement with comics are distinct and meant for their affective relationship with comics. The following study directly engages with racialized women. Doing so centers intersecting identities, rather than have race be an add-on to the project, and generates insight into counter-hegemonic fan practices that do not depend on visibility.

Methodology

This project interviewed WOC comic fans about their lived experiences in comics fandom. There were two components to participant recruitment. Firstly, I drew on my positionalities as a comics fan, Asian woman, and researcher to circulate my call for participants. I used Twitter and Instagram, where my fandoms were located, in August 2021 to post my call and welcomed online peers to circulate my post. Secondly, self-identification was a key point in the call. Recruitment materials called for participants who identify as women of color and as comic book fans. Terms like Black, Indigenous, People of Color (BIPOC) and Women of Color (WOC) are often used within comics fandom. However, I recognize that these terms can be essentializing. Tomi Ajele (2021) for the *CBC* and Constance Grady (2020) for *Vox* note that terms like BIPOC and WOC can generalize systemic inequality that each racialized community experience. Instead, being specific is more effective and accurate when discussing the systemic issues related to race and/or gender. The tensions regarding terminology, especially in addressing racial inequality and marginalization, indicate how language is also a site for contestation (Harmon 2021).

The racialized women who participated in my study came from diverse communities and racial and ethnic heritages. They used different terms to articulate their identities, and when asked how they self-identify, used words that were specific. Some examples include: Black cis-gender woman; Brown woman; Taiwanese-Canadian; Black Christian Woman; Pakistani, woman, Muslim; and woman of color, immigrant. However, their responses and engagements with my study indicates that terms like "WOC" can also have a place and function in the context of comics fandom. Therefore, in this chapter when I am addressing participants I interviewed, or racialized women within the context of comics fandom, I will use the phrase "WOC fans." Lastly, I will contextualize participants with their respective identity terms to provide specificity whilst maintaining their anonymity.

Fan studies often examines digital content produced by fans (Booth 2017), such as fanart (Dennis 2010; Scott 2015; Hetrick 2018) or fanfiction (Hellekson and Busse 2014; Busse 2017; De Kosnik 2019). While fan-produced content is a rich body of primary data, to have greater understanding of WOC fans' lived experiences and their perspectives, I conducted ethnographic interviews. Ethnographic interviews "…elicit talk in order to provide a window into…" people's lived experiences in cultural worlds (Woo 2021: 99). More importantly, ethnographic interviews enable participants to share as much as they are comfortable with, and support reflection and elaboration. From August to November 2021, I conducted interviews with 14 self-identifying WOC comics fans. Participants resided in the United States and Canada, were fluent in English, and were at least 18 years old; all had experience with online fan communities, especially as a result of the Covid-19 pandemic. To provide anonymity to the interview participants, they either chose a pseudonym or were assigned one, which I use below when I refer to them. Each interview was recorded on Zoom and transcripts were produced from the recordings.

Thematic analysis (Guest et al. 2012; Braun and Clarke 2021) of the transcripts was conducted in two rounds to assemble overarching and specific insights. The first round of analysis produced overarching similarities between WOC fans' experiences, and the second round of analysis developed insight into differences within emerging themes. Below I highlight two themes that provide insight into how WOC fans experience comics fandom. The first theme illustrates how many participants credited their love for reading as a catalyst to comics fandom. The second theme highlights how reflection is a practice WOC fans use to maintain personal affective relationships with comics fandom. Together, the two themes illustrate how WOC navigate around "gatekeepers" in order to participate in comics fandom on their terms.

(For the) Love of Reading

Similar to a lot of hobbies, many WOC comics fans experienced a learning curve when becoming a fan. My journey into comics fandom was the cumulation of growing up with superhero transmedia, reading Japanese manga, and fostering a love of reading through fanfiction and Young Adult (YA) fiction as a teen. A general love for reading was expressed and shared by many WOC comics fans I interviewed. Participants expressed how a love for a particular genre in one medium, such as novels, helped them segue into comics. For example, Maryam, who self-identified as a "colored immigrant Muslim woman," spoke of her love for fantasy fiction, her background in literature, and how it led to becoming a fan of the *Sandman* comic book series. Despite disliking horror, the series also has elements of fantasy and folklore in its narrative which won her over in being a fan. Similarly, Hanna, a Black woman, also spoke of how she is a "...big science fiction, fantasy, speculative fiction person, so I can be wooed into reading something if it's in that vein," and of how despite not being able to watch horror movies, she is able to read and enjoy, "...a really good horror comic." In other words, WOC fans are leveraging their interests in other areas of art, literature, and culture to form their affective relationships with comics. And through this, their foundation in comics fandom is rooted in passions that were formed outside of comics, but are now interconnected with one another. This kind of comics fandom, one that is rooted and interconnected with other interests, results in navigating comics fandom according to their personal compass.

In doing so, WOC fans experience personal fulfillment in their experience with comics that can be lasting and empowering. For instance, Jupiterjulep24, a Black cis-gender woman, recounted how her family knew she was an avid reader as a young girl, and how it is now easier for her to be open about her fandom because there is more representation, such as the *Black Panther* (2018) movie. When the movie was released, her extended family remembered her love of comics and are now more understanding and interested in her fandom, too. Hence, her enduring comics fandom and love for reading supports a form of bonding in her family. In terms of empowerment, Rhona reflected on how her comics fandom also started in a love for reading, and how she has grown as a comics fan. She identified as Guyanese-Canadian from a lower-middle class immigrant family and said,

> I love the format, like I've always loved to read, but I love looking at the illustrations and the way stories are told. Very exciting and interesting. And I've also noticed a shift in what I read when I first started out to what I read now. That's been interesting – seeing or figuring out what I actually like instead of reading what everyone tells me to read. A lot of people like to do that when you first start reading comics.

Rhona's reflection describes a form of gatekeeping in comics fandom, specifically the unsaid expectation of reading "the right" comics. However, her reflection highlights a contrast between when she started reading comics and her current understanding of herself as a comics fan. More specifically, the contrast is between her personal satisfaction and empowerment of knowing the kind of comics she enjoys and how that has led her to prioritizing comics created by women. She cites the *Ms. Marvel* (2014) series, written by G. Willow Wilson with art by Adrian Alphona, as being one of the first comics that guided her in that direction. For Jupiterjulep24 and Rhona, a love of reading drew them into comics fandom. Moreover, a love of reading formed the basis for their comics fandom, and it has contributed meaningfully to other components of life, like family bonding and self-assurance. Their experiences highlight how WOC fans reflect on their positionalities and how they participate in fandom. This practice of reflection not only helps maintain a meaningful and affective relationship with comics, but also lends to WOC fans becoming critical of comics, and more broadly of popular culture.

Reflection as a Fan Practice

As mentioned earlier, a key characteristic of fandom is how it facilitates intellectual and emotional stimulation. Through this experience, fans form greater emotional investments in, and bonds with, their fan objects. In this case, WOC comics fans' practice of reading comics leads to a practice of reflection, especially with comics that mirror or represent their positionalities as racialized women. Lina, who identified as "Pakistani, Muslim, and Canadian," reflected on how being a fan of the *Ms. Marvel* (2014) comic book series meant a lot to her because she identified with Kamala Khan/Ms. Marvel's social location. She said,

> …with Ms. Marvel it's because of the representation… I had never, growing up, seen a Muslim, let alone a Pakistani character… anywhere. I connected with anybody that had brown skin… I didn't see myself, but I could relate to being different, or two, not seen yourself as often so I was like, 'I need to see more of that and maybe one day it'll be me,' so I want to support that.

Feeling represented in *Ms. Marvel* motivated her to support and advocate for inclusive representation in comics and media. She is also a teacher, and described how this motivation and advocacy for inclusive representation is not only for herself, but also for her students and nieces and nephew. This deeply affective motivation has resulted in other forms of fan engagement by Lina, such as cosplaying and podcasting. Similarly, Cecilia, who identified as second-generation Canadian of Chinese ethnicity, noted how her reflections and emotions for superhero comics motivate her to support BIPOC creatives and greater inclusivity in her field of work. She shared how, "…I had never seen Asian women led comics. At the time, it was really only *Ms. Marvel* and *Silk* as the only women of color leads for like any of the Marvel series so like those are what are attracted me to Marvel, in general, and those are the two series I stuck with… ." The production and circulation of digital content is often interpreted as a form of engagement and affective expression by fans. And while that remains an indicator of fan participation, WOC fans' practice of reflection also indicates the depths of their emotional and intellectual bonds with comics, and how the nuances of their fandom are interconnected to their positionalities. Their positionalities, as related to the multiplicities of their identity, inform how they navigate comics fandom so that it is emotionally and intellectually fulfilling. In short, whether it is the production of fan-content or advocacy in other parts of life, WOC fans engage in reflection to maintain a meaningful and fulfilling relationship with comics so that they can mobilize their values.

While reflection as a fan practice helps deepen personal affect for comics, it can also help in understanding external events. Another participant described how reading comics encouraged her to reflect on geopolitics and inequality. Tina, who identified as an Asian woman, spoke of how the space-opera fantasy series *Saga* by Brian K. Vaughn and Fiona Staples was impactful on her. She specified that she is a fan of comics as a creative medium because she was artistic as a student. She admired the creative craft demonstrated in the comic's storytelling, but was also greatly intrigued by the comic's multiple plot lines and how it explored power. She described her reading experience as,

> So, I think there's a lot of, at least, I can see reflections of what's happening in *Saga* reflected in our global politics, geo-conflicts now. I think that was also very intriguing, because you have the main story of the family together, and that's basically, the driving force, but you also have the political small stories going on the undercurrent, and that's the whole reason why they're on the run because they are politically inconvenient for those that are in power.

Tina's reading of *Saga* highlights how the practice of reflection extends beyond her personal experiences and sense of self. Reflecting on *Saga* prompted intellectual and emotional connections with the broader socio-cultural landscape, too. Jupiterjulep24, mentioned earlier, similarly engages in this reflection practice. Based on her love of reading, she reflected on comic book publishers' roles in making comics accessible to communities across socio-economic backgrounds:

> ...what if there was a place in your community that [publishers] would send things to and convert people, early readers, and just maybe do some other things in terms of access to their artists, access to their writers, to the editors and also bringing a face to the people that create these things, and these people can be you.

Jupiterjulep24's reflection considers the role of comics and the industry in context to local communities, especially those that might not be near a local comic bookstore or do not have the means to access comics culture. Both Tina and Jupiterjulep24's reflections highlight how being a fan can be an internal and personal experience that engages with issues of inequality in the broader world. Overall, reflection as a fan practice connects back to an enjoyment and engagement with comics as a fan object, text, and medium. For WOC fans, the practice of reflection is not only personal but one that centers them, and their interests and values, so that they can form and maintain space for themselves within fandom and their broader communities.

Conclusion

By focusing on WOC comics fans' experiences, I illustrated how we have a comics fandom that is specific and meaningful to us. Comics fandom has always been demographically diverse and this chapter illustrates this in three ways. Firstly, this chapter offers a picture into racial diversity in comics fandom. This is reflected in the variety of terminology and phrasing used by participants to self-identify. Secondly, rather than viewing racialized women through one axis of power, which can be reductive and generalizing, this study accounts for the intersection of race and gender. This chapter's intersectional framework highlights shared experiences between WOC fans and potential insight into solidarity between racialized women (Bilge 2013). Moreover, this framework extends fan studies and comics studies into direct engagement with racialized women as fans and readers, which enables nuanced analysis of their voices and experiences.

Lastly, this chapter expands fan studies focus on what fan participation can look and be like. By using ethnographic interviews, this chapter illustrates how fan participation does not need to be visible for others, within or outside of the fandom, in order to be meaningful for WOC fans. This is reflected by WOC fans drawing on interests outside of fandom, such as their love of reading, to navigate racial and gendered gatekeeping. Instead of appeasing gatekeepers, WOC fans leverage their positionalities and interests, such as genres, geopolitics, or socio-economic barriers to comics, to experience comics fandom on their terms. This, therefore, displaces whiteness and masculinity, rendering gatekeeping ineffective. Moreover, the practice of reflection highlights how WOC fans evaluate and locate comics in their personal, professional, and social lives and spaces. For comics studies, this chapter builds insight into how comics are situated and read by racialized women as readers, especially in light of fluctuating attitudes to racial and gender representation and inclusion. This chapter's scope is limited to the intersectionality of race and gender. I encourage further engagement with intersectionality in fan studies and comics studies research so that greater nuances of marginalized fans' social locations and lived experiences with fandom and the medium are reflected in scholarship.

References

Ajele, T. (2021) *OPINION | Here's why "BIPOC" doesn't do it for me | CBC News*, [online] Available from: www.cbc.ca/news/canada/calgary/road-ahead-why-bipoc-doesn-t-do-it-for-me-tomi-ajele-1.6067753 (Accessed: 27 November 2022).

Bilge, S. (2013) INTERSECTIONALITY UNDONE: Saving Intersectionality from Feminist Intersectionality Studies, *Du Bois Review: Social Science Research on Race*, 10(2), pp. 405–424, doi: 10.1017/S1742058X13000283.

Booth, P. (2017) *Digital Fandom 2.0: New Media Studies*, Second edition, New York: Peter Lang.

Braun, V. and Clarke, V. (2021) *Thematic Analysis: A Practical Guide to Understanding and Doing*, First edition, Thousand Oaks: Sage Publications.

Busse, K. (2017) *Framing Fan Fiction: Literary and Social Practices in Fan Fiction Communities*, Chicago, Iowa City: University of Iowa Press.

Carbado, D.W., Crenshaw, K.W., Mays, V.M. and Tomlinson, B. (2013) INTERSECTIONALITY: Mapping the Movements of a Theory, *Du Bois Review: Social Science Research on Race*, 10(2), pp. 303–312, doi: 10.1017/S1742058X13000349.

Cocca, C. (2016) *Superwomen: Gender, Power, and Representation*, New York: Bloomsbury Academic.

Crenshaw, K. (1991) Mapping the Margins: Intersectionality, Identity Politics, and Violence against Women of Color. *Stanford Law Review*, 43(6), pp. 1241–1299, doi: 10.2307/1229039.

De Dauw, E. (2021) *Hot Pants and Spandex Suits: Gender Representation in American Superhero Comic Books*, First edition, New Brunswick: Rutgers University Press.

De Kosnik, A. (2019) Relationshipping Nations: Philippines/US Fan Art and Fan Fiction. *Transformative Works and Cultures*, 29, https://doi.org/10.3983/twc.2019.1513

Dennis, J.P. (2010) Drawing Desire: Male Youth and Homoerotic Fan Art, *Journal of LGBT Youth*, 7(1), pp. 6–28, doi: 10.1080/19361650903507734.

Duffett, M. (2013) *Understanding Fandom: An Introduction to the Study of Media Fan Culture*, American First edition, New York: Bloomsbury Academic.

Fu, A.S. (2015) Fear of a Black Spider-Man: Racebending and the Colour-line in Superhero (Re)Casting, *Journal of Graphic Novels & Comics*, 6(3), pp. 269–283, doi: 10.1080/21504857.2014.994647.

Grady, C. (2020) *Why the Term "BIPOC" is So Complicated, Explained by Linguists*, [online] Available from: www.vox.com/2020/6/30/21300294/bipoc-what-does-it-mean-critical-race-linguistics-jonathan-rosa-deandra-miles-hercules (Accessed: 16 May 2023).

Griffin, M. and Van den Bulck, H. (2022) Of Superheroes and SJWs: Media and Fans Framing the Impact of Diversity in 2010s Comic Books, *Journal of Popular Culture*, 55(1), pp. 11–35, doi: 10.1111/jpcu.13100.

Guest, G., MacQueen, K.M. and Namey, E.E. (2012) *Applied Thematic Analysis*, Thousand Oaks, CA: SAGE Publications.

Guynes, S. and Lund, M. (2020) Not to Interpret, but to Abolish: Whiteness Studies and American Superhero Comics. In: Sean Guynes and Martin Lund (eds.), *Unstable Masks: Whiteness and American Superhero Comics*, Columbus: The Ohio State University Press, pp. 1–16.

Harmon, A. (2021) BIPOC or POC? Equity or Equality? The Debate Over Language on the Left, *The New York Times*, [online] Available from: www.nytimes.com/2021/11/01/us/terminology-language-politics.html (Accessed: 27 November 2022).

Hellekson, K. and Busse, K. (2014) *The Fan Fiction Studies Reader*, Iowa City: University of Iowa Press.

Hetrick, L. (2018) Reading Fan Art as Complex Texts, *Art Education (Reston)*, 71(3), pp. 56–62, doi: 10.1080/00043125.2018.1436357.

Kashtan, A. (2020) "Wow. Many Hero. Much Super. Such Girl": Kamala Khan and Female Comics Fandom. In: Jessica Baldanzi and Hussein Rashid (eds.), *Ms. Marvel's America: No Normal*, Jackson: University Press of Mississippi, pp. 191–206.

Kidman, S. (2019) *Comic Books Incorporated: How the Business of Comics Became the Business of Hollywood*, Oakland: University of California Press.

Martin, R.J. and Van Gunten, D.M. (2002) Reflected Identities: Applying Positionality and Multicultural Social Reconstructionism in Teacher Education, *Journal of Teacher Education*, 53(1), pp. 44–54. doi: 10.1177/0022487102053001005.

McMillan, G. (2013) *Marvel Unveils New Muslim 'Ms. Marvel.'*, [online] Available from: www.hollywoodreporter.com/movies/movie-news/marvel-unveils-new-muslim-ms-653870/ (Accessed: 4 May 2023).

Misawa, M. (2010) Queer Race Pedagogy for Educators in Higher Education: Dealing with Power Dynamics and Positionality of LGBTQ Students of Color, *International Journal of Critical Pedagogy*, 3(1), p. 26.

Pande, R. (2018) *Squee from the Margins: Fandom and Race*, Iowa City: University of Iowa Press.

Pande, R. (2020) How (not) to Talk About Race: A Critique of Methodological Practices in Fan Studies, *Transformative Works and Cultures*, 33, https://doi.org/10.3983/twc.2020.1737

Pustz, M.J. (2000) *Comic Book Culture: Fanboys and True Believers*, Jackson: University Press of Mississippi.

Scott, S. (2013) Fangirls in Refrigerators: The Politics of (In)Visibility in Comic Book Culture. *Transformative Works and Cultures*, 13, doi: 10.3983/twc.2013.0460.

Scott, S. (2015) The Hawkeye Initiative: Pinning Down Transformative Feminisms in Comic-Book Culture through Superhero Crossplay Fan Art. *Cinema Journal*, 55(1), pp. 150–160, doi: 10.1353/cj.2015.0075.

Scott, S. (2019) *Fake Geek Girls: Fandom, Gender, and the Convergence Culture Industry*, New York: New York University Press.

Shoemaker, P.J. and Vos, T. (2009) *Gatekeeping Theory*, Florence: Taylor & Francis Group.

Stanfill, M. and Lothian, A. (2021) An Archive of Whose Own? White Feminism and Racial Justice in Fan Fiction's Digital Infrastructure, *Transformative Works and Cultures*, 36, https://doi.org/10.3983/twc.2021.2119

STITCH. (2021) *Who Actually Gets to "Escape" Into Fandom?*, Teen Vogue, [online] Available from: www.teenvogue.com/story/who-actually-gets-to-escape-into-fandom-column-fan-service (Accessed: 27 March 2023).

STITCH. (2022) *Revisiting Escapism: Fandom is Far More Than Just a Head-Empty Hobby*, [online] Available from: https://stitchmediamix.com/2022/04/18/revisiting-escapism-fandom-is-far-more-than-just-a-head-empty-hobby/ (Accessed: 5 November 2022).

Wanzo, R. (2015) African American Acafandom and Other Strangers: New Genealogies of Fan Studies, Transformative Works and Cultures, 20, https://doi.org/10.3983/twc.2015.0699

Warner, K.J. (2017) (Black female) Fans Strike Back: The Emergence of the Iris West Defense Squad. In: Melissa A. Click and Suzanne Scott (eds.), *The Routledge Companion to Media Fandom*, New York: Routledge, pp. 253–261.

Woo, B. (2017) The Invisible Bag of Holding: Whiteness and Media Fandom. In: Melissa A. Click and Suzanne Scott (eds.), *The Routledge Companion to Media Fandom*, New York: Routledge, pp. 245–252.

Woo, B. (2021) ASKING FANS QUESTIONS: The Ethnographic Interview. In: Booth, P. and Williams, R. (eds.), *A Fan Studies Primer: Method, Research, Ethics*, Iowa City: University of Iowa Press, pp. 97–110.

Yodovich, N. (2022) *Women Negotiating Feminism and Science Fiction Fandom: The Case of the "Good" Fan*, Cham, Switzerland: Palgrave Macmillan.

25
FINDING THE NATIONAL IN TRANSNATIONAL

Mapping Identities and Power in K-pop Fandoms

Celeste Oon

Introduction

In 2022, the Korea Foundation reported that there were over 156 million Hallyu fans, or fans of the Korean Wave, in the world – a 17-fold increase in the past decade, with the Americas experiencing the largest growth of 102% (Molina and Young 2002). Among the myriad Korean cultural products being distributed, K-pop has exploded as a popular cultural export, with several K-pop groups such as BTS and BLACKPINK becoming household names. With the industry as massive as it is now, it is difficult to imagine a world wherein K-pop and its fans are not making headlines. K-pop fans are famously, and at times notoriously, known for their ability to mobilize for any cause, showcasing a strong unified presence across global and cultural lines. As consumers of K-pop, an industry that aims to appeal to the international market, such a transcendence of global boundaries is seemingly par for the course.

However, a closer look at the network of K-pop fandoms reveals significant fragmentation. As fans attempt to make sense of their relationships amongst themselves, so do they begin to stratify and categorize one another based on identities and practices. As Gray et al. (2007: 6) mention, fandom is "embedded in the existing economic, social, and cultural status quo," and fans are "agents of maintaining social and cultural systems of classification and thus existing hierarchies." Most strikingly, a polarity emerges among K-pop fans during conflict, one that produces two fundamental categories: domestic fans and international fans. Domestic fans are typically understood as ethnic Korean fans who live in South Korea, whereas international fans are non-Korean fans outside of South Korea.

But what would seem a simple classification breaks down once such groups interact, making it clear that each side is instead delineated by a particular set of attitudes, knowledges, and behaviors. Bitter fan wars erupt along these lines, as both sides vie for power to verify their authenticity as fans. The association of external characteristics with ethnic and national identities, then, results in racist, xenophobic, nationalist, and classist sentiment, which further drives both groups apart and increases their affinity to their own in-groups.

Thus, this chapter outlines conflicts that illuminate the subnetworks of transnational K-pop fans, identifies the criteria used to mold their fan identities, and analyzes how they negotiate power and relationships in their networks. I argue that despite K-pop fandoms' transnational nature, fans, in an attempt to regain a sense of identity and order within an amorphous network that has "erased" boundaries, make efforts to redefine and rechart hierarchies, therefore relocating themselves within a structured and regionally defined network.

K-pop Fandom: Towards a Transnational Community

I begin by surveying the landscape of literature that speaks to the transnational and transcultural aspects of K-pop and its fandoms. In terms of production, the global-local-global (G-L-G) strategy has long been utilized, wherein K-pop companies outsource production to international talent, refine the creative process in-house with Korean companies, and subsequently distribute finished products to worldwide audiences (Oh 2013). Within the past decade, K-pop's global sights have broadened as it has gained increasing popularity. The glocalization strategy, then – wherein the industry localizes its globalized output to accommodate local tastes where its products are distributed – has taken precedent as a way to cater to clearly diverse audiences (Oh and Jang 2020). In doing so, K-pop is able to overcome cultural, linguistic, and geographic barriers to appeal to the masses, while still deeply embodying its cultural origins through its presentation of East Asian, and specifically Korean, characteristics. This hybridization positions it as both culturally-specific and culturally "odorless," and therefore prime for mass consumption as it attracts local and global audiences (Chan 2002).

As a result, K-pop fandoms span a geographically wide demographic. These global consumers interact with one another daily on social platforms, bringing their vastly different cultural upbringings and lived experiences to the table when engaging in fan activities and extracting meaning from their fan objects. Given that they are able to come together in shared spaces despite their differences, one way of conceptualizing fandom is theorizing it as an imagined community. Benedict Anderson (2006) originally conceived of this idea in reference to nationalism. Anderson proposed that a nation is an imagined community because its members "will never know most of their fellow-members, meet them, or even hear of them, yet in the minds of each lives the image of their communion" (6). Thus, it is a fabricated shared sense of identity that binds members of the nation together and creates a sense of common ground, despite not knowing one another personally.

Anderson's theory can be expanded to include fandom and its online communities, as Morimoto and Chin (2007: 174) posit that online fandom spaces offer a "simultaneous, shared pop culture experience" that transcends geographic and cultural boundaries. In this way, fans from all walks of life may come together within a community centered around a common fan object and feel a sense of camaraderie, bonding with other fans who would otherwise be strangers across the globe. The imagined communities approach has often been used to analyze transcultural fan objects and fandoms in particular because of the ways in which both its objects and audiences surpass physical boundaries. The transculturality of these phenomena arises through the "affinities of affect between the fan, in [their] various contexts, and the border-crossing object" (Morimoto and Chin 2013: 93). This makes the framework apt for analyzing K-pop, as the use of the G-L-G model and the targeted generation of a global audience create a transcultural community held together by shared affect.

However, as one would imagine, a completely harmonious meeting ground between people of global cultures, who have distinct sets of beliefs and practices, is a far-fetched fantasy. The transnational and transcultural aspect of fandom is precisely what causes it to also function as a contact zone for potential conflict (Morimoto and Chin 2007: 182). Online fandoms can be thought of as "social spaces where cultures meet, clash, and grapple with each other, often in contexts of highly asymmetrical relations of power" (Pratt 1991: 34). Fandom, much like greater society, is structured by hierarchical notions, with power deriving from perceived authenticity and authority built from a variety of factors. This is precisely why it is important to analyze discourse – and particularly *discord* – between fans in their online spaces, given that they must continuously align and realign their fan- and personal-identities to make sense of their relationships with fan objects and fellow co-fans.

K-pop fandoms add an interesting perspective into grappling with power as they provide insight into the dynamics of non-Western fan culture, which has been underrepresented in fan studies. Non-Western media subjects have historically been othered in the literature, while power has often been explored with ideas of "whiteness" as the epicenter, and rarely through a transcultural lens. Hence, this chapter seeks to enrich the current literature by examining non-Western media. By using K-pop fandoms as a case study, we can further expand our understanding of power struggles in fandom that largely decenter white-, Western-, and anglo-centered hegemony.

No Money, No Opinion: Power Struggles and Underlying International Tensions

Power struggles within transnational fandoms are most salient when conflict arises and fans must choose sides. Though disputes do not always explicitly unfold along national lines, there are often unspoken understandings about who deserves to be heard that interplay with geographic realities. To illustrate an example of this phenomenon, I turn to the mobile app Lysn.

Lysn was a social media platform that launched in 2018[1] and was originally created by SM Entertainment, one of the largest media conglomerates in the K-pop industry and home to top artists like EXO, NCT, and Aespa. The platform housed the official fanclubs of SM's associated artists, allowing for fans to congregate and engage in discussion over their favorite celebrities. There were two membership types in each fanclub: 1) a basic membership, which was free and open to any user who joined; and 2) an ACE membership, open only to those who paid an annual membership fee. Each user's membership status was displayed in a tag next to their username, and in the case of ACE members, this tag also indicated how long they had been subscribed to the fanclub by adding numerals, such as "ACE II" for second-year members.

The visible subscription system created an explicit hierarchy within the fandoms on the platform. This hierarchy was exacerbated and enforced discursively by fans when disputes emerged on the Lysn bulletin boards (community forum) located within each artist's fanclub hub. It was not uncommon to witness heated debates, name-calling, and vitriol such as the following[2]:

- Prove your opinion by signing up ACE (*heart emoji*)
- No Ace No Voice

- NO MONEY NO VOICE
- The opinions of ACE fans should be respected. If you want to come up with an opinion, pay for it.
- Please turn basic into ace before you express your opinion (*heart emoji*)
- Sis you ain't even a ace member. You got no opinion
- Ace members have freedom of opinion

On the surface, this rhetoric seemed purely classist and based on a clear and direct connection between money and power. Fans with ACE memberships asserted that because they financially supported the celebrity, they had the right to express their opinions about them, while those that did not invest money had no such power. In this case, authority appeared to be predicated solely on the basis of financial capital and buying power. But in reality, rather than entirely hinging on possessing or spending money, fans' perceptions and subsequent policing of economic decisions were heavily linked to their geographic circumstances. This was a direct result of the nature of an ACE membership. ACE membership benefits were threefold: 1) every ACE member received an ACE kit each year, which was a box of official celebrity merchandise; 2) ACE members received exclusive access to view and comment on posts uploaded by celebrities that were not available to basic users; and 3) ACE members could attend ACE-only events – typically album signings or special exhibitions – and received priority access in purchasing tickets for general events, such as concerts.

While the perks were, in theory, distributed to all ACE members, in practice they did not impact everyone equally. Obtaining the ACE kit was required in the first year, but for fans living overseas, the shipping and customs fees almost always amounted to more than the membership itself, typically doubling or tripling the price. And while exclusive posts should have only been available to ACE members, the nature of the internet meant that almost instantly, every ACE post was re-uploaded to various social media platforms. This was despite fan protests that this information should not be available to everyone, and that sharing posts was against the terms of Lysn to begin with. Lastly, many fans living overseas did not have the financial means to travel abroad to take part in in-person experiences, which were mostly held in South Korea. Despite having exclusive access to special priorities and ACE events, they could not realistically attend them, even had they acquired a ticket. Consequently, these circumstances placed overseas fans at an automatic disadvantage and significantly reduced their benefits from an ACE membership.

For the aforementioned reasons, many overseas fans believed that purchasing an ACE membership was not worth the price, especially because they had to pay more money for less return. Due to the disproportionate costs and inequitable circumstances among fans around the world, there grew to be a prevailing sentiment that ACE memberships were mostly held by fans living in South Korea, while basic memberships were mostly held by fans outside of South Korea. One of the largest issues with this broad binary was how closely fans' locations patterned with national and cultural identities, creating a schism between domestic Korean fans as an ethnic and national group, and non-Korean fans outside of South Korea, broadly labeled as "international" or "foreign."

Though the latter two terms are characterized by a general "non-Koreanness," in practice the term "international" is typically coded to refer to fans outside of East Asia, and sometimes exclusively refers to Western or anglophone fans. Exact definitions vary across individual fans, though there is a general sense that the farther one travels away from South Korea, the more the label of "international" becomes pertinent. Non-Korean Asian countries, then, tend to occupy an in-between space, which will be discussed in a later section.

In short, debates over money, which are actually quite common across fandoms of all types, frequently take a different form in transnational fandoms. Despite presenting as a purely economic issue on Lysn, fans were able to identify underlying implications and eventually ascribed their differences to nationality, ethnicity, and culture. However, this false attribution led to broader, harmful generalizations of fans simply due to their belonging to these groups, and laid the groundwork for more explicit regional conflicts later.

No Korean, No Opinion: National Ties and Cultural Proximity

As time went on, interactions on Lysn grew increasingly turbulent. Global tensions became less concealed as fans shed euphemisms and indirect language, opting for overtly nationalist and xenophobic sentiment on both sides. As the bitterness heightened, one could imagine that the boundaries defining both groups grew much more pronounced, creating an even larger split between them and simultaneously strengthening in-group belonging. Such hostility on Lysn led to gatekeeping that emerged on explicitly cultural lines:

- NO KOREAN NO OPINION. Get outttt
- It's so lucky and so fortunate to be born in the same country and speak the same language (*dancing kaomoji*)
- NO KOREAN PASSPORT NO VOICE. Foreign cockroaches be quiet
- [celebrity name] is a korean artist and his principal audience are korean people, just a reminder (*smiling emoji*) so no korean no opinion

There are several key takeaways from the comments above. Firstly, debates over fan power pattern similarly across issues, with matching rhetoric used to assert prescribed power structures. Authority is always drawn from possession of a form of capital, whether it is economic capital, cultural capital, so on and so forth.

Secondly, from the data presented, it is actually unclear what factor(s) fans utilize to define "Koreanness." The comments refer to the knowledge of a language, the possession of a passport, a geographical place of residence, ethnic heritage, and so on, but do not specify to what extent one must possess these qualities. This raises questions as to whether, for example, a Korean-American or a foreign resident of South Korea would be accepted into this group. This ambiguity could potentially afford non-ethnic Korean fans power in particular circumstances, should they possess one of these traits.

Thirdly and most importantly, there are subtle cues in the language of these fans that indicate their identities are only valuable because they match the celebrities'. To quote the language above, these fans are "born in the *same* country and speak the *same* language [as celebrities]" (emphasis added), and as Korean people, they are the primary audience that Korean artists cater to. Thus, the power that being Korean holds, in this case, is not derived from an objective superiority as compared to other cultures and ethnicities, but rather, is through its *cultural proximity* to the celebrity. This is a significant distinction, because it displays power as a product relative to the source.

The concept of cultural proximity, distinguished from its use in discussing audience preferences for media built on shared cultural backgrounds (Moeran 2001: 58), can be defined as the degree of culture one shares with the source site – in this case, the celebrity and the industry. By living in the same time zone and country, speaking the same language, and sharing the same culture, fans within the domestic Korean subnetwork feel that they have greater command in matters pertaining to the Korean celebrity. These traits are viewed as lending authenticity and authority to this group of fans because only *they* have particular knowledges and shared experiences with the celebrities that may inform their logic in times of dissension.

Thus, geographic and cultural proximity are incredibly valuable as tools for power-wielding in transnational fandom. Interestingly, proximity generates a type of power that relies on intrinsic and often unchanging attributes of the self, such as ethnicity, yet its value fluctuates based on the object (celebrity) it is fixated around. Using identity as a weapon in battles over power, then, creates deeply personal attacks that fans interpret not as petty jabs, but as xenophobia, nationalism, racism, and classism.

The Foreign Cockroach: Western Hegemony Strikes Again

While the discourse shown in previous sections seems to denote blatant bias and discrimination, it is false to suggest that this rhetoric derives solely from an innate sense of superiority. In reality, some of this sentiment represents a resistance to what Korean fans interpret as imposed *Western* superiority. Over the years, domestic Korean fans have cited many gripes against international fans that are based on larger cultural dynamics. This is evidenced by the characteristics attributed to the term "foreign cockroach," a popular derogatory slang term in online K-pop fan communities in South Korea. The following description, translated from Korean, is sourced from the Korean language wiki Namuwiki, and it provides examples for the conditions under which Korean fans typically use the term:

Foreign Cockroach

- 'eng sub plz' coercion – Go to the Twitter or Instagram of an idol you support and suddenly demand 'Please write in English so that we can understand.'
- [Livestream] terror – … a case where comments are spammed on [livestream] broadcasts saying you don't understand what they're talking about and 'eng plz.'
- Pride in being more 'objective' or 'reasonable' than domestic fans – A tendency to be quietly chauvinist/supremacist and discriminatory towards Asians… The reality is that you only see English comments… unconditionally criticizing Korea.
- Unconditional bias towards [celebrities] and shielding their own celebrities' incidents/accidents – They come in and set the premise that their [celebrity] is absolutely correct and should be treated as royalty, and with no care to understand the domestic situation, defend the incidents/accidents that [celebrities] cause while criticizing all (Korean) internet citizens who criticize [the celebrity]… Due to a lack of understanding about Korean society and history, and accurate (Korean) public opinion and legal processes, there is the behavior of criticizing Korean people sharply based only on superficial aspects.

As indicated by these descriptions, the term "foreign cockroach," as claimed by Korean internet users, typically applies to English-speaking international fans who are ignorant, offensive, and act inappropriately. This may be contained within fan culture itself, but more often than not speaks to larger sociocultural dynamics. The first half of the listed characteristics pertains to language – domestic fans frequently voice their outrage over foreign fans coming into Korean spaces and telling Korean people to speak English. The latter half alludes to the unwanted imposition of fans who involve themselves in global affairs, commonly taking the form of non-Korean people speaking on Korean matters without proper knowledge. This issue frequently arises when Korean celebrities become embroiled in scandals or issues that generate criticism from Korean citizens. Domestic Korean fans do not feel that non-Koreans have the right to comment on incidents in Korean society, nor do they have the right to criticize Korean people for their reactions – in fact, this is interpreted as discriminatory, ignorant, and racist. Moreover, cultural differences between South Korea and other countries frequently lead to clashes as cultural and societal norms may be incompatible.

When one considers the history between South Korea and the West, and particularly with the United States, the sentiment expressed by domestic fans aligns with longtime societal frustrations. From the institution of English as a required language in higher education and workplaces, to the heavy presence of the US military in the country, to the involvement of the US government in Korean affairs which has heightened geopolitical tensions in East Asia – these factors and many more have contributed to grievances over Western, and specifically American (cultural) imperialism. Fandom as a subculture in South Korea is simply a microcosm that reflects these widespread sentiments. Returning to Anderson's (2006) concept of imagined communities, one can see that the attitudes and beliefs held by citizens of globalized nations are carried over to subcultural communities as individuals attempt to relocate and enforce their own in-groups.

Perhaps most striking about this phenomenon is that it also illustrates the tension between two competing forces: that power in K-pop fandom spaces is based on proximity to Korean culture, and yet, Western and anglophonic hegemony remain as invading influences. Though K-pop fandom certainly provides a unique window into what power may look like outside of a structure that centers whiteness, Western hegemony inevitably leaks in as an opposing framework. This issue is only exacerbated as K-pop expands globally, integrating more international fans into fandom networks and creating increased opportunities for cultural clashes.

The Third Space: Shifting and Undefined Powers

Lastly, it is important to consider the position of individuals who fall outside of the system discussed in this chapter. With such a strong focus on a rigid binary – with domestic Korean fans on one end and non-Korean international fans on the other – there seems to be little consideration of fans who may not fit into either category, yet occupy a significant presence. As mentioned earlier, consider other populations such as non-Korean fans who live in South Korea, who likely have knowledge of Korean society and culture; diasporic Koreans who may or may not be knowledgeable about their home cultures; or non-Korean Asians who have shared histories and culture with South Korea. Individuals in these groups share traits with both the domestic and international subnetworks of fans, but often do not feel completely accepted into either.

Such fans seem to occupy an in-between space, a shifting and amorphous landscape wherein power is equally as fluid. In considering how to conceptualize such fans, the theories of hybridity and the third space may be fruitful (Bhabha 1994). These concepts have long been used to convey experiences faced by immigrants, diasporic communities, and globalized citizens. Such individuals, through intercontinental movement and intercultural contact, find themselves struggling to "make sense of [their] identity in relation to prevailing notions of self and cultural practices" (Gutiérrez et al. 1999: 288), because such standards have been built on discrete cultural ideals. Instead, the third space they inhabit is wholly their own, one that is formed at the cusp of other cultures. In the case of K-pop fans, struggles to articulate what is "Korean" enough to merit a voice parallel struggles among populations whose identities are in constant flux, and are marked by a unique hybridization of many groups.

Nevertheless, rather than necessarily being a hindrance to their belonging as fans, I posit that the third space may afford individuals a unique flexibility in power. Such fans may move smoothly between subnetworks while reaping the benefits of both sides. For example, a non-Korean fan who can speak Korean may retain their identity as an international fan, which affords them intimacy with other international fans and strengthens their in-group, while simultaneously gaining access to exclusive information by maneuvering through online Korean spaces. Such fans may also be shielded from criticism by either side due to their ability to navigate the norms of both groups.

Although a robust discussion of these "hybridized" fans is outside the scope of this chapter, their existence spurs questions with regard to what extent power structures can be manufactured among subnetworks that have no set boundaries, despite fans' attempts at delineating them. As will be proven time and time again, those in the margins will always resist and find alternative ways of acquiring power, rendering attempts at gatekeeping and strict hierarchies rather ineffective.

Conclusion

K-pop shows no signs of slowing down, and as the industry continues on its mission of global expansion, disputes will become increasingly common. Particularly within the past several years, there has been a growing concern among domestic fans that they are being left behind in favor of Western audiences (Yoon 2023), which may create ripples in the domestic market that will be felt overseas. Regardless, one thing is for certain: with more opportunities for fans to clash within the contact zones of online communities, self-made hierarchies built from forms of capital will become more robust. And while struggles for power are not unique to transnational and transcultural fandoms by any means, such environments present a complex entanglement of sociocultural and geopolitical factors at a heightened level.

My aim in highlighting K-pop fandoms is to partially provide a counter case to narratives that portray transnational communities as solely unified fronts that do not contend with the realities of conflicting cultures and beliefs. K-pop fandoms are additionally a prime illustration of the intricate dynamics of fandoms that center non-white and non-Western objects, yet which still grapple with Western hegemony within alternative systems of power. Ultimately, K-pop fans, in order to make sense of their identities in relation to global fans with whom they share communities, redraw lines along national, ethnic, and cultural boundaries, thereby relocating the national in transnational.

Notes

1. Although the Lysn app still exists, the fanclubs it housed, as well as the social functions described in this chapter, have been moved onto another platform and are no longer available on the app. ACE memberships were also dissolved in favor of a new fanclub service.
2. All comments were sourced from the Lysn app across its community forums from February to March of 2021, though the comments themselves date back to as early as January 2020. Comments were not attributed to specific users in order to protect the privacy of fans.

References

Anderson, B. (2006) *Imagined Communities: Reflections on the Origin and Spread of Nationalism*, Revised ed, New York: Verso.

Bhabha, H. (1994) *The Location of Culture*, London: Routledge.

Chan, J. M. (2002) "Disneyfying and Globalizing the Chinese Legend Mulan: A Study of Transculturation," in J. M. Chan and B. T. McIntyre (eds.) *In Search of Boundaries: Communication, Nation-States and Cultural Identities*, New York: Ablex Publishing, pp. 225–248.

Gray, J. et al. (2007) "Introduction: Why Study Fans?" in J. Gray et al. (eds.) *Fandom: Identities and Communities in a Mediated World*, New York: New York University Press, pp. 1–16.

Gutiérrez, K. D., Baquedano-López, P. and Tejeda, C. (1999) "Rethinking Diversity: Hybridity and Hybrid Language Practices in the Third Space." *Mind, Culture, and Activity*, 6(4), pp. 286–303.

Moeran, B. (2001) "Introduction: The Field of Asian Media Productions," in B. Moeran (ed.) *Asian Media Productions*, 1st ed, Honolulu: University of Hawai'i Press, pp. 1–35.

Molina, E. and Young, Y. H. (2002) "No. of Global Hallyu Fans Sees 17-fold Jump to 150M in 10 Years." *Korea.net*, [online] 4 March. Available at: www.korea.net/NewsFocus/Culture/view?articleId=211458 [Accessed 24 July 2023].

Morimoto, L. H. and Chin, B. (2007) "Reimagining the Imagined Community: Online Media Fandoms in the Age of Global Convergence," in J. Gray et al. (eds.) *Fandom: Identities and Communities in a Mediated World*, 2nd ed, New York: New York University Press, pp. 174–188.

Morimoto, L. H. and Chin, B. (2013) "Towards a Theory of Transcultural Fandom." *Participations: Journal of Audience & Reception Studies*, 10(1), pp. 92–108.

Namuwiki. "Oekwi 외퀴 (Foreign Cockroach)." *Namuwiki*, [online] N.d. Available at: https://namu.wiki/w/외퀴 [Accessed 28 July 2023].

Oh, I. (2013) "The Globalization of K-pop: Korea's Place in the Global Music Industry." *Korea Observer*, 44(3), pp. 389–409.

Oh, I. and Jang, W. (2020) "From Globalization to Glocalization: Configuring Korean Pop Culture to Meet Glocal Demands." *Culture and Empathy*, 3(1–2), pp. 23–42.

Pratt, M. L. (1991) "Arts of the Contact Zone." Profession, pp. 33–40.

Yoon, J. (2023) "In K-Pop's Quest for Global Growth, Korean Fans Feel Cast Aside." *NYTimes.com*, [online] 5 April. Available at: www.nytimes.com/2023/04/04/business/sm-entertainment-kakao-hybe-kpop.html [Accessed 1 August 2023].

26
CHARTING LATINX FANDOM

Jillian M. Báez

This essay provides a survey of the burgeoning work on Latinx[1] fandom. Although not always labeled as fan studies, there is a growing literature on how Latinx fans and audiences interact in pleasurable ways with various forms of media and popular culture. Contemporary mainstream and Spanish-language media industries invest billions of dollars to woo the Latinx market, and yet, we still know little about Latinx audiences (Dávila 2012; Báez 2018). Latina/os are the largest minority population in the US and are a growing demographic, especially amongst youth (U.S. Census Bureau 2023). More specifically, apart from the work of Eion Devereux and Melissa Mora Hidalgo (2015), myself (Báez 2015), and Michelle Rivera (2011), Latina/o studies is seldom in direct dialogue with the fan studies literature. In this essay, I call for more studies of Latinx fan communities not only to remedy erasure in the field, but also because they can offer us theoretical frameworks to more deeply understand how fans might experience transnationalism, hybridity, and intersectionality in their consumption and creative practices.

There is little work on Latinx fans partly because most of the burgeoning research on Latinx reception suggests that audiences have an ambivalent relationship to media. Similar to African Americans (see Wanzo 2015), Latinx audiences often experience frustration when consuming media (Báez 2018; Valdivia 2000). Latinx audiences' frustration is experienced in consumption of both mainstream and Spanish-language media because representations in both these media markets often reproduce longstanding stereotypes that homogenize Latinidad.[2] Historically, fan studies foregrounds audiences who not only have a sustained relationship to a media form, but also experience immense pleasure in consuming it and engaging in what Henry Jenkins (2006) calls a participatory culture. More recently, scholars are paying more attention to "anti-fandom" (cf. Gray 2003; Jones 2015; Rivera 2011). According to Jonathan Gray (2003), anti-fans are audiences "who strongly dislike a given text" and who are "variously bothered, insulted or otherwise assaulted by its presence" (70). Rebecca Wanzo (2015) argues that African Americans are largely ignored in fan studies because of their relationship to mainstream media images, that is, representations that often flatten and marginalize Black experiences. As a result, most reception studies of African Americans tend to focus on audiences' frustration, disgust, and resentment regarding Black media representation. Nonetheless, Wanzo asserts that an overt inclusion of African Americans in fan studies necessitates new methodologies (i.e., archival research of newspapers that document African Americans' fraught media relationship) and complicates how we think of fandom in only pleasurable terms. Racialized minorities might be critical fans, anti-fans, or in many cases, enjoy problematic media through what Frances Aparicio (1998) calls "re-writing pleasure." In her study of salsa music, Aparicio finds that women salsa listeners engage in "re-writing pleasure" through alternative or oppositional readings of patriarchal lyrics by changing the words when singing along and reappropriating the sexualized images on album jackets as ones of agency, not domination. As such, if one is to study racialized minorities or other subjugated groups through a fan studies approach, one must be mindful of the troubled relationship these audiences have to media and the practices in which fans engage to make media more palatable. Moreover, Latinx audiences share an ambivalent relationship not only to mainstream media, but also to Spanish-language and ethnic media.[3]

This essay serves as a cursory introduction to the scholarship on Latinx fandom. Although Latinx audiences certainly have been frustrated by media representations, there are numerous forms of media that Latina/o audiences consume regularly and find immensely pleasurable. Latinx fandom thrives in both expected (i.e., fans of the late Tejana singer Selena and *telenovelas* in general) and unexpected (i.e., Mexican American devotees of rock singer Morrissey) sites. While some burgeoning research on Latinx fans of comics, radio, film, video games, and sports exists (i.e., Aldama 2009, 2013; Bodey et al. 2009; Casillas 2014; Jensen 2012; Seiter 2007; Thornton 2010), this essay focuses on Latinx music fandom and *telenovela* viewership since the majority of the scholarship in this area is centered on music and television. In exploring musical and televisual Latinx fandom, I demonstrate new ways of thinking about fan creativity and agency that account for multiple generations and multiple linguistic media outlets. In particular, Latinx fandom illuminates how cultural hybridity and transnationalism shape media consumption and participatory cultures.

Latinx Music Fandom

Music created, performed, and consumed by Latinx communities is central to the Latinx experience in the US (Kotarba, Fackler, and Nowotny 2009). This heavy engagement with music is facilitated by Latinx audiences' longstanding use of radio since the medium's inception (Castillas 2014). Latinx communities enjoy both traditional musical forms from Latin America (i.e., regional Mexican, salsa, merengue, and bachata) and US and British genres like pop, rock, punk, R&B, and hip hop. In particular, second and third generation Latinx musicians and fans take pleasure in producing and consuming hybrid forms of music that meld Latin American and US styles as exemplified in Tejano music and Nuyorican salsa of the 1960s and 1970s (Flores 2016; Negrón 2015; Pancini Hernandez 2010; Valdez and Halley 1991). Dating back to the nineteenth century, Tejano music melds Texan and Mexican music together with lyrics in Spanish. Nuyorican salsa was created and performed by Puerto Ricans in New York and incorporated Cuban son rhythms, Puerto Rican folkloric music, jazz, and disco among other musical styles.

Latinx communities engage in music to connect to their home country (in the case of immigrants) or ethnic heritage (in the case of later generations). Latina/os also produce, listen to, and dance to US musical styles. Latinx fans' heterogeneous musical tastes are indicative of the communities' cultural hybridity. Angharad Valdivia (2003b) reminds us of the "radical hybridity" of Latina/os who encompass a myriad of nationalities, racial mixtures, religions, and languages and dialects. Latinx music and its attendant fan practices reflect this heterogeneity. As Deborah Pancini Hernandez (2010) states,

> Far from being defined by or limited to musical aesthetics associated with particular national groups, Latino music making has always entailed crossing musical, geographic, racial, and ethnic boundaries. The result has been a dazzling variety of musical practices – many of them not usually identified as Latino – each with its own intricate genealogy and each giving voice to the quintessentially blended and layered qualities that characterize the experience of being Latino in the United States (2).

In other words, Latinx musical production and consumption is emblematic of Latina/os' experiences of cultural hybridity in the US, particularly in navigating multiple cultures and languages. As Stephen Joseph Loza (1993) and Ruth Glasser (1995) document, Latinx musicians were expected to know Latin American traditional music styles in addition to popular US genres in order to both perform and record their music.

There is a robust scholarship exploring Latinx music, particularly the genres of Mexican regional (Paredez 2009; Vargas 2014), salsa (Aparicio 1998; Flores 2016, Negron 2015; Valdivia 2003a), reggaetón (Báez 2006; M. Rivera 2011; P. Rivera 2015), pop (Cepeda 2010), and hip hop (Flores 2000) and even some work on less conventional genres such as punk (see Habell-Pallan 2005). In addition to the scholarship, overviews of Latin music are also available for general readers. These include John Storm Robert's book *The Latin Tinge* (1999) and Ed Morales' *The Latin Beat* (2003). PBS's series *Latin Music USA* (2009) also explores the history of Latin music in the US for a general audience. Studies of Latin music tend to focus on the content of music (i.e., tone, arrangement, and lyrics) alongside the musicians who produce and perform music. Most treatments of Latin music mention fans, but they are seldom the focus with a few notable exceptions.

One area of Latina/o music fandom that is explored extensively in the literature is rock and roll music. Chicana/os in particular have heavy engagement with rock and roll – both as musicians and fans (Pancini Hernandez 2010). For example, Eion Devereux and Melissa Hidalgo (2015) document Chicana/o fans of the rock star Morrissey. In their analysis of "Moz Angeles" – an imagined space where Los Angeles Chicana/o fans engage with Morrissey – Devereux and Hidalgo find that these fans express their cultural hybridity through their participatory culture. Chicana/o fandom surrounding Morrissey might not seem like an obvious connection until one takes note of Morrissey calling attention to material realities they face. Put another way, Chicana/o Morrissey fans identify with the ethnic and class critiques within the rock star's lyrics and interviews. Chicana/o Morrissey fans reincorporate lyrics and images of the musician and his music into Chicana/o iconography. For example, images of the Virgin of Guadalupe, and typesetting used in Chicana/o cultural production and the borderlands, are invoked in fan merchandise distributed and worn by Chicana/o Morrissey fans.

Keta "Marie" Miranda (2005) also explores Chicana/o rock fandom. Studying teenage girl fans of boy bands of the 1960s in East Los Angeles, Miranda contests myths of fan girls as hysterical and boy crazy and recasts female fans as central to the boy bands' creative output. She argues that these boy bands' music and performances meld mainstream and

Chicana/o alternative sounds that reflect the cultural hybridity of their audiences. Building on Homi Bhabba's and Emma Perez's conceptualizations of "third space," Miranda demonstrates that the adolescent girls' dancing and mod style of dress reflected their aspiring class status (moving from working class status to a middle class lifestyle), while not easily adhering to cultural or ethnic assimilation. In this way, Miranda debunks myths of teenage girls as fanatics and instead positions them as creative negotiators of shifting ethnic and class identities.

Regional Mexican music is another area scholars have explored in terms of fandom. Regional Mexican music, which includes genres like banda, ranchera, mariachi, conjunto, and norteño, continues to be the highest grossing Latin musical format. One important early study of fans of Regional Mexican music is Avelardo Valdez and Jeffrey Halley's (1991) comparison of working class and middle class Mexican American fans. Valdez and Halley document differences in the genres and themes of lyrics that appeal to these two class segments of Mexican American fandom. They also illustrate how entry into the middle class cannot be simply dismissed as ethnic assimilation. Middle class Mexican Americans continue to listen and dance to Mexican musical genres despite their upward bound class mobility.

In addition to class distinctions amongst fans of Regional Mexican music, gender is also a significant axe of difference. In the germinal book *Selenidad: Selena, Latinos, and the Performance of Memory* (2009), Deborah Paredez explores the fandom surrounding the late Tejana singer Selena who was killed at the age of 23 by her fan club manager in 1995. After her death, there was a huge outpouring of Mexican American and other Latina/o fans who mourned her loss. Paredez finds that Selena's fandom was an expression of both grief and hope – grief for the slain star and also hope for more recognition and inclusion of Latina/os in mainstream US society. Chicana filmmaker Lourdes Portillo also explores Selena's fans in her documentary *Corpus: A Home Movie* (1999). The film spans across various sectors of Selena fandom including the young girls, mothers, grandmothers, and drag queens that adore the young singer. Portillo also interviews academics about Selena's iconicity and questions fans' adoration of Selena because the star was ensconced in largely normative notions of Latina femininity and womanhood (i.e., provocative dress, heterosexual marriage at a young age, under the watchful eye of her father as her manager, etc.).

Keeping in mind the memory of Selena and her devoted fans, Deborah Vargas' (2014) more recent essay on another deceased Mexican American singer, Jenni Rivera, presents an alternate form of fandom. Rivera died in a plane crash in 2012 at the age of 43. Unlike Selena whose lyrics and performances largely fit within heteronormative, dominant notions of Latina womanhood, Rivera challenged conventional norms of femininity. Rivera was very outspoken in interviews, especially about her experiences of domestic violence. In addition, Rivera's lyrics discussed women's empowerment and her early involvement in a drug cartel. In this way, Rivera was not steeped in the same politics of respectability that framed Selena. Instead, Vargas demonstrates how fans embraced Rivera because of her transparency and expansion of what it means to be a Mexican American woman, particularly in the realm of Regional Mexican music which continues to be a male dominant space.

Some of the more revealing studies of Latinx fandoms (even if not located within fan scholarship) are studies of dance amongst music audiences. Going beyond listening, this scholarship explores how fans deeply engage with music through the body. Dance allows for its own creative expression – it is a dialogue between the music, performer, and other fans. Like fanfiction and other forms of fan production, dance is a fan text that constitutes a participatory culture. A handful of scholars have studied salsa dancing amongst both Latinx and non-Latinx communities. Since at least the 1990s, salsa has been exported globally and is one of the most popular Latin music genres worldwide. One noteworthy study of Latinx salsa dancers is Patria Roman-Velazquez's book *The Making of Latin London: Salsa Music, Place, Identity* (1999) which explores how Latinx communities are formed vis-à-vis salsa dancing in London. Building on Roman-Velazquez's work, Angharad Valdivia (2003a) explores salsa dancing in a small Midwestern community she calls Corn Soya. Within this community, salsa is way of engaging in and embodying Latinidad within a space that is not overtly marked as Latinx.

Studies of salsa dancing within Latinx communities not only show how fan communities are created through dance, but also are sites for intercultural and gender tensions. For example, in the ethnography *Salsa Crossings: Dancing Latinidad in Los Angeles* (2013), Cindy Garcia documents the ways that ethnicity and class are inscribed on the dance floor by non-Latinx dancers (often middle and upper middle class) and working class Latinx dancers. Garcia argues that "choreographies of belonging" are constantly performed on the dance floors of salsa clubs in Los Angeles that re-inscribe social hierarchies. In other words, salsa fans on the dance floor enact and challenge ethnic and class tensions that also exist outside the terrain of the dance club. Similarly, in her study of salsa dancing in Chicago, Frances Aparicio (2010) finds similar intercultural tensions alongside gender issues. Patriarchal heterosexual pairings structure salsa dancing leaving women to negotiate, and sometimes challenge, these structures while enjoying the music. In her study of Nuyorican salsa in the 1960s and 1970s, Marisol Negrón (2015) similarly notes that "women [salsa dancers] participated in the social hierarchies of the dance floor while centering their own desires… [women dancers] developed their reputations as skilled dancers, evaluating men's dexterity and stylistic choices, and determined where other dancers fit into New York's cultural matrix of salser@s" (295). Thus, ethnicity, class, and gender are mapped onto salsa dance floors, and become contested spaces that expose fissures within fan communities.

It bears noting that anti-fans are also important to understanding Latinx fandom. Michelle Rivera (2011) explores how Latin Americans reject and distance themselves from the genre reggaetón because it has been marketed within the discourse of "Latin urban authenticity." Reggaetón is a hybrid musical form that melds Jamaican reggae, US and Puerto Rican rap, and various Spanish Caribbean beats. The genre is largely associated with urban youth, particularly from Puerto Rico and the US. In the mid-2000s, reggaetón crossed over into the mainstream with the wide appeal of artists like Daddy Yankee. While reggaetón's fandom spans across Latinx, Latin American, US and European markets, it has also generated a large backlash. Rivera (*ibid.*) argues that anti-fans of reggaetón are often Latin Americans and Latina/os who want to distance themselves from music that represents poor, working class, and disenfranchised communities. In addition, anti-fans deem reggaetón as culturally inferior – a form of low culture – only for audiences that have little taste. As such, anti-fans demonstrate the tensions with Latinx fandoms (and non-fandoms) and the ways that low and high culture continue to shape the contours of fan communities.

Latinx music has longstanding fan communities that are heterogeneous and transnational. Studying Latinx music fandoms offers an entryway into exploring how fans use media texts to express their cultural hybridity, build community, and also distinguish themselves from others (even within the Latinx community). At present most of the research on Latinx music does privilege the study of musical form, content, and performance at the expense of fandom. The few studies that do center on fandom teach us much about the significance of music for people's sense of community and belonging. As such, we need more studies of Latinx music fandom because fans are central to the proliferation and distribution of music in everyday life. In addition, fans cultivate communities not only of consumption, but also production (i.e., dance) through music.

Latinx *Telenovela* Fans

In addition to music, Latinx audiences have heavily consumed broadcast media since the inception of radio and television technology (Casillas 2014). Spanish-language television broadcast stations, namely Univision and Telemundo, have been available in the US since the 1950s. *Telenovelas* are one of the most popular television formats in Spanish-language television across the hemisphere. *Telenovelas* are often likened to US soap operas, but the former are aired on primetime television and have a finite running time (usually a few months long). In addition, while soap operas are generally considered a woman's format initially created for housewives, *telenovelas* are consumed intergenerationally in families. While the melodrama is central in the genre of *telenovelas* and is also feminized in Latin American and Latinx culture, men and boys commonly watch alongside women family members. As such, traditionally *telenovelas* are watched as a group, in contrast to individual consumption of television. Certainly, with the advent of digital streaming technologies that allow for viewers to watch episodes at any space or time, *telenovela* viewing is increasingly becoming both a solitary and group activity (Avilés-Santiago and Báez, forthcoming 2025).

There is growing research on *telenovela* viewing among Latina/o audiences. Diana Rios (2003) and Vivian Barrera and Denise Bielby (2001) find that Latinx families watch *telenovelas* for a number of reasons that include Spanish-language maintenance, bonding across generations, and keeping in touch with Latin American culture. In her study of Latina/o television viewing in San Diego, California, Kristin Moran (2011) finds that both parents and children watch *telenovelas* together. The family viewing of *telenovelas* is especially poignant because most of the children tend to be English-dominant and otherwise prefer English-language media. As such, *telenovelas* provide a space for bonding across generations.

Telenovela viewing is a family affair not only for nuclear and extended Latinx families in the US, but also across national borders. Both Vicki Mayer (2003) and Lucila Vargas (2009) find that Latinx youth watch *telenovelas* partly in order to stay in touch with family members living in Latin America. Both Mayer's and Vargas' ethnographies indicate that youth talk on the phone with family members in Mexico and other parts of Latin America about the latest and most popular *telenovelas*. Because *telenovelas* broadcast in the US, they tend to be released at a much later date than in Latin America. Therefore, US Latinx audiences sometimes learn about future episodes from family members abroad. In this way, *telenovela* fandom facilitates transnational connections between families in the US and Latin America.

It should be noted that *telenovelas* yield fan communities beyond Latinx and Latin American audiences (Castañeda and Rios 2011). Latin American and Miami produced *telenovelas* are exported throughout the globe through dubbing and subtitling. One noteworthy example is *Los Ricos Tambien Lloren*, a *telenovela* that aired in the 1970s in Mexico and became very popular in Russia in the 1990s (Baldwin 1995). Adaptations of *telenovelas* are also quite common today. The Colombian series *Yo soy Betty la fea* (1999–2001) was adapted for numerous countries including Mexico, China, Russia, and the US (Donoghue 2011). Yeidy Rivero's (2003) study of Latinas' readings of the original *Yo soy Betty la fea* indicates that the series served as a springboard for fans to discuss expected gender norms with Latin American and US cultures, especially in terms of beauty ideals for women. My research (Báez 2018) on Latina audiences of the US adaptation *Ugly Betty* (2006–10) are consistent with Rivero's findings on the Colombian version of the series in terms of gender. However, I also found that the US version generated additional questions of Latina belonging in the US in terms of race and class. It bears further inspection how non-Latin American and non-Latinx audiences make sense of the numerous *Betty* iterations.

Since the late-2000s, US television networks have had several moderately successful adaptations of *telenovelas*, such as Lifetime's *Devious Maids* (2013–16), Free Form's *Chasing Life* (2014–15), and the CW's *Jane the Virgin* (2014–). My study (Báez 2015) on fans of *Devious Maids* reveals that there are different fan communities for the series. Some fans include non-Latinx audiences in the US who watch because they are fans of the creator's (Marc Cherry) earlier hit series *Desperate Housewives* (2004–12). These fans tend to enjoy the show based on its format alongside its invocation of familiar archetypes of Latinas. There are also Latinx fans, many who are women, who find pleasure in the agency of the working class, Latina maids on screen who talk back to their Anglo, wealthy employers. At the same time, the show generated a considerable amount of Latinx anti-fans who were frustrated with the show's depiction of Latinas as hypersexual maids. What this research suggests is that Latinx televisual fans are reading these adaptations very differently than mainstream audiences.

In sum, *telenovelas* generate fan communities that cut across gender, generation, language, and nation. For Latinx fans, these series enable them to maintain their Spanish-language skills and provide visual and audio reminders of their (or their parents' or grandparents') home country. *Telenovela* viewership is not only intergenerational within the household, but also connects US viewers to family and friends living in Latin America. *Telenovela* fandom teaches us important lessons about the potential intercultural and transnational connects within fan communities. In a media landscape that is increasingly globalized, we have much to learn from Latinx *telenovela* fans.

Conclusion

A review of the scholarship on Latinx music and *telenovela* fans demonstrates that there is much to glean from research on Latinx fandom, especially in terms of hybridity, the borderlands, and transnationalism. The complexities within Latinidad are evident in the fandom formations and practices of Latinx communities. Latina/os can be fans of English-language, mainstream media, such as the Morrissey fans discussed earlier in the essay, who hybridize Morrissey iconography in fan texts that link the British star to Latina/o images and sounds. Latinx fandom also occurs in transnational Spanish-language media that ties US fans to friends and family in Latin America. These types of fan practices can also inform studies of non-Latinx fans given that migration from the Global South is intensifying at the same time that media production and content is increasingly globalized. Viewing fandom through a Latinx lens also pushes fan studies scholars to heed to Sam Ford's (2014) call to diversify the kinds of texts/media outlets/genres, and perhaps even the types of active audience engagement, usually explored in fan studies. Given that Latinx fandoms are often intersectional and cut across race, ethnicity, generation, class, gender, nation, and sometimes sexuality, studies of these fans offer us a template to understand the nuances within contemporary fandoms.

While this essay is primarily concerned with charting Latina/o fandom as a necessary step to understanding the scope of this emerging area, it also urges Latina/o media scholars to branch outside of music fandom into other forms of media and popular culture, particularly video games and social media. Studies of televisual fandom should include streaming content. Gaming and social media are both highly interactive and studies of Latinx fans seem fitting given that Latina/os are the majority of digital content makers (Negrón-Muntaner et al. 2014). Fan studies scholars would find it helpful to review the Latina/o Studies scholarship on fandom. Likewise, Latina/o Studies scholars could engage more directly with the fan studies scholarship. Overall, a Latinx perspective on fandom offers us a more transnational, culturally hybrid, and intersectional register that can benefit the overall field of fan studies.

Notes

1. Latinx refers to communities of Latin American descent living in the US. Latinx is preferred over the more widely used term Latina/o because it is gender neutral and inclusive of non-conforming gender and transgender individuals. At times, however, I will use the term Latina/o in order to not be redundant in my writing. It should be noted that the terms Latinx and Latina/o are rooted in experiences in the US and are not synonymous with Latin American.
2. Latinidad refers to "the culture produced by Latina/os and the practices of being Latina/o" (Valdivia 2003b: 115 fn. 1) that places people of Latin American descent in the US into one pan-ethnic category. Latinidad is a term that is debated and contested amongst Latina/o studies scholars because it can be both transgressive and problematic. On one hand, Latinidad can be a unifying term that signals social and political solidarities across Latinx groups. At the same time, when applied in broad strokes Latinidad can be homogenizing and erase differences (i.e., of nationality, language, gender, sexuality, and religion) between Latinx groups. See Aparicio 2003, Báez 2007, and Flores 2000 for more extensive discussions of the possibilities and dangers of Latinidad.
3. Latinx audiences' complex relationships to Spanish-language media are discussed in Dolores Ines Casilla's (2014) study of radio and Vivana Rojas' (2004) work on television audiences. Ethnic media, which include mostly English-language outlets catered to second and third generation Latinx audiences, are also fraught with problematic images. See my chapter on audiences' responses to the longstanding magazine *Latina* (Baez 2018). It should be noted that many Latinx audiences, particularly youth, also consume black media like BET (see Vargas 2009).

References

Aldama, F. (ed.) (2013). *Latinos and Narrative Media: Participation and Portrayal*. New York: Palgrave.

Aldama, F. (2009). *Your Brain on Latino Comics: From Gus Arriola to Los Bros Hernandez*. Austin: University of Texas Press.

Aparicio, F. (2010). "From Boricua Dancers to Salsa Soldiers: The Cultural Politics of Globalized Salsa Dancing in Chicago." In *Inside the Latin@ Experience: A Latin@ Studies Reader*, edited by Norma E. Cantú and María E. Fránquiz. New York: Palgrave.

Aparicio, F. (1998). *Listening to Salsa: Gender, Latin Popular Music, and Puerto Rican Cultures*. Hanover, NH: University Press of New England.

Avilés-Santiago, M. and Báez, J. (2025, forthcoming). *Spanish-Language Television: Language, Race, and Industrial Shifts*. Austin, TX: University of Texas Press.

Báez, J. (2018). *In Search of Belonging: Latinas, Media, and Citizenship*. Urbana, IL: University of Illinois Press.

Baez, J. (2015). "Television for All Women?: Watching Lifetime's *Devious Maids*." In *Cupcakes, Pinterest, and Ladyporn: Feminized Popular Culture in the Early 21st Century*, edited by Elana Levine. Urbana, IL: University of Illinois Press, pp. 51–70.

Baez, J. (2007). "Towards a Latinidad feminista: The Multiplicities of Latinidad and Feminism in Contemporary Cinema." *Journal of Popular Communication* 5.2, pp. 109–128.

Baez, J. (2006). "'*En mi imperio*': Competing Discourses of Identity in Ivy Queen's Reggaetón." *CENTRO: Journal of the Center for Puerto Rican Studies* 18.2, pp. 62–81.

Baldwin, K (1995). "Montezuma's Revenge: Reading *Los Ricos También Lloran* in Russia." In *To Be Continued…:Soap Operas Around the World*, edited by Robert C. Allen. London & New York: Routledge.

Barrera, V. and Bielby, D. (2001). "Places, Faces, and Other Familiar Things: The Cultural Experience of Telenovela Viewing Among Latinos in the United States." *Journal of Popular Culture* 34.4, pp. 1–18.

Bodey, K., Judge, L., Steward, M. and Gobel, T. (2009). "Researching Hispanic Fans: Professional Sports' Use of Spanish Language on the Internet." *Journal of Research*, 4, pp. 58–63.

Brannon Donoghue, Courtney. (2011). "Importing and Translating *Betty*: Contemporary Telenovela Format Flow within the United States Television Industry." In *Soap Operas and Telenovelas in the Digital Age: Global Industries and New Audiences*, edited by Diana I. Rios & Mari Castañeda. New York: Peter Lang, pp. 257–274.

Casillas, D. (2014). *Sounds of Belonging: U.S. Spanish-Language Radio and Public Advocacy*. New York: New York University Press.

Cepeda, M. (2010). *Musical ImagiNation: U.S.-Colombian Identity and the Latin Music Boom*. New York: New York University Press.

Cepeda, M. (2008). Survival aesthetics: U.S. Latinas and the negotiation of popular media. In *Latina/o Communication Studies Today*, edited by A. N. Valdivia. New York: Peter Lang, pp. 237–256.

Dávila, A. (2012). *Latinos, Inc.: The Marketing and Making of a People* (2nd ed.). Berkeley and Los Angeles: University of California Press.

Devereux, E. and Hidalgo, M. (2015). " 'You're Going to Need Someone on Your Side': Morrissey's Latino/a and Chicano/a Fans." *Participations: Journal of Audience & Reception Studies* 12.2, pp. 197–217.

Flores, J. (2016). *Salsa Rising: New York Latin Music of the Sixties Generation*. New York: Oxford University Press.

Flores, J. (2000). "The Latino Imaginary: Meanings of Community and Identity." In *From Bomba to Hip Hop: Puerto Rican Culture and Latino Identity*. New York: Columbia University Press, pp. 191–203.

Ford, S. (2014). "Fan Studies: Grappling with an 'Undisciplined' Discipline." *Journal of Fandom Studies* 2.1, pp. 53–71.

Garcia, C. (2013). *Salsa Crossings: Dancing Latinidad in Los Angeles*. Durham, NC: Duke University Press.

Glasser, R. (1995). *My Music is My Flag: Puerto Rican Musicians and Their New York Communities, 1917–1940*. Berkeley and Los Angeles: University of California Press.

Gray, J. (2003). "New Audiences, New Textualities." *International Journal of Cultural Studies* 6.1, pp. 64–81.

Habell-Pallan, M. (2005). *Loca Motion: The Travels of Chicana and Latina Popular Culture*. New York: New York University Press.

Hull, K., Kim, J. K., and Stilwell, M. (2018). Fotos de Béisbol: An Examination of the Spanish-language Instagram Accounts of Major League Baseball Teams. *Howard Journal of Communications* 30.3, pp. 249–264. https://doi.org/10.1080/10646175.2018.1471756

Jenkins, H. (2006). *Convergence Culture: Where Old and New Media Collide*. New York: New York University Press.

Jensen, R. (2012). "Why Hispanic Fans Are the Lifeblood of Major League Soccer." In *Sports Fans Identities, and Socialization: Exploring the Fandemonium,* edited by Adam C. Earnheardt, Paul M. Haridakis, and Barbara S. Hugenberg. Landham, MD: Lexington Books, pp. 191–202.

Jones, B. (2015). "My Little Pony, Tolerance is Magic: Gender Policing and Brony Anti-Fandom." *Journal of Popular Television* 3.1, pp. 119–125.

Kotarba, J., Fackley, J., and Nowotny, K. (2009). "An Ethnography of Emerging Latino Music Scenes." *Symbolic Interaction* 32.4, pp. 310–333.

Loza, S. (1993). *Barrio Rhythm: Mexican American Music in Los Angeles.* Urbana, IL: University of Illinois Press.

Mayer, V. (2003). "Living Telenovelas/Telenovelizing Life: Mexican American Girls' Identities and Transnational Novelas." *Journal of Communication*, September, pp. 479–495.

Miranda, K. (2005). "'The East Side Revue, 40 Hits by East Los Angeles' Most Popular Groups!': The Boys in the Band and the Girls Who Were Their Fans." In *Beyond the Frame: Women of Color and Visual Representation,* edited by Angela Y. Davis and Neferti X.M. Tadier. New York: Palgrave Press, pp. 13–30.

Moran, K. (2011). *Listening to Latina/o Youth: Television Consumption within Families.* New York: Peter Lang.

Negrón Muntaner, F. with Abbas, C., Figueroa, L., and Robson, S. (2014). *The Latino Media Gap: A Report on the State of Latinos in U.S. Media.* New York, NY: National Association of Latino Independent Producers, The Center for the Study of Ethnicity and Race at Columbia University, and National Hispanic Foundation for the Arts. Available at: www.columbia.edu/cu/cser/downloads/Latino_Media_Gap_Report.pdf (Accessed 8 November 2024).

Negrón, M. (2015). "Fania Records and its Nuyorican Imaginary: Representing Salsa as Commodity and Cultural Sign in *Our Latin Thing.*" *Journal of Popular Music Studies* 27.3, pp. 274–303.

Pacini-Hernandez, D. (2010). *Oye Come Va: Hybridity and Identity in Latino Popular Music.* Philadelphia: Temple University Press.

Paredez, D. (2009). *Selenidad: Selena, Latinos, and the Performance of Memory.* Durham & London: Duke University Press.

Rios, D. (2003). "U.S. Latino Audiences of 'Telenovelas.'" *Journal of Latinos and Education* 2.1, pp. 59–65.

Rios, D. and Castañeda, M. (eds.) (2011). *Soap Operas and Telenovelas in the Digital Age.* New York: Peter Lang.

Rivera, M. (2011). "The Online Anti-Reggaetón Movement: A Visual Exploration." In *Seeing in Spanish: From Don Quixote to Daddy Yankee: 22 Essays on Hispanic Visual Cultures,* edited by Ryan Prout and Tillman Altenberg. Cambridge: Cambridge Scholars Publishing, pp. 281–299.

Rivera, P. (2015). *Remixing Reggaetón: The Cultural Politics of Race in Puerto Rico.* Durham, NC: Duke University Press.

Rivero, Y. (2003). "The Performance and Reception of Televisual 'Ugliness' in *Yo Soy Betty La Fea.*" *Feminist Media Studies* 3.1, pp. 65–81.

Rojas, V. (2004). "The Gender of Latinidad: Latinas Speak about Hispanic Television." *The Communication Review* 7.2, pp. 125–53.

Román-Velásquez, P. (1999). *The Making of Latin London: Salsa Music, Place, and Identity.* Aldershot, England: Ashgate.

Seiter, E. (2007). *The Internet Playground: Children's Access, Entertainment, and Mis-Education.* New York: Peter Lang.

Thornton, N. (2010). "YouTube: Transnational Fandom and Mexican Divas." *Transnational Cinemas* 1.1, pp. 53–67.

U.S. Census Bureau. (2023). "Quick Facts." July 3, 2023. www.census.gov/quickfacts/fact/table/US/RHI725222

Valdivia, A. (2003a). "Salsa as Popular Culture: Ethnic Audiences Constructing an Identity." In *Media Studies Companion,* edited by A. N. Valdivia. Oxford: Blackwell.

Valdivia, A. (2003b). "Radical hybridity: Latina/s as the paradigmatic transnational post-subculture." In *The Post-Subcultures Reader,* edited by David Muggleton and Rupert Weinzierl. New York: Berg, pp. 151–165.

Valdez, A. and Halley, J. (1991). "The Popular in Conjunto Tejano Music: Changes in Chicano Class and Identity." *Tonantzin*, 7.2, pp. 16–17.
Vargas, D. (2014). "Un desmadre positivo: Notes on how Jenni Rivera Played Music." In *Contemporary Latina/o Media*, edited by Arlene Davila and Yeidy Rivero. New York: New York University Press.
Vargas, L. (2009). *Latina Teens, Migration, and Popular Culture*. New York: Peter Lang.
Wanzo, R. (2015). "African American Acafandom and Other Strangers: New Genealogies of Fan Studies." *Transformative Works and Culture* 20, accessed at http://journal.transformativeworks.org/index.php/twc/article/view/699/538.

27
EVERYDAY COSTUME
Feminized Fandom, Retail, and Beauty Culture

Elizabeth Affuso

> *Today I have a very exciting video because I get to geek out over makeup. It's like my dream come true... geek stuff and makeup... like they had a baby, they created this collection. It's the MAC Star Trek collection.*
>
> – vlogger Laura Neuzeth (2016)

As fandom has become more visible in recent years, we have seen a proliferation of retail tie-ins that extend beyond the traditionally associated action figures, memorabilia, and T-shirts into fashion forward spaces. Fan fashion is no longer limited to venues directly associated with fandom and fan practices (cons, niche retailers, etc.), but rather is widely available in mass-market chains like Target, Kohl's, and Sephora. This new visibility comes with a destigmatization of fan products that is directly related to the mass appeal of comic book franchises and the reframing of nerds in contemporary culture. One of the core places this trend emerges is with makeup lines linked to specific media products and targeted at female fans for everyday cosplay. Examples of these include the Covergirl x *Star Wars* collection, the Benefit Cosmetics Marvel Spygal collaboration, the NBA x Colourpop collection, and MAC's *Star Trek* at 50 lines. The move of branded fan merchandise into this feminized market speaks to the dominance of female fans in contemporary fan cultures and the distinctive needs of this group. The move into more subtle spaces like makeup also reflects a desire to integrate fan practices into everyday life and speaks to a marking of the body in intimate – and often less visible – terms.

Using these makeup lines as a frame, this chapter examines the changing nature of gender in fandom. It is especially focused on the branded targeting of female fans as related to the mass marketing and mainstreaming of fandom. In examining these topics, I consider what it means for fan products to move out of subcultural or subversive spaces and into mainstream ones. In particular, the move into beauty culture speaks to the ways that fandom can be indoctrinated into cultural values, such as those related to appearance, and illuminates that as fan practices become more gender inclusive, they often simultaneously reinforce gender divides. I am additionally focused on how these makeup brands circulate in the affective, sharing economy of digital culture in spaces like YouTube makeup tutorials, haul videos, #makeuptok, and Tumblr posts. Mass-market brands rely on fans to circulate their products in these spaces to get free targeted advertising. Female fans – especially teenagers and young women – are among the most productive in these spaces, so brands target these consumers quite aggressively to tap into their networks in the crowded digital space. Using formal and textual analysis of the makeup products and related advertising and social media discourse, this chapter investigates the implications of branded fan fashion objects for contemporary fan practices.

"Courage, Confidence, and Charisma": Fandom-oriented Makeup Lines

As female fans have become a more visible market within fan communities, there has been an expansion of products branded towards explicitly feminine spaces.[1] Nowhere is this more apparent than in branded makeup tie-ins around sports, sci-fi, and comic book franchises that are more commonly associated with male fans. In 2012, Benefit Cosmetics partnered with Marvel to produce an exclusive comic called *Spygal: Thrills, Frills, and Espionage* featuring Phil Noto artwork – Marvel's *X-Force* and *Black Widow* – that was free with a $30 purchase and distributed as a promotion at New York Comic-Con. This Comic-Con promotion points toward an attempt to promote brand awareness of Benefit, but also to the cultures of collecting that are a central part of the con marketplace. Collecting, especially of rare or exclusive objects, can give fans positions of legitimacy in the hierarchies of fandom. As Avi Santo (2025) notes, "merchandise can help fans establish their legitimacy within particular communities while also functioning as a status symbol that reinforces hierarchies and differences within that community." The makeup lines discussed in this chapter are all limited edition collections feeding into ideas of rarity and exclusivity that are hallmarks of collecting culture. This exclusivity creates a secondary market for the objects in spaces like eBay, but also promotes interest in them for digital circulation, which I will discuss later in this chapter. Thus, the makeup lines function both as mass-market objects and as rare ones at the same time with limited edition functioning as a branding strategy to drive interest in product. The limited edition comic *Spygal* turns existing Benefit products into the tools of spy craft with SpyGal using nail polishes that transform into climbing ropes and blush compacts that turn into X-rays. The press materials stated:

> SpyGal is a witty secret agent decked in blue mod threads and equipped with a pore-zapping ray gun and touch-up pro case as her primary weapons. With an entire catalog of skincare products that provide instant beauty solutions and prevent pores from resembling Ben-Day dots, Benefit Cosmetics easily lends itself to be a viable artillery for both makeup enthusiasts and super-spies alike. (Felon 2012)

The narrative of the comic itself imagines Benefit products as tools of feminine superpower, indoctrinating readers into a postfeminist logic of consumer feminism where girl power is a commodity to be bought and sold. The logic also speaks to a weaponizing of beauty culture as what the prepared lady needs for any situation they might encounter.

This Marvel collaboration piggybacked DC's 2011 *Wonder Woman* MAC Cosmetics collaboration, which featured packaging designed by Mike and Laura Allred of *Madman* fame. Promotions for the line invited women to:

> Banish any thought of being a Plain Jane: MAC and Wonder Woman have joined forces! For Spring 2011, take a trip to Paradise Island with a legendary line up of super-sized Mineralize Skinfinish, bold Eye Shadow quads, Pigment,... Nail Lacquer and Lash inspired by the larger-than-life Bold Babe. Dashing and dazzling, the iconic super heroine reminds us that inside every woman is a Mighty Aphrodite full of courage, confidence and charisma. Kaboom! Mission Accomplished! (*Temptalia* 2011)

As with the Benefit SpyGal collaboration, the makeup is being positioned as a tool of empowerment that is in line both with the superhero character that the products are being associated with and contemporary beauty culture, which seeks to position beauty as a tool of neoliberal feminine empowerment. The branded makeup lines extend beauty products into fannish spaces, turning notions of beauty into tools of fan engagement, which I will address later in this chapter to talk about the rise of everyday cosplay and digital circulation's role in it. The push into this market reflects the acknowledgement on the part of companies like Marvel and DC that there is a significant female audience for their products and that these audience members are fashion forward and image conscious with money to spend. This is distinct from the oft-targeted children 4–14 group that Avi Santo (2025) mentions in "Fans and Merchandise," as makeup is generally targeted at the teen and older markets.

In both cases, the branding and the objects themselves are placed within the contemporary popular feminist discourse of girl power. Makeup is seen as tool that can help women unleash their powers, not over men, though that is implicit, but rather through conventionally feminized products. The comic industry has long sought female consumers, as evidenced by the popularity of romance comics in the postwar period. In fact, the romance comic panels that were inspirational to pop artist Roy Lichtenstein serve as a visual reference point for Allred's art for the *Wonder Woman* MAC collaboration, pointing to the high cult associations that a fashion forward brand like MAC is seeking.

The success of the MAC *Wonder Woman* line – among others – led to additional movie collaborations including the MAC *Star Trek 50* collection released for the 50th anniversary of *Star Trek*. The objects in this line featured a wide array of products referring to episodes and characters across the franchise's motion pictures and television shows with an emphasis on products related to female characters such as Uhura, Deanna Troi, Vina, Seven of Nine, and Orion Girl. This explicit focus on female characters could be seen as a response to the #wheresrey campaign after the release of *Star Wars: The Force Awakens* and Rey's absence from merchandise including the *Star Wars* x CoverGirl line (Scott 2017). As with the Benefit Marvel collaboration, *Star Trek 50* had a con tie-in, with MAC developing a *Star Trek* Experience at Comic-Con with:

> a huge, sectioned, spherical and very Trek-like station that features a Ten Forward area, an interactive transporter section (yes, you can beam up and down), and an

engineering warp core, along with Trek music, atmospheric smoke, view screens, computer terminals and more. (Malik 2016)

This presentation is in line with the experiential previews that Comic-Con visitors expect and with the retail branding strategy of the pop-up shop once again pointing toward issues of collection and rarity in how fans are being sold to.

For the 2015 release of *Star Wars: The Force Awakens*, CoverGirl released *Star Wars* x CoverGirl in stores nationwide. In line with *Star Wars*' broad appeal, CoverGirl is a drugstore makeup brand that retails at a low price point compared with the mid-range department store pricing associated with Benefit and MAC. For the launch of this line, Covergirl released six looks – Jedi, Mystic, Droid (light side) and Storm Trooper, Dark Apprentice, Chrome Captain (dark side) – on a dedicated Tumblr inviting women to consider whether they were light side or dark side, a play on the good girl vs. bad girl trope and an acknowledgment of makeup's power to transform wearers and enable fantasy. In CoverGirl's classic branding practice of using celebrities to promote its products – thereby turning all women into cover girls by association – CoverGirl enlisted famous *Star Wars* fans such as Janelle Monáe to promote the products with the hashtag #ForceBeauty. By aligning beauty with the force, CoverGirl was implying that beauty was a tool of power just as "The Force" is in the *Star Wars* films. Using the terminology of force also created associations with the squad – 2015's biggest girl trend – with both using militarized language in a feminized solidarity. Of squads, Megan Garber (2015) has written:

When a squad is presented as a #squad, it is transforming itself, via the logic of media, from a social circumstance into a social product. It's transforming the generality of a group of friends – a collective that can expand or contract, organically – into a specific, and defined, thing. A branded thing. A #squad is a clique, commodified.

The language of both squads and force points to a banding together of femininity that represents a modern clique, as Garber notes, and points to empowerment via this banding together. Additionally, the linking of fans to notions of the clique points to feminine fandoms' new position, as not the province of geeks, but rather a hallmark of coolness. The geeks, who were once marginalized by the clique, are now the aspirational clique. Being interested in sci-fi and comics no longer points to geekiness, but rather to mainstream cultural interests that exist in fashion forward feminized spaces. In no place is this turn more embodied than Rodarte's *Star Wars* evening gowns for their Fall 2014 Ready to Wear collection worn by Kirsten Dunst to the Met Gala, or "Fashion Prom" as it is colloquially known, that same year (Lamerichs 2023).

It is important to note that makeup has a clear use value that is inherently different from other fan-branded products such as memorabilia and that the personal intimacy of these products allows for forms of everyday cosplay, as it's not immediately apparent that a fan is wearing a *Wonder Woman* MAC lipstick even to consumers in the know. This also opens up forms of fan wear for people who might not be comfortable wearing a branded T-shirt or performing cosplay. It makes it possible for fans to wear fan products in a context – such as work – where they might not otherwise be appropriate, as makeup is seen as a feminine expectation in nearly every context. In Colourpop's branding for their NBA line, they suggested that makeup could be worn "to go to the game or watch it at home."

Additionally, desire for flattering shades might push consumers to purchase products from tie-in lines that they do not have a fan association with. MAC, CoverGirl, Colourpop, and Benefit are all banking on the wide appeal of flattering shades and cool packaging to draw in consumers regardless of fan associations. In a #makeuptok video reviewing the Dallas Mavericks Colourpop x NBA palette, TikToker Kassandra Sisk stated, "Once again I'd like to point out I know nothing about basketball, just a love for makeup." On #makeuptok, brands like Colourpop sometimes get critiqued for using their normal range of products in their fan-branded collaborations. Makeup TikToker Bobby Jean Spears noted that the "Vampire Skin" highlighter in Colourpop's 2023 *Twilight* collection was just another shade of their Supershock highlighter for $1 more. However, by keeping the price point of goods in these lines consistent with other products, the broad appeal is further expanded. A MAC nail polish in the *Star Trek* line costs $14, while a regular polish costs $13, which represents a markup small enough to be insignificant to many consumers. Fans of the products themselves are likely happy to have additional shades regardless of the fan branding.

Digital Circulation: Fan Labor as Advertising

The *Star Wars* x CoverGirl Tumblr positioning pointed to an understanding of the spaces where fan communities exist and a desire to use the sharing economy of fandom as a core mode of marketing the products, using the tools of fan production for explicitly branded purposes. The rise of amateur digital culture also opens up the spaces of fandom for women who might have been otherwise invisible or not part of conventional fan subcultures, especially for comic book and sci-fi products. Fan content around makeup is among the most lucrative because of makeup's core relationship to consumption cultures, branding, and structures of capital. This can be seen in the click-through shopping experiences on social media sites where feminine fans collect and share beauty culture to followers. This represents a feminized form of collecting that is in stark contrast to its masculine forms so often discussed in fan studies around collecting comic books, action figures, or models. These branded makeup products and the collection/consumption discourse around them indoctrinate female fans into both the ideologies of fandom and of postfeminist consumer citizenship. Of this postfeminist consumer citizenship, Angela McRobbie has written that there is a:

> need for women, particularly those who are under age 50, and thus still of potential value to the labour market, to come, or move forward, as active participants in these labour markets, and also in consumer culture, since the disposable income permits new realms of buying and shopping. Both of these activities, working and spending, become defining features of new modes of female citizenship. (2008: 124)

Spaces like Tumblr, YouTube, Pinterest, and TikTok allow for women to participate in consumption and labor at the same time, turning them into ideal postfeminist citizens.

In addition to sharing taste via digital collection and curation, female fans also share skills via YouTube and TikTok. These makeup lines are part of a growing trend in media fandoms toward everyday cosplay. On YouTube and TikTok, everyday cosplay is embodied by makeup tutorial videos, which teach fans how to the get the looks featured in their favorite franchises or worn by their favorite stars in their real life using commercially available products. While some of these videos fall into the realm of cosplay instruction – *The Walking Dead* zombie makeup, for example – the vast majority are teaching components of the look that are about bringing fandom into everyday life. They teach viewers how to get Katniss' *Hunger Games* braid or Daenerys' *Game of Thrones* makeup not to create an accurate reproduction for cosplay, but to learn to emulate a look for integration into everyday life. This creates a quotidian fan practice that is about subtly wearing your fandom in ways that are not clearly marked and it suggests a slippage between fan and character/celebrity. The branded makeup lines take this a step further by providing a form of wearable fan merchandise that is even less visible than what is being invoked by the makeup tutorials, as these brands are asking *Star Wars* fans not to dress up like a Storm Trooper, but rather to evoke them and the franchise's themes overall by wearing Storm Trooper-inspired lipstick. The branding for Colourpop x NBA 2021 NY Knicks palette states that it is, "A winning 9-pan palette with a mix of cobalt blue, soft orange with a high-impact metallic duo chrome finish and essential neutrals for everything from everyday looks to super glam beats!" The palette is designed specifically to appeal not just to game day, but to everyday, with only the wearer knowing that the neutral shade is called "Knickerbockers."

Matt Hills has examined "why the cult fan's costuming and impersonation appears to be so threatening to hegemonic and non-fan cultures" (2012: 167). This threat typically relegates the practice of cosplay to sanctioned spaces, namely the con. The hair and makeup videos enable fans to integrate the elements of costuming and interpretation into their lives in a manner that strips the codes of cosplay, thus protecting them from ridicule or skepticism from more mainstream forms of culture by making this work distinct from the idea of costuming. However, these videos are still linked to what Hills (2002) calls "performative consumption" through their use of imitation and impersonation, but they work to conceal the imitation by removing the visible signs of costume to create a form of costume that is recognizable only to the wearers themselves.

Digital culture allows fans to perform their consumption in a multitude of ways, from Instagram pics to tweets to haul videos, all of which demand a performative, affective consumption practice. It produces a sharing economy of consumption where fans review products and provide tutorials on how to use them. Social media opens up spaces for inclusive and resistant fan activity, with tutorials providing adaptive measures for women of all ages, races, and body types to get in on the action. This adaption is in line with other trends of postfeminist beauty culture that position inclusion as a way of indoctrinating larger numbers of women to opt-in to consumer citizenship. As Shani Orgad and Rosalind Gill note, "confidence cult(ure) opens up the promise of a more intersectional address that is attentive to power and difference, only to close this down, returning us to a 'one-size-fits-all' message" (2022: 7). This practice also aligns with the girl power and body positivity elements that are such a significant part of branding the female body in contemporary culture. We can see these practices play out in numerous different ways in mainstream culture – Dove Real Beauty, *Sports Illustrated* Swimsuits 2016 cover, Mattel's Barbie Fashionista collection – and fandom is responding to this larger trend.

"Performative consumption" is at the core of how makeup is sold on social media. For the CoverGirl *Star Wars* line, the brand partnered with popular makeup vloggers – Shameless Maya, From Head to Toe, Tasha Leelyn, and Madeeyewlook – to release five tutorial videos promoting the products in an attempt get free advertising and to associate their products with the influencer economy. The brand additionally placed product with other YouTube vloggers, such as Sonjdradeluxe, resulting in thousands of tutorials for the CoverGirl *Star Wars* line.

For the *Star Trek* 50 line, MAC relied on its devoted cult fan base to circulate and review the products, especially on the multitude of channels devoted to making haul videos of MAC products. At the time of this writing, 4,860 of 2,890,000 MAC haul videos on YouTube were devoted to *Star Trek* 50 hauls. Haul videos are the practice of showing off your purchases or "hauls" in social media video. These videos have exploded in the post-recession era and provide a space for viewers to participate in the experience of shopping without having to make purchases themselves. They additionally turn shopping into a commodity spectacle and entertainment in its own right, while providing free advertising for the brands that the haul videos are focused on. The rise of items like makeup haul videos enable fans to participate in practices of consumption whether they can afford the goods or not, as these videos function as simulated shopping. For fans who are purchasing the makeup as a collection practice, the objects are relatively inexpensive – falling primarily in the $5–30 range – by comparison with other collectible items associated with fan culture. For brands like MAC with a large digital following, there has been an increased push into alliances with other fandoms in digital space, hence the associations with mass media products like *Star Trek*, cult objects like *Rocky Horror Picture Show*, and the emerging micro celebrity market with their 2017 influencer collaboration.

Because of their relationship to branded products, makeup tutorials and haul videos have become some of the most popular – and in many cases profitable – forms of vlogging. The decision about what looks are made into tutorials or what hauls are showcased by vloggers generally comes from what is popular in pop culture at large and therefore might yield the most searches, solidifying their own personal vlogging brands through high numbers of page views, subscriptions, and follows. The other motivation comes from community feedback. Viewers can request tutorials from vloggers using the feedback functions that are built into YouTube and TikTok, creating the intimacy that is a hallmark of vlogging. In the case of these videos, the intimacy is not only fostered by the intimacy of the camera, but also the intimacy of the actions in question: entering the private space of the vloggers – often a bedroom – and sharing in the private act of putting on makeup or looking at personal hauls. In the fandom-oriented tutorials, this connection is further fostered through shared interest.

Commodity Feminism and Female Fans

This intimacy reflects a form of commodity feminism that falls within a category that Sarah Banet-Weiser has termed the "interactive subject," of which she writes, "the interactive subject participates in and through interactive technology; she 'finds' a self and broadcasts that self, through those spaces that authorize and encourage user activity. These two cultural formations – postfeminism and interactivity – both enabled by advanced capitalism, make self-branding seem not only logical, but perhaps necessary" (2012: 56). This self-branding is explicitly important both for the vloggers and the viewers of these videos who themselves self-brand via their digital and physical presence. And in the case of the aforementioned videos, this self-branding gets tied to fandom and its affective communities. These makeup tutorials and haul videos reflect a larger, recession-generated turn in postfeminism towards DIY and sharing models reflected on YouTube, TikTok, Pinterest, and Tumblr.

Commodity feminism falls explicitly into a postfeminist culture that, as Diane Negra and Yvonne Tasker have noted, "works in part to incorporate, assume, or naturalize aspects of feminism; crucially, it also works to commodify feminism via the figure of woman as empowered consumer" (2007: 2). These ideologies are spelled out in both the production and circulation of fan-branded makeup lines. The brands place themselves into a narrative of girl empowerment where purchasing a *Wonder Woman* lipstick speaks to empowerment by association with Wonder Woman's position as a superhero. Meanwhile, the vloggers who are circulating these products in makeup tutorial and haul videos are using the tools of neoliberal, postfeminist entrepreneurship to leverage feminized knowledge and media literacy into a brand community. These videos speak to a postfeminist production of labor that is decidedly different from second-wave feminist iterations of it, which sought to consider the oppressive and limiting aspects of beauty culture. Beauty culture is now seen as something that is opted into and a place where labor is required. This new expansiveness of beauty culture speaks to the fact that, "for all the gains that various women's movements have made possible, rigidly prescribed, predominantly white beauty standards are one site where time has not revolutionized our thinking. Concurrently, it's also where the expansion of consumer choice has made it possible to bow to such standards in countless ways," as Andi Zeisler (2016: 221) has noted. This new expansiveness is exactly the market that the fan-branded makeup lines and their digital circulation are playing to. This speaks to makeup as a transnational commodity product that is pitched at varied audiences. The videos teach consumers how to adapt the looks for a range of types, so that the norms and standards are not only attainable, but also required for women regardless of race, class, weight, gender, sexuality, skill, and so forth. This new indoctrination is coming largely from women themselves, which speaks to the ways in which beauty culture is situated within postfeminist discourse. As magazines have become less popular, these beauty standards have been taken up by digital culture and beauty vloggers are at the core of this.

The labor also speaks to the ways that fans are media literate and the ways that media literacy is deployed for personal branding and counted on by retail companies and media franchises. Fans are targeted as a branding opportunity for makeup lines because they represent a built-in audience as consumers and as circulators. Creators are aligning themselves with popular branded content to be found within the sea of material on social media. Franchises like *Star Trek* and *Star Wars* are already the subject of thousands of tutorials timed to the release of new franchise entries in order to build the personal brands of influencers. Companies are exploiting this by providing opportunities for a multitude of types of videos, whether it's get-the-look makeup tutorials, review videos, or haul videos, which function in a mutually beneficial relationship where makers get more hits by associating themselves with mainstream brands and socially networked marketing strategies – such as #ForceBeauty or #Colourpop – while brands get targeted advertising by influencer brands for limited financial outlay on their part. At most this might be the cost of placing their products within the hands of the right influencers. This is an extension of Suzanne Scott's (2014) idea of the "fan-trepreneur," where rather than creating fan-made merchandise for sale to other fans, these vloggers use their knowledge and skills in feminized activities to gift knowledge to other fans, while simultaneously building up influencer brands that can be leveraged into careers in the influencer economy. At the highest levels of influencer success, this means becoming a Michelle Phan-level vlogger making Dr. Pepper ads and launching her own makeup line built on the backs of teaching fans how to do *Game of Thrones* and Lady Gaga makeup.

Conclusion

Fandom's built-in consumption market makes it a ripe area for brands looking to expand reach and move product. It becomes increasingly difficult to parse actual fandom in the makers of these videos, who may or may not be fans of the franchises and products they are shilling, but may instead be using fannish associations to increase the visibility of their own brand, as Phan did to launch herself into stardom. There is a sense that fandom is profitable in broad strokes, which speaks to what Avi Santo calls "the reconstitution of fandom as a lifestyle category" (2025). The digital literacies of these communities make them additionally ripe for exploitation by major brands. Since the community around beauty and shopping videos on YouTube is robust, female fans become key targets of branded merchandise, playing into long-standing conceptions of shopping as feminine practice. These practices are distinct from masculinized discourses of collecting that are used to categorize male fans' consumption practices. It is also important to point out that with fandom's emergent position as a site of fashion forwardness, as embodied by these makeup lines, fan studies' reliance on thinking about consumption as a "starting point" for fan participation might need to be retargeted, as Santo (2025) also points out. The reliance on this logic of making seems to bypass a lot of what fans actually do with goods they purchase and it bypasses some of the capital logic that makes fans and the franchises they support valuable in the first place. Makeup may be purchased for collection purposes, as indicated by the limited nature of these collections, but once it is used up it no longer exists, so it has an ephemeral use-value that makes it distinct from other forms of collecting. The products also expire, making them somewhat undesirable as collectibles for collecting's sake. This licensed merchandise is also linked to an explicitly adult audience, making it distinct from the juvenilia so often thought to be the target of fan-branded merchandise. This may point to a distinction of female fans from male fans, where collecting is not viewed as a way to hold on to childish objects via consumptive collecting, but rather a sense that fandom and fan-branded products can co-exist with the desire to be sophisticated, adult, and fashion forward. It also removes some of the public-facing agenda of many products in that these objects, once worn, are not designed to be recognized as fan-oriented products, allowing fans to participate in an everyday cosplay that only they are aware of. Personal pleasure has always been a core part of the practice of consumption and placing fan consumption into a politicized practice separate from other forms of capital is a problematic distinction, as these makeup lines elucidate.

Notes

1   Makeup has historically been targeted at female consumers, though there has been a move toward more gender inclusive branding with CoverGirl's use of James Charles as "male ambassador" for the brand and in MAC's ongoing collaboration with RuPaul, Dame Edna, and several other drag icons.

References

Banet-Weiser, S. (2012) *Authentic: The Politics of Ambivalence in Brand Culture*, New York: NYU Press.
Covergirl (2016) *Star Wars Makeup Collection*, YouTube videos (5), October 18. Available from: www.youtube.com/playlist?list=PL1_vRQKoHSnx07kFIm593C8z9j4DxdTV3.
Covergirl (2015) Covergirl Star Wars, Tumblr.
Felon, B. (2012) "Marvel and Benefit Cosmetics' 'SpyGal' Sports Gorgeous Phil Noto Artwork," *Comics Alliance*, May 18. Available from: http://comicsalliance.com/spy-gal-phil-noto-marvel-benefot-cosmetics-high-resolution-preview-artwork/.
Garber, M. (2015) "The Summer of the #Squad," *The Atlantic*, July 23. Available from: www.theatlantic.com/entertainment/archive/2015/07/the-summer-of-the-squad/399308/.
Hills, M. (2002) *Fan Cultures*, London: Routledge.
Lamerichs, Nicolle (2023) "Droids on the Runway: Fandom, Business, and Transmedia in Star Wars Luxury Fashion," in *Sartorial Fandom: Fashion, Beauty Culture, and Identity*. Edited by Suzanne Scott and Elizabeth Affuso, Ann Arbor: University of Michigan Press. 99–113.
Malik, T. (2016) "Star Trek Makeup by M-A-C beams into San Diego Comic-Con," *space.com*, July 23. Available from: www.space.com/33524-star-trek-makeup-beams-into-sdcc-2016.html.
McRobbie, A. (2008) *The Aftermath of Feminism*, London: Sage.
Negra, D. and Tasker, Y. (2007) *Interrogating Postfeminism*, Durham: Duke University Press.
Neuzeth, L. (2016) *MAC Star Trek Collection*, YouTube video, July 24. Available from: www.youtube.com/watch?v=eek4OXg8Pg4.
Orgad, S. and Gill, R. (2022) *Confidence Culture*, Durham: Duke University Press.
Santo, A. (2025) "Fans and Merchandise," in *The Routledge Companion to Media Fandom*. Edited by M. Click and S. Scott. 2nd edition, London: Routledge, 2025.
Scott, S. (2014) "Talking the Walk: Enunciative Fandom and Fan Studies Industrial Turn," Society for Cinema and Media Studies Conference, Seattle, March 19–23.
Scott, S. (2017) "#wheresrey?: Toys, Spoilers, and the Gender Politics of Franchise Paratexts," *Critical Studies in Media Communication* 34 (2): 138–147. doi:10.1080/15295036.2017.1286023.
Sisk, K. @kassandrasisk (2023, March 4) @colourpopco NBA palette featuring @dallasmavs [Video]. TikTok. Available from: www.tiktok.com/t/ZTLLCeoJG/.
Sonjradeluxe (2015) *CoverGirl Star Wars Lightside vs Darkside Tutorial*, YouTube Video, November 18. Available from: www.youtube.com/watch?v=gtj0AGeDF8M.
Spears, B.J. (2024, January 21) #*stich with Manny Mua Again. Lets stop rewarding beands [sic] for mediocrity* [Video]. TikTok. Available from: www.tiktok.com/t/ZTLLQoseJ/.
Temptalia (2011) "MAC Wonder Women Collection for Spring 2011—Official Information, Photos, Prices," *Temptalia*, January 14. Available from: www.temptalia.com/mac-wonder-woman-collection-for-spring-2011-official/.
Zeisler, A. (2016) *We Were Feminists Once*, New York: PublicAffairs.

28
WATCHING THE SERIES OF THE ENEMY

The Reception of Turkish Soap Operas by Greeks

Dimitra Laurence Larochelle

Transcultural flows can no longer be understood according to models that describe the structural relationship between an "advanced" center and a "less developed" periphery (Appadurai 1996). On the contrary, they ought to be comprehended through a more fluid model of transnational cultural flow in which the United States do not have the leading role but constitute a node in this complex system (ibid.). Thus, contemporary global television culture goes hand in hand with the proliferation of new versions of modern culture that highlight particular identities that are different from hegemonic Americanism (Ang 2007). In this context, the hegemonic role of the United States as the cultural avatar of contemporary modernity seems to be declining in favor of the emergence of new forms of modernity that are more familiar and/or close to American modernity for some countries (Iwabuchi 2002). The global dissemination and consumption of media conveying alternative modernities has drawn the attention of fan studies scholars who have examined, among other things, the potential of these products as mechanisms through which nations can effectively promote their culture to international audiences (e.g., Jenkins 2004; Kim 2014; Annett 2014; Morimoto 2014, 2018). Nevertheless, studies often overlook how real-world events shape fan practices and perceptions of media content. Specifically, little attention has been given to transcultural fandoms of media products in countries that maintain long-enduring rivalries with the producing country. Through this study, focusing on the Greek fandom of Turkish soap operas, I aim to illustrate how fans in non-Western settings engage with and interpret transnational media content, as well as how they navigate their cultural identities and affiliations through their interaction with media content.

How do Greek fans negotiate long-enduring negative stereotypes about Turks through the viewing of Turkish soap operas? What are the limits of this process? Should the popularity of these soap operas in Greece be interpreted as the success of Turkish *soft power* in the neighboring country as many journalists and several researchers have claimed? Finally, what are the factors that determine the reception of cultural products originating from a perceived "enemy" country?

The results presented in this chapter are based on 50 in-depth interviews with individuals that took place during the period 2016–2018. The vast majority of the participants were women. More precisely, among the 50 interviewees there were only three men. This over-representation of women is consistent with related literature observations about the "female" characterization of serial fiction, whether in terms of choice of subjects, type of narration, or audience profile (Hobson 2003). Interviewees were of various socio-economic backgrounds residing in different geographical areas in Greece (Athens, Thessaloniki, Chalcis, and Komotiní) aged from 17 to 89 years old. Interviewees were recruited on a voluntary basis and through the snowball method. The important majority of my interviewees were recruited by replying to the announcement I posted within several online fan communities. Although they exhibit varying degrees of fandom, many of them are involved in activities that demonstrate their commitment to the common object of admiration (e.g., group travels, fanart, fansubbing, etc.). At the time of the research, they all have been watching Turkish series for at least five years. The thematic areas discussed during the interviews were as various as the representation of gendered identities, of love and marital relations, of Turkish society, of social classes, etc. In the following pages, I first consider the relations between Greece and Turkey and the viewing of Turkish soap operas in Greece within this context. I then present the results of my empirical research on the reception of Turkish dramas by Greek fans.

From Global to Local: The Importation of Turkish Series in Greece and the Fear of Cultural Alienation from the Products of the "Enemy"

In recent decades, Turkey has become one of the central nodes of global television culture as the second-largest exporter of TV series (Khan and Won 2020). First distributed in countries that formerly comprised parts of the Ottoman Empire (i.e., the Balkans and the Middle East), Turkish soap operas have quickly attracted heterogeneous audiences, accrediting to the Turkish serial industry a leading role on the international media scene (Öztürkmen 2018). The dramas in question propose a fantasy world of globalized consumerism and romantic love that defies national boundaries (Olson 2000). However, at the same time, Turkish soap operas propose an alternative modernity characterized by traditional family structures and gender roles (Buccianti 2010). It is this element that differentiates the soaps in question from the American prototype. The consistent worldwide appeal of Turkish series has led to a rise in scholarly inquiry not only into the reception of these cultural products but also into their potential influence in terms of *soft power* (e.g., Fisher Onar 2009; Anaz and Purcell 2010; Salamandra 2012; Al-Ghazzi and Kraidy 2013; Ağırseven and Örki 2017; Elitaş and Kir 2019; Berg 2017; Anaz and Özcan 2016; Algan and Kaptan 2021).

Over the last few decades, Greece has been one of the countries systematically importing Turkish soap operas (Larochelle 2023). The success of Turkish soap operas in terms of audience ratings in Greece has often been analyzed as a triumph of Turkish foreign policy, favoring the logic of textual determinism. However, these claims don't pay attention to the socio-historical conditions of reception and have never been supported by empirical evidence.

The reception of these cultural products by Greek audiences is a complex phenomenon that has yet to be sufficiently discussed. On this point, it is worth mentioning that Greece and Turkey constitute an "antagonistic dyad," and their relationship is characterized by a classic enduring conflict between neighbors (Heraclides 2010). More specifically, following the advent of nationalism, in order to establish themselves as a nation-state, Greeks had to differentiate themselves from the Ottoman Empire in order to assert their singularity. In this context, Greek national identity was defined in opposition to Turkish identity (Couroucli 2002). It was at this point that the modern Greeks identified themselves as descendants of the ancient Greeks and wanted to join their "natural family," i.e., Europe (ibid.). This process led not only to the establishment of myths and positive self-representations, but also to the "demonization" of the *Other*, i.e., the Turk (Millas 2001). Since then, the Turk has come to embody the *Other* of the Greeks, representing everything the Greeks are not, or rather everything they don't want to be (Theodossopoulos 2006).

School textbooks, historiography, the media, the family, literature, and everyday language are all institutions that reproduce and crystallize stereotypes about Turks (Millas 2001; Özgünes and Terzis 2000; Terzis 2008; Mini 2017). The same is true of Turkey, where similar stereotypes about Greeks persist (Yilmazok 2018). In Greek public discourse, Turks are stereotyped as enemies of the Greek nation, with "barbaric" characteristics. However, we must take into consideration that these images are due to the process of constructing national identities, which by definition requires the existence of an *Other* to whom *We* are opposed in principle (Smith 1991). Greek national identity was the invention of rising romantic nationalism in the nineteenth century (Plumyène 1979), as were the categories used by Greeks to describe *Others*. In the Greek collective imaginary, Turks are therefore an abstract and vague category, self-made to designate the *Other*, and as such have more to say about their authors than about their protagonists (Kirtsoglou and Sistani 2003).

Within this specific context, the broadcast of Turkish soap operas in Greece has been accompanied by numerous negative reactions in the field of the public sphere. These critics have most often focused their objections on the supposed cultural "invasion" and "alienation" of the working classes through the cultural products of the "enemy" (Larochelle 2023).

(Re)Discovering the Other Through Soap Operas

The success of Turkish soap operas in Greece seem to be due to the cultural proximity (Straubhaar 1991) between the two neighboring countries. Turkish soap operas convey an alternative modernity characterized by several elements in common with Greek popular culture. The respect accorded to the heteronormative family, the representation of heteronormative romantic relationships and/or marital structures, and the importance given to religion and tradition are some of these elements. Linguistic affinities between Greece and Turkey – and the cultural representations they incorporate – are other elements that make Turkish serial dramas familiar to Greek viewers. Moreover, daily life in Turkey seems to be characterized by habits and traditions that are also valid in Greece. In this sense, elements portrayed in Turkish soap operas, such as eating habits, musical traditions, superstitions, and wedding traditions, are also part of the cultural baggage of the popular classes in Greece. In addition, it should not be overlooked that some of the themes addressed by Turkish soap operas – such as the rivalry between rich and poor, the stereotypes of the "poor but happy and honest" and the "rich but unhappy and dishonest," or the victory of good over evil, etc. – are universal and thus likely to appeal more or less to all viewers, regardless of their ethnic background.

In this context, it seems that these elements enabled some of the fans who took part in my study (17 of them) to realize the cultural affinities between their own *imagined community* (Anderson 1983) and the *Other* (the Turk), and to question some of the negative representations they held for their neighbors. Through Turkish soap operas, the Turk ceases to be an abstract, vague figure and becomes a human being who is not radically different from *Us*. In opposition to the widespread orientalist (Said 1978) representation of the Turkish male in Greece, the man in Turkish soap operas is handsome and noble, in most cases he loves and doesn't abuse women, he sacrifices himself for his beloved ones, he puts his honor and his family first, he respects his elders, he eats the same things as *Us*, he listens to the same music as *Us*, he speaks like *Us*, he has the same superstitions as *Us*; he is hurt, he suffers, he carries out his own battles to restore justice, he is also a victim of the capitalist system like *Us*. In other words, Turkish soap operas convey a "humanized" image of the *Other*, whom Greek audiences have learned from an early age to perceive in a negative way. In this sense, the figure considered de facto to be opposed to *Us*, becomes a very familiar figure. The Turk thus becomes a man who not only has weaknesses and sensitivities, but also resembles *Us*. In this sense, a 52-year-old German teacher declared:

> The Turks have a lot in common with us. I recognize myself in these series. I recognize my values. We have the same appearance, the same values, the same traditions... even the way we cook... the hospitality, the importance given to religion.... I'm finally realizing how much we've borrowed from the Turks, and how much they've also borrowed from us, of course.[1]

Similarly, a 64-year-old housewife said:

> By watching Turkish (series), I realized that as nations, as people, we have many more similarities than differences.... What I like is that I see pieces of us in them. I see a lot of similarities... I mean a lot... Let's say the institution of the family, the food, even their dining table is the same, the role of mother and father, they're just like us! Also, religious faith is something we have in common, not religion but faith, the role religion plays in our lives. Even the scenes in these series remind me of Greece. The blue of the sea reminds me of Greece... it's as if I can see *Us*.

By watching Turkish soap operas, viewers are invited to question official Greek discourse and recognize the cultural affinities between Greeks and Turks. The idea that national cultures are distinct from one another was imposed with the advent of nationalism. However, it would be wrong to consider that nationalist ideology gradually led to the eradication of cultural affinities between nations that – until very recently – belonged to the same cultural and geopolitical entities. So, while on an official level Greeks are supposed to be radically different from Turks, everyday life in Greece has many elements in common with Turkish culture. Gastronomic culture, linguistic affinities, worldview, and the similar way in which the two populations deal with their feelings are some of the elements identified by the social subjects interviewed as constituting the cultural proximity between Greeks and Turks. As illustrated by the following interview extract, taking similarities into account gradually leads some interviewees to question certain stereotypes about the *Other*:

> Turks are becoming nicer through these series... how can I explain that? I had a different image of them before. But through these series, I've realized that we're very

close... they show their civilization. Their way of living, their cleanliness... They show that they're not underdeveloped (entrepreneur, 57 years old).

Sultan Erdoğan and the Greeks

Although some of my interviewees have challenged a number of the negative stereotypes they held of Turks through their viewing of Turkish serial dramas, I argue that it would be wrong to equate this process with the supposed success of Turkish cultural diplomacy. More precisely, many of those who took part in my survey seem to be somehow suspicious of the Turkish government. The process of intercultural communication through Turkish soap operas is thus limited, and Greeks' attitudes towards their neighboring country seem unchanged despite the popularity of Turkish soap operas in Greece. More specifically, 46 out of 50 respondents said they perceived representations of Turkish culture, history, and way of life in Turkish soap operas as unrealistic, partly or completely biased. Some of those interviewed even detected a bias for propaganda and, in the case of Greece, an anti-Greek discourse. In other words, even though watching Turkish soap operas enabled some people to grasp the cultural affinities between Greeks and Turks, they were at the same time quite critical of the messages conveyed by the soap operas in question. In this context, a large majority of interviewees pointed out that Turkish historical soap operas present a version of history that does not correspond to reality, and whose aim is to promote a positive image of Turkey in general and its imperial past in particular, both inside and outside Turkey. In this sense, according to the interviewees, some historical soap operas intend to present Turkey's imperial past in a phantasmagorical and idealized way. For this reason, they declared that they didn't appreciate this kind of serial drama.

A representative example of this phenomenon is the following statement:

I chose not to watch Suleiman[2].... Listen, many times they alter history... they tell what they want! They are narrating history as they know it, not as everyone else knows it.... It's more about things related to the Greeks. I'm surprised that women in Greece watched this series. I remember saying to them 'are you aware of what you're watching?' It was a production, like all other Turkish productions for that matter, based on Turkish nationalism. As a Greek, I don't accept watching something like that.... Well, it's true that we like Turkish series, but there are limits... we mustn't exaggerate either (journalist, 31 years old).

This interview extract is representative of the fact that fans decode the series according to their historical knowledge, and reject what they see as the Turkish rewriting of history, or even revisionism and propaganda. The last sentence of the aforementioned verbatim is particularly important – "Well, it's true we like Turkish series, but there are limits... we mustn't exaggerate either." This sentence illustrates the selection process carried out by fans of these products. This selection is determined by several factors.

The first factor concerns the *veracity of the representations* projected, especially when it comes to dramas dealing with historical facts. Greek fans' "love" for Turkish soap operas is therefore not unconditional or limitless, but rather in accordance with the collective memory of the Greeks: the decoding of serial fiction is thus done with reference to the *imagined community* that constitutes the nation, and more precisely to the representations of its history that this community maintains. In addition, a large number of viewers interviewed during our survey were quite sensitive to the representation of their ethnic identity in Turkish soap operas, not only in historical and/or military soap operas, but also in other series. Greeks are so vigilant about the portrayal of their national identity in Turkish media productions, because for Greeks, Turks (and the Turkish state) are still enemies who seek to slander and devalue the nation in the eyes of international society. In this sense, on the rare occasions when a Greek is portrayed in Turkish soap operas, Greek fans seem to be rather suspicious of the representation accorded to them by their neighbors. Overall, almost all the interviewees were fairly critical of the representations of Greece conveyed by Turkish soap operas, and several of them made a clear distinction between their appreciation of Turkish soap operas and their view of Turks and Turkey. The vast majority of Greek fans interpret the content they watch according to their own historical, cultural, and ideological dispositions and prisms, which are largely trans-generational, imprinted in the collective memory, or even in "popular wisdom" as demonstrated by the following declaration of a 51-year-old woman who has been unemployed since the closure of the company where she worked due to the economic crisis:

Interviewee: You know what they say: "If you have a Turkish friend, you have to carry a big knife."
Interviewer: What does this mean for you and how does it relate to your viewing?
Interviewee: I liked the series, but not the Turks.

Therefore, even if some fans have declared that they have been influenced in their image of Turks, it seems that for most of them, there is no direct link between their taste for a cultural product and the transformation of their perception of another country. Reciprocal visions are rooted in history, and thus are stronger than serial fiction narratives. This is especially true concerning Greek fans of Turkish soap operas as they are – like fans elsewhere in the world (Jenkins 1992) – experts interested in every detail of their object of admiration. In fact, they seek out and share information with each other on all aspects related to their object of admiration (e.g., the duration and details of contracts signed between actors and production companies, sources of funding for Turkish serial fictions, links between government agents and actors, etc.), and are very familiar with narrative mechanisms and their ideological underpinnings. More precisely, the historical prism is not the only one to influence reception. Knowledge of the contemporary geopolitical situation in general, and of political and social life in Turkey in particular, also plays a role. In this sense, some interviewees believe that Turkish soap operas are a tool in the hands of the President of the Turkish Republic aiming to impose Muslim values on the neighboring population. An example of this is the following statement of a 63-year-old woman who, since the economic crisis, has been unemployed, whereas previously she held the position of marketing director for an advertising company:

> I notice that due to the political situation in Turkey, the most recent Turkish soap operas are not good, and this is because Sultan Erdoğan[3] wants everything to be in line with Muslim values. He doesn't want things to move towards the Western way of life. He wants them (the Turks) to go back to headscarves and prayers.... That's why for the last two years, following the 2016 coup, he banned 150 TV channels....

Turkey has 80 million inhabitants and he [Recep Tayyip Erdoğan] has to offer them *bread and circuses*... most of them are uneducated. Educated people living in large urban centers are only a small minority. Most of them are an uneducated mass, and he castrates them through the series. I read a lot about Turkish series every day, and I see which series he has interrupted and which he funds. He promotes all nationalist series, those that don't encourage people to think in a Western way. He makes propaganda through Turkish series.

For other fans, the norms conveyed by soap operas in order to encourage international acceptance are too far from reality to be credible. For the majority of the subjects interviewed, Turkish soap operas aim to promote a positive image of contemporary Turkey, that of a modern, economically and politically developed country, which does not correspond to the reality of the country (or at least to their knowledge of the reality of the country). In this sense, some of the women interviewed consider that certain Turkish soap operas have an educational vocation for Turks. For this purpose, however, they mobilize narratives and representations that, in their view, do not correspond to the reality of the country. In other words, the representations projected through Turkish dramas contradict their knowledge of the situation of social life in Turkey. This knowledge forms the basis on which Turkish soap operas are evaluated. According to the interviewees, these soap operas aim to project an image of a democratic Turkey, where meritocracy as well as respect for women prevail. However, as they point out, this image of the Turkish state is far from their understanding of reality, and is therefore rejected.

In this sense, the appeal of Turkish soap operas or the realization of cultural affinities between Greeks and Turks should not be equated with a supposed submission of the receiver of meaning to the message conveyed by the media text. Although some of the persons interviewed identified several affinities between their own culture and the culture of the *Other*, Turkish society seems to remain a distinctly different society, with very different structural characteristics to Greek society, according to the vast majority of those interviewed. In the same way, the interviewees seem particularly attracted by Turkish soap operas and the alternative modernity they convey, but they remain aware that the serial fictions they watch constitute creations whose production process is ideologically determined.

The final parameter influencing Greek reception of transnational products is the diplomatic situation between the producing and receiving countries. Thus, periods of diplomatic tension between Greece and Turkey result in lower audience ratings for Turkish soap operas. This was the case in July 2020, when the Turkish government announced its decision to convert the museum (formerly the Orthodox Basilica and later the National Museum) of Saint Sophia in Istanbul into a mosque. Following this decision, the channels which broadcast Turkish soap operas (STAR CHANNEL and SKAI) suffered a significant drop in their audience ratings. Furthermore, the backlash against Turkey and the country's cultural (and other) products has been so virulent that ANTENNA has announced the permanent removal of Turkish soap operas from its programming. One year later, however, the channel in question has returned to broadcasting numerous Turkish soap operas. Thus, the success of Turkish serial dramas is not helping diplomatic relations between Greece and Turkey. On the contrary, it is rather the state of diplomatic relations that influences the reception of Turkish dramas in Greece: audience success is "vulnerable" to diplomatic and geopolitical conflicts.

Conclusion

The objective of this study was to shift away from the traditional emphasis on Western media and illustrate how fans in non-Western settings engage with and interpret transnational media content. Through this case study, I examined how Greek fans navigate their cultural identities and affiliations through their interaction with media content, thus apprehending fan communities as arenas for identity negotiation and construction. The results of my research reveal the complexity of the reception process. On the one hand, the reception of Turkish soap operas by Greeks sheds light on the potential of fan engagement to disrupt established cultural narratives and foster intercultural comprehension, as well as underscoring the significance of media fandom as a platform for critical reflection and dialogue concerning issues of cultural representation and identity. On the other hand, this study challenges the notion of media influence as a one-way process, showing how real-world events influence fan practices and perceptions of media content. By examining assertions about the perceived *soft power* of Turkish media in Greece, this study questions simplistic assumptions regarding the impact of media on cultural attitudes and behaviors and emphasizes the necessity for a nuanced understanding of the interplay between media consumption, national identity, and geopolitical dynamics.

Notes

1 The verbatims have been translated into English by the author.
2 Referencing the historical soap opera *Muhteşem Yüzyıl* (2011–2014), which deals with the life of Sultan Suleiman the Magnificent.
3 Reference to Turkish President Recep Tayyip Erdoğan.

References

Ağırseven, N., & Örki, A. (2017). Evaluating Turkish TV Series as Soft Power Instruments. *OPUS International Journal of Society Researches*, 7(13), 838–853.
Algan, E., & Kaptan, Y. (2021). Turkey's TV Celebrities as Cultural Envoys: The Role of Celebrity Diplomacy in Nation Branding and the Pursuit of Soft Power. *Popular Communication*, 19(1), 1–13.
Al-Ghazzi, O., & Kraidy, M. M. (2013). Neo-Ottoman Cool 2: Turkish Nation Branding and Arabic-Language Transnational Broadcasting. *International Journal of Communication*, 7, 2341–2360.
Anaz, N., & Özcan, C. C. (2016). Geography of Turkish Soap Operas: Tourism, Soft Power, and Alternative Narratives. In I. Egresi (Éd.), *Alternative Tourism in Turkey. Role, Potential Development and Sustainability* (Vol. 121, pp. 247–258). Springer International Publishing.
Anaz, N., & Purcell, D. E. (2010). Geopolitics of Film: Valley of the Wolves—Iraq and its Reception in Turkey and Beyond. *Arab World Geographer*, 13(1), 34–49.
Anderson, B. (1983). *Imagined Communities: Reflections on the Origin and Spread of Nationalism*. New York: Verso.
Annett, S. (2014). *Anime Fan Communities: Transcultural Flows and Frictions*. Palgrave Macmillan.
Ang, I. (2007). Television Fictions Around the World: Melodrama and Irony in Global Perspective. *Critical Studies in Television*, 2(2), 18–30.
Appadurai, A. (1996). *Modernity at Large. Cultural Dimensions of Globalization*. University of Minnesota Press.
Berg, M. (2017). Turkish Drama Serials as a Tool for Soft Power. *Participant Journal*, 14(2), 32–52.

Buccianti, A. (2010). Dubbed Turkish Soap Operas Conquering the Arab World: Social Liberation or Cultural Alienation. *Arab Media and Society*, 10(2), 4–28.

Couroucli, M. (2002). Le nationalisme de l'Etat en Grèce. In A. Dieckhoff & R. Kastoryano (Éds.), *Nationalismes en mutation en Méditerranée Orientale* (pp. 41–59). CNRS Éditions.

Elitaş, T., & Kır, S. (2019). Reading Turkey's New Vision Based Real Policies through an Identity and their Presentation in Series as a Soft Power: A Study on the Series, Resurrection-Ertugrul. *Journal of Social Sciences*, 8(1), 41–62.

Fan, Y. (2008). Soft Power: Power of Attraction or Confusion? *Place Branding and Public Diplomacy*, 4(2), 147–158.

Fisher Onar, N. (2009). *Neo Ottomanism, Historical Legacies and Turkish Foreign Policy* (3; Discussion Paper Series). EDAM /German Marshall Fund.

Heraclides, A. (2010). *The Greek-Turkish Conflict in the Aegean. Imagined Enemies*. Palgrave Macmillan.

Hobson, D. (2003). *Soap Opera*. Polity Press.

Iwabuchi, K. (2002). *Recentering Globalization: Popular Culture and Japanese Transnationalism*. Duke University Press.

Jenkins, H. (2004). Pop Cosmopolitanism: Mapping Cultural Flows in an Age of Media Convergence. In M. M. Suárez-Orozco & D. B. Qin-Hilliard, *Globalization: Culture and Education in the New Millennium* (pp. 114–140). University of California Press.

Jenkins, H. (1992). *Textual Poachers. Television Fans and Participatory Culture*. Routledge.

Khan, M., & Won, Y. (2020). Transnationalization of TV Serials: A Comparative Study of the Exportation of Korean and Turkish TV Serials. *European Journal of Social Sciences*, 59(2), 193–208.

Kim, J. (2014). *Reading Asian Television Drama: Crossing Borders and Breaking Boundaries*. I. B. Taurus.

Kirtsoglou, E., & Sistani, L. (2003). The Other Then, the Other Now, the Other Within: Stereotypical Images and Narrative Captions of the Turk in Northern and Central Greece. *Journal of Mediterranean Studies*, 13(2), 189–213.

Larochelle, D. L. (2023). Transnational Soap Operas and Viewing Practices in the Digital Age: The Greek Fandom of Turkish Dramas. *International Communication Gazette*, 85(3-4), 233–249.

Millas, H. (2001). *Images des Grecs et des Turcs—Manuels scolaires, historiographie, littérature et stéréotypes nationaux*. Alexandreia (en grec).

Mini, P. (2017). The Image of the Turk in Greek Fiction Cinema: An Overview. *Etudes balkaniques LIII*, 1, 55–66.

Morimoto, L. (2018). Transnational Media Fan Studies. In M. Click & S. Scott (Éds.), *Routledge Companion to Media Fandom* (pp. 280–288). Routledge.

Morimoto, L. (2014, février 22). *Yukata!batch Goes Global: Japanese Entertainment Booms in the Age of Social Media*. ACA/ PCA Southwest Conference.

Nye, J. (2004). *Soft Power: The Means to Success in World Politics*. Public Affairs.

Olson, S. R. (2000). The Globalization of Hollywood. *International Journal on World Peace*, 17(4), 3–17.

Özgüneş, N., & Terzis, G. (2000). Constraints and Remedies for Journalists Reporting National Conflict: The Case of Greece and Turkey. *Journalism Studies*, 1(3), 405–426.

Öztürkmen, A. (2018). "Turkish Content": The Historical Rise of the Dizi Genre. *TV/Series*, 13, 1–12.

Plumyène, J. (1979). *les Nations romantiques, histoire du nationalisme: Le dix-neuvième siècle*. Fayard.

Said, E. (1978). *Orientalism*. Pantheon Books.

Salamandra, C. (2012). The Muhannad Effect: Media Panic, Melodrama, and the Arab Female Gaze. *Anthropological Quarterly*, 85(1), 45–77.

Smith, A. D. (1991). *National Identity*. Penguin Books.

Straubhaar, J. (1991). Beyond Media Imperialism: Assymetrical Interdependece and Cultural Proximity. *Critical Studies in Media Communication*, 8, 39–59.

Terzis, G. (2008). Journalism Education Crossing National Boundaries: Demainstreaming Binary Oppositions in Reporting. *Journalism*, 9(2), 141–162.

Theodossopoulos, D. (2006). Introduction: The « Turks » in the Imagination of the « Greeks ». *South European Society & Politics*, *11*(1), 1–32.

Tutal-Cheviron, N., & Çam, A. (2017). La vision turque du « soft-power » et l'instrumentalisation de la culture. In D. Marchetti (Éd.), *La circulation des productions culturelles. Cinémas, informations et séries télévisées dans les mondes arabes* et musulmans (Centre Jacques-Berque, pp. 125–147).

Yilmazok, L. (2018). Persistent Othering in Turkish Cinema: The Stereotyped and Gendered Greek Identity. *Turkish Studies*, *20*(1), 120–139.

29
AGING, FANS, AND FANDOM

C. Lee Harrington and Denise D. Bielby

What does it mean to be a 40-year-old *Once Upon a Time* (ABC) fan who live-tweets each episode? Or a 60-year-old *Lord of the Rings* enthusiast who curates an online catalog of fan art? Or an 80-year-old who collects Spice Girls dolls, not for their profit potential or nostalgia's sake but out of deep emotional attachment? In short, how are fans and fandoms shaped by age? As scholars have expanded their scope of inquiry to examine how fandom is influenced by multiple aspects of social identity—including not only gender and sexuality but now also race, ethnicity, and national identity—we advocate for the importance of highlighting *age* and *aging* in fan scholarship. Fandom in youth and adolescence has received considerable attention over the years from industries and scholars alike, reflecting both the profit potential of the youth market and long-held associations between fan practices and childhood development. In contrast, fandom in late(r) life remains underexamined, even as a rapidly aging global population and increased consumer spending by older adults signal its growing importance to media landscapes (Tedeschi 2006). For example, in the US context, about 35% of movie-goers are now 45 or older (Nielsen 2013), the most active concert-goers are middle-aged (35 to 54; Mazur 2015), and about 45% of all ad-supported cable television (TV) networks have median audience ages of 50 or older (Sternberg 2015). These trends are expected to continue in the future—how might they impact fan identities and practices?

This chapter builds on an earlier project (Harrington and Bielby 2010a) in which we introduced insights from gerontology—the interdisciplinary study of age and aging—into fan studies. Our project reviewed the prior two decades of fan studies to examine treatment of issues related to fans and aging. We found numerous scholars who wrote about fandom in later life, but their research rarely engaged gerontological knowledge that helps clarify how fan objects and experiences become positioned in life trajectories, transformations of fandom over time, and experiences of fandom in later life. We proposed that fans' identities, practices, and interpretive capacities have more age-related structure than was previously addressed and explored that thesis through four issues: (1) fandom and life milestones; (2) changes in the fan self over time; (3) age norms in fandom; and (4) changes in fan objects over time.

Over the past few years, fan scholars have increasingly examined age-related issues in fandom as well as more generalized processes of change and adaptation. They have also begun to more fully integrate fan studies with gerontological scholarship. This chapter thus has two aims: First, to revisit how fan studies can account for fandom over time and to update our prior thesis through incorporation of recent literature; and second, to highlight emergent areas of research in the field of aging, fans, and fandom. As noted, given rapid processes of global aging currently underway, swiftly changing demographics of media audiences worldwide, and rising industry interest in cultivating fan-consumers, it is important to understand how age and aging modifies the experiences of fans both individually and collectively. We begin with an introduction to media and the life course.

Life Course and Media

Understanding the life course is about "understanding lives through time" (Fry 2003: 271). Life course scholars are interested in the social and historical changes that impact a particular generation at a particular point in time and shape the ways that "members of that generation make sense of a presently remembered past, experienced present, and anticipated future" (Cohler and Hostetler 2003: 557). Sociologists tend to use the term *life course* whereas psychologists prefer the term *life span*, but both approaches focus on issues of time and timing, intersections of social context and personal biography, interdependent lives, and the importance of human agency (George 2003: 672). The difference in terminology reflects the amount of emphasis placed on internal aspects of development (life span approach) versus social influences on human development (life course approach).

The life course is conceptualized within this framework via general patterns of stability and transition rather than evolutionary or hierarchical stages. Since life journeys can follow unexpected paths, the task for scholars is to "simultaneously do justice to long-term patterns of change and stability and to the heterogeneity of those patterns" (George 2003: 675). Though unscripted, different life phases tend to be marked by distinct opportunities and challenges, and our engagement with them shapes our development from infancy through childhood, adolescence, adulthood, and late life. Each individual life course is also guided by culturally and historically bound ideals of how lives "should" unfold, offering normative pathways against which we evaluate our own personal trajectories. These ideals are undergoing significant transition in the US and elsewhere but continue to influence how we understand our lived experiences.

Popular media such as music, comics, and TV are thoroughly implicated in life course processes, offering representations of normatively appropriate (and inappropriate) identities and activities, producing so-called "rock-and-roll," "TV," and "YouTube" generations, altering expectations for how publicly lives can or should be lived, and transforming relatively non-mediated lives in earlier historical eras into thoroughly mediated ones today. Media texts and technologies help unite cohorts, define generations and cross-generational differences, and give structure and meaning to our lives as they unfold. In our earlier article (2010a) we found that fan scholars discussed a wide variety of age-related *issues* but rarely utilized *theories* of age and aging to ground their analyses. In this chapter, we revisit the four age-based issues noted earlier—fandom and life milestones, changes in the fan self over time, age norms within fandom, and changes in the fan object over time—and illustrate how a life course/life span perspective informs these experiences. Next, we discuss emergent areas of research in the study of aging, fans, and fandom.

Issue I: Fandom and Life Milestones

Life course scholars explore how lives unfold by examining factors that cause our current path to shift direction. Stability in one's life journey can be interrupted by age-graded life transitions (e.g. graduating college), physiological changes (e.g. andropause), or significant turning points such as transformations in self-awareness or involvement in new social roles. In terms of physiological changes, scholars have been most interested in fandom and puberty, specifically in adolescents' engagement with fan objects to help them interpret their changing bodies and emergent sense of self. Analytic focus in this literature is on the links between gender, sexuality, and fan identity in adolescence (e.g., Ehrenreich, Hess, and Jacobs 1992), with more recent research examining intersectional identities (age/gender/sexuality) explicitly in the context of adult fans (e.g. Scodari 2014).

Physiological changes associated with later life phases—such as changes in physical stamina, sexual arousal patterns, and physical appearance—are only now being explored in fan studies. For example, older music (punk) fans declare that they "paid their dues" in their youth and can now bypass certain aesthetic or performative aspects of fandom (day-glo Mohawks, mosh pits etc.) they adhered to when younger (Bennett 2006). Relatedly, older soap opera fans debate whether real-world issues associated with aging (erectile dysfunction, receding hairlines, perimenopausal hot flashes) can be entertainingly told in soap storylines (Harrington and Brothers 2010a), and 60-something Patti Smith fans question what it means to retain libidinal desire and sexual agency in late-life fandom (Lavin 2015).

If the impact of bodily aging on fan identities and practices remains underexamined, we know even less about the impact of cognitive aging. Brooker (2002) offers a fascinating discussion of how age shapes the *Star Wars* fandom by positioning fans in radically different interpretive communities. A fan's experiences of *Star Wars* are shaped by when she or he first encounters the narrative, given that the first episode, produced in 1977, was later positioned as the fourth installment of the franchise; as a result, older fans tend to "read" *Star Wars* differently than younger ones. However, Brooker's discussion does not capture the aspect of cognitive aging that most interests gerontologists and geriatricians: changes in functional capacity. Research on media engagement and cognition is located outside of media/fan studies (in neurology, epidemiology, biostatistics, etc.) and finds that some forms of media consumption may be cognitively damaging. For example, Fogel and Carlson (2006) report cognitive impairment among older adults who watch talk shows and soap operas. While a *contra* body of research suggests that greater engagement in media-related activities actually slows down cognitive decline (e.g. Ghisletta, Bickel, and Lovden 2006), the overall relationship between aging bodies, aging minds, and fan practices is ripe for research.

From both methodological and ethical perspectives, there can be challenges in studying older adults. Most of the nascent research on late(r)-life fandom includes participants who are members of "adult" (18–64 years) or "young–old" (65–74) age groups, to use categorizations typical within gerontology. Fan studies on the "middle-old" (75–84) or "old–old" (85+) seem largely nonexistent, even though humans continue to develop throughout the *entire* life course (George 2003). Older fans may be less likely than younger fans to be active online, posing challenges to scholars who prioritize networked fandom (see Sandvoss and Kearns 2014). Moreover, conducting interviews and/or focus groups with middle-old and old-old fans raises concerns given higher risks of fatigue, stress, and frailty (physical and cognitive) among these populations (Morgan and Kunkel 2016: 44). There has been interesting work in celebrity studies on the meanings of celebrities for nursing home residents (Claessens 2014), but within fan studies research on the oldest groups of fans calls for attention.

In addition to physiological changes, age-graded transitions and major life turning points also shape fandom. For example, reaching the legal age to drive opens up new possibilities for attending fan events, becoming a parent re-shapes the time one has to devote to fandom, and retirement from paid labor allows for new investments in personal interests (e.g. Davis 2012). For committed fans, discovering or losing their fan object is a major turning point that rewrites identities, daily activities, and life trajectories. Becoming-a-fan narratives are central to fan studies—attachments to Beyoncé or *Game of Thrones* or PewDiePie so deeply meaningful that fans feel reborn or rebooted. Long-term fandom provides structure to life narratives, as fans use specific cultural texts to segment their lives into different phases—"before" and "after" Harry Potter or Bruce Springsteen entered the picture (e.g. Brunner 2016; Cavicchi 1998). Becoming a fan thus redirects the life course, gives new meaning and structure to specific life stages, and marks periods of one's past: hallmarks of what gerontologists consider a major life milestone.

Issue II: The Aging Self

The second life course issue relevant to fandom involves the aging self. While there are continuities in the self from infancy to adulthood, the self changes in reasonably predictable ways due to developmentally related challenges and opportunities associated with each life phase. Long-term identity changes can emerge in the characteristics associated with an identity, a shift in the importance of one identity versus another (e.g. fan versus employee), or the gain or loss of an identity (Deaux 1991). Fan identities are also influenced by age norms, the larger sociocultural expectations of how we "should" behave (or be) at different life stages. In broader historical context, claiming a fan identity has shifted over time from the "loser" stereotype that marked twentieth-century fandom to the more widespread acceptance, public visibility, and industry cultivation of fandom today. However, the public understanding of fans remains predominantly associated with certain identity characteristics, such as youth, gender, and sexuality, while overlooking others. Rebecca Wanzo (2015) advocates for a new genealogy of fan studies that accounts for both fans and acafans of color, and our own scholarship obviously emphasizes the relevance of age, aging, and life course perspectives for a full understanding of fan experiences. Unlike many identities or group memberships, fan identities are always acquired and elective and thus can be abandoned at any point. As fan objects are picked up and discarded, the nature of fan identity—and thus our broader "overall" identities—shifts in important ways (e.g. Hills 2005).

Participating in fandom also aids adults in navigating disjunctures between chronological age (number of years lived) and subjective (or "felt") age. In general, younger adolescents feel older than their age, older adolescents feel younger than their age, and this disconnect intensifies across adulthood with adults feeling increasingly younger than what their chronological age signifies (Montepare 2009: 42). How older adults perceive themselves and how they are perceived by others is thus often mismatched. For example, in her study of women over 50 in the *Sherlock* (BBC) fandom, Petersen (2016) finds that subjective aging is negotiated in particular ways through social media and fan practices. Analysis of email interviews reveals that fandom shapes how women negotiate their subjective age specifically in relation to fandom as "youth culture" alongside cultural expectations of adult female passion and creativity. In short, older female fans engage in both self-legitimizing and self-othering practices in regard to different meanings of age in fandom.

The self also changes due to general processes of human development. While many developmental theories only address childhood and/or adolescence, adulthood and later life are strategic sites for self-examination amongst the challenges posed by the very process of getting old (George 1998: 139). Erikson's (1959) classic eight-stage model of maturation, with each stage including a distinct challenge that represents an opportunity for personal growth or failure, is potentially useful to fan scholars (albeit with the reminder that contemporary gerontologists reject rigid stage models of aging). For example, the challenge associated with early adulthood—intimacy versus isolation—is implicit in numerous fan studies that examine the emotional authenticity and/or social implications of adult fans' attachments to media objects (e.g. Bennett 2006; Cavicchi 1998; Stevenson 2006). See the large literature on parasociality in media psychology or early historical analyses of fandom that assumed fan attachments merely compensated for social isolation (e.g. Giles 2002; Horton and Wohl 1956). Here, the young adult fan "fails" the developmental challenge because emotional intimacy with cultural objects was long perceived by scholars as deluded.

In contrast, evidence of successful negotiation of the mid-adulthood challenge—generativity versus stagnation—is evidenced in the various mentoring practices of older fans. For example, see Harrington and Bielby (1995) on intergenerational soap opera viewing, Brooker (2002) on adult fan apprenticeship, and Smith (2012) on the familial transfer of subcultural capital in the British Northern Soul scene. Finally, evidence of the developmental challenge associated with late life—integrity versus despair—can be seen in the contemplative dimension of older adults' positioning of fandom in their life course (e.g. Harrington and Bielby 2010b). Here, fans' reflection of their fandom across time—and their own aging selves within fandom—results in a gradual repositioning of their place in various fan communities. For an example of how Erikson's model of adult maturation might be applied within fan studies, see our prior study of older soap opera fans (Harrington and Bielby 2010b).

Issue III: Changing Age Norms

The third relevant life course issue, noted earlier, involves age norms within fandom. Age norms—the benchmark against which we evaluate ourselves and are evaluated by others as behaving age appropriately or inappropriately—change over time and are influenced by the disjuncture between chronological and subjective age discussed above. Age norms change for us as individuals (what is appropriate at 15 is different at 45), they change historically (what is appropriate for a 15-year-old today is different than for a 15-year-old in 1960), and their overall impact changes over time (age norms are more powerful in some life phases than others). Age norms faced by individuals have received the most attention in fan studies. For example, adult pop music fans are regularly accused of being in "arrested development" (Bennett 2006; Vroomen 2004) and older soap opera fans routinely hide their fandom due to age considerations (what is acceptable for adults) as well as the genre (the low social value of soaps; Harrington and Bielby 1995). However, the twenty-first-century mainstreaming of fandom allows once-stigmatized communities to legitimize their practices in light of broader cultural trends. For example, adult toy collectors have developed concrete strategies to justify their interests, such as rhetorically disguising their interest in toys *as* toys (items to be played with) under the more socially acceptable guise of collecting (e.g. Heljakka 2017). In general, there continue to be disparities in how adult fans experience and express their fandom in public, due in part to age norms.

Age norms are also relevant in terms of late-life role models provided by aging celebrities and fictional characters (e.g. Lavin 2015), the use of older spokespersons to promote a healthy "senior" lifestyle (e.g. Marshall and Rahman 2015), and the growing interest in alternative and/or radical images of aging (e.g. Loos and Ekstrom 2014). Interestingly, as long-term fans make sense of aging through the models provided by aging celebrities, those celebrities must negotiate their own aging process simultaneously with their construction or embodiment of an aging cultural text (Harrington and Brothers 2010b). As such, media performances that might provide one kind of age-based role modeling for fans might generate very different outcomes for performers.

Issue IV: Changing Fan Objects

Finally, the fact that fan objects themselves change over time shapes fans' experiences with aging. Fan texts age as fans do—unpredictably. It is a complicated task, however, to assess the interactions between self-unfolding-across-time and fan-object-unfolding-across-time—and even when fan objects do *not* seem to transform with age (such as the seemingly static nature of movie dialogue or sporting event outcomes), their meaning is always different because the fan has changed. For example, Cavicchi (1998) examines the changing meanings of Springsteen songs across fans' life journeys and Kuhn (2002) explores how movie fans' selective memory of scenes and characters reflects who they were at earlier life stages. When fan objects *do* change with time, such as the re-imaginings of cult TV series like *Doctor Who* (BBC) or *American Horror Story* (FX), fans are forced to renegotiate their fan identity with each new iteration (Hills 2016).

In his examination of the social psychological basis of fandom, Sandvoss (2005) suggests that fan objects come to form "part of the self, and hence function as its extension" (100). Fans' relationship with cultural objects, in which fans "superimpose attributes of the self, their beliefs and value systems, and, ultimately, their sense of self on the object of fandom" (104), becomes more complicated over time. To borrow from Harrington and Brothers' study of soap opera actors and the aging process (2010b), it seems that fans' *existence* is gradually transformed into *texistence*—the self develops in ongoing dialogue with the media texts that help define and sustain it. This concept is comparable to that of "charactor" in celebrity studies which refers to the blending of actor and character over time. Our observations here point to a rich potential research trajectory for scholars focusing on how texts age from a life course perspective (life course analysis of a media text) or how aspects of human development might illuminate this duality of self-aging and text-aging.

Emergent Research on Aging, Fans, and Fandom

Interest in aging and fandom has expanded rapidly since the publication of our original essay (2010a) and in this section, we feature three emergent areas of research. First, scholars are increasingly interested in broad processes of change and adaptation in fan communities (e.g. Williams forthcoming). For example, Whiteman and Metivier (2013) explore zombie fan cultures, or online communities "that have entered into a state of atrophy, decline or impending demise" (270). Situating their analysis in prior work on post-object fandom (Williams 2011; see also Williams 2015), they examine how two fan sites (City of Angel and the Sugar Quill) "reached a state of exhaustion and/or degeneration" (290) and how fan responses to these endings reveal the formation of fan subjectivity online. Whereas Williams (2011) emphasizes how endings can generate efforts to stabilize and reaffirm fan engagement, Whiteman and Metivier (2013) are more interested in the permanent rupturing of fannish involvement.

In another approach to fan adaptation, Deller (2014) studies fans of two different British music acts to explore how they "respond to changes in technology, changes in the careers of the acts and changes in personal circumstances" (237). Revisiting communities she first studied a decade earlier, Deller examines how fan discourse, group norms, and relationship-building transforms over time and with age. Additional research on fan adaptation includes Davis (2012) on how punk fans adapt to the expectations of adulthood, Adams and Harmon (2014) on how aging fans of the Grateful Dead adapt how they participate in the community to allow continuity in their Deadhead identities, and Click (2017) on how Martha Stewart fans modified their identities following her incarceration for securities fraud.

A second promising research trajectory focuses on collective memory, which "defines the relationships between the individual and society and enables the community to preserve its self-image and transfer it over time" (Zandberg 2015: 111). Scholars of collective memory typically address societies at the macro-level but their principles apply equally to fan communities. For example, Kuhn's (2002) study of men and women growing up in the 1930s reveals the crucial role of memory at both the personal and group level in defining the existence of a film-going fandom. In contrast, Hills (2014) analyzes texts produced by *Doctor Who* fans and introduces the term "fanfac" to refer to "fans' factual writings on their own fan experiences, memories and communities" (32). Fanfac comes to circulate as an everyday element within the fandom, "acting to bind fans into a collectivity of recognizable experience" (37). Taking a different approach, our own project (Bielby and Harrington 2017) explores the production of collective memory within the *Glee* (Fox) fandom following the death of actor Cory Monteith. Situating our analysis in theories of grief, loss, and collective memory, we show how fans' efforts at commemoration played an important role in their adaptation to Monteith's death and to the creative choices made by the show's production team.

The final research trajectory we highlight encompasses new work on the concept of generations, first defined by Mannheim (1928 [1952]) as comprising both the category of persons born within a specific era of history as well as a shared world view (generational consciousness) distinct from that of other generations. Whereas our chronological and subjective ages shift over time, our generational belonging stays with us forever. Casual reference to media generations has been present in fan studies for decades but the concept has come under heightened scrutiny lately. For example, contemporary work on generational objects in fandom (e.g. Harrington and Bielby 2013; Hills 2016) has drawn on the influential writings of Christopher Bollas, and a recent book on millennial fandom (Stein 2015) examines the evolving relationship between fan and millennial. Acknowledging that the term "millennial" has grown to reference more than a generational group—it now also refers to "a vision of the ideal multiplatform cultural participant" (2015: 3)—author Louisa Stein explores millennial "feels culture" in terms of its competing discourses: millennial hope versus millennial noir.

Generation was also the focus of a recent issue of *Participations* (Volume 11, Number 2, 2014) that featured a special themed section aimed at "illustrating how the cultural concept of generations may help scholars in describing the contemporary audience fragmentation and in exploring the complex interrelations between audiences, technologies and cultural settings" (Siibak, Vittadini, and Nimrod 2014:102). In one of the featured articles, Napoli (2014) explores social media use and generational identity, asking (among other questions) whether social media impacts peer-to-peer and cross-generational relationships. Interested in how culture and media such as fan objects function to bind generations together, she finds that social media strengthens ties both across and within generations. In another featured article and in the context of TV fandom, Urresti (2014) explores the intergenerational status of television in four different age groups: 18–34 ("Youngs"), 35–49 ("Adult 1"), 50–64 ("Adult 2"), and 65+ ("Elders"). The project finds intriguing differences in how age groups approach television, with Youngs seeing it as something to "fill the void," the two Adult groups valuing it due to the rarity and value of free time, and Elders relating to TV "with a sense of wonder and amazement that cannot be found in other age groups" (2014: 142). This holds interesting implications for TV-fan relationships at different points in the life course and may refer to the developmental opportunities and challenges unique to each life stage (e.g. Erikson's model).

Conclusion

Our goal in this chapter has been to revisit and extend our earlier article on the value of a life course perspective for fan scholars. Given a rapidly aging global population and thus rapidly aging audiences/consumers across a range of entertainment landscapes, understanding how age and aging shape fandom is of vital importance. Through a particular focus on the age-related structure implicit in fan identities, practices, and interpretive capacities, we aim to highlight the rich developmental issues raised by participating in fandom. Our focus on adult fans reflects the fact that they remain under-theorized and under-studied by media scholars. A key element of the storying of fans' lives is the integration and revisiting of media texts with fans' own self-constructions over time such that those texts inform their aging process—both who they become as they grow older and how it is that they grow older. Media fans' life narratives might thus be said to comprise complex interactions between their "real" life (biography), their autobiography (storying of their life), and the media texts which help construct, give meaning to, and guide the relationship between the two—and that age along with them (Harrington and Bielby 2010a: 444).

The interplay between these elements may be experienced differently by long-term fans of a singular fan object than by cyclical fans, and differently based on genre of fan object. For example, one of the most compelling themes in research on long-term fans is the extent to which fan objects serve as touchstones or lifelines as fans age. From a life-course perspective, this emotional anchoring is crucial in an era characterized by the rapid dismantling of normative adult life, as has been observed by human development scholars in the suspension of traditional timetables for life transitions, the increasing lack of synchrony among age-related roles, and the growing absence of clear life scripts (Settersten 2007). As normative adult life destabilizes, fan objects increasingly provide a reference point for navigating the trajectory through adulthood and later life. Scholarship on age, aging, and fandom has thus never been more timely and relevant.

Acknowledgement

Some material in this chapter has been repurposed from a prior publication (Harrington and Bielby 2010a). We thank Sage Publications for their permission to do so.

References

Adams, R. G. and Harmon, J. T. (2014) "'The Long Strange Trip' Continues: Aging Deadheads," in C. L. Harrington, D. D. Bielby and A. R. Bardo (eds.), *Aging, Media, and Culture*, Lanham, MD: Lexington Books, pp. 107–119.

Bennett, A. (2006) "Punk's Not Dead: The Continuing Significance of Punk Rock for an Older Generation of Fans," *Sociology*, 40(2), pp. 219–235.

Bielby, D. D. and Harrington, C. L. (2017) "The Lives of Fandoms," in J. Gray, C. Sandvoss and C. L. Harrington (eds.), *Fandom: Identities and Communities in a Mediated World* (2nd edition), New York: New York University Press, pp. 205–221.

Brooker, W. (2002) *Using the Force: Creativity, Community and Star Wars Fans*, New York and London: Continuum.

Brunner, A. (2016) "The Harry Potter Generation: Growing Up and Growing Older with Harry Potter," presentation at symposium on Ageing Celebrities and Ageing Fans in Popular Media Culture, Copenhagen, Denmark.

Cavicchi, D. (1998) *Tramps like Us: Music and Meaning among Springsteen Fans*, New York and Oxford: Oxford University Press.

Claessens, N. (2014) "Social Meanings of Celebrities in the Everyday Lives of Nursing Home Residents: An Exploratory Study," in C. L. Harrington, D. D. Bielby and A. R. Bardo (eds.), *Aging, Media and Culture*, Lanham, MD: Lexington Books, pp. 77–90.

Click, M. A. (2017) "Do All 'Good Things' Come to an End? Revisiting Martha Stewart Fans After ImClone," in J. Gray, C. Sandvoss and C. L. Harrington (eds.), *Fandom: Identities and Communities in a Mediated World* (2nd edition), New York: New York University Press, pp. 191–204.

Cohler, B. J. and Hostetler, A. (2003) "Linking Life Course and Life Story: Social Change and the Narrative Study of Lives over Time," in J. T. Mortimer and M. J. Shanahan (eds.), *Handbook of the Life Course*, New York: Kluwer Academic/Plenum Publishers, pp. 555–576.

Davis, J. R. (2012) "Punk, Ageing and the Expectations of Adult Life," in A. Bennett and P. Hodkinson (eds.), *Ageing and Youth Cultures: Music, Style and Identity*, London and New York: Berg, pp. 105–118.

Deaux, K. (1991) "Social Identities: Thoughts on Structure and Change," in R. C. Curtis (ed.), *The Relational Self: Theoretical Convergences in Psychoanalysis and Social Psychology*, New York: Guildford Press, pp. 77–93.

Deller, R. A. (2014) "A Decade in the Life of Online Fan Communities," in K. Zwan, L. Duits and S. Reijnders (eds.), *Ashgate Research Companion to Fan Cultures*, Surrey, England: Ashgate Publishing, pp. 23–34.

Ehrenreich, B., Hess, E., and Jacobs, G. (1992) "Beatlemania: Girls Just Want to Have Fun," in L. A. Lewis (ed.) *The Adoring Audience: Fan Culture and Popular Media*, New York: Routledge, pp. 84–106.

Erikson, E. H. (1959) *Identity and the Life Cycle: Selected Papers*. New York: International Universities Press.

Fogel, J. and Carlson, M. C. (2006) "Soap Operas and Talk Shows on Television are Associated with Poorer Cognition in Older Women," *Southern Medical Journal*, 99(3), pp. 226–233.

Fry, C. L. (2003) "The Life Course as a Cultural Construct," in R. A. Settersten, Jr. (ed.) *Invitation to the Life Course: Toward New Understandings of Later Life*, Amityville, New York: Baywood Publishing, pp. 269–294.

George, L. (1998) "Self and Identity in Later Life: Protecting and Enhancing the Self," *Journal of Aging and Identity*, 3(3), pp. 133–152.

George, L. (2003) "Life Course Research: Achievements and Potential," in J. T. Mortimer and M. J. Shanahan (eds.) *Handbook of the Life Course*, New York: Kluwer Academic/Plenum Publishers, pp. 671–680.

Ghisletta, P., Bickel, J-F., and Lovden, M. (2006) "Does Activity Engagement Protect against Cognitive Decline in Old Age? Methodological and Analytical Considerations," *Journal of Gerontology: Psychological Sciences*, 61B(5), pp. 253–261.

Giles, D. C. (2002) "Parasocial Interaction: A Review of the Literature and a Model for Future Research," *Media Psychology*, 4, pp. 279–302.

Harrington, C. L. and Bielby, D. D. (1995) *Soap Fans: Pursuing Pleasure and Making Meaning in Everyday Life*, Philadelphia, PA: Temple University Press.

Harrington, C. L. and Bielby, D. D. (2010a) "A Life Course Perspective on Fandom," *International Journal of Cultural Studies*, 13(5), pp. 1–22.

Harrington, C. L. and Bielby, D. D. (2010b) "Autobiographical Reasoning in Long-Term Fandom," *Transformative Works and Cultures*, 5, published online.

Harrington, C. L. and Bielby, D. D. (2013) "Pleasure and Adult Development: Extending Winnicott into Late(r) Life," in Annette Kuhn (ed.), *Little Madnesses: Winnicott, Transitional Phenomena and Cultural Experience*, London and New York: I.B. Tauris, pp. 87–101.

Harrington, C. L. and Brothers, D. (2010a) "Constructing the Older Audience: Age and Aging on Soaps," in A. De Kosnik, S. Ford and C. L. Harrington (eds.), *The Survival of Soap Operas: Strategies for a New Media Era*, Jackson, MS: University Press of Mississippi, pp. 300–314.

Harrington, C. L. and Brothers, D. (2010b) "A Life Course Built for Two: Acting, Aging and Soap Operas," *Journal of Aging Studies*, 24, pp. 20–29.

Heljakki, K. (2017) "Toy Fandom, Adulthood, and the Ludic Age: Creative Material Culture and Play," in J. Gray, C. Sandvoss and C. L. Harrington (eds.), *Fandom: Identities and Communities in a Mediated World* (2nd edition), New York: New York University Press, pp. 91–105.

Hills, M. (2005) "Patterns of Surprise: The 'Aleatory Object' in Psychoanalytic Ethnography and Cyclical Fandom," *American Behavior Scientist*, 48(7), pp. 801–821.

Hills, M. (2014) "Returning to 'Becoming-a-Fan' Stories: Theorising Transformational Objects and the Emergence/Extension of Fandom," in L. Duits, K. Zwaan, and S. Rejnders (eds.), *The Ashgate Research Companion to Fan Cultures*, Farnham, England: Ashgate, pp. 9–21.

Hills, M. (2016) "Cult Revivals from *Doctor Who* (2005) to *The X-Files* (2016): The 'Generational Consciousness' of Ageing alongside Fan Objects," presentation at symposium on Ageing Celebrities and Ageing Fans in Popular Media Culture, Copenhagen, Denmark.

Horton, D. and Wohl, R. R. (1956) "Mass Communication and Para-social Interaction: Observations on Intimacy at a Distance," *Psychiatry*, 19, pp. 215–229.

Kuhn, A. (2002) *An Everyday Magic: Cinema and Cultural Memory*, London and New York: I.B. Tauris Publishers.

Lavin, M. (2015) "Aging, Fandom, and Libido," *Transformative Works and Cultures*, 20, published online.

Loos, E. and Ekstrom, M. (2014) "Visually Representing the Generation of Older Consumers as a Diverse Audience: Towards a Multidimensional Market Segment Typology," *Participations*, 11(2), pp. 258–273.

Mannheim, K. (1928 [1952]) "The Problem of Generations," in K. Mannheim, *Essays in the Sociology of Knowledge*, London: Routledge & Keegan Paul, pp. 276–320.

Marshall, B. L. and Rahman, M. (2015) "Celebrity, Ageing and the Construction of 'Third Age' Identities," *International Journal of Cultural Studies*, 18(6), pp. 577–593.

Mazur, K. (2015) "Millennials and Boomers Love Experiences, But Who Attends More Concerts?" *Billboard*, August 24, www.billboard.com/articles/business/6671232/millennials-and-boomers-love-experiences-but-who-attends-more-concerts.

Montepare, J. M. (2009) "Subjective Age: Toward a Guiding Lifespan Framework," *International Journal of Behavioral Development*, 33(1), pp. 42–46.

Morgan, L. A. and Kunkel, S. R. (2016) *Aging, Society, and the Life Course* (5th edition), New York: Springer.

Napoli, A. (2014) "Social Media Use and Generational Identity: Issues and Consequences on Peer-to-Peer and Cross-Generational Relationships—An Empirical Study," *Participations*, 11(2), pp. 182–206.

Nielsen. (2013) "Popcorn People: Profiles of the U.S. Moviegoer Audience," January 29, www.nielsen.com/us/en/insights/news/2013/popcorn-people-profiles-of-the-u-s-moviegoer-audience.html.

Petersen, L. N. (2016) "'The Florals': Fans over Fifty in the *Sherlock* Fandom," presentation at Ageing Celebrities and Ageing Fans, Copenhagen, Denmark.

Sandvoss, C. (2005) *Fans: The Mirror of Consumption*, Cambridge: Polity Press.

Sandvoss, C. and Kearns, L. (2014) "From Interpretive Communities to Interpretive Fairs: Ordinary Fandom, Textual Selection and Digital Media," in L. Duits, K. Zwaan, and S. Reijnders (eds.), *The Ashgate Research Companion to Fan Cultures*, Surrey, England: Ashgate, pp. 91–106.

Scodari, C. (2014) "Breaking Dusk: Fandom, Gender/Age Intersectionality, and the 'Twilight Moms'," in C. L. Harrington, D. D. Bielby and A. R. Bardo (eds.), *Aging, Media, and Culture*, Lanham, MD: Lexington Books, pp. 143–154.

Settersten, R. A. (2007) "The New Landscape of Adult Life: Road Maps, Signposts, and Speed Lines," *Research in Human Development*, 4(3–4), pp. 239–252.

Smith, N. (2012) "Parenthood and the Transfer of Capital in the Northern Soul Scene," in A. Bennett and P. Hodkinson (eds.), *Ageing and Youth Cultures: Music, Style and Identity*, London and New York: Berg, pp. 159–172.

Stein, L. E. (2015) *Millennial Fandom: Television Audiences in the Transmedia Age*. Iowa City, IA: University of Iowa Press.

Sternberg, S. (2015) "Will All TV Median Ages Soon Be Over 50?" *MediaDailyNews*, April 30, www.mediapost.com/publications/article/248728/will-all-TV-median-ages-soon-be0over-50.html.

Stevenson, N. (2009) "Talking to Bowie Fans: Masculinity, Ambivalence and Cultural Citizenship," *European Journal of Cultural Studies*, 12(1), pp. 79–98.

Tedeschi, B. (2006) "Older Consumers Flex Their Muscle (and Money) Online," *New York Times*, June 12, www.nytimes.com/2006/06/12/technology/12ecom.html.

Urresti, X. L. (2014) "Television as an Intergenerational Leisure Artefact: An Interdisciplinary Dialogue," *Participations*, 11(2), pp. 132–155.

Vroomen, L. (2004) "Kate Bush: Teen Pop and Older Female Fans," in A. Bennett and R. A. Peterson (eds.), *Music Scenes: Local, Translocal, and Virtual*, Nashville, TN: Vanderbilt University Press, pp. 238–253.

Wanzo, R. (2015) "African American Acafandom and Other Strangers: New Genealogies of Fan Studies," *Transformative Works and Cultures*, 20 (online journal).

Whiteman, N. and Metivier, J. (2013) "From Post-Object to 'Zombie' Fandoms: The 'Deaths' of Online Fan Communities and What They Say about Us," *Participations*, 10(1), pp. 270–298.

Williams, R. (2011) "'This Is the Night TV Died': Television Post-Object Fandom and the Demise of *The West Wing*," *Popular Communication*, 9(4), pp. 266–279.

Williams, R. (2015) *Post-Object Fandom: Television, Identity, and Self-Narrative*, London: Bloomsbury.

Williams, R. (ed.) (Forthcoming) *Transitions, Endings, and Resurrections in Fandom*, Iowa City, IA: University of Iowa Press.

Zandberg, E. (2015) "'Ketchup is the Auschwitz of Tomatoes': Humor and the Collective Memory of Traumatic Events," *Communication, Culture & Critique*, 8(1), pp. 108–123.

30
SOUNDING QUEER FANDOM
Podfic and Nonbinary Theory

Olivia Johnston Riley

Introduction

Fan studies has spilled a great deal of ink on gender and sexuality, but almost exclusively from a limited, binary, cisnormative perspective. The field must come to terms with its structural repression of non-feminine genders and all the nonbinary and trans queer potential discarded with this choice. Renewed attention to gender/sexuality can revivify the concept of "queer fandom," an academic idea which has at times taken too narrow a view, with only limited forms of queerness qualifying, and at others taken too broad a reach, disconnecting the concept from the politically grounded stakes of queer people's lives. Queer fandom in regard to trans and nonbinary fans, texts, and practices remains deeply understudied and therefore holds great promise (Duggan and Fazekas 2023). For instance, this chapter will explore the gendered potentialities produced by podfic (fanfiction read aloud, recorded, and shared online), an understudied community whose structures of performance and reception encourage trans and nonbinary possibility. I place the terms "trans and nonbinary" in a phrase to encourage recognition of their overlap, as "trans" can potentially encompass any experience outside the assigned-at-birth cisgender binary, including nonbinary identity. "Nonbinary" as an identity position can involve expanding existing binary male/female gender categories into a more diverse spectrum inhabited fluidly and plurally, creating a third category or space of gender, or rejecting gender altogether (Monro 2019). The use of both terms in sync and individually gestures to their shared political commitments and exclusions from queer thought and theory, while still maintaining space for specifically "trans" and "nonbinary" experiences.

I take up recent calls from Duggan (2022) and Leetal (2022) to interrogate the absence of trans and nonbinary gender from the field of fan studies, examining not just the harm caused by ignoring these voices but the consequences of basing fan studies' central theoretical tenets on their absence. Trying to recoup women's fannish contributions, communities, and creative practices against a patriarchal backdrop has entrenched a cisnormative binary that pins many of fandom's political achievements on the assumption that its participants are – and must be, for these arguments to stand – women. This obscures the marginalization of gender minorities in fandom, making this a pressing issue of harm reduction as the assertion of female/feminine status injures nonbinary, gender queer, and trans men fans who should not have yet another layer of misgendering violence pressed upon them by academics. Disrupting this assumption allows us to interrogate other static conclusions, begin untangling fan studies' complicity in various marginalizations, and reimagine what contributions a more equitably queer fan studies can offer. This chapter first summarizes the existing queer and trans fan studies literature, then explores queer genders in fandom, addressing how nonbinary queerness requires theoretical shifts in binary frameworks like transformative/affirmative fandom. It concludes with a case study of podfic to illustrate how nonbinary fan studies can produce new, critical, queer insights by exploring how these marginalized sonic performances playfully eschew stable gender categories and thereby queerly extend fans' imaginative, identificatory horizons.

Literature Review

Early fan studies focused almost entirely on female fans and their fiction (Click and Scott 2018) and to this day gender is the single most studied axis of fan identity (Pande 2018), though predominantly in the context of a fairly rigid gender binary (Duggan and Fazekas 2023). As early as 1983, Janice Radway's study of women readers of romance (a text often understood as a precursor to official fan studies) positioned women as marginalized, tactically resisting patriarchy through the use of media as a space for self-care and private rebellion. Russ' (2014 [1985]) study of Kirk/Spock originary slash fic described the practice as "pornography written 100% by women for a 100% female readership" (85), Bacon-Smith (1992) lovingly mythologizes the "ladies" of fandom, and Penley (1992) positions fandom as "almost completely female and heterosexual" (483). Contemporary fan studies has cohered around the "fan" as a white, middle-class, US American woman (Lothian, Busse, and Reid 2007) who engages in transformative fanworks, where both the participant and her practices are gendered female.

There are obvious feminist benefits to this focus as, for example, it allows scholars to claim that fanfiction is a liberatory practice that's part of "an open archive of women's culture" (De Kosnik 2015: 123). Fan studies has often assumed that the feminine character of its normative subject assured a marginalized position, especially when combined with the stigma historically attached to fans (Jenkins 2012 [1992]). Coppa (2014), for instance, argues that fanfiction's association with women and embodiment are at the root of the medium's cultural denigration. Yet, the aggressive policing of the femininity of the fan studies fan in the name of progressive alignment with women as marginalized subjects harms the field's critical potential. For example, Bury's (2005) virtual ethnography explicitly occluded lesbian and non-female participants, speaking as if the fans under observation were all straight (occasionally bisexual) women despite sharing survey results that demonstrated otherwise, positioning non-women as "exceptions" to the rule rather than evidence of its untenability. Further, this claim of fan subversiveness has motivated fan studies to keep quiet on its own inequalities – such as structural whiteness – as this would make it harder to claim marginal or progressive status (Stanfill 2019).

Despite this non-intersectional gender myopia, fan studies claims queer theory as a foundational tenet, such as in Henry Jenkins' (2012 [1992]) landmark study of slash practices. The female gendering of the fan intersects with an odd bifurcation in the study of queerness and fandom: that of fandom itself as queer/ing, such as the queer literary practice of slash, and fans themselves as queer. In regard to the former, Lothian, Busse, and Reid (2007) proposed the "queer female space" of online slash fandom. These authors built on queer theory to disrupt the one-to-one relationship of fan identity and the queerness of their practice, and posit "slasher" as contingent fan sexual identity. The work celebrates the queer potential in (mostly though not exclusively) straight women writing about queer male sexual encounters, but doesn't assert that fandom is therefore inherently transgressive or immune to problems like reinforcing homonormativity. Busse and Lothian reflected on this work in 2017 to describe how slash studies has since opened up from the early "straight women writing gay men" model to one more cognizant of queer lives and representation, with space for more diverse queer genders and sexualities.

Contemporary queer fan studies attends to queer fans as well as queer fan practices. Due to the lingering assumption of womanhood and presumed absence of gay men, studying fans who are queer has led to femslash (e.g., stories about and usually written by queer women), a practice neglected both by broader fandom and fan scholars. Russo (2017) argues that although fan studies has felt pressure to temper investment in fandom-as-queer because of corporate exploitation, queer women and their works are still not a major commercial market, and therefore queer women doing femslash *is* a meaningful queer intervention in pop culture discourse. She also argues that scholars shouldn't use a scarcity framework to study these fan interventions, even though current fandom stats indicate femslash still lags far behind slash in sheer quantity of content. Fan studies is complicit in the lack of attention to queer women's fanworks because this sexist homophobia is shielded by the valorization of fandom *itself* as queer practice. This perspective allows scholars and fans to erase the work of queer women (see again Bury's buried lesbians) in pursuit of claiming the political capital of queer subversion for what scholars historically argued were primarily straight ciswomen. Yet, this critique also requires nuancing, as it doesn't question the underlying assumption that fandom is almost exclusively populated by women (queer or no) and fan practices are therefore inherently feminine. Centering neglected trans and nonbinary perspectives can help uncover lost lesbian and bisexual fandom as well as other marginalized queer genders and orientations by leading us out of the cis-quagmire of binary frameworks.

Many of fan studies' key questions (such as the infamous "why do straight women want to read and write about gay male sex?") and assumptions (fans are subversive because they're women marginalized in a patriarchal society) are only sensible from a hegemonic sex and gender position that assumes fans have a stable, binary identity which also maps neatly onto their preferences for fiction. One mode of disrupting this hegemonic perspective is to focus not just on the "sexually queer" but on trans and nonbinary genders (Duggan 2022: 706). Duggan (2023) provides an excellent literature review on the state of trans fan studies, beginning with scholarly investigations of the (trans)gendered implications of fanfic genres like genderswap/genderfuck and omegaverse and mpreg, noting how they can both reinforce stereotypes and essentialist biological narratives and also provide a reparative imaginary space. Fandom is important for queer youth exploring their identities, especially trans and nonbinary fans, who can begin to address a dearth of media representation through their online fan communities (Duggan 2023) and collectively add to cultural archives of transmasculinity (Rose 2020). As with femslash, transfic has been hailed as "a compelling form of fan activism" (Beazley 2014: 57). And as slash fanfic can allow straight readers to experience a queer affect, transfic can develop a trans affect for cis people as "transing" becomes an intersecting corollary to "queering" media (Duggan 2023).

Nonbinary identity experiences an even greater lack of study than binary trans identity. Even well-intentioned queer scholarship and activism often exacerbate the problem by subsuming trans, gender-nonconforming, and other nonbinary experiences under a broader umbrella of generic "LGBT" issues, where the documented problem of ignoring transgender narratives renders nonbinary stories "doubly silent" (Fiani and Han 2019: 181). In fan studies specifically, Leetal's (2022) literature review of nonbinary fan studies wonders at the scope of contributions from nonbinary and trans fans and scholars that have been ignored and lost. Even Willis' (2016) landmark piece on trans-ing gender and fanfiction exclusively discusses slash written by "women" and about "men," although she goes on to complicate these categories and makes it clear this is a choice of scope not intended to erase the existence of male and nonbinary slashers. Thus, even trans fan studies has neglected to reckon with nonbinary gender and how centering nonbinary gender drastically changes the foundational set-up of major fan studies concepts.

Theorizing Queer Gender in Fandom

The cisnormative foundations of fan studies prevent us from reckoning with the most obviously queer aspect of fandom: gender. Creative fan desire produces a delicious confusion of genders, which has not gone unnoticed but instead been anxiously investigated and labeled, from Joanna Russ' fear of being seen as "lesbian" (2014 [1985]: 95), to Lothian, Busse, and Reid's (2007) slasher as sexuality, to Russo's (2017) reality-and-fiction-matched queer woman identities. Yet, these approaches all name this palimpsest of gendered affect *as* sexuality, rather than centering the queering of gender itself. Leetal (2022) posits that the precise natures of these fan sexualities are impossible to pin down in the binary because the women in question aren't only/always/entirely women and the men are only sometimes/partially/uneasily men. Fan experiences require a nonbinary lens because of the overlapping multiplicity of genders present in the form of (at least) 1) the fanwork creator, 2) the characters, and 3) the fanwork audience. Fans and fanworks aren't just being "read" as nonbinary, they *are* nonbinary, as in, they have multiple genders and are producing nonbinary effects in the fan space such as disrupting stable notions of binary gender and attraction.

Nonbinary fan genders and sexualities open up a new mode of queer fandom that doesn't rely on first nailing down a binary gender position from which to locate possible "same-sex" attractions in order to qualify such people or practices as queer. Nor does it flatten and de-politicize real-world experiences of queerness, as some arguments about slash run the risk of centering straight women fans as themselves marginalized and queer, despite such a position bearing virtually none of the brunt of actual queer marginalization. Nonbinary and trans approaches can guide us towards the "infinite potential" of queer fandom suggested by scholars such as Lothian, Busse, and Reid (2007), opening up queer possibilities in the politically valuable sense of rejecting normative orientations towards the self, others, and media objects, not just in the problematically de facto queerness sometimes assigned to transformative practices. In other words, nonbinary theory can help us avoid the pitfalls of abandoning marginalized queer experiences without expanding the queer umbrella so wide that "anything" becomes queer, thus evacuating the term of meaning.

Nonbinary and trans perspectives are not new to fandom or fan scholarship, as "transing has always been an integral part of fanfiction, which has long hinged on subverting and playing with gender expressions and embodiments" (Duggan 2023: 1.4). Leetal's (2022) investigation of nonbinary gender in fanfiction uncovers the trans and nonbinary possibilities contained within landmark early fan texts like Bacon-Smith's *Enterprising Women* (1992) and argues this potential has been "continually disregarded." This is a particularly apt phrasing that gestures to how fan studies as a field has had to repeatedly, in each new article and book and wave of theory, shunt aside the nonbinary and trans data that demonstrably exists in the margins of so many canonical fan studies texts when it does not support the field's dominant cisgender version of feminism and/or queerness. Regarding this ignored data, older scholarship that precedes the modern wave of "fandom is queer" writing contains the seeds for a variety of interesting projects about how fans and scholars may have imagined fannish gender-play in nonbinary and trans ways, sometimes precisely due to their somewhat limiting and limited language. For instance, early gender-swap scholarship initially only makes sense within a hegemonic cisgender framework, where "women" and "men" are categories self-contained enough to allow for a "swap." Yet, scholarship that clumsily asked questions like "what does it mean for real women to write fictional men as imaginary stand-ins for women?" contains clear gender-fluid possibility, even as the answer it fumbles for remains out of reach within an ideology that understands only binary gender.

Invoking a nonbinary framework draws to the fore the entrenched binaries which animate so much of fan studies, including straight/gay, creator/audience, authentic/performative, and especially affirmative/transformative as aligned with male/female. "Affirmative" and "transformative" may sometimes be useful markers; for example, Scott (2019) acknowledges the terms' arbitrary natures but explains that they can still usefully explain feminist and industrial logics at play in fandom in her discussion of gender. However, the longer these terms remain in use, they more they sediment binary and essentialist meanings rather than encourage analysis. Wanzo's (2015) landmark analysis of race and fan studies lays the groundwork for this argument, as she describes how fan studies' valorization of non-commerciality structurally disregards the political significance of many popular modes of Black fandom, such as financial support of marginalized creators. Because such fans and fan practices don't fit the (binary) model, they're not included in fan studies' purview, and thus the limited model remains unchallenged.

We must therefore interrogate what assumptions and imaginaries of power are engrained in the use of this binary. What forms of resistance and harm have been obscured by this terminology? For example, Pande (2018) critiques the "transformative" racism of the Star Wars Kylux fandom, which re-wrote the canon text in order to marginalize the franchise's lead characters of color and center secondary white male characters. Calling works "transformative" with the assumption that this equates to "critical" has at times acted as a cover for the re-entrenchment of harmful ideologies in fandom (Johnson 2019). Concurrently, how has "affirmative" been wielded against marginalized fans, painting them with the same brush as the corporate dupes that scholars like Jenkins worked so hard to differentiate from "transformative" fans? For example, *The Flash* fandom group the Iris West Defense Squad "affirms" this Black female lead character's canonical centrality in the face of mainstream and fandom racism that seeks to sideline her, including through transformative works that pair her canonical white male love interest with other white, often male characters (Warner 2017). The Squad's efforts are not read as "subversive" through the traditional binary lens of fan studies, yet they are contributing meaningfully to anti-racist discourse. These examples demonstrate the limits of working within binaries, especially for the stakes of scholarly arguments.

Nonbinary Performance in Podfic

The categoric reliance on transformative fandom has eclipsed the value of "affirmative" queer, disabled, and/or anti-racist fan practices. However, the solution is not to dive from one pigeonhole to the other and "re-affirm" affirmation, but to reckon with whether these terms are still useful. The practices that "affirmative" and "transformative" indicate cannot be meaningfully separated from each other, as to affirm can be to transform and vice versa, an apparent paradox demonstrated by this chapter's case study of podfic. Podfic is notably a transformative work: it transforms a textual piece of fanfic into a vocal recording, adding new emotional layers through performance and sharing the text with a new audience. Yet, it's also indelibly affirmative: podfic "affirms" the queerness of fanfic in its affectively charged remediation of the text as podfic performers and listeners affirm their love of the original fanwork through re-making and re-living it. This transformative affirmation is not intelligible within the binary. Instead, podfic urges scholars to develop a nonbinary approach.

Podfic is a space where identity and performance blur in accidental and conscious, serious and playful, subversive and problematic ways. There are gender and sexual identities at work but also fan and creator identities, as podfic performers layer speaker/author/poacher and other positionalities through their vocality. Podfic is structurally queer, as the sheer multiplicity of positionalities precludes straight, normative relationships of desire, in addition to each of these layers individually containing the potential for queerness of identity and content (Riley 2020). Podfic frustrates binaries and necessitates complex engagements with fans' queer positionalities, especially trans, nonbinary, and genderqueer identities and orientations towards fandom. Of course, there is no single podfic community but rather an evolving mosaic of overlapping archives, Discord servers, Twitter threads, IRL convention groups, and more. When I use the term "podfic" or "podfic community" here, I'm using it as a shorthand to indicate the podfics and podficcers I've been able to study, which are primarily stories and users drawn from the major fan repository Archive of Our Own (AO3) and particularly a set of 25 podfic fan interviewees (Riley 2024). I located these participants via a digital call distributed on Twitter and in a popular podfic Discord server, and interviewed them over Zoom in 2020 about their experiences first with podfic broadly, and then about podfic, disability, accessibility, and identity. The participants were diverse in age, gender, and nationality, and interpersonally connected through a loosely bounded digital community. My research found that podfic adds to the already queer potential of fanfic and provides an opportunity to deepen the relationship between these queer experiences and the queer/ed physical body through vocal performance, disrupting staid binary norms through embracing the unknowability of digitally mediated genders. Nonbinary frameworks developed through this study can allow scholars to better capture the diversely queer realities of fandom and reckon with the times fandom replicates mainstream oppressions.

Fandom can provide a creative alternate route of exploring gender that does not necessarily offer "finished" identities but rather a space for fans to make, explore, and try on different gender performances in playful, low-stakes environs through writing, reading, drawing, vocal performance, cosplay, and more. Podfic, like drag, illuminates a spectrum of performance in such fan expressions of gender. Some participants focus most on the creative aspect: many podficcers see their craft as a creative outlet similar to theater or stand-up, but find the fandom space safer and more accepting of non-normative identity and of amateurism than more public, professionalized performance spaces. Other participants explicitly use podfic to experiment with their gender identity: they use the performance of characters to feel out alternate modes of gender expression and explore the gendered dimensions of the voice (Zimman 2018). Leetal (2022) draws on Judith Butler's classic gender theory to suggest that fans' repeated gender performances through fanfiction communities and archives – that is, "doing gender" in a supportive social setting that allows for gender codes outside the norm to seed and develop – allow for nonbinary possibilities. Podfic fandom specifically allows for an embodied and consciously performative exploration of gender that fans can build away from the binary, increasingly referencing their own fan-community-created gender imaginaries instead of normative ones.

The performative freedom of podfic extends our gendered possibilities as the soundscape allows us to reimagine the affordances of our lived gender worlds, particularly in trans and nonbinary directions. Fanfiction also allows fans to explore non-cis lives and bodies as "something both normal and desirable" (Duggan 2022: 11); podfic provides the added opportunity to actually perform those genders in/on/though the body. Cosplay studies have begun the work of studying such embodied fan genders (Lamerichs 2011), and podfic research will complement that field by focusing on more digital, private, and vocal performances. My interviewees frequently commented that they enjoy podfic because it offers a space of performance that is safely online and home-based, allowing them creative, queer freedom without risking bodily safety or demanding they navigate often inaccessible physical convention or theatrical environments. Further, the profusion of layered genders at play in podfic spaces offers particular interest for nonbinary fans. Leetal describes narrating podfic as "one of the very few times I felt gender euphoria" (2022: 4.6); "[a]s I tasted for nonbinary gender in my characters' words, in my throat and on my lips, people who make podfic of my stories may echo, taste, shift, or reinvent them" (2022: 4.12).

The structurally nonbinary inclinations of podfic can help spur a nonbinary theoretical framework which rejects unhelpful questions of category, such as whether or not fan performances of gender in podfic are "real/authentic" or "just fun/play/pretend." For instance, podfic has structurally developed a mode of performance that rejects the division between authenticity and playfulness. This is most noticeable in how podfic differs from professional audiobooks, which often seek mimicry as they cast performers whose gender and accent match the lead character of the book they'll be reading. Podficcers cannot and do not consistently "match" their characters' canonical identities, and as such, the art form has developed different, queerer standards of value more to do with evoking "feels" (e.g., producing a positive affective state in the listener through the emotional skill of the performance) than with canonical fidelity. Therefore, podfic as a community medium rejects normative definitions of "realness" when it comes to performance, instead taking a nonbinary approach where reality and play are inseparable and gender need not be normatively legible.

Gender in podfic is often unknowable, as the performer and original fic author's genders may remain a mystery even to those motivated to seek out their profile and search for pronouns or other identity clues. The audience's genders are equally obscure, and the genders of the characters being performed are multifaceted due to the well-studied layering of intentionality and interpretation. Gender is therefore inherently indeterminate even in the case of a single podfic, much less when approaching a broader podfic community, archive, or fandom. We as listeners cannot know these genders, therefore, we as scholars must theorize from a place of not-knowing. This approach frees us from standard fan studies binaries and assumptions to instead ask new questions and make new claims. As the preceding section demonstrated, setting aside the gendered implications of the transformative/affirmative binary reveals novel approaches to creation, subversion, and normativity. In the vocal realm of podfic, scholars can much better capture an imprint of reality when we don't start from the mistaken assertion that fans are women and the characters they play with are men, and instead are open to the diverse gender work actually being done.

A nonbinary approach can allow us to explore structurally neglected queer possibilities, such as the affirmation of trans identities through vocal performance of the same, the transformation of normative masculinity through non-male readers' performance of such, and the invisibilized participation of asexual and aromantic fans. Regarding this last example, several of my interviewees noted joy at the increasing popularity of A-spec (on the spectrum of asexual and aromantic identity) works in general and podfic in particular as a space to explore such experiences which are often marginalized both by dominant and queer cultures. A nonbinary gender lens allows us to recognize these especially marginalized asexual fans as queer without framing them in terms of explicit sexual attraction. The queerness of nonbinary gender isn't limited to a set of non-straight allosexual orientations, but instead involves a political and tactical use of "queer" to indicate non-normative and politically marginalized relationships to dominant sexual norms – including an absence of sexual attraction.

In addition to increasing inclusivity, nonbinary frameworks can help make fan studies more equitable by holding it accountable for its role in ongoing marginalizations. For example, Leetal (2022) points out how nonbinary fans have been left out of scholarly and fan queer arrangements of sexual orientation, refusing room for nonbinary people to desire or be desired, a lacuna which nonbinary theory addresses directly. Such theory can similarly help address homophobia and gender essentialism in fandom. One of my interviewees noted occasional "gender BS" in the way some podficcers performing slash would give one character, perceived as the more "masculine" of the pair, a deeper voice and give the other character, consequently labeled more "feminine," a higher voice, regardless of the pitch of those characters' canonical voices. This spotlights an ongoing problem wherein some fans interpret queer pairings according to heteronormative standards and then impress those standards on their fannish creations. These problematic assumptions are dramatized and indelibly encoded in podfic performance, and can be rendered particularly noticeable in relief against a nonbinary theoretical framework. Such a framework frees scholars from binary arguments about whether fandom "is" subversive or oppressive and instead allows us to explore the inseparable mechanisms of both.

Conclusion

Binary thought has structured much of fandom scholarship, from a persistent focus on women fans to the splitting of fandom as either transformative or affirmative along gendered lines. Bringing a trans and nonbinary framework to fan studies can help disrupt these problematic assumptions by spotlighting and re-valuing sidelined non-feminine and queer fans. Podfic fandom particularly renders audible gaps and contradictions in binary fan studies concepts through indelibly nonbinary performances which center neglected queer genders and reject binaries such as authentic/performative in favor of queer play with vocal identity. Future fan studies should continue experimenting with trans and nonbinary frameworks to explore fan identity, theory, and practice beyond the binary.

References

Bacon-Smith, C. (1992) *Enterprising Women: Television Fandom and the Creation of Popular Myth*, Philadelphia: University of Pennsylvania Press.

Beazley, M. (2014) "'Out of the Cupboards and Into the Streets!' Harry Potter Genderfuck Fan Fiction and Fan Activism," MA Thesis at Concordia.

Bury, R. (2005) *Cyberspaces of Their Own: Female Fandoms Online*, Peter Lang.

Busse, K. and A. Lothian. (2017) "A history of slash sexualities," in C. Smith, F. Attwood, and B. McNair (eds) *The Routledge Companion to Media, Sex, and Sexuality*, New York: Routledge.

Click, M. A. and S. Scott. (2018) "Introduction," in M. A. Click and S. Scott (eds) *Routledge Companion to Media Fandom*, London: Routledge, pp. 1–6.

Coppa, F. (2014) "Writing Bodies in Space Media Fan Fiction as Theatrical Performance," in K. Hellekson and K. Busse (eds) *The Fan Fiction Studies Reader*, Iowa City: University of Iowa Press, pp. 218–238.

De Kosnik, A. (2015) "Fifty Shades and the Archive of Women's Culture," *Cinema Journal* 54(3), pp. 116–25.

Duggan, J. (2022) "'Worlds...[of] Contingent Possibilities': Genderqueer and Trans Adolescents Reading Fan Fiction," *Television & New Media* 23(7), pp. 703–720.

Duggan, J. (2023) "Trans Fans and Fan Fiction: A Literature Review," in J. Duggan and A. Fazekas (eds) special issue, *Transformative Works and Cultures*, 39, https://doi.org/10.3983/twc.2023.2309.

Duggan, J. and A. Fazekas. (2023) "Trans Fandom," in J. Duggan and A. Fazekas (eds) special issue, *Transformative Works and Cultures*, 39, https://doi.org/10.3983/twc.2023.2521.

Fathallah, J. M. (2017) *Fanfiction and the Author: How Fanfic Changes Popular Cultural Texts*, Amsterdam: Amsterdam University Press.

Fiani, C. N. and H. J. Han. (2019) "Navigating identity: Experiences of binary and non-binary transgender and gender non-conforming (TGNC) adults," *International Journal of Transgenderism* 20(2-3), pp. 181–194, https://doi.org/10.1080/15532739.2018.1426074.

Jenkins, H. (2012) *Textual Poachers: Television Fans and Participatory Culture*, New York: Routledge.

Johnson, P. (2019) "Transformative Racism: The Black Body in Fan Works," *Transformative Works and Cultures*, 29, https://doi.org/10.3983/twc.2019.1669.

Lamerichs, N. (2011) "Stranger Than Fiction: Fan Identity in Cosplay," *Transformative Works and Cultures*, 7, https://doi.org/10.3983/twc.2011.0246.

Leetal, D. (2022) "Revisiting Gender Theory in Fan Fiction: Bringing Nonbinary Genders into the World," *Transformative Works and Cultures*, 38, https://doi.org/10.3983/twc.2022.2081.

Lothian, A., K. Busse, and R. A. Reid. (2007) ""Yearning Void and Infinite Potential": Online Slash Fandom as Queer Female Space," *English Language Notes* 45(2), pp. 103–111.

Monro, S. (2019) "Non-binary and genderqueer: An overview of the field," *International Journal of Transgenderism* 20(2–3), pp. 126–131, https://doi.org/10.1080/15532739.2018.1538841.

Pande, R. (2018) *Squee from the Margins: Fandom and Race*, Iowa City: University of Iowa Press.

Penley, C. (1992) "Feminism, Psychoanalysis, and the Study of Popular Culture," in L. Grossberg, C. Nelson, and P. A. Treichler (eds) *Cultural Studies*, New York: Routledge, pp. 479–500.

Radway, J. (1983) "Women Read the Romance: The Interaction of Text and Context," *Feminist Studies* 9(1)(Spring), pp. 56–68.

Riley, O. J. (2020) "Podfic: Queer Structures of Sound," *Transformative Works and Cultures*, 34, https://doi.org/10.3983/twc.2020.1933.

Riley, O. J. (2024) "Podfic: Cultural Accessibility through Digital Community," *Participations* 20(1), pp. 94–116.

Rose, J. A. (2020) " 'My Male Skin': (Self-)narratives of Transmasculinities in Fanfiction," *European Journal of English Studies* 24(1), pp. 25–36, doi:10.1080/13825577.2020.1730044.

Russ, J. (2014) "Pornography by Women for Women, with Love," in K. Hellekson and K. Busse (eds) *The Fan Fiction Studies Reader*, Iowa City: University of Iowa Press, pp. 82–96.

Russo, J. L. (2017) "The Queer Politics of Femslash," in M. A. Click and S. Scott (eds) *Routledge Companion to Media Fandom*, London: Routledge, pp. 155–164.

Scott, S. (2019) *Fake Geek Girls: Fandom, Gender, and the Convergence Culture Industry*, New York: NYU Press.

Stanfill, M. (2019) *Exploiting Fandom: How the Media Industry Seeks to Manipulate Fans*, Iowa City: University of Iowa Press.

Wanzo, R. (2015) "African American Acafandom and Other Strangers: New Genealogies of Fan Studies," *Transformative Works and Cultures*, 20, https://doi.org/10.3983/twc.2015.0699.

Warner, K. J. (2017) "(Black Female) Fans Strike Back: The Emergence of the Iris West Defense Squad," in M. A. Click and S. Scott (eds) *Routledge Companion to Media Fandom*, London: Routledge, pp. 253–261.

Willis, I. (2016) "Writing the Fables of Sexual Difference: Slash Fiction as Technology of Gender," Parallax 22(3), pp. 290–311, https://doi.org/10.1080/13534645.2016.1201920.

Zimman, L. (2018) "Transgender voices: Insights on identity, embodiment, and the gender of the voice," *Language and Linguistics Compass* 12(8), https://doi.org/10.1111/lnc3.12284.

31
BOYS LOVE MEDIA ACROSS ASIA
Theorizing the Role of Queer Affect in Transcultural Fandom

Thomas Baudinette

For the first six months of 2023, I spent almost every Friday evening and Saturday morning engaging with fans on social media who had just finished watching a Boys Love (hereafter, BL) series produced by Thailand's youth-oriented television station, GMMTV. Each week, we shared our enjoyment of either the high school romance *My School President* (2022–2023, *Faen Phom Pen Prathan Nak-Rian*, "My Boyfriend is the Student Council President), the office comedy *A Boss and A Babe* (2023, *Cho Ka Che Khun Kan*, "Gun and Cher are Together"), or the time-travel saga *Be My Favorite* (2023, *Botkawi Khong Pisaeng*, "Poetry of the Lightyear"). As media depicting the romantic and sexual relationships between beautiful male youths (McLelland and Welker 2015: 3), originally emerging as a genre of *manga* comics marketed to young women in Japan, since the late 1980s BL media has spread across East, Southeast, and South Asia to inform a variety of local fandoms (Welker 2022: 1). As such, BL has developed into a pan-Asian queer popular culture form that includes not only print comics, but also live action television series (such as the Thai series listed above), webnovels and fanfictions, video games, audio dramas on CDs and podcasting services, and online graphic novels known as webtoons (Welker 2022: 3). Possessing a diverse fandom active across not only Asia, but the rest of the world, BL has emerged into a significant popular culture phenomenon which is strongly influencing how fans understand not only gender and sexuality, but also their broader positioning in the world *as* fans (Baudinette 2023a).

For both the fans with whom I interacted on social media and myself, Thai BL series stoked fannish imaginations to celebrate not only the romances depicted within the series themselves, but also the homoerotic potentials produced by the interactions between each series' stars off the screen (see Baudinette 2023a). Our social media conversations ranged from articulate discussions of each series' cinematography and their stars' acting prowess to excited ramblings concerning how attractive the stars appeared in each episode, especially when circulating videos and image stills of scenes in which the characters these stars portrayed hugged, kissed, and even had sex. Uniting our conversations were the emotions evoked by BL media culture, which we expressed openly through our impassioned debates via Twitter DMs or Facebook messages. While our tastes in actors and stories differed significantly, and we came from a variety of different backgrounds, we were all ultimately united into a single community of fans grounded in a shared culture of affect. By affect, I refer to the cognitive process that philosopher Brian Massumi (2002: 35) considers a preconscious intensity generated by an individual's engagement with another body (whether that be another person, object, or even abstract idea/concept). Within their discussion of the Japanese female idol industry, media theorists Patrick Galbraith and Jason Karlin conceptualize affect as shared intimacies and resultant emotional reactions through which fans interpret media and subsequently make them meaningful (2020: 29–33).

In this chapter, I take the fandom for BL media across Asia as a case study to unpack and theorize the role of queer affect within a community of fans with differing backgrounds, expectations, and experiences. Drawing upon the seminal work of queer theorist David Halperin (1997: 67), I understand queerness to represent a deconstructive force or process which challenges and/or subverts social norms, most notably the positioning of heterosexuality as natural and compulsory within contemporary global culture. As I will argue throughout this chapter, BL fandom generates queer affects designed to challenge heteronormative expectations surrounding gender and sexuality across Asia's diverse media markets.

To make sense of the queer affective potentials of the community of fans across Asia who consume a variety of different kinds of BL media, the concept of transcultural fandom developed by fan studies scholars Bertha Chin and Lori Morimoto (2013) is particularly useful. Chin and Morimoto (2013: 95) introduced their theory of transcultural fandom to push back against the privileging of the "nation" as the primary frame of reference through which fan behaviors and motivations were conceptualized in previous media studies research. In their pointed criticism of Koichi Iwabuchi's (2002) structuralist work on the "transnational" spread of Japanese media, for example, Chin and Morimoto argue that it is the affective experience of fandom itself and its potential to satisfy consumers' individual desires that is most significant to theorizing fandom for globalized media. Chin and Morimoto (2013: 95) strongly reject Iwabuchi's theory that Japanese media's popularity is grounded in its ability to be adapted to meet the cultural expectations of specific national contexts (2002: 58), correctly suggesting that such a top-down theorization focused on commodity production fails to consider fans' diverse understandings of the role of media in their everyday lives. Rather than assuming that fans are united by particular expectations which have been produced through their interpellation as subjects within a unified national media market (Iwabuchi 2002: 58–59), Chin and Morimoto instead argue that the shared affects generated through fandom act to unite fans who possess disparate personal expectations and backgrounds into a transcultural space of mutual exchange (2013: 95–96).

Within a transcultural approach, the national contexts of both media production and consumption are thus less important to understanding fandom than the individual aspirations and experiences of those who come together to form a community grounded in shared affects (Chin and Morimoto 2013: 96). As I will argue below, diverse fans' utilization of both the BL media which they consume and the emotional connections between each other produced by this fannish consumption to actively challenge heteronormativity as it is expressed in everyday life are fundamental to BL's transcultural affective community (Baudinette 2022: 48–49). It is for this reason that I have insisted throughout my ethnographic work on various BL fandom communities across Asia that this genre of queer popular culture is best theorized as a "resource of hope" which acts as a concrete tool which consumers can deploy to queer mainstream society's broader ideological systems and social structures (see Baudinette 2022, 2023b). It is my hope that readers of this chapter similarly take up the methods of transcultural fandom studies to ensure that their work on fandom cultures – whether grounded in queer popular culture or not – attends to the emancipatory work of affective, transcultural fandom.

What is BL and Who Are its Fans?

To understand the affective engagement of BL media fans across Asia, it is necessary to briefly cover the history of this media genre and profile its fans. I draw upon three principal case studies conducted between 2013 and 2023: Chinese gay male fans of Japanese BL *manga* (see Baudinette 2022a), LGBTQ+ Philippine fans of Japanese BL *manga* (see Baudinette 2023b), and diverse fans of Thai BL series from China, Japan, the Philippines, and Thailand (see Baudinette 2023a).

As historian James Welker notes in the introduction to the edited collection *Queer Transfigurations: Boys Love Media in Asia*, BL represents a pan-Asian form of popular culture that unites diverse consumers possessing different cultural, gendered, national, religious, and sexual backgrounds into a collective based in shared fantasies and aspirations for queer representation, queer expression, and queer political activism (2022: 2). As such, BL is playing an important political role in "transfiguring" how queer sexuality is articulated within Asian media culture, giving rise to fandom spaces tied to the consumption of Japanese BL *manga* which Welker argues are broadly affirming of LGBTQ+ individuals (2022: 3). Significantly, the contributors to Welker's edited collection unpack how the generic logics of Japanese BL *manga* and their particular reading practices – grounded in BL's ties to *shōjo bunka* (Japanese girls' culture) – have transformed local understandings of queerness across Asia. While Welker's edited collection mostly focuses on the spread of Japan's BL *manga* across Asia, the globalization of BL has diversified the genre's production beyond Japanese models. In the 2020s, BL media is no longer restricted to Japanese *manga* and now encompasses the text-based BL novels (often published online) of China, Thailand, and Vietnam, the BL television and web series of the Philippines, South Korea, Taiwan, and Thailand, and the BL comics of the Philippines and South Korea.

Within Japan, BL emerged from young women's consumer culture and has therefore primarily been understood and theorized as a media genre that is principally consumed and produced by heterosexual cisgender women, typically in their teens or 20s, who understand BL as a space of escapist fantasy (McLelland and Welker 2015: 3). When I reflect on the demographics of the fans of Thailand's BL series with whom I regularly interacted each week in the first half of 2023, however, a more expansive image of the diversity of contemporary BL fandom emerges. For instance, while it is indeed the case that some of my fannish interlocutors were cisgender women, many also expressed that they were not heterosexual, instead openly identifying as bisexual, lesbian, or queer. Likewise, a large number of my interlocutors were bisexual, gay, or queer cisgender men who – like myself – had come to appreciate that BL media represented a space through which men could explore their romantic and sexual desires for other men (see Baudinette 2022). I also frequently conversed with fans who identified as genderqueer or trans, indicating that members of the broader LGBTQ+ community across a variety of national contexts – the fannish interlocutors with whom I most frequently interacted were variously located in China, India, Ireland, Japan, the Philippines, Thailand, Vietnam, and the US – identified as BL fans. Further, while the typical BL fan has been previously understood to be in their teens or 20s, and many of my interlocutors were indeed from these age groups, I also regularly engaged with fans in their 30s, 40s, and 50s during my weekly social media conversations throughout the first six months of 2023. This is unsurprising considering the fact that BL first emerged in the 1970s and thus many fans (particularly in Japan) have aged along with the genre.

While impressionistic accounts of my own personal fan networks on social media may not provide a statistically generalizable description of BL's typical audience, they clearly indicate that the axiomatic argument produced in previous scholarship centered on Japan that BL is only ever consumed and enjoyed by heterosexual women no longer holds true in the 2020s. Indeed, both my own work (Baudinette 2021) and the work of media theorist Mizoguchi Akiko (2015) reveal that Japanese gay men and lesbian women have been consuming BL *manga* since the genre's emergence in the 1970s. Recent large quantitative surveys of fans by Satō Mai and Ishida Hitoshi (2022) in the Japanese context and Poowin Bunyavejchewin and Natthanont Sukthungthong (2021) in the Thai context also highlight statistically significant engagement with BL *manga* among LGBTQ+ readers, particularly cisgender gay and bisexual men, since at least the 1980s. In fact, the argument which dominated previous scholarship that BL's popularity was grounded in the demographic background of the audience to which it was typically marketed (that is, heterosexual women) was perhaps reflective of previous scholars' assumptions about BL's supposedly fraught relationship with gay male media ecologies (see Baudinette 2023a: 58–61). That is, these previous arguments may have emerged from the misogynistic expectations of gay male activists and scholars who dismissed the political agency and queer potentials of female readers of BL (see Santos and Baudinette 2024). The axiomatic argument that BL media fandom only ever represented a fandom culture based in the views and values of cisgender heterosexual women in their teens and 20s was thus never empirically true in the first place, even if this demographic may remain the primary audience to which BL media is marketed in some (but not all) contexts.

BL's Queer Affective Literacies

BL's historical grounding in Japanese women's media culture does remain significant, however, when considering the genre's narrative conventions and the dominant reading practices which have emerged among fans of this pan-Asian queer popular culture. This is because fans in a variety of local contexts have, through their engagement with BL, learnt to read media via particular "literacies" which cultural historian Kristine Michelle Santos (2020) argues emerge from Japanese women's culture, but which have become adapted to form part of the queer "fantasy work" of diverse fans around Asia, including LGBTQ+ audiences (Baudinette 2023b: 55). Expanding on the theories of literary scholar Tomoko Aoyama (2012) concerning the fundamental intertextuality which guides Japanese women's engagement with *shōjo bunka*, Santos (2020: 82) reveals that BL media are specifically structured to produce certain pleasures tied to the genre's narrative conventions and typical characterizations. Known as the BL *ōdō* (noble path of BL), these narrative and character conventions privilege a fairly formulaic romantic storyline that typically ends happily, and which focuses on the developing relationship between two archetypical characters known as the *seme* and the *uke* (Santos 2020: 83). In the classic BL *ōdō*, the *seme* (attacker) represents the dominant and stereotypically masculine partner in a male-male couple, whereas the *uke* (receiver) represents the passive, feminized partner who is swept up into a relationship by the *seme*'s all-encompassing and uncontrollable romantic and sexual desires (Santos 2020: 83). For Santos, BL fans develop particular generic expectations or "literacies" through their reading and decoding of this BL *ōdō*, with the ultimate pleasure of consuming BL media deriving from fans' affective response to how well an author is able to manipulate the *seme-uke* paradigm to produce a satisfyingly romantic story (2020: 83). These affective entanglements between fans and BL media, Santos further suggests, are ultimately queer due to their grounding in the appreciation of the emotional and romantic potentials of male-male relationships (2020: 84).

But these affective entanglements possess a queerness that extends beyond fans' engagement with BL media themselves. This is because fans can apply the literacy practices of BL to other texts, especially texts which hint towards the potential of homoeroticism through their focus on intense male relationships, often called *nioi-kei* BL (loosely, "texts which smell like BL") by Japanese BL fans (see Aoyama 2012). This then facilitates BL fans' recognition and appreciation of the intense pleasures to be gained from actively queering mainstream media, extending their queer affective literacies beyond the world of formal BL media, and subsequently producing a more expansive fandom experience. As I unpack in a following section, this application of the queer affective literacies of BL consumption is especially significant to LGBTQ+ fans' fantasy work.

The following examples of the application of BL literacy practices by fans are particularly instructive. Santos (2020: 80–81) discusses, for instance, how the queer affective literacies of Japanese BL fans have given rise to a subculture of derivative works known as *dōjinshi* (self-published zines) within which fan artists re-imagine the male characters appearing in popular *manga* marketed to young boys in romantic and sexual relationships. In his research on Japanese BL consumers' socialization with each other as fans, Galbraith (2015) likewise highlights that a significant form of BL fan sociality in Japan is *moe-banashi* (affective talk), a practice where fans debate who would represent an ideal *seme* or *uke* within a fictional male-male pairing (both within and without canonically BL works). Within the Thai context, I have argued that the cinematographic conventions of early BL series such as 2014's *Lovesick, The Series* created a specific gaze which actively transformed mainstream viewers into BL fans, thus educating consumers who were only familiar with the heteronormative conventions of Thai media at the time about how to pleasurably consume male-male romance (Baudinette 2023a: 66–69). This queer gaze is then applied to how fans make sense of the interactions between the actors who perform the male-male romances within these BL series, thus producing a significant fandom culture of imagining the celebrities active in the Thai BL industry in romantic relationships (Baudinette 2023a: 69).

Importantly, within all of the examples of fan behavior introduced above, the affective literacies of BL provide fans with the ability to "queer" a variety of mainstream, heteronormative media, uniting them together into a community based in the enjoyment of queer romance. Put simply, BL fandom operates as a community of shared affect which is structured by disparate fans' queer literacy practices. Consumers with diverse backgrounds, possessing various expectations conditioned by their own subjective experiences as media consumers located around the world, thus are bound together as BL fans through these queer affects, producing a transcultural fandom community.

While these literacy practices historically emerged from Japan's *shōjo bunka*, this does not limit their queer affects to the heterosexual women who represent the normative market for such media. These ways of viewing and discussing BL, centered explicitly in queer affective practice, are open to participation by any consumer of BL media. Indeed, deriving a sense of identity from the shared enjoyment of such queer affective literacies is one of the key sites through which BL fan identity could be said to be produced (see Galbraith 2015: 155). For example, the weekly conversations which I had with fans of GMMTV's BL series each week in the first half of 2023 could be considered instances of the affective practice of *moe-banashi*. This is especially true since a frequent topic of conversation among my fellow fans was determining whether the stars appearing within each of these BL series had the requisite chemistry and acting prowess to perform their roles as *seme* and *uke* characters, with our *moe-banashi* drawing us together even if we did not necessarily agree. Likewise, in my work on Chinese gay male and Philippine LGBTQ+ fans of Japanese BL *manga*, I learnt that many of these fans drew upon the queer affective logics of the BL *ōdō* as part of articulating and making sense of both their queer sexuality as well as their identities as fans (Baudinette 2022, 2023b).

In many ways, one could even consider these fans' detailed reflections on their sexualities through the lens of the BL *ōdō* during their formal interviews with me, an academic and fellow BL fan, as another example of *moe-banashi*. As a practice, *moe-banashi* (or perhaps, more simply put, "fan discourse") represents a key instance where fannish enjoyment cuts across demographic backgrounds and unites BL fans into the shared community of affect typical of transcultural fandom. This represents a very concrete example of how attention to transcultural affective work allows us to theorize what brings fans together into a community of practice grounded in pleasure and enjoyment (as well as, in some instances, less positive emotions). In the following section, I build upon this transcultural affective framework to demonstrate how it can be practically applied to theorizing BL fandom's queer emancipatory politics.

Theorizing Queer Media Fandom in Asia via Transcultural Affect

Having theorized the transcultural nature of BL fandom through careful attention to its shared affects, I now turn my attention to considering how this theory can be drawn upon by fan studies scholars and media theorists interested in exploring queer media fandom within Asia. I will reveal that focusing analysis on the agency of LGBTQ+ fans of BL to engage in fantasy work through their consumption of this pan-Asian popular culture provides fruitful avenues for conceptualizing the queer political potentials of fandom, challenging the applicability of structuralist theories of queer media consumption emerging from Western contexts.

Since the 1990s, when mainstream media producers in North America and Western Europe began to increasingly depict LGBTQ+ subjects within their works, many media theorists and fan studies scholars alike have turned to the concepts of "queerbaiting" and "pinkwashing" to critique what they often deemed facile visibility politics (Brennan 2019: 1–2). For these theorists, queerbaiting represented the practice of including tokenistic representations of LGBTQ+ characters within a media product – or producing marketing which hinted toward queer content that was never fully actualized within the work itself – without engaging in political questions relevant to the liberation of oppressed sexual minority communities (Brennan 2019: 3). Pinkwashing likewise referred to the practice of depicting queerness within a mainstream work, often produced by individuals from outside the LGBTQ+ community, for the purposes of exploiting LGBTQ+ (and other) consumers economically (Brennan 2019: 3). Significantly, such theoretical approaches developed to make sense of how the introduction of legal protections for LGBTQ+ individuals in a variety of Western contexts had led to the production of apolitical media which simply integrated LGBTQ+ consumers into pre-established capitalist and hetero-patriarchal social systems that had previously excluded them (Chasin 2000: 184). That is, scholars sought to understand why the expansion of LGBTQ+ rights in some Western societies supposedly led to a decrease in radical queer challenges to the status quo within media culture (Chasin 2000: 185). It is important to note that similar criticisms were also raised in the 1990s by gay activists in Japan (see Ishida 2015). These Japanese criticisms, however, were often framed via the axiomatic argument that BL was only ever consumed by cisgender heterosexual women and thus failed to appropriately consider the fact that BL's audience did in fact include LGBTQ+ fans who found the genre meaningful and representative of their lived experiences and romantic lives (Baudinette 2021: 108–113).

Rather than simplistically assuming that BL media engages in a so-called pinkwashing agenda that is always already detrimental to consumers, approaching BL fandom as a transcultural community grounded in affect can instead help theorists appreciate how queerness can be performed and actualized through fannish consumption in Asia. This is particularly useful since most Asian societies lack legal protections for LGBTQ+ people – with some states even actively censoring depictions of LGBTQ+ people or criminalizing queer sexual practices – and thus differ greatly from the Western contexts where the theories of queerbaiting and pinkwashing were initially developed. Many of the LGBTQ+ fans of BL who I have interviewed throughout my ethnographic work on BL media fandom strongly insisted that BL played a socially significant role in raising the visibility of LGBTQ+ people and therefore challenged negative stereotypes concerning queer sexuality which circulate in many Asian societies (Baudinette 2022, 2023a, 2023b). This sense of satisfaction with finally seeing LGBTQ+ people positively depicted in media, whether it be locally produced or foreign, is in turn tangled into the queer affective literacies which structure BL consumption, enhancing the pleasure and enjoyment derived from participating in BL's transcultural fandom. Within the Philippines, for instance, LGBTQ+ fans of Japanese BL *manga* and Thai BL series alike would often enthusiastically respond to depictions of queer romance in BL with the youth slang term "*sana all*" (see Baudinette 2023b, 2023b). This emotionally charged expression of spontaneous pleasure was deployed by fans – almost without thinking, according to some of my interviewees (Baudinette 2023a: 147) – to not only vocalize their enjoyment of BL but also their hopes that the positive depictions of queer romance found therein could be actualized within the Philippine's hetero-patriarchal society (see Baudinette 2023b: 57).

Philippine LGBTQ+ BL fans' use of the phrase *sana all* to articulate their aspirations for utopian futures represents just one of many instances where fans active within this transcultural fandom mobilize their affective engagement with BL to engage in queer fantasy work. By queer fantasy work, I refer to the mobilization of affective engagement with media texts in the active production of new ways of being, doing, and knowing in the world designed to carve out a space of acceptance and liberation for oppressed LGBTQ+ subjects living under systems of hetero-patriarchy (Baudinette 2022: 44).

More than representing a simple form of aspirational consumption (Baudinette 2022: 50), however, considering BL media and its queer affective literacies as resources of hope for diverse BL fans can help fan studies scholars and media theorists re-center the investigation of queer media fandom back on the agency of fans. Even within production systems dominated by so-called queerbaiting and pinkwashing, media texts can be used by subjects to actively insist upon the legitimacy of their own queer aspirations, dreams, and hopes, especially when located within social contexts such as Asia's dominated by homophobia, transphobia, and a systematic lack of legal protections (Baudinette 2022: 51). As an example of BL being actively used as a resource of hope in this way, many Philippine LGBTQ+ fans of Japanese BL *manga* that I have interviewed believed that their fandom represented a form of "necessary" activism in a society where they lack basic rights and freedoms (Baudinette 2023b: 57). Some fans even sought to visibilize their BL fan identities when engaging in formal activist practices such as attendance at Pride parades, arguing that BL fan positionalities were more effective in engaging youth for whom this popular culture is both recognizable and relevant (Baudinette 2023b: 57).

For this reason, when considering BL media's circulation within Asian media markets, I believe it is premature to focus too firmly on structuralist theories such as queerbaiting which would always already dismiss the queer potentials of a media genre such as BL. My insistence on paying attention to the queer affective work of BL from the perspective of transcultural fandom ultimately represents a call for theorists of queer media's reception to remember Stuart Hall's (1980) seminal argument that consumers possess the fundamental agency to decode media texts in ways which challenge the messages encoded in them by their producers. While it is certainly important to question the production logics and representational politics of BL media across Asia, failing to pay attention to the queer affects which structure transcultural fandom has led many previous theorists of BL to neglect the important emancipatory politics strategically and explicitly produced by BL fandom's increasingly diverse participants.

Queer theory is ultimately grounded in both the critical and reparative work of excavating spaces for LGBTQ+ liberation (Halperin 1997), a point which many seeking to investigate BL fandom have often overlooked in their insistence on criticizing the heterosexual women for whom this genre was supposedly produced (see Santos and Baudinette 2024). A transcultural theory of fandom and its centering of fans' fantasy work represents a powerful conceptual approach which directly aligns with queer theory's broader political mission and thus addresses a significant gap in fan studies scholarship on BL. It recognizes that all fans, regardless of their gender or sexuality, can draw upon their affective entanglements with media such as BL to collectively engage in fandom behaviors which queer the status quo.

References

Aoyama, T. (2012) "BL (Boys' Love) Literacy: Subversion, Resuscitation, and Transformation of the (Father's) Text," *US-Japan Women's Journal* 43, pp. 63–84.

Baudinette, T. (2023a) *Boys Love Media in Thailand: Celebrity, Fans, and Transnational Asian Queer Popular Culture*, New York: Bloomsbury.

Baudinette, T. (2023b) "Japanese Queer Popular Culture and the Production of Sexual Knowledge in the Philippines," in S. Tang & H.Y. Wijaya (eds.), *Queer Southeast Asia*, London: Routledge, pp. 47–62.

Baudinette, T. (2022) "BL as a 'Resource of Hope' among Chinese Gay Men in Japan," in J. Welker (ed.), *Queer Transfigurations: Boys Love Media in Asia*, Honolulu: University of Hawaii Press, pp. 42–54.

Baudinette, T. (2021) *Regimes of Desire: Young Gay Men, Media and Masculinity in Japan*, Ann Arbor: University of Michigan Press.
Brennan, J. (2019) "Introduction: A History of Queerbaiting," in J. Brennan (ed.), *Queerbaiting and Fandom: Teasing Fans through Homoerotic Possibilities*, Iowa City: University of Iowa Press, pp. 1–23.
Bunyavejchewin, P. & Sukthungthong, N. (2021) *Lok khong wai*, Bangkok: Thammasat University Institute of East Asian Studies.
Chasin, A. (2000) *Selling Out: The Gay and Lesbian Movement Goes to Market*, New York: St Martin's Press.
Chin, B. & Morimoto, L. (2013) "Towards a Theory of Transcultural Fandom," *Participations: Journal of Audience and Reception Studies* 10(1), pp. 92–108.
Galbraith, P.W & Karlin, J.G. (2020) *AKB48*, New York: Bloomsbury.
Galbraith, P.W. (2015) "Moe Talk: Affective Communication among Female Fans of *yaoi* in Japan," in M. McLelland, K. Nagaike, K. Suganuma & J. Welker (eds.), *Boys Love Manga and Beyond: History, Culture, and Community in Japan*, Jackson, MI: University Press of Mississippi, pp. 153–168.
Hall, S. (1980) "Encoding/Decoding," in Centre for Contemporary Cultural Studies (ed.), *Culture, Media, Language: Working Papers in Cultural Studies, 1972–79*, London: Hutchinson, pp. 128–138.
Halperin, D. M. (1997) *Saint Foucault: Towards a Gay Hagiography*, Oxford: Oxford University Press.
Ishida, H. (2015) "Representational Appropriation and the Autonomy of Desire in *Yaoi*/BL" (trans. Katsuhiko Suganuma), in M. McLelland, K. Nagaike, K. Suganuma & J. Welker (eds.), *Boys Love Manga and Beyond: History, Culture, and Community in Japan*, Jackson, MI: University Press of Mississippi, pp. 210–232.
Iwabuchi, K. (2002) *Recentering Globalization: Popular Culture and Japanese Transnationalism*, Durham, NC: Duke University Press.
McLelland, M. & Welker, J. (2015) "An Introduction to 'Boys Love' in Japan," in M. McLelland, K. Nagaike, K. Suganuma & J. Welker (eds.), *Boys Love Manga and Beyond: History, Culture, and Community in Japan*, Jackson, MI: University Press of Mississippi, pp. 3–22.
Massumi, B. (2002) *Parables of the Virtual: Movement, Affect, Sensation*, Durham: Duke University Press.
Mizoguchi, A. (2015) *BL shinka-ron: Bōizu rabu ga shakai o ugokasu*, Tokyo: Ōta Shuppan.
Santos, K. M. L. (2020) "Queer Affective Literacies: Examining 'Rotten' Women's Literacies in Japan," *Critical Arts* 34(5), pp. 72–86.
Santos, K. M. L. & Baudinette, T. (2024). "Exploring Debates over "Boys Love" Media in the Philippines: From Misogynistic Backlash to Queer Emancipation," *Feminist Media Studies*. Online first: https://doi.org/10.1080/14680777.2024.2345198.
Satō, M. & Ishida, H. (2022) *BL dokusha/hi-dokusha ni tai suru chōsa: Chōsha-hyō to tanjun shūhei-hyō*, Tokyo: Japanese Society for the Promotion of Science.
Welker, J. (2022) "Introduction: Boys Love (BL) Media and its Asian Transfigurations," in J. Welker (ed.), *Queer Transfigurations: Boys Love Media in Asia*, Honolulu: University of Hawaii Press, pp. 1–16.

32
ADVANCING TRANSCULTURAL FANDOM
A Conversation

Bertha Chin, Aswin Punathambekar, and Sangita Shresthova

While the chapters in this section demonstrate the importance of studying race and transcultural fandom, these areas of fan studies remain underdeveloped. We asked Bertha Chin, Aswin Punathambekar, and Sangita Shresthova to help illuminate the benefits, pitfalls, and future directions of these areas of study. Bertha Chin serves on the board of the Fan Studies Network and the editorial board of the Journal of Fandom Studies; she has written widely about social media, crowdfunding, and science fiction fandom. Aswin Punathambekar writes about media and political culture with a focus on South Asia and the South Asian diaspora, and his book, *From Bombay to Bollywood: The Making of a Global Media Industry*, explores the transnational growth of the Bombay media industry, including a discussion of fandom; he is co-editor of *Global Bollywood*, *Television at Large in South Asia*, and associate editor of *Media, Culture and Society*. Sangita Shresthova is director of the Media Activism & Participatory Politics (MAPP) project based at the University of Southern California and the founder of Bollynatyam's Global Bollywood Dance Project; she has written about Bollywood dance culture in her book, *Is It All About Hips? Around the World with Bollywood Dance*, and about youth activism, popular culture, new media, and civic life in numerous publications. These three scholars discuss the challenges that language, citational practices, and immersion present to the practice and impact of transcultural scholarship; the merits of ethnography for transcultural fan studies; the ways a more robust incorporation of transcultural scholarship into fan studies would broaden and strengthen scholarship on fan cultures; and future directions for race and transcultural scholarship in fan studies.

With the exception of a few early studies, fan studies scholarship on race and transnational fandom is less referenced and cited, leaving these valuable subjects relatively invisible. What are the challenges and stumbling blocks to these areas of study?

Bertha Chin: For me, the biggest challenge is language. I often wonder if academic works on fandom are actually being produced in say, for instance—pertaining to my own research interests and cultural background—Chinese/Korean/Japanese, but because of my own mono-lingualism, I have no knowledge and access to these works. Language is also a challenge for very practical reasons. For a while I was playing with the idea of doing a bit of research on *Arrow* fans in China after learning that Warner Brothers had sent Stephen Amell, the lead actor, to do some promotional work in Shanghai and Beijing. I contacted fans on Tumblr who had posted reports of Amell's events in China, and got very generic responses (e.g. how long he was there, what those events involved, how many fans attended the events). But as soon as I tried to engage them in more in-depth discussions, or to ask for recommendations to other fans who were active online, the ranks immediately closed once they determined I didn't speak Chinese. For them, the lack of language skills immediately signals me as the outsider in their community, even if fans were active on Tumblr.

Sangita Shresthova: The Bollywood fandoms I have studied are often only visible to those involved with them, which becomes a real challenge for researchers not directly involved with them on an ongoing basis. They may be primarily performative and non-verbal. They may also be intricately woven into the everyday lives of the fans in ways that make extracting "fannish" behavior as a separate category difficult. For Bollywood in particular, performativity (often live and impromptu) plays is a crucial expressive, and by definition ephemeral, medium. To effectively study it, a researcher would need to be trained to recognize and analyze performance as fandom. They would need to be able to unpack the distinction between mimicry, appropriation, and remix within performance, and they would need to have enough knowledge of the source material and the cultural context to situate said performance within a particular cultural context. When I started studying Bollywood dance more than a decade ago, finding dancers engaged in fandom through dance was challenging because of the informal nature of when it manifested—at family celebrations, family gatherings, after dinner. I found that I needed to spend a lot of time with my potential subjects just to arrive at an understanding of what Bollywood fandom looks like in these particular contexts.

Aswin Punathambekar: In addition to the question of language and performativity that Chin and Shresthova have raised, I would point to citational practices as a major problem for fan studies and more generally, for media studies writ large. To this day, scholars in media studies simply do not take up theoretical insights developed from studies of fans (and more generally, audiences) in non-Western contexts. Dipesh Chakrabarty's trenchant observation regarding the marginal status of non-Western histories – "only 'Europe', the argument would appear to be, is theoretically knowable; all other histories are matters of empirical research that fleshes out a theoretical skeleton that is substantially 'Europe' "—is pertinent to media studies as well. Consider, for instance, S. V. Srinivas' pathbreaking work on fan cultures, performance, and political culture(s) in south India. There is much we can learn about links between stardom and the mediatization of politics from Srinivas' work that would help make sense of, for instance, populist figures like Trump. The only way to push for change on this front is by reflecting on our reading and writing practices, by making a concerted effort to seek scholarship from well outside the immediate context(s) we live and operate in, and incorporating scholarly voices that are otherwise relegated to the margins.

Bertha Chin: I agree—those are good points raised by Sangita and Aswin. The issue of invisibility needs to be solved within fan, media, and cultural studies at large. There's a sense that anything beyond UK/US/Europe is always considered "fringe," and therefore not applicable to fan practices in the Western context, even though discussions of race, ethnicity, and whitewashing are becoming more of a concern for fans now. This invisibility is also part of the reason why Lori Morimoto and myself talked about these fandoms from a transcultural perspective rather than a transnational or regional perspective, but as Aswin points out we also need to be inclusive in our own reading and writing practices to push for more inclusivity, that these concerns are applicable to media fandoms at large rather than within regional specificity. Furthermore, with social media becoming more prominent and platforms like Tumblr changing the ways fans take to texts (visually rather than textually), exposure to fans who are familiar with different conceptualizations of (fan) practice and norms now make it more crucial for those of us working in fan, media, and cultural studies to embrace works which we are not necessarily familiar with.

Sangita Shresthova: I completely agree, Bertha. We also need to consider how the axis of visibility and invisibility are defined. As Aswin points out, scholarly work relevant to our understanding of transnational fandoms is likely being done outside the easily acceptable spaces. Searching for fandoms that "look and feel" like those commonly identified in the West is effectively creating blinders that may systematically overlook expressions of fandom that do not fall within these recognized parameters. I once again return to my work on Bollywood dance fandom to reiterate how challenging it can be to identify, let alone, understand such fandoms.

In what ways are studies of fan communities and practices that normalize national, Western-based fandoms limiting fan studies' understandings of fan cultures?

Bertha Chin: I think it denies us layers of complexities in understanding fan cultures (as well as industrial practices) in different national and cultural contexts. Even within Western contexts, there's an assumption of homogeneity in fan practices (e.g. fan practices are the same in Australia as they are in the United States, which obviously isn't necessarily the case), so acknowledging the diversity of fan practices across different national cultures could help encourage a wider engagement of variety of concepts and perspectives—or even fan practices, source texts, etc.—in fan studies. I also think, in concentrating on national, Western-based fandoms (and really, it's mostly white, American or British fandoms), we may end up exoticizing and eroticizing other fan cultures, as Susan Napier (2001) has commented on the West's continued fascination with anime, as if that is the only representation of non-Western fan culture or that Japan immediately equals (East) Asia, thus giving us a one-dimensional view of pop culture and fandom outside the West.

Sangita Shresthova: Approaches to fandom rooted in Western-based perspectives run the danger of making an implicit and/or explicit assumption about the traditions and practices that they aim to unpack. They may assume particular expectations about audiences and the norms associated with engaging with media texts. If we simply transpose these approaches on to other cultural contexts we run the risk of imposing cultural blinders on the ways that fans connect to existing traditions and practices. We may also miss moments when they are, in fact, actually borrowing from other culturally rooted practices if we force a comparison to Western-based fandoms.

Aswin Punathambekar: One of the fundamental issues, I would argue, is the continued mis-reading of pleasure when it comes to audiences in the non-Western world. And this has to do, in turn, with the fact that "audience studies" has simply not been major focus for academic study in the non-Western world. Where international communication (with a political economy bent) never had any patience for audience studies, global media studies (since the 1990s) has tended to focus on media industries and production cultures. With the exception of path-breaking work by scholars like Purnima Mankekar (India) and Lila Abu-Lughod (Egypt), we simply do not have good ethnographic and historical accounts of fans and audiences. In this context, fandom in the non-Western world ends up being framed as something extraordinary. The struggle, in other words, is to render fandom as something that can also be profoundly ordinary, as woven into the rhythms of everyday, mediatized lives. We are beginning to see this shift in scholarship on Korean popular culture, for instance, and its incredible transnational appeal. But we have a long way to go and I would argue that the most important task is to develop good historical accounts of audiences and reception within which we can properly situate fan practices as well.

Bertha Chin: I agree that there's a shift, with Korean wave scholarship leading the debates. I'm certainly starting to see push back from early career researchers now, especially those working in Asia, who are incorporating popular culture and fandom into their research or teaching. But I think there's also institutional resistance in place, in terms of research funding and expectations (as in institutional expectations of researchers), that media or communication research—if they are done—should have a political economy bent, because it's perceived to be more valuable than research into popular culture or fandom. And this again comes from Western indoctrination of popular culture (and by extension, fandom) as feminized and thus, devalued.

Sangita Shresthova: I agree. I encounter this institutional resistance when I present my work on Bollywood dance at conferences outside the United States. In these contexts, I often encounter a push back regarding my choice to focus on Bollywood dance fans and their live performed dances. I am often asked why I don't instead choose to focus on the history and political economy of song-and-dance production, with the implied critique that my focus on Bollywood dance fandom is somehow less able to yield important insights into Bollywood dance, a dance style that, in my view, owes its very existence to fans.

Are particular methodologies or "best practices" better suited for studies that focus on race and transcultural fandom? And what levels of cultural knowledge and competency are ideal for work that engages race and transcultural fandom?

Bertha Chin: I don't think there is necessarily a "best practice"—I could be wrong. I think outsider perspectives could be valuable in certain situations, as long as we're sensitive to the issues that we're writing about. But, as I mentioned earlier, access can be an issue as the fan communities may consider the lack of language skills (or perhaps similarities?) as a disadvantage, with heightened possibilities that their practices could be misrepresented.

Sangita Shresthova: I am going to reveal my own methodological bias here and state that I am a big advocate of ethnography as an entry point method when it comes to studying fandom. I do, however, believe in supplementing ethnography with other methods. In my view, ethnography allows the researcher to approach the multifaceted nature of fandom and how it plays out in the lives of individuals and in the building of communities and networks. Ethnography is also well suited to approaching fandom with the understanding that we can never adequately plan for what the research will reveal. It explicitly places the researcher in the position of perceiving, listening, and observing, leading them to note behaviors, beliefs, connections, and expressions that they may not have picked up on if they had entered through interviews or surveys. Once initiated, ethnography can be supplemented through other research methods, like the already mentioned interviews and surveys to validate and deepen ethnographic findings. I also always complement such researches through a media (and/or performance) analysis of the source materials and the materials created by the fans themselves.

Aswin Punathambekar: I could not agree more with Shresthova that an ethnographic approach is the best way forward. The first step for any researcher has to be immersion, both with the media texts in question and the broader cultural context. Beyond this, any researcher would do well to read widely in the history and culture that relates to the object of study and, of course, to commit to learning the language if need be. It calls for a lot of patience and hard work, and calls on scholars to accept that some projects do take time. The temporalities of contemporary academic work being what they are—the demands on publishing that we all struggle with—this kind of slow, immersive work assumes greater importance.

Sangita Shresthova: I feel we are all in agreement here. Researching dancers involved in the Bollywood dance competitions, I have also started to experiment with more participatory approaches to researching Bollywood dance fandom that move between in-person encounters and online spaces. After conducting initial research using ethnographic and other qualitative research tools, I transition to working with specific dancer fan communities to surface additional insights and collect media artifacts they create. While it certainly raises considerations that need to be dealt with in terms of ethics and attribution, I have found that this approach actually yields crucial insights as it allows me to work with the researched community to surface aspects of their fandom that may not have been apparent to me without their support.

How does a transcultural lens offer critical depth to topics including politics, economics, activism, and industry?

Bertha Chin: We live in an increasingly globalized world (which sounds a bit trite nowadays), and platforms like Tumblr are allowing for more participation from fans from different parts of the world. Likewise, networks such as Netflix are also expanding globally, making a lot of creative content available to global audiences at the same time as their US counterparts. This is happening with increasing frequency—Netflix has the streaming rights for *Riverdale*, for instance, which is shown on the CW Network in the United States, so the show is available to Netflix markets outside of America 24 hours after its first airing. And in Malaysia, the local satellite television, Astro, airs *Game of Thrones* at the same time HBO is airing it in the United States. These kinds of arrangements enable fans to engage with the texts they're watching at the same time, especially on social media as fans respond immediately to the episode as it airs. This isn't to say that this didn't already happen prior to Netflix, but fans now have the option of obtaining the content legitimately and participate more actively in conversations happening on Tumblr and social media. Lori Morimoto (2015) has talked about how Tumblr creates what Mary Pratt calls "contact zones," "social spaces where cultures meet, clash and grapple with each other, often in contexts of highly asymmetrical relations of power," moving the argument and focus away from fandom to be conceptualized merely as a community. Is this allowing for a different level of "just-in-time fandom" that Matt Hills proposed in 2002? I think it makes us realize that we have to diversify our conceptualization of fan cultures beyond the United States and United Kingdom to allow for more perspectives to intervene on a scholarly level, as well as take into account fan voices from different perspectives who may experience social, cultural, sexual, and racial identity differently from what is considered the majority in the United States, United Kingdom, and Western Europe. I think it also exposes us to different issues, and enables us (as academics as well as fans) to participate in different forms of activism beyond our own "backyard," in a way. Take the *Veronica Mars* crowdfunding campaign in 2014, for instance—the producers did not anticipate the global interest or response from fans, and eventually had to accommodate for donations to come in from different parts of the world.

Sangita Shresthova: The work that we at the Henry Jenkins's Civic Paths Group at the University of Southern California do, has, at times, explicitly focused on the relationship between activism, politics, and fandom. The first stage of our work focused predominantly on the United States and revealed a range of findings about fans leveraging their fandom towards social justice causes (as is the case of the Harry Potter Alliance) and activists recognizing that fandom, as a set of practices rooted predominantly in the cultural realms, can have an important role to play in mobilizing for political change (foregrounding Superman as an undocumented immigrant to advocate for immigration reform). As we shift to a more transnational focus, we recognize that the connections between fandom, activism, and politics will play out very differently. For one, when and how fandom is politicized differs significantly from region to region, country to country, community to community.

Ethan Zuckerman (2014) demonstrates the importance of a nuanced approach to transnational fandoms through his discussion of Pharrell Williams's song "Happy" and tribute music videos it inspired:

> When the residents of Toliara, Madagascar, make their version of "Happy," they're making a statement that they're part of the same media environment, part of the same culture, part of the same world as Pharrell's LA ... Happy in Damman, Saudi Arabia, features wonderfully goofy men, but not a single woman. Beijing is happy,

but profoundly crowded and hazy—intentionally or not, the video is a statement about air pollution as well as about a modern, cosmopolitan city.

In hindsight, I can also speak to this as one of the (former) organizers of the Prague Bollywood Festival. When we established the festival in 2003, we essentially wanted to create a space to collectively experience Hindi films in a city that did not have any formal or informal distribution structures for such films at that time. As we organized this festival for the better part of a decade, we came to realize that post-1990 Bollywood fandom in the Czech Republic was intertwined with existing, problematically orientalizing, assumptions regarding Indian cultures. A young Indian-American journalist, Rudra Vasquez, who found the way Czech audiences laughed during film screenings at the Prague Bollywood Festival captured this realization when she narrated her experience of watching the film *Taal* (1999) in an article she later wrote for India Currents, a monthly Indian community magazine published in California:

> The movie began, and within the first ten minutes, the audience was giggling ... In the row in front of us, two women in their early 20s were intermittently convulsing with loud, cringe inducing laughter. I knew there were some moments of comedy in the film, intentional funny scenes and dialogues and expressions, but the audience seemed to all be laughing at something that I could not figure out ... Memories of the first time I had ever seen *Taal* rushed back to me. I had been in college, sitting on the floor in a *desi* friend's tiny dorm room ... I questioned myself: had I laughed too. No, surely not. That was impossible.

To me, Vasquez's observation drove home the imperative need a deeper understanding of how transnational fandom, that is fandom that crosses national, and other boundaries, needs to be examined on multiple levels that include connections to power dynamics, cultural contexts, and ultimately political meaning.

Aswin Punathambekar: I have already alluded to this when I discussed the importance of reading and writing (citation) practices. In response to this question, I would also say that a transcultural lens will help us question what we mean by fandom in relation to, as you put it, topics such as politics and activism. In our quest to show links between the domains of fandom and the political in non-Western contexts, I fear that we have, far too hastily, cast aside the sociable dimensions of participation. We need to develop accounts of participatory culture that take the sociable and everyday dimensions of participation in and around popular culture more seriously while remaining attuned to the possibility that such participation might, in rare instances, intersect with broader civic and political issues and movements. It is worth reminding ourselves that the world of "public life" is not limited to questions of citizenship or civic engagement. Moments of participation surrounding popular culture need to be understood by first asking questions about sociability and everyday life. Progressive ideals and expectations about participatory cultures encouraging and informing civic/political engagement are well and good, but only if they are grounded in an understanding of and deep appreciation for what an immense challenge it is to create and sustain spaces of sociability.

Sangita Shresthova: I am so glad that Aswin brought up the need to value the "sociable dimensions of participation." I still often return to the conversation that I had with Aswin years ago when we founded the Civic Paths group at the University of Southern California. In that specific conversation, Aswin challenged us to expand our frame to recognize that the sociable spaces created through fannish engagements need to be valued, particularly in contexts where participation is often *assumed* to be political. In such spaces, sociable engagement does important work precisely *because* it evades political interpretation.

What are the promising directions of scholarship on race and transcultural fandom? The troubling absences?

Bertha Chin: I do think there's more interest in issues of race, not just within fandom itself such as recent articles like Rebecca Wanzo's (2015) piece in *Transformative Works and Cultures*; and Rukmini Pande has been thinking and writing a lot about race as well. I think the fact that fans are calling out content producers and the media industry on social media about misrepresentations and non-representations are encouraging more fan studies scholars to look at the ways in which we're also perpetuating a white, Western, homogenous fan culture. I think a lot more conversations need to happen, not just with scholars who are strategically placed in the "right" geographical region or happen to be the "right ethnicity" to talk about race. I think as long as the conversations or the knowledge being produced are by non-white academics, we're still maintaining some sort of status quo which posits us as "Other." I'm not in the United States, so I can't say I'm privy to the racial tensions that I see and read on the media, but I often feel when we talk about transcultural fandom (in the context of East Asian pop culture, in my case), it's often dismissed as being too "different," too "foreign," and too impenetrable because of language and cultural barriers.

There's a need on our part, particularly for scholars working on issues of race or those interested in fandom in Asia to also acknowledge that the region exists beyond Japan and Korea. Each of these countries approach race issues differently. What may be considered as whitewashing in the West, to fans familiar with Western concepts of fandom, may not be viewed as such in Asia. Box office returns and industry reports have suggested that *Ghost in the Shell* performed relatively well in Japan and China (in comparison to the United States), with fans less concerned about accusations of whitewashing than American fans were. So, we need to acknowledge the cultural differences in the ways we approach issues of race, and ask—no matter how uncomfortable it may seem—if the concerns of whitewashing and representation may be another way in which the West wants to speak for the "Other" to justify a cause. I'm not advocating that this is necessarily the case, but I think we certainly need to explore this possibility, and enable other voices and other conceptualizations of the issue to take place here rather than assume that everyone should have the same opinion about whitewashing, representations, and/or race.

Aswin Punathambekar: The most promising directions, I think, come from entirely new circuits of media production and circulation that by-pass and de-center the United States. There are two cases I would point to here: the circulation of Hindi-language Bollywood films and film music in, for example, Nigeria; and the trans-national circulation of Korean popular culture over the past decade. The Bollywood case is fascinating, as Brian Larkin has so richly detailed, because it defies any ideas about "cultural proximity" that we might, retrospectively, read into the Nigerian social context. For what is far more interesting is the ways in which films and film music from a particular era seemed to offer a "parallel modernity"—one that wasn't defined by the "West"—that was both alluring and meaningful for Nigerian audiences. In a similar vein, the K-Pop case makes it clear that we live in a multi-polar media world today and that a global phenomenon can completely by-pass the Anglophone media capitals and set up circuits of fandom that scholars based in the Anglophone academy do not understand very well at this point.

Sangita Shresthova: This is not my area of expertise, so I defer to Aswin and Bertha on this. In terms of my own work, I have been drawn to popular online projects that map fandoms of specific media content across geographies. Often situated outside the academy, these projects currently tend to map (or at least curate) fan-driven media production inspired by "Western" content and are usually shared through user-generated platforms like YouTube. As such their scope and reach is clearly limited when we consider issues of circulation and access. Still, I see these efforts as a sneak peek into the incredibly rich insights that mapping transnational fandom could yield if expanded. I also see these projects as invitation to explore their underlying production practices, the specific communities that created them, and how, if at all, they connect to the others who were also inspired by this specific media content.

References

Hills, M. (2002) *Fan Cultures*. London: Routledge.
Larkin, B. (2008) *Signal and Noise: Media, Infrastructure, and Urban Culture in Nigeria*. Durham, NC: Duke University Press.
Morimoto, L. (2015) "Fandom in/as Contact Zone," *The Fan Meta Reader*. Available at: https://thefanmetareader.org/2015/05/28/fandom-inas-contact-zone-by-tea-and-liminality/ (Accessed: 3 May 2017).
Napier, S. (2001) *Anime from Akira to Princess Mononoke: Experiencing Contemporary Japanese Animation*. New York: Palgrave Macmillan.
Srinivas, S. V. (2013) *Politics as Performance: A Social History of the Telugu Cinema*. New Delhi: Permanent Black.
Vasquez, S. R. (2008) "Bollywood on Parade," *India Currents* (April), 68.
Wanzo, R. (2015) "African American Acafandom and other Strangers: New Genealogies of Fan Studies," *Transformative Works and Cultures*, 20. http://dx.doi.org/10.3983/twc.2015.0699.
Zuckerman, Ethan (2014) "YouTube Parody as Politics: How the World Made Pharrell Cry," *Atlantic* (May 21). www.theatlantic.com/technology/archive/2014/05 /youtube-parody-as-politics-how-the-world-made-pharrell-cry/371380/.

PART IV

Industry and Labor

Introduction: Industry and Labor

When media fan studies first emerged in the late 1980s and early 1990s, it was common to position media industries (or media producers) and media fans as locked in a conflict for textual and ideological ownership over media objects. As fans have increasingly become a desirable demographic media in a landscape that values (both literally and figuratively) precisely the sort of franchise loyalty and engagement emblematic of fan communities, the power dynamic between industry and fans has shifted. While fans unquestionably have more avenues available to speak back to industry (either directly, through an array of social media platforms, or indirectly through the capacity to widely disseminate transformative fan works), it would be equally problematic to claim that the conflicts and power differentials that once defined this relationship have evaporated alongside the rise of digital media. As fan labor and content creation has increasingly become a cornerstone of industry promotional strategies, this section explores the alternately fraught and friendly relationship between media industries and media fans, as each side attempts to negotiate the evolving terms of their relationship.

This section contains five chapters reprinted from the first edition. Avi Santo's chapter, focused on fandom as an emerging lifestyle brand and the wide array of functions fan merchandise serves for fans, has emerged as a foundational work for a growing body of scholarship focused on the intersections of fandom, fashion, and merchandising. Alisa Perren and Laura Felschow's chapter brings media industry studies into more active conversation with fan studies. Focusing on the comic book industry, and through a comparative analysis of DC Comics and Image Comics, Perren and Felschow utilize interviews to address how creators imagine and navigate their relationship with both company executives and fans. Shifting focus from comic books to comic conventions, Anne Gilbert explores the tensions surrounding San Diego Comic-Con as a site of both fan community and industrial promotion. Derek Johnson expands his early work on "fantagonsism" to explore reactionary fan responses (such as outcry over the recent all-female Ghostbusters reboot) and how media industries attempt to manage growing concerns around fan "entitlement." Finally, Kristen J. Warner examines the other side of fan advocacy around representation, examining how the Iris West Defense Squad mobilized through Twitter to apply pressure to the producers of Warner Brothers' film version of *The Flash* and ensure that a Black actress was cast as Iris West. Two chapters originally featured in the first edition have been revised: First, Mel Stanfill revisits their consideration of how corporate and for-profit fanfiction platforms poses a potential threat to fan culture's longstanding gift economy, addressing how the emergence of AI-generated fanfiction further complicates these tensions. Similarly, Melanie Kohnen revisits their consideration of transmedia and immersive marketing campaigns, building on their work on experiential marketing and fan activations at San Diego Comic-Con.

This section on fan/industry relations and fan labor also features four new chapters. Eve Ng, synthesizing and building on the work of their 2022 book *Cancel Culture: A Critical Analysis*, explores an array of motivations for "cancelling" (ranging from celebrity misconduct to problematic media content) as well as responses to it (including deplatforming). While Anne Gilbert's chapter in this section focuses on San Diego Comic-Con as a preeminent site of interaction between media industries and fans, Guillermo Aguilar Vázquez and Ana Fabiola Vidal Fernández focus on "frikis" (a term used by Mexican fans to self-identify as avid media consumers) and the various conventions and fan retail spaces operating within Mexico City. In particular, their work sheds light on both the impact of the North American Free Trade Agreement (NAFTA) has had on Mexican fan culture, as well as the role that class plays in limiting fan practices and participation. Charlotte Howell considers how the streaming service DAZN's coverage of women's football courted global fans of the sport, and how this produced mixed results for women fans. While DAZN succeeding in not treating women's football as a niche market, it also erased some of the specific community concerns and spaces that had been cultivated by women's soccer fandom. Finally, in "So Strike We All: Union Action and Cosplay on the Picket Line," Kate Fortmueller and Suzanne Scott address how the 2023 WGA and SAG-Aftra union strikes deployed an array of fannish tactics to gain visibility and build allyship with media consumers on social media.

Further Reading

Affuso, E and Suzanne Scott. (2023). *Sartorial Fandom: Fashion, Beauty Culture, and Identity*. Ann Arbor: University of Michigan Press.
Affuso, E. and Avi Santo (eds.). 2018. "Film and Merchandise." Special issue, *Film Criticism* 42 (2).
Allison, R. (2018) *Kicking Center: Gender and the Selling of Women's Professional Soccer*. New Brunswick, NJ: Rutgers University Press.
Ang, I. (1991). *Desperately Seeking the Audience*. New York: Routledge.
Banks, M., Conor, B. and Mayer, V. (eds.) (2015) *Production Studies, The Sequel! Cultural Studies of Global Media Industries*. New York: Routledge.
Cherry, B. (2011) "Knit One, Bite One: Vampire Fandom, Fan Production and Feminine Handicrafts," In G. Schott and K. Moffat (eds.) *Fanpires: Audience Consumption of the Modern Vampire*. Washington DC: New Academia Publishing, pp. 137–55.
Chin, B. (2013) "The Fan-Media Producer Collaboration: How Fan Relationships are Managed in a Post-Series X-Files Fandom," *Science Fiction Film & Television*, 6(1): 87–99.
Clarke, M. J. (2012) *Transmedia Television: New Trends in Network Serial Production*. London and New York: Bloomsbury Academic.
Click, M. (ed.). (2019) *Anti-Fandom: Dislike and Hate in the Digital Age*. New York: New York University Press.
Couldry, N. (2000) *The Place of Media Power: Pilgrims and Witnesses of the Media Age*. New York: Routledge.

Evans, E. (2011) *Transmedia Television: Audiences, New Media, and Daily Life*. New York and London: Routledge.
Evans, E. (2020). *Understanding Engagement in Transmedia Culture*. New York: Routledge.
Fortmueller, K. and Luci Marzola (2024) *Hollywood Unions*. Chicago: Rutgers University Press.
Gabilliet, J.-P. (2009) *Of Comics and Men: A Cultural History of American Comic Books*. Trans. Bart Beaty and Nick Nguyen. Jackson, MS: University of Mississippi Press.
Geraghty, L. (2014) "It's Not All About the Music: Online Fan Communities and Collecting Hard Rock Caf. Pins," *Transformative Works and Cultures*, 16, http://dx.doi.org/10.3983/twc.2014.0492.
Gray, J. (2010) *Show Sold Separately: Promos, Spoilers, and Other Media Paratexts*. New York: New York University Press.
Hebdige, D. (1979) *Subculture: The Meaning of Style*. London: New York, Routledge.
Hills, M. (2002) *Fan Cultures*. London: Routledge.
Hoebink, D., Reijnders, S. and Waysdorf, A. (2014) "Exhibiting Fandom: A Museological Perspective," *Transformative Works and Cultures*, 16, http://dx.doi.org/10.3983/twc.2014.0529.
Jenkins, H., Ford, S. and Green J. (2013) *Spreadable Media: Creating Value and Meaning in a Networked Culture*. New York: NYU Press.
Johnson, D. (2007) "Fan-tagonism: Factions, Institutions, and Constitutive Hegemonies of Fandom," in J. Gray, C. Sandvoss and C. L. Harrington (eds.) *Fandom: Identities and Communities in A Mediated World*. New York: New York University Press, pp. 285–300.
Johnson, D., Kompare, D. and Santo, A. (eds.) (2014) *Making Media Work: Cultures of Management in the Entertainment Industries*. New York: NYU Press.
Kustritz, A.M. (2022). "Transmediating Difference: Fictional Filter Bubbles and Transmedia Storytelling." *Convergence* (28:3): 699–713.
Lewis, L. A. (ed.) (1992) *The Adoring Audience: Fan Culture and Popular Media*. London: New York, Routledge.
McClearen, J. (2021) *Fighting Visibility: Sports Media and Female Athletes in the UFC*. Chicago, IL: University of Illinois Press.
Schaffar, W. and P. Wongratanawin. (2021). "The #MilkTeaAlliance: A New Transnational Pro-Democracy Movement Against Chinese-Centered Globalization?," *Advances in South-East Asian Studies* 14(1): 5–35.
Urbanski, H. (2013) *The Science Fiction Reboot: Canon, Innovation and Fandom in Refashioned Franchises*. Jefferson, NC: McFarland.
Williams, R. (2020). *Theme Park Fandom: Spatial Transmedia, Materiality and Participatory Cultures*. Amsterdam: Amsterdam University Press.
Woo, B. (2015) "Erasing the Lines between Leisure and Labor: Creative Work in the Comics World" *Spectator* 35(2): 57–64.

33
FANS AND MERCHANDISE

Avi Santo

Introduction

Despite Benjamin Woo's recognition that "things are the sine qua non of fandom, that without which it remains only potentiality and not a realized capability" (2014: 1.3), the relationship between fandom and merchandise has received very little critical attention from scholars. Matt Hills theorizes that this diminished focus is due to the perceived relationship between merchandise and consumerism that has dogged fan cultures and which fan scholars have worked so hard to recuperate by emphasizing fan productivity at the expense of fan consumption practices (2014: 1.1). Hills also suggests that "material fandom" has traditionally been gendered male and been seen as complicit with official media industry conceptualizations of acceptable fan behavior (i.e. filial devotion to reproducing the text; loyalty to corporate brand owners and licensed merchandise), while fan scholarship has largely been informed by feminist approaches that focus on the work done by marginalized communities in challenging and disrupting the scriptural economy (1.3-1.4). Only very recently has there been a turn toward studying "object-oriented" fans, though the tendency has been to focus on maker and craft communities (see Rehak 2013, Hills 2014, Godwin 2015) rather than the role of merchandise within fan culture. There has also been general disregard for how some crafty fans have emerged as "fan-trepreneurs" (Scott 2014) seeking to capitalize on their fandom by—among other things—developing businesses that sell 'fan-made merchandise' to other fans (See Jones 2014 for exception).

Ultimately, the aversion to taking material fan practices seriously has led to large gaps in studying what fans actually do with the merchandise they acquire and how these material objects function as veritable sites of struggle and negotiation over what constitutes fandom and who can gain access to/status within a particular community. Moreover, merchandise constitutes one of the key components through which media industries have redefined their relationship with fan culture and have sought to define fandom not only in consumerist terms but also within existing frameworks for consumer product extension: namely the reconstitution of fandom as a lifestyle category rather than a communal experience. In turn, this has led to the commissioning of fan-oriented objects that celebrate fans' supposed continued embrace of juvenility and rejection of adulthood's stifling of creativity and play (precisely the opposite way fans were formerly derided by mainstream institutions as stuck in a perpetual adolescence). In so doing, the media industries have attempted not only to delimit what fans do with merchandise, but also to define what types of merchandise might be considered fannish.

Finally, as the mainstreaming of fandom has led to an overproduction of merchandise for fans and the "regifting" (Scott 2009) of material fandom back to its constituents, 'fan-made merchandise' (i.e. objects built or crafted by fans and then either sold to fans or marketed as authentically fannish) has emerged as a contested practice for both buttressing against industry-sanctioned fans and cultivating a niche market invested in its own exclusivity. While fan-made merchandise challenges the role of a gift economy in tethering and sheltering fan communities, it does so not only by introducing market-driven transactionality into fan exchanges, but also by placing great emphasis on acquiring "One-of-a-Kind" (OOAK) objects that set individual fans apart within their respective communities, altering how status and cultural capital have typically operated. Even as marketing for fan-made merchandise relies upon a particular rhetorical positioning of maker and buyer as sharing fannish dispositions, increasingly, in terms of production, the line between fan-made merchandise and fan merchandise produced by official licensees is becoming blurred. In the following pages, I unpack each of these ideas further while synthesizing the small but significant body of scholarship turning its attention to the intersections of fandom and merchandise.

Collecting as Sharing within Fan Communities

Fandom's relationship to merchandise is complicated. Merchandise can be an outlet for demonstrating financial and emotional investment in a franchise or brand's "lovemarks" (Jenkins 2006) but it is also an approach typically understood as shallow compared to other fan practices. Owning licensed merchandise is often seen as merely a starting point for fans, who quickly move from buying things to making them as a more authentic display of engagement (see Rehak 2012, Hills 2002, Jenkins 1992). While I do not refute the possibility that some fans see the acquisition of merchandise as merely a starting point for participation (and perhaps one that needs to be outgrown to become a fully fledged member of a given fan community), the leap from buying to making bypasses a wide range of things that fans actually do with the things they buy.

Dorus Hoebink, Stijn Reijnders, and Abby Waysdorf suggest that part of the problem lies in the language used to describe the investment by fans in merchandise, which places too much emphasis on their consumption of commodities rather than their acquisition of objects. The latter not only implies a purposefulness attached to attaining material objects denied to so-called victims of consumer culture, but it also points to "an understanding that physical things have a life in the possession of their owner after purchase and are not discarded after they have been used, read, or seen" (2014: 2.1). In short, acquiring and/or collecting objects places emphasis on fan agency in selecting particular items while also granting those items purpose within fan practices. Those purposes might include opportunities to engage in "tactile transmediality" (Gilligan 2012) wherein a media text is extended into the material world through "feelies" (Peters 2014) and other tangible products, creating opportunities for fans to continue exploring a storyworld even as their homes (or other places where their fandom resides) become part of said world. Tactile transmediality implies that material objects need to be considered part of the transmedia storytelling experience that many cult media franchises embrace and encourage, but more than that, the concept gestures at the opportunity made available by such objects for fans to reach out and grab hold of the story for the purposes of telling their own (albeit with impositions found in packaging and design features that attempt to narrow the scope of the storytelling scenarios) (See Gray 2010, Bainbridge 2010).

While merchandise can lend itself to forms of textual extraction and extension that are key components of fan engagement, it is also important to note that the acts of acquiring and collecting media-oriented objects are also an integral part of how individuals express their identity and individuality within a consumer society. Merchandise can materially encapsulate their acquirer's memories of a particular event or experience, bits of their biography, or elicit affect tied to nostalgia or a sense of place that is only tangentially related to the text upon which an item is based. For example, a *Buffy the Vampire Slayer* action figure might serve as a tactile encapsulation of its owner's allegiance to a particular form of feminism, or it might be a reminder of how their participation in a particular viewing community summons up hard-to-place feelings reminiscent of childhood. Cornel Sandvoss notes, "fans give their consumption an inherently private and personal nature that removes their object of consumption from the logic of capitalist exchange" (2005: 116), while Mihali Csikszentmihalyi (1995) asserts that material objects express identity within a physical space. Csikszentmihalyi's claim captures how mass-produced merchandise can be transformed into personalized objects of self-expression through curatorial work done by fans within the confines of their own homes.

Indeed, Hoebink, Reijnders and Waysdorf claim that fan curatorial work, while often done in private, must be recognized as transformative because the very act of placing items in any sort of systematic or personalized order necessarily changes their original meaning (though not always in progressive or transgressive ways). Borrowing from museology, they contend that fan collecting is often curated in ways that either emphasize personal (souvenir), object-oriented (fetishistic/devotional) or context-oriented (systematic) organizational schemas. Acquired objects can stand in for places their collector has visited as part of their fandom, like Comic-Con exclusives or Hard Rock Cafe pins (see Geraghty 2014), or they can exemplify their owner's investment of money, time, effort in acquiring objects that carry cultural capital within a particular fan community (and serve as totems representing a member's status within that community), or they can be organized according to their encapsulation of particular socio-historic practices related to the franchise's development or adaptation (as well as offering opportunity for their owner to share their knowledge about the production, distribution, and/or marketing of such an artifact).

Of course, many people own objects—some based on media and popular culture—that represent aspects of their identity, but of which they are not fans. What distinguishes the fan collector from the non-fan variety is typically their desire to share these objects along with the stories that surround their production, acquisition, and display with other members of a fan community who will appreciate an item's cultural and social value as much as if not more than its economic worth. Lincoln Geraghty (2014, 2014a) asserts that community is formed around *stories* told about collectibles, not the items themselves; a possibility greatly enhanced by Web 2.0's facilitation of sharing images and video among fans that can in turn transform items displayed in one's living room into a semi-public curated collection.

Geraghty (2014a) also suggests that sharing images of and stories about collectible merchandise mediates fan abilities to both stand out and fit in within their respective communities, offering opportunities for some fans to distinguish themselves and enhance their social and cultural capital. Thus, merchandise can help fans establish their legitimacy within particular communities while also functioning as a status symbol that reinforces hierarchies and differences within that community. This potential for divisiveness is exacerbated by what Woo points to as the "constraints of materiality" (2014: 1.5), namely the cost of acquiring (which can include the expense of traveling to places where objects can be acquired), housing and taking care of collectible objects, which often separates fans from one another based on real world socioeconomic differences. Indeed, class differences are among the most understudied dimensions of fandom. As Josh Stenger (2006) notes concerning Buffy fans' reactions to the prices paid by a small contingent for costumes and props from the series that were auctioned on eBay, differences in disposable income were sources of great frustration, with poorer fans repeatedly questioning the allegiances of those outbidding them. When fans found out that the money spent on Buffy costumes and props went back into 20th Century Fox's coffers rather than to charity, they proudly denounced the process as exploitative framing those who had spent big dollars on these items as either complicit with or duped by the industrial machine. In essence, Buffy fans reproduced the same negative discourse about fandom's hyper-consumerism but used it to label those who could afford to bid on auctioned items as inauthentic fans.

Buying into the Fan Lifestyle

The claim that fandom has become inundated with pretenders is fueled to some extent by the term's reclamation by the entertainment industries over the past two decades. Simply put, there has been a clear shift in the way entertainment industries address fans that can be characterized as a movement from derisive dismissal to active cultivation. This change in attitude is partly in response to industrial and cultural convergence, which has led on the one hand to a privileging of intellectual property (IP) as the entertainment industry's core asset and, on the other hand, to a recognition that the boundaries separating producers and consumers have dissolved granting fans a "contested utility" (Murray 2004) as brand evangelists and grassroots marketers. Merchandise plays an important role in forwarding both agendas. Branded t-shirts, backpacks, and cell phone covers may transform fans into walking promotional platforms for particular franchises, but they also fulfill the entertainment industry's objective in creating veritable touch points for IP that integrate them into consumers' daily routines as branded lifestyle products.

Lifestyle brands infuse mundane and functional things with personality, whereby a character or franchise's attributes become signifiers of their owners' unique identity. This is at the heart of how the entertainment industries have re-branded fandom: as a lifestyle in search of products that allow individuals to express affinity with particular brands (and through those brands with one another). Fandom as lifestyle doesn't merely place greater emphasis on consumption, but on individuals using branded products as forms of self-expression and even self-promotion in order to establish their value in a reputational economy (see Banet-Weiser 2012). Acquiring media objects is still seen as productive, but productivity is no longer defined by how fans curate those objects but instead by how they use them as self-branding opportunities (while simultaneously serving as brand advocates). Similarly, community is not abolished as part of the fan lifestyle, but rather its function is re-purposed so that participation is contingent on a kind of competitive popularity. This can be evidenced in the way marketing for branded merchandise often suggests that others will envy the person possessing it. Significantly, this person is typically envisioned as a child, as most licensed merchandise is still directed at kids aged 4–14.

Fandom's historical relationship to children's culture is fraught with accusations that fans had failed to enter adulthood and were stuck in a kind of protracted adolescence (see Jenkins 1992). Yet, there can be little doubt that entertainment franchises repeatedly position children as fans and increasingly seek to use lifestyle merchandise categories to extend that relationship into adulthood, especially for men. Where male fans had previously been ridiculed for their childlike obsessions with toys, comic books, and other worthless ephemera, there is now a distinct market-driven celebration of male fan refusals to abandon youthful pursuits as a form of rebelliousness against the status quo (see Kimmel 2009, Cross 2010).

And though so-called "geeks" may embrace their supposed outsider status, from an industry perspective it is abundantly clear that they are not only a lucrative market for licensed merchandise, but a market envisioned as a direct extension of preformed product and consumer categories. For example, Disney's consumer products division is divided into five teams organized according to age, gender, and lifestyle. They have an infant and children's team, a boys and geeks team, a girls and tweens team, and an adult team. The organizing principles not only normalize gendered expectations for branded products, but they also position both "geeks" and "tweens" as categories with expiration dates that will eventually give way to adulthood (though "geek" is assuredly less bound by actual age ranges than "tween," whose very label implies a physiological endpoint. Boys can choose to remain "geeks" forever, but hormones will eventually age girls out of products directed at "tweens").

While the implication is that "geeks" will continue to consume products that appeal to "boys," the reality is that by binding these imagined consumer groups together, the industry has simply mapped fan-directed merchandise onto preexisting product categories with established sales records at retail. That the vast majority of products sold as fan items directed at geeks take the shape of action figures, toys, games, t-shirts, and boxer shorts is a byproduct of licensors and licensees needing to slot items onto retail shelves according to the organizing principles that most store buyers already adhere to.

Brand owners are increasingly encouraged to see the retailer as the ultimate client and to position products "from the outside in" by visualizing how they help retailers to "fill out their assortment" (Parham 2015). In other words, merchandise developed and sold as part of a fan lifestyle reflects consumer product divisions investment in manufacturer and retailer needs more than any deep commitment to understanding what fans want or an attempt to differentiate wants among fandoms for different media franchises. Indeed, the opposite is true. There is a marked effort to shoehorn fan consumption into established consumer categories and patterns.

Fan-Made Merchandise

The entertainment industries' recent revaluation of fans has led to the manufacturing and marketing of merchandise tailored specifically for their 'lifestyle.' Though responses to this new-found recognition have been mixed, one area of fandom that has grown partly in response to the mainstreaming of "fans" is fan-made merchandise. Fan-made merchandise is stuff made by fans and sold to fans as authentic expressions of fannishness. Fan-made merchandise combines craft culture's fetishistic embrace of hand-made items with claims to authenticity rooted in the crafter's allegiance to and membership within particular fan communities. Fan-made merchandise has also proliferated due to the opportunities afforded by digital platforms like Etsy.com for crafty fans to set up virtual storefronts as well as in conjunction with the circulation of neoliberal ideologies that encourage the monetization of leisure, pleasure, and relaxation-based activities.

To be clear, fans have made things for other fans for a very long time. Some of those things have even required an exchange of money. What separates fan-made merchandise from these earlier exchanges is the placement of these items in virtual stores that compete with one another for fan business. Also distinct, is the sense that many of these virtual storefronts are operated by individuals for whom the sale of fan-made merchandise is more than a hobby or a side business but rather their primary means of making a living (or at least that they'd like it to be). Brigid Cherry asserts that a site like Etsy serves as "an extremely commercial niche for entrepreneurial fans" (2011: 137). Though the notion that earlier generations of fans either gave freely to other fans or paid money for a piece of fan art merely as a symbolic gesture of appreciation or solidarity (or only to help cover the artist's expenses) romanticizes how capital functions within reputational economies and ignores how the pre-internet gray economy of fan convention booths, newsletter advertorials, and deals for space on comic book store shelves operated, current efforts by "fan-trepreneurs" (Scott 2014) to monetize their creativity have been met with concern over how they disrupt fan allegiance to the "gift economy."

While Abigail De Kosnik (2009) supports the idea of fans being paid by other fans for their work as preferable to that work being appropriated and sold back to fans by mainstream media producers, Karen Hellekson (2009) has expressed concern that this transaction-based model will undermine the gift economy's emphasis on reciprocity and obligation that cement relationships and reinforce fan community social structures via the free exchange of artifacts. The De Kosnik/Hellekson debate has largely focused on the potential impact of commercialization on fan fiction community norms and standards. Bethan Jones (2014) points out that these debates are far less fervent when it comes to the exchange of fan art, jewelry, t-shirts, and other objects because the latter are understood as forms of brand identification rather than community participation and thereby do not lose their fannish quality just because they are bought and sold. For Jones, fan fiction is a participatory experience wherein fans read multiple drafts and offer both revision and plot suggestions that the writer then incorporates into the work. Fan-made merchandise supposedly has no such reciprocal process to begin with and is therefore exempted from debates over whether or not it should have a price tag attached to it.

Without entering too deeply into this debate, I do need to push back slightly against Jones' assertion that fan-made merchandise does not undergo a process of co-creation, albeit a somewhat different one than fan fiction. It is actually quite common for fans to commission work from shop owners on sites like Etsy. Most shops say they accept inquiries for custom requests, but in actuality, many shop owners will only take on custom requests for characters and franchises they have personal affinities for. Placing a request is part of an initial back-and-forth through which shop owners and fans negotiate and even collaborate on the design process, but also share personal stories connected to their fandom.

For example, when I commissioned a set of peg dolls based on characters from *The Wiz* for my children, I sent a note explaining the film's significance to our family, including photos of us dressed up as some of the characters for a local comic-con convention. It was important to me that the designer understood the depth of our love for the film. Their enthusiastic response, which included mentioning that my note had inspired them to re-watch the film with their own kids, was far more important than their agreement to take on the project or their monetary quote. Once they received payment, they felt obligated to share sketches of their design with me and seek my input about certain characters, resulting in our mutual decision to make the character of The Wiz into an Amigurimi figure instead of the standard peg doll. Though the shop owner certainly asked that positive feedback be left on their page, they also requested photos of the items on display in my house and asked my permission to share those images on their personal blog.

Though this example is purely anecdotal, I believe it to be typical of how a lot of fan-made merchandise gets commissioned. The terms of transaction are folded in with demonstrations of fannish affinity. The process bears similarity to the gift economy model for fan fiction in that it engenders a good deal of reciprocity and feelings of obligation on the part of the fan-creator to seek input and share design ideas before the item is actually constructed (though obviously money has already been exchanged, which generates a different type of obligation as well). While a closer comparison might be to artist/patron relationships, there was nonetheless a sense of co-creation that was both integral to the experience and antithetical to the acquisition of store-bought merchandise. The interest expressed by the designer in seeing how their creations were ultimately displayed might be understood as both extending the relationship beyond the point of sale and tying back to the social function of curating within certain fan communities. It also certainly served as a way for them to promote their fannish sensibilities to other potential clients.

Suzanne Scott has argued that it is increasingly difficult to discuss the gift economy in isolation from "commodity culture" targeting fan communities. Scott suggests that this is because mainstream industries have "selectively appropriated" aspects of "the gift economy's ethos for its own economic gain" (2009: 1.1). Though Hellekson notes that the gift economy has served as a type of protection for fan creators against threats of copyright and trademark infringement precisely because it places emphasis on the free exchange of items, there is plenty of evidence that IP owners and manufacturers look to fan creations as sources of merchandising inspiration and selectively threaten legal action typically only when licensed versions of similar items enter the market. Such was the case when 20th Century Fox awarded ThinkGeek a license to sell *Firefly*-inspired knitted hats worn by the popular character Jayne. Such hats had previously circulated widely on sites like Etsy by and for members of *Firefly*'s Browncoat fan community. Once ThinkGeek began selling the licensed version, fan stores like Firefly Cargo Bay had their listings deactivated by Etsy's legal department who had received cease and desist letters from Fox. No opportunity to claim fair use was provided (see Hall 2013).

While it is certainly the case that IP owners have sought to emulate fan creations (while seeking to eliminate fan creators), the opposite is also true. It is increasingly difficult to differentiate between fan-made merchandise and its mass-produced cousin. This is partly the result of companies like Funko that produce "designer" figures that mimic fan styles, but it is also due to changes brought about by platforms like Etsy, which now allow designers to partner with manufacturers to increase merchandise volume (see Norton 2014). Similarly, RedBubble.com takes original fan design work and prints it onto a range of generic objects from coffee mugs to t-shirts, in effect replicating the logic of lifestyle branding (see Jones 2014). Meanwhile, media giants like Disney and Cartoon Network have begun exploring the possibilities of online IP licensing portals for fan-made merchandise wherein shopkeepers can obtain exclusive rights to certain designs for products currently not licensed to commercial manufacturers. This is billed as granting some fans a competitive edge within craft circles, while also ensuring corporate oversight of how their IP is being crafted (interview with Alice Cahn, former vice president of Development & Acquisitions for Cartoon Network, 2016).

Faced on the one hand with a glut of mass-produced merchandise directed at a fan lifestyle and, on the other hand, with an increasingly murky distinction between fan-made merchandise and its commercial equivalent, many fans have looked to acquire OOAK items that offer assurances of authenticity. On the surface, OOAK items—like *The Wiz* peg dolls—seem to reject the mainstreaming of fandom while also holding Etsy designers accountable to the promise of "hand-made." And OOAK items do share something in common with fan collecting practices in that they are rare items that fan curators can utilize to demonstrate their commitment to the fandom. But OOAK items also transform the functions of merchandise among fans. Because they are typically commissioned, not found, OOAK items foreground the taste and personality of the person who commissioned them over that of the media property's communal meanings and value. In this sense, OOAK items and lifestyle brands are not so different. Moreover, the stories of discovery that typically accompany curating collectibles are redirected away from the archaeological dimensions of finding a rare artifact toward the process of finding work-for-hire capable of capturing an individual fan's vision. In this sense, OOAK items grant a kind of authorial status to their owners not all that different from the one corporations claim over their IP, even as others—including fans—do the creative work in reproducing these assets.

References

Bainbridge, J. (2010) "Fully Articulated: The Rise of the Action Figure and the Changing Face of 'Children's' Entertainment," *Continuum*, 24(6), pp. 829–42.

Banet-Weiser, S. (2012) *Authentic: The Politics of Ambivalence in a Brand Culture*, New York: NYU Press.

Cahn, A. (2016) Interview. March 25.

Cherry, B. (2011) "Knit One, Bite One: Vampire Fandom, Fan Production and Feminine Handicrafts," in G. Schott and K. Moffat (eds.) *Fanpires: Audience Consumption of the Modern Vampire*, Washington, DC: New Academia Publishing, pp. 137–55.

Cross, G. (2010) *Men to Boys: The Making of Modern Immaturity*, New York: Columbia University Press.

Csikszentmihalyi, M. (1995) "Why We Need Things," in S. Lubar and W.D. Kingery (eds.) *History from Things: Essays on Material Culture*, Washington, DC: Smithsonian Institution Press, pp. 20–29.

De Kosnik, A. (2009) "Should Fan Fiction Be Free?" *Cinema Journal*, 48(4), pp. 118–24.

Geraghty, L. (2014) "It's Not All About the Music: Online Fan Communities and Collecting Hard Rock Café Pins," *Transformative Works and Cultures*, 16, http://dx.doi.org/10.3983/twc.2014.0492.

Geraghty, L. (2014a) *Cult Collectors: Nostalgia, Fandom and Collecting Popular Culture*, New York: Routledge.

Gilligan, S. (2012) "Heaving Cleavages and Fantastic Frock Coats: Gender Fluidity, Celebrity and Tactile Transmediality in Contemporary Costume Cinema," *Fashion, Film & Consumption*, 1(1), pp. 7–38.

Godwin, V. (2015) "Mimetic Fandom and One-sixth-scale Action Figures," *Transformative Works and Cultures*, 20, http://dx.doi.org/10.3983/twc.2015.0689.

Gray, J. (2010) *Show Sold Separately: Promos, Spoilers and Other Media Paratexts*, New York: NYU Press.

Hall, E. (2013) "Firefly Hat Triggers Corporate Crackdown," *Buzzfeed News*, April 9, www.buzzfeed.com/ellievhall/firefly-hat-triggers-corporate-crackdown?utm_term=.dfYem6ZnOw#.prRvmW1Eok.
Hellekson, K. (2009) "A Fannish Field of Value: Online Fan Gift Culture," *Cinema Journal*, 48(4), pp. 113–118.
Hills, M. (2002) *Fan Cultures*, New York: Routledge.
Hills, M. (2014) "From Dalek Half Balls to Daft Punk Helmets: Mimetic Fandom and the Crafting of Replicas," *Transformative Works and Cultures*, 16, http://dx.doi.org/10.3983/twc.2014.0531.
Hoebink, D., Reijnders, S., and Waysdorf, A. (2014) "Exhibiting Fandom: A Museological Perspective," *Transformative Works and Cultures*, 16, http://dx.doi.org/10.3983/twc.2014.0529.
Jenkins, H. (1992) *Textual Poachers: Television Fans & Participatory Culture*, New York: Routledge.
Jenkins, H. (2006) *Convergence Culture: Where Old and New Media Collide*, New York: NYU Press.
Jones, B. (2014) "Fifty Shades of Exploitation: Fan Labor and Fifty Shades of Grey," *Transformative Works and Cultures*, 15, http://dx.doi.org/10.3983/twc.2014.0501.
Kimmel, M. (2009), *Guyland: The Perilous World Where Boys Become Men*, New York: Harper.
Murray, S. (2004) "'Celebrating the Story the Way It Is': Cultural Studies, Corporate Media and the Contested Utility of Fandom," *Continuum*, 18(1), pp. 7–25.
Norton, E. (2014) "True Handmade: Exploring the Negotiations over the Subcultural Ideology of Authenticity within the Etsy Community," MA Thesis, Utrecht University.
Parham, J. (2015) "How to Win at Retail: The 5 Rules," *LIMA Licensing University Roundtable Session*, June 10.
Peters, I. (2014) "Peril-Sensitive Sunglasses, Superheroes in Miniature, and Pink Polka-Dot Boxers: Artifact and Collectible Video Game Feelies, Play, and the Paratextual Gaming Experience," *Transformative Works and Cultures*, 16, http://dx.doi.org/10.3983/twc.2014.0509.
Rehak, B. (2013) "Materializing Monsters: Aurora Models, Garage Kits, and the Object Practices of Horror Fandom," *Journal of Fandom Studies*, 1(1), pp. 27–45.
Sandvoss, C. (2005) *Fans: The Mirror of Consumption*, Cambridge: Polity Press.
Scott, S. (2009) "Repackaging Fan Culture: The Regifting Economy of Ancillary Content Models," *Transformative Works and Cultures*, 3, http://dx.doi.org/10.3983/twc.2009.0150.
Scott, S. (2014) "Talking the Walk: Enunciative Fandom and Fan Studies' Industrial Turn," *Society for Cinema and Media Studies Conference*, Seattle, March 19–23.
Stenger, J. (2006) "The Clothes Make the Fan: Fashion and Online Fandom When 'Buffy the Vampire Slayer' Goes to eBay," *Cinema Journal*, 45(4), pp. 26–44.
Unknown (2015) "MAGIC: Marvel Amps Up Fashion Presence," *License Global!* February 18, www.licensemag.com/license-global/magic-marvel-amps-fashion-presence.
Woo, B. (2014) "A Pragmatics of Things: Materiality and Constraint in Fan Practices," *Transformative Works and Cultures*, 16, http://dx.doi.org/10.3983/twc.2014.0495.

34
THE FANFICTION GOLD RUSH 2.0
After/AI

Mel Stanfill

"Fanfiction, as it's known, can be big business," announced a 2022 newspaper article (Kerridge 2022). Just how big is it? In 2021, publishing platform Wattpad, which has fanfiction as a main category of content, was purchased for $600 million (Grady 2022). Fan creative production and its attendant value creation – in terms of meaning, commitment, and promotion – are as old as fandom itself, but the 2010s saw a shift to move these forms of amateur production into the market that has only continued to escalate in the 2020s. I argue that new forms of commercialization of fanfiction driven by sites like Wattpad differ dramatically from previous modes of fannish production. They are, first, a notable departure from fandom's historical organization as a gift economy. Additionally, these new forms of monetization diverge from older routes to making money from fan labor, as they have been transformed by both the runaway success of *Fifty Shades of Grey* (James 2012) – which began its life as *Twilight* (Meyer 2006) fanfiction "Master of the Universe" – as well as the platformization of fanfiction. The fanfiction gold rush has increasingly been normalized, but tensions persist between older, more communitarian models of fandom and new individualistic, market-based ones that may be crowding out previous traditions.

Historical Fandom Norms

As the monetization of fanfiction began to ramp up in the early 2010s with the advent of things like Amazon's Kindle Worlds platform (2013–2018) – which allowed authors to sell fanfiction e-books for certain intellectual properties for which Amazon had negotiated licenses – there was often resistance to these developments from previous generations of fans whose social norms differed. Fandom has historically functioned largely as a gift economy. Participants in gift economies use gift-giving – as opposed to capitalism's market exchange – to circulate goods and services. This economy is not simply friendly and voluntary in the way that "gifts" are colloquially understood as freely chosen expressions of affection, but quite structured. Giving in a gift *economy* is, first, hierarchical – in fandom, as in the Indigenous North American practice of potlatch (Mauss 2000; Boyle 2003; Hyde 2007), giving more produces status. Producing a lot of stories, or a story perceived as a great contribution to the community, provides one major way to become a Big Name Fan – that is, one with status. The effusive commenter on fanfiction is also seen as a good contributor, while there is less regard for the person who either writes only sporadically or begins a story and doesn't finish it (this will become important later). Additionally, giving and returning gifts is obligatory in a gift economy (Mauss 2000; Pearson 2007; Hellekson 2009). Because the gift of creative production normatively obliges the recipient to provide feedback, under this model of exchange the "lurker" who reads but does not write stories or comment can be seen as a freeloader or "leecher" (Jenkins et al. 2013: 63).

This gift economy is thus clearly distinguishable from the market economy. Part of the reason for this is that fan work has often remained firmly noncommercial out of a fear of legal censure (Hellekson 2009; Scott 2019); gift economies are thought to be less likely to attract legal action (though by the letter of the law, noncommercial uses can still be judged unfair). However, beyond avoiding legal risk, some fans actively reject commercialism. Hellekson (2009: 118) describes fandom has having its own "field of value" that "specifically excludes profit, further separating their community from the larger (male-gendered) community of commerce." What is it that fans value instead? One key reason to engage in fan production is recognition from the community (Tushnet 2007; Lothian 2009; Chin 2014) or to support or contribute to the community (Jones 2014, Turk 2014). Fandom runs on fan labor, and this work produces enjoyment, collectivity, and the various material and immaterial goods that give fandom shape as a practice, community, or culture. For example, fan work made the Organization for Transformative Works' (OTW) fanfiction archive, the Archive of Our Own (AO3). As with all such archives, fans contribute its content, but fans also built AO3 and maintain it as a platform. Indeed, the labor of creating AO3 was recognized with a Hugo Award for Best Related Work in 2019 (Romano 2019).

Perhaps most importantly, fan work creates fan community – fandom itself – through the production and maintenance of affective ties. Bethan Jones (2014: 2.3) describes these forms of creative production as communal because "fans do not simply upload art, fic, or vids; they also beta read [edit] each other's work, correspond with readers and other writers in mailing lists and discussion forums, respond to challenge communities," and make other contributions. These norms permit "those engaged in fannish production to bounce ideas off each other; it also allows them to work collaboratively to create stories, art, music and vids" (Jones 2014: 2.3) – which Tisha Turk and Joshua Johnson (2011) have described as an ecology of interdependent roles. While a specific author (or authors) has produced any given fan work, the idea that fanfiction writers produce with help from the community is relatively uncontroversial within this tradition. Fans much more directly acknowledge that every author draws from and builds on existing cultural materials than mainstream culture, where the ideology of the lone author is stronger (Busse 2013). Fan work is also shared freely among community members. In all of these ways, then, anglophone fandom traditions are rather sharply distinguished from market exchange. (As Nele Noppe (2015) notes, in Japan there has been a long tradition of selling fanworks, so this is certainly not a universal norm.) Given these norms, the question "Is it really fanfiction?" is often raised about attempts to monetize.

Kindle Worlds is Dead, and We're Living in a Wattpad World

The monetization of fanfiction began to increase in the early 2010s, and by the end of the decade it had exploded. In some ways, this has been just an intensification of previous tendencies. In other ways, it has been significantly new. There is a long tradition of writers honing their skills in fandom and then becoming paid writers of officially licensed tie-in novels, which share fanfiction's exploration of nooks and crannies of a fictional universe but are tightly controlled in order to fit within the official trajectory of the corporate story world. Others have leveraged their fan work to "go pro" in the media industry, becoming screenwriters, filmmakers, special effects workers, or other creative professionals after learning relevant skills in fandom. It's important to recognize, then, that fandom isn't isolated from market values – and not merely because it tends to respond to capitalist-produced media. However, historically the norm was that those things were kept apart, and especially there was a norm against directly selling fanfiction for one's own benefit (Jones 2014).

In 2007, a site called FanLib sought to directly profit from fanfiction. They ran contests collecting fanfiction for specific partner media organizations and even at times specific desired narratives. These contests offered prizes like T-shirts and "proximity to media creators" in return for writing, and moreover required that fans surrender their intellectual property rights (Scott 2019: 117). This was fundamentally a fill-in-the-blanks model of fanfiction, as evidenced by the name "FanLib" riffing on "MadLibs" (Scott 2019), and it narrowly recruited particular stories under specific terms rather than the freer play of the fanfiction community. FanLib generated huge backlash from fans because it fundamentally misunderstood the existing culture and motivations of fan writing, and consequently it was short-lived (Russo 2010; Scott 2019).

Just five years later, however, the runaway success of *Fifty Shades of Grey* sparked what I call the fanfiction gold rush. The 2010s commercialization of fanfiction, in functioning by book publishers seeking out fanfiction – at times explicitly ("the next *Fifty Shades*") – is unlike either the gift economy or previous forms of commercialization. Importantly, E.L. James and other fan authors had to "file off the serial numbers" – remove identifying marks that the stories were originally fanfiction – in order to publish their work as "original" novels. This is not something that was imposed, for example, on Alice Randall's (2001) *The Wind Done Gone*, a critical response to *Gone With the Wind* (Mitchell 1936). Though Randall's publisher was sued (*Suntrust Bank v. Houghton Mifflin Co.* 2001), they prevailed, and I would argue that the fact that her work was not framed as fanfiction, despite its structural similarities as engaging with and reworking an existing work of fiction, had much to do with this outcome. The need to hide is another indication of fan publishing being treated as lesser than "real" publishing, and to an extent it continues today, with One Direction singer Harry Styles known as "Hardin Scott" (Todd 2014), "Hayes Campbell" (Lee 2017), and "Hayden" (DeVos 2019) in various novels that originated as fanfiction.

If *Fifty Shades* had been the model early on, in the late 2010s and early 2020s, Anna Todd's *After* series, which originated as real-person fiction about the band One Direction, became the paradigmatic case of the new model of fanfiction monetization. After Todd published on Wattpad, "Within months she had 544 million readers and a publishing deal with Simon & Schuster," and the film rights were also acquired (Roach 2019), with five films made as of 2023. Wattpad is far and away the biggest player in this segment of the economy as of 2023, though there are also others such as Dorian (Chan 2021) and Postype (Ock 2021). In particular, Wattpad fanfiction is being picked up into the professional publishing ecosystem. While various forms of using fandom to gain skills have longer histories, one key difference since the mid-2010s is the increasing openness on the part of both authors and publishers about the value of fanfiction for developing into a professional creator. Fanfiction is now often recognized as "a pivotal training ground for emerging young adult novelists" (Kembrey 2019). In these new publishing models, fan origins can be a selling point and not something to hide; as one author said, "I love that my publisher never tried to hide that it was fanfiction," and press sources note that "It's quite common to see published novels being marketed by reference to common fanfic tropes" (The Straits Times 2022). Indeed, the fact that one romance writer sued another in 2020, seeking more than $1 million in damages over claimed ownership of the "Omegaverse" trope (Alter 2020) – which was not original to either author but rather first popularized in fanfiction for television show *Supernatural* (WB 2005–2006, CW 2006–2020) – shows that there can be a lot of money at stake in fanfiction tropes. Fanfiction has made its way into many corners of the publishing ecosystem, as "outlets like BookRiot are beginning to publish fanfiction recommendations" (Marsden 2022). The size of the market is demonstrated by the fact that Wattpad offers five-figure stipends to authors of popular stories and "boasts of its partnerships with leading publishers (Macmillan, Penguin Random House)" (Kerridge 2022).

Beyond this means of going pro by moving from fanfiction to traditional novels, however, the decade that began with Kindle Worlds's launch in 2013 has seen significant changes. Much like *After* and its sequels, Wattpad and its ilk have systems in place to turn fanfiction into other media. In an interview, Wattpad CEO Jeanne Lam said, "The opportunities are endless because every form of entertainment starts with a story. Writers can build their careers and have giant fandoms. That translates into huge franchises and writers making many millions of dollars and really enabling the future of entertainment" (Grady 2022). This includes partnerships with companies like Sony, Hulu, and NBCUniversal to create film and TV from fanfiction. This pipeline is developed enough that one "literary scout for film and television companies... makes it her business to keep an eye on the likes of Wattpad and AO3" (Kerridge 2022).

Platformization has also been a significant shift in the monetization of fanfiction. As Noppe (2011: 1.2) contends, "now that new technologies allow individuals to create media of a quality that makes them economically viable one of the main reasons for any sharp separation between sharing and commercial economies is steadily losing its significance." Notably, in Kindle Worlds, fan authors were offered less favorable contract terms than professional writers usually secure (Hellekson 2013). Additionally, Kindle Worlds was very restrictive in terms of content, forbidding explicit sexuality and crossovers between different narrative universes in general as well as imposing particular restrictions specific to each intellectual property. In this sense, Kindle Worlds was, as Hellekson (2013) notes, closer to tie-in novels than the ways fanfiction is constrained only by community norms. However, despite these restrictions, people did publish fanfiction on Kindle Worlds, though it's not clear to what extent these authors were coming from existing fan communities as opposed to aspiring or already published authors looking for a promising revenue stream. However, by 2018, Kindle Worlds was no more, "and some authors told Business Insider they lost thousands of dollars in monthly income" (Clark 2020), thus calling attention to the pitfalls of relying on corporate platforms that had led to founding of the AO3 in the first place (De Kosnik 2016).

What is distinctive about Wattpad in particular is its intense use of datafication, which is made possible by being both the platform and the broker with the media industry. News reports indicate that Wattpad analyzes "data on its stories – including sentence structure, vocabulary, readers' comments, and popularity – in an effort to deduce exactly what makes a book succeed. In time, it may try to automate the editing process" (Bosker 2018). In fact, in mid-2023 some fans began posting screencaps of messages they'd received from Wattpad nudging them to complete stories that said "Our system indicates that you have a story which hasn't been updated in a while," which these fans found pushy and creepy. Other fans, however, could well respond positively.

The fanfiction gold rush represents a significant, and important, departure from historical norms in fan communities. If fandom has often been described as a gift economy, then leveraging gifts made in the fannish economy in the market economy has usefully been termed a "regifting economy" by Suzanne Scott (2009, 2019). Spinning fanfiction into gold, in all its variants, regifts fan work, taking it out of the communal gift economy for individual and especially corporate gain, which has not come without resistance.

Shifting Norms, or Whose Fandom Is it Anyway?

The rapid expansion and uptake of fanfiction monetization inherently conflicts with older gift economy norms. People who were in fandom before social media, or who first joined fandoms with many people who had been in fandom before social media, have been exposed to and/or acculturated into the gift economy. This set of practices and values has had some continuity. They're vague, loose, and vary in important ways from fandom to fandom, to be sure, but there are through-lines. This is a tradition in which there are shared norms about fanfiction being noncommercial, as well as about genres, styles, and other characteristics of the texts themselves. However, the fact that fanfiction was historically organized this way does not mean it will continue to be; as Noppe (2011: 3.5) points out, "Fannish practices and mindsets are just as susceptible to change as those of companies, so the fact that certain concerns have been dominant among fans up to now doesn't mean they will always remain so."

Multiple norms are now shifting within fanfiction. For example, the reciprocity of feedback as payment for creativity seems to be diminishing, with pleas or demands for feedback appended to chapters of serialized works, often as a condition of continuing, suggesting a decline of the norm that response is freely given. Similarly, Leora Hadas (2009: 5.2) has described the contemporary attitude in the context of Doctor Who fandom as the sense of a "basic right" to create and post fic, pointing to prioritizing individual desire to create over any sense of obligation to produce something others want to read. These tensions over individual pleasure vs. community responsibility have intensified in recent years. In particular, there has been conflict around both sexuality and race. On one hand, in what I have elsewhere called the Fandom Anti Wars (Stanfill 2024), individuals who oppose particular categories of fanfiction and fanart, such as works that include rape, or particular preferences for relationships between characters, such as works that feature underage sex or incest, have tried to prevent such fiction from being written or posted. This is an attempt to impose their individual taste and judgment on the entire community. On the other hand, there has been contestation over racist fanfiction, which white fans have tended to be unwilling to see as a matter of inclusive community norms rather than as question of individual taste. Overall, it is unclear whether fans who are departing from historical communitarian ideas of fanfiction know that older modes of fandom exist and reject them; or whether the influx of new people into fandom was too great to socialize them into how it was done before; or whether contemporary fans don't know this history because searchability allows finding fanfiction outside of community or knowing how it has traditionally been done, but the shifts in norms are quite apparent. In all, various aspects of contemporary fan practice point to increasing individualism as opposed to sharing a communitarian focus.

Historical fan resistance to monetization is also shifting. Some champion paying fans to prevent labor exploitation. De Kosnik (2012: 99) notes: "We are at a ripe moment for establishing the fact that fandom is a form of free labor and for calling upon fans, scholars, and the corporations that benefit from fan activity to seriously consider the question of whether fans should be compensated for their work." Noppe (2011: 1.4) argues more forcefully, "It is time to consider how we can ensure that commodification of fan work ends up benefiting fans first." Accordingly, fandom may have hit a tipping point (which it hadn't at the time of FanLib) with a critical mass of people who see these kinds of corporate-driven commercialization as legitimate. The benefits of these new models of fanfiction publishing are real. Moving into the formal economy allows the work fans have always done without financial gain to become paid. While it surely benefits capital more than labor – as all work does – the capacity to have compensation for labor should not be devalued. On the other hand, the gift economy affords community, nonmarket values, and more freedom to create, unhindered by the need to be market-viable or licensing restrictions, which simply cannot be replicated by commercialized fanfiction. These arguments, in operating from different values, are incommensurable and thus tend to come to an impasse.

These questions about who and what fanfiction is for are playing out especially acutely with generative AI tools like ChatGPT. Some fans are using such tools to generate content, including finishing incomplete fanfictions, sparking controversy in fandom beginning in March 2023 (Adarlo 2023). Generative AI is kicking off a gold rush of its own generally, and in fandom, companies are trying to leverage it to do things like create chatbots in the voice of a character as a more interactive form of fanfiction (Rosenberg 2023), though there has been pushback against such tools as missing the point of fanfiction. AI tools have also faced resistance due to the fact that AO3 is believed to have been scraped as part of training their models (Eskici 2023), taking fan work for corporate gain without permission or compensation, and one source of evidence for this claim is that AI tools seem to know what Omegaverse is (Eveleth 2023). Further, there was a controversy when a member of OTW's legal team expressed excitement about the possibilities of AI-generated fanfiction (Klosek 2023, Update to OTW Signal 2023). These fights over AI in fanfiction show both the way norms are a moving target and the way different fandom generations (which, as Bridget Kies and Megan Connor (2022) note, map uneasily onto the real ages of their participants) have developed increasingly divergent norms in a number of ways.

Risks and Rewards of Commercializing Fanfiction

As the fanfiction gold rush continues into its second decade, it's important to recognize that, much like other forms of incorporation of fandom into media industry logics (Scott 2019; Stanfill 2019), there are real limitations. For all the ways news articles announce that "amateurs" are "rewriting Hollywood's script – and turning 'fanfiction' into gold" (Kerridge 2022), fanfiction remains marginal in many ways. First, some of the ways that fanfiction is being capitalized on are those that mock fans, from a webseries that films fanfiction while parodying its queer content (Hess 2017), to Star Trek actor Brent Spiner writing a semiautobiographical mystery novel about "a murderously obsessive fan" (Fan Fiction 2021), to "The Really, Really Rude Puppet Show" featuring celebrities reading erotic fanfiction about themselves (Tonks 2023). Fanfiction has also continued to face prohibition, from a BBC FAQ announcing that fanfiction can't be posted online (Baker 2021) – despite the fact that the show has been helmed by fanboy auteurs such as Steven Moffat (Salter and Stanfill 2020) – to Netflix's lawsuit over the Unofficial Bridgerton Musical (Kerridge 2022). Fanfiction websites were also banned in Malaysia and Indonesia in 2017 (@FictionPress 2017) and China in 2020 (Feng 2020), and there was a petition for government intervention against K-pop real person fiction in Korea in 2021 (Ock 2021).

The monetization of fanfiction has undoubtedly produced benefits, but what benefits, to whom they accrue, and how they are apportioned remain essential questions. It's important to recognize the validity of fans' nonmarket reasons for production and not see them as foolish or backward for participating in the gift economy even while critiquing the uneven distribution of market reward. Fan nonmarket values are legitimate. They are also perhaps at risk of being lost. Not everyone knows that this new, individualist, commercialized model isn't the only option, and while the benefits are clear, one must know and value fandom history in order to recognize the tradeoffs they require. As these new forms of fandom gain ascendancy, older forms may fall out of use and cease to be an option – if fans no longer have an awareness that fanfiction could be otherwise, they will be unable to make an informed decision about which kind of fandom they want to have. This potential for inventing a new mode of fanfiction at the expense of fannish traditions should concern us. The creation of new models isn't inherently bad, unless they crowd out the old one and become the only way to be a fan, or unless rights holders deploy legal measures to insist that all fanfiction be done in these confined, commercial ways. The battle for the future of fandom can only fairly be fought if fans know what's at stake.

References

Adarlo, S., 2023. Writers Furious When Fanfiction Site Won't Ban AI-Generated Work [online]. *Yahoo Finance*. Available from: https://finance.yahoo.com/news/writers-furious-fanfiction-won-t-182802720.html [Accessed 29 Jul 2023].

Alter, A., 2020. In a Fanfic Feud, Deep (and Kinky) Questions Emerge. *The New York Times*, 24 May, p. 1.

Baker, E., 2021. "Doctor Who" and the Army of Fan Fiction Writers. *i-Independent Print Ltd*, 13 May.

Bosker, B., 2018. The One Direction Fan-Fiction Novel That Became a Literary Sensation. *The Atlantic*.

Boyle, J., 2003. The Second Enclosure Movement and the Construction of the Public Domain. *Law and Contemporary Problems*, 66 (1/2), 33–74.

Busse, K., 2013. The Return of the Author: Ethos and Identity Politics. In: J. Gray and D. Johnson, eds. *A Companion to Media Authorship*. New York, NY: John Wiley & Sons, 48–68.

Chan, J.C., 2021. Lionsgate Partners with Storytelling Platform Dorian to Create User-Generated Games. *The Hollywood Reporter*.

Chin, B., 2014. Sherlockology and Galactica.tv: Fan sites as gifts or exploited labor? *Transformative Works and Cultures*, 15.

Clark, T., 2020. Authors Describe Losing Thousands of Dollars in Monthly Income when Amazon Quietly Shut Down its Fan-Fiction Service – and How They Bounced Back. *The Business Insider*, 15 Jan.

De Kosnik, A., 2012. Fandom as Free Labor. In: T. Scholz, ed. *Digital Labor: The Internet as Playground and Factory*. New York, NY: Routledge, 98–111.

De Kosnik, A., 2016. *Rogue Archives: Digital Cultural Memory and Media Fandom*. Cambridge, MA: The MIT Press.

DeVos, M., 2019. *Anarchy: The Hunger Games for a New Generation*. London, UK: Orion.

Eskici, 2023. AI and Data Scraping on the Archive | Organization for Transformative Works. *Organization for Transformative Works*.

Eveleth, R., 2023. *The Fanfic Sex Trope That Caught a Plundering AI Red-Handed*. Wired.

Fan Fiction: A Mem-Noir: Inspired by True Events, 2021. *Kirkus Reviews*, 1 Sep.

Feng, E., 2020. "China Blocks Website After Complaints About Fan Fiction Story On a Celebrity." NPR, October 28, 2020, sec. Asia. www.npr.org/2020/10/28/928805796/china-blocks-website-after-complaints-about-fan-fiction-story-on-a-celebrity.

@FictionPress, 2017. Malaysia has Joined Indonesia as the Only Two Countries on Earth that has Blocked Access to http://FanFiction.Net.😂 [online]. Twitter. Available from: https://twitter.com/FictionPress/status/918411647152033792 [Accessed 29 Jul 2023].

Grady, L., 2022. How Wattpad boss Jeanne Lam is Helping Aspiring Writers Give Up Their Day Jobs. *The Star*, 25 Oct.

Hadas, L., 2009. The Web Planet: How the Changing Internet Divided 'Doctor Who' Fan Fiction Writers. *Transformative Works and Cultures*, 3, n.p.

Hellekson, K., 2009. A Fannish Field of Value: Online Fan Gift Culture. *Cinema Journal*, 48 (4), 113–118.

Hellekson, K. 2013. "Kindle Worlds and Fan Fiction." 23 May 2013. http://khellekson.wordpress.com/2013/05/23/kindle-worlds-and-fan-fiction/.

Hess, A., 2017. When Fan Fiction and Reality Collide. *New York Times*, 22 Jun.

Hyde, L., 2007. *The Gift: Creativity and the Artist in the Modern World*. New York, NY: Vintage.

James, E.L., 2012. *Fifty Shades of Grey*. New York: Vintage Books.

Jenkins, H., Ford, S., and Green, J., 2013. *Spreadable Media: Creating Value and Meaning in a Networked Culture*. New York, NY: New York University Press.

Jones, B., 2014. Fifty Shades of Fan Labor: Exploitation and Fifty Shades of Grey. *Transformative Works and Cultures*, 15.

Kembrey, M., 2019. Fact: Fan Fiction is the Real Deal. *Sunday Age*, 21 Jul, p. 14.

Kerridge, J., 2022. Fanfiction Gold. *National Post*, 10 Dec, p. WP2.

Kies, B. and Connor, M., eds., 2022. *Fandom, the Next Generation*. Iowa City: University of Iowa Press.

Klosek, K., 2023. "Applying Intellectual Property Law to AI: An Interview with Betsy Rosenblatt - Association of Research Libraries." 23 February 2023. www.arl.org/blog/applying-intellectual-property-law-to-ai-an-interview-with-betsy-rosenblatt/.

Lee, R., 2017. *The Idea of You*. First Edition. New York: St. Martin's Griffin.

Lothian, A., 2009. Living in a Den of Thieves: Fan Video and Digital Challenges to Ownership. *Cinema Journal*, 48 (4), 130–136.

Marsden, H., 2022. How a 557,000-Word, 'Woke' Harry Potter Fanfic Took on JK Rowling. *The Telegraph*, 1 Jan.

Mauss, M., 2000. *The Gift: The Form and Reason for Exchange in Archaic Societies*. New York, NY: W. W. Norton.

Meyer, S., 2006. *Twilight*. New York, NY: Little, Brown Books for Young Readers.

Mitchell, M., 1936. *Gone with the Wind*. New York, NY: Macmillan.

Noppe, N., 2011. Why we should talk about commodifying fan work. *Transformative Works and Cultures*, 8, n.p.

Noppe, N., 2015. Mechanisms of Control in Online Fanwork Sales: A Comparison of Kindle Worlds and Dlsite.com. *Participations*, 12 (2), 218–237.

Ock, H., 2021. "Controversy Grows over 'real Person Slash' Sexualizing Male K-Pop Idols." *The Korea Herald*, January 13, 2021.

Pearson, E., 2007. Digital Gifts: Participation and Gift Exchange in LiveJournal Communities. *First Monday*, 12 (5–7), n.p.

Randall, A., 2001. *The Wind Done Gone: A Novel*. Boston, MA: Mariner Books.

Roach, V., 2019. Fan Fiction Romance makes 50 Shades of Grey Look Intellectual. *The Daily Telegraph*, 7 Jul.

Romano, A., 2019. 4.7 Million Fanfics Are Now Hugo Winners, Thanks to the Archive of Our Own [online]. *Vox*. Available from: www.vox.com/2019/4/11/18292419/archive-of-our-own-wins-hugo-award-best-related-work [Accessed 29 Jul 2023].

Rosenberg, A., 2023. Custom AI Chatbots are Quietly Becoming the Next Big Thing in Fandom [online]. *The Verge*. Available from: www.theverge.com/23627402/character-ai-fandom-chatbots-fanfiction-role-playing [Accessed 29 Jul 2023].

Russo, J.L., 2010. *Indiscrete Media: Television/Digital Convergence and Economies of Online Lesbian Fan Communities*. Providence, RI: Dissertation. Brown University.
Salter, A. and Stanfill, M., 2020. *A Portrait of the Auteur as Fanboy: The Construction of Authorship in Transmedia Franchises*. Jackson: University Press of Mississippi.
Scott, S., 2009. Repackaging Fan Culture: The Regifting Economy of Ancillary Content Models. *Transformative Works and Cultures*, 3, n.p.
Scott, S., 2019. *Fake Geek Girls: Fandom, Gender, and the Convergence Culture Industry*. New York: NYU Press.
Stanfill, M., 2019. *Exploiting Fandom: How the Media Industry Seeks to Manipulate Fans*. Iowa City: University of Iowa Press.
Stanfill, M., 2024. *Fandom Is Ugly: Networked Harassment in Participatory Culture*. NYU Press.
SunTrust Bank v. Houghton Mifflin Co., 268 F.3d 1257 (11th Cir. 2001).
The Straits Times, 2022. From Fan Fiction to Books of Their Own: Fandom Authors Make it Big in Publishing. *The Daily Star*, 14 Feb.
Todd, A., 2014. *After*. New York: Gallery Books.
Tonks, O., 2023. Kerry Katona and Martin Kemp 'Sign Up for The Really, Really Rude Puppet Show Which Will See them Read Out Steamy Fan Fiction About Themselves'. *MailOnline*, 7 Feb.
Turk, T., 2014. Fan Work: Labor, Worth, and Participation in Fandom's Gift Economy. *Transformative Works and Cultures*, 15.
Turk, T. and Johnson, J., 2011. Toward an Ecology of Vidding. *Transformative Works and Cultures*, 9, n.p.
Tushnet, R., 2007. Payment in Credit: Copyright Law and Subcultural Creativity. *Law and Contemporary Problems*, 70 (2), 135–174.
Update to OTW Signal, May 2023, 2023. *Organization for Transformative Works*.

35
FANDOM AND THE POLITICS OF CANCEL CULTURE

Eve Ng

Media fandoms have been a prominent part of what has been discussed – and often condemned – as "cancel culture." As this chapter will cover, there are several important political dimensions to cancel culture as it pertains to fandom, which vary across different cultural and national contexts. These include the factors that precipitate cancel events, how fans are involved in initiating or perpetuating cancelling, the dynamics between fans and institutional actors, and the sociopolitical effects of these cancel events.

What is labeled "cancel culture" is a set of phenomena with multiple origins. One important line stems from Black communicative practices intended as in-group criticism, and another from a broader realm of digital activism around issues such as sexual misconduct, racism, and other progressive concerns (Clark 2020; Ng 2022). Thus, **cancel agents** enact **cancel practices** against the **cancel targets**, with the **cancel triggers** typically involving conduct or speech deemed problematic. **Cancel discourses** are instances of commentary about the primary cancel event or additional commentary, such as evaluations of the cancel agents and cancel practices involved (Ng 2022).

In the popular culture domain, cancel targets are often performing artists, especially actors and musicians, though may also be those behind the camera such as writers, directors, producers, and executives. When cancel culture shot to prominence in 2018–2019, the use of **cancel language** in online comments and hashtags often clearly marked a cancel event, e.g., "James Franco is cancelled," or the #DemiIsOverParty hashtag when Demi Moore was a target in 2020. However, cancelling does not necessarily involve explicit cancel language; rather, the defining characteristic is the goal of diminishing the popularity and public profile of the cancel target. Cancel practices by individuals include withdrawing support on social media and through consumer behavior, and otherwise publicly disavowing or cutting ties with the target. Fans might also advocate for a cancel target to be removed from the production of a film or television show. Institutional cancel agents, such as studios, digital platforms, or government bodies, can enact other measures, such as cancelling production completely, suspending a target's social media accounts, or taking down their performances (Ng 2022).

Cancel triggers vary, especially when looking at cancel events in different cultural contexts. In the US and other Western environments, triggers have often arisen from fan assessments of misbehavior around interpersonal "drama," but also include more problematic speech and behavior, such as racist expression or sexual misconduct. However, in China, celebrities have been cancelled for reasons that do not typically provoke cancelling in the West, such as financial improprieties, drug use, soliciting prostitutes, and – often most damagingly – being perceived as transgressing nationalist positions, such as the One China Principle, which holds that Hong Kong and Taiwan belong to the PRC (see Li and Ng 2025). Fans are often the ones initiating such cancellings, but the state sometimes plays this role as well.

With these possible variations, then, a grassroots-led fan effort against a showrunner for producing problematic content, for example, has different valences from a state-supported cancelling against an individual deemed to be insufficiently patriotic. The case studies discussed below, of fandom cancellings spurred by celebrity misconduct, media content and its creators, and mainstream political issues, illustrate how the key characteristics of cancelling – the cancel triggers, agents, and practices – shape the political significance of each cancel event and of cancel culture more generally.

Scholarly research on cancel culture and fandoms has made use of various methods. A number of studies have examined relevant posts on Twitter/X and other cancel discourse data, using content analysis, qualitative textual analysis, or discourse analysis to identify user sentiments and common thematic threads (e.g., Geusens et al. 2023; Han and Liu 2024; Lewis and Christin 2022). Some scholars have conducted more extensive studies of relevant online spaces, comprising digital ethnography (Lee and Abidin 2021), or interviewed fans who have participated in cancelling or observed cancel events (Driessen 2023; Huang et al. 2023). And, while most research has been confined to a single national context, there are recent studies providing a transnational comparison, such as between China and the West (Huang et al. 2023).

Celebrity Misconduct

One of the most common types of cancel event involving fans is triggered by celebrity misconduct. This may be due to interpersonal "drama," typically involving other celebrities; other perceived failures of character, such as relationship infidelity or questionable financial activities; and actions that are more seriously harmful to others (and often illegal), such as online harassment, hate speech, and sexual assault.

One celebrity "drama" saga that attracted substantial popular attention occurred within beauty advice blogging in 2019, precipitated by a set of YouTube video posts and responses between US beauty influencers James Charles and Tati Westbrook that came to be dubbed Dramageddon 2.0 (a 2018 conflict in the YouTube beauty community had been labeled "Dramageddon"). Westbrook, over a decade older than Charles, had been a parent-like mentor to him, and the conflict included accusations of Charles betraying their relationship by promoting a rival's wellness products, as well as sexting with teenagers.

Fan cancel practices primarily involved unfollowing and criticizing Charles online, and no longer purchasing the products Charles had endorsed or was associated with; some users posted dramatic videos of themselves destroying Charles' eyeshadow palette. There were longer videos responding to the controversy as it played out over several weeks, thus constituting additional fan-produced content that comprised the cancel discourses and "contribut[ing] value to the content producers and the platforms hosting them" (Ng 2022: 22). Conducting a content analysis of over 40 YouTube drama channels and interviews with some of the channel creators, Lewis and Christin (2022) argued that while there were viewers invested in holding Charles accountable, whether for his perceived wrongdoing against Westbrook or the more serious sexual misconduct, the fact that pertinent videos about Drameggedon 2.0 and similar cases of "platform drama" were sources of income often led creators "to maximize the entertainment value of their content and minimize genuine accountability practices" (1644); this sometimes even involved manufacturing fake conflicts or otherwise "stirring up drama," as Geusens et al. (2023) also discussed. Thus, being cancelled did not necessarily have long-lasting negative consequences for the targets. Charles had dramatic decreases in the number of followers at the outset of the Drameggedon 2.0 events, but within a couple of years, he had even more followers on YouTube, Instagram, and TikTok than before (Ng 2022).

Sometimes celebrities do stay cancelled, such as when the misconduct is judged to be too severe. For example, in 2021, when American actor Armie Hammer was accused by multiple women of emotional, physical, and sexual abuse, also made public were text messages where Hammer expressed cannibalistic desires in explicitly sexual ways. Hammer was criticized and mocked by fans and other commentators, lost all his acting roles, and was dropped by his publicist and talent agency (Kirchick 2023). To date, he has not returned to the entertainment industry, presumably due to his cannibalistic kink, since being accused or proven guilty of even serious assault has not had the same outcomes for other male celebrities (e.g., musician Chris Brown, whose 2009 assault on his girlfriend Rihanna was documented in widely circulated photos, or actor Johnny Depp, accused by Amber Heard of various instances of abuse in 2022).

Some cancel targets may also remain cancelled while others regain public support due to how the cancel triggers interact with other factors determining the targets' popular appeal. Lee and Abidin (2021) analyzed the cases of two female South Korean influencers who were cancelled when it came to light that they had accepted "backdoor advertising" money, despite consistently proclaiming that they received no compensation for product promotion. While both influencers apologized, only one of them won back fan allegiance, after she announced that she was using the money to support her family; she was also more conventionally feminine in appearance and demeanor (though both were subject to misogynistic comments), demonstrating how gender norms partly shaped the trajectories of these cancel events.

There has been other research on how fans respond to cancelling, seeking to better understand the character of cancel events as well as the dynamics of digital interaction more broadly. For example, Pereira de Sá and Pereira Alberto (2022) conducted a content analysis of a tweet critical of English pop musician Morrissey and all the over 600 responses to it after Morrissey was cancelled for wearing a pin of a far right British political party. In finding several themes, most but not all of which supported Morrissey's cancelling, the authors argued for viewing "the fan as a type of guard,... the gatekeeper of coherent perceptions about a certain artist" (1101). In another case, Driessen (2023) interviewed fans of Dutch singer and voice coach Marco Borsato after he was cancelled due to sexual misconduct allegations. Driessen discussed how, although some fans maintained their support of Borsato, others became more circumspect about expressing their fan attachments, and the complex dynamics of how the fandom negotiated the "everyday political and cultural consequences" (1) of being a fan or ex-fan provide insights into the development of polarized views online. Thus, modes of fan engagement around popular media and celebrities, which tend to be overlooked in literature about politics in digital spheres, serve as important examples of how personal politics are negotiated in specific communities (Driessen 2023).

The role of the state in determining cancel outcomes is also important in certain contexts, particularly China. The Chinese government is well-known for tight control over media content and production (e.g., see Bai and Song 2015), but it also regulates the conduct of performers. In 2014, the State Administration of Press Publication, Radio, Film and Television (SAPPRFT) proclaimed that artists guilty of behavior such as hiring prostitutes and illicit drug use would be subject to having their performances made unavailable. SAPPRFT (now the National Radio and Television Administration) and other regulatory bodies, including the Cyberspace Administration of China (CAC), have followed up with additional statements about measures to be taken against performers with problematic ideological positions or moral character (see Li and Ng 2025), including "lapsed morals" or "behavior such as drug addiction, gambling, drunk driving, indecent assault, tax evasion and fraud" (Global Times 2022: para. 5).

Given these state dictates, fans and the state may work in concert in particular celebrity cancellings. Sometimes the state initiates the cancel event, particularly for financial misconduct such as tax evasion, since it is government authorities that typically have access to the relevant records. For example, popular actors Fan Bingbing and Deng Lun were both publicly criticized and fined by the state for tax evasion (to the tune of tens of millions of dollars) in 2018 and 2022 respectively, and both had their social media accounts suspended (Myers 2018; Chen 2022). While some fans remained supportive, a large proportion cancelled the actors online, expressing outrage at their offenses and approval of the government actions.

Other celebrities have had their misconduct first highlighted by regular social media users, and then the state has joined the fray. Thus, in 2021 the singer and actor Leehom Wang was accused by his wife Li Jinglei on social media of repeated cheating and emotional abuse, and she called for women to demand better living conditions as spouses. Many Chinese netizens criticized Wang, calling for him to face consequences, and the large amount of online discourse likely spurred Chinese Communist Party media outlets to publish their own commentary, which was supportive of Li. Wang's performances were temporarily taken down from Chinese TV and streaming platforms (Mengshenmumu 2021) and he lost numerous endorsements (Han and Liu 2024).

Media Content and Creators

Earlier scholarship has documented fans organizing to push content creators towards better representation (e.g., see Jenkins and Shresthova 2012), but fan-led cancel events triggered by finding media content problematic instead involve disengagement or actions to diminish the popularity of the pertinent texts. An illustrative case occurred around the youth-oriented sci-fi series *The 100* (CW, 2014–2020), which attracted a passionate queer fandom for the relationship between the lead character, Clarke, and her love interest, Lexa, in Season 2. However, in a mid-Season 3 episode, just after the two made love for the first time, Lexa was killed off. Calling for a social media blackout, many fans stopped following showrunner Jason Rothenberg or using any hashtags about the show and its producers on Twitter, downvoted the episode in which Lexa was killed at sites like imdb.com, and urged CW advertisers to pull their spots from *The 100* episodes (see Ng 2022). While these actions did not have an impact on the fate of Rothenberg or the show – it ran for another four seasons with Rothenberg at the helm – the fan campaign helped raise the profile of the "Bury Your Gays" trope, with several mainstream entertainment and news outlets providing coverage about the problematic narrative on *The 100* and the subsequent fan responses.

Sometimes, writers or producers face cancel actions not for the content they create but for their problematic conduct. For example, Joss Whedon had been the admired showrunner of *Buffy the Vampire Slayer* (WB/UPN, 1997–2003), building a strong fan following as well as attracting significant scholarly attention. While there had been some critiques of gender and racial representation on Whedon's shows, it was a series of accusations in 2020–2021 by actors who had worked with Whedon detailing abusive and misogynist treatment that left fans "grappling with whether to cancel Whedon and his shows" (Whitmore 2021: para. 29). He experienced some professional repercussions in 2020, with HBO removing him as showrunner for its series *The Nevers* and Warner Bros. launching an investigation into Whedon, since some allegations concerned the *Justice League* movie set. Amongst Whedon's academic fans, the Whedon Studies Association, formed in 2009 to study Whedon's creative works, renamed itself the Association for the Study of Buffy+ in 2022 and revised its mission statement to remove all references to Whedon (see "About the Association for the Study of Buffy+ (ASB+)" n.d.).

These kinds of cancel actions, motivated by fan concerns about the treatment or representation of traditionally marginalized groups, coexist with fan campaigns arising from resistance to increased diversity in popular media, the goals of which may also involve diminishing the popularity of particular media texts or targeting performers on social media. Notably, a number of science fiction films or television series with women and people of color as leads have been subject to organized downvoting at online sites, and actors in those roles have experienced sexist and/or racist attacks on social media, such as around the 2016 *Ghostbusters* remake with a cast of women (Blodgett and Salter 2018) and a range of superhero movies (see Driessen 2022). Although the triggers are quite different in these latter instances compared to cases like *The 100* or Joss Whedon, it is hard to draw a conceptual distinction between what we would readily label "cancelling" on the one hand and trolling or online harassment on the other. This also becomes apparent in examining cancel events centered around political issues, since the triggers can arise from different parts of the political spectrum.

Political Triggers

Performers are judged by fans not just for their behavior, but for their political beliefs and positions, and have faced consequences well before the social media era. For example, in 2003, soon after the US had invaded Iraq under the leadership of President George W. Bush, Natalie Maines, a member of the Dixie Chicks (later, The Chicks) – at the time the most popular women's band in the US – commented at a concert, "we're ashamed the president of the United States is from Texas." Many politically conservative fans were outraged, and the band's loss of popularity was reflected in their number 1 single at the time ("Travelin' Soldier") falling over 60 spots on the country sales charts, a significant decrease in the band's airplay, some radio stations organizing events for destroying Dixie Chicks CDs, as well as protests at their concerts and death threats; animosity against the group remained in evidence for years after the incident, most likely affecting the sales of their subsequent albums (Moss 2020).

More recently, pop star Taylor Swift experienced cancelling after endorsing Democratic candidates and voicing liberal perspectives about racism, women's rights, and LGBTQ rights in 2018; conservative fans posted online about burning their Taylor Swift CDs and boycotting her concerts, including white nationalists who had previously seen her as an icon abandoning their support (see Huang et al. 2023). For different political reasons, *Harry Potter* author JK Rowling has also been cancelled, for transphobic comments as well as writing a novel using a transphobic trope (a male serial killer donning women's clothing as a disguise). Fans trended an #ripjkrowling hashtag in 2020, and have sought to pursue their fandom activities without supporting Rowling personally (see Ravell 2023; Schott 2023).

At a more general level, as Huang et al. (2023) noted, fan studies scholars have pointed out similarities between the practices of fan cultures and mainstream politics, like voting and organizing against opponents. A distinct manifestation of such dynamics is what Liu (2019) termed "fandom nationalism" in China, when fandom passions intersect with nationalist sentiment, so that fans who "love their nation the way they love an idol" (142) apply practices previously used in support of a favored celebrity to bolster their nation against identified antagonists. Fandom nationalism may also manifest when celebrities are cancelled for perceived violations of patriotic conduct, and, just as for cases where the trigger is personal misconduct, the state often plays a key role, both in carrying out cancel actions against the target and with respect to the regulation of media content and the cultural domain.

An early case of nationalist cancelling occurred in 2001–2002 against Chinese singer and actor Zhao Wei, after she wore a dress with a pattern that resembled a Japanese military flag. Angry netizens, pointing out how much China had suffered under Japan's occupation during World War II, advocated for no longer consuming Zhao's music, television, or films; she also experienced physical attacks and had feces thrown towards her when she was performing shortly after the controversy erupted (see Rosen 2003). Since then, a veritable parade of popular performers have been cancelled in China due to nationalist triggers, whether also being insufficiently sensitive to Japan's historical wrongs against China, such as actor Zhang Zhehan in 2021 after old photos of him posing at two Japanese shrines surfaced (e.g., see Huang and Xie 2021); being seen as challenging the One China Principle, such as Taiwanese singer Tzuyu in 2016 (Yang 2019) and Thai actor Vachirawit Chivaaree in 2020 (Dedman and Lai 2021); or otherwise insulting China, such as director Chloé Zhao shortly after winning accolades for her film *Nomadland* in 2021 (Feng 2021).

The Chinese government has often encouraged the mass cancel actions; in some of these cases, Chinese state organs are themselves cancel agents. For example, state media harshly criticized Zhang Zhehan, and media regulators ensured that all of his work became unavailable on platforms based in China, even after he apologized; similarly, the previously state-approved release of *Nomadland* in China was abruptly cancelled after netizens discovered interview comments Chloé Zhao had made critical of her homeland. On the other hand, the state may also seek to temper fan outrage; some government-aligned commentators defended Zhao, and Chinese state officials also tried to defuse any diplomatic fallout from the Vachirawit Chivaaree cancelling after this broadened into a loosely organized online "Milk Tea Alliance" pitting fans in several Asian countries against Chinese nationalists

Fandom and the Politics of Cancel Culture

(Ng 2022). Still, in the Chinese digital sphere, nationalist sentiment tends to dominate, even though "not all Chinese pop culture fans work to promote state interests," with many "advocating for women's rights or LGBTQ rights, for example," but state "censorship and repression of these sensitive subjects" means that they do not attain the online prominence of nationalist expression (Chen 2021: para. 14).

Indeed, institutional actors are often crucial to cancel events not just as agents who directly enact cancel actions, but through their roles in shaping the cultural contexts where cancelling plays out.

As part of its control over popular culture, the Chinese government has increasingly targeted the online domain, but until recently, numerous fan spaces operated almost entirely outside of official attention. However, in the last few years, fan cultures have attracted specific regulatory measures (Wang and Ge 2023). For example, in 2015 the Cyberspace Administration of China (CAC) launched a campaign against content deemed harmful to minors such as "pornography, violence, terror and superstition" (see Global Times 2015). In 2016, the CAC announced a "Clean Up Campaign" (晴朗行动 *qínglǎng xíngdòng*), where the initial focus was misinformation; by 2019, amongst the 12 "harmful aspects" identified was "trolling and toxic behavior" (see Sun 2019). In 2020, the CAC and other Chinese state organs began issuing statements criticizing celebrity culture and fan practices centered on celebrity idols, and in June 2021, the CAC announced a "purification and fan circle disorder" clean-up campaign, pointing to phenomena such as fans attacking each other or otherwise "trolling and igniting wars" against disfavored targets – practices that are often part of cancel events (see Li and Ng 2025).

Although media fandoms are often characterized as resisting mainstream authority, in China fans have at times recruited state regulators into fandom disputes – an instance of what Wang and Ge (2023) note as "reporting culture" – with an especially consequential case involving a popular singer and actor, Xiao Zhan. Xiao's fandom included two major factions, and in 2020, one faction reported fanfiction about Xiao that they disapproved of to the CAC, on the basis that its "explicit erotic descriptions of illegal prostitution could have an extremely detrimental influence on juveniles" (Wang and Ge 2023: 365), thus highlighting areas that Chinese authorities were already aiming to restrict. The fanfiction had been posted on An Archive of Our Own, and the reporting led the government to block this site altogether – a significant loss to readers in China. Many upset fans then organized to cancel Xiao Zhan, spurning the media texts and products associated with him and downvoting his shows, as well as seeking to have the social media accounts of the fans who had initiated the reporting blocked (Huang et al. 2023; Wang and Ge 2023). This major dispute helped precipitate subsequent state actions against Chinese fans (Wang and Ge 2023), compelling fans to explicitly negotiate the relations between their "neo-tribal" fan affiliations and their "conventional political identities" as Chinese citizens (Huang et al. 2023: 1431).

The trajectories of fan-initiated cancellings can also depend on the policies of the digital platforms where these actions occur. Notably, after US businessman Elon Musk purchased Twitter (which he later renamed X) in October 2022, he explicitly stated that he would be combatting cancel culture. Within a few weeks, Musk reinstated accounts that had been suspended or banned under the previous ownership (see Tiffany 2023), including those that Twitter's content moderators had earlier judged to be sexist, homophobic, racist, or otherwise forms of hate speech, such as the account of rapper Ye (formerly known as Kanye

West). Since deplatforming is one of the most consequential types of cancel practice, Musk's actions underscored how platform governance can significantly influence the outcomes of cancel events (Ng 2025).

Conclusion

Because celebrities are common targets of cancelling, fans are often the initiators of cancel events, calling attention to perceived wrongdoing through social media content that goes viral. Examining the specific triggers and sociopolitical contexts reveals that similar cancel practices can be involved in cancel events that vary in their political characteristics and import. For example, in China, fan cancelling is affected by state actors in several key ways. When government entities participate as cancel agents, fans sometimes collaborate with the state. Popular fandom in China is also significantly shaped by nationalist discourses, with the latter sparking many instances of celebrity cancelling, and by state regulatory policies. Having previously been supportive of several fandom nationalist online campaigns, the Chinese government currently frames fans as prone to excesses in favor of or against particular idols, and seeks to constrain fandoms accordingly. These aspects of Chinese cancel culture have no exact parallel in the West, but platform governance is another crucial element for the trajectories of cancel events, as demonstrated by the changes Elon Musk enacted at Twitter/X after purchasing the site. Also, not all fans are supportive of cancelling: many elect not to participate in collective actions against a target, or negotiate their positions by separating the art from the artist, disavowing a cancelled creator while continuing to consume their content or pursuing fan creations.

Future scholarship could productively investigate cancelling in fandoms based outside of the West, examining both the specifics of the cancel events and the cultural and sociopolitical conditions under which they occur. More research about the nuances of differences in fan responses should also provide greater insight into the dynamics of fandom interaction, including attention to how these are structured by gender, race, and other social hierarchies, and help situate fan cancelling within a broader constellation of collective fan actions.

References

About the Association for the Study of Buffy+ (ASB+) (n.d.) *Association for the Study of Buffy+*, www.whedonstudies.tv/about.html.
Bai, R. and Song, G. (2015) *Chinese Television in the Twenty-First Century: Entertaining the Nation*, New York: Routledge.
Blodgett, B. and Salter, A. (2018) "*Ghostbusters* is for Boys: Understanding Geek Masculinity's Role in the Alt-Right," *Communication, Culture & Critique*, 11(1), pp. 133–146. https://doi.org/10.1093/ccc/tcx003.
Chen, C. (2022, March 16) "Pop Star Ordered to Pay Big Tax Bill," *China Daily*, https://global.chinadaily.com.cn/a/202203/16/WS623145cfa310fd2b29e512b3.html.
Chen, S. (2021, May 8) "How Chinese Fans Enforce Chinese Nationalism on the World," *The Diplomat*, https://thediplomat.com/2021/05/how-chinese-fans-enforce-chinese-nationalism-on-the-world/.
Clark, M. D. (2020) "DRAG THEM: A Brief Etymology of So-Called 'Cancel Culture'," *Communication and the Public*, 5(3–4), pp. 88–92. https://doi.org/10.1177/2057047320961562.

Dedman, A. K. and Lai, A. (2021) "Digitally Dismantling Asian Authoritarianism: Activist Reflections From the #MilkTeaAlliance," *Contention*, 9(1), pp. 97–132. https://doi.org/10.3167/cont.2021.090105.

Driessen, S. (2022) "'For the Greater Good?' Vigilantism in Online Pop Culture Fandoms," in D. Trottier, R. Gabdulhakov, and Q. Huang (eds.) *Introducing Vigilant Audiences*, Open Book Publishers, pp. 1–20. https://doi.org/10.11647/OBP.0200.02.

Driessen, S. (2023) "The Participatory Politics and Play of Canceling an Idol: Exploring How Fans Negotiate Their Fandom of a Canceled 'Fave'," *Convergence*, 30(1), pp. 395–409. https://doi.org/10.1177/13548565231199983.

Feng, J. (2021, March 9) "Following Nationalist Backlash, Chloé Zhao Finds No Place in China for her 'Nomadland'," *The China Project*, https://thechinaproject.com/2021/03/09/following-nationlist-backlash-chloe-zhao-finds-no-place-in-china-for-her-nomadland/.

Geusens, F., Ouvrein, G., and Remen, S. (2023) "#Cancelled: A Qualitative Content Analysis of Cancel Culture in the YouTube Beauty Community," *The Social Science Journal*, Advance Online Publication, https://doi.org/10.1080/03623319.2023.2175150.

Global Times (2015, April 23) "China to Clean Up Cyberspace for Minors," *Global Times*, www.globaltimes.cn/content/918356.shtml.

Global Times (2022, November 1) "Tighter Guidelines Introduced for Celebrity Endorsements," *Global Times*, www.globaltimes.cn/page/202211/1278422.shtml.

Han, L. and Liu, Y. (2024) "#metoo Activism Without the #MeToo Hashtag: Online Debates Over Entertainment Celebrities' Sex Scandals in China," *Feminist Media Studies*, 24(4), pp. 657–674. https://doi.org/10.1080/14680777.2023.2219857.

Huang, L. and Xie, J. (2021, August 13) "Chinese Actor Zhang Zhehan 'Pays Heavy Price' by Posing at Japan's Notorious Yasukuni Shrine; 'All Brands End Cooperation'," *Global Times*, www.globaltimes.cn/page/202108/1231431.shtml.

Huang, Q., Driessen, S., and Trottier, D. (2023) "When Pop and Politics Collide: A Transcultural Perspective on Contested Practices in Pop Idol Fandoms in China and the West," *International Journal of Communication*, 17, pp. 1425–1444. https://ijoc.org/index.php/ijoc/article/view/17255.

Jenkins, H. and Shresthova, S. (eds.) (2012) "Transformative Works and Fan Activism" special issue, *Transformative Works and Cultures* 10, https://journal.transformativeworks.org/index.php/twc/issue/view/12.

Kirchick, J. (2023, February 4) "Armie Hammer Breaks His Silence," *Airmail*, https://airmail.news/issues/2023-2-4/armie-hammer-breaks-his-silence.

Lee, J. and Abidin, C. (2024) "Backdoor Advertising Scandals, Yingyeo Culture, and Cancel Culture Among YouTube Influencers in South Korea," *New Media & Society*, 26(1), pp. 405–425. https://doi.org/10.1177/14614448211061829.

Lewis, R. and Christin, A. (2022) "Platform Drama: 'Cancel Culture,' Celebrity, and the Struggle for Accountability on YouTube," *New Media & Society*, 24(7), pp. 1632–1656. https://doi.org/10.1177/14614448221099235.

Li, X. and Ng, E. (2025) "'Block (封杀)!'": State-Netizen Constructions of Cancel Culture in China," *Television & New Media* "Digital Platforms and Cancel Culture" special issue, 26(1), pp. 104–118. https://doi.org/10.1177/15274764241277478.

Liu, H. (ed.) (2019) *From Cyber-Nationalism to Fandom Nationalism: The Case of Diba Expedition in China*, London: Routledge.

Mengshenmumu (2021, December 19) "Leehom Wang Is Being Blocked, CCTV Urgently Switching Music, Co-Stars Are Affected and Works Are Taken Down [王力宏开始被封杀，央视紧急替换音源，合作明星遭殃作品或被下架]," *163.com*, www.163.com/dy/article/GRJ31B3O05179RJN.html.

Moss, G. (2020, January 22) "The Dixie Chicks Were Cancelled for Criticizing the President. Now, They're Heroes," *Refinery29*, www.refinery29.com/en-us/dixie-chicks-cancelled-president-bush-controversy.

Myers, S. L. (2018, October 2) "Fan Bingbing, China's Most Famous Actress, Faces Huge Fines in Tax Evasion," *New York Times*, www.nytimes.com/2018/10/02/world/asia/fan-bingbing-tax-evasion-china.html.

Ng, E. (2022) *Cancel Culture: A Critical Analysis*, Cham, Switzerland: Palgrave Macmillan.

Ng, E. (2025) "The Complexities of 'Cancel Culture': A Manifesto on Its Practices and Politics," in S. Eckert and L. Steiner (eds.) *We Can Do Better: Feminist Manifestos for Media and Communication*, New Brunswick, NJ: Rutgers University Press.

Pereira de Sá, S. and Pereira Alberto, T. (2022) "Bigmouth Strikes Again: The Controversies of Morrissey and Cancel Culture," *American Behavioral Scientist*, 66(8), pp. 1091–1105. https://doi.org/10.1177/00027642211042291.

Ravell, H. (2023) "#RIPJKRowling: A Tale of a Fandom, Twitter and a Haunting Author Who Refuses to Die," *Public Relations Inquiry*, 12(3), pp. 239–270. https://doi.org/10.1177/2046147X231180501.

Rosen, S. (2003) "Chinese Media and Youth: Attitudes Toward Nationalism and Internationalism," in Chin-Chuan Lee (ed.) *Chinese Media, Global Contexts*, New York: Routledge, pp. 96–116.

Schott, C. (2023) "Harry Potter and Cancel Culture: Responding to Fallen Heroes," *Journal of Fandom Studies*, 11(1), pp. 19–36. https://doi.org/10.1386/jfs_00069_1.

Sun, T. (2019, January 4) "Fresh Campaign Launched to Clean Up Cyber Environment," *Chinanews.com*, www.ecns.cn/news/2019-01-04/detail-ifzcitha9950511.shtml.

Tiffany, K. (2023, January 10) "Twitter Was the Ultimate Cancellation Machine. If the Platform Dies, How Will People Find Quick Justice?" *The Atlantic*, www.theatlantic.com/technology/archive/2023/01/twitter-cancel-culture-hashtags/672684/.

Wang, E. N. and Ge, L. (2023) "Fan Conflicts and State Power in China: Internalised Heteronormativity, Censorship Sensibilities, and Fandom Police," *Asian Studies Review*, 47(2), pp. 355–373. https://doi.org/10.1080/10357823.2022.2112655.

Whitmore, A. (2021, May 19) "Whedon, Fandom, and Cancel Culture," *The Geek Anthropologist*, https://thegeekanthropologist.com/2021/05/19/whedon-fandom-and-cancel-culture/.

Yang, G. (2019) "Performing Cyber-Nationalism in Twenty-First-Century China: The case of Diba Expedition," in Hailong Liu (ed.) *From Cyber-Nationalism to Fandom Nationalism: The Case of Diba Expedition in China*, New York: Routledge, pp. 1–12.

36
CONSPICUOUS CONVENTION
Industry Interpellation and Fan Consumption at San Diego Comic-Con

Anne Gilbert

Conventions are a concentrated experience of fandom. Fan conventions are immersive, shared spaces in which fannish pursuits can become codified, reinforcing both the behaviors and significance of fan practice. Conventions create entry points to the fan community (Bacon-Smith 1992) and erect physical spaces, albeit ephemeral ones, that shape how fans relate to one another, to media properties, and to industrial forces. The details that structure a fan convention—how it is organized, how it is covered, the fans and creative producers who choose (and are able) to participate, and what that participation looks like—also structure the material practices of fandom. The experience of a fan convention is generated in the planning, navigating, enjoying, and archiving of the event itself, but it is not limited to those in attendance. As the ephemera of convention participation are increasingly digital, and as industry professionals are increasingly invested in the practices of fans, conventions exert an influence of how fandom is understood that extends beyond the event boundaries.

San Diego Comic-Con (SDCC) is arguably the most influential of conventions, in part for its size and longevity, but also because of the attention it receives from media content producers, entertainment news outlets, and fans themselves. SDCC started in 1970 and is run by Comic-Con International, a small not-for-profit that organizes this and two other annual events dedicated to "creating awareness of, and appreciation for, comics and related popular arts" (Comic-Con International 2015a). In recent years, SDCC has also become a major marketing event for film studios, television networks, and game distributors. Comic-Con brings more than 130,000 ticket-holding fans to downtown San Diego each July (Comic-Con International); since 2010, tickets to the event have sold out within minutes. The increase in attendee interest has accompanied a rising industry profile, with A-list celebrities, major film and television properties, and entertainment news media all making SDCC a focus. Thus, SDCC is comprised of both grassroots communities and corporate-sponsored interests, operating in tandem.

The focus of this chapter is on the economics of industrial participation at SDCC. Fans in attendance do enjoy a number of affective benefits from the convention—engagement with a community of like-minded, self-identified geeks; the cachet of privileged access at the event; and the direct attention of media producers courting fan interest, for example. Yet it is important to note that the fandom that is practiced at SDCC is deeply imbricated in industry interest: attendees are effectively idealized as a palatable, industrially sanctioned version of media fandom.

Industry participation at SDCC should be understood as an effort to construct an identity of a "good fan," and to incorporate attendees into that identity. Industry rhetoric often echoes the conventional wisdom, celebrated but also critiqued in this volume and elsewhere in fan studies, that fans are the most productive, engaged, and powerful audiences in participatory culture. In reality, however, industrial involvement at SDCC is less concerned with fan agency than with reinforcing the role of conspicuous consumption as central to the fan identity. At SDCC, attendees are encouraged to be consumers first, to prioritize visible consumption practices for themselves and to understand consumption in general as a key component of status and achievement in fan culture. The practices of industry at San Diego Comic-Con cultivate fan participation that values loyalty to mainstream geek culture and access to entertainment media—and that is unconcerned with the level of commodification and industrial control that accompanies these benefits.

While specific to SDCC, these industry practices are significant because they interpellate individuals—both those in attendance and those who follow the convention from afar—into a restricted fan identity that ultimately benefits industrial economic aims. Louis Althusser's (1971) concept of interpellation argues that social institutions shape individual identity by "hailing" participants; when those participants respond, they implicitly take on the characteristics those institutions embed within the call. Individuals consent to this process, and are willing (if not necessarily explicitly aware) participants in the ideological framing of their identity. In other words, the practices of corporate media industries at SDCC encourage and valorize particular behaviors—watch the show, see the film, tell your friends, like and share us on social media—as activities that mark "attendees" as "fans." In doing so, attendees willingly further the commodification of popular culture and strengthen the fan's role as consumer. Simply by participating at the convention, therefore, attendees are invited into a fan identity that is constructed by industrial interest, and that has implications beyond the visible behaviors.

SDCC is a large scale, heterogeneous event, and can be difficult to characterize by any limited set of its practices. But industrial presence is marked at SDCC: major media conglomerates mix with small-scale business operations, and though independent vendors are not as easily identifiable as industrial contributions, they likewise shape fans' affective behaviors. This chapter considers the most visible influences of industrial interest at SDCC, the programming and content of the panel presentations and the giveaways and autograph lotteries on the convention's trade floor. I argue that these elements may invoke the rhetoric of participatory culture, but in fact legitimate a fan identity that reinforces industrial dominance and traditional audience behavior. In effect, the practices of industry at SDCC create a culture of fandom in which participation is structured as consumption.

Navigating SDCC

SDCC is a fan convention on a grand scale. The event takes over the San Diego Convention Center as well as neighboring hotels, restaurants, theatres, and businesses, for five days of fan gatherings, media presentations, games, screenings, costumes, parties, and celebrity sightings. As part of the event, SDCC hosts, among other activities, an animation festival, an academic conference, fan club recruitment tables, and a cosplay Masquerade. The most popular—and significant—features of SDCC are its panels and its exhibition floor. On the floor, small-press comic vendors operate next to promotional booths from DC and Marvel; Mattel, Hasbro, and LEGO have pop-up shops selling collectibles and exclusive merchandise; and independent vendors and artists sell geeky artwork, apparel, memorabilia, games, and collectibles. The trade floor is also the site of some of the most visible industry participation: Hollywood studios erect displays to market films and give away t-shirts, bags, or posters to passersby; television networks build interactive replicas of show sets; and video game makers offer the chance to play new products prior to their release. The programming schedule of panel presentations offers a similar range of activities. In the smallest panels are intimate discussions of fan culture and geek media; in the largest halls, Hollywood distributors parade stars to promote films and television. Panels and the exhibition floor are major events, with thousands of attendees spending their convention time in—or in line for—one of these.

Attempts by industrial interests to channel fan activity toward corporate gain are not unusual; fans' investment in popular culture has led them to become a target market and industry-demarcated demographic (Stein 2011). Engagement with participatory culture has meant, in some instances, that "marketers have simply found creative ways to harness the enthusiasm of active media audiences in order to sell to them more effectively" (Bird 2011: 507). Henry Jenkins sums up the ambivalence of industry interest in fan practice: "to be desired by the networks is to have your tastes commodified" (Jenkins 2006: 62). Jenkins notes that the commodification of consumers who are deemed to matter by media industries presents an inevitable paradox, as this commodification is a form of exploitation, but at the same time it is an indication of the economic value and larger cultural visibility of a group. However, fans are always already implicated as consumers of popular culture, and their investment in media properties is, by necessity, a support of the corporate practices of production and promotion that create these properties. SDCC's industrial hailing of fans does not entail the co-optation or appropriation of fan interest for economic gain, but rather indicates that fans' existing consumer behaviors are being targeted, shaped, and valorized as a useful proponent of promotion in corporate popular culture.

SDCC presents an opportunity to consider fans as community members and consumers simultaneously, where these behaviors do not assemble a hierarchical or segmented version of fandom, but instead collude in the fan identity. Industry presence is designed to reward fan consumption, reinforce it as essential to the fan identity, and guide consumer behaviors toward particular practices and value systems. Attendees are directed toward longstanding, traditional models of exhibition and consumption: watching television (TV) shows when they air on broadcast networks, lining up for and purchasing tickets to movies in theatres, buying copies—often physical ones—of books and comic books to read. Industry promotion at SDCC is also designed to valorize fans who wait, and connects anticipation and hype with loyalty. Producers and distributors of media build exclusivity and access into their presence at SDCC, encouraging attendees to, essentially, brag to friends not in attendance about the content they previewed at the convention; wait to watch or play or read through legitimate, traditional avenues; and to then bring others along when doing so. This is how fandom is structured at SDCC, conscripting attendees into the promotion of media enterprises, thus implicating them into systems of hype and interpellating fans into an understanding of loyalty as marketing strategy.

Convention Panels: Programming Fandom

Panel programming at SDCC is a massive operation, four full days of up to 18 concurrent panels host presentations, screenings, workshops, and question and answer (Q&A) sessions. The largest rooms are the domain of Hollywood film and television programs, and offer sneak peaks of mainstream geek culture: Presentations, for example, featuring the actors from the latest *Star Wars* film or every superhero from the Marvel films slated for the next three years, or conversations with the cast and creators of *Doctor Who* or *Supernatural*. Newsworthy announcements from the presentations are rebroadcast by entertainment news outlets and fan circuits alike, and the panel content, minus any footage or visual material, are likewise recorded and shared online. Despite opportunities to access the information elsewhere, attendees line up for hours and even days to be in the room during one of the major panel presentations; though the largest panel room at SDCC, Hall H, holds more than 6,000 people, it also supports a line to get in that can easily include double that number and starts more than 24 hours in advance. In contrast are panels held in the smaller rooms. These presentations and workshops cover an array of fan interest, from cosplay techniques to debating the state of women in gaming to learning how to run a comic book store or become a geek blogger. Small panels outnumber the large ones, often have little to no wait, and offer an interactive conversation in which panelists and audience members share perspectives on geek culture.

Despite their differences, panels of all sizes should be understood as an opportunity for industrial players to infuse media consumption with a sense of exclusivity, anticipation, and scarcity, and to steer fan interest in directions that, ultimately, can translate to economic gain. Some of these efforts are built in to the organization of the panels: the programming schedule is only released a couple of weeks prior to the event, and even then, details can be vague. While some panels list the celebrities who will be present and the media properties promoted, others simply list, for example, a 90-minute block during which Warner Bros. promises a "'sneak peek' at a few upcoming features" (Comic-Con International 2015b: 72). Fans compete to buy limited tickets months before programming is announced and, even while at the event, must make educated guesses, based on conjecture as well as information gleaned from celebrity Twitter feeds and entertainment news reports, about who will be at the event. Attending panels involves some degree of faith, in convention programmers and media institutions, that the presentations will be on-brand and live up to fans' expectations.

Film and television producers take advantage of this system to guide attendees toward new properties. In film distributors' programming blocks, presentations for highly anticipated comic book features are interspersed with those for films looking to generate advance buzz by making a splash at the convention. TV distributors program advance screenings and exclusive access to shows to cultivate a viewership from among SDCC's loyal attendees. Implicitly, industry programming encourages fans of one media property to explore three or four new ones as well—in effect, to consume ever more media.

In addition to the anticipation of panel content, the structural characteristics of SDCC's panel programming builds in scarcity, because for attendees to participate in these events necessitates a degree of selection and sacrifice. SDCC's size means that desirable properties are often programmed concurrently, and waiting to attend a Marvel television panel means fans miss out on *Game of Thrones* entirely. SDCC also does not empty out rooms between presentations, though breaks between panels do allow attendees to leave, enter, or vie for a more desirable seat. Fans use the no-clearing policy as a strategy, electing to sit through other presentations to ensure being present for the panel they want. Effectively, attending the convention also means missing the convention, as fans wait in line and through presentations long enough to miss events, panels, and entire days of SDCC.

Industrial involvement at SDCC consolidates the anticipation and scarcity of the event into a sense of exclusivity, constructing an explicit aura of privilege and casting panel presentations as an opportunity to "give back" to loyal fans. Some of this is expressed in direct dialogue: celebrities and producers who are on SDCC panels effusively thank fans for showing up, they take pictures of the size of the crowds, they praise attendee questions, and generally express amazement and gratitude at the dedication of their viewers. Industry rhetoric valorizes fans' choice to attend panel programming, and fans are assured that what they are watching is privileged material, available only to those who made the sacrifice of time, money, and energy to be in the room for a particular presentation. Though discussions and Q&A with the celebrity guests are recorded, any filming of exclusive content presented at SDCC is forbidden, and security patrols aim to prevent media leaks of advance footage. It is largely irrelevant that piracy remains rampant and little SDCC "exclusive content" remains truly exclusive for any length of time; what matters is that industry representatives perpetuate the notion that the footage is a reward for the fans who are in the room.

The practices of praise and the reward of exclusivity implicitly encourage behaviors that ultimately provide economic benefit for film, television, and game producers that can be quantified according to traditional industry metrics. In effect, fans are engaged in "speculative consumption" (Gray 2010) at the convention, watching early footage, advance trailers, and screenings that can translate attendee interest in July to eventual fan loyalty in the form of box office receipts, ratings numbers, and sales—or such is the industry goal. In the panel presentations, fans are given carefully curated promotional information, like details on casting or plot points from early episodes of an upcoming season; their interest is then explicitly guided to, later, purchasing movie theatre tickets or DVDs, tweeting about upcoming properties with authorized hashtags, and setting a reminder to watch broadcast airings of new episodes. These presentations tease but do not spoil future releases—panels do not reveal the outcome of a pending of a cliffhanger, offer cheats to a new game, or discuss critical plot points of upcoming film releases. Instead, industry participation in SDCC is an investment, one that relies on attendees' long-term willingness to purchase and view content in sanctioned, traditional avenues in order to see a return. The content of panels is therefore designed to complement and encourage consumption, but not replace it.

Panel programming illustrates some of the ambivalence of how fandom is structured at SDCC: though they are more popular and receive greater attention, there is also a perception that larger panels, and the individuals who flock to the convention for them, are perhaps missing out on the authentic Comic-Con experience by spending time with corporate media presentations rather than in smaller workshops and discussions. However, while the industrial presence is more visible in the larger panels, all panel programming has a role in reinforcing the constructed identity of fans as consumers. In instructional workshops, fans are shown how to enter the geek market and generate audience interest by becoming viable comic artists, store owners, bloggers, or cultural commentators. In discussions that critique representation or a lack of diversity in geek culture, participants are encouraged to make their voices heard through buying behaviors—buy the books, films, and games that do better, and thus influence industry practice. Small fandom and geek culture panels often feature peer-to-peer recommendations, helping other attendees find new media properties to consume. As such, even in smaller panels, fandom is commodified and fan practice is steered toward consumptive behaviors.

Industry participants take advantage of programming structures to develop a sense of privilege in attending panel presentations; fans' dedication to popular media is reinforced through direct praise and by fostering an aura of anticipation and scarcity to industrial content. Fans at SDCC are offered access to exclusive footage that does not replace paid-for content, but instead urges them to be both voracious and omnivorous in their media consumption. Panel presentations encourage media participation that has economic advantages and reinforce the notion that the identity of the best fans is one of loyalty and consumption.

Acquiring the Fan Experience: Giveaways and Autographs

The trade floor at San Diego Comic-Con is primarily a commercial space. Though it is also a site of community, where fans mingle with fellow attendees, people-watch, and take photos of cosplayers, the dominant function of the exhibition hall is retail: the free and paid-for merchandise at the convention render attendance a commodity to be acquired. Major toy companies use events like SDCC to market exclusive, limited edition toys, and other vendors offer exclusive art, apparel, and collectibles; these do make a robust aftermarket reselling opportunity that relies upon the prestige of convention exclusivity even as it challenges the accuracy of the products' limited availability. Vendors of comic books, memorabilia, toys, and collectibles line the floor, making the convention an ideal space for fans to augment and curate their collections (Geraghty 2014). To walk the floor at SDCC is to browse opportunities for consumption, both for items to purchase and for new books, games, comics, films, or television shows to check out.

Booths for artists or a small, independent retailer may be little larger than a table, but these are effectively storefronts at which small business owners pedal their geeky wares to a receptive audience.

On the other hand, booths for the largest film distributors, television networks, game producers, and comic book creators have a footprint of several hundred square feet and are themselves architectural spectacles. These booths feature exhibits of movie costumes and props, elaborate LEGO sculptures and original artwork, models of sets, characters, and special effects, and even second-story VIP party areas for celebrities that provide curiosities and photo opportunities for fans passing by.

Few of the major film studios, networks, or game companies, however, operate these large-scale booths as retail spaces. Instead, major industry booths are designed as marketing tools at which exhibitors give away promotional material, both as tangible goods and as interactive experiences. With the former, the experience of SDCC is heavily punctuated by swag: from convention registration, which includes the receipt of giant collectible bags, branded by Warner Bros. and badge lanyards, sponsored by Showtime, fans are given promotional merchandise to wear, carry, or collect as they approach and navigate the convention.

Some of these giveaways happen in the panel presentations, where fans receive a ticket to redeem for t-shirts, posters, bags, or other items that are branded in connection to that show or film. Others happen, however, on the trade floor, when booth workers hand out

Conspicuous Convention

Figure 36.1 Small comic book retail booth on the SDCC trade floor.

similar swag to passersby, creating substantial crowds and, at times, increasing the desirability for some items that are coveted by fans but cannot be purchased and are only handed out at random intervals. Interactive experiences on the trade floor are similar: Fans can play advance versions of new video games, have green screen photos taken with film villains, be chased by zombies, or peruse recreations of TV show sets. These experiences always have long lines and, because of fire codes and crowd management in a convention space filled to capacity, the lines are often full and closed to new entrants, even those willing to wait.

With the giveaways of both material and immaterial goods, producers and distributors are structuring consumer practice for attendees. Like the exclusive content released in the panel presentations, these giveaways do not replace the consumer goods fans are asked to buy; the giveaways do not include DVDs of the last season of a show or tickets to a film yet to be released. Rather, these giveaways are of branded material that can only be acquired as a gift, so that attendees actually vie to be able to get new stuff—stuff that renders them walking advertisements for upcoming media properties. In sharing photos of SDCC's interactive experiences, in wearing branded merchandise that is not available for retail, fans are engaged in viral marketing for media industry properties that is never fully articulated as such. Access to these items and experience is not restricted by price or even by merit, but by limits of quantity and space. Fans at SDCC are not rewarded with increased interactivity, engagement, or ownership for their participation in the convention. Instead,

Figure 36.2 Warner Bros.' large-scale booth on the SDCC trade floor, during a signing for HBO's *Silicon Valley*.

industry giveaways afford fans more opportunities to act as consumers, and thus participation in industrial promotion is constructed as aspirational—desirable, but not necessarily attainable.

Industrial offerings also take the form of autographs, which are likewise often disbursed through lottery, but offer an intangible sense of access to celebrity along with their material rewards. Autograph opportunities are varied at the convention: some are paid transactions, in which memorabilia booths on the exhibition floor bring in celebrities, often established fixtures on the convention circuit, to sign autographs at a set price, a fee that serves as direct—and sometimes generous—compensation for the celebrities involved (Goldberg 2016). Some autograph signings are actually giveaways attached to panel presentations, with random fans at the panel awarded a ticket that allows them access to a later event at which the celebrities on the panel sign posters or branded merchandise. Most commonly, however, autographs are remarkably similar to exhibit floor giveaways and panel presentations: run as lottery or as rewards for those who wait. SDCC organizers have a full slate of autographs, populated by artists and authors as well as actors, for which fans wait in line or for a ticket in the autograph area of the convention center. Autograph events operated by film distributors and television networks are held in the booths on the exhibition floor, and feature many of the high-profile celebrities that headline the biggest panel

Conspicuous Convention

Figure 36.3 Attendees study convention maps with their SDCC bags. Souvenir bags are sponsored by Warner Bros., and distributed to attendees at registration.

presentations. For these, attendees wait in line to be given a ticket, which enters them in a lottery for the autograph event. A challenge for fans is the fact that these lottery lines are separate from, but concurrent with, lines for the panel presentations for the same show or film, so vying for an autograph is often done at the expense of seeing the panel.

Though autograph signings are not long affairs in which fans engage in a conversation with a celebrity, they are desirable opportunities. The autograph program schedule provides ephemeral access to celebrities for a brief interaction, photos, personal contact, and an autograph to take away, access to the media world and its prestige that is not readily available elsewhere. Some booths on the exhibition floor post schedules or make announcements when the cast of this show or that film will be on hand to sign autographs. This is, of course, somewhat misleading, as opportunities for fans to take part in the signings have long since been given away by the time announcements are made, but it does offer a representation of the type of social stratification upon which autograph signings (and giveaways) rely. Fans on the convention floor can move toward booths conducting signings in the hope of catching a glimpse or snagging a photo of a celebrity, but they are generally not permitted to congregate in the walkways of the floor and must keep moving—whereas fans ticketed for the event stand in line in precisely those desirable locations to await their turn. Exclusive access to celebrities and convention experiences reinforce to attendees the rewards of privileged consumption by giving validation to a hierarchy in which those fans who participate—vie for giveaways and autographs, compete for opportunities of consumption—are held up as the ideal fans.

Autograph signings are again opportunities in which fans must sacrifice time and attention, and are rewarded with effusive thanks, exclusive access to industry professionals, and both an immaterial interactive experience and a material takeaway that reinforce the legitimacy of industrial dominance and celebrity culture. These are rewards that cannot be bought, but must be earned through loyalty, devotion, and luck. Most importantly, these are rewards that are predicated on the fan's role as consumer; whereas theoretical models of participatory culture often emphasize the blurring of distinctions between producer and consumer, access to celebrity is only rewarding if the boundary between celebrity and fan remains intact. Fans at SDCC, therefore, are idealized as consumers, those who are willing to wait for fleeting engagement with industry in the form of an autograph or a branded material giveaway.

Culture of Consumption

The practices outlined here represent those undertaken by representatives of multinational media conglomerates at SDCC; the convention is the site of a spectrum of media work, and while the most visible interests might be those of major film studios and television networks, industry efforts at SDCC also include retailers, media properties, and producers of a variety of sizes. While practices of these interests may differ somewhat from those of high profile corporate industry—and the influence wielded by them may be likewise different—the efforts of small and independent business interests at SDCC still contribute to a consumer-focused fan identity and perpetuate a culture of fandom that is fully incorporated in commodity politics.

Autograph signings that do not originate with major film studios or television distributors nevertheless similarly promote a celebrity culture that peddles access to actors, authors, artists, and significant cultural figures. The vendors on the exhibition floor who offer paid autograph signings are often small and independent business owners, but are also contributing to a brisk economy in which fan participation becomes a commodified experience with a fixed price. The smallest panels perpetuate a geek culture that endorses the implicit messages of the largest program spaces. Promotional film and television giveaways on the trade floor are surrounded by small retailers of geek merchandise, and complemented by the flyers and promotions that blanket the neighborhoods surrounding the convention. Industrial practices, in other words, are not limited to industrial players, but the behaviors serve a similar function whether coming from a major Hollywood studio or an independent t-shirt vendor: they establish SDCC as a venue in which fan consumption is shaped, validated, and codified.

For attendees at SDCC, even if it were possible to distinguish between types of media work represented in practices at the convention, it is not necessarily productive to do so. The experience of the convention interweaves interests of multinational corporate industry and independent start-ups and those in between, such that all ask the same of fans, and offer similar rewards. The culture of consumption at SDCC is reinforced by industry at all levels, because it constructs the mainstream geek identity as a loyal, productive consumer.

Industry presence at SDCC first constructs and then interpellates attendees into this identity of the "good fan." SDCC presents an opportunity for industry to harness fan loyalty and investment and funnel it into particular behaviors that valorize fans' sacrifices of time and attention, their practices of consumption, marketing, and proselytizing for media properties, and their willingness to value privileged access to content and people. Industry involvement at the convention is designed to capitalize on the structures of the event and the investment of attendees to reinscribe these practices as desirable and productive behaviors. At SDCC, fans are hailed as collaborators in efforts to reinforce the value of celebrity and media content; that exclusive content and access to industrial insiders are framed as rewards for fannish devotion legitimates that devotion while at the same time reinforcing the dominance of industry interests in a corporate entertainment culture. Industry participation at San Diego Comic-Con constructs an identity of fans as consumers, encouraging them to be loyal audiences of mainstream geek culture and to represent a sanctioned version of fandom that, through the cultural prominence of the convention and its participants, comes to stand in cultural conversations for the most visible and readily accessible fan identity.

References

Althusser, L. (1971) "Ideology and Ideological State Apparatuses." In L. Athusser (ed.), *Lenin and Philosophy and Other Essays*, New York: Monthly Review Press.

Bacon-Smith, C. (1992) *Enterprising Women: Television Fandom and the Creation of Popular Myth*, Philadelphia: University of Pennsylvania Press.

Bird, S. E. (2011) "Are We All Produsers Now?" *Cultural Studies*, 25(4–5), pp. 502–516.

Comic-Con International. (2015a) "About Comic-Con International." [ONLINE] Available at: www.comic-con.org/about [Accessed 21 March 2016].

Comic-Con International (2015b) *Events Guide*, San Diego: Comic-Con International.

Geraghty, L. (2014) *Cult Collectors: Nostalgia, Fandom and Collecting Popular Culture*, London: Routledge.

Goldberg, L. (2016) "Stars Getting Rich Off Fan Conventions: How to Take Home 'Garbage Bags Full of $20s'," *Hollywood Reporter*. [ONLINE] Available at: www.hollywoodreporter.com/live-feed/stars-getting-rich-fan-conventions-933062 [Accessed 20 December 2016].

Gray, J. (2010) *Show Sold Separately: Promos, Spoilers, and Other Media Paratexts*, New York: New York University Press.

Jenkins, H. (2006) *Convergence Culture*, New York: New York University Press.

Stein, L. E. (2011) "'Word of Mouth on Steroids': Hailing the Millennial Media Fan." In M. Kackman et al. (eds.), *Flow TV: Television in the Age of Media Convergence*, London: Routledge, pp. 128–143.

37

(BLACK FEMALE) FANS STRIKE BACK

The Emergence of the Iris West Defense Squad

Kristen J. Warner

June 15, 2016 marked a big day for the Twitter section of the Iris West Defense Squad (IWDS). In response to the news that Warner Bros. was moving forward with the pre-production for their *The Flash* movie after hiring Rick Famuyiwa to direct,[1] IWDS set out one of their monthly pre-emptive campaigns for their eponymous character to be portrayed by a Black woman as she has been on the hit CW network's series of the same name. #KeepIrisBlack emerged as fans of the televised version of the character realized that similar to how the film's lead varied from his television counterpart, it was possible the feature could not only choose a different actor but a differently raced character. Television's Iris West, #KeepIrisBlack argued, increased the diversity of representation for Black women within the DC comic universe thus, it would be in the best interest of the studio to continue casting Iris as Black in the film. A type of fancasting, where fans of a particular text collectively organize to suggest possible casting choices for producers and casting directors alike, the hashtag tagged Famuyiwa and DC Comics with various rationales for Iris's Blackness. Attaching photos and Twitter accounts (when available) of up and coming Black actresses who could fit the Iris West type, these hashtagged tweets were designed to worldwide trend as evidence of their importance. While I am certain that this campaign, much like most fancasting, was not designed to actually force the studios into casting a specific actress, its goal was no less ambitious: get the powers that be to both acknowledge the possibility that Iris could be Black as well as owning the responsibility should they choose to go with a white actress.

A campaign of this type is a key aspect of the IWDS. Self-tasked with the responsibilities of protecting and defending the blackness of the television character as well as the actress who portrays her, these fans transformed their adoration of their love object into something of a political action. Understanding this allegiance and pledge of fealty to a fictitious character, to an actor, or to a text, is a worthwhile exploration; adding to this quest identity variables such as race and gender only enriches the field of inquiry. Considering how a predominantly online Black membership group, already functioning in the margins of fandom, not only exists but finds sustenance in publicizing and fighting for their convictions is the focus of this chapter. Through a historicizing of IWDS' antics through the lens of fan studies as well as a discursive analysis of the fandom at work on Twitter, I illustrate a fandom driven by dual functions: the typical love of their fan object intertwined with a desire for racial visibility onscreen that when put into action mobilizes them to fight for good characterization both within the series and as an identificatory model of their Black female selves.

Making the Virtual Defense Squad Visible

Louisa Stein posits that the labor fans employ for their love objects results in voluminous waves of creative work across the digital landscape.

> Media fans have come to be known as digitally resourceful (and/or overdependent) and community oriented. Inspired by their love of a specific media text or of media culture in general, fans use digital networks like LiveJournal, YouTube, Tumblr, and Polyvore to build communities and to share and respond to their creative work. Fans often use digital tools in unexpected and unintended ways, creating interactive narrative via linked online journals or constructing fannish narrative worlds out of unaffiliated world-building games such as *The Sims*. Fans also coordinate with each other to raise charity, to campaign for cancelled shows, or to increase the visibility of their favorite series. Although media fans may make up only a small percentage of film and TV viewers, fan modes of engagement have become increasingly visible.
> (Stein 2015, 3)

Put simply, the ways fans behave as prosumers of content illustrate a set of ever-expanding possibilities that tether their love labor to a set of collective agendas they aim to accomplish. What's more, that these fans have become more strategic about the manner with which they engage with producers and one another online points to the integration of this labor into their everyday lives. Their obsessions are reified into literal labors "of love" work that is attended to in such uniform fashions it becomes mundane. That said, it would be imprecise to suggest that the mundane work these fans participate in are without passion. In their discussion of the impact of Pinterest in relationship to the "mamasphere," Julie Wilson and Emily Chivers Yochim cite Kathleen Stewart's notion of "ordinary affects" to explain the affective payoff the women within these shared communities experience participating in the uniformly mundane activities necessary for engagement on social media.

> The varied, surging capacities to affect and to be affected that give everyday life the quality of a continual motion of relations, scenes, contingencies and emergencies ... They happen in impulses, sensations, expectations, daydreams, encounters, and habits of relating ... in publics and social worlds of all kinds that catch people up in something that feels like something. Their significance lies in the intensities they build and in what thoughts and feelings they make possible.
> (Wilson and Chivers Yochim 2015, 236–237)

Stewart's characterization of ordinary affects fits the tone of the prosumer fan within the fandom working to prove the legitimacy of her ship or the importance of her favorite character—the intensities of feeling brought to their labor correlate to the expectations of change, growth, and success with what they hope to see onscreen. That hope indeed catches them up in service of a goal that feels like something meaningful.

The connection between affect and fandom communities doing work is useful for considering the manner by which fans structure their in-group status as well as corporately decide how to publicly "feel." Lauren Berlant's notion of intimate publics illustrates how both of these drives emerge within these closed off, hierarchical spaces. Berlant posits that what makes an intimate public intimate lies in "the expectation that the consumers of its particular stuff already share a worldview and emotional knowledge that they have derived from a broadly common historical experience (Berlant 2008, viii)." Berlant continues:

> An intimate public is an achievement. Whether linked to women or other non-dominant people, it flourishes as a porous, affective scene of identification among strangers that promises a certain experience of belonging and provides a complex of consolation, confirmation, discipline, and discussion about how to live as an x.
>
> (Berlant 2008, viii)

Berlant's characterization easily fits the notion of fan communities as a place where strangers with shared affinities come together to safely meet and decide how to protect their love object while also forming factions that self-regulate. The factions discipline and confirm within their alliances but also across alliances resulting in what Derek Johnson describes as "fantagonisms" (Johnson 2007, 287). In this sense, fantagonisms are underpinned by the intimate public an affinity text generates through affective ties enabling them to affirm, fight, align, and discuss with one another with full knowledge that skirmishes, while often problematic, are par for the course.

Bringing the "Black" Back into Fandom

Up until this point I have been laying the groundwork for a consideration of the defense squad as a naturally emerging facet of online fandoms. Piecemealing a corpus of literature thus becomes an exercise of locating the concepts that generally apply and filling in the context. However, in the case of this chapter, fleshing out context increases twofold because not only am I filling in the gaps for a phenomenon not yet accounted for but I am also wedging Black women into the equation—a group who are not often considered in manners of fandom. As I have argued in relationship to Black female fans of ABC's *Scandal*, both in the research area of fan studies as well as in the world of fandom-at-large, this identity group remains invisible. I argued then:

> While the stereotype of women in fandom generally precludes women of color as participants and producers of content, it is nevertheless true that Black and Brown female bodies do exist in fan communities. Producing content is a necessary act of agency for women of color who strive for visibility in a landscape that favors a more normative (read: white) fan identity that often dismisses and diminishes the desires of its diverse body to see themselves equally represented not only on screen but in the fan community at large.
>
> (Warner 2015, 34)

Yet, the basis of work in fan studies functions at nearly every level *except* for the intersections of race and gender. Alexis Lothian describes the necessity of an intersectional approach to discussing race and fandom as it best encapsulates how people of color—most often women of color—are left out of the debate. "The intersection of race and gender is crucial to a lot of the terminology that comes up in discussions of race in fandom, particularly because much of the discussion takes place in online spaces that are dominated by white women (Lothian 2009, 4.1)." Extrapolating from Lothian's point, trying to find space in those dominated and often-times hierarchical communities compels women of color to develop their own spaces. But how do these spaces function within fandom?

Despite the rampant invisibility afforded to them as fan laborers, Black female fandom continues to thrive in spite of the ways their spaces are relegated to the background. In fact, part of what may strengthen these pluralist communities is the fact that they are left alone to create their own safe spaces for interaction and creative labor. Returning to Berlant's interrogation of intimate publics, the desire of belonging to these shared communities is so strong, marginalized groups strategize ways to co-exist. Expanding Berlant's point, because of a lack of resources, Black women have long had to "make do" and consequently will recalibrate the limits of fandom experience to suit their own need for participation and community amongst themselves.

Inserting Blackness into a mode of engagement it has not been explicitly tethered to is a political act not unlike the epochs where making [white] women's fandom experience visible was the goal. Ironically, the one marginalized group that has never been considered as part of the unshackling are white female fans. Much of the work of fan studies has focused on foregrounding the place of women in fandom. As Henry Jenkins and Camille Bacon-Smith posit in their seminal texts on fandom, the role of female fans is one of making their desires and labor visible. From discussions on the role of fantasy and pleasure for female fans, including slash fiction, to various other kinds of fan labor, articulating the intimate pleasure of fandom is of central importance. Affirming this point, Darlene Hampton argues that digital culture continues to reinforce male privilege thus rendering women's labor as simplistic. "Raising awareness of the gendered nature of online space is an important endeavor because this gendering contributes to the ongoing subordination of women under patriarchy by marginalizing or dismissing their concerns, labor, and cultural tastes" (Hampton 2010, 3). For Hampton, decentering the ways that male fans dismiss female fans online is the primary goal. She's not wrong in exploring that work. However, that formulation implicitly leads to white men and women being solely understood as those who are marginalized.

And this is why the politics of Black female fandom must be unpacked. While not specifically engaging Black women and fandom, in her seminal work—and, for the record, still the only book that specifically examines Black women's reception to media—Jacqueline Bobo argues that Black women form interpretative communities as a kind of political resistance. "Black women within an interpretive community are also part of this movement. As cultural producers, critics, and members of an audience the women are positioned to intervene strategically in the imaginative construction, critical interpretation, and social condition of black women" (Bobo 1995, 27). When applied to their objects of desire, these Black women's acts of labor can thus represent signs of mainstream fan behavior. However, if these pluralist online fandoms created by and for Black women exist, under what principles might they operate?

Emergence of the IWDS

When it was announced that the CW was expanding its DC Universe from *Arrow* to include *The Flash*, online fans seemed to be excited about the possibilities. Opting to diversify the original source material, executive producers Greg Berlanti, Andrew Kriesberg, and Geoff Johns cast Detective Joe West as African-American. Of course, this casting decision generated a domino effect, ultimately redesigning the racial types of West's family line. So, when Candice Patton was announced as Iris West it should not have come as a surprise. A cursory glance at message boards and industry trade articles circulating Patton's announcement suggested the sentiment around a Black Iris West was mixed. On one hand, fans celebrated DC stepping up to make a more diverse story world with its supporting characters; on the other, loyalists concerned with the perils of adaptation worried that switching the race of the West family would adversely affect the narrative. There is truth to both perspectives. It is advantageous for the series as well as for the network that hosts it to increase the visual diversity of its cast. However, to many industry professionals race is "heavy" and, for them, acts as a yoke around their neck rather than functioning as a beneficial and organic additive. Especially in a televisual space where racialized bodies are not present, incorporating them into these narratives presents more problems than the diversity seal of approval granted by minority watchdog groups seems worth. Moreover, the notion of race as heavy indicates an awareness on the part of many creative industry professionals that there is no simple fix with the colorblind casting diverse bodies in a kind of "dipping white bodies in chocolate," mode of hiring. Despite the fact that nothing about the character has to change save the skin color, implicit in race blind casting is the knowledge that racialized bodies have histories that when presented without adjustment can reproduce terrible, racist stereotypes. Of course, the benefit of colorblind casting is that when the blind-casted actor takes the part, the writers are shielded from whatever accidental tropes her character falls into because they wrote that part for "anyone"; thus, the trope is unintentional and the interpretation lies solely with the viewer making the accusation. This means that when these tropes emerge within the narrative or when a blind-cast character's screen time is reduced, for fans who wish to cry foul, claims of indirect racism are difficult to prove. Add to that that because the character is blind cast not only are the writers blameless but many of the fans—who likely were not interested in racializing the characters in the first place—could push back against those charges because these shows are not about race. Perhaps the powers imbued in the characters are metaphors for deep insecurities they harbor—but not race. Thus the messiness that occurs when fans attempt to make those claims seems to only reinforce the race as heavy discourse for those affiliated with these shows, culminating in a cycle of self-fulfilling prophecies that often result in intentional vacancies of diversity within series and a bitterness and resentment within the fandom-at-large.

Still, for the audience member who clusters with others to form a fandom around the character who, for them, grants them representational access to a world within the comics universe they have never been previously allowed, the messiness of fighting back against bad representation of their character is necessary. Locating the specific origin story of the IWDS is challenging because there are no clear starts. According to a Tumblr blog post, the first mentions of the IWDS in mainstream articles came in 2015 from one of Angelica Jade Bastien's weekly write-ups on *The Flash* for *Bustle* magazine. In a sub-section of the article called, "Racism in the Fandom," Bastien (Bastien 2015) writes that she hopes the writers wouldn't couple *The Flash* lead, Barry Allen, with one of the supporting characters, Caitlin Snow (shippers refer to them as SnowBarry), before giving Barry and Iris (WestAllen) a chance. Acknowledging the tensions between fans around the possibility of this match, Bastien embeds a few tweets that illustrate the strain of racism present in the fandom not fond of an interracial couple and then offers the emergent IWDS and their "clapbacks" as recourse. Citing the IWDS Tumblr as a base location for these warriors, the article introduced the IWDS as a concrete response to these attacks.

In a long response outlining the importance of the IWDS, Tumblr page "Posts from Under the Bridge" defines the squad as a group:

> Formed to fight against the hate that Iris and her actress, Candice Patton, received online. Both fans and Candice herself have received a near constant litany of hate for her character. Most of it is racial.
>
> (Posts from Under the Bridge 2015)

Indeed, on many of the fan posts about Iris West, there is a common narrative that the fan—and perhaps even the powers that be— told Patton not to join social media or read the comments on articles about her on the show. While having a Twitter account has become a part of the job of actors tasked with promoting their series, reading the comments in response to her Twitter presence is certainly not required. Asked about it in an MTV interview, asserting that whenever they post clips about the WestAllen pairing or an alternative, WestAllen fans "go nuts," Patton confirms she heeds the warnings. "Listen, I try and stay away from my comment section on Twitter. But for the most part, the response that I get usually is very positive (Benal 2015)." She continues this response in a *TVLine* interview: "I try not to read too many comments ... The haters can be ... they can really get on your nerves, I guess. I don't mind people talking badly about me or whatever; it's when I feel like it has to do with race that really kind of bothers me" (Mitovich 2015). The quotes reveal the self-fashioning of an actress who has to be cautious of how she speaks about the fans of this show because the DC Universe looms larger than her subject position can ever be allowed.

What's more, Patton has to not only sell the importance of her blind-cast diverse representation as a character where race is not important but paradoxically must praise the producers for allowing Iris to be Black—for others.

> I think people love the character of Iris West. I think a lot of fans are also excited that Iris West is now African–American ... It's so weird because when I was thinking about pilot season before I went in for *The Flash*, I just remember saying to myself, "I would love to get a role that changes the landscape of being an African American woman in television and film." And lo and behold I got *Flash*, playing a traditionally white character, and I didn't realize what would come with that. It's been incredibly difficult, but at the same time I've been in a position to give a lot of young actors that look like me hope that more characters are going to be written like Iris West and Joe West. I get comments all the time on Twitter, and fan mail about how amazing it is to see me play Iris West: a strong woman. It's not really about her being black, she just happens to be black.
>
> (Benal 2015)

Patton moves between enjoying the responsibility that comes with being chosen to racialize Iris West and navigating the difficulty associated with the pushback of her portrayal. That she ends by diminishing the blackness of the part—she's a woman first who happens to be black—may indicate that that is the best, most unprovocative, light she can imagine her character being seen. If she is allowed to be a "strong woman" and not a strong Black woman, Patton may imagine, she can normalize the racial difference so that it really won't make a difference. But it does make a difference—to the Black women fans who care about her and her character.

#IrisWestDeservesBetter: IWDS at Work

Previously, I mentioned the origins of the IWDS, but it is crucial to see how this fandom develops not simply to protect but to fight back. The "Talking Diaries" Tumblr page lays out a rationale of emergence predicated upon the knowledge if they did not act, the blind-cast Black love interest would be sidelined:

> The IWDS originated from backlash Candice Patton received when she got cast as Iris West simply because "she didn't look like comic book!Iris." Which is code for: she's not white. As soon as this happened, people watched the approx. (sic) 30 sec trailer of the show and immediately—without any context beyond "I need you to pee in a cup"—started shipping Barry with Caitlin. When you have people choosing to completely erase this history [of Iris's importance to the comics] by immediately giving that role [of love interest] to Caitlin without any context other than she "looks like Iris" [from the comics] which is code for—you guessed it—she's white, is problematic. This is when the IWDS began building itself, though, at the time, the (sic) we didn't have a name or even a full group of members.
>
> (Talking Diaries 2015)

What the IWDS knows is that whoever gets to be the male lead's love interest, gets to have the storylines. "Shipping" thus becomes a major facet of fandom because as I have argued elsewhere, "establishing the legitimacy of a character can be easily crafted by placing her in a relationship with a lead" (Warner 2015, 40). Of course, Iris is already a lead based on her billing in the comics; yet for these fans who have seen Black female leads be quickly reduced to supporting parts, there was enough precedent to merit the need for a plan.

Talking Diaries pushes forth the necessity of shipping WestAllen (WA) for the betterment of Iris West:

> The origins of the IWDS is very much related to shipping and it's not because we wanted it that way, it's how the problem began. The birth of SB (Snowbarry) and their fans' incessant need to erase Iris's importance in the narrative henceforth—is why the squad reiterates the importance of WA in Iris's defense. Not only do we ship them because we love them as a pair, we see the importance that the relationship has on the overall story and the characters themselves. But mainly we defend Iris West because she's a black woman and we've seen it way too often in fandom where the

black female character is often sidelined, erased, ripped apart and written off as a love interest and we weren't going to stand for that.

(Talking Diaries 2015)

The IWDS identifies shipping as a traditionally effective strategy for maintaining the centrality of its female lead. Shipping also obviously allows for representations of romance—something not often allowed for Black women characters. Thus, shipping WA becomes a bifurcated position where Black women fans can both support their character and their larger representational politics at once. In response to a query about why members of the IWDS supported WA, Talking Diaries reinforces this as a critical point of what makes Black women's fandom implicitly political.

The reason why saying we can't care about both is a problem is because it's asking underrepresented women to choose one way to engage in fandom. Women are still individuals while in a romantic relationship. It doesn't make her less-than. It also doesn't make her fans any less of a fan to want to see her in a relationship with another character they love. It's especially a problem for WoC because you're asking us to choose representation over romance when those things shouldn't be mutually exclusive especially when white fangirls don't have to choose.

(Talking Diaries 2015)

Black women reminding fans that all fan and fan objects are not treated equally within fan culture is a point of connection across fandom that unites them to work together in similar pursuits. "Posts from Under the Bridge" details how the IWDS gained popularity by lending its influence to other maligned Black female fandoms such as that of the Abbie Mills defense squad within the *Sleepy Hollow* fandom:

They gained popularity, most notably when [former *Sleepy Hollow* cast member] Orlando Jones reached out to them and asked to team up with Sleepyheads and help a trending event to Renew *Sleepy Hollow*. In fact Iris West fans have been acknowledged and reached out to by several fandoms for trending [on Twitter] worldwide nearly every week. The most successful run was 6 worldwide trends in 5 weeks. Since then they've been talking to members of other fandoms, scheduling trends with the explicit goal of uplifting and protecting black women on TV.

(Posts from Under the Bridge 2015)

While it is more than likely that many Iris West fans are also Abbie Mills fans and, quite possibly, Bonnie Bennett of *The Vampire Diaries* fans, it is equally plausible that the need to collaborate on protecting their heroines is shared from a frustration of invisibility within their fandoms. Fighting against that invisibility through the labor of building Trending topics on Twitter pushes their mutually constitutive cause of Black female representation to the fore. Hashtags like #IrisWestDeservesBetter work because the Abbie Mills Defense Squad fans used it first to gain attention both within the fandom and with the producers and pop culture writers. In that instance, Black female fans rejected Mills' being sidelined in favor of a white supporting character and created the #AbbieMillsDeservesBetter hashtag that trended on Twitter for days. IWDS fans Kerri Evans and Britta Darling wrote an op-ed on Black female fans like themselves and described the result of that campaign: "Ratings tanked as they tuned out. As the show teetered on the brink of cancellation, executives promised their black women fan base that in the coming episodes Abbie would regain her lead status and be included in important plotlines again" (Evans and Darling 2015).

Similar to the gains the Abbie Mills Defense Squad earned, the IWDS' use of social media to connect with the cast and crew of *The Flash* also has seen visible spoils for their labor. Evans and Darling assert that they would "spend time voting [for awards and nominations] and promoting endlessly. They've held all-night voting parties, during which those fans get little to no sleep. They spend more time promoting the show on social media than the interns that the CW pays to do the same" (Evans and Darling 2015). The time expended by the IWDS, even writing this op-ed piece that lays out the goals and missions of Black women fandoms, is the very definition of affective labor generated because the community who participates in this long suffering does so with pride, believing that their strong desire to identify with someone who looks like them—just like the white women have—will be rewarded in the long run.

Epilogue: The IWDS and Slippery Slopes

Returning to the opening of this chapter, the IWDS's campaign to #KeepIrisBlack for the film version of the comic franchise stayed in full swing for much of summer 2016. Possibly attributable in some small measure to their efforts, on June 25, 2016, *Variety* announced that Black actress, Kiersey Clemons, booked the role of West. Contrary to expectations of excitement and joy from all members of the IWDS, it seemed the reaction splintered between those content with the selection and those who rejected the choice outright because the actress is light skinned. Asserting an argument of colorism, that is, the phenomenon where lighter skinned African-Americans are considered to be better and more attractive than their darker skinned counterparts, these disgruntled fans claimed that Hollywood's consistent employment of lighter skinned actresses disproportionately kept a large segment of Black women out of work. While there is validity to the claim, the fact remains that Clemons is not only a woman of color but, more specifically, honors their campaign to Keep Iris Black. Regardless of the push-pull emotive tugs between negotiation and ambiguity, the IWDS membership will always agree on one foundational point: Iris West is best written as a Black woman and as such, she must be protected from the subtle and not-so-subtle effects of white supremacy on her character—even from themselves if need be. And even while there is discord within Black women's fandom concerning if the tactics of Defense Squads are actually bullying, the central cornerstone is that striking back against attacks on Iris West and Candice Patton is a support of Black womanhood. It is, in a sense, them standing up for themselves and modeling how they want to be defended and protected. The same battles they fight as the IWDS are in many ways similar to the battles they face in their everyday lives.

Note

1   As of October 31, Famuyiwa left the film production.

References

Bastién, Angelica. "Barry & Caitlin Shouldn't Be A 'Flash' Couple, No Matter How Flirty They Get." *Bustle.com*. N.p., 2017. Web. 22 Feb. 2017.

Benal, Zal. "'The Flash' Star Candice Patton Tearfully Inspires Comic Book Fans to Look Beyond Race." *MTV News*. N.p., 2017. Web. 22 Feb. 2017.

Berlant, Lauren Gail. *The Female Complaint*. Durham: Duke University Press, 2008. Print.

Bobo, Jacqueline. *Black Women as Cultural Readers*. 1st edition. New York: Columbia University Press, 1995. Print.

Darling, Britta and Kerri Evans. "The Power of Black Women in Fandom." *Black Enterprise*. N.p., 2017. Web. 22 Feb. 2017.

Hampton, Darlene. "Beyond Resistance: Gender, Performance, And Fannish Practice in Digital Culture." Ph.D. University of Oregon, 2010. Print.

Johnson, Derek. "Fan-Tagonism: Factions, Institutions, And Constitutive Hegemonies of Fandom." *Fandom: Identities and Communities in A Mediated World*. Jonathan Gray, Cornel Sandvoss and C. Lee Harrington. 1st edition. New York City: New York University Press, 2007. 287. Print.

Lothian, Alexis. "Editor". *Journal.transformativeworks.org*. 4.1, 2017. Web. 22 Feb. 2017.

Mitovich, Matt. "The Flash's Candice Patton Cheers 'Badass' Iris of Earth-Two and The Progressive Support For 'Westallen'." *TVLine*. N.p., 2017. Web. 22 Feb. 2017.

Posts from Under the Bridge. "Blackgirlnerd Perpetuates Misogynoir in Fandom." *posts from under the bridge*. N.p., 2017. Web. 22 Feb. 2017.

Talking Diaries. "The Thing About the IWDS Is That Sometimes I Think …" *Talking Diaries*. N.p., 2017. Web. 22 Feb. 2017.

Warner, Kristen. "ABC's *Scandal* and Black Women's Fandom." *Cupcakes, Pinterest, And Ladyporn: Feminized Popular Culture in The Early Twenty-First Century*. Elana Levine. 1st edition. Champaign: University of Illinois Press, 2015. 37–40. Print.

Wilson, Julie and Emily Chivers Yochim. "Pinning Happiness: Affect, Social Media, And the Work of Mothering." *Cupcakes, Pinterest, Ladyporn: Feminized Popular Culture in The Early 21st Century*. Elana Levine. 1st edition. Champaign: University of Illinois Press, 2015. 236–237. Print.

38
FANTAGONISM, FRANCHISING, AND INDUSTRY MANAGEMENT OF FAN PRIVILEGE

Derek Johnson

In August 2016, media trade publication *Variety* reported that fans of the widely panned summer blockbuster *Suicide Squad* had launched a petition to "shut down" review aggregation website *Rotten Tomatoes*. Thanks to professional critics' complaints about "muddled plot, thinly written characters, and choppy directing," *Rotten Tomatoes* awarded *Suicide Squad* a very low "approval rating"—34% initially and even less more recently (McClendon 2016, "Suicide Squad," *Rotten Tomatoes* 2016). Some fans of the film, however, took this as an insult to their own aesthetic sensibilities, with tens of thousands signing a Change.org petition that initially called for the dissolution of *Rotten Tomatoes* for propagating "unjust bad reviews"; later, the campaign pivoted to intervene in the "disconnect between critics and audiences" by demanding that viewers "Please Don't Listen to Film Criticism" (McClendon 2016, Coldwater 2016). These fans moved to exclude critics from the unspoken category of "real" audiences and "real" fans, claiming greater authority to represent popular tastes, and to speak with fan understanding of established intellectual properties. Paramount in this populist critique was the perceived anger behind it. On *Browbeat*, columnist Sam Adams (2016) characterized the "Anti-Rotten Tomatoes Movement" as indicative of a more insidious dynamic in contemporary fan cultures in which opposing perspectives must be shouted down with extreme prejudice: "The 'Crush the Tomato' faction wants to live in a world where other opinions don't exist, or at least they don't have to hear about them." Pointing to the mainstream ascendance of "geek" taste, Adams opines that such fans have "inherited a once-marginalized subculture's grudges despite the fact that … they effectively control the culture: Any threat to their dominance … has to be met with maximum force, repelled like an unwanted invader." The *Suicide Squad* case, then, represents not just activist fan attempts to intervene in powerful cultural institutions like film criticism, but also a more complex and ambivalent line of tension over privilege in fandom and domination over cultural value and meaning.

In contrast to celebrations of fandom as "beautiful" (Gray et al. 2017), dynamics like these have invited recent commentators to reflect upon forces of entitlement and oppression working through fan engagement more broadly than *Suicide Squad* alone. Most visibly, David Faraci's (2016) essay "Fandom is Broken" (discussed by Ivan Askwith, Britta Lundin, and Aja Romano in this collection) charges that the "ubiquity of social media" has created a toxic environment in which fans use easy access to one another and producers to demand satisfaction of their consumer desires and spew hate-filled speech at those who dare propose other possibilities. From #GamerGate to discussions of potential queerness in *Frozen*, Faraci offers numerous examples in which fan debates take troubling turns toward harassment and threats of violence. At the same time, he identifies the consumerist position of fans—"the customer is always right"— as a factor reinforcing these fissures and putting a sense of righteousness behind fan desires. Here and in many other opinion pieces too, this broken, "dark side" of fandom is described as "rabid" and "petulant" (Bramesco 2016, Penny 2014, Hassenger 2016). *CBC News*' Eli Glasner (2016) emphasizes the impact of this "fan fury" on media industries, claiming from interviews with industry professionals that content producers are definitely responsive to fans empowered by social media, even employing social media research firms like Fizzology to monitor what fans are saying. At stake in this discourse, therefore, is not just hostility and harassment within fandom, but also the potential receptivity of industry—artists and money-minded studios alike—to the demands of fans' often-enraged consumer activism.

To explore these tensions within fandom and tease out their impact on the world of media industries, this chapter will first revisit and rework early claims about "fantagonism" and its centrality to relationships among media fans and industries by considering how the "antagonistic ways fans relate to one another, producers, and the text" (Johnson 2017) intersect with collective organization and activist struggles (even in reactionary forms). By framing fantagonism as a potential force in the push for—or more often in this chapter, against—media *change*, we can grasp how industries manage and incorporate those competing pressures into new strategies and corporate practices. Although I do not share Faraci's view that all fan demands come equally from a place of consumer "entitlement" (fans communities from marginalized backgrounds fight for recognition long denied them by consumerism), I do find it productive to consider the politics of cultural loss in which some fans perceive threats to their consumer sovereignty and privilege from the potential improvement of service to other consumers. For against this "zero sum geek" premise, the logics of media franchising (Johnson 2013) manage fan texts as multiplicative industrial product ranges in which a number of different spin-offs and parallel market appeals can be made simultaneously to reach different kinds of consumers. Exploring this tension between the zero sum geek conflicts of fantagonism and the multiplicative potential of franchising, this chapter reveals not just the frequent opposition of factionalized fantagonism to industry forces, but also its market utility. Considering the case of the 2016 *Ghostbusters* reboot, I argue that such oppositions allow media industries to identify market opportunities, incorporate competing consumer demands into new product offerings, and play all sides of the struggles between different fandoms. While popular discourse on rabid fandom wrings its hands over the possibility that small but vocal fans may sway creative and market decision making, what we see here instead is the way in which industry manages fan outrage and activism in hegemonic forms of incorporation, absorbing it into franchise strategy rather than being disrupted by it.

Fantagonism Redux

This wave of claims about fan entitlement and consumer attempts to reshape the decisions of creators and studios demands a revisiting of the "fantagonism" concept. I initially defined fantagonism as the "ongoing, competitive struggles between both internal factions and external institutions to discursively codify the fan-text-producer relationship according to their respective interests" (2017). My concern was with how fan communities debated the aesthetic history of television series, generating a hegemonic interpretative consensus that established commonsense claims about the text. Having secured this discursive power, dominant fan factions could then mobilize challenges "to the productive power of outside institutional/industrial forces" (294). Building on the work of Pamela Wilson (2004), Melissa Scardaville (2005), and more recently, Christina Savage (2014), who frame fan engagement in these terms, fantagonism explicitly invokes an *activist* struggle to intervene in industry worlds (Johnson 2017). Yet a third dimension of fantagonism considered the power of television producers to deploy the text itself as a means of disciplining fan engagement, representing fandom onscreen through characters that rearticulate "distinctions between normative audience and Othered fan, professional and amateur, producers and consumer" (298). Fantagonism thus captures tensions within fandom, the fans struggle to shape the production of the text and meaning from it, and the ability of producers to respond to and incorporate these struggles into serial reproduction over time, disciplining any petulance or rabidity.

Other scholars have since explored the dynamic antagonistic and activist relationships among fans, factions, and producers with more nuance. Lori Lopez and Jason Lopez coin the term "oppositional fandom" to describe "fandoms that are temporarily defined by their position in opposition to another fandom," where controversies around social justice in the world of entertainment create opportunities for some fans to engage meaningfully with the idea of political change while others are "digging in against change" (Lopez and Lopez 2017). Their study of conflicts over racist sports mascot imagery is legible as fantagonism, but they reveal how privileges of race, class, and gender feed into oppositions of "activist" versus "authentic" that bring harassment and delegitimation to the former. Suzanne Scott (2017) also pushes fantagonism to a more productive interrogation of its intersectional dynamics by interrogating the resistance of female fans to that potential appropriation of "fangirl" identity by male, African-American industry professional Orlando Jones. Meanwhile, in both her essay in this volume and in previous work, Anne Gilbert offers a more nuanced insight into the complicated relationship between industry and fan audiences than the binary logic that fantagonism suggests. In her study of the cooperative but hierarchically uneven relationship between fans and industry at San Diego Comic Con (2017), Gilbert's model suggests the possibility of symbiosis as much as struggle.

Considering these complexities, the continued utility of fantagonism comes not in its suggestion of two-sided conflict, but instead in the multiple axes of interaction it imagines among fans, other factions of fans, and media industries. On the one hand, this focus on fandom as factionalized refuses any universalizing conception of fandom in the singular. On the other, it recognizes that some factions, at some times and in some moments, take up positions of oppositional intervention in relation to the industries that produce and distribute media texts. From this, we might push one step further to reason that fan positions in relation to media industries are nearly always positions taken in opposition to other fan factions with their own positions in relation to industry. Any fan/fan and fan/industry antagonisms can thus be closely intertwined. Furthermore, these fantagonisms can be productively understood in relation to the industrial logics and practices of media franchising—the "ongoing generation, exchange, and use of shared cultural resources" across multiple markets, media platforms, as well as historical contexts of production (Johnson 2013: 7). If media franchising focuses, among other things, on the reproduction of intellectual properties across multiple industry moments and successive sites of creativity, then franchise fandom may most often co-exist with franchise "anti-fandom" (Gray 2003) as fans of one iteration in that sequence of reproduction are often simultaneously anti-fans of other divergent iterations. The temporalities of franchising, in other words, prompt fans to negotiate their positions in relation to the past, the present, as well as imagined futures that have not yet come to pass for objects of interest that have been and will continue to be constantly remade and reworked by industry—much as Melissa Click (2017) encourages us to consider fans' changing orientations in the dynamic "texistence" of media objects. The industrial dynamics of media franchising thus feed fantagonism, reproducing popular culture in an iterative manner that, gradually or radically, aims media texts at a multiplicity of new markets, audiences, tastes, and forms of fan engagement.

Taking a page from Gilbert (2017), we might also argue that fantagonism in turn serves the needs of media franchising in a truly symbiotic sense, despite the clear potential for opposition to the industrial forces managing fan texts. As Michael Curtin (1996), Joseph Turow (1997), and others argue, the world of segmented, niche marketing requires marketers to clearly communicate who they do *not* want to be a part of the target audience. As much as gathering the right audiences, segmented marketing depends on exclusion, division, and sometimes opposition between market segments. With that in mind, fan factionalization carves audiences into smaller, manageable, targetable segments to which different, co-existing product lines in an ever-expanding media franchise might offer individualized appeals. This multiplicity and simultaneity of franchised cultural reproduction allows media industries to expand their appeals to new markets without changing existing targets. In the space that remains, therefore, I want to suggest that fantagonism holds new relevance to our understanding of struggles over social justice and the possibility of effecting change in popular media industries, while also grasping how those cultural struggles feed the franchising logics that seem to propel fantagonism in the first place.

Who you Gonna Call (Out)?

In October 2014, Sony Pictures announced that *Bridesmaids* director Paul Feig would helm a new *Ghostbusters* film breaking with the 1984–1989 continuity to center around an all-female cast (Zuckerman 2014). While the backlash from avowed fans of this media franchise began almost immediately, the January 27, 2015 announcement of the cast (Kristin Wiig, Melissa McCarthy, Leslie Jones, and Kate McKinnon) created more tangible targets. While some Twitter user comments aggregated in reports by *The Daily Edge* praised this "awesome" and "amazing" casting, others users perceived to be "mostly men" appeared "worried the remake would 'ruin' the classic" (O'Connor 2015). Ruination emerged as a key theme in this discourse, as the irate Tweets featured in this story made implicit demands of the film industry to "stop ruining Classic movies" as well as to "stop ruining my childhood!" To blame, in this threat to the childhoods of this vocal group of male-identifying fans, were certainly creative professionals like Paul Feig (who was "killing the Ghostbusters franchise for everybody Who grew up with the original") but also more broadly the politics of feminism, as the remake was unflatteringly described as a "#Feminist Ghostbusters" serving "soccer moms," "feminist bimbos," and "angry feminists." Such responses included fan art like the Ghostbusters logo with the familiar white ghost extending his middle finger to scold: "Feminists. This isn't about women. This isn't about misogyny. It's about our childhoods. Stop making it about you!" (O'Connor 2015). Attacks directed specifically at African-American cast member Leslie Jones, meanwhile, put hostility toward feminism in intersection with racial epithets (Heugel 2016). These sexist and racist expressions of antagonism set a dominant tone for the reception of the film, with the image of the middle-finger ghost, for example, circulating widely enough to be the subject of retort in several other feminist blog spaces (McEwan 2015, Wheedston 2015).

The release of the first trailer on March 3, 2016, presented an opportunity for angry fans to make their oppositionality more measurably felt by Sony. By May, the two-minute preview of the film had become "most disliked Movie Trailer to ever appear on YouTube" (Cornet 2016), somewhat marring the studio's effort to market the film. At a point in May by which this trailer had received 624,461 thumbs down votes of dislike on YouTube, *Hollywood Reporter* looked to user comments as evidence of significant coordination and organization rather than a casual disinterest. YouTube users sought to recruit others to the cause with comments like "You too can be apart [sic] of history by hitting that dislike button" (McMillan 2016). All attempts to build publicity for the film also met with this same organized resistance and hostile rejection—even the cast's in-costume visit to Tufts Medical Center to cheer up sick children (Dickens 2016).

While utterly reactionary, the organized, activist character of this antagonism was most legible on sites like *Return of Kings*, where avowedly anti-feminist bloggers devoted to the principles of "neomasculinity" ("About") quite predictably viewed the film's potential empowerment of women within the franchise as a development to be opposed at all costs. Writing from both ultra-conservative anxiety about lost masculine power and a fan position of nostalgic concern for loss of cherished childhood experiences, essays on *Return of Kings* claimed that the feminist agenda of the in-development film would damage the cultural value of the franchise. The language used in the article made clear the threat to perceived inheritance, legacy, and entitlement, mixed with a claim to lost masculine power. The new "neuter[ed]" film was "ruining the memory" and "eliminating the history" of the earlier films, showing disrespect those invested in the franchise "by creating a new franchise from the raped carcass of the original" (Unwin 2015). At the release of the trailer, therefore, the site called explicitly for a boycott, arguing that if these changes to the franchise found box office success, they might determine the course of future entertainment product in this culture war (Brown 2016a).

Measuring industry response to and management of this kind of antagonism is tricky. Most obviously, we might consider the way in which industry strategists and analysts tracked the box office performance of the film against these organized attempts to ensure its failure. After all, when the film made only $46 million of its over $200 million production and marketing costs in its first weekend, David Brown (2016) at *Return of Kings* took a victory lap to "bask in the frustrations of our enemies." While the small readership of *Return of Kings* suggests little potential for direct impact, the effect of the larger fan backlash undoubtedly troubled Hollywood analysts in the wake of the film's release. For *Hollywood Reporter*, a film project like *Ocean's Ocho* should now be considered a "risky" venture in its attempt to launch "an all-female spinoff of a beloved franchise" (Siegel 2016a). The burden was now on *Ocho* producers to offer assurances that "the *Ocean's* [*Eleven*] franchise is better poised for the gender swap than *Ghostbusters*, given that it is a frothy heist film aimed at adults rather than a fanboy-skewing action property with supernatural elements based on a movie that some now consider sacrosanct" (Siegel 2016). Digs at the immaturity of entitled fans notwithstanding, these assurances took seriously the box office threat of fantagonism.

Taking a more longitudinal view, however, we can see how industry forces sought not just to respond to this fantagonism's potential box office impact, but also to *manage* it along the way. For creative talent, fantagonism represented a threat to reputation and professional worth (not to mention safety and sanity) and thus required reassertion of professional authority over fans. Melissa McCarthy disqualified repeated fan claims about "ruined childhoods" in a *Guardian* interview: "really, four women doing any movie on Earth will destroy your childhood?" (Freeman 2016). Her more gentle suggestion that fans reconsider the intensity of their claims (made indirectly to a journalist) stands in contrast to Feig's attempts to directly match fan combativeness. Perhaps most exemplary of that dialogue: "You've been ranting at me and my cast for months with misogyny and insults. So go fuck yourself" (Damore 2015). Yet the *Ghostbusters* film text itself also provided Feig and his cast a platform to push against fantagonism and discipline fan interpretation and practice. Critic Matt Zoller Seitz (2016) reads the film as meta-commentary on these online conflicts with male fans; the villain Rowan, in particular, offers "a blatant satirical jab at the comic book-worshipping woman-hater, the sort of guy who'd spam the mentions of anyone who didn't like the latest Marvel or DC film … while denigrating an all-girl 'Ghostbusters' remake as a 'cash grab.'" In such a reading, Rowan—a creepy social outcast who plans to unleash a horde of ghosts upon New York City to get back at all those who have denied him respect—serves to channel the fantagonism of the film's detractors, providing a narrative representation of misogyny for the protagonists to defeat. The gender politics of this are overt in many instances, including Rowan's misogynist taunt that the Ghostbusters "shoot like girls." Looking at the protagonists' relationships to other male characters who challenge their authority and ghost-hunting expertise as well, Seitz perceives "a disquieting but fascinating sense of Erin, Abby, Jillian, and Patty fighting to assert a right to exist within a franchise which is itself uncomfortable with the very idea of allowing women to fill leading roles." The film also takes time to speak back to the online hate surrounding the film when Kristin Wiig's Erin character reads a tweet in response to her ghostbusting enterprise "Ain't no bitches gonna hunt no ghosts" to which Melissa McCarthy's Abby responds: "Don't pay attention to stuff crazy people write in the middle of the night online." From Rowan to fictional twitter users, these male antagonists thus join a long tradition of characters that allow professional creators to comment upon fandom while prescribing proper orientations toward the creators in industrial control of cult texts (Johnson 2017).

Yet, while creative talent took oppositional positions in relation to this confluence of misogynistic cultural conservatism and fannish sense of loss, Sony and the professionals in charge of promoting the film simultaneously courted the very sense of zero sum geek nostalgia driving fantagonism. Endorsements and cameos from the surviving cast members and producers of the original 1984 film anchored a campaign meant to lend more legitimacy to the new female cast. Credited as a producer on the new film, Dan Akyroyd described his new role as one of a cheerleader (in an interesting gender reversal), promising that "this one with the four girls is going to be massive ... It hits the right notes, and I'm really excited about it" (Huver 2015). But beyond cheerleading, these public statements allowed male actors to play skeptic, initially unsure whether their female successors were up to the task and at such pains to defend that female talent that they revealed and affirmed ongoing questions about it. Ernie Hudson displayed this kind of ambivalence when he insisted the new cast was "extraordinarily funny and there's a great chemistry with them ... I was really pleasantly surprised to see how the women kind of gelled together" (Damore 2016). This testimonial praised the cast while nevertheless treating as legitimate any concern or surprise at the possibility that four women could lead a comedy franchise. So central was the power of male authority to the marketing that quotes from the original cast dominated the visual real estate of the official film website. The main banner at the center of the site alternated between pictures of the new cast and quotes from Akyroyd, Hudson, Bill Murray, as well as director Ivan Reitman, who promised "the movie is going to be quite *wonderful*, because I know the *cast works*. The ladies in this film are in every way as *talented* as that original group of actors were." Akyroyd, meanwhile, remained "*delighted* by this inheritance of the Ghostbusters torch & by these most *magnificent* women in comedy" (Sony 2016a, emphases in original). These conciliatory promotional efforts treated seriously concerns about the worthiness of the female cast to inherit (in Akyroyd's term) the *Ghostbusters* mantle. If an oppositional Feig treated antagonistic fans as a group that should go fuck themselves, these testimonials welcomed them back to the fold.

Beyond welcoming angry fans back into the market for the Feig film, strategies at the level of the larger *Ghostbusters* franchise seemed more intent on turning that rejection of the reboot into a market for other new products. On the one hand, the very conceit of a female-oriented *Ghostbusters* film works from this principle, envisioned as a way to extend the target audience for the franchise brand. As explained to *License Global* by Greg Economos, senior vice president of Sony Global Consumer Products, "The female cast allows us to actually expand the demographics of who we think will buy product" (David 2015). On the other hand, Sony by no means abandoned its interest in male consumers, masculinized markets, or the merchandising of the original film. Noting the many deals made by Sony with licensees like Mattel and LEGO to produce merchandise based on the original cast in addition (or instead) of the new cast, *License Global* recognized that "Sony plans to continue its successful merchandising program for the classic Ghostbusters films alongside the new movie and any future content" (David 2015).

Comparing LEGO's product offerings confirms this sense of distinct consumer markets as well as potential hierarchies between them. While LEGO produced an ECTO-1 construction set with Abby, Erin, Jillian, and Patty mini-figures that retailed for $59.99 to accompany the new film, that new item joined another $49.99 ECTO-1 with Peter, Ray, Egon, and Winston still in production from 2014 as well as (brand new for 2016) a $349.99 Ghostbusters Firehouse Headquarters set based on the 1984 film. With LEGO typically retiring older product before introducing newer models of similar size and theme, the co-existence of two ECTO-1s indicates the premium placed on serving multiple facets of the *Ghostbusters* franchise and types of consumers simultaneously. Moreover, the high collector's price tag on the Firehouse suggests a willingness to invest greater resources on one side of that equation than another. As Vivianne Waisman, executive director for retail development at Sony, explained to *License Global*, "The style guide is so versatile that it allows us to accommodate for mass and specialty without having them conflict with each other" (Davis 2015). In this case, while Sony and its partners sought to build a wider, more gender-inclusive mass market, it sought at the specialty level to maintain focus on the arms of the franchise that could support $350 purchases from nostalgic fans.

This carving up of the *Ghostbusters* market into distinct, even opposed, segments could also be seen at a production level as Sony announced in March 2015 the creation of Ghost Corps, a new production company charged with "the mission to scare up branding opportunities" for the franchise at a scope much larger than a single film. Instead of gauging the success of or taking cues from the 2016 film, "the first order of business" at Ghost Corps was "an action-centric comedy that is a counterpart to the Paul Feig-directed film" (Fleming 2015). Earliest reports suggested a search for new franchise talent in contrast to Feig and his cast. *Deadline* reported promises of a film directed and produced by Joe and Anthony Russo (*Captain America: The Winter Solider* and *Community*), written by Drew Pearce (*Iron Man 3*), and starring Channing Tatum (*21 Jump Street*). The fanfare surrounding Ghost Corps revolved around promises of a forthcoming, testosterone-driven antidote to what ailed vocal fans in the backlash. Ivan Reitman explained that as the head of Ghost Corps, "My primary focus will be to build the Ghostbusters into the universe it always promised it might become. The original film is beloved, as is the cast, and we hope to create films we will continue to love" (Fleming 2015). Reitman makes an appeal to the love fans feel, but in articulating that love to the original (amid the onslaught of abuse directed at the new film), he effectively dog whistled at disgruntled fans with the promise of an alternative.

As the development of the Feig film continued, however, Reitman carefully backed away from some of these promises. By July 2015, he insisted that "There is only one new 'Ghostbusters' movie and that is the Paul Feig-directed version coming next July, presently filming and going fantastically. The rest is just noise" (Melrose 2015). Yet managing the whole of a franchise, Reitman remained sensitive to the possibility that the fans so angry now might become a viable market focus down the road. In contrast to Feig's combativeness and the courtliness of studio promotions, Reitman took an empathetic (if very negotiated) public position in relation to angry, misogynistic, and racist fans. Reitman carefully established some distance for himself in allowing that those fan responses "surprised me a little bit," while also adding "but then I realized many of the people who are writing were about eight or nine years old when the 1984 *Ghostbusters* movie came out. It was kind of a seminal moment in their lives." So while the testimonials and cameos from the original cast legitimized the female talent Feig assembled for the new film, here Reitman lent legitimacy to the fans that antagonized the 2016 production. Indeed, he tried to deny that any hostility or abuse emerged from gender and racial privilege, but instead endorsed the same idea of lost childhood lamented by fans. "I wouldn't put it at that," Reitman noted of these fans' alleged gender biases, "as much as some sense of disappointment for people who went through this experience themselves" (Jang 2016). Reitman thus granted the angry fan a stronger claim to authentic fandom, having had the singular nostalgic experience that trumps newer audiences' experiences. Reitman made comprehensible as authentic fandom the sexist and racist antagonism that would otherwise read as simple abuse and hate.

Conclusion

As the manager of a franchise, Reitman's position is almost comprehensible. In the search for multiple profit centers across different culture industries and over successive years and decades, fantagonism might be managed to create the segmentation and definition of distinct consumer demands that organize and give unique purpose to different product offerings underneath the shared franchise. Rather than combat fantagonism, like Feig and company in the face of intense, personal attacks, Reitman and studio marketers seemed intent on harnessing it, transforming fan demands that were activist in their orientation toward industry into consumer demands for the franchise extensions to come in the future. To do that, however, those demands must be significantly rehabilitated at the same time, made understandable as nostalgic *activism* rather than the abusive terrorism that they really represented in their sexist and racist manifestations. In other words, the threat posed by angry fans might be less to the success of a single film like *Ghostbusters*, and more the ability of Sony to continue to envision fans as a profit center rather than a hate group.

While fantagonism asks us to consider fans' oppositional positions in relation to each other and their activist positions in relation to media industries, that struggle should not blind us from considering the ways in which angry fans and industries work in tandem. Particularly in the case of media franchising, where the ongoing multiplication of product and reproduction of culture across an unending series of markets and platforms thrives upon the creation of divisions and segmentations, angry fans can prove to be as much a boon as a challenge to industry power. Of course, the perceived failure of *Ghostbusters* at the 2016 summer box office following fan backlash to its female cast was hardly a victory for Sony; yet, the existence of that backlash, and the ability to empathize with its worst impulses and rationalize it as fandom, offers a potential path for future development as the exploitation of the franchise continues inevitably into the future. The struggle between fans to determine who and what pleasures count as real fandom gives franchise managers a flexibility to both choose between service to competing claims based on their potential marketability and support multiple profit centers by keeping each side of the struggle in tension.

In arriving at the conclusion that we might consider fantagonism not in terms of activism, but the terrorism of racist and sexist harassment (as well as industry management and service of it, sometimes), we must ask whether we are even talking about fandom anymore, but instead something far more sinister. Particularly when such media fandom becomes articulated to the larger anti-feminist, racist, and reactionary political projects of something like *Return of Kings*, it seems that we may need to question the ability of a concept like fantagonism to adequately capture all the struggles in play. It would be very easy to conclude that the vocal online trolls who send abusive tweets to actors and creators because they do not endorse their creative vision for a franchise are not actually real fans, just bigots who have stumbled into and twisted the world of fandom; yet such a conclusion would ironically work to police "real" fan identity and authority in the same way that many angry fans themselves have. Instead, we need to recognize the moments in which fandom overlaps and informs these larger structures of domination. Moreover, as the growth of media franchising helps to make fandom a more mainstreamed dimension of identification, we may have to increasingly pay attention to the moments and spaces in which politics and struggles of all kind come to imperfectly overlap with our competing hopes for the inevitable, industrially managed futures of the media objects in which we have invested ourselves.

References

"About" (n.d.). Return of Kings, www.returnofkings.com/about.

Adams, Sam (2016). "The Anti-Rotten Tomatoes Movement Is Key to Understanding Angry Comic Book Fan Culture Overall." *Browbeat*, August 5, www.slate.com/blogs/browbeat/2016/08/05/the_anti_rotten_tomatoes_movement_is_key_to_understanding_angry_comic_book.html.

Bramesco, Charles (2016). "How Suicide Squad Showcases the Nasty Side of Fandom in 2016." *Rolling Stone*, August 9, www.rollingstone.com/movies/news/how-suicide-squad-showcases-nasty-side-of-fandom-in-2016-w433407.

Brown, David (2016). "Feminist Ghostbusters Film Bombs Despite Hysterical Attacks Against Its Critics." *Return of Kings*, July 26, www.returnofkings.com/91699/feminist-ghostbusters-bombs-despite-hysterical-attacks-against-its-critics.

Brown, David (2016a). "The World is Revolting Against Hollywood's Awful Feminist Remake of Ghostbusters." *Return of Kings*, March 7, www.returnofkings.com/56056/the-new-ghostbusters-movie-will-be-ruined-by-the-feminist-agenda.

Click, Melissa (2017). "Do 'All Good Things' Come to An End?: Revisiting Martha Stewart Fans After ImClone." In Jonathan Gray, C. Lee Harrington, and Cornel Sandvoss (eds.), *Fandom: Identities and Communities in a Mediated World*, 2nd Edition, 191–204. New York: New York University Press.

Coldwater, Abdullah (2016). "Don't Listen to Film Criticism." *Change.org*, August 5, www.change.org/p/don-t-listen-to-film-criticism/u/17486237.

Cornet, Roth (2016). "'Ghostbusters' Has Become 'Fun Summer Movie: The Battleground for Internet Politics.'" *Hitfix*, May 19, www.hitfix.com/the-dartboard/ghostbusters-has-become-fun-summer-movie-the-battleground-for-internet-politics.

Curtin, Michael (1996). "On Edge: Culture Industries in the Neo-Network Era." In Richard Ohmann (ed.), *Making and Selling Culture*, 181–202. Hanover: Wesleyan University Press.

Damore, Meagan (2015). "'Ghostbusters' Director Paul Feig Strikes Back at Haters." *Comic Book Resources*, September 24, www.cbr.com/ghostbusters-director-paul-feig-strikes-back-at-haters/.

Damore, Meagan (2016). "Ernie Hudson Talks 'Ghostbusters' Cameo, Calls the New Cast 'Extraordinarily Funny.'" *Comic Book Resources*, February 24, www.cbr.com/ernie-hudson-talks-ghostbusters-cameo-calls-the-new-cast-extraordinarily-funny/.

Davis, Nicole (2015). "Giving Ghostbusters New Life." *License Global*, June 1, www.licensemag.com/license-global/giving-ghostbusters-new-life.

Dickens, Donna (2015). "Sexist Dudes Can't Believe These Uppity 'Ghostbusters' Dames Visited Sick Kids." *Hitfix*, August 3, www.hitfix.com/harpy/sexist-dudes-cant-believe-these-uppity-ghostbuster-dames-visited-sick-kids.

Faraci, David (2016). "Fandom is Broken." *Birth, Movies, Death*, May 30, http://birthmoviesdeath.com/2016/05/30/fandom-is-broken.

Fleming, Mike Jr. (2015). "Sony Plans New 'Ghostbusters' Film with Russo Brothers, Channing Tatum & 'IM3' Scribe Drew Pearce." *Deadline Hollywood*, March 9, http://deadline.com/2015/03/ghostbusters-channing-tatum-joe-and-anthony-russo-drew-pearce-ivan-reitman-dan-aykroyd-1201388917/.

Freeman, Hadley (2016). "Melissa McCarthy: 'I Love a Woman Who Doesn't Play By the Rules'." *The Guardian*, May 28, www.theguardian.com/film/2016/may/28/melissa-mccarthy-love-woman-doesnt-play-rules-ghostbusters.

Gilbert, Anne (2017). "Live from Hall H: Fan/Producer Symbiosis at San Diego Comic Con." In Jonathan Gray, C. Lee Harrington, and Cornel Sandvoss (eds.), *Fandom: Identities and Communities in a Mediated World*, 2nd Edition, 354–368. New York: New York University Press.

Glasner, Eli (2016). "Fan Fury, Fan Power: The Changing Relationships Between Creators and Consumers." *CBC News*, July 15, www.cbc.ca/news/arts/fan-fury-ghostbusters-the-100-1.3678897.

Gray, Jonathan (2003). "New Audiences, New Textualities: Anti-Fans, and Non-Fans." *International Journal of Cultural Studies* 6 (1): 64–81.

Gray, Jonathan, C. Lee Harrington, and Cornel Sandvoss (2017). "Introduction: Why Still Study Fans?" In *Fandom: Identities and Communities in a Mediated World*, 2nd Edition, 1–26. New York: New York University Press.

Hassenger, Jesse (2016). "Ghostbusters, Frozen, and the Strange Entitlement of Fan Culture." *AV Club*, May 25, www.avclub.com/article/ghostbusters-frozen-and-strange-entitlement-fan-cu-237139.

Heugel, Abby (2016). "'Ghostbusters' Star Leslie Jones Speaks Out About the Racial Abuse She Received on Twitter." *Twenty-Two Words*, June 20, http://twentytwowords.com/ghostbusters-star-leslie-jones-speaks-out-about-the-racial-abuse-shes-received-on-twitter/17/.

Huver, Scott (2015). "Dan Akyroyd Promises 'Ghostbusters' Reboot 'Hits the Right Notes'." *Comic Book Resources*, June 17, www.cbr.com/dan-aykroyd-promises-ghostbusters-reboot-hits-the-right-notes/.

Jang, Meena (2016). "'Ghostbusters' Director Ivan Reitman Says Reboot Criticism Stems From Nostalgia Over Original Film." *Hollywood Reporter*, June 30, www.hollywoodreporter.com/news/ghostbusters-backlash-ivan-reitman-defends-907653.

Johnson, Derek (2013). *Media Franchising: Creative License and Collaboration in the Culture Industries*. New York: New York University Press.

Johnson, Derek (2017). "Fantagonism: Factions, Institutions, and Constitutive Hegemonies of Fandom." In Jonathan Gray, C. Lee Harrington, and Cornel Sandvoss (eds.), *Fandom: Identities and Communities in a Mediated World*, 2nd Edition, 369–386. New York: New York University Press.

Lopez, Lori and Jason Lopez (2017). "Activating Oppositional Fandoms: The Redskins Controversy and the Potential for Sports Fan-Activism." In Jonathan Gray, C. Lee Harrington, and Cornel Sandvoss (eds.), *Fandom: Identities and Communities in a Mediated World*, 2nd Edition, 315–330. New York: New York University Press.

McClendon, Lamarco (2016). "'Suicide Squad' Fans Petition to Shut Down Rotten Tomatoes Over Negative Reviews." *Variety*, August 3, http://variety.com/2016/film/news/suicide-squad-fans-petition-rotten-tomatoes-bad-reviews-shut-down-1201829631/.

McEwan, Melissa (2015). "Ain't Afraid of Ghosts. Terrified of Women." *Shakesville*, January 29, www.shakesville.com/2015/01/aint-afraid-of-ghosts-terrified-of-women.html.

McMillan, Graeme (2016). "Is the 'Ghostbusters' Reboot Trailer Really That Disliked?" *Hollywood Reporter*, May 2, www.hollywoodreporter.com/heat-vision/ghostbusters-reboot-youtube-trailer-is-889438.

Melrose, Kevin (2015). "Ivan Reitman Shoots Down Talk of Second 'Ghostbusters'." *Comic Book Resources*, July 30, www.cbr.com/ivan-reitman-shoots-down-talk-of-second-ghostbusters/.

O'Connor, Amy (2015). "Some Men are Really Angry About the All-Female Ghostbusters Remake." *The Daily Edge*, January 28, www.dailyedge.ie/all-female-ghostbusters-reaction-1907535-Jan2015/.

Penny, Laurie (2014). "On Nerd Entitlement." *The New Statesman*, December 29, www.newstatesman.com/laurie-penny/on-nerd-entitlement-rebel-alliance-empire.

Savage, Christina (2014). "Chuck Versus the Ratings: Savvy Fans and 'Save Our Show' Campaigns." *Transformative Works and Cultures* 15: 1–14.

Scardaville, Melissa (2005). "Accidental Activists: Fan Activism in the Soap Opera Community." *American Behavioral Scientist* 48 (7): 881–901.

Scott, Suzanne (2017). "The Powers That Squee: Orlando Jones and Intersectional Fan Studies." In Jonathan Gray, C. Lee Harrington, and Cornel Sandvoss (eds.), *Fandom: Identities and Communities in a Mediated World*, 2nd Edition, 387-401. New York: New York University Press.

Seitz, Matt Zoller (2016). "Women's Work: The New 'Ghostbusters'." *MZS*, July 16, www.rogerebert.com/mzs/womens-work-man-babies-and-the-new-ghostbusters.

Siegel, Tatiana (2016). "All-Female 'Ocean's Eleven' Spinoff Looking to Avoid 'Ghostbusters'-Type Backlash." *Hollywood Reporter*, August 11, www.hollywoodreporter.com/news/sandra-bullock-anne-hathaway-all-918828.

Siegel, Tatiana (2016a). "Anne Hathaway, Rihanna Join All-Female 'Ocean's Eleven' Spinoff." *Hollywood Reporter*, August 10, www.hollywoodreporter.com/news/female-oceans-eleven-reboot-cast-news-ocho-918642.

Sony Pictures Entertainment (2016). "'Ghostbusters' Official Trailer." *YouTube*, www.youtube.com/watch?v=w3ugHP-yZXw.

Sony Pictures Entertainment (2016). *Ghostbusters* Official Website, www.ghostbusters.com/.

"Suicide Squad" (2016). *Rotten Tomatoes*, September 5, www.rottentomatoes.com/m/suicide_squad_2016/.

Turow, Joseph (1997). *Breaking Up America: Advertisers and the New Media World*. Chicago: University of Chicago Press.

Unwin, Jack (2015). "The New Ghostbusters Movie Will Be Ruined by The Feminist Agenda." *Return of Kings*, February 19, www.returnofkings.com/56056/the-new-ghostbusters-movie-will-be-ruined-by-the-feminist-agenda.

Wheedston, Lindsey (2015). "Fuck Your Childhood." *Not Sorry Feminism*, January 30, www.notsorryfeminism.com/2015/01/fuck-your-childhood.html.

Williams, Rebecca (2011). "'This is the Night That TV Died': Television Post-Object Fandom and the Demise of The West Wing." *Popular Communication* 9 (4): 266–279.

Williams, Rebecca (2015). *Post-Object Fandom: Television, Identity, and Self-Narrative*. New York: Bloomsbury.

Wilson, Pamela (2004). "Jamming *Big Brother*: Webcasting, Audience Intervention, and Narrative Activism." In Susan Murray and Laurie Ouellette (eds.), *Reality TV: Remaking Television Culture*, 323–344. New York: New York University Press.

Zuckerman, Esther (2014). "Paul Feig Confirms He's on Board for 'Ghostbusters' with 'Hilarious Women.'" *Entertainment Weekly*, October 8, www.ew.com/article/2014/10/08/ghostbusters-reboot-paul-feig.

39
FRIKI CONVENTIONS
Comic-Cons, Expos, and Fandom in Mexico City

Guillermo Aguilar Vázquez and Ana Fabiola Vidal Fernández

Since the signing of the North American Free Trade Agreement (NAFTA) (1991–1994), Mexico has predominantly assumed the role of a consumer within the global media economy, particularly in foreign cultural industries and primarily those produced or distributed by the United States. Science fiction films, comic books, video games, television programs, and cartoons resonated with Mexican audiences, predominantly among children and young people of that era, who have now transitioned into adulthood. This consumer trend has expanded to encompass new productions originating from Asian countries such as Japan, South Korea, and China, which have identified a lucrative opportunity in the Mexican market. Products such as manga, anime, Korean dramas (or "doramas"), and K-pop have evolved from niche interests consumed by a small group of "frikis" to becoming a trend among contemporary Mexican adolescents and young adults. The term "friki" is commonly used by Mexican fans to identify themselves as enjoyers and consumers of any kind of mass media.

This chapter analyzes the "friki-identity" and comic-cons held in the metropolitan area of Mexico City. We argue that the main characteristic of these Mexican frikis is that their consumption and media thematic interests extend beyond geographical origins (both of the fans and the products). Instead, they are directed toward the characters, plots, themes, esthetics, and other components of cultural products that capture the attention and imagination of frikis. These elements are adapted and adopted to their social and cultural contexts, giving rise to new subjectivities, identities, and social relationships. In particular, class and gender exert a direct and profound influence on how frikis perceive themselves and others.

Mexican Television and NAFTA

To comprehend Mexican consumers of entertainment, it is imperative to delve into the history of Mexican television. While much of the current content consumed by frikis may not be directly associated with this medium, broadcast television remains one of the most significant cultural industries in the political, economic, and cultural life of the Mexican populace. Mexico's initial exposure to Asian media content occurred through broadcast television, with the transmission of programs such as *Heidi* (1978–1998) and *Candy Candy* (1980–1987). Nevertheless, their widespread popularity and integration into the preferences of the Mexican population, particularly among younger audiences, burgeoned during the 1990s due to two pivotal events: the signing of the North American Free Trade Agreement (NAFTA) and the advent of cable television (Pareja 2010; Mejía 2007).

During the NAFTA negotiations (1991–1994), at the behest of the United States, a section of the entertainment industry and its trade among the three countries was incorporated. Noteworthy provisions within this segment addressed content produced and broadcast in Mexico, including the mandate to dub foreign productions into Spanish for transmission in Mexico, the requirement for the broadcast of 30% of Mexican films in the other two countries, the streamlining of requirements and procedures for granting radio and television concessions to foreign citizens in Mexico, and the potential for direct negotiations between entertainment industry entrepreneurs from the three nations without the need for governmental intervention (Gómez 2004).

These changes were warmly welcomed by entrepreneurs, particularly those from the United States and Mexico. The Americans sought to expand beyond their borders, while the Mexicans aimed to diversify their content catalogs and acquire knowledge about production and marketing techniques. The needs of Mexico's two largest television networks, Televisa and TV Azteca, stemmed from their initiation of a competition to capture viewers' attention. As the preferences of the Mexican population began to evolve and cable television started to proliferate within the country from the northern border, particularly in the states of Baja California and Nuevo León (Alejandro 2004; Pareja 2010; Mejía 2007), the urgency to cater to these changing dynamics prompted Mexican entrepreneurs to hasten the opening of the entertainment industry. Consequently, they began procuring foreign content for transmission on their various channels.

Competition has prompted television networks in Mexico to reorganize their channels and content transmission based on age groups. Channels 13 (owned by TV Azteca) and 5 (owned by Televisa) were designated for children's audiences. These channels featured a combination of domestic programs such as *El Chavo del 8* (1973–1980 aired by Televisa) and *Otro Rollo* (1997 aired by Televisa), as well as foreign content comprising a blend of American series, cartoons, and anime, including *Dragon Ball* (1995–1999, aired by Televisa), *Malcolm in the Middle* (2002–2006 aired by Televisa), and *The Simpsons* (1991–, aired by TV Azteca). Similarly, cable channels such as Cartoon Network, Nickelodeon, and Fox Kids transmitted a variety of content specifically designed for the youth demographic (Alejandro 2004; Pareja 2010; Lozano 1996; Lozano 2000). The rationale behind airing these programs was that they were deemed "child-oriented" by the television networks. Notably, this occasion marked the first time that the youth market was recognized as distinct viewers, departing from the traditional "family-oriented" content model.

As the new millennium approached, anime became common content for viewers. The association with Asia, particularly Japan, began with the success of *Pokémon*, despite objections from conservative segments of the population. Moreover, cable channels, notably Cartoon Network, broadcast *Sakura Card Captor* (2002–2007) and *InuYasha* (2002–2007), thereby diversifying program options beyond traditional broadcast television. These programs garnered significant favor among the young populace, especially children, owing to their presentation of fresh narratives, novel nomenclature, intricate characters, and values with which viewers could identify.

Amalgamation of Content: The Friki-Identity

The commercial opening that occurred after NAFTA allowed a myriad of foreign productions to reach Mexico, particularly those originating from Asia, thereby reaching new audiences and fans. Consequently, Korean dramas (doramas), Turkish soap operas, Thai Boys Love (BL) series, Chinese webnovels, and K-pop music joined Japanese anime and manga in gaining popularity. The convergence of all these elements had a direct impact on Mexican fans, influencing their identity, social relationships formed based on preferences, activities undertaken, and the venues they attended, such as conventions and expos. This phenomenon can be discerned through the meaning of the term "friki."

The term "friki" is an adaptation of the English word "freaky." Although its precise origin in Spanish-speaking countries is not well-documented, its widespread usage led to its official integration into the Spanish language by the Real Academia Española (RAE) in 2001. RAE official dictionaries define it as an adjective used to describe someone as "eccentric, strange, or uncommon" or "a person who engages excessively and obsessively in a hobby." Consequently, in Spain, Mexico, and other Latin American countries, the term is commonly employed to refer to enthusiasts of a movie, series, cartoon, novel, video game, or music band, who invest considerable time, effort, and financial resources in following, consuming, and actively participating in anything related to their preferred subject. In other words, it is associated with the old pathologized conception of the fan that Jenkins describes in *Textual Poachers* (1992).

It is imperative to delve into some aspects regarding the term. First, this designation does not pertain to any specific fandom. A "friki" encompasses any fan of movies, television series, role-playing games, video games, anime, manga, cartoons, science fiction books, fantasy, or horror novels, irrespective of their nature or origin (Camacho 2021). Similarly, it does not allude to any particular fan activity, as a "friki" encompasses individuals engaged in cosplay, attending conventions, writing fanfiction, creating fanart, or collecting memorabilia of any kind. It is also noteworthy that terms such as otaku, geek, or nerd are not unfamiliar in Mexico. Moreover, more specific concepts referring to fans of a particular franchise, such as "marvelita" (fans of Marvel comics) or "warsie" (fans of the Star Wars franchise), are also prevalent. The critical distinction lies in the fact that the term "friki" enjoys greater recognition among Mexican audiences to the extent that it is not uncommon for people to use "friki" as a blanket term encompassing all types of mass media fans. During an interview with José Reyes, a young reseller of used toys, when asked about the meaning of the word otaku he said, "I mean, all otakus are 'frikis,' but not all 'frikis' are otakus. But even though there are some differences, in the end, we are all 'frikis,' whether you like anime, *Spider-Man*, or *Star Wars*." In other words, "friki" is employed to denote fans of mass media, their activities, and relations they create in an indiscriminate manner.

Drawing on interviews that we conducted during 2022 and 2023, there are examples that clearly illustrate this distinction. Israel Pérez is a nursing student from Mexico City who engages in cosplay as part of his fan activities. Although he initially portrayed characters from anime, over the past two years, he has developed an interest in cosplaying characters from Western cartoons such as *Amphibia* (2019–2022) or *The Owl House* (2020–2023). This preference has led him to connect with other fans and even participate in small gatherings and meetups focused on these two Disney productions. Another example is Karol Villa, a high school student whose hobby is collecting manga. On several occasions, she mentioned that what drew her to Japanese comics was Korean pop music.

Her friends who introduced her to this musical genre are also avid readers of the *Demon Slayer* manga. Now, Karol reproduces some panels from these manga on glass to give away and sell to her school friends. Similar to José Reyes, when asked if they identified as otakus, both Israel and Karol responded that they had no issue with being categorized as otakus. However, they mentioned that they actually identify as "frikis" because they do not limit themselves to consuming a specific type of content or engaging in a singular activity. Instead, they remain open to enjoying any form of entertainment that appeals to them or undertaking various activities. These examples illustrate that, despite the pathological and stereotyped usage of the term "friki," individuals over time have gradually appropriated the term, reclaiming and modifying certain elements that constitute it. The outcome has been the emergence of a friki identity, which, akin to other fandoms, is positioned in a convergence of media, interests, and discourses that permeate the way in which they perceive themselves and establish social relationships.

With these testimonies, the question we then asked ourselves was, "What makes a production appealing to 'frikis'?" Although we initially thought the answers would vary significantly, we found two elements that were consistently mentioned. According to our informants, the way the plot of the story is constructed and the characteristics of the characters are the main features that make any movie, comic, anime, cartoon, video game, or novel attractive to them. Let us take the words of our informant Michell Porras, a cosplayer who often attends various conventions to sell prints of herself posing in different costumes. Her repertoire includes characters from both anime and manga, as well as Western cartoons, all equally popular within the small fan community that Michell has built around her. When asking her about what drives her to choose the characters she plans to portray, her response was clear and direct: she selects them only if she feels she identifies with them. For Michell, cosplaying is not only a way to embody the character and show them respect but also a means of embracing the values and ideals they represent. Heroic, selfless, and protective attitudes motivate her, making characters like Rengoku from *Demon Slayer* or Ladybug from *Miraculous Ladybug* her favorite cosplays.

The fact that characters or stories are significant aspects for frikis when consuming any type of entertainment not only provides them with a wide variety of media and content to choose from, but also makes the shared taste for these elements the core of their identity as a friki. If we follow Stuart Hall's (2003) proposal about identity, we can understand that this "friki-identity" is a point of social attachment and exclusion, constantly shaped by the subjects' tastes and appreciation for characters and stories produced by various entertainment industries. Under this premise, the distinguishing elements that create an idea of "us/them" among different frikis are not related to the origin of the entertainment productions but rather social aspects such as class, gender, or age.

Finally, we would like to point out that the recognition of this "friki-identity" is an idea that has spread to various sectors of the population in Mexico, which has both negative and positive ramifications for frikis. Negatively, there are the stereotypes associated with them, portraying them as antisocial individuals obsessed with the unreal, incapable of relating to other people, and unclean with poor hygiene. On the other hand, frikis have sought to overturn these stereotypes, constructing a series of activities and discourses that use the word as a source of pride and identity, with the most visible result being "El Dia del Orgullo Friki" (Friki Pride Day). Every May 25th, different groups of frikis gather in plazas, conventions, and parks to engage in activities like cosplay or group dances, aiming to express their love and appreciation for the stories and characters they hold dear. Social media is not an exception, as platforms like Instagram, Facebook, or Twitter (now X) are filled with videos, images, and memes emphasizing not feeling ashamed to identify as frikis. Perhaps one of the most popular gatherings occurs at Frikiplaza, a commercial plaza located in downtown Mexico City dedicated to the purchase and sale of all kinds of merchandise related to the world of entertainment and popular culture, from licensed products to piracy or fan-made items. The plaza organizes contests and raffles, and often invites local celebrities or voice actors. All these activities attract frikis from diverse backgrounds.

Conventions in Mexico City: Fractures of the "Friki-identity"

During July 2022, a video posted on Twitter with the description "attending an anime-con in Mexico has been added to the bucket list," caught the attention of many users. The video showcased the band "Los Shinigamis del Norte" performing the song "Butter-Fly", the opening theme of the anime *Digimon*, with a rhythm of Northern Mexican cumbia at the convention "El Mercado Otaku." This danceable musical genre is typical of Northern Mexico and is characterized by narrating the misfortunes of various public figures (corridos), featuring an accordion as the main instrument. Reading through the different comments, most of which were written in English, many mentioned how surreal the conventions in Mexico appeared to them and how fun it was to see characters from various origins dancing to Mexican music. This ranged from anime characters like Akko Katsuragi from *My Little Witch Academia* to Din Djarin and Grogu from *The Mandalorian*, and even characters from Mexican animations like Miss Heed from *Villanos*. They also highlighted the appearance of the band members, who were dressed in Akatsuki organization robes from *Naruto* with cowboy hats.

The above example perfectly describes how many conventions and expos in Mexico are composed of an amalgamation of content, characters, and stories from different productions and media, which are adapted and embraced by frikis who enjoy, identify with, and relate to these elements in their own context. If we follow what has been presented so far, it will seem that the "friki-identity" is a solid union without fractures or divisions, but the reality is quite different. The ethnographic fieldwork conducted at various conventions in Mexico City allowed us to observe firsthand the ways and effects of these aspects.

The aspect that stood out the most was class, particularly in terms of access to both media texts and related merchandise. While in the first part of this chapter we emphasized that NAFTA allowed for a greater flow and consumption of foreign content, this was not the case for everyone. For many frikis, legal access to movies, series, or anime proves to be very challenging and, in some cases, impossible. This is mainly due to the precarious labor conditions and low wages that most of the population in Mexico face. According to data from INEGI, the state organization responsible for censuses and population studies in Mexico, the average salary for workers in Mexico is 7,380 pesos per month (approximately $441), where the main expenses are food and beverages (38% of total expenses), transportation and communication (18.6% of total expenses), and housing and services (11% of total expenses), leaving leisure activities with only 7.7% of expenses (INEGI 2020). This situation has led many frikis to resort to various strategies to access the stories and characters they love.

While we can list different ways in which frikis approach this scenario, the main one is piracy, or accessing the desired entertainment illegally and for free. Frikis resort to various means and technologies, such as websites like Animeflv, TuMangaOnline, or Cuevana3 that allow them to watch anime, manga, and movies with Spanish subtitles made by other frikis. Another way is through ripping content, which is subsequently shared through messaging applications like Telegram or WhatsApp. Finally, although physical formats are not as popular anymore, it is still possible to find pirated DVDs with seasons of some anime or doramas at the Frikiplaza and some conventions. Although there are increasingly more legal options to access this content, such as Crunchyroll or Netflix, the economic situation of many frikis makes piracy never completely ruled out as a mode of accessing content.

A similar situation occurs with related merchandise, mainly toys, collectible figures, or plushies. There are few stores that sell these types of products, and those that do often sell them at high prices to recover transportation and customs costs, ultimately making them expensive to obtain. This has led to the proliferation of a wide market for pirated and fan-made merchandise. Many of these pirated products are distributed through wholesale centers like Izazaga, commercial plazas dedicated to the wholesale of various items of Chinese origin. As for fan-made products, these are items that fans produce to sell to other fans at conventions or through social media. Within this category, we can find all kinds of objects, ranging from the simplest and easiest to produce, such as T-shirts, posters, and keychains, to those that require a more specialized technical knowledge, such as backpacks, ceramic mugs, phone cases and rag dolls, which can cost from a few pesos to several hundreds.

The way frikis access content and the market for original, pirated, or fan-made merchandise has a direct effect on the social relationships that these subjects build around themselves, generating divisions and fractures within friki-identity. It is common to read on social media or hear at some conventions comments that belittle those who buy fan-made or pirated merchandise, accusing them of being lazy and irresponsible with money, of not saving to buy licensed or original products, which ultimately harms the industries that produce these contents. The main response to these accusations usually involves arguments that bring to the table the fact that not all frikis have the same possibilities, that each friki has the freedom to appropriate stories and characters in any way they can, and that without the existence of these non-legal options, no entertainment production would have its current success.

These different discussions and perceptions about access to entertainment and related merchandise materialize in a physical space, the conventions. Within the circuit of friki events that occur in Mexico City, some are constantly the subject of ridicule because their exhibitors are fan-stores that trade in pirated and fan-made products, and their guests are local celebrities such as non-professional cosplayers, influencers, and voice actors. This has led them to being labeled as events of low quality, mediocre, and "for the poor." Clear examples of this are expos like COMACOJU or Expo Juibo, conventions that occur in the historic center of Mexico City, specifically at the Salón Ferrocarrileros. In our field observations, we noticed that, despite constant criticism, these events are very popular, with their main attendees being frikis who use them as a meeting place with friends, children, and teenagers with their families looking for affordable collectibles, and frikis with small businesses seeking to gain exposure. As Rudy Gallardo, a 22-year-old university student and regular attendee at these conventions, told us, "At these conventions, you come to relax, to hang out with friends, not to buy expensive toys and collectibles, because there are none; you come to fully enjoy being a 'friki'."

As mentioned earlier, an important part of these conventions is the businesses that provide all these non-legal items. For the owners of these businesses, conventions represent not only a place of socializing but also a place to work, a space where they can showcase their products, which often serve as a significant source of income. This is the case of Ross and her online store "BeMineCS," where she sells mugs, stickers, and plush toys with her own designs inspired by cartoons, anime, movies, series, and even soap operas. She started the project with her sister with the goal of making extra money to complement their salaries. However, the Covid-19 pandemic transformed the entire landscape. Her sister left the project, Ross lost her job as a designer, and the few available jobs were poorly paid temporary projects. This led her to invest more time in her store, which became her main source of income. Now, she regularly attends conventions, bazaars, and expos to promote her business and expand her customer base. When asked if she identified as a friki, she answered affirmatively, and not just because of her store. "If I didn't feel any affection for these cartoons and anime characters, I wouldn't enjoy drawing them to print on the mugs," she said.

In contrast to these events, there are conventions like La Mole, considered the largest, most important, and expensive comic-con in Mexico City. The first major difference with the mentioned expos is that there is an admission fee of 500 pesos per day (approximately $30) for a three-day event. The second difference lies in the exhibitors, as they mainly consist of large toy companies like Hasbro or Figma as well as entertainment companies like Crunchyroll, and although there are some individual businesses, they are very few due to the high cost of the venue. Marlene García, owner of an Asian food stall that attends several conventions, mentioned that at small events, the cost per table ranges from 600 to 1,000 pesos ($35 to 60), while La Mole can charge from 10,000 to 20,000 pesos ($600 to 1100) depending on the table size and type of business. As for the guests, they are usually professional cosplayers, famous actors, and internationally renowned artists, who also charge for their items, photos, and greetings. Due to these costs, La Mole is often seen as an inaccessible convention reserved for the wealthy, or one in which you must save money for a long time to enter. Because of this, a common joke among frikis who cannot attend La Mole is that you buy a ticket to enter a place to spend more money.

Conclusions

The conventions, events, and comic-cons held in Mexico City are excellent examples of class differences in the formation of the Mexican friki-identity. Mexico's role as an entertainment consumer since the 1990s has seen fans seeking diverse means to access their preferred programs and related merchandise in diverse ways and spaces. These comic-cons are access points for desired products. This phenomenon can be considered an indicator of how class permeates frikis' identification and how it distinguishes them from other fans. The variability in prices, both for access and for the products offered, limits attendance, causing conventions to become meeting places for fans of the same social class, thus acting as markers and distinctions among the enthusiasts themselves.

References

Alejandro, M. (2004). La apertura de la telesvisión privada en México. *Política y Sociedad*, 41(1), pp. 89–93.

Camacho, N.P. (2021). La identidad friki-yucateca y sus prácticas culturales. *Historieta, manga y cultura popular: México y Japón a través de la cultura popular contemporánea*, 1(1), pp. 19–25.

Gómez, R. (2004). TV Azteca y la industria televisiva mexicana en tiempos de integración regional (TLCAN) y desregulación económica. *Comunicación y Sociedad*, 1(1), pp. 51–90.

Hall, S. (2003). Introducción ¿Quién necesita "identidad"? in Hall, S. and Du Gay, P. (eds.), *Cuestiones de Identidad Cultural*, Buenos Aires: Amorrortu Editores, pp. 13–39.

INEGI. (2020). *Encuesta Nacional de Ingresos y Gastos de los Hogares (ENIGH)*. www.inegi.org.mx/programas/enigh/nc/2020/

Jenkins, H. (1992). *Textual Poachers. Television Fans & Participatory Culture*, New York: Routledge.

Lozano, C. (1996). Oferta y recepción de televisión extranjera en México. *Comunicación y Sociedad*, 1(1), pp. 259–284.

Lozano, C. (2000). Oferta y consumo de contenidos televisivos transnacionales en México. *Estudios sobre las Culturas Contemporáneas*, VI(12), pp. 111–126.

Mejía, F. (2007). Historia mínima de la televisión mexicana (1928–1996). *Revista de Comunicación y Cultura*, 1(1), pp. 1–26.

Pareja, N. (2010). Televisión y democracia. La televisión abierta y su oferta en la Ciudad de México. *Andamios. Revista de Investigación Social*, 7(14), pp. 101–135.

Patrick, G. and Lamarre, T. (2010). Otakuology: A Dialogue. *Mechademia Second Arc, Fanthropologies*, 5(1), pp. 360–374.

40
FANNISH AFFECT, "QUALITY" FANDOM, AND TRANSMEDIA STORYTELLING CAMPAIGNS

Melanie E.S. Kohnen

In advance of *Game of Thrones*' premiere in 2011, HBO launched a multi-platform marketing campaign that included an online video game, a weather app, a multi-week online puzzle, food trucks, and a finely crafted wooden box containing scents of Westeros sent to TV critics and bloggers. The campaign reached out to fans of the books on which the series is based, invited new viewers to explore the storyworld, and most of all, aimed to convince HBO subscribers that a fantasy series could fit into the channel's "quality TV" brand (Bourdaa 2014: 23). *Game of Thrones* became one of HBO's most successful programs, leading at least those involved in the initial marketing to believe that the intense courting of old and new fans played a role in this success (Campfire 2012). HBO's marketing campaign embodies transmedia storytelling, "a process where integral elements of a fiction get dispersed systematically across multiple delivery channels for the purpose of creating a unified and coordinated entertainment experience" (Jenkins 2011). Transmedia storytelling balances marketing and world-building, often in uneasy ways, and is part of the shifting relationship between industry and audiences in the convergence era. Crucially, transmedia success depends on fans' emotional investment in a text. Only someone who has a strong emotional attachment to a narrative universe will invest time in decoding puzzles on a website, or spend hours lining up in the cold to participate in a DVD release party like HBO's "Take the Black" event in New York City in February 2013, which offered fans Westeros-inspired food, a live performance of the show's score, and an exhibit of props and costumes (Carberry 2013).

The "Take Back the Black" event signals a shift in transmedia promotion that occurred during the 2010s as streaming platforms rose to prominence. Transmedia storytelling originally developed as a tool to bring viewers back to linear TV when on-demand viewing and social media were in their early stages of development in the mid-2000s (Mittell 2015: 294). While online transmedia extensions still exist, and experienced a revival during the early days of the Covid-19 pandemic, in-person experiences that promise to immerse fans into the world of their favorite shows have risen to prominence, especially at events like San Diego Comic-Con (Kohnen 2021). For example, at Comic-Con 2023, fans were invited to stroll down the "Street of Immortality," recreating a core setting of AMC's *Interview with the Vampire* (2022–), replete with actors who engaged attendees in conversation (Figure 40.1).

As part of experiential marketing, these "activations" shift transmedia from storytelling to "storyliving," a concept that marketing scholar Wided Batat sees as the next step in branded promotion (2019: 229). Subsequently, I will use "transmedia storytelling" and "transmedia marketing activations" to distinguish older vs. newer forms of diegetic expansions for marketing purposes. I focus on officially produced transmedia campaigns for TV series and blockbuster franchises, and the way these campaigns invite fans to participate.

Fannish affect takes on a contradictory role in transmedia campaigns. On the one hand, the appeal to audiences' emotional investment in media texts fuels transmedia engagement and is consequently a necessary component of transmedia storytelling and marketing. A core tenet of experiential marketing is that memorable, affective in-person experiences will create brand loyalty (Batat 2019: 43). On the other hand, transmedia producers are also wary of too much affect because it is unpredictable and not quantifiable; it might evade the profitable paths set out in official transmedia. While affect is thus a prerequisite for transmedia engagement, the industry seeks the "right," i.e., predictable and commodifiable, response from fans. Particularly fans whose investments go against the grain of the diegesis (e.g., slash fandom) or fans who create their own transmedia are met with skepticism, and, in some cases, cease-and-desist letters (for example, when a fan created an Alternate Reality Game for *The Hunger Games* that too closely imitated a planned official ARG, Lee 2011). Audience engagement via transmedia blends old and new industrial strategies: it builds on the TV industry's practice of selling audiences to advertisers by quantifying viewers' attention via Nielsen ratings and it incorporates the platform economy's reliance on free labor and user demographics as currencies that make social media profitable. Activations in particular rely on these tactics. As they are often "free" to attend, their ROI is social media buzz generated by fans and personal data collected via sign-ups for photo opportunities and swag.

In reaching out to fans, the media industry seeks and legitimates certain forms of fannish affect while rejecting others. This process of legitimation and rejection is often gendered: masculinized fan practices structured around a passionate yet intellectual investment are embraced by official transmedia, while feminized practices centered on (seemingly)

Figure 40.1 *Interview with the Vampire* activation at SDCC 2023. Photos by the author.

unbridled exuberance are denigrated as youthful excess or excluded altogether. I argue that masculinized affect is thus embraced as "quality fandom" that is desirable to the industry, and feminized affect is rejected or simply ignored in transmedia. This contradictory process is part of a broader pattern of legitimation that characterizes media and audiences in the 2000s.

Fans, Industry, and Transmedia Storytelling

The creation of a narrative universe across multiple media precedes the convergence era, but transmedia storytelling and marketing is a defining feature of the current relationship between industry and fans. At a time of audience fragmentation, the film and TV industry feels compelled to provide multiple entry points into a narrative universe. The multiplication of media platforms and concentration of media ownership in the 2000s first led to a push toward multiple touch points for audience engagement and to build ongoing, long-term engagement with a TV show rather than the one-time or once-a-week appointment model of the network and multi-channel eras (Jenkins et al. 2013: 137). Transmedia marketing represents a further step: in addition to promoting single TV shows, activations in the 2020s also center on a streamer or corporate brand as umbrella for a variety of content. At a time when TV shows can disappear from streamers overnight (C-Scott 2023), channeling fan affect toward a brand rather than a singular storyworld is a more effective promotional tool. Transmedia can take on a variety of forms, ranging from elaborate promotional campaigns like the one designed for the premiere of *Game of Thrones*, *The Lost Experience*, a global ARG keeping fans engaged with *Lost* during the summer hiatus of 2006, or Amazon Prime's 2019 Comic-Con activation, which transformed a 60,000 square-foot parking lot into immersive experiences for upcoming series. The earliest examples of coordinated transmedia storytelling include *The Blair Witch Project* (1999) and *A.I.: Artificial Intelligence* (2001) for film and *Dawson's Creek* and *Homicide: Life on the Street* for TV. Denise Mann notes that TV networks backed away from transmedia storytelling like *The Lost Experience* after the 2007 Writers Guild of America Strike and pulled this kind of labor back into their own marketing departments (Mann 2014: 119). This move foreshadows the rise of activations in the 2010s, which are almost exclusively planned by marketing departments and agencies.

While many fans embrace transmedia storytelling and activations, Suzanne Scott has argued that one could see all of transmedia "as a more covert form of cease and desist letters, temporally and ideologically (rather than legally) discouraging fans from certain interpretations of or elaborations on the text" (Scott 2013: 325). Transmedia fills in gaps in media texts that fans often use to insert their own interpretations into canon. From Scott's point of view, transmedia aims to direct fans' engagement with the text toward a preferred reading – one that not incidentally leads to consumption. On the one hand, transmedia storytelling can be an invitation to fans to develop a deeper understanding of a narrative world, but on the other hand, fans are only invited in restricted and predetermined ways that often favor masculinized fan practices over feminized ones. As Kristina Busse puts it, "certain groups of fans can become legit if and only if they follow certain ideas, don't become too rebellious, too pornographic, don't read too much against the grain" (Busse 2006). Fans themselves have theorized the double-edged sword of industry recognition that welcomes some fans while excluding others, distinguishing between masculinized "affirmational" fan practices that move within canonical boundaries and feminized "transformational" practices that "twist" the text according to fans' desires, e.g., in the form of erotic fanfiction (obsession_inc 2009). The distinction between affirmational and transformational fans has made its way into fan studies literature due to its succinct definition of the industry's gendered way of valuing fan practices (Jenkins et al. 2013: 150; Scott 2013: 327; Stanfill 2019). Regarding the industry's management of fans, Mel Stanfill remarks that "consumption norms pitch intensive engagement so fans get what they desire in ways that (conveniently enough) do not challenge industry interests – financial or reputational" (Stanfill 2019: 102). As I will discuss later, the structure and address of transmedia are more welcoming to affirmational than to transformational fans.

Fannish affect and emotional investment are central to transmedia storytelling. For the most part, I use "affect" in the sense of "strong emotional attachment" rather than the way affect theory uses the term (i.e., as a involuntary, pre-cognitive, bodily reaction, Seigworth and Gregg 2010: 2). Joanne Garde-Hansen and Kristyn Gorton argue that in online communities, "affect is a sort of glue that binds and connects those ideas, values, and objects, and as such we might come to view media objects that transmit ideas and values as affective in nature" and that "affect also functions as collective energy that initiates and sustains gatherings of people and ideas" (Garde-Hansen 2013: 33). In other words, affect connects fans to texts and to each other. Affect is also a central element in experiential marketing as it aims to create "sensory, emotional" experience in immersive environments (Schmitt 1999: 57). Even though transmedia can provide, in the words of transmedia creator Andrea Phillips, a "persistent emotional connection," fannish affect is most valuable for the industry when it can be channeled toward quantification and consumption (Knowledge@Wharton 2012).

Quantifying Fannish Affect

Transmedia campaigns call on fans' emotional investment in a narrative universe in two key ways: by promising a deeper insight into the diegesis, and/or by giving fans an experience that invites them to participate in creating the text. Ideally, a transmedia experience pays off in two ways: for fans, it allows a deeper involvement in a beloved text, and for the industry, it delivers quantifiable engagement in the form of clicks, hashtags, etc., and fans' increased loyalty to a series, film, or brand.

Returning to *Game of Thrones*, HBO launched the website mywatchbegins.com as a promotion of the Season 2 DVDs in 2013. The site invited fans to "[a]dd your voice to the chorus of the Night's Watch" by recording themselves reciting an oath, and subsequently sharing this experience on Twitter with the hashtag #taketheblack. Fans were also asked to return to the website "over the coming weeks to hear our chorus grow stronger." Participation allowed fans to imagine themselves as members of the Night's Watch, but were also called upon to spread the word about *Game of Thrones* via their personal social media accounts. Fans' emotional investments were channeled toward quantifiable results: it is easy to track how many fans recorded their voices or used the hashtag. The encouragement to translate participation into social sharing becomes ubiquitous in transmedia marketing: activations act as "giant multiplier" that translate a few thousand attendees into millions of desirable social media impressions (Salkowitz 2018).

Prompting fans to make themselves quantifiable via social media is a precarious moment: transmedia campaigns need to deliver tangible results to count as industrial success, but fans need to believe that there is something more at stake for them than becoming data for profitable purposes. At least, the benefits of the transmedia experience need to outweigh the cost of rendering yourself trackable. Fans who participate in official transmedia events are aware of the commercial interests driving these events and experiences, and they are willing to subject themselves to these interests as long as the experience makes it worthwhile. Consider the following statement by Jefferson Carberry discussing the *Game of Thrones* Season 2 DVD release event in NYC:

> This was it. A hardcore fan dressed as a Black Brother, interacting with a prop in front of a display of *Game of Thrones* Blu-rays. This was the photo PR wanted tweeted, along with the YouTube oaths, to stoke sales and bloat the fandom. Let us not forget that, from a cynical point of view, the event was all about selling things. But that view only goes so far. Building and promoting a fanbase by asking fans to do what they love is hardly a raw deal. (Carberry 2013)

Here, Carberry argues that fans participating in the release event did what they would do anyway, including cosplaying as a member of the Night's Watch, and were recognized and rewarded for their enthusiasm. From this point of view, the industry embraces existing fan practices, and performing these practices for the industry in exchange for perks like a DVD release party seems like a small price to pay. In this case, fan interests and industry interests converge. This convergence is the goal of most mainstream transmedia campaigns. Official transmedia experiences are designed to keep a loyal audience interested in established series, to build an audience before the premiere of a show, or to confirm the value of a streaming subscription. Transmedia campaigns' conversion of emotion into quantifiable information is a new version of an old TV business practice (providing TV "for free" by selling audience's attention to advertisers). It also aligns transmedia with the platform economy that depends on users' free labor and voluntary surrender of demographic information.

Inclusions and Exclusions in Transmedia Storytelling

Ideally, a transmedia campaign caters to fan and industry investments. But not all fan practices map easily onto industry interests. The industry tends to reward affirmational fan practices, especially when these practices take place in spaces created by the industry (Scott 2007). Transformational fan practices are not as welcome. In transforming a text, fans' affective investments result in a vast variety of fanart and fiction that transcend genre boundaries and intertextual limitations. For example, in gif sets on Tumblr, fans use images from cast members' previous roles to transport characters from *Game of Thrones* into our contemporary reality, or they reimagine major male-skewing franchises like the Marvel Cinematic Universe with an all-female and/or all non-white cast. Moreover, as Louisa Stein argues, fans' transformative engagement with canon decenters the original text – while it may have served as the original spark for fan engagement, fans more frequently engage with other fans' creations than the source text, in part because fannish production vastly outweighs the pages or minutes contained in canon (Stein 2016).

This irreverent engagement with the source text rarely happens in official transmedia. Due to industrial constraints, official transmedia can never be as vast or as exhaustive as fan creations. Consider the transmedia campaign for *The Hunger Games* (2012). Official transmedia had to offer material about the world of *THG* that appeared new and exciting to fans of the novel on which the film is based; at the same time, this material could not

Fannish Affect, "Quality" Fandom, and Transmedia Storytelling

give away too many details about the film itself. Working within these constraints leads to transmedia elements that focus on exploring places and settings rather than on expanding plot or characterizations. Consequently, a core element of *THG*'s transmedia campaign was a virtual tour of the capitol of Panem. As a perfect example of official transmedia storytelling, it provided new insights about the world of *THG* without spoiling the film or diverging from the novel. In contrast, fans were free from the constraints of avoiding spoilers and adhering to canon. In fact, most fan creations delve deeply into the lives of central characters, envisioning moments before, during, and after canon. When fans' playful exploration of the storyworld encroaches on official transmedia, they are often met with resistance. This was the case with *Panem October*, a fan-authored ARG that allowed fans to become citizens of Panem. It came dangerously close to the website capitol.pn, the centerpiece of the official campaign that also revolved around a "citizens of Panem" theme (Figure 40.2).

The fan-created ARG was shut down with a cease-and-desist letter from Lionsgate (Lee 2011). While Lionsgate's decision to shut down *Panem October* might have been motivated by copyright concerns, it could also stem from the worry that fans might only be interested in one ARG. This line of thought fundamentally misunderstands fandom: fans embrace multiple versions of a story – one could argue that the desire to have more than one version of the same narrative universe is the primary motivation behind fan creations. While the industry is often invested in scarcity, fandom is invested in plenitude (Coppa 2009). The shutdown of *Panem October* is also interesting because fans did not infringe upon the core text, i.e., the film, but rather a transmedia extension. This underlines transmedia's perceived importance as point of entry into a franchise.

While Panem October did not fit into Lionsgate's vision of *The Hunger Games*, other fan-run transmedia projects appeal to the industry. One example is Lostpedia, a fan-run wiki that documents the universe of *Lost*. It is an exercise that aligns with the way quality TV imagines itself – as gripping and intellectually stimulating storytelling. Showrunner Damon Lindeloff stated that "when we've visited the site [Lostpedia] we are incredibly

Figure 40.2 Panem October screenshot on the left, capitol.pn screenshot on the right.

impressed with sort of the level of detail" (qtd. in Mittell 2009). Here, Lindeloff offers his unofficial approval of this particular fan practice.

Lostpedia's inclusion in industry-approved transmedia depends on exclusionary tactics. Jason Mittell details the Lostpedia editors' deletion of all content that did not strictly adhere to *Lost* canon, like parody and slash (2009). This example shows that official transmedia campaigns and spaces are not alone in regulating fan engagement with texts. Indeed, self-policing is not unusual among fans. As Kristina Busse has pointed out, "[a]ccusations of being too attached, too obsessed, too invested get thrown around readily, and all too often such affect is criticized for being too girly or like a teen" (Busse 2010). Thus, even among fans, overtly affective fan investment is suspect and associated with the exuberance of a teen girl, a cultural figure that has long been maligned in mainstream culture. An extreme example of self-policing was the denigration of *Twilight* fangirls, especially when they entered highly masculinized fandom spaces such as San Diego Comic-Con (SDCC). An *L.A. Weekly* article about *Twilight* fangirls at SDCC 2009 included a picture of a white male fan holding a "Twilight Ruined Comic-Con" sign and speculated whether a "gender war" was taking place at the convention (Ohanesian 2009). Melissa Click argues that popular press articles use "Victorian era gendered words like 'fever,' 'madness,' 'hysteria,' and 'obsession' to describe Twilighters and Twi-hards" (Click 2009).

The dismissal of fangirls is a concentrated form of the dismissal that fandom at large experienced not too long ago. The mainstreaming of fandom over the past two decades – helped in part by self-identified "fanboy" auteurs leading cult series like *Doctor Who* – has allowed certain fan practices to become socially acceptable (such as the detailed discussion of TV series plots), but fan engagement too rooted in affect or perceived as too feminine continues to be dismissed (Scott 2019: 21). Judgment of *Twilight* fangirls is also connected to the negative connotation of the source text – *Twilight* is not a "quality" film. In contrast to fantasy texts like *Game of Thrones*, which HBO has successfully branded as both "quality" TV and masculine, *Twilight*'s emphasis on teen romance marks it as a non-quality text; similarly, *Twilight* fans' investment in romance is also not considered a form of "quality fandom." As the *Twilight* and Lostpedia examples show, fan communities and transmedia creators apply similar standards to embracing or rejecting fan practices: rational, masculinized, affirmational fandom is valued over exuberant, feminized, transformational fandom. This does not mean that young female fans are never courted by transmedia campaigns. *The Hunger Games* launched *Capitol Couture*, a fashion blog that showcasing characters' clothing; likewise, male-skewing franchises like *Star Wars* or the MCU release tie-in makeup to address female fans, like the 2022 ColourPop x Star Wars palette inspired by *A New Hope*. These canon-compliant products address fans in gender-normative ways aimed at consumption.

While *The Hunger Games*, *Lost*, and *Twilight* examples are shaped by actively curtailing affective fan practices, boundary-policing by official transmedia makers does not have to take the form of overt censorship of too much affect or too much fan initiative; it can also manifest through absence. Non-canonical interpretations of storyworlds can elicit fans' strong affective investment, but there is no space for them in transmedia campaigns. Consider slash, a way of approaching pop culture that has a long history in female fan communities. Slash is almost entirely absent from transmedia storytelling. When it makes an appearance, it often comes in the form of queerbaiting, "a strategy by which writers and networks attempt to gain the attention of queer viewers via hints, jokes, gestures, and symbolism suggesting a queer relationship between two characters, and then emphatically denying and laughing off the possibility" (Fathallah 2015: 491). For example, MTV's *Teen Wolf* posted a video featuring actors Dylan O'Brien and Tyler Hoechlin cuddling on a boat in order to encourage fans to vote for the show in the Teen Choice Awards poll, thus seemingly recognizing fans' investment in "Sterek," the portmanteau for the Stiles/Derek ship (Fonseca 2012). One might say that instead of rejecting fans' counter-diegetic affective investment in Sterek, showrunners mobilize it toward a quantifiable target. *Teen Wolf*'s niche status may explain this overt acknowledgement of slash fans. As a teen drama on MTV, the series needed its most enthusiastic fans, excessive affect and all. But in the context of the *Teen Wolf* showrunners' tease-without-payoff dance around "Sterek," the video seems more like an exploitation than a genuine embrace of fannish affect. While some slash fans want to keep their creations away from showrunners to keep the fourth wall intact, absences and exclusions nevertheless indicate that the industry does not value fannish perspectives traditionally rooted in female communities, and thus implicitly rejects practices that often have at least the potential to question the socially normative storyworlds.

An interesting exception to this pattern is the relationship between fans and producers of the NBC drama *Hannibal* (2012–2015). *Hannibal* did not have official transmedia storytelling, but the producers, especially showrunner Bryan Fuller, catered to fan-produced extensions of the text on social media. Fuller often tweeted using the fan-created hashtag "#Hannigram", a portmanteau of "Hannibal" and "[Will] Graham," and shared fanart depicting main characters Will Graham and Hannibal Lecter in romantic poses. In contrast to other texts with a large female fan base, *Hannibal* was perceived as "quality" TV in mainstream press discourse (Sepinwall 2015; Zoller Seitz 2015). Moreover, showrunners and actors embraced rather than rejected female fans' queer and affective reading of the text; for example, fans' transformational romantic reading of the relationship between Will and Hannibal ended up being an affirmational reading by the series' end. Discussing this development, Fuller expressed his awareness of fans' transformational reading and explained that the canonical acknowledgment of love shared by Will and Hannibal "was felt to be an authentic, logical extension of everything we'd been doing thus far" (Dibdin 2015). *Hannibal* itself upended expectations for what quality TV can be: it morphed from a masculinized procedural into a queer melodrama. The transmedia interactions around *Hannibal* thus mirror other mainstream transmedia storytelling efforts in that industry and audience interests converged, but in contrast to most other examples I have discussed in this essay, *Hannibal* catered to feminized fan practices, and did so without resorting to queerbaiting. *Our Flag Means Death* (2022–2023) and *Good Omens* (2019–) followed a similar trajectory of showrunners welcoming transformational queer readings of relationships between male characters that eventually turned into canon romances.

Conclusion: Transmedia Storytelling and "Quality" Fandom

Reading transmedia through the lens of affect enables a nuanced understanding of how and why certain fan practices are embraced or rejected by official transmedia campaigns. Fans display intense attachment to a text, but this display of affect is evaluated by both industry and audiences in divergent ways depending on the form of fans' enthusiasm and the perceived quality of the revered text. Understanding these differing modes of evaluation through the lens of affect complicates the idea that all fans are welcome and valued participants of transmedia storytelling. The uneven inclusion of fannish affect slots into larger patterns of convergence-era media, particularly television. As Elena Levine and Michael Newman discuss, the legitimation of television as a quality medium depends on a rejection of TV's feminized, mass-media origins (2011: 10). Thus, premium cable drama and single-camera sitcoms were elevated as "quality TV" (and even as art) while prime-time soaps and teen television are still excluded – and they are often excluded precisely because of their mobilization of affect (2011: 99).

The negotiation of fannish affect in transmedia campaigns constitutes another process of legitimation. Thus, transmedia campaigns legitimate "quality fandom" – the masculinized and intellectual engagement with TV storyworlds via official transmedia. This legitimation crucially depends on the denigration of (often female or feminized) fans that are perceived as unpredictable and overly emotional.

This essay includes material previous published here:
http://blog.commarts.wisc.edu/2012/05/11/creating-a-spark-official-and-fan-produced-transmedia-for-the-hunger-games/

References

Batat, W. (2019). *Experiential Marketing: Consumer Behavior, Customer Experience, and the 7Es.* New York: Routledge.

Bourdaa, M. (2014). "This is Not Marketing. This is HBO: Branding HBO with Transmedia Storytelling." *Networking Knowledge: Journal of the MeCCSA Postgraduate Network* 7(1), pp. 18–25.

Busse, K. (2006). "Podcasts and the Fan Experience of Disseminated Media Commentary". http://flowtv.org/?p=109

Busse, K. (2010). "Geek Hierarchies, Boundary Policing, and the Good Fan/Bad Fan Dichotomy." Antenna. http://blog.commarts.wisc.edu/2010/08/13/geek-hierarchies-boundary-policing-and-the-good-fanbad-fan-dichotomy/

C-Scott, M. (2023). "Streaming Services Are Removing Your Favorite TV and Films." *The Conversation.* https://theconversation.com/streaming-services-are-removing-original-tv-and-films-what-this-means-for-your-favourite-show-and-our-cultural-heritage-208746 Accessed August 7, 2023.

Campfire (2012). "Game of Thrones Case Study." https://vimeo.com/29285256

Carberry, J. (2013). "Take the Black Event Wrap-Up," *Winter Is Coming.* https://web.archive.org/web/20130529203458/ https://winteriscoming.net/2013/02/take-the-black-event-wrap-up/ Accessed May 26, 2016.

Click, M. (2009). "'Rabid,' 'Obsessed,' and 'Frenzied': Understanding Twilight Fangirls and the Gendered Politics of Fandom," Flow, 11(04). http://flowtv.org/2009/12/rabid-obsessed-and-frenzied-understanding-twilight-fangirls-and-the-gendered-politics-of-fandom-melissa-click-university-of-missouri/

Coppa, F. (2009). "Things We Don't Have in the Future and How Fan Arts Can Help," *Talk at the University of the Arts, Philadelphia.* www.criticalcommons.org/Members/fcoppa/clips/things-we-dont-have-in-the-future-and-how-fan-arts/view Accessed June 3, 2016.

Dibdin, E. (2015). "Hannibal: Bryan Fuller Talks Season 4, Sexual Fluidity, and How Will Became Clarice Starling," Digital Spy. www.digitalspy.com/tv/hannibal/interviews/a667077/hannibal-bryan-fuller-talks-season-4-sexual-fluidity-and-how-will-became-clarice-starling/ Accessed June 3, 2016.

Fathallah, J. (2015). "Moriarty's Ghost: Or the Queer Disruption of the BBC's *Sherlock*," *Television and New Media* 16(5), 490–500.

Fonseca, N. (2012). "Sterek fans it's time to vote!!! Teen Choice Awards here we go!!!": www.youtube.com/watch?v=aeYBGm2En5I Accessed June 3, 2016.

Garde-Hansen, J. and K. Gorton (2013). *Emotion Online: Theorizing Affect on the Internet.* London: Palgrave-Macmillan.

Jenkins, H. (2011). "Transmedia 202: Further Reflections," *Confessions of an Aca-Fan.* http://henryjenkins.org/2011/08/defining_transmedia_further_re.html Accessed May 30, 2016.

Jenkins, H., S. Ford, and J. Green (2013). *Spreadable Media: Creating Value and Meaning in a Networked Culture.* New York: NYU Press.

Knowledge@Wharton (2012). "Transmedia Storytelling, Fan Culture and the Future of Marketing (an interview with Andrea Phillips, author of A Creator's Guide to Transmedia Storytelling)." http://knowledge.wharton.upenn.edu/article/transmedia-storytelling-fan-culture-and-the-future-of-marketing/

Kohnen M.E.S. (2021). "The Experience Economy of TV Promotion at San Diego Comic-Con," *International Journal of Cultural Studies* 24(1), 157–76. DOI: 10.1177/1367877920935888.

Lee, M. (2011). "Panem October Aftermath: Rowan the Gamemaster Speaks Out About Lionsgate Issue." www.movieviral.com/2011/09/22/panem-october-aftermath-rowan-the-gamemaster-speaks-out-about-lionsgate-issue/ Accessed May 30, 2016.

Mann, D. (2014). "The Labor Behind the Lost ARG: WGA's Tentative Foothold in the Digital Age." In: D. Mann (ed). *Wired TV: Laboring Over an Interactive Future.* Brunswick, NJ: Rutgers University Press, 118–140.

Mittell, J. (2015) *Complex TV: The Poetics of Contemporary Television Storytelling.* New York: NYU Press.

Mittell, J. (2009). "Sites of Participation: Wiki Fandom and the Case of Lostpedia," *Transformative Works and Cultures* 3(4). http://journal.transformativeworks.org/index.php/twc/article/view/118/117

Newman, M. and E. Levine (2011). *Legitimating Television: Media Convergence and Cultural Status.* New York: Routledge.

Obsession_inc. (2009). "Affirmational vs. Transformational Fandom," http://obsession-inc.dreamwidth.org/82589.html Accessed May 20, 2016.

Ohanesian, L. (2009). "Comic-Con's Twilight Protests: Is There a Gender War Brewing?" L.A. Weekly, July 28. www.laweekly.com/comic-cons-twilight-protests-is-there-a-gender-war-brewing/ Accessed May 20, 2016.

Salkowitz, R. (2018). "How Brands Are Making Their Own Fan Con Outside the Convention Center," Forbes. www.forbes.com/sites/robsalkowitz/2018/08/24/how-brands-are-making-their-own-fan-con-outside-the-convention-center/ Accessed August 4, 2023.

Schmitt, B. (1999). "Experiential Marketing," *Journal of Marketing Management.* 15, 53–67.

Scott, S. (2019). *Fake Geek Girls: Fandom, Gender, and the Convergence Culture Industry.* New York: NYU Press.

Scott, S. (2013). "And They Have a Plan: *Battlestar Galactica*, Ancillary Content, and Affirmational Fandom." In: Thompson, E. and J. Mittell (eds). *How to Watch Television.* New York: NYU Press, 320–330.

Scott, S. (2007). "Authorized Resistance: Is Fan Production Frakked?" In: Potter, T. and C.W. Marshall (eds). *Cylons in America: Critical Studies in Battlestar Galactica,* 210–224.

Seigworth, G.J. and M. Gregg (2010). "An Inventory of Shimmers." In: Gregg, M. and G.J. Seigworth (eds). *The Affect Theory Reader.* Durham, NC: Duke University Press, 1–28.

Sepinwall, A. (2015). "Series Finale Review: 'Hannibal'- 'The Wrath of the Lamb': Hannibal vs. the Great Red Dragon?" Hitfix. https://web.archive.org/web/20150912041755/http://www.hitfix.com/whats-alan-watching/series-finale-review-hannibal-the-wrath-of-the-lamb-hannibal-vs-the-great-red-dragon Accessed June 3, 2016.

Stanfill, M. (2019). *Exploiting Fandom: How the Media Industry Seeks to Exploit Fans.* Iowa City: University of Iowa Press.

Stein, Louisa. (2016). "Fandom and the Transtext." In: M. Bourdaa and B. Derhy Kurtz (eds). The Rise of Transtexts: Challenges and Opportunities. New York, NY: Routledge.

Zoller Seitz, M (2015). "*Hannibal* Redefined How We Tell Stories on Television," Vulture. www.vulture.com/2015/08/hannibal-redefined-how-we-tell-stories-on-tv.html Accessed June 3, 2016.

41
DAZN'S COVERAGE STRATEGIES OF THE UEFA WOMEN'S CHAMPIONS LEAGUE

Growing the Game Through Women's Football Fandom

Charlotte E. Howell

The Beautiful Game. The World's Sport. Soccer. Football. There are many names for the game, and many more ways of being a soccer fan. Generational and regional fandom are key aspects to European soccer fandom, with many people claiming allegiance to the league team with the nearby stadium or the one their parents and grandparents supported. In the United States, there is a much shorter history of top-level professional soccer leagues, so much more attention has been cultivated through allegiance to National Teams, especially the dominant US Women's National Team (USWNT). But as the 2010s rolled into the 2020s, more stability and investment in women's domestic leagues in both the US and Europe have led to a growing fanbase for women's soccer. No longer relegated to major tournaments or poorly broadcast league play, the media industries have started to see significant value in the growing fanbase of women's soccer and have invested in leagues like the National Women's Soccer League (NWSL) in the US and the Women's Super League (WSL) in the UK and multi-country competitions like the UEFA Women's Champion League (UWCL). Access for global fans had been expanding, but it was often contained by the norms of domestic women's sport coverage. That is, until DAZN (an OTT streaming service, pronounced "Da Zone") strategically focused on global access to coverage that treated women's football as football to build the fanbase for its UWCL coverage. Free games, streamed live on YouTube, and multiple language options with experts focused on the football rather than the gender of the players gave many women's soccer fans just what they were clamoring for. The idea was to slowly move games behind a paywall, banking on cultivating a fanbase willing to pay for this level of coverage. However, as I argue, this media industry strategy minimizes the power of the specific (and progressive, often queer) communities of women's soccer fans in order to target affluent global soccer fans more broadly.

The statistical discrepancies between media coverage for women's sports and men's sports is a well-known point of inequality: only 4% of sports media coverage discusses women's sports (UNESCO 2018) and even during major sporting events, the percentage rarely breaks 10% (Bowes 2020). Although that number has been changing since the statistic spread in news and advertising in the late 2010s, the qualitative findings contingent with the quantitative headline have largely persisted: coverage of women's sports tends toward stories and commentary that focus on the athletes as "women first and athletes second" (UNESCO 2018). This aligns with sports media studies of sportswomen in both corporate sports media and in the increasingly significant space of social media (Bruce 2016; Howell 2021; Sturm 2019; Vann 2014). Specifically in the realm of women's professional soccer/football (I will use the two terms interchangeably), scholars Rachel Allison (2018) and Beth Fielding-Lloyd, Donna Woodhouse, and Ruther Sequerra (2020) have done in-depth studies of top leagues in the United States and the United Kingdom, respectively, and found a fundamental tension between league framing and targeting of heteronormative family appeal over reliance on sport appeal in and of itself, specifically because it was women playing. The critique of this unbalanced requirement of gendered appeal and presumption of a specifically girl-oriented fanbase placed on women athletes is best summed up by Sophie Lawson (2022), a reporter for the women's soccer-focused blog *All for XI*: "Stop making 'inspirational' a requirement for women to play sport."

This kind of sexist coverage flows from a fundamental assumption about women's sports fans that sports studies and fan studies scholarship – as well as the lived experiences of women's sports fans – have tried to counter: that women particularly need more incentives than the actual sport to watch. Scholars like Victoria K. Gosling (2007) and Victoria E. Johnson (2016) have critiqued the ways that masculine sports fan culture and the National Football League have assumed women need appropriately feminine appeal for them to become fans of sports they were already watching. Coverage of women's sports have faced similar stultifying assumptions about who is watching and why, shaping its coverage and stories. The imagined women's sports fan can be: heterosexual male sports fans leading to sexualized framing prevalent in the 1990s (Cooky et al. 2021: 358), mothers and girls looking for inspiration (but not overt feminism) (Allison 2018: 74), or only recently and still somewhat marginally LGBT+ fans who want to see their community embraced (Allison 2018: 140; Hardin and Whiteside 2010; Schultz 2019; Parkinson 2019).

Building Fan Appeal and Access to Women's Soccer Broadcasts

One approach to fan appeal beyond the sport itself is the utilization of melodrama to amplify identification and emotional investment with the televised sport. Many media scholars (Jenkins 1997; Rose and Friedman 1997) have analyzed the increasingly melodramatic televisual framing of sport, with Victoria E. Johnson arguing that "though sports TV spans a continuum of program types, its dominant mode is fundamentally melodramatic" (2021: 14). The melodrama perpetuated in the variety of male-dominated sports TV – game footage, highlights packages, analyst programs, shoulder content, and behind-the-scenes documentary series like *All or Nothing* (Amazon, 2016–), *F1: Drive to Survive* (Netflix, 2019–), *Full Swing* (Netflix, 2023–), and *Hard Knocks* (HBO, 2001–) build in more stories about male athletes' family lives, backgrounds, struggles, and relationships. But women's sports have very few examples of this kind of expansive content, with DAZN's *One Team, One Dream: This Is Chelsea* (2022–), *Angel City* (HBO Max, 2023), and the Netflix series following the US Women's National Team (USWNT) at the 2023 World Cup as a few of the only docuseries following top-level women's teams. These types of docuseries have proven invaluable in pulling new fans into a sport as well as providing a separate media space for attention to interpersonal storylines that can deepen fan investment in the athletes and the sport. For women's soccer broadcasts that already are often constrained by the narrow ideas of who a women's sports fan can be and what they want, this has meant that broadcasts favor an audience believed to want more personal stories than tactical analysis, a distinct and criticized difference from coverage of men's soccer.

Women's soccer, especially in the US despite its reputation as the forefront of the women's game, has often faced criticism for underfunding that has led to both technological issues and analysts who lack in-depth league knowledge and thus focus on off-the-field stories more than on-the-field play (Murray 2013; Anderson 2023). From the first year of its broadcasts, the NWSL has utilized analysts and commentators that are either more broad sports analysts with little specific knowledge of soccer or soccer experts who lack in-depth league and team knowledge even if they're familiar with the USWNT (Murray 2013). The results have often been coverage focused more on the few national team players and their stories than a solid understanding of even player numbers or correct name pronunciations let alone tactics. Significant investment in rights, coverage, team compensation, and studio analysis in 2021 (Wrack 2021) and 2022 (Whyatt 2022) from the BBC and Sky Sports for the WSL in the UK set that league up for claims of the best domestic broadcasts. However, the much-lauded Sky Sports broadcasts of games and analysis – praised specifically for the goal of "treat[ing] women's football in the same way that we treat men's football" (Whyatt 2022) and thus appealing to viewers as football fans first and foremost – were not available outside the country. Global women's leagues like the WSL, Division 1 Féminine in France, the Frauen-Bundisliga in Germany, or the W-League in Australia have not seen the global rights deals that the analog men's leagues have, leaving fans of global women's soccer navigating streams without commentary, VPNs, and pirate streams and live-chats to find decent coverage in a language they understand with knowledgeable analysts. Although the early 2020s saw increased licensing across regions for many of the top European leagues, global women's soccer fans still struggled to find consistent, top-level, live broadcasts and analysis. That's what DAZN set out to provide when it acquired UEFA Women's Champions League rights in 2021 (Yossman 2021).

DAZN's Women's Champions League Strategy

DAZN launched in 2016 as a primarily European over-the-top (OTT) sports-based streaming service; its goal was to be the "Netflix of sport" (Williams 2016). In its first few years, DAZN focused on acquiring rights to out-of-market sports and building its European subscriber base (Lawson 2018), and in 2018 the platform started acquiring major combat sports (boxing and MMA in particular) as it expanded into the United States (Rafael 2018; Wetzel 2018). A major global expansion plan was briefly paused in 2020 (Hayes 2020), and 2021 marked a significant shift into global soccer rights first by poaching Serie A rights from Sky Sports (Vivarelli et al. 2021) then investing heavily in UWCL rights for four years, focusing on building the fanbase through free access and quality productions then hopefully translating that to subscribers as games gradually move behind a paywall (Linehan 2021). The Women's Champions League rights align with DAZN's global expansion goals because the high level of play and cross-region appeal mirror a key benefit of the Men's Champions

League, as it "offers a standardized product of universal availability, dimensions of time and place are eroded" (Sandvoss 2003: 120). For DAZN's coverage of the UWCL, the emphasis on simultaneous global access was further emphasized by their two-stage strategy, banking on access to grow the game and build a transnational fanbase willing to pay.

One of the clearest ways that DAZN sought to address the extant women's football fanbase and reach out to football fans more broadly has been through their digital promotional and social media arms. One of the selling points to both sides of the audience was to integrate women's football and men's football into a singular Twitter feed, @DAZNfootball. While most other women's sports broadcasters, such as Sky Sports' coverage of the WSL (@SkySportsWSL) or the ESPN-W (@ESPNW) digital vertical, tend toward separate channels for women's leagues and coverage, DAZN's social media approach explicitly categorized women's football as football. Moreover, the posts on the feed approach gender equity, switching between women's and men's football topics frequently. For example, in the off-season for European Leagues on June 17 and 18, 2022, one engagement-ready post featured a post asking for reactions to Lieke Martens' five years at FC Barcelona Feminil as she prepared to transfer to Paris Saint-Germain, followed the next day by Manchester City's Jack Grealish kissing a trophy and asking for Premier League predictions (DAZN Football 2022a; DAZN Football 2022b). In other words, the DAZNfootball Twitter handle actively rejects the "one and done" gender disparity norm of both traditional sports media and general sports social media where "a single women's sports story [is] partially eclipsed by a cluster of men's stories that precede it, follow it, and are longer in length" (Cooky et al. 2021: 366). Fans of women's soccer wouldn't have to wade through multiple posts about men's football to get to the one post about women's football in their social media feeds. Football-forward coverage led to equity in both social media strategy and the sense of what types of fans are welcomed by DAZN.

This treatment of UWCL as equal to and covered similarly to men's football flowed into the actual broadcasts on YouTube, even though that platform did have a separate channel specifically for UWCL coverage. As Cooky et al. (2021) have shown through their longitudinal studies of women's sports coverage, the norm, when not overshadowed by men's coverage, is shying away from engaging, high-energy commentary in favor of bland, boring, but "respectful" language and delivery (359). For DAZN's UWCL coverage, however, deeply engaged and knowledgeable analysis as well as exciting commentary was the norm over the 2022 and 2023 competitions.

DAZN featured top level commentators in each language, assuring the global access and brand unity of approach. For example, when Arsenal's Frida Maanum scored what would be voted goal of the tournament in their March 29, 2023 quarterfinal game against Bayern Munich Frauen, the broadcasters displayed the approach that DAZN promoted: top-level, multi-lingual, and as-good or better-than terrestrial regional broadcasters. The English-language play-by-play analysts were: Pien Meulensteen, an experienced Premier League sports broadcaster with Sky and BBC, and Lucy Ward, a former player with Leeds United who's worked in British sports broadcasting since 2007. And in German: Christoph Fetzer, a journalist and commentator for La Liga in Germany, and Almuth Schult, a goalkeeper for the German Women's National team. At the goal Meulensteen yelled, "What a finish from Frida Maanum! That is the response that Arsenal needed!" and on replay analysis, Ward added, "This is all about Arsenal pressing high... that's a stunning strike, hardly any backlift!" In German, Fetzer and Schult were equally emotional and exclamatory at the strike while also offering their own detailed analysis of how it happened and what it meant for the game. The level of enthusiasm, analysis, and entertainment displayed by these broadcast teams for DAZN offers fans of women's football precisely what they've been asking for: knowledge, emotion, and soccer-specific focus and framing that treats the game, and more specifically, its fans with respect instead of condescension.[1]

Broadcasts were simulcast in multiple languages: English and at least one other language (Spanish, German, or French) for each game, creating multiple contact zones for transcultural fans. Each broadcast had a live chat function that was dominated by the language of the commentators but also featured many other languages, indicating viewers from multiple countries and backgrounds. The DAZN UWCL coverage on YouTube illustrates how "within the contact zones of online fandom, the normative fandom of shared affinities and even aspirations is, in its intrinsic transculturality, always already a site of difference" (Morimoto and Chin 2017: 182). DAZN's UWCL channel embraced the transculturality of women's football fans as part of its unique appeal. However, as Morimoto and Chin (2017) note, affinity can sometimes lead to hegemonic norms that exclude those within a transcultural online fandom who do not adhere to these norms (182). For DAZN to grow its fandom through appeal to wider football fans, the drive for improved access and coverage may discount some of the unique elements of women's football fandom.

The Appeal and Cost of "More Eyes" for Women's Soccer Fandom

The key promotional video campaign to promote the UWCL on DAZN, "We ALL Rise With More Eyes," (2021) struck an ambivalent tone as it showed women's football and its fans as expressions of high-level sport and its culture while also clearly acknowledging the need to coax more football fans to watch the competition. Starting with close-ups of women's eyes of a variety of races, ages, and ethnicities, the video intercuts between key plays and players from the UWCL and images of everyday women playing football and participating in football culture. The types of players, fans, and ways of engaging with the sport are presented as expansive. To emphasize this, a young woman performs a spoken-word poem about visibility in a British accent, aurally presenting the cosmopolitan and multicultural appeal of European football while stating the step-by-step strategy of DAZN's emphasis on (initial) free access. The first part of the video explicitly positions fandom as the foundation of this strategy. The speaker states: "The more eyes. The more eyes, the more likes. The more likes the more tweets. The more tweets, the more fans, and more fans fill more seats [images of full stadia, flares, and supporters' groups]. A full house means more noise. More heads getting turned [images of players heading the ball]." This section emphasizes how fans online lead to fans at matches, and fans at matches get more media attention, becoming even more explicit in how a visible and active fandom is necessary for increased coverage. The narrator goes on: "More cameras, more angles, more pundits, more press, more headlines, more airtime, more billboards, more big time, more sponsors, more shoots. More signature boots." The video, as with every major women's sport, does emphasize the inspiration-for-little-girls aspect of the league, but it is at least framed more as gender-ambiguous sport achievement instead of vague women's empowerment: "More little shirts and more little leagues [images of young kids, mostly girls but not all, in jerseys with names of UWCL stars on their backs] with big dreams of golden gloves or golden balls [images of women's football stars when they were kids]. Well done kid." Then the video transitions to talking about more players, coaches, referees, and pitches; essentially saying watching the UWCL on DAZN will help build the infrastructure of European women's football from the five-on-five pitches in cities to women's leagues of all ages to multiple paths for careers for women in football both on and off the pitch. The poem ends with the tagline for DAZN's campaign, "We all rise with more eyes," and the video ends with a victorious score under the final text: "DAZN brings you UEFA Women's Champions League 2021–2025 free for the world to see on YouTube." The framing exemplifies the idea that DAZN is giving the gift of the game to football fans, and that their faith – if you show it, fans will watch – is the foundation for women's football broadly. The video speaks to women's football fans who would already understand and know the players, teams, and images of the UWCL, while also saying they are not enough, that growing the fandom of women's football is the fundamental goal. But DAZN's rights strategy is not a gift, and the way it promotes UWCL and speaks to women's football global fandom illustrates the good and ill of treating women's football as football.

Ultimately, DAZN made a business decision that lines up with both long-tested television sports rights logic of exposure leading to increased viewership and the growing domain of subscription-free streaming and FAST (free ad-based streaming television) (Bridge 2022). Free access is only temporary because global football fans are recognized (or at least perceived) as a consumer base willing to pay for access (Collet 2017; Burham 2023). This is the fundamental tension in DAZN's strategy: using global women's football fans to leverage more global women's football viewership that lessens the power and influence of those original fans. DAZN's UWCL digital rights strategy is indicative of media industries' increasing hailing of fans "as a flexible concept describing certain intensive audience practices (and not others)" (Stanfill 2019: 5). More specifically, we see in DAZN the value as well as the price of using the specific fandom that has formed around women's football – progressive, inclusive, and willing to challenge unjust norms of sports fan culture (Howell 2022) – being potentially overwritten by broader football fan norms. In other words, as Suzanne Scott (2019) argues regarding geek fan culture, masculine-associated fan practices often align with sanctioned fan practices within both industry and fan discourses in ways that discipline and potentially displace feminine-gendered "nonsanctioned modes of engagement" (39). Active viewing, paying for subscriptions, focusing on the sport, and promoting the sport and platform on social media are all sanctioned ways of engaging with football as a fan, but they also can obscure the sexism, racism, xenophobia, homophobia, and entrenched structural issues faced by specifically women's football and its fans.

More eyes also mean less specific attention and shared community concerns. General football fans watching women's global soccer on DAZN might be disappointed their favorite players are injured and have slightly less incentive to watch, but women's football fans might understand the epidemic of ACL tears in the 2020s as indicative of the sport extending beyond its resources, including lack of study of women footballers' body mechanics (Wright 2023). General football viewers might not understand the structural inequalities being recreated among the women's tournament as major men's teams are creating "super clubs" for both genders that hides resource discrepancies within women's leagues (Valenti et al. 2023). As sports fandom scholar Erin C. Tarver (2017) argues, "Some forms of women's sports fandom… involve practices that constitute significant resistance to misogyny, racism, and heterosexism and thus give reason to nuance our analysis of the social functions of sports fandom" (172). Because women's sports fans have had to create their own communities at the margins and work into spaces of visibility and market power, they can provide distinct perspectives on the sport and its fan practices. For example: women's football supporters' groups like the Rose City Riveters (fans of the NWSL Portland Thorns) have organized protests against their team owners who allegedly covered up sexual abuse and harassment (Zirin and Boykoff 2022), and other women's supporters' groups across the NWSL regularly attend matches with signs to protect trans kids and support queer people. But a fandom that can thread the needle of supporting the players and critiquing larger structures is a much more complicated form of fandom than the one being cultivated by DAZN, which promises success and growth through traditional sports media means. Jennifer McClearen (2021) argues for more caution and "questioning the presumption that visibility is a panacea for gender inequality in sports" in her book on female UFC fighters because "visibility… can actually be detrimental for female fighters because media exposure offers promises of success, fame, and fortune that it cannot deliver for most athletes within the current structure" (4). While global women's football promises different things than UFC and has different guardrails due to its governing bodies and team structures, the promise of exposure leading to greater success for the sport and players is central to DAZN's branding. It is a promise built on the foundation – or stepping stone – of appealing to the specific digital fan communities of global women's football, possibly at the expense of the specific and often alternative sports fan characteristics cultivated for the beautiful game.

Note

1 The January 2023 announcement of shifts in access partially behind a paywall, increased geoblocking, diminished language options, and necessity of the DAZN app for some games was met with fan disappointment on social media, indicating the high-quality expectations DAZN had cultivated (DAZN Football 2023).

References

Allison, R. (2018) *Kicking Center: Gender and the Selling of Women's Professional Soccer*. New Brunswick, NJ: Rutgers University Press.
Anderson, J. (2023) "NWSL Weekend Take-Off: Broadcasting Woes and New Wrinkles for Reign, Red Stars," *Pro Soccer Wire*, 18 April. Available at: https://prosoccerwire.usatoday.com/lists/nwsl-take-off-broadcast-problems-ol-reign-chicago-red-stars/ (Accessed: 1 June 2023).
Bowes, A. (2020) "Coverage of Women's Sport is Pathetic at the Best of Times – The Lockdown Has Made It Even Worse," *The Conversation*, 15 June. Available at: http://theconversation.com/coverage-of-womens-sport-is-pathetic-at-the-best-of-times-the-lockdown-has-made-it-even-worse-140593 (Accessed: 15 June 2023).
Bridge, G. (2022) "The Meteoric Rise of Free Streaming FAST Channels: A VIP+ Special Report," *Variety*, 1 December. Available at: https://variety.com/2022/streaming/news/rise-free-streaming-fast-channels-special-report-1235441193/ (Accessed: 25 June 2023).
Bruce, T. (2016) "New Rules for New Times: Sportswomen and Media Representation in the Third Wave," *Sex Roles*, 74(7), pp. 361–376. Available at: https://doi.org/10.1007/s11199-015-0497-6.
Burhan, A. (2023) "Converting Visibility Into Value Key As Dazn Move UWCL To Pay TV Model," *Forbes*, 23 May. Available at: www.forbes.com/sites/asifburhan/2023/05/23/converting-visibility-into-value-key-as-dazn-move-uwcl-to-pay-tv-model/ (Accessed: 1 June 2023).
Collet, C. (2017) "Soccer, Politics and the American Public: Still 'Exceptional'?" *Soccer & Society*, 18(2/3), pp. 348–367. Available at: https://doi.org/10.1080/14660970.2016.1166766.

Cooky, C. et al. (2021) "One and Done: The Long Eclipse of Women's Televised Sports, 1989–2019," *Communication & Sport*, 9(3), pp. 347–371. Available at: https://doi.org/10.1177/2167479521 1003524.

DAZN Football [@DAZNFootball] (2022a) "How Would You Describe Lieke Martens' 5 Years at @FCBfemeni? ↓ https://t.co/PexZ6dpXiJ," *Twitter*, June 17. Available at: https://twitter.com/DAZNFootball/status/1537842511984570368 (Accessed: 29 June 2023).

DAZN Football [@DAZNFootball] (2022b) "7 Weeks Until the Premier League is Back... Your best 2021/22 moment was _____. https://t.co/5uQCxdqHXU," *Twitter*, June 18. Available at: https://twitter.com/DAZNFootball/status/1538119111656624129 (Accessed: 29 June 2023).

DAZN Football [@DAZNFootball] (2023) "The only thing better than watching football, is watching it for FREE 😃😃 DAZN is offering fans A NEW DEAL FOR WOMEN'S FOOTBALL. 📋 Register on the link and watch for free: https://dazn.com/womensfootball #NewDealforWomensFootball," Twitter, January 23. Available at: https://t.co/6R2SQHlwwv (Accessed: 28 January 2024).

DAZN UEFA Women's Champions League (2021) *We All Rise With More Eyes*. June 30. Available at: www.youtube.com/watch?v=qxF40zSjFCw (Accessed: 15 June 2023).

Fielding-Lloyd, B., Woodhouse, D. and Sequerra, R. (2020) "'More Than Just a Game': Family and Spectacle in Marketing the England Women's Super League," *Soccer & Society*, 21(2), pp. 166–179. Available at: https://doi.org/10.1080/14660970.2018.1541799.

Gosling, V.K. (2007) "Girls Allowed? The Marginalization of Female Sport Fans," in J. Gray, C. Sandvoss, and C.L. Harrington (eds) *Fandom: Identities and Communities in a Mediated World*. 1st edn. New York, NY: NYU Press, pp. 250–260.

Hardin, M. and Whiteside, E. (2010) "The Rene Portland Case: New Homophobia and Heterosexism in Women's Sports Coverage," in H.L. Hundley and A.C. Billings (eds) *Examining Identity in Sports Media*. Thousand Oaks, CA: Sage, pp. 17–36.

Hayes, D. (2020) "DAZN Reactivates Global Expansion Plan, Updates Strategy for Sports Streaming in COVID-19 Comeback," *Deadline*, 28 October. Available at: https://deadline.com/2020/10/dazn-global-streaming-sports-200-countries-anthony-joshua-1234602714/ (Accessed: 1 June 2023).

Howell, C.E. (2021) "A Touch More with Megan Rapinoe and Sue Bird: Authenticity, Intimacy and Women's Sports Celebrity on Instagram Live," *Celebrity Studies*, pp. 1–16. Available at: https://doi.org/10.1080/19392397.2021.1958694.

Howell, C.E. (2022) "'The American Outlaws Are Our People': Fox Sports and the Branded Ambivalence of an American Soccer Fan at the 2019 FIFA Women's World Cup," *Television & New Media*, 23(8), pp. 900–916. Available at: https://doi.org/10.1177/15274764211053219.

Jenkins, H. (1997) "'Never Trust a Snake': WWF Wrestling as Masculine Melodrama," in A. Baker and T. Boyd (eds) *Out of Bounds: Sports, Media, and the Politics of Identity*. Bloomington, IN: Indiana University Press, pp. 48–78.

Johnson, V.E. (2016) "'Together, We Make Football': The NFL's 'Feminine' Discourses," *Popular Communication*, 14, pp. 12–20. Available at: www.tandfonline.com/doi/abs/10.1080/15405702.2015.1084622 (Accessed: 6 June 2023).

Johnson, V.E. (2021) *Sports TV*. New York: Routledge.

Lawson, A. (2018) "Business Interview: DAZN Tech Boss Tempts Fans with Spotify for Sport," *Evening Standard*, 14 December. Available at: www.standard.co.uk/business/business-interview-simon-denyer-dazn-the-london-tech-boss-tempting-fans-with-a-ps3bn-spotify-for-sport-a4017781.html (Accessed: 1 June 2023).

Lawson, S. "Stop making 'inspirational' a requirement for women to play sport. *SBNation*, June 16, 2022. www.allforxi.com/2022/6/16/23170570/stop-making-inspirational-a-requirement-for-women-to-play-sport.

Linehan, M. (2021) "UEFA Women's Champions League Inks Four-year DAZN Deal," *The Athletic*, 30 June. Available at: https://theathletic.com/2681299/2021/06/30/uwcl-dazn-youtube-broadcast-deal/ (Accessed: 8 June 2023).

McClearen, J. (2021) *Fighting Visibility: Sports Media and Female Athletes in the UFC*. Chicago, IL: University of Illinois Press.

Morimoto, L.H. and Chin, B. (2017) "Reimagining the Imagined Community: Online Media Fandoms in the Age of Global Convergence," in J. Gray, C. Sandvoss, and C.L. Harrington (eds) *Fandom: Identities and Communities in a Mediated World*. Second Edition. New York, NY: NYU Press, pp. 174–188.

Murray, C. (2013) "Assessing Year 1, Future of NWSL Livestreams," *Equalizer Soccer*, 14 August. Available at: https://equalizersoccer.com/2013/08/14/assessing-year-1-future-of-nwsl-livestreams/ (Accessed: 1 June 2023).

Parkinson, H.J. (2019) "Love All: How Megan Rapinoe and Other Gay Players Are Taking Sport to a Higher Level," *The Guardian*, 4 July. Available at: www.theguardian.com/sport/shortcuts/2019/jul/04/love-all-how-megan-rapinoe-and-other-gay-players-are-taking-sport-to-a-higher-level (Accessed: 16 May 2020).

Rafael, D. (2018) "Hearn Has Big U.S. Plans with $1B DAZN Deal," *ESPN.com*, 10 May. Available at: www.espn.com/boxing/story/_/id/23465848/eddie-hearn-matchroom-boxing-plans-big-things-us-streaming-service-dazn-revenue (Accessed: 1 June 2023).

Rose, A. and Friedman, J. (1997) "Television Sports as Mas(s)culine Cult of Distraction," in A. Baker and T. Boyd (eds) *Out of Bounds: Sports, Media, and the Politics of Identity*. Bloomington, IN: Indiana University Press, pp. 1–15.

Sandvoss, C. (2003) *A Game of Two Halves: Football Fandom, Television and Globalisation*. London: Routledge.

Schultz, K. (2019) "WNBA Leads Other Sports Leagues in LGBTQ Inclusion," *Outsports*, 22 July. Available at: www.outsports.com/2019/7/22/20701939/wnba-lgbtq-inclusion-pride-night-los-angeles-sparks-womens-basketball (Accessed: 24 September 2020).

Scott, S. (2019) *Fake Geek Girls: Fandom, Gender and the Convergence Culture Industry*. New York: New York University Press.

Stanfill, M. (2019) *Exploiting Fandom: How the Media Industry Seeks to Manipulate Fans*. Iowa City: University of Iowa Press.

Sturm, D. (2019) "'I Dream of Genie': Eugenie Bouchard's 'Body' of Work on Facebook," *Celebrity Studies*, 10(4), pp. 583–587. Available at: https://doi.org/10.1080/19392397.2019.1601808.

Tarver, E.C. (2017) *The I in Team: Sports Fandom and the Reproduction of Identity*. Chicago, IL: University of Chicago Press.

Valenti, M., Scelles, N., Morrow, S. (2023) "The Impact of 'Super Clubs' on Uncertainty of Outcome in the UEFA Women's Champions League," *Soccer & Society*, 24(4), pp. 509–519. Available at: https://doi.org/10.1080/14660970.2023.2194514.

Vann, P. (2014) "Changing the Game: The Role of Social Media in Overcoming Old Media's Attention Deficit Toward Women's Sport," *Journal of Broadcasting & Electronic Media*, 58(3), pp. 438–455. Available at: https://doi.org/10.1080/08838151.2014.935850.

Vivarelli, N., Keslassy, E. and Lang, J. (2021) "Streaming Services Like DAZN Are Shaking Up Sports in Europe," Variety, 8 May. Available at: https://variety.com/2021/global/news/streaming-dazn-sports-europe-1234968092/ (Accessed: 31 May 2022).

Wetzel, H. (2018) "DAZN Makes its U.S. Debut," *Awful Announcing*, 11 September. Available at: https://awfulannouncing.com/dazn/dazn-makes-its-u-s-debut.html (Accessed: 1 June 2023).

Whyatt, K. (2022) "'The Vision Was to Treat Women's Football the Same Way We Treat Men's Football': Inside Sky's WSL Coverage," *The Athletic*, 6 May. Available at: https://theathletic.com/3295551/2022/05/06/the-vision-was-to-treat-womens-football-the-same-way-we-treat-mens-football-inside-skys-wsl-coverage/ (Accessed: 6 June 2023).

Williams, C. (2016) "Blavatnik's Perform Group Rebuffs Tech Investors to Build 'Netflix for Sport,'" *The Telegraph*, 20 August. Available at: www.telegraph.co.uk/business/2016/08/20/blavatniks-perform-group-rebuffs-tech-investors-to-build-netflix/ (Accessed: 1 June 2023).

Wrack, S. (2021) "The New WSL Broadcast Deal is the Perfect Riposte to the 'No One Cares' Brigade," The Guardian, 22 March. Available at: www.theguardian.com/football/2021/mar/22/the-new-wsl-broadcast-deal-is-the-perfect-riposte-to-the-no-one-cares-brigade (Accessed: 6 June 2023).

Wright, K. (2023) "Why Do So Many Female Footballers Get ACL Injuries?," *BBC Sport*, 21 April. Available at: www.bbc.com/sport/football/64032536 (Accessed: 27 June 2023).

Yossman, K.J. (2021) "UEFA Women's Champions League Soccer Lands on Global Sports Streaming Platform DAZN," *Variety*, 30 June. Available at: https://variety.com/2021/sports/news/uefa-womens-champions-league-soccer-dazn-1235008325/ (Accessed: 1 June 2023).

Zirin, D. and Boykoff, J. (2022) "Portland Soccer Feels the Power of Protest," *The Nation*, 30 March. Available at: www.thenation.com/article/society/portland-timbers-merritt-paulson-rctid/ (Accessed: 27 June 2023).

42
THE BIGGER PICTURE
Drawing Intersections between Comics, Fan, and Industry Studies

Alisa Perren and Laura E. Felschow

For decades, American comic books have attracted one of the most dedicated, active fandoms (Duncan & Smith 2009; Smith 2011; Steirer 2011). And since the early 2000s, Hollywood has perceived comic book fans to be especially valuable consumers and promoters of their products. Although the roughly $1 billion in revenue generated each year in sales of single issues, graphic novels, and digital issues by the American comic book industry (Griepp 2015) is miniscule in comparison to the roughly $11 billion generated annually by Hollywood theatrical film releases (MPAA 2016) and $70 billion from US television advertising (Lynch 2016), the comic book industry has evolved to become a central source of intellectual property and franchise development for the media industries more generally. Increasingly, the media landscape has been dominated by superhero television series, films, and video games generated by the "Big Two" publishers, DC Comics (owned by Time Warner; 31.30% share of market as of November 2016) and Marvel Comics (owned by Disney, 39.46% share as of November 2016) (Diamond 2016). But comics are more than superhero properties. Indeed, with growing regularity, comic book adaptations are coming from independent, entrepreneurial publishers including Dark Horse (*Hellboy* 1993–; 2.85% share as of November 2016), BOOM! Studios (*Two Guns* 2007–, 1.66% share as of November 2016), and Image Comics (*The Walking Dead* 2003–, 9.06% share as of November 2016) (Diamond 2016).

Concurrent with the expansion of the comic book industry and the diversification of the types of comics produced and mined as intellectual property (IP), there has been a burgeoning body of scholarship on the topic in fan studies, media industry studies, and comics studies. Although work in each of these fields is thriving in its own right, more could be done to put such work in conversation. This chapter seeks to undertake just such a task. In the pages that follow, through case studies of how fans are imagined, targeted, engaged, and valued by two different comic book publishers—mainstream DC Comics and independent Image Comics—we illustrate the utility of a more nuanced analysis of the industry-creative-fan relationship. Drawing from trade publications, corporate marketing materials, and interviews with executives, writers, and artists working for both of these companies, we show how variations in corporate structures and business models impact the types of stories that are told as well as the kinds of relationships that exist between diverse stakeholders. By first discussing how executives at the two companies describe their relationships with both creatives and fans, and then shifting to consider how creatives working for each of these companies perceive their relationships with both executives and fans, we complicate the often-monolithic industry–fan (or producer–fan) binary that has dominated many studies of convergence culture.

Building a Dialogue: Fan Studies, Industry Studies, Comics Studies

Since the early 1980s, scholars—especially those drawing from cultural studies traditions—have looked at the diverse behaviors and practices of comic book fans from a variety of perspectives. Dominant areas of emphasis include analysis of fan activity in physical spaces such as conventions (Hanna 2014; Kohnen 2014; Swafford 2012) and retail stores (Woo 2011) as well as in diverse online spaces; and the cultural politics of race, class, gender, and sexuality of comic book fandoms (Brown 2000; Putsz, 2000; Healey 2009). Many of these studies have approached comics from the bottom up, relying on ethnographic methods such as interviews and observation, sometimes combined with ideological or formal analyses of comic book texts. Often the comic book industry, when discussed in such work, is either marginalized or presented oppositionally—as something fans have been reacting against. Such a stance, dominant in the 1980s and 1990s, was emblematic of the first wave of fan studies scholarship. More broadly, this stance conformed to the schism between political economic and cultural studies scholarship evident in American media and cultural studies during that time period.

Until the last decade, industry-oriented scholarship on comics has been rather limited in output. Much of what was produced mostly was either historical in nature—situating key companies, creatives, and executives within the larger sociocultural context of the twentieth century (Wright 2001; Jones 2005; Gabilliet 2009)—or it took a macro-level, top-down, political economic approach, emphasizing issues such as ownership, structure, business strategy, and mode of production (McAllister 2001; Meehan 1991; Rogers 2006; Steirer 2011). Fans were largely absent from such studies; instead, such work spoke in terms of broader categories such as readers, consumers, and markets. Even recently, when fan-industry dynamics have been discussed in a single publication, such as in the many case studies focusing on Batman (Pearson and Uricchio 1991; Brooker 2012; Burke 2013), the relationship between industry and fandom is reified in terms of top-down/bottom-up framework. A striking exception comes in work by Jeffrey A. Brown, who explores the shifting cultural status of the fan as constructed by and in relation to the comic book industry (1997).

Notably, while industry-oriented scholars may not have had much interest in studying fans until the early 2000s, fans have published prolifically for—and to—the comic book industry. For example, fans produced buyers' guides and collectors' guides that subsequently were taken up by publishers and retailers (Light 1971–2013; Overstreet 1970–present). Meanwhile, comic book industry writers, artists, and executives produced a range of books targeted to fans wishing to break into comics (Lee and Buscema 1984; McCloud 2006; Rhoades 2007). Certainly, one of the most distinctive traits about the comic book industry, as will be discussed below, is the extent to which it has attracted workers who proudly self-identify as fans.

Shifts in larger economic, creative, technological, and cultural conditions during the 2000s corresponded with changes in how industry studies and fan studies scholars analyzed comics. As Henry Jenkins and Joshua Green (2013) argue, industrial, technological, and cultural convergence have impacted how producers and consumers interact, in turn necessitating new ways of integrating industry studies with fan studies. Building on work by such participatory culture scholars, comics studies scholars such as Suzanne Scott (2013) and Liam Burke (2015) have further complicated the discussion of industry-fan relationships in notable ways: Scott, by examining how the comics industry privileges a young, white male fandom; Burke, by considering how comic book fans communicate their opinions regarding comic book adaptations to the films' producers.

Below, we push the study of industry-fan relations further by moving beyond the top-down/bottom-up binary that continues to dominate much work on convergence culture. We do so in two key ways: first, we illustrate the complex power dynamics at work within and across the comic book industry through a comparative study of mainstream publisher DC Comics and independent publisher Image Comics. Such an approach is informed by recent work in the cultural studies of production (Mayer, Banks, and Caldwell 2009) and on cultural intermediaries (e.g. creative and marketing executives) (Johnson, Kompare, and Santo 2014). Through such a framework, we can see how key stakeholders—executives, creatives, and fans—exercise varying levels of agency and control. Second, through this comparative analysis, we can understand how varying levels of agency are enabled or constrained by different business models favored by different companies. In other words, how DC and Image executives and creatives imagine, cultivate, and engage with their fans is in part a function of how these different companies are structured.

A Tale of Two Business Models: DC Comics and Image Comics

Most scholarship as well as most journalistic coverage of the American comic book industry has focused on Marvel and DC Comics. To an extent this is understandable, as together, these two companies take in roughly 70% of the share of the domestic market; our screens and store shelves are dominated primarily by IP generated by these two comic book companies. Image, with roughly 9% of the market, is the next major player. No other publisher earns more than 5% of the share of the market (Diamond 2016; Miller 2016). Nonetheless, in recent years, Image, along with other independent publishers such as Valiant and BOOM!, gradually have increased their profile in the marketplace. Before understanding how and why these companies have grown, and how Image in particular operates, it is important to first briefly discuss DC Comics' business model.

DC Comics is the comic book publishing arm of DC Entertainment. DC Entertainment, in turn, is focused on managing DC's brand identity and controlling DC's content as it travels throughout parent company Time Warner's film, television, consumer products, home entertainment, and games divisions (DC Entertainment 2016). As a small division within an integrated conglomerate, DC Comics is primarily designed to produce IP that feeds into its larger corporate structure. The publishing division's business model prioritizes *character, continuity*, and *collection*. Rarely does a single DC Comics book earn that much money. Yet, maintaining a regular publishing schedule—with key characters such as Superman and Batman featured across many different books and pitched to readers in several different demographics—sustains an existing fanbase and, ideally, helps to grow a new one. As one DC Comics executive explained:

> Once [readers] come in with one character, they start to spread and pick up things for other reasons. You come to reading our comics through *Batman*, you enjoy reading the [Scott] Snyder *Batman* books, then you seek out the other things that Snyder writes. At the same time, you seek out other *Batman* books, which then lead you to other books, because Batman's in *Justice League*. And then you read *Justice League*, and get engaged with Wonder Woman, and then you go and read *Wonder Woman* ... A DC fan doesn't just buy one book. A DC fan is committed to multiple books and, it is my core belief that the DC fan really likes continuity—really likes to see the books interrelate, and take place within the same world.

Wonder Woman writer Greg Rucka reinforces the extent to which creatives are constrained by the DC business model, maintaining that with

> The Big Two, if you read *Batman*, you read *Batman*. And it doesn't really matter who's writing it. People can talk about "Well, I really like this artist" or "I really like this writer." But if you collect *Batman*, you collect *Batman*. When you're at a place like Image, people don't collect [his Image-authored] *Lazarus*. They're reading it.

In other words, within the DC Comics business model, the type of fandom that is especially valued is the collector-fan. Indeed, an ideal fan might be one who buys multiple copies of the same issue—a digital copy to read, a single-issue copy to "buy and bag" to preserve value, and perhaps even a hardcover graphic novel for display on their bookshelf (DC Comics Executive 2016). Of course, this same fan also will be engaged with the characters across multiple media forms.

This is not to say that other types of fandom (and consumption) aren't welcomed and encouraged by DC (and Marvel), of course. But it does indicate that some types of practices are encouraged over others, both on the part of creators and fans. And, in turn, some types of fans—and creators—have embraced the DC model more enthusiastically. Although DC's readership has diversified in recent years, and DC executives have made a concerted effort to attract more diverse writers and artists, historically, white men (now moving into middle age) have been the company's core readership. This core audience, of course, is also the one most aggressively (and successfully) pursued by DC content across other media (e.g. *Suicide Squad* in film, *Arrow* in television, *Batman: Arkham Night* in games).

While character, continuity, and collection represent priorities for DC Comics-cum-DC Entertainment, Image Comics' corporate structure and business model prioritizes *creators*, *consumption*, and *cultivation* of new readers. Launched in 1992 by seven Marvel-based artists who grew dissatisfied with their working conditions, Image originally served primarily as a publisher housing these artists' partner studios (Image Comics 2016; Dean 2000). Jim Lee (*WildC.A.T.s* 1994–1995), Rob Liefeld (*Youngblood* 1992), and Todd McFarlane (*Spawn* 1992–1998) were among the founders of the company, which developed a business model that favored creatives. In Image's creator-owned model, control over copyright remained with talent; Image simply charged talent fixed fees for distribution and marketing expenditures. Although select top-tier talent at DC Comics might strike creator-owned deals, these arrangements have been far less common and are not nearly as favorable as what Image offers. According to the creatives interviewed, in most instances, DC strikes work-for-hire deals and compensates talent via page rates and with royalties if sales reach particular performance thresholds.

Whereas DC Comics is a small division employing approximately 250 people within a global media conglomerate that employs roughly 25,000 people worldwide, Image Comics' staff totals fewer than 25 people, all of whom are involved directly in the comics publishing business (DC Comics Executive 2016; Time Warner 2016). During Image's first decade in operation, it functioned essentially as Marvel on steroids, publishing what writer Kelly Sue DeConnick (*Captain Marvel* 2012–2015, Image's *Bitch Planet* 2014–) calls "hypermasculine" comics that were "aggressively anti-women and aggressively marketed to a perspective that grossly centered the male heterosexual reader and marginalized and objectified women" (DeConnick 2016). Image initially appealed primarily to the same young white male fanbase targeted by the Big Two. However, as the 2000s continued, and much of the talent initially affiliated with the company moved on, Image began to publish different types of books. The success of books such as *The Walking Dead* (2003–), *Wanted* (2003–2005, via Top Cow), and, more recently, *Saga* (2012–) helped elevate Image's profile.

Equally important to Image's expansion, was the explosion of comic book properties as IP during the 2000s. In fact, the same forces that enabled comic book franchises to become a primary focus for the media industries facilitated the growth of Image. As DC and Marvel increasingly favored established characters and multimedia franchises with global appeal, many successful artists and writers who worked for the Big Two felt creatively constrained by them. Concurrently, Marvel and DC deprioritized their investment in their creator-owned imprints. Changing compensation deals at the Big Two, along with the possibility of more back-end income, greater creative control, and the ability to retain film and television rights, all contributed to making Image more attractive to writers and artists. These writers and artists, in turn, began to develop properties that the Big Two could not or would not produce, including crime comics (*Criminal* 2006–), fantasy books (*Saga*), and romance comedies (*Sex Criminals* 2013–).

As creatives have flocked to Image, the company has cultivated a specific brand identity and grown its own distinctive fanbase. While Image's readership runs from teenagers to baby boomers, according to Image publisher Eric Stephenson, in recent years the company's product has become especially popular with teens and twentysomethings—especially women and people of color in that age group. According to Stephenson, "You have people who are seeking out that material. They want something like *Saga* where it's kind of genre-based and fun, and has action, but at Image it's not like a cookie-cutter Marvel book."

Image increasingly has thrived by differentiating itself as a place where more inclusive stories can be told (Rucka 2016). Through this emerging identity, Image appeals to a particular taste culture and its brand carries a degree of cultural capital for a specific contingent of fans. This reputation also attracts certain types of creators—ones willing to undertake the additional labor required to market and promote their books through Image in exchange for the possibility of greater financial reward and cultural status. As Kat Salazar, director of PR and Marketing for Image Comics, observes, "From the moment Image was first founded, its success was about the *fans following the creators* [italics added]. It's not about the big properties or about it being 'Image Comics'—it's about the creators who publish some of their career-best here because they're given the freedom to do what they want." Image no doubt benefits from drawing established talent from DC and Marvel—talent that carries some of their fans with them. These new readers, according to Salazar, find the books appealing precisely because they aren't "required to know decades of back-history and continuity." When you consume Image, you consume a book and a brand—not a transmedia storyworld and a multiverse of characters. The hard work of attracting, engaging, and retaining fans, however, falls to a much greater extent on the creatives involved. These creatives, like the companies for which they work, frequently operate with only a vague sense of their fans.

Imagining Audiences, Engaging Fans

Much of the knowledge that both executives and creatives have about their readership is anecdotal in nature. Industry employees are notoriously tight-lipped about the data they collect, and, unsurprisingly, those we spoke with were hesitant to disclose much information regarding the demographics of their readership. Creatives' knowledge, meanwhile, is based primarily on their own experiences engaging with fans through physical and online spaces; they are not privy to the market research conducted by distributors and retailers. What's more, relatively little of publishers' proprietary research is shared with the press or public. Regardless of the granularity of the demographic data about *readers* that publishers possess, in general, it is evident that companies' conceptions of *fandom* are not clearly conceptualized or articulated.

Fan behaviors such as the purchasing, reading, collecting, and trading of comic books, as well as fan-production practices, are not widely catalogued or quantified. As is the case with other industry measurement systems such as television ratings (Ang 1991; Gitlin 2000), data collection is a fraught process that involves a delicate dance between retailers, distributors, and publishers. Executives often profess to making production, distribution, and marketing decisions by relying on their instincts and tastes, or by turning to qualitatively oriented data gained through interactions on social media and at conventions. Surveys undertaken by comics retailers are limited in number and also based largely on anecdotal evidence from store owners, such as the annual studies done by *Publisher's Weekly* (O'Leary 2015). Other studies, such as the work completed monthly by *Graphic Policy*, are methodologically problematic, as they are restricted to the demographic makeup of self-identifying comic book fans on Facebook only (Schenker n.d.).

Significantly, the perception that the primary readership of comics is between the ages of 18 and 34, young, white, and male continues to hold much power into the present. The turn during the 1980s toward masculine hyperviolence and overt sexuality with books such as *Spawn* (1992–), *Lady Death* (1994–2004), and *Sin City* (1991–2000) coupled with the siloing off of the comics market to direct market stores, solidified this direction for the comic book industry for decades. This compatibility of the target audience for comics with the target audience for motion pictures in Conglomerate Hollywood further facilitated a mutually reinforcing production cycle (Schatz 2009). Meanwhile, as noted above, Image has grown its market share in part through a product differentiation strategy that involved appealing to previously underserved readers—including people of color and women. In addition to the aforementioned books such as *Saga*, *Black Magick* (2015–), and *Lazarus* (2013–), other Image titles such as *Paper Girls* (2016–), *Pretty Deadly* (2013–), and *Monstress* (2015–) appeal to female fans (Asselin 2015). Further, the availability of comics through digital platforms have drawn in new readers who are either unable to travel to comic book stores or who find retail outlets inhospitable spaces to enter (DC Comics Executive 2016).

As noted above, to the Big Two, of utmost importance is actively pursuing those "core" customers who consume their characters in as many platforms and products as possible. Creatives that we interviewed, meanwhile, expressed limited interest in knowing details about the demographic data collected by the Big Two. The audience here is understood by creatives to be a distant bloc with set expectations based on years and years of backstory. Many of the creatives we interviewed preferred not to think about the interests or desires of their fans while they wrote, drew, inked, or colored, as they believed that such considerations interfered with the authenticity of the creative process (DeConnick 2016; Rucka 2016). Nonetheless, when working for an independent publisher such as Image, some of them conducted (unscientific) market research periodically to better understand who was reading their books. Both Kieron Gillen and Jamie McKelvie of *The Wicked + The Divine*, and Brian K. Vaughn and Fiona Staples of *Saga* have conducted their own research into the makeup of their readership via online surveys or write-in forms at the back of their books, respectively. However, Gillen recognized that the sample sizes for their surveys were quite small and unlikely to accurately reflect the demographic makeup of their total readership: "Only 57% of our readership identify as straight, according to [our survey] numbers. [...] Even I in my wildest fantasies could not believe that that's the demographics of our audience" (Gillen 2016). According to Gillen, the first collected volume of *The Wicked + The Divine* sold 100,000 copies, and the response to their online survey was about 1,500. Although these sample sizes are modest relative to the sales figures for their titles, through these surveys, they better came to understand their readership. And, if they wished to do so, they could recalibrate their stories moving forward in response to their survey results.

Building and Managing Identities on and Offline

Given DC's corporate structure and investment in brand maintenance, as well as fan expectations bound to the company's characters, creatives are limited in terms of what they can do. Creatives working for DC Comics are usually freelancers assigned to a specific run of one character for a set number of issues. Their positions are precarious and so they must be careful not to engage with fans in ways that the company would deem inappropriate. Further, the conventions of the industry demand that the dictates of the Big Two take priority. This means that the creatives have little stake in the overall publication process; they do not have to worry about procuring advertisements for the issue, for example, or developing marketing strategies for the issue's release. In short, creatives working for DC Comics need not be concerned with the fan to a large extent because it is ultimately the company's responsibility to reach their audience. The companies have designated marketing and social media teams whose job it is to promote their product and connect with audiences. While creatives are encouraged by DC to engage with fans directly, their behavior is proscribed by well-established industrial and cultural norms.

The situation at Image is quite different. As a result of the work being creator-owned, creatives need to wear multiple hats throughout the process, from development to release. A writer or artist publishing with Image might shift between varied identities including entrepreneur, market researcher, brand name, and mentor to fans. As Kieron Gillen points out, "The thing with Image is you have to be a bit more hands-on. [...] It means you have to take on some of the roles that distribution would traditionally take" (Gillen 2016). When developing creator-owned work for Image, most of the onus falls upon the writer and artist to juggle artistic and entrepreneurial objectives.

Importantly, regardless of whom they are working for, creatives often are explicit about their own identities as comic book fans (Woo 2015). For instance, authors like DeConnick and Gillen built their own names by posting on writer Warren Ellis's forums before launching their careers in the industry. Their own history as well as their ongoing positionality as comic fans shapes the ways they interact with their own fans. In recent years, many creatives have taken advantage of the increased number of fan conventions and the greater ability for real-time interaction through digital technologies to make connections. Some even collect their own fans' creations: Fiona Staples numbers and catalogs gifts such as fan art or fan crafts, keeping them in what she refers to as a "treasure chest"; in essence, she acts as a fan of her fans, respecting and collecting their work as they might do hers.

The comics industry has a long history of fans becoming professional writers or artists, and in the past, this often was a direct result of the fan being taken under the wing of an established creative. These types of relationships still develop. For example, DeConnick's current assistant initially came to DeConnick's attention through her cosplay skills. Now they are co-writing a story together. However, fear of litigation limits how much advice or constructive criticism writers feel they can offer. Particularly, when working for the Big Two, reading or evaluating a fan or amateur's writing increases the chances of potential lawsuits and makes taking on a mentorship role particularly difficult. As such, this practice has declined over the years. While comic book fandom is traditionally associated with the convention, interactions with fans are limited by the time creatives have available to engage in these spaces. Fans at conventions are often discouraged from bringing their own work for evaluation, but they may bring items for autographs, offer their own fan-made objects as gifts, or commission specific work from artists for a fee. How amenable professional artists are to portfolio reviews at such venues varies from person to person. Regardless of publisher, writers and artists use these conventions as opportunities to promote their personal brand with fans, to network with other creators, and to pursue new work opportunities.

Personal brands—and personal relationships with fans—are also cultivated in online spaces in a variety of ways. Some, like DeConnick, use Skype to visit with classrooms and book clubs reading her work. Many of the creatives we spoke with were active on Twitter, Tumblr, and Instagram, although most were clear that they established boundaries around how they engaged with fans through social media. This included turning off the ask functions on Tumblr and direct messaging functions on Twitter, and opting for liking or re-tweeting items from fans. Although some expressed concern about social media management becoming another full-time job, others were more willing to take on extra hours online. Gillen and McKelvie were especially notable for being active in helping cultivate an online fandom for *The Wicked + The Divine*, specifically starting the #WicDiv hashtag to avoid the potentially offensive acronym #TWATD. Gillen also offers writer's notes and music playlists related to *The Wicked + The Divine* on his personal blog, while he and artist McKelvie discuss their creative process on Twitter, making them both visible online personalities (Gillen 2016).

Other creatives prided themselves on channeling fans into offline modes of engagement. Vaughn and Staples, for example, have discouraged readers from using email to respond to *Saga*. Instead, they only accept hard copy letters. In doing so, they hope to cultivate a certain type of fan, one who thinks critically and offers a thoughtful response rather than a gut-reaction Tweet. As Staples explains:

> If you have to sit down and take the time to write it out and then make a trip to the post office, buy a stamp, maybe you'll have cooled off a bit by then and you don't want to send your angry rant about how much you hate us. Because most of the mail is positive. There's still definitely critical letters from people that don't like the book or don't like something about it and we've run a few of those. But at least they're well-reasoned. People took their time with them.

Exercising a greater degree of control over engagement with fans via Image's letter sections is one key way that distinctions in a publisher's business models impact industry–creative–fan dynamics. While DC has public relations PR and marketing teams specifically to do the majority of the work in appealing to fans, creatives at Image can decide for themselves how they will or will not engage with fandom. Likewise, producing work for Image also enables the creative team to conduct research regarding their readership as they see fit, and to develop and market their books in a manner they feel is best suited for their imagined audience. In contrast, market research for DC is most often not accessible by creatives, and development and marketing is not under their purview.

Conclusion and Areas for Future Research

The comparison between Image and DC enables us to bring into relief the similarities and differences between how mainstream and independent comics publishers and their creative teams conceive of and interact with fans. Calling attention to the corporate structures and industrial practices of the comic book industry leads us to consider about the contexts and conditions under which fans are imagined and engaged with differently by distinct publishers—as well as by the creatives that work with these different publishers. More broadly, this study pushes us to think through the instances in which corporate structures, business models, and institutional relationships matter, shaping stakeholder relationships in significant ways.

Looking at the intersection of comics studies, industry studies, and fan studies enables fresh ways of thinking through the industry–creative–fan relationship and further nuances the industry–fan binary. More specifically, this case study demonstrates that the relationships between comic book executives, creatives, and fans in some cases are differentiated along company lines. In other cases, however—such as when creatives approach their work from their own position as fans—variations in business models can have less of an impact on the stories that are told or the ways fans are engaged with by creatives and executives. There remains a need for scholars to more fully consider how the comic book industry cultivates, imagines, and connects with fandom. Especially valuable would be more studies that move beyond top-down political economic/bottom-up cultural studies approaches that tend to reify fandom as oppositional to industry. More such work would be welcome not only within scholarship focused on comics, but also within media industry studies more generally. We also welcome further research that considers how and why different social, economic, cultural, and regional contexts might lead to fans being perceived, engaged with, and valued differently by diverse industry stakeholders.

References

Ang, I. 1991. *Desperately Seeking the Audience.* New York: Routledge.
Asselin, J. 12 June 2015. For Second Year in a Row, Female Readers are a Growing Market. *Comics Alliance*. [online] Retrieved from http://comicsalliance.com/female-readers-growing-market/ [31 December 2016].
Banks, M., B. Conor, and V. Mayer (eds.) 2015. *Production Studies, The Sequel! Cultural Studies of Global Media Industries.* New York: Routledge.
Brooker, W. 2012. *Hunting the Dark Knight: Twenty-First Century Batman.* London: I.B. Tauris.
Brown, J. 1997. Comic Book Fandom and Cultural Capital. *Journal of Popular Culture* 30 (4), 13–31.
Brown, J. 2000. *Black Superheroes, Milestone Comics and Their Fans.* Jackson, MS: University of Mississippi Press.
Burke, L. (ed.) 2013. *Fan Phenomena: Batman.* Intellect.
Burke, L. 2015. *The Comic Book Film Adaptation.* Jackson, MS: University of Mississippi Press.
DC Comics Executive. 2016. Interviewed by Alisa Perren on 13 August 2016. Los Angeles, CA.
DC Entertainment. 2016. Welcome to DC Entertainment. [online] Retrieved from www.dcentertainment.com/ [31 December 2016].
De Connick, K. S. 2016. Interviewed by Laura E. Felschow on 12 August 2016. Telephone.
Dean, M. April 2000. The Image Story Part One. *Comics Journal* (222), 11–14.
Diamond Comics Distributors. 2016. Publisher Market Shares: November 2016. *Diamond Comics*. [online] Retrieved from www.diamondcomics.com/Home/1/1/3/237?articleID=187694 [31 December 2016].
Duncan, R. and M. Smith. 2009. *The Power of Comics: History, Form & Culture.* New York: Continuum International Publishing Group, Inc.
Gabilliet, J.-P. 2009. *Of Comics and Men: A Cultural History of American Comic Books.* Trans. Bart Beaty and Nick Nguyen. Jackson, MS: University of Mississippi Press.
Gillen, K. 2016. Interviewed by Laura E. Felschow on 17 August 2016. Skype.
Gitlin, T. 2000. *Inside Prime Time.* Oakland, CA: University of California Press.
Griepp, M. 30 June 2015. Comics and Graphic Novel Market Sales Hit New 20-Year High. *ICv2*. [online] Retrieved from http://icv2.com/articles/markets/view/31916/comics-graphic-novel-market-sales-hit-new-20-year-high [31 December 2016].
Hanna, E. 2014. Making Fandom Work: Industry Space and Structures of Power at the San Diego Comic-Con. Dissertation. The University of Michigan.
Healey, K. 2009. When Fangirls Perform: The Gendered Fan Identity in Superhero Comics Fandom. In Ndalianis, A. (ed.) *The Contemporary Comic Book Superhero*. New York: Routledge, 144–163.
Image Comics. 2016. Frequently Asked Questions. [online] Retrieved from https://imagecomics.com/about/faq [31 December 2016].
Jenkins, H., and J. Green. 2009. The Moral Economy of Web 2.0: Audience Research and Convergence Culture. In Holt, J. and A. Perren (eds.) *Media Industries: History, Theory, and Method*. Wiley-Blackwell, 213–225.
Johnson, D., D. Kompare, and A. Santo (eds.) 2014. *Making Media Work: Cultures of Management in the Entertainment Industries.* New York: NYU Press.
Jones, G. 2005. *Men of Tomorrow: Geeks, Gangsters, and the Birth of the Comic Book.* New York: Basic Books.
Kohnen, M. 2014. The Power of Geek: Fandom as Gendered Community at Comic-Con. *Creative Industries Journal* 7 (1), 75–78.
Lee, S. and Buscema, J. 1984. *How to Draw Comics the Marvel Way.* New York: Touchtone.
Light, A. 1971–2013. *Comics Buyer's Guide.* Iola, WS: F+W Media.
Lynch, J. 6 June 2016. PwC: Internet Advertising Will Overtake Broadcast Advertising in the U.S. Next Year. *Adweek*. [online] Retrieved from www.adweek.com/news/television/pwc-internet-advertising-will-overtake-broadcast-advertising-us-next-year-171871 [3 January 2017].

McAllister, M.P. 2001. Ownership Concentration in the U.S. Comic Book Industry. In McAllister, M. P., Sewell, Jr, E. H., and Gordon, I. (eds.) *Comics and Ideology*. New York: Peter Lang, 15–38.

McCloud, S. 2006. *Making Comics: Storytelling Secrets of Comics, Manga, and Graphic Novels*. New York: William Morrow Paperbacks.

Meehan, E. 1991. 'Holy Commodity Fetish, Batman!': The Political Economy of a Commercial Intertext. In Pearson, R. and W. Uricchio (eds.) *The Many Lives of Batman*. New York: Routledge, 47–65.

Miller, J. 16 September 2016. More Than 10 Million Comics Ordered in August, Most Since 1996; Harley Quinn is #1. *Comichron*. [online] Retrieved from http://blog.comichron.com/2016/09/more-than-10-million-comics-ordered-in.html [31 December 2016].

MPAA. 2015. Theatrical Market Statistic. MPAA. [online] Retrieved from www.mpaa.org/wp-content/uploads/2016/04/MPAA-Theatrical-Market-Statistics-2015_Final.pdf [4 January 2017].

O'Leary, S. 5 June 2015. Comics Retailer Survey: Good Sales Get Better in 2015. *Publisher's Weekly*. [online] Retrieved from www.publishersweekly.com/pw/by-topic/industry-news/comics/article/67045-comics-retailer-survey-good-sales-get-better-in-2015.html [31 December 2016].

Overstreet, R. 1970–present. *Comic Book Price Guide*. Timonium, MD: Gemstone Publishing.

Pearson, R. E., and W. Uricchio. 1991. *The Many Lives of the Batman: Critical Approaches to a Superhero and His Media*. New York: Routledge.

Pustz, M. 1999. *Comic Book Culture: Fanboys and True Believers*. Jackson, MS: University of Mississippi Press.

Rhoades, S. 2007. *Comic Books: How the Industry Works*. New York: Peter Lang.

Rogers, M. 2006. Understanding Production: The Stylistic Impact of Artisan and Industrial Methods. *International Journal of Comic Art* 8 (1), 509–517.

Rucka, G. 2016. Interviewed by Laura E. Felschow on 12 August 2016. Telephone.

Salazar, K. 2016. Interviewed by Alisa Perren on 11 August 2016. Email.

Schatz, T. 2009. Film Industry Studies and Hollywood History. In Holt, J. and A. Perren (eds.) *Media Industries: History, Theory, and Method*. Malden, MA: Wiley-Blackwell.

Schenker, B. n.d. Demo-graphics. *Graphic Policy*. [online] Retrieved from https://graphicpolicy.com/tag/facebook-fandom/ [31 December 2016].

Scott, S. 2013. Fangirls in the Refrigerator: The Politics of (In)visibility in Comic Book Culture. *Transformative Works and Cultures*, [online] 13. Available at http://journal.transformativeworks.org/index.php/twc/article/view/460/384 [Accessed 2 January 2017].

Smith, G. M. 2011. Surveying the World of Contemporary Comics Scholarship. *Cinema Journal* 50 (3), 135–147.

Staples, F. 2016. Interviewed by Laura E. Felschow on 13 September 2016. Telephone.

Steirer, G. 2011. The State of Comics Scholarship: Comics Studies and Disciplinarity. *International Journal of Comic Art* 13 (2), 263–285.

Stephenson, E. 2016. Interviewed by Alisa Perren on 11 August 2016. Los Angeles, CA.

Swafford, B. 2012. Critical Ethnography: The Comics Shop as Clubhouse. In: Smith, M. and R. Duncan (eds.) *Critical Approaches to Comics: Theories and Methods*. New York: Routledge, 291–302.

Time Warner. 2016. About Us [online] Retrieved from www.timewarner.com/company/about-us [31 December 2016].

Tryon, C. 2013. *On-Demand Culture: Digital Delivery and the Future of Movies*. New Brunswick, NJ: Rutgers University Press.

Woo, B. 2011. The Android's Dungeon: Comic-Bookstores, Cultural Spaces, and the Social Practices of Audiences. *Journal of Graphic Novels and Comics* 2 (2), 125–136.

Woo, B. 2015. Erasing the Lines between Leisure and Labor: Creative Work in the Comics World. *Spectator* 35 (2), 57–64.

Wright, B. 2003. *Comic Book Nation: The Transformation of Youth Culture in America*. Baltimore, MD: Johns Hopkins University Press.

43
SO STRIKE WE ALL
Union Action and Cosplay on the Picket Line

Kate Fortmueller and Suzanne Scott

The press conference officially announcing the SAG-AFTRA strike on July 13, 2023 closed with a question focused on potential fan response to the strikes, directed at the union's President, actress Fran Drescher. When asked, "What is your message to fans and consumers who aren't interested in the nuance that we are discussing here today, they just want their favorite TV shows or they want to go to the movies?," Drescher bristled and pushed back. After pointedly asking, "Well, what makes you think they aren't interested in what's happening here?," Drescher went on to state that fans felt an "allegiance" with creatives (Washington Post 2023). And Drescher was correct: there is a long history of fans advocating for and with creatives against "The Powers That Be," or the studio suits and corporations more focused on commerce than craft. From fan-run "Save Our Show" campaigns dating back to *Star Trek* in 1966, to more contemporary fan critiques of media representations, fan activist efforts have reflected both a growing understanding of how to most effectively manipulate both the mechanics of industry (Savage 2014) and the attention economies of social media (Warner in this collection, Navar-Gill and Stanfill 2018).

This chapter focuses on fan "allegiance" with Hollywood talent during the 2007–8 WGA strike and the 2023 WGA and SAG-AFTRA strike. While fans expressed their solidarity in both of these strikes in various ways, ranging from joining the picket lines, to paying to fly banners over studios, to supplying food and supplies to striking workers, we will be focusing on displays of fannishness from striking workers on the picket lines. Specifically, we are interested in how the use of theme days and cosplay evolved alongside industrial and technocultural shifts that were both the driving force behind the strikes, but also reflect the centrality of fans and the visibility tactics developed in fan communities on social media to the contemporary industry landscape.

In addition to fan support, solidarity from other unions and support from the public provide essential support for striking workers. In the videos of picket lines and the reporting of the 2023 strikes, picketers were often heard ending their chants with the phrase: "L.A. is a union town!" This was apparent in 2023 as the Writers Guild of America (WGA) and Screen Actors Guild – Association of Film, Television, and Radio Artists (SAG-AFTRA) shut down film and television for a total of 187 days. Hollywood is more than the actors, writers, and directors known by their credits, interviews, and red carpet photos; it also consists of thousands of other crew members, drivers, and electricians who help make movie magic, and in the case of the 2023 strike, stopped all work. As the writers and actors walked the sidewalks in front of studios, they were joined by other union workers, many of whom had recently been on strike, including nurses, flight attendants, teachers, Local 11 hotel workers (who were also on strike), as well as fans and aspirants during "hot labor summer." The show of labor solidarity across the industry and city was historic, and demonstrated that the labor culture of Los Angeles has changed tremendously since 1910 when studios relocated to Los Angeles to escape the unions and organizers on the East Coast.

Both fans and the Hollywood unions have ambivalent relationships with the studios and networks that own the rights to intellectual property and fund the production of media, but their antagonistic relationships have different origins. Studios have long sought to control both fans and workers; in the case of fans, studio PR often tried to direct fans to engage with media strictly as consumers, or activate them as an evangelizing promotional force. In the case of workers, the studios sought to keep wages low, despite the importance of media workers. Unions, as the collective bargaining agents for workers, have antagonistic relationships with employers – this is what the fledgling Hollywood studios wanted to avoid. Throughout the 1910s and 1920s, various groups focused on organizing crew members and eventually achieved a contract in 1926 (Horne 2001; Fortmueller and Marzola 2024). Theater actors tried to organize in Hollywood fairly early on, but it was immediately clear that film actors had different problems and needs than those of the stage (Clark 1995; Holmes 2013; Prindle 1988). The audience attachments to film stars were also different; theater actors were famous, but film technologies such as the close-up and the wide distribution of films allowed for broader appeal and attachments with film actors beginning in the silent era (Barbas 2001; Stamp 2000). Studio heads did not want audiences to see images of beloved stars on the picket lines, and even though the actors unionized amid proposed Depression-era belt-tightening in 1933, it would be almost thirty years before stars would walk out of negotiations.

The film and television industries offer some of their workers fame, but in reality the percentage of people who are able to make a good living working in film and television is small. The role of the Hollywood unions is to collectively bargain on behalf of their members for improved working conditions and terms such as minimum pay increases, health and pension benefits, and residuals (payment for the replay of television shows or films). All of these terms are renegotiated every three years, but residual payments are the most contentious. 2023 was not the first time a Hollywood union had gone on strike. The WGA walked out of negotiations seven times prior to 2023 and SAG left the table during two previous negotiations in 1960 and 1980 over their film and television contracts. Historically, Hollywood strikes have either been about working conditions (which were more common in the beginning of the twentieth century) or related to residual payments tied to changes in distribution.

Within the context of fandom and fan studies, the term "labor" is used in far more expansive terms, though often with a similar overarching aim to acknowledge fans as laborers through their own creative production of fanworks (fanfiction, fanart, etc.). Accordingly, the term "fan labor" might be used to describe anything from the value produced through consuming media content, along the lines of Dallas Smythe's conception of the "audience commodity" and how it has evolved (Caraway 2011), to the myriad ways in which digital fan engagement is measured and monetized by the media industries (Napoli 2003; Barker 2022). Fan scholars such as Mel Stanfill have also drawn on theories of affective and emotional labor to characterize much of the work that fans do as a form of "lovebor," or "the work of loving the object of fandom and showing that love," in ways that may or may not ultimately generate value for the industry (Stanfill 2019: 151–153). While some fan scholars have advocated for the importance of fans being able to profit from their labor (De Kosnik 2009; Willard 2020), there are few examples of direct advocacy for remuneration or unionization in response to industrial exploitation of fan labor.

Perhaps the most noteworthy example of the tensions surrounding the monetization of fan labor is the short-lived fanfiction site Fanlib. Founded in 2007 by a variety of media companies (from Simon & Schuster to Showtime), the site sought to commoditize the production and distribution of fanfiction in exchange for proximity to media creators. Fans quickly pushed back on this effort to capitalize on existing fan gift economies, and it exists today only as a notable example of a failed attempt by "(male) venture capitalists to profit financially from (female-generated) fan fiction" (Hellekson 2009: 117). Still, these incidents, as well as the growing centrality of fans as a grassroots marketing force for media industries on social media, have provoked comparisons to other forms of precarious labor in Hollywood and the ways they are increasingly enmeshed with broader digital gig economies.

Thus, while "union labor" and "fan labor" must be approached as distinct, and even possibly divergent, concepts, fans and workers have both been subject to attempts at studio control. Fans and workers have relationships to studios, networks, and streamers, but those are connections born out of necessity and often antagonistic. The 2007–8 and 2023 strikes highlight these connections, both in terms of how fan audiences were imagined within the broader industrial shifts that provoked the strikes, and through the adoption of fan performances on the picket line. The two strikes of the twenty-first century were both inspired by the expansion of digital distribution technologies and their relationship to promotion. In the case of the 2023 strike, the unions demonstrated that they were just as, if not more, adept at using Hollywood's shifting strategies of engagement and promotion to connect the strike to a broader public. In doing so, they drew upon digital fan community and activist tactics to promote their positions, as well as long-standing cosplay practices to increase their visibility on social media platforms.

The rise of digital ecosystems has generated debates around labor and fair compensation for fans and media workers alike. In the case of fans, digital media have been a boon for fans' creative practices but also invariably raised questions around professionalization and compensation for practices and communities rooted in a gift economy model of exchange. For union members, the emergence of digital platforms and streaming media have been incredibly disruptive to long-developed payment structures. Film and television are expensive to make, but media companies take advantage of economies of scope and scale to generate their sizable profits. In the early 2000s, what this meant was releasing film and television to be mass produced as VHS tapes and DVDs, licensed for toys and other merchandise, and also to air on broadcast, cable, and premium cable networks. Studios, networks, and producers made a great deal of profit when films or television shows were sold as VHS/DVD or licensed for rebroadcast because at this point production costs had been spent long ago.

Because films and television shows generate profit even when media workers are unemployed, residuals have been negotiated to fill those revenue gaps created by the freelance nature of media work. Screen residuals were inspired by royalties in music and were an early conversation for the unions as television found its footing as a medium (Porst 2021). Residuals inspired the first writers' strike in 1952, were one of the reasons for the WGA and SAG's first dual strike in 1960, and subsequent strikes in the 1980s onward were tied to residuals for new media. Digital distribution of media does not require the production costs of video and DVD and allows for more replays. For media workers, this combination of factors has allowed for studios to make more money from their film and television shows without compensating their talent accordingly. As studios reaped more profit and extracted more promotional work from talent, unions have turned their attention to negotiating contract terms to appropriately compensate this work – ongoing changes to distribution methods and departures from traditional film and television formats were some of the core issues in the 2007–8 WGA strike and 2023 WGA and SAG-AFTRA strikes.

When the writers walked out in 2007, digital distribution was in its infancy, but for the unions its potential to revolutionize film and television distribution was clear. Tech companies demonstrated the potential of digital video when the free (and now ad-supported) YouTube launched in 2005, followed by Amazon Prime Video in 2006 and Netflix in early 2007. Although Hollywood talent missed out on residuals for the films and shows licensed to these platforms, traditional film and television jobs made up the bulk of paid work for professional writers and digitally born writing consisted of short webisodes rather than full series episodes. However, it was precisely the increased slippage between webisodes and other forms of ancillary web content aimed at fans, and canonical narrative content valued by fans, that created solidarity between writers and television fans during the 2007–8 strike. Transmedia storytelling and franchising trends, industrially motivated by horizontal integration and the growing valuation of second screen "engagement" as an audience metric, were key drivers of the 2007–8 strike.

Writers like *Battlestar Galactica* showrunner Ronald D. Moore decried studio efforts to paint webisodes and other ancillary narrative web content created by union writers, directors, and actors as purely "promotional," and thus uncompensated, work. Speaking from the WGA picket lines in 2007, Moore argued that this stance was "undercutting everything that the writers have built up in other media" (qtd. in Goldman 2007). On this point, fans were a clear source of solidarity, both as the desired target audience for the emergent forms of ad-supported content, and as a collective that similarly viewed "The Resistance" webisodes that premiered online before Season 3 of the *Syfy* series as core canonical narrative content. For fans, Moore's picket line prediction that "Your television and your computer are going to become the same device within the foreseeable future" (qtd. in Goldman 2007) was already a reality for many participatory fan cultures.

Fast forward to 2023, and many of the key industry players are the same but the production and distribution landscape has caught up to Moore's 2007 prediction. Amazon, Netflix, and now Apple are not simply licensing and circulating content from legacy studios and networks, but are producing and distributing their own films and television shows. For Hollywood workers and their residuals this is an important distinction, as residuals are calculated based on platform of release and platform of replay. Despite its prominence in the media landscape, streaming companies have insisted that digitally born content was less profitable and thus the residual rates should be low. Fans were also more actively caught up in the 2023 strikes, which for the first time included guidelines for social media influencers, signaling that the social media promotion landscape had also changed considerably since 2007–8. The further mainstreaming and professionalization of fan identities and performances in the intervening years meant that cosplayers and fan influencers who had struck deals with Hollywood studios to promote content had to seriously weigh their own aspirations to someday join Hollywood labor unions. Even within amateur fan creator communities, concerns about performing solidarity with striking workers quickly arose, with some fans suggesting they would not promote any struck work until the strike was resolved.

Reflecting the growing melding of fan and media worker concerns, comic book and television writer Julie Benson observed in a tweet on May 24, 2023, "The Superhero Day picket line at Warner Bros was like San Diego Comic Con. And at this rate, SDCC will probably be like picket day at Warner Bros. See you there with my sign, fellow geeks!" Benson's prediction was only partially realized: with SAG-AFTRA strike authorization occurring mere days before San Diego Comic-Con 2024, many fans expressed solidarity with striking writers and actors, as well as a willingness to join picket lines at the fan convention. Despite a brief appearance from SAG-AFTRA strikers for a photo-op with signs and a few cosplayers recruited to mark the event, the con never resembled a studio picket line. Studio picket lines in 2023, however, *did* resemble a fan convention, replete with "theme days" centered around specific genres and media properties, cosplay, and cast "reunions" (ranging from nostalgic 1990s fare like *Boy Meets World,* complete with a special in-character message from Mr. Feeny on the WGA Instagram, to buzzy contemporary hits like Apple+'s *Severance*, whose season had been delayed by the strike). Or, at least, this is what much of the social media strategy for the strike foregrounded, banking on the increased visibility of fannish spectacle and fan engagement with these posts to keep the strike in the headlines.

In reality, the vast majority of striking workers, not unlike the bulk of Comic-Con's 125,000 annual attendees, wore functional outfits consisting of statement T-shirts, jeans, and sneakers – a necessary uniform for those who spend a great deal of time walking and standing. Writing about an early rally in front of Fox in 2007, journalist Cynthia Littleton described the strikers: "The dress code for the morning was the new picket-line chic: jeans, crimson WGA T-shirts, sneakers, and baseball caps. Some wore T-shirts specially made for the occasion with messages decrying corporate greed, studio bosses, and, in a few cases, the Bush administration" (Littleton 2013). Similarly, many on the picket lines in 2023 donned union T-shirts along with hats and shorts to beat the summer heat. Also similar to Comic-Con, the most visible people in news and social media coverage were the ones who displayed the most creativity, whether this was through costumes, toys (e.g., Chucky dolls), or illustrations or humorous commentary on picket signs.

The potential for media coverage of fannish spectacle to draw public attention and build fan support for the broader conditions and stakes for striking workers was noted in a 2007 *Los Angeles Times* article. Covering *Star Trek* Day, reporter Deborah Netburn (2007) opened the article with a conventionally pathologizing tone ("One never knows what those crazy 'Star Trek' fans might do.") before wearily acknowledging, "Let's face it, the town is five weeks into the strike, so an inspired, theme-dressing event can only help attract attention now that newer and more scandalous headlines are winning over the fight for prime placement." Noting that "a few Klingons in the crowd would make a nice photo-op.

Or, at the very least, somebody in one of those skin-tight crew member outfits," Netburn disappointedly reported that "all we got were roughly a fifth of the 150 strikers wearing special WGA-issued 'Star Trek' tees." While this event was framed as "not a total washout" for fans, who mingled with and snapped photos of the franchise's actors and writers, Netburn's palpable disappointment in the lack of fan spectacle is revealing. By 2023, the WGA and SAG-AFTRA had recognized the power of social media traction, and codified themed pickets as a cornerstone of their awareness raising strategy (see Figure 43.1).

On this point, it is illustrative to compare the design and coverage of horror theme days from the 2007–8 and 2023 strikes. On November 27, 2007, a small collective of film horror writers gathered to perform an "exorcism" of Warner Bros. Studios. A solo saxophone player performed the theme to *The Exorcist* and other iconic horror scores, and a handful of writers dressed as priests and nuns gathered outside the Warner Bros. gates to "undertake the expulsion of diabolical infestation from this studio and its masters" (wgaamerica 2007). Sprinkling "holy water" to cast out the "enemy of the guild, originator of corporate greed, robber of internet residuals," the cosplaying "priest" led the crowd in chants of "Out, demons, out!" The vast majority of participants merely wore horror-themed T-shirts and carried picket signs with the slogan "We eat scabs." Thus, while costumes on the picket line were used sparingly in the 2007–8 strike to both perform

Figure 43.1 Screengrab of themed picket schedule posted to the WGA's Instagram Stories.

fan attachment to particular genres and media texts as well as draw the attention of fans and reporters, writers more actively took advantage of the technologies fans were using to create community and share news. WGA members wrote on blogs, updated websites, and posted often humorous YouTube videos to share their message, which was a counter to the Alliance of Motion Picture and Television Producers' (AMPTP) expensive anti-strike ads in newspapers and business trades (Banks 2010). This was an effective tool, but may have further demonstrated the value of digital media to studios.

In 2023 the unions made ample use of the technological affordances and culture of social media as well as existing fan networks on these platforms. Rebekah McKendry, one of the organizers of two horror-themed strikes, put a great deal of care into her themed strikes. McKendry (2024) explained: "Everything that we did with these strikes, especially the two that I organized. It was all very strategically planned, like it wasn't just show up and show Netflix that you're angry. [We asked ourselves] How do we get press there? How do we make a lot of noise? How do we draw attention to ourselves?" To get attention McKendry drew on her time as director of marketing at *Fangoria*, a well-established horror fan magazine, and reached out to her favorite press outlets, influencers, and the hosts of the YouTube channel *Dead Meat* to come take pictures and cover the picket.

Speaking about the first 2023 horror picket, McKendry (2024) described it as a beautiful mix, including "people who have made $200,000 horror films in their backyards, people who were shooting stuff for *SyFy*, all the way up to Mike Flanagan and Brian Fuller." Beyond a mix of writers, the crowd was populated with composers, musicians who had brought along instruments, fans (including one who had driven from Vegas to show his solidarity with the people who make his favorite films) and of course, people sporting horror T-shirts, carrying themed signs, and dressed like nightmare-inducing characters including Michael Myers, Samara (Figure 43.2), and the Art the Clown. The picket line was a who's who of horror writers, directors, and actors showing off their creativity in the only way they could in the summer of 2023. The result was widespread coverage that went viral beyond industry trades as horror fans shared and reshared images of the horror picket lines. As McKendry (2024) explained, this demonstrated widespread support: "It's one thing if they [the AMPTP] think the writers are angry. It's another thing if they know that the horror fans are angry too."

The themed pickets also reflected union members' own fannish predilections and participation in fan practices. One of the theme days that more explicitly encouraged cosplay, or dressing up and embodying a particular character from a media text, was the *Bridgerton* picket outside of Netflix on July 18, 2023. Framed as an invitation from Lady Whistledown herself to "spill the tea on the AMPTP," the widely circulated call to participate in the themed picket promised afternoon tea and instructed workers to "Come dressed in your Regency best and protest the bureaucracy of the ton." In addition to being thematically resonant (*Bridgerton*, after all, is a show preoccupied with financial security, social status, and various power imbalances), the primary reason this particular themed picket garnered so much media coverage was its visible cosplaying contingent of striking workers (Figure 43.3). Baseball hats were replaced by parasols and delicate fans emblazoned with the words "ON STRIKE." Striking workers took to Instagram to show off their costumes, coupled with captions that bridged performances of fan affect for the series with consciousness raising: "a truly *scandalous* day on the picket line. did you hear? they're even trying to starve us out of homes. what horror! lady whistledown must know…" The bulk of these

So Strike We All: Union Action and Cosplay on the Picket Line

Figure 43.2 Picketer dressed as Samara from *The Ring* during the 2023 horror-themed picket during the WGA strike.

Instagram posts tagged the user's respective guild and strike slogans (e.g., #wga, #wgastrike, #wgastrong), along with theme day-specific slogans (#quillsdown) and #bridgerton, clearly aiming to cross over with fans searching the show's tag on social media.

Notably, several of the listed organizers of the *Bridgerton* picket line had existing ties to fan cosplay communities. Writer Brittney Jeng's personal statement in their WGA directory profile speaks explicitly and extensively to how their fandom has been central to navigating both their professional and personal identity. Specifically, Jeng cites discovering fandom and cosplay as a revelatory experience:

> Behind my costume, I felt free and confident to truly be my nerdy silly self. My costume became my armor.... The only things my fellow cosplay enthusiasts cared about was my dedication to the character and craft of my costumes – which they always

Figure 43.3 Screengrab of WGA Instagram post coverage of the *Bridgerton* themed picket.

praised me for. I reveled in the joy I found in cosplay. Because for the first time, I got to choose who I wanted to be instead of allowing others to decide for me.

Jeng's reflection echoes scholar Nicolle Lamerich's description of the embodied experience of cosplaying as an "affective process," offering the fan a space to mutually work through their own identity and their relationship to a fictional world or character, culminating in a "supreme moment" in which the costume is worn in public at a convention (2018: 208). Cosplay on the picket line, in the case of union members like Jeng already fannishly involved in the practice, might function similarly. However, for other striking workers the affective process of choosing to cosplay on the picket line and the "supreme moment" it produces, is unique. For example, a consideration of the May 18, 2023 *Newsies* picket outside of Disney would need to take into account how the 1992 film's overt themes about labor unions, the Walt Disney Company's long history of aggressively protecting their intellectual property, nostalgia for the film amongst WGA members, and the ease of cosplaying the film's characters (vests and flat caps), converged to produce a particular "supreme moment."

Similarly, while some union members might partake in a themed picket as part of an affective process tied to either their own fan connection to a particular media property or cosplay as a practice, others view themed pickets as essential to maintaining the momentum within the movement. One of the other organizers of the *Bridgerton* themed picket, genre writer and IATSE member Pepper Reed, recalled in a May 2024 interview that Jeng approached her on the picket line about the possibility of co-coordinating a *Bridgerton* theme day because she was walking the line wearing a Regency style dress. Reed (2024) doesn't self-identify as a cosplayer, but rather someone who enjoys making and wearing historically inspired fashion in daily life. According to Reed, Jeng, along with many of the other picketers in cosplay, already owned Regency dress because they had attended the "The Queen's Ball: A *Bridgerton* Experience," a paid fan activation held in major cities across America in 2022. Donning a Regency dress at a fan activation versus engaging in labor activism on the picket line creates two diametrically opposed "supreme moments," one focused on immersion in a fictional world and the other designed to disrupt real-world public space.

Just as the immersive "Queen's Ball" fan experience was timed to promote and capitalize on the fan activity around the release of Season 2 of *Bridgerton*, Reed (2024) credits the timing of the themed picket (on the heels of the release of *Queen Charlotte: A Bridgerton Story*) as well as the location for its success, as streamer Netflix was known for having the largest media coverage presence of any of the studios during the strike. Quipping that more people had seen her reel of the *Bridgerton* picket on Instagram than short films she has written and directed, Reed acknowledged that the themed pickets and tagging posts with broader media properties certainly helped to garner visibility with both news media and reaching fan audiences. However, Reed ultimately claims that the themed picket "wasn't for that," but rather "It was for us," for those walking the line. Reed, who walked the line for all but 6 of the 187 days of strikes, noted:

> It's a grind. It's a lot to get up every morning and go to the picket line and walk.... It's about giving some kind of joy, some kind of excitement, to something that's really hard.... So, it definitely got a lot of attention, but it wasn't for outside, it was because we all loved *Bridgerton*.... Anytime people could go dressed up... it just gave a little bit of a lift to something that was exhausting. (Reed 2024)

What Reed is describing is certainly, like cosplaying, an embodied experience driven by affective process, and one where "the affective reception of fans cannot be divided from the social community that thrives around these texts" (Lamerichs 2018 207).

Speaking to the differences between the 2007–8 and 2023 strikes, both Rebekah McKendry (2024) and Reed (2024) noted the importance of community on the picket line. McKendry described the horror pickets as a wide range of fans, workers, and aspirants and noted that both in person and on social media, "the fans got involved a lot more than they did in the prior one [2007–8]." For Reed, the affective experience of the strike was also about her own position in the industry and her belonging within it, which increased palpably during the 2023 strike. One of the binding factors on the picket line, according to Reed, was a fannish investment in media: "The biggest thing is... we just love film and television and we want to be able to do it, we are fans of the stuff that we write... it's really hard to make a living in the industry, so we're all here because we love it... We love our fandoms."

The core issues workers go on strike for, which include the nuances of working conditions and remuneration, can often be seen as irrelevant to those outside the industry. The 2023 pickets revealed that the distinctions between professional and fan identities can often blur. Looking at how fan activities became intertwined with labor action is one way of understanding the increasingly porous boundaries between fan and professional within digital cultures and media industries that continually seek to exploit passion.

References

Banks, M. (2010) "The Picket Line Online: Creative Labor, Digital Activism, and the 2007–2008 Writers Guild of America Strike." *Popular Communication* 8(1), pp. 20–33.

Barbas, S. (2001) *Movie Crazy*. New York: Palgrave.

Barker, C. (2022) *Social TV: Multi-Screen Content and Ephemeral Culture*. Jackson: University Press of Mississippi.

Benson, J. (2023) [Twitter/X] May 24. Available at: https://x.com/TheJulieBenson/status/1661482076837920769 [Accessed May 1, 2024].

Caraway, B. (2011) "Audience Labor in the New Media Environment: A Marxian Revisiting of the Audience Commodity," *Media, Culture & Society* 33(5), pp. 693–708.

Clark, D. (1995) *Negotiating Hollywood: The Cultural Politics of Actors' Labor*. Minneapolis: University of Minnesota Press.

De Kosnik, A. (2009) "Should Fan Fiction Be Free?," *Cinema Journal* 48(4), pp. 118–124.

Fortmueller, K. and Marzola, L. (2024) *Hollywood Unions*. New Brunswick, NJ: Rutgers University Press.

Goldman, E. (2007) *Battlestar Galactica Producer Talks Strike*. IGN 14 May. Available at: www.ign.com/articles/2007/11/08/battlestar-galactica-producer-talks-strike [Accessed May 1, 2024].

Hellekson, K. (2009) "A Fannish Field of Value: Online Fan Gift Culture," *Cinema Journal* 48(4), pp. 113–118.

Holmes, Sean P. (2013) *Weavers of Dreams, Unite!: Actors' Unionism in Early Twentieth-Century America*. Urbana: University of Illinois Press.

Horne, G. (2001) *Class Struggle in Hollywood, 1930–1950: Moguls, Mobsters, Stars, Reds, and Trade Unionists*. Austin: University of Texas Press.

Jeng, B. (n. d.) *Personal Statement*. Available at: https://directories.wga.org/member/brittneyjeng [Accessed May 17, 2024].

Lamerichs, N. (2018) *Productive Fandom. Intermediality and Affective Reception in Fan Cultures*. Amsterdam: Amsterdam University Press.

Littleton, C. (2013) *TV on Strike: Why Hollywood Went to War Over the Internet*. Syracuse: Syracuse University Press.

McKendry, R. (2024) *Interview with Kate Fortmueller*. May 22, online.

Napoli, P.M. (2003) *Audience Economics: Media Institutions and the Audience Marketplace*. New York: Columbia University Press.

Navar-Gill, A. and Mel Stanfill (2018) "'We Shouldn't Have to Trend to Make You Listen': Queer Fan Hashtag Campaigns as Production Interventions," *Journal of Film and Video* 70(3–4), pp. 85–100.

Netburn, D. (2007) 'WGA's 'Star Trek' day: Live long and picket,' *Los Angeles Times* 10 December. Available at: www.latimes.com/archives/blogs/show-tracker/story/2007-12-10/wgas-star-trek-day-live-long-and-picket [Accessed May 1, 2024].

Porst, J. (2021) *Broadcasting Hollywood: The Struggle Over Feature Films on Early TV*. New Brunswick, NJ: Rutgers University Press.

Prindle, D. (1988) *The Politics of Glamour: Ideology and Democracy in the Screen Actors Guild*. Madison: University of Wisconsin Press.

Reed, P. (2024) *Interview with Suzanne Scott*. May 23, online.

Stamp, S. (2000) *Movie-Struck Girls: Women and Motion Picture Culture After the Nickelodeon*. Princeton: Princeton University Press.

Savage, C. (2014) "*Chuck* versus the Ratings: Savvy Fans and 'Save Our Show' Campaigns." In "Fandom and/as Labor," edited by Mel Stanfill and Megan Condis, Special Issue, Transformative Works and Cultures, no. 15. https://doi.org/10.3983/twc.2014.0497.

Stanfill, M. (2019) *Exploiting Fandom: How the Media Industry Seeks to Manipulate Fans*. Iowa City: University of Iowa Press.

Wgaamerica (2007) *The Exorcism of Warner Bros.* Youtube [Online Video]. Available at: www.youtube.com/watch?v=kl2f8Duqdyw [Accessed May 20, 2024].

Washington Post (2023) *WATCH: Actors union holds news conference on pending strike*. Youtube [Online Video]. Available at: www.youtube.com/watch?v=H-OpxNr87jk. [Accessed May 17, 2024].

Willard, L. (2020) *From Hobby to Side Hustle: Fan Artist Professionalization in the Post-Network Era*. PhD Thesis. University of Texas at Austin.

INDEX

AAVE *see* African American Vernacular English (AAVE)
Abbey Road Studios 145
ABC Studios 301, 386
academics 108; activism by 336; misgendering by 313; non-white 338; politicization of 106; *see also* acafans
acafans 11, 17, 36, 243; of color 304; *see also* African American Acafandom
ACG *see* anime-comics-games (ACG)
adolescence 301–303, 305, 346
aesthetic: forms and language 178; modes 183; musical 272; on Tumblr 178; traditions 175
affect 417, 420–421; for comics 256
affection 2, 35, 118, 133, 161, 209, 354
affective: consumption practice 286–287; entanglements fans and BL media 326–328; experience 182, 323, 453; expression 256; language 184
affiliations, neo-tribal 369
affirmational 416–418, 420, 421
African American Acafandom 217
African American Vernacular English (AAVE) 234
age 155–156, 285–286, 301–308
AI *see* artificial intelligence (AI)
Alliance of Motion Picture and Television Producers (AMPTP) 450
Alternate Reality Game (ARG) 415–416, 419
alternative modernity 292–293, 297
Amazon 126, 232, 354, 447
American: comic books 433–439; cultural imperialism 267; fans 72, 338
American film: history of 91–93; industry 96
American Horror Story 306
Americanization 112, 198–199
American/Western fan networks 32–39
AMTP *see* Alliance of Motion Picture and Television Producers (AMTP)

An Archive of Our Own (AO3) 23–24, 34, 37–38, 60, 81–82, 84, 86, 159, 176, 193, 240, 355, 359; and femslash 240; Hugo award 2
Anderson, B. 73, 262, 267, 293, 426
Android 194
Ang, I. 72, 76, 233, 291, 438
Anglo-American: communities of shared interest 76; contexts and traditions 61; fandom 46; media industries 71
anime 77, 145–146, 333, 407; and frikis 410–411
anime-comics-games (ACG) 46
animeflv 411
ante-fandom 41–42, 44–45, 47
anti-Blackness 27
anti-fandom 24–25, 100, 116, 270, 397
anti-fans 24, 147, 152, 270–271, 274, 397
anti-racism 24–26
AO3 *see* An Archive of Our Own (AO3)
AoIR *see* Association of Internet Researchers (AoIR)
API *see* application programming interface (API)
Apple 447–448
application programming interface (API) 84–86
archives (rogue) *see* rogue archives
ARG *see* Alternate Reality Game (ARG)
artifact: artistic 14; fannish 15
artificial intelligence (AI): AI-generated fanfiction 342, 359; ChatGPT 86, 359; DALL-E 86; Midjourney 86; models 86
Association of Internet Researchers (AoIR), 12–14, 83; Principles for Internet Research 83
audience: black 156; children's 407; engagement 415–416; studies 334
autobiography 124, 308
autographs 380–382, 440
Avatar: The Last Airbender 157, 159, 236
Ayanga 208–214

456

Bacon-Smith, C. 1, 31–35, 72, 112, 115, 227, 233, 242, 313, 316, 373, 387
Banet-Weiser, S. 287, 348
Barbie 1, 286
barriers: economic 233; geographic 262; language and cultural 112, 133, 135, 139, 338; of communication and participation 62, 137; to participation for disabled fans 188–189
Battlestar Galactica 200, 447
BBC 129, 146, 426–427
beauty 228, 276, 289; Benefit Cosmetics 281–283; #Colourpop 288; CoverGirl 228, 281, 283–287; culture 281–286, 288–289; #ForceBeauty 284, 288; YouTube 364
behaviors: affective 374; anti 24; comic book fans 434, 438; consumer 375, 377–378, 382; decoding 8; destructive 165; fanatical 165; fannish 93; lurking 62; of fan tourists 144, 148; political 367; prosocial 103, 108; psychiatric 65; Shifting 165, 168; toxic 101, 369
Bennett, A. 151–152, 154–157, 159–161, 303, 305
Bielby, D. D. 227, 275, 301, 305, 307–308
Big Name Fans 200
#BillionGirlSummer 1–2
Biltereyst, D. 245
binge-watching 120–121
Black, Indigenous, People of Color (BIPOC) 254
BL *see* Boy(s) Love (BL)
Black 154–161, 254, 414; audience 156; fandoms 251, 316, 386–387, 391–392; lead character 161, 253, 316, 342, 384, 388–392; media 271; women 251, 384, 391–392; Women of Color (WOC) 254–255
Black Lives Matter (BLM) 3, 27
Black Panther 255
Black, R. 134, 136
Black Spider-Man 253
Black Widow 282
The Blair Witch Project 416
BLM *see* Black Lives Matter (BLM)
blockbuster 159, 415
bloggers 398, 414
Blumer, H. 93, 237
Blu-ray 126, 130, 418
Bobo, J. 156, 387
Bollywood: Bollynatyam's Global Bollywood Dance Project 331; dance 331; fandoms 332–335, 337; films 338; Prague Festival 337
BOOM! Studios 433, 435
Booth, P. 44, 116, 178
bots 85, 105–106, 359
Bourdieu, P. 118, 231, 236–237

Bowie, David 124
Boy(s) Love (BL) 32–33, 133, 228, 322–328, 408
Boys Love Manga and Beyond 32
brand 438–439; awareness 282–283; community 288; corporate 345, 416; culture 73, 437; franchise 346, 400; identification 350, 435, 437; lifestyle 341, 348; loyalty 415, 417; maintenance 439; merchandise 348; owners 349; personal 440; TV- 414; unity 427
branding 22, 147, 251, 282–289, 348, 351, 401
British cultural studies 72, 153, 242
broadcast: airings 377; DAZN 428; league play 424; media 275; networks 375; television 406–407; Turkish soap operas 297; women's soccer 425–427
BTS 261
Buffy the Vampire Slayer 129, 160, 242, 247, 347–348, 367
"Bury your Gays" trope 246, 367
Bush, Kate 52–55, 57
Busse, K. 120, 175, 178, 182, 223, 235, 244–245, 254, 313–315, 355, 416, 420

CAC *see* Cyberspace Administration of China (CAC)
cancel culture 342, 363–369; agents 363, 368; China 364, 366, 368–369; combatting 369; deplatforming 342; discourses 363–364; events 363–367, 369; Joss Whedon 367; politics 363–369; practices 363; targets 363, 365; triggers 363–365; Xiao Zhan 369
canon 15–16, 43, 116, 124, 126, 128, 132–138, 159–161, 200, 316, 416, 418–421
capital: cultural 44, 61, 200, 265, 268, 346–348, 437; economic 265; financial 264; linguistic 234; political 314
Captain America 221, 401
Captain Marvel 251, 437
Cartoon Network 351, 407
casting 2, 155, 157–159, 161, 236, 377, 384, 397; colorblind 388; fan- 159, 384
Cavicchi, D. 90–91
celebrity fans 112, 208, 212–213; Chinese 112, 207–213
children 91–92, 155, 275, 349, 406–407, 411; of color 155
Chin, B. 74, 323
Cho, A. 177, 181–182
cisgender 36, 63–64, 198, 241, 312, 316, 324–325, 328
class 146, 153, 156, 237; differences 348; economic 232, 252–253, 274, 276, 288; frikis 406; in sport 342; middle 36, 92, 127, 198, 233–235; privileges of 396; social aspects of

Index

78, 93, 292, 409; working 242, 273–274, 276, 293
classic 217, 284, 292, 305, 318, 326
Click, M. A. 100, 313, 397, 420
collectibles 289, 347, 375, 378, 411
collecting: cultures of 282; fanfiction 356; feminized 285; male 289; neo- 22, objects 346–347, 408
colonialism 65, 67
comic book: fans 231, 252–254, 433–435, 438, 440; franchises 281–282; industry 441; IP 437; publishers 257; series 255–256; stores 439
commercial: exploitation 146; market 130, 314; media 33, 182, 243; promotion 125; spaces 144; value 2
commodification 66, 92, 143–144, 244, 359, 374–375
commodity 287, 323; "audience" 445–446; culture 351; feminism 287–289; girl power 282; politics 382
communal: activity 45, 62; creative production 355; culture 172; experience 345; gift economy 358; practices 146; relations 116, 119
communities 39; affective 287, 323; female 235, 421; participation 125, 350; pluralist 251, 387; transcultural 263, 328
consumer(s) 2, 244, 252, 301, 374, 382, 396, 406; activism 395; audience as 288; behavior 363, 375; culture 92–93, 285, 324, 346–347, 382; feminism 282, 285; of K-pop 261; of media object 3; products 94, 349, 379, 400, 435
consumerism 292, 345, 348, 395
conventions 32, 36, 91, 124, 127, 233, 247, 350, 373–382; friki 342, 409–411; SDCC 420, 448
convergence culture 4, 434–435
Coppa, F. 32, 35–36, 38, 60, 62–63, 127, 172, 187, 202, 313, 419
cosplay 155, 170, 192, 197, 281, 284–286, 289, 318, 342, 375–376, 408–409, 440, 444
counterpublic 156, 245
crip theory 8, 63–64
crowdfunding 331, 336
cult: fan 286–287; fashion 283; film 130; geographies 142; media 235; music 130; series 420; texts 200, 399
cultural: affinities 297; appropriation 42, 245; capital 44; criticism 232, 236; diversity 236; imperialism 73; invasion 293; politics of race 434; practices 268; products 297; proximity 265–266, 338; systems 74, 261; theory 92; value 190–191
Cumberbatch, Benedict 7, 75–77

CW Network 336, 384, 388, 392
Cyberspace Administration of China (CAC) 366, 369

Dallas 72, 76
data scraping 8, 81–82, 84
DAZN 342, 424–429
DC Comics 341, 384, 433, 435–437, 439
decoding 8, 47, 125, 153, 295, 326
decolonization 28, 61–62, 66
DeConnick, Kelly Sue 437, 439, 440
De Kosnik, A. 82, 350, 359
Deller, R. 51, 307
demographics 1, 241, 302, 324, 400, 415, 436, 438–439
DeviantArt 86, 175–176, 203
digital: activism 363; circulation 282, 285, 288; collection 285; community 317; content 254, 256; culture 282, 285–228, 288, 387; ethnography 364; fan communities 446; following 287; forums and fan-fiction repositories 234; humanities 81, 108; literacies 289; media 46, 100, 126, 193, 341, 446, 450; networks 385; platforms 243, 350, 363, 369, 438; rights 429; streaming 275; technologies 243–244, 440
Digital Millennium Copyright Act (DMCA) 219
disability 60–67, 187–193, 241, 253, 317; decolonial approach to 61–63, 66–67; *see also* mental disability; *see also* neurodiversity
Disney 130, 144, 148, 159, 184, 242, 349, 351, 408, 433, 452
DMCA *see* Digital Millennium Copyright Act (DMCA)
Doctor Who 47, 66, 107, 126, 129, 138, 147, 306–307, 358, 376, 420; *Profeta no Brasil* 135, 138
dōjinshi/doujinshi 33
Douban 112, 208, 212–213
Dreamwidth (DW) 75, 175–176, 182, 193
Duffet, M. 147–148, 252
Duggan, J. 245, 312–316, 318
Dungeons & Dragons 200, 237
DW *see* Dreamwidth (DW)

empirical: evidence 116, 292; research data 51, 292, 332; whiteness 232; work 43–44
encoding-decoding 41–43; 153, 157
ephemera 91, 94–96, 128–129, 349, 373
ethics: of fan studies 11–18; of fan tourism 149; of scraping Facebook data 85; survey 51–57
ethnic 268; assimilation 273; background 293; boundaries 272; diversity 152; heritage 253–254, 265, 271; identity 296–297; media 271; minorities 65, 204, 233

Index

ethnicity 78, 93, 111, 126, 157, 159, 227, 232, 235, 237, 265–266, 274, 338; Chinese 256; social identity 301; and whitewashing 333

ethnography 313; ethnographic interviews 252, 254; fan research 18; for fan studies 51, 335; for transcultural fan studies 331; in cancel culture 364; virtual 313

ethos 14, 190, 351

European: fandom 197, 242; football 424, 426, 427–429; markets 274

Facebook 12, 25, 39, 82, 85, 117–118, 190, 204, 323, 409–410, 438

factions 369, 386, 396

fan communities 175–178, 181, 184, 187–193, 198–199, 201, 204, 207–213, 218, 227, 231–234, 236–237, 242–243, 282, 285, 292, 303, 305–307, 314, 335, 341, 346–348, 350–351, 357–358, 386, 396, 420–421, 444; Ayanga and Yunlong 209, 213; celebrity 212; Chinese celebrity 214; Latinx 228; Polish 197, 199, 205

fan conventions: Comic-Con 282–284, 341–342, 347, 350, 414, 416, 420, 448; Comiket 33; Mexico City 410–411; San Diego 373–382; Wiscon 240

fan curation 125, 167–168; curation history of 127–130; *curators* 124–125, 347

fan research 52, 81; scholars 22, 26, 28, 81; scholarship 60; studies 7–8, 235

fan studies 124, 142–143, 148–149, 187–188, 194, 197–198, 217, 220, 227–228, 231–235, 237, 240–245, 253–254, 257–258, 271, 277, 291, 304, 312, 316, 327, 341, 387, 434

fan(s) 3–4; activism 245–246, 314; activities 74, 95, 152, 201, 208, 233, 262, 408; aging 227, 301–308; allegiance 350, 365; amateur 129; and fan object 46, 391; and interface 175; anti- 44, 152; appeal 425; archives 33, 37; -art 159, 203, 211; artists 159, 178; association 285; audience 57, 446, 453; authors 60, 128, 356; autobiography 124; behaviors 95, 165, 199, 202–203, 323, 373, 438; blogs 15, 42; -branded collaborations 285; Brazilian 133; business 350; campaign 367; cancel practices 364; canons 130; -casting 159, 384; Chinese 112, 369; circle disorder 369; -clubs 32, 36, 129, 199, 263; collector 347; combativeness 399; communication 175; culture 1, 3, 22–23, 25, 28, 37–39, 46, 51, 53, 56–57, 62, 72, 74, 90–91, 93–96, 111, 126, 143–144, 177, 201–202, 204, 228, 246, 251, 263, 266, 286–287, 333, 338, 342, 345, 374–375, 391, 425, 429; demands 395; descriptors 61; discourse 66, 207, 212, 232, 307, 327, 429;

discussion 120, 241; entitlement 156, 341, 394–396, 398; experience 183–184, 211, 326, 387; -fiction 354, 356; -fashion 281–285; follower 62; *gatherings* 124; globalization 198; history of 32–33, 36, 44, 82, 85, 90, 96, 125, 128; and film exhibition history 94; hyper-consumerism 348; identities 213; identity politics 28; in youth and adolescence 301; is broken 395; Korean (South) 32, 228, 261, 264, 266–267; Latinx 270–271, 276; lingua franca 203; magazines 92–96; makeup lines 282; nationalism 368; networks 267; norms 157; on Tumblr 182; parasocial relations 45; pilgrimage 146; Polish 199, 204; racism 316; spaces 11, 14, 24–27, 60, 81–82, 232, 285, 314, 318, 324, 420; tourism 142–149; toxic 101

fanboy(s) 197, 235, 237, 399, 420

fandom: affirmational 420; aging 301–308; algorithm 36–38; anti- 24; Anti Wars 358; Asia 7, 228, 338 *see also* Boy(s) Love (BL); authentic 401; Black female 384–391 *see also* Iris West Defense Squad (IWDS); BL media 323; China 369; comic book 440; combativeness in 25; conventions 373–379; disabled 66–67; feminized 281–289; femslash 243–247; gatekeeping 252–257; gatherings 127; Greece 291–297; killjoy 25; K-pop 262–263 *see also* K-pop; Korean *see* K-pop, *see also* Boy(s) Love (BL); Latinx 270–276; media 33–39, 41–46; merchandise 345–351; mental health 67; Mexico City 407–411; movie 90–97; norms 354–359; older 303–308; online 440; pathologies 165–166; pilgrimage 143; platformized 43, 45, 354; Poland 197–204; politics of cancel culture 363–369; practices, protective 46; privilege in 394–401; quality 415–417, 419–421; queer 312–319; reactionary fandom 26; *Sherlock* 75–78; soccer 424–429; surveys 51–58; toxic 100–109; transcultural 21–28, 331–339; transnational 74–77; white male 435; whiteness of 235–237

fanfiction 13–14, 18, 39, 228, 350–351; fanfiction.net 81, 203, 234; podfic 228, 312–320; qualitative analysis of 112

fangirl(s) 272, 396

FanLib 356

fannish 36, 41–42, 102, 124, 126, 176, 346; activity 52, 56; affect 182, 414–421; allegiance 47; artifacts 15; BSO's 217; co-decoding 41; collective 182; commentary 15; community 74; constructing 385; consumption 125, 323, 328; engagement 72, 338; fannishness 349, 444; history 16, 157; identities 63; imagined 316; investment

459

72, 453; micro-celebrities 46; narrative worlds 385; -ness 349, 444; object 124, 130; online spaces 17; platforms 15; predilections 450; poaching 42; practices 117, 192, 358; pseudonyms 14; pursuits 373; uncertainty principle 16
fanon 26, 43, 160, 247
fantagonism 394–401; redux 396
fantasy 125, 129, 228, 237, 255, 257, 284, 408
fanvids *see* vidding
fanzines 32, 37, 127–129, 201, 234
fashion 281, 283–284, 289, 341–342
Feig, Paul 397, 399, 400–401
female: audiences 92; body 286; cast 399–400; -centered melodramas 92; characterization 292; characters 151, 228, 245–246, 251, 283; characters, black 391; citizenship 285; comics fandom 252; fans 1, 281–282, 285, 287, 289, 305, 313, 387, 396, 420–421, 438; fans, racialized 251–253; female pairing 240; gendering 313; media fans 234; pleasure 220; readers 325
feminine 1, 137, 216–217, 253, 282, 314, 319, 365, 420, 426
feminism 63, 182, 217, 282, 287–288, 316, 347, 398
feminist 1, 8, 25, 44, 63, 82, 100, 182, 216–219, 220, 233, 236, 242, 243, 316, 345, 398; Frequency YouTube channel 126; media studies 1; science fiction 218
feminized: fandom 281; fan practices 421; forward spaces 284
femslash 223, 228, 240–243, 245–248, 314
Fifty Shades of Grey 354, 356
film 72, 92–96, 156, 223, 236, 342, 356, 376, 378, 380, 392, 394, 397–398, 445, 449; and television 129, 242, 357, 375–376, 385, 416, 437, 445–447; exhibitors 95; music 338; -induced tourism 149
Firefly 351
Fiske, J. 231, 234
The Flash 316, 342, 384, 388–389
forums 14, 95, 100, 107, 119, 121, 129
franchise 3, 161, 165, 217, 235, 285, 288–289, 303, 316, 341, 346, 348, 350, 357, 392, 395, 397–401, 408, 415, 419, 433; *Bond* 219; multimedia 437
franchising 394–401, 447
friki conventions 406–412; -identity 342, 406, 408–410
Frozen 395

Galaxy Quest 201
Game of Thrones 147, 188, 286, 289, 304, 336, 377, 414, 416–418, 420

GamerGate 26, 100–102, 105, 107–108, 120, 236, 395
gaming 100, 376; culture 100, 102
gatekeeping 169, 252, 265, 268
geek 193, 200, 232, 235, 376, 378, 382
The Geek Girl Chronicles 126
gender 92–93, 100, 126, 131, 134, 137, 153–156, 202, 216, 228, 231–232, 234, 240, 243–245, 246–247, 252–254, 257–258, 276, 281, 312–313, 315–319, 424, 429; and sexuality 234, 247, 301, 312, 322; binary 247, 315–316; cis- 36, 63–64, 198, 235, 241, 312, 316, 324–325, 328; diversity 251; identities 246; norms 276, 365; politics 399; studies 90
genre 27, 92, 126–128, 154, 252, 272–275, 322–323, 325, 328
Geraghty, L. 126, 347–348
gerontology 301, 303
Ghostbusters 341, 367, 395, 397–402
GIFs 111, 130, 178, 180–184, 188–189, 418
gift economy 26, 66, 71, 116, 120, 342, 346, 350–351, 354–356, 358–359, 446
Gillespie, T. 72, 187, 194
Gledhill, C. 156, 161
global 67, 291–292, 426; access 424, 427; Bollywood 331; cultures 73, 227, 263, 323; fan cultures 28, 77; fandom 78, 429; fans 148, 268, 342, 424
globalization 197–198, 204, 324; BL 324
Gone With the Wind 356
Google 2, 86, 118, 126, 129; Forms 54
Granger, Hermione 151, 157, 159–161; as non-white 154–155
Graphical Interface Format *see* GIFs
Gray, J. 43, 125, 270
Greece 228, 291–297
Greek: fandom (Turkish soap operas) 291–297; national identity 292–297

Hall, S. 42–43, 45, 72, 135, 153–154, 156, 161
Hallyu *see* Korean Wave
Hamilton 180–181
Hannibal 184, 421
harassment 23–24, 102, 395–396
Harry Potter 66, 145, 151, 159, 161, 164–167, 169, 172, 202, 204, 304, 368; books 124, 154; fandom 38; mud-blood 154; *see also* Hermione Granger; shifting 164–172; tour 147
hashtag 119, 165, 175–178, 180, 182–184, 188, 190, 192, 209, 211, 284, 363, 366, 384, 417, 421
hate speech 364, 369
HBO 120, 142, 147, 367, 380, 414, 417, 420, 425

Index

hegemonic 61, 64, 67, 74, 100, 253, 286, 314, 316, 395–396; Americanism 291; anti- 72, 73; norms 428
Hellekson, K. 11, 14–15, 18, 34–35, 350, 351, 357
heteronormative 63–64, 247, 273, 293, 323, 326; romantic relationships 293; standards 319
heterosexual 235, 240, 273, 313, 324, 425; cisgender women 324; marriage 273
heterosexuality 64–65, 323
hierarchies 116, 240, 243, 247, 263, 268, 282, 348, 382
Hills, M. 142–144, 286, 307, 345
historical: accounts 334; anthropology 90; approach 224; contexts 94, 111, 160, 397; fandoms 90–91
Hogwarts 145, 147, 155, 164, 166, 170
Hollywood 72, 93, 95–96, 156–158, 392, 433, 444–447; casting 159; films 72, 376; labor unions 448
homoerotic 32–33, 322
homophobia 25, 116, 245, 314, 319, 329, 429
homophobic 101, 103, 369
homosexuality 65, 244
The Hunger Games 154, 286, 415, 418–420
hybridity 271–274

Image Comics 341, 433, 435–439
industry 4, 341–342, 406, 434, 441; and audiences 414, 421; and fans 304, 341, 395–396, 416, 429, 434; game 108; streaming 3; transmedia 420
influencers 287–288, 365, 411, 450
Instagram 85, 176, 189–190, 203, 254, 266, 365, 410, 440, 450–451, 453; pics 286
intellectual property (IP) 348, 354, 357, 397, 433, 435, 437, 445, 452
Internal Review Boards (IRBs) 12, 14, 105–106
internet 51, 103–104, 128–130, 197–199, 201–202, 204; and China 212, 360, 369; fandom 71; meme 181; Poland 201, research 8, 83, 106–107
intersectionality 28, 253, 270
interviews 51, 55, 94, 210–211, 254, 272–273, 303–304, 327, 335, 408, 414, 434, 453
intimacy 45, 143, 182, 210, 268, 287, 305; on Weibo 210
IP *see* intellectual property (IP)
IRBs *see* Internal Review Boards (IRBs)
Iris West Defense Squad (IWDS) 251, 316, 342, 384–392

Jamison, A. 32, 38, 134
Japanese: anime and manga 35–36, 406, 408–409, 411; BL 324, 326–328; BL *manga* 324; Comiket 33, 36; fans 71, 75; media 323, 325

Jenkins, H. 34–35, 42–43, 72–74, 116–118, 133, 153, 167, 198, 232–233, 237, 242, 346, 375, 387, 417, 435
Jones, B. 42, 350, 355

Kindle Worlds 23, 355, 357
Korean (South) 22, 77, 134, 136, 138, 228, 261–268, 331, 334, 338, 365; dramas 406, 408–409; *see also* K-pop
Korean Wave 71, 261
K-pop 24, 134, 138, 228, 261–268, 406; BLACKPINK 261; BTS 261; Jungkook 136

labor 288, 304, 341–342, 355, 359, 385, 387, 391–392, 416, 445–446
Lady Gaga 45, 55, 57, 289
language: acquisition 136; barrier 133, 135, 136, 140, 198; competencies 135, 137
The Last Airbender 157, 159, 236
Latinidad 270, 274, 276
Latinx 270, 272, 274–276; communities 271, 274–276; fandoms 270, 273–274, 276; fans 228, 270–271, 276; Latina femininity 273; music 271–275; salsa 274; *Telenovela* 275–277
Lazarus 436, 438
legitimacy 116, 153–154, 168–170, 245, 247, 282, 348, 382, 385, 390, 399
LEGO 375, 378, 400
lesbian 63, 223, 241–242, 246, 313–315, 324–325; Poussey 247
#LexaDeservedBetter 246
LGBTQ 100, 102, 192–193, 199, 223, 227, 240–241, 324–329; rights 204, 368–369
lifestyle brands 348–349
LiveJournal (LJ) 14–15, 23, 31, 34, 37, 72, 75, 81–82, 127, 130, 241, 385
LJ *see* LiveJournal (LJ)
Lothian, A. 82, 244, 387
Luminosity 218, 224
lurker 62, 119, 355
The L Word 242
Lysn 263–265

MAC Cosmetics: collaboration 283–287, 289; drag icons 289; fan-branded cosmetics 228, 281; squad 284; *Star Trek* Collection 283–284, 287; *Wonder Woman* 283–284
McCarthy, M. 397, 399
McCracken, A. 96, 182, 192
McRuer, R. 64–66
mainstream: audiences 276; culture 64, 286, 355, 420; DC Comics 433; entertainment 367; fan behavior 387; fanfiction 2; geek culture 374, 376; music 272
makeup 281–289, 439; tutorials 285–288; *The Walking Dead* zombie 286

461

Index

male 316, 325, 420; -dominant 273; fans 63, 96, 115, 197, 252, 282, 289, 324, 349, 387, 399, 420
marginalization 64, 154, 189, 228, 233, 236, 247, 253–254, 312–313, 319
marginalize 233, 253, 270, 316
marginalized groups 26–28, 60, 100, 367, 387
Marvel: and DC 435–437; Cinematic Universe 418; Comics 126, 251, 408, 433, 437; efforts to diversify 158; fandom 66, 376; *Ms. Marvel* 251, 256; Netflix 236; *SpyGal* 282–283; *Wonder Woman* 284, 436
masculinity 100, 121, 243, 252, 319; fan practices 415–416; neo- 398, trans- 314
mass: market 281–282, 351; media 287
media 31–33, 73–74; apolitical 328; artifacts 335; audiences 302, 375, 416, BL 322–329; capitalist 356; celebrities 7; companies 4, 144, 263, 446; consumers 326, 342; consumption 61, 72, 74, 142, 271, 291, 303, 378; content 117, 228, 291, 364, 366, 368; cult 235; culture 125, 183, 246, 328, 385; *encyclopedic* 124, 126, 130, 168; engagement 303; fan cultures 1, 74, 241; fandom 1, 26, 31–32, 35–37, 45, 73, 78, 199, 245, 333–335, 409–410; fans 32–34, 36, 43, 142, 204, 219, 227, 232–233, 235–236, 308, 341, 385, 395; forms 124–125, 127, 227, 270, 436; franchises 288, 347, 349, 395, 397; generations 307; giants 351; geek 375; globalized 72–73, 323; heteronormative 326; influence 298; Japanese 323–324; landscape 2, 3, 152, 242, 276, 301, 433, 447; Latinx 270–271; lesbian 246; mainstream 326; mass 243, 247, 406, 408; objects 2–3, 74, 90–91, 96, 176, 181, 305, 315, 341, 397, 417; platforms 33, 192, 397, 416; popular 302; producers 1–2, 74–75, 158, 234, 341; psychology 305; queer 247, 315, 327–329; regulators 368; social- 308, 322–323, 331; sports 427; studies 332, 334, 341; texts 302, 308, 328, 335; Thai 326; trans- 342
melodrama 275, 425
memorabilia 281, 284, 375, 378
mental: disorders 65; disability 65; health 65, 67; illness 60, 62, 65–66; wellbeing 165
merchandise 94, 117, 282–289, 345–352, 378, 380, 400, 410–411, 446; fan-made 345–346, 349–350; geek 382
metaphors 64, 159, 388
Mexican: American 271, 273; fan culture 342; fans 342, 406, 408; music 271–273, 410; television 406–407
middle class 92, 232, 243, 273–274

millennial 112, 202–203, 307; fandom 307
misogyny 398–399, 429
Ms. Marvel 251, 256
monetization: of fanfiction 74, 354–358; of fan labor 446
Morimoto, L. 74, 133, 323, 336
Morrissey 271–272, 276, 365
Motion Picture Association of America (MPAA) 219
movie theaters 75, 94–95
MPAA *see* Motion Picture Association of America (MPAA)
MTV 389, 421
music 35–36, 218, 220, 222, 235, 271–275, 355; K-pop 408; Mexican 271, 410; "pirated" 130; royalties 447; videos 128; videos on YouTube and TikTok 223
myths 104, 154, 243, 293

NAFTA *see* North American Free Trade Agreement (NAFTA)
narrative 117, 133–135, 144, 147, 181, 216, 219–220, 222, 240, 246, 251, 255, 282, 288, 296, 303, 325, 357, 385, 388–390, 399, 414, 416–417, 419, 447
nationalism 78, 262, 266, 292, 294
neoliberal: commodification of difference 66; feminine empowerment 283; ideologies 350; postfeminist entrepreneurship 288
Netflix 27, 120, 126, 247, 335–336, 411, 425–426, 447, 450
neurodiversity 65–66; movement 65
NHF *see* Northeast Historic Films (NHF)
niches 397, 406
nickelodeon 92
nonbinary 54, 228, 241, 312–320; Nonbinary Theory 312–319
non-Western 71, 76, 187, 198, 228, 263, 268, 291, 332–334, 337
non-white 61, 65, 192, 227, 236–237, 418; fans 62; Hermione 154; race and disability 61
Noppe, N. 74, 355, 358–359
North American Free Trade Agreement (NAFTA) 342, 406–408, 410
Northeast Historic Films (NHF) 94
nostalgia 301, 347, 399, 401, 452

The 100 246, 366–367
online 62, 117–119, 124–125, 127, 203–204, 268, 384; behavior 104–107; fan gift culture 446; IP licensing portals 352
Organization of Transformative Works (OTW) 23, 34, 37, 84–85, 359
OTW *see* Organization of Transformative Works (OTW)

Index

Pande, R. 8, 36, 61, 155–156, 177, 198, 243, 316
parasocial relations 41, 45, 48
paratexts 44, 125, 247
paratextual discourse 45, 242
participation 53, 60, 62, 115–118, 191, 252, 337–338, 346–348, 373–374, 379–380, 417
participatory: culture 115–117, 119, 270–272, 337, 374–375; experience 350; fans 3, 62; types of media 191
patriarchy 271, 274, 312, 314; hierarchies 243; social systems 328; societies 328
Patton, Candice 388–389, 392
Payne Fund Studies 93
Penley, C. 33, 72
performance 52, 143, 169, 172, 273, 317–319, 332
Philippines 324–325, 328; *sana all* 328
Pickford, Mary 92, 94, 216
pilgrimage 111, 142–143, 145–147
Pinterest 176, 285, 288, 385
piracy 377, 410–411
platformized fandom 43, 45, 354
platforms 23, 31, 34, 38, 54, 82, 85–86, 103–106, 108, 111–112, 115, 117–118, 164, 169, 171–172, 187–193, 203, 207–210, 212–213, 263–264, 341, 426–427, 446–447; AO3 23, 31, 38, 81–82, 86 *see also* An Archive of Our Own (AO3); Dreamwidth 23 *see also* Dreamwidth (DW); -driven research 81; Etsy 350–351; Facebook 82, 410 *see also* Facebook; Instagram 85, 410 *see also* Instagram; Kindle Worlds 23, 357 *see also* Kindle Worlds; LiveJournal 23, 31, 81 *see also* LiveJournal (LJ); Mastodon 188–191; Pillowfort 193; Reddit 85 *see also* Reddit; TikTok 86 *see also* TikTok; Tumblr 15, 62, 81, 333, 335 *see also* Tumblr; SnapChat 85; Twitter 15, 23, 81, 85, 369, 410 *see also* Twitter/X; Wattpad 22–23 *see also* Wattpad; YouTube 339 *see also* YouTube
podcasts 42, 47, 166, 168
podfic 228, 312–319
Polish 199–201, 203–204; conventions 201; fan culture 202, 197–204; fans 199, 204; media fandoms 202; zines 200
politics: angle 245; change 336, 396; campaigning 231; injustices 3; strategizing 73, 367
pop cosmopolitanism 73, 133–134
pop culture 151, 219, 222, 287, 333, 420; and fandoms 333
popular media 1, 152, 235–236, 240, 302, 366–367
populist: critique 394; Trump 332
pornography 64, 176, 369; by women for women 313

postfeminism 287–288
Presley, Elvis 144, 146
privacy 14–16, 209
production 328, 375, 396–398, 400–401, 407, 409, 411, 418, 434–435, 438, 445–447
pseudonymous 12–15

QAnon 26, 100–101
queer 63–64, 182, 242, 244–247, 323–328, 421, 424; affect 228, 322; and pinkwashing 328; -baiting 228, 242, 327–328, 420–421; community 181; content 27, 327, 359; fandom 227, 246, 312, 315–316; fans 177, 242, 246, 314; marginalization of 315; practices 228, 244, 314; *see also* femslash; *see also* slash; romance 326, 328; sexuality 314, 324, 327–328; theory 247, 313–314; trans 312
Quileute reservation 144

race 25, 61–62, 152, 154–161, 227, 231–237, 257, 276, 331, 333–334, 338, 387–389; and culture 160; and ethnicity 16, 93, 232; and fandom 387; and gender 252, 384; and racialization 67, 227, 231, 236–237; and racism 25, 253; and whiteness 235; -bending 42, 111, 151–161; in comics 251–254
RaceFail '09 26
racial: animus 236; diversity in comics fandom 257; identity 25, 159, 232, 336
racialized 61; bodies 236, 388; community experience 254; minorities 271
racism 22, 24–25, 105, 116, 159, 243, 252–253, 266, 316, 363, 368, 389, 429; flagrant 247; implicit and explicit 236; in AO3 24, in comics 253; indirect 388; in women's football 429; systemic 22, 25; transformative 316
Raiders of The Lost Ark 216
real-person fiction (RPF) 133–134, 136
reception 1, 76, 93, 95, 152–153, 199, 291–292, 312, 334, 398
Reddit 85–86, 119–121, 169; subreddits 119–120, 168
reproduction 125, 128, 153, 286; franchised cultural 397; of culture 402
Return of Kings 398, 402
rhetoric 22, 243, 264–265, 374, 377
risk 13, 17, 33, 36, 83, 198, 203, 303, 315, 333, 359; of bodily safety 318; of isolation 165; legal 355
rock (music) 218, 271–272, 302
Rocky Horror Picture Show 287
rogue archives 82–85
romantic: desires 324–325; love 292; nationalism 293; relationships 77, 293, 322, 326, 391; story 326; transformational 421

Index

Rowling, J. K. 154–155, 161, 164, 368
RPF *see* real person's fiction (RPF)
RRR (2022) 27

SAG-AFTRA strike 444
salsa (music) 271, 274
Sandvoss, C. 125, 142, 347
science fiction (SF) 32, 35–36, 39, 125, 127, 199, 217, 233, 235–236, 255
Scott, S. 252–253, 416, 435
scrapbooks 91–92, 94
Selena (singer) 273
semiotic: codes 153; guerrillas 74; insufficiency 155, 160
Sense 8 22, 27
sexism 25–26, 100, 102, 105, 192, 252, 429; in comic fandom 252–253
sexuality 63–64, 100, 223, 232, 234, 244–245, 247, 303–304, 314–315, 322–323; and gender 100, 245; and race 358; female 63
sexual: abuse 365; arousal 303; assault 166, 364; attraction 319; autonomy 169; behaviour 247; content 193, 210; desires 63, 324, 326; identities 63, 153, 246, 314, 317, 336; indeterminacy 247; minorities 245–246, 327–328; misconduct 168, 363, 365; norms 319; orientation 157, 319; practices 328; relationships 32, 322, 326; subordination 253
SF *see* science fiction (SF)
Sherlock 7, 66, 75–78, 146, 160, 304
shifting 111–112, 164–173
ShiftTok 164–172
shipping 25, 245, 264, 390–391
shōjo bunka 324–325, 327
showrunners 246, 364, 367, 421
silent film 90, 92
The Simpsons 43, 407
Sin City 438
slash 63–64, 202–203, 223, 240–247, 313–315, 319, 387, 415, 420–421
Sleepy Hollow 391
soap operas 35–36, 275, 293, 295, 297, 303
soccer/football 342, 424–430
social justice 22, 28, 217, 220, 253, 336, 396–397
social media 2–3, 8, 38–39, 41–43, 45–48, 117, 286, 322, 336, 358, 366–367, 392, 410–411, 414–415, 427, 429, 444; discourse 282; influencers 448; networks 182; platforms 23, 31, 82, 115, 117–118, 164, 189, 207–208, 263–264, 341–446
sociology 12–13, 18, 103
soft power 74, 76–77, 133, 291–292
Spanish-language media 270, 276
Spawn 436, 438
Spider-man 184, 236, 253, 408

sports 103, 152, 212, 235, 271, 282, 342, 425–426, 428–429; fans 46, 235, 425, 428–429; fandoms 26, 429; media 425, 427, 430; women's 425, 428
Spotify 126
Springsteen, Bruce 304, 306
Squid Game 22
Stanfill, M. 25–26, 35, 61, 82, 100, 156, 190, 233, 243, 245–247, 253, 313, 342, 358–359, 417, 429, 444, 446
stanning 45–46
Star Trek 76, 115, 126, 128–129, 131, 146, 200, 202, 217, 235, 281, 283, 287–288; inspired strike 448; MAC collection 281, 283, 285, 287
Star Wars 72, 125, 130, 144, 165, 200, 281, 283–288, 303, 376, 408, 420; Covergirl makeup collection 284
Stein, L. 187, 385
stereotypes 138–139, 270, 293–294, 314, 386, 409; disability 60; gendered 115, loser 304; reductive 64
strike (*Bridgerton* themed) 450–454
subcultural 23, 242, 281; capital 144, 305
subculture(s) 13, 31, 36, 267, 326; in South Korea 267; marginalized 242; self-identified vidding 223; supportive 243
Succession 120, 142
Suicide Squad 394–395, 436
superhero/ine 251, 288, 376
superheroes 154–155, 158, 251
Supernatural 135, 139, 182, 184, 357, 376
Superstandard English 234
surveillance 165, 168–169
surveys 51–58; data analysis 57; design 54–56; ethics 52–53; representation 56–57
sustainable fan travel 148
Swift, Taylor 2, 45, 192, 368

teenagers 104, 202, 282, 364, 411, 437
Teen Wolf 421
Tejano (music) 271
telenovelas 228, 271, 275–276
television (TV) 115–116, 118–119, 126, 308, 331, 377–378, 435–436, 444–447; ad-based streaming 429
textual poaching 41–42, 116
Thai BL industry 326; series 322, 324, 328
third space 267, 273
TikTok 164–172, 192–193, 285, 287–288, 365; shadowbanning 192
Time Warner 433, 437
Tokyo Revengers 137–138
transcultural 8, 21, 24, 26, 74, 132–133, 262, 327; fandom 21–22, 132–139, 262–268, 291, 322–328, 331–339, 428

trans fans/fandom 74, 77, 177, 313–319
Transformative Works and Cultures (TWC) 11, 338
transmedia 342, 414–419; campaigns 415, 417–420; creators 420; elements 419; marketing activations 415–418; producers 415; storytelling 346, 414–421
transnational 21, 24–26, 75, 77, 261–263, 265, 267–268, 274, 276, 291, 323, 333; fandom 21, 24–28, 75, 276, 291, 323, 333; K-pop 262–268; media fan studies 71–77; *Sherlock* 75–77; streaming platforms 23
trolling 104, 367, 369
Tumblr 13–15, 23, 81–82, 175–178, 180–184, 190–193, 203–204, 240, 332–333, 335–336, 440
Turkey 292–293, 295–297
Turkish soap operas 292, 297; Greek fandom of 228, 291–296, 298
TV *see* television (TV)
TWC *see Transformative Works and Cultures* (TWC)
Twilight 144–146, 285, 354, 420; and Colourpop collection 285
The Twilight Zone 126
Twitter/X 43–44, 81, 85, 117, 188–189, 364, 369, 389, 391–392, 410, 427, 440

UEFA Women's Champions League (UWCL) 424–429
Uncertain Destiny 134, 136, 138
Union of the Physically Impaired Against Segregation (UPIAS) 62–63
USENET 33–34, 117, 129–130
UWCL *see* UEFA Women's Champions League (UWCL)

The Vampire Diaries 391
vidding 111–112, 223; algorithmic effect on 222; and identity 111, 217–225; communities 13, 216; fandoms 217; female 216–224; networks 218; queer 223–224
video games 33, 100, 126, 271, 322, 379, 406, 408–409, 433
vloggers 287–288

Wanzo, R. 152, 231, 235, 237, 253, 270–271, 316
Warner Brothers 332, 342, 367, 376, 378, 384, 448–449

Warner, K. J. 177, 188, 251, 317, 341, 386, 390, 444
Wattpad 23, 354–358
WeChat 112, 210–213; and Douban 208
Weibo 23–24, 112, 208–213; algorithm 207, 209
Western: culture 127, 200; fan cultures and objects 3; hegemony 266–268; indoctrination 334; societies 328
West, Iris 342, 384, 388–392
WGA *see* Writers Guild of America (WGA)
whiteness 22, 25–26, 28, 61, 154–156, 217, 227, 243, 247; and media fandom 231–237; of media fandom 233; of popular media 236
white: people 61, 158–159, 232, 235, 237; supremacy 22, 26, 392
whitewashing 333, 338
wikis 82, 124
women 63–65, 72, 75, 92, 101, 103; abuse 294; as consumer group 2; bisexual 246; empowerment of 273, 398, 428; black 156, 251, 384, 386–387, 391; heterosexual 325, 327; of color 247, 251–252, 254, 256, 386–387; queer-identified 244; racialized 253–254, 256; straight 314; white 387, 392
Women of Color (WOC) 228, 251–257, 386–387, 391; fans 251–257
women's football fandom 424–429
Wonder Woman 436; MAC Cosmetics collaboration 283–284, 288
Woo, B. 345, 348
Writers Guild of America (WGA) 3, 416, 444

Xena: Warrior Princess 242, 245, 247
The X-Files 117, 143–144, 234, 242

YA *see* young adult (YA)
Yahoo 72, 129, 176
yaoi see Boy(s) Love (BL)
Yin, Y. 45–46, 208–209, 214
young adult (YA) 255, 305, 357, 406
YouTube 26, 126, 169–170, 222–223, 285, 287–289, 424, 427–429, 447, 450; channel 450; makeup tutorials 282; videos 166, 450; vloggers 287

Zheng, Yunlong 208–213

9781032438009